Pavarotti

Technician and Magician

JOSEPH TALIA OAM

AUSTRALIANACADEMICPRESS

Other books by this author:
A History of Vocal Pedagogy: Intuition and Science
Vocal Science for Elite Singers
Italian Bel Canto in the Age of Vocal Science

First published 2024 by:
Australian Academic Press Group Pty. Ltd., Australia
www.australianacademicpress.com.au

Copyright © 2024 Joseph Talia

Copying for educational purposes
The Australian Copyright Act 1968 (Cwlth) (Act) allows a maximum of one chapter or 10% of this book, whichever is the greater, to be reproduced and/or communicated by any educational institution for its educational purposes provided that the educational institution (or the body that administers it) has given a remuneration notice to Copyright Agency (CA) (www.copyright.com.au) under the Act.

For details of the CA licence for educational institutions contact:
Copyright Agency, Level 12, 66 Goulburn St. Sydney NSW 2000.
E-mail info@copyright.com.au

Production and communication for other purposes
Except as permitted under the Act, for example a fair dealing for the purposes of study, research, criticism or review, no part of this book may be reproduced, stored in a retrieval system, or transmitted in any form or by any means electronic, mechanical, photocopying, recording or otherwise without prior written permission of the copyright holder. For all enquiries, contact the Publisher.

 A catalogue record for this book is available from the National Library of Australia

ISBN 978-1-925644-82-1 (paperback)
ISBN 978-1-925644-86-9 (hardback)
ISBN 978-1-925644-87-6 (ebook)

Publisher and Editor: Stephen May
Typesetting: Australian Academic Press
Printing: Lightning Source

The Raison d'être for this Book

- To promote the art of singing and nurture the love for opera by conducting a detailed analysis of the artistic and technical development of one of the greatest tenors of all time, Luciano Pavarotti.

- To obtain practical empirical knowledge that can be described in the language of the old school but also informed by contemporary scientific knowledge of anatomy and physiology. Singing teachers should have all these tools at their disposal and use whichever device and language most likely resonates with the particular student.

- To establish criteria such as breathing technique, resonance balancing and register blending, and vocal quality by which we may judge great singing.

- To advocate for specific techniques depending on prevailing circumstances, particular voice types, temperament, psychology, and varying operatic styles.

- To establish aesthetic principles and dramatic criteria by which we may adjudicate both musical and dramatic performances.

- To examine the influence of originating time and place on the artist as well as family and community influence on the psychology of the artist or the student.

- To develop a cohesive strategy and an appropriately coordinated elaboration of this aggregate knowledge so that it may be utilised as a systematic educational tool for career development and for the promotion and enjoyment of the art of singing and the melodrama which is opera.

- To use the result of these findings to establish objective patterns and methods by which we may rank Pavarotti's development and standing among the great singers of the twentieth century.

- Finally, I hope that this combined paradigm that utilises the precepts of the old Italian school in combination with contemporary scientific and physiological knowledge will become the objective standard by which great singing will be judged. I also encourage young singing teachers to train and develop their ear rather than resort to technology all the time. It is all right to check yourself occasionally, but not to become reliant on technology. Your hearing and your knowledge are your technology. I am proud that no part of any analysis in this book has been subjected to technology; instead, it is about hearing the sound and visualising the muscular physiology.

Joseph Talia, 2024

Contents

The Raison d'être for this Book iii

About the Author viii

Chapter 1: An Introduction 1

Chapter 2: The Pavarotti Family During The War Years 19

Chapter 3: The Prevailing Cultural Conditions in Italy in 1954 33

Chapter 4: Italian Vocal Technique During Pavarotti's Youth and Beyond 39

Chapter 5: The International Italian School and the Modenese Chapter 51

Chapter 6: The Three Amigos, Pavarotti, Freni and Magiera 59

Chapter 7: To Mantova and Ettore Campogalliani 65

Chapter 8: Family and Friends Rally in a Crisis 75

Chapter 9: The Sostegno System of Breath Management 83

Chapter 10: Arrigo Pola's Belief in Si Canta Come si Parla 89

Chapter 11: Mori on Vocal Registers and Passaggio 99

Chapter 12: Success at the Achille Peri Competition, 1961 109

Chapter 13: Pavarotti's Debut as Rodolfo in La Boheme, 1961 115

Chapter 14: Rigoletto and Serafin, Teatro Massimo Palermo, 1962 155

Chapter 15: Comparison of the 1967 RAI and the 1971 Decca Rigoletto 169

Chapter 16: Comparison of La Bohème, London 1963 and Modena 1967 ...173

Chapter 17: Joan Sutherland and Lucia di Lammermoor 183

Chapter 18: Lucia Di Lammermoor, Scotto/Pavarotti/Pradelli, 1966 187

Chapter 19: La Traviata, Modena, Pavarotti, Freni, Magiera, 1965.................201

Chapter 20: Sutherland and Pavarotti, Australia 1965 213

Chapter 21: La Sonnambula, Sutherland and Pavarotti, Sydney 1965 213

Chapter 22: The Appoggio System of Breath Management 231

Chapter 23: I Capuletti E Montecchi, 1966...241

Chapter 24: Beatrice di Tenda, Sutherland, Pavarotti, Decca 1966..............247

Chapter 25: La Fille du Regiment, Pavarotti, Sutherland, July 1967 251

Chapter 26: L'Amico Fritz, Mascagni, Pavarotti, Freni, Gavazzeni, 1968 263

Chapter 27: La Bohème, Pavarotti, Freni, Schippers RAI, July 1969 271

Chapter 28: L'elisir d'amore, Pavarotti, Sutherland: January–June, 1970.......277

Chapter 29: La Traviata at the Metropolitan Opera, 1970...............................285

Chapter 30: La Bohème, Pavarotti, Freni, Karajan, 1973 287

Chapter 31: La Fille du Regiment, 1972/73..293

Chapter 32: A Change of Direction..305

Chapter 33: L'elisir d'amore, The Metropolitan Opera, Rescigno, 1981 317

Chapter 34: Un Ballo in Maschera, Pavarotti, Tebaldi, Bartoletti, 1970..........339

Chapter 35: Rigoletto, Sutherland, Pavarotti, Bonynge, June 1971 349

Chapter 36: Lucia, Sutherland/Pavarotti, June–July 1971................................355

Chapter 37: L'Elisir d'amore, Pavarotti/Battle/Levine 1990..............................363

Chapter 38: I Puritani, Pavarotti/Sutherland/Bonynge, May–July 1973..........367

Chapter 39: La Favorita by Donizetti, Pavarotti/Cossotto/Ghiaurov, 1974.....383

Chapter 40: Maria Stuarda, 1975/1976 403

Chapter 41: Pavarotti's Struggle with Depression 411

Chapter 42: Cavalleria Rusticana, Mascagni, 1976 417

Chapter 43: I Pagliacci: Pavarotti/Freni 1977 423

Chapter 44: Turandot, Pavarotti/Sutherland/Mehta 431

Chapter 45: Ballo in Maschera, Pavarotti/Solti May–June 1982 441

Chapter 46: Conclusion — An Everlasting Legacy..449

Bibliography..453

About the Author

For over 40 years Joseph Talia has sung, directed, conducted, and taught opera, as well as achieving a PhD from La Trobe University on the topic of cultural hegemony and the economics of the performing arts. He began his career in Melbourne, studied in Milan, was engaged to sing at the Teatro Eliseo in Rome, and has performed as a concert artist in Milan, and Vercelli. His repertoire consists of over 50 major tenor roles. He has been involved in over 140 opera productions and has directed such masterpieces as La Boheme, Carmen, Andrea Chenier, Tosca and La Rondine. Dr Talia was artistic director of the Globe Opera Company for ten years, followed by the Melbourne City Opera from 1997 to 2015, and formed the Millennium Opera in 2015. He was awarded the Order of Australia Medal in 2007 for his dedicated service to opera. He currently maintains a successful voice studio in Melbourne where apart from his regular students, he teaches visiting students from New Zealand, Europe, Japan and Korea. He is also in high demand as an adjudicator of international competitions, such as the Paolo Tosti, in Ortona, the Mattia Battistini International in Rieti, and The Izmir International in Turkey. He regularly conducts International master classes, in Australia, New Zealand, Spain, Italy, Belgium and Austria.

Chapter 1

An Introduction

At the age of twenty-five, Luciano Pavarotti was in total despair. He had been studying singing for over six years and had yet to earn a penny. His entire family had sacrificed so that he could study and now they had nothing to show for it except a voice that had cracked under pressure in the final of an international competition.

At that time, he refused to discuss the source of his despair with anyone. His childhood friend Mirella Freni, who was like a sister to him, tried desperately to talk him into resuming lessons and getting back on the stage, but he would have none of it. He loved her like a sister, but even that love could not disguise the fact that her success was a constant reminder of what could be achieved in an operatic career. They were the same age and came from the same socio-economic, educational and cultural backgrounds. Yet, Mirella had begun her career as Micaela in Carmen at the age of nineteen. Moreover, although only twenty-five, Mirella had, for the last six years, graced the operatic stages of Europe and the United Kingdom.

By comparison, Pavarotti was still singing concerts with piano at provincial music societies. Mirella was always the sweetest and the staunchest of his supporters, and he could not help but be thrilled for her success. Nonetheless, the contrast was stark, and the more he thought about it, the more difficult it became to understand why his own career had failed to ignite. Nobody knew then why he had withdrawn from life in general and music in particular. Time would reveal, however that in his mind, he had not so much renounced his singing as his singing had deserted him. What good is a tenor without a reliable head register? He felt publicly humiliated by his failure and privately disappointed with himself.

His teacher Campogalliani and his friend and coach Leone Magiera tried to get him involved, but to no avail. These events particularly affected Mirella and Leone Magiera. Leone and Luciano had been working together on his singing and artistry for years: always engaged, hearts filled with hope, and mischief on their minds. They couldn't wait to complete their work, raid the fridge, and create havoc. Now those glorious carefree days seemed so far away; so distant in fact that they took on the glow of the halcyon days of their friendship. Everyone was miserable, but Luciano most of all.

The only person he would communicate with was his fiancée, Adua Veroni. They had been together since high school and she would have married him right there and then, but Luciano felt that it would be irresponsible to ask her to marry whilst his career was so nebulous and insecure. Adua was an intelligent young woman, an independent but caring spirit who would prove to be a tower of strength in adversity. Theirs had been a tempestuous relationship, punctuated by arguments, misunderstandings, and separations, including one that lasted twelve months. However, over the years, their love had matured into a very deep and stable relationship. They wanted nothing more than to marry, but they had no money, no property, and now it would appear, no prospects.

However, after all these years, the mystery remains unsolved. What was it that plunged one of the most optimistic and gifted young tenors of his generation into such depths of despair, forcing him to give up his dream?

I know that these issues are always more complicated than they seem, so I put these questions to his friend and coach Leone Magiera. If anyone knew the facts that preceded this dark chapter of Pavarotti's life, then surely the man facing me on the other side of the coffee table would. Reluctantly, being still protective of his friend, he agreed that there were two decisive events within a short period of time that forced the young Pavarotti to reconsider his career options. The first occurred when he decided to engage a manager to help him with his career, a good decision in principle you would think. However, when you are as driven and ambitious as the young Pavarotti you quickly realise that it cannot be just any manager — it had to be the best. Mirella Freni for instance was very happy with her manager, Alda Finzi. She was not as powerful as her former mentor Liduino but she had the happy task of casting many opera festivals in Europe and the United Kingdom. Finzi's preparation for a career as an artist manager was impeccable. In many respects, she was the most intellectual and cultured of all the agents operating in Italy at that time, and she had been courting Luciano. Finzi really believed in him and was keen to develop his career but Luciano always found some excuse to delay joining her.

He had convinced himself that if he were to sign with a manager, the latter would have to be Italy's most powerful and influential manager. That accolade belonged to Liduino Bonardi. His roster of clients reads like a Who's Who in Opera in the 1950s and 1960s. Although a completely unknown artist, Pavarotti set out to impress Bonardi, but attaining an audition with him was not as simple as he had imagined. Fortunately, Pavarotti's teacher Arrigo Pola knew Bonardi very well and was predisposed to help. On the designated day the three musicians from Modena adjourned to Liduino's studio where, with Magiera at the piano and Pola talking up his student's potential, Pavarotti began singing *'Che gelida manina'*. Magiera recalls that:

> Luciano was producing a lovely tone and Liduino was quickly engaged in the performance, if only because he could already envision the potential for making a lot of money. The first B flat on *'chi son'* was an excellent ringing tone, and 'suddenly Liduino's shark's eyes seem to light up'. However, by the time Luciano arrived at *'Talor del forziere'* his voice stuck in his throat, producing an unexpected and jarring false note. Liduino shot out of his chair, slamming the door as he left the room, muttering that he did not need short tenors and time wasters [Magiera, 2008:31].

This experience left the young Pavarotti wounded and traumatised, feeling that he had little control over his singing career and even less over his life. Unfortunately, worse was to come.

The second adverse event came in the spring of 1960 when Pavarotti submitted himself to the rigorous judgement of the adjudicators at the Achilli Peri international competition for young singers. Among the highly qualified adjudicators were the great baritone Mariano Stabile (arguably the finest Falstaff ever) and the superb soprano Mafalda Favero. Pavarotti sang his way into the final, and everything seemed to be going to plan. He had reason to be positive, having correctly assessed that the adjudicators liked him and his singing.

On the evening of the final, Pavarotti was singing well, and everything was progressing as expected. It helped immensely that he had his good friend and coach, Leone Magiera, at the piano. Magiera had been his coach from the beginning and had married Pavarotti's childhood friend, the young soprano Mirella Freni, who was already making a considerable international reputation for herself. The three of them had become inseparable, often staying up half the night to discuss some fine point of vocal production and interpretation, and it was a source of comfort for Pavarotti to have Magiera at the piano. They had rehearsed the program in great detail, and for the final, they selected the famous aria *'Ah fouyez douce image'* from Manon by Massenet. He reached the aria's climax comfortably and with an excellent sense of style, but suddenly, the Pavarotti curse struck again, and his voice began cracking on both B flats. The audience was shocked, but the adjudicators, feeling great empathy, willed him to sing the repeat sequence correctly. Although in a sweaty panic, Pavarotti pulled himself together and appeared to recover until the repetition of this sequence, during which the same thing happened. The audience saw the embarrassment written all over his face, but what they could not see, which cut much deeper, was the shattering of his dreams. Ever since he was a boy, he had dared to dream that one day he would win a major competition, thus launching a successful career. His most vivid recollections were associated with singing. He had never been as happy as when the *Corale Rossini* entered the choral Eisteddfod in Wales and unexpectedly won first prize. He knew then that singing was what he wanted to pursue.

It had been very difficult for him to resign himself to not being a singer. For three months, his confidence remained shattered and his grief inconsolable. He spoke to no one avoided all human contact except for Adua. He refused food, which was of great concern to those around him, but he remained unaware. His closest relationship at that time, apart from fiancee Adua Veroni, was with his grief, an unshakable sense of loss seemed to have taken hold of him, and he couldn't extricate himself from it.

Consequently, I can honestly say that the purpose of this book is not to criticise Pavarotti but rather to examine in detail how this traumatised young tenor found the strength of character to transform himself into arguably the greatest lyric *bel canto* tenor of all time. This was an incredible journey, a wondrous achievement for a young boy brought up in public housing. Once he got it right, his voice proved his ultimate weapon. He combined his bright, silvery, harmonically vibrant voice with a velvety roundness, a honeyed tone and a hauntingly beautiful natural bloom. In short, it perfectly balanced and represented the *chiaro/scuro* qualities so prized by the old Italian masters.

However, I must stress that whilst Pavarotti's voice was undoubtedly an enormous natural gift, the artistic and technical perfection he achieved resulted from diligent, intelligent and persistent hard work. It was also fortuitous that he was born into a loving, musical and supportive family that was part of a larger community that loved great tenors at least as much as they loved sporting heroes and footballers.

This duality created a certain tension for the young and athletic Luciano Pavarotti. There was a time when he was seriously conflicted between being a professional footballer and becoming an opera singer.

Throughout this period, the gramophone at the Pavarotti house rang out with the glorious sounds of Caruso, Martinelli, Schipa, Gigli, Bjorling and later Di Stefano. This was like a siren song for him, and his passion for singing soon overcame his love for football. Now that he was taking it more seriously, that love asserted itself most emphatically. When he was a little boy, he climbed up on the kitchen table, took centre stage, and began singing his rendition of *'La Donna e Mobile,'* after which he announced that he would become a professional tenor when he grew up. As a boy, one of Pavarotti's favourite rituals was walking hand in hand with his father, himself a fine amateur tenor, to the church of San Bartolomeo, where they sang vespers. When Luciano was a young adult, they walked together to the *Corale Rossini,* where music was a living, dynamic organism. Its members sang to their hearts' delight and dissected the strengths and weaknesses of all the great singers, especially the tenors.

The streets of Modena rang with the sound of operatic music, whether on a radio or on a gramophone blaring through somebody's window, a young man serenading his sweetheart or a group of young women singing as they rode bicycles on their way to work or school. In short, Modena was a city in which singing rarely stopped.

In Pavarotti's case, it was significant that he possessed such a muscular and athletic physique, combined with a marvellous voice and sensitive musicality.

Leone Magiera who was one year older and had played football with him at school before participating in his artistic development throughout their adult life would recall that:

> From an early age, Pavarotti was a big, muscular young man, very athletic, with enormous muscles and a colossal chest. He was built like a tree trunk. All of which provided him with an immense respiratory capacity. He also had a naturally protruding mandible, a bit like Sutherland, which he used naturally as a secondary means of shaping and supporting the vowel sounds [Personal interview, Magiera: 2019].

Pavarotti was that rare blend of nature and nurture, being blessed with enormous talent, intelligence, perseverance, persistence and willpower, which qualities were associated not just with great artists but also with sports stars. As a result of these characteristics Herbert Von Karajan was moved to declare that Pavarotti was the greatest tenor of all time, going as far as to suggest that his *'vocal cords were kissed by God.'*

Richard Bonynge, who had intimate knowledge of great voices including that of his wife Joan Sutherland, recalled that in the case of the young Pavarotti 'it didn't take a great deal of knowhow to understand immediately that this was a voice from God. It was a natural voice, an easy voice: a voice that comes along once every century.

Montserrat Caballe recalled that the characteristic that left the deepest impression on her was not Pavarotti's art but rather his personality — 'the man himself, the richness of his humanity'. Luciano was a world apart, another dimension, it was like being close to and speaking with a type of angel, or a god, a benevolent god.

Jose Carreras asserts that: 'No one in the world, speaking of the last generation of tenors, possessed this colour, this sunny timbre in the voice, and this power of communication. Only Luciano!'.

Renata Scotto, one of his famous leading ladies, believed that there were two great pillars of Italian tenor singing: 'The first was Caruso at the beginning of the twentieth century and the second was Pavarotti in the latter part of the twentieth century. Scotto contends that 'Pavarotti's voice was fantastic, the greatest Italian voice since Caruso'.

The music critic Norman Lebrecht drew a similar conclusion, but whereas Scotto's evaluation is based predominantly on vocal quality and technique, Lebrecht's comments are unashamedly slanted towards popularity and fame. However, this does not preclude vocal excellence; on the contrary, it assumes it. Lebrecht contends that:

> Outside of the opera world, Enrico Caruso became the first tenor with really universal fame, and that is because he was the first voice that was credible on record. He was the first bestseller. Half a century after Caruso's death, along comes Pavarotti who redefined that model for the mass public. There has been nobody between these two titans as pillars of what a tenor means to the general audience that does not generally go to the opera or even listen to an opera on the radio. For them, the tenor is defined at one extreme by Caruso and at the other by Pavarotti [Lebrecht, the last tenor DVD].

It is hard to argue with any of these sentiments but perhaps the most compelling tributes came from his two great contemporary, Placido Domingo.

On the other hand, Domingo considers that: 'It was one of the most beautiful and important voices ever: a voice for the Ages'.

Whilst there is universal agreement that Pavarotti's voice was one of the greatest tenor voices of all time, it is left to Placido Domingo to recognise Pavarotti's personal contribution to his own success. Domingo lauds him for bringing his great gifts to fruition as well as nurturing them with extreme intelligence and wisdom. Here are Domingo's thoughts on the occasion of the fortieth anniversary of Pavarotti's debut:

> The first thing that comes to mind when someone says 'Luciano Pavarotti' is that yours is one of the most beautiful voices in operatic history — a voice with which you still thrill millions of people all over the globe today and a voice that will remain 'unmistakably Pavarotti' even when you will be 90 years or older. Yes, the vote was God-given, but you deserve the most significant credit for taking care of it with love and wisdom. History will prove that yours is a voice for the ages and that for future generations, it will stand as a role model thanks to your splendid recordings [Domingo, in Pavarotti: *Quarantanni per La Lirica*, 2001: 42].

Domingo has identified the crux of the matter concerning Pavarotti, which is that most fans and critics praise his astonishing natural gifts. In so doing they unwittingly diminish his technical and artistic achievements and the superb manner with which he conducted his career.

Contrary to popular opinion, Pavarotti was one of many young tenor in postwar Italy to have a God-given voice. We never hear about the others because they failed to bring their potential to fruition. Many others enjoyed their moment in the sun but, like a shooting star, they shone brightly for an instant only to be quickly extinguished. By comparison, Pavarotti was inspired to nurture his vocal instrument to an astonishing level of perfection. Even more miraculous was the fact that he was able to maintain his finely tuned voice for over 40 years. That is an accomplishment that should neither be taken for granted nor underestimated. Dr. Umberto Boeri, Pavarotti's boyhood friend, illustrates my point with a most delightful recollection that not only speaks to this point but remains instructive in terms of context and perspective. Boeri recalls an opera excursion to the Roman Amphitheatre in Verona to see Di Stefano in Ponchielli's *La Gioconda*.

The following is his account of the event:

> The performance was beautiful, and during the trip back to Modena that night everyone's spirits ran high on the bus home. There was a lot of singing. Some of it was group singing, but there were also many solos. I wouldn't say I like admitting it, but Luciano's voice wasn't the only reasonable voice on that bus that night. Still, his high Bs were extraordinary. I was impressed that this popular, good-looking, town boy could sing like that [Boeri in Wright, 1981: 22].

Pavarotti remains adamant that perfecting his voice was a laborious process over many years, and part of a never-ending quest for artistic and technical perfection.

When we decipher the different opinions and recollections, analysing them with an objective turn of mind, we conclude that right from the very beginning, Pavarotti possessed a wonderful gift from God. However, it is equally true that this gift was by no means complete: it was, from all accounts, a very small, voice, lacking roundness and power. According to Magiera, Pavarotti's voice 'was extraordinarily beautiful. It was a bright voice, but a little voice. A voice that didn't have the necessary roundness and power, but which possessed all the essential characteristics to become an important voice.' [Personal interview with Magiera]. Nonetheless, Magiera recalls that the first time he heard the young Pavarotti, his singing made an immense impression. Sixty years later, during our interview, he was still moved by the remembrances of that occasion. He would recall that Luciano's voice 'was so hauntingly beautiful that I found it difficult to sleep that night' [Leone Magiera, personal interview].

In summary, it is clear that whilst Pavarotti was the possessor of a wonderful natural gift, his instrument required considerable development in order to withstand the rigours of an international career. It also occurred to me during the research for this book that much of the art we have come to take for granted was not there at the beginning of his career, let alone at the beginning of his training. I think it is fair to say that whilst he was naturally musical, the technical aspects of his musicianship were of a primitive nature.

Another reason why Pavarotti's vocal development should not be taken for granted is supported by the fact that many great voices before and since have been ruined by inferior teaching, lousy advice and impatient students who want to run before they can walk. Anybody who has ever been entrusted with the task of developing a vocal instrument knows that every day brings new decisions and choices about technique, repertoire and the timing of incorporating new roles and new challenges. For instance, every technical choice leads to a different physiological and artistic outcome, and often, unless the teacher is highly skilled, the singer does not achieve the intended result. Unfortunately, it remains a fact that a lack of technical and objective knowledge, incorrect choices and ill-informed artistic decisions ruin many gifted voices. There is no doubt that the gods loved Pavarotti, for he was twice blessed — firstly, to have been born with the most beautiful voice, and secondly, to have gathered around him the Right people to provide him with inspiration and technical, artistic and career guidance. It is worth recalling that he enjoyed a quasi-paternalistic relationship with his first teacher, Arrigo Pola. His second teacher Ettore Campogalliani, was also a wonderful mentor and very fond of Luciano. However, the most constant, the most significant and most enduring relationships after Pola left Italy were the ones he enjoyed with Mirella Freni and Leone Magiera. Their devotion to each other and the art of singing and opera was extraordinary, their constructive arguments about singing often lasting until dawn. Pavarotti's team was later completed by the influential tenor Alessandro Ziliani, who was to become his first agent and mentor. These people possessed an intimate knowledge of the vocal instrument, a monumental understanding of the repertoire and its technical demands, and an intuitive knowledge of a particular role's character and emotional requirements. Armed with this knowledge, they were able to guide him towards role the were particularly well suited to his voice and persona. They also had an exquisite sense of timing and an excellent understanding of the sequencing of roles — what should precede and follow a particular position. For instance, at the very beginning of his career, La Scala offered Pavarotti a production of *I Puritani* or *William Tell*, for which they were prepared to pay a great deal of money, way above his normal fee. He was human enough to be tempted, not as much by the money (which would have been a great boon at that stage of his career), but by his passionate desire to make his debut in Italy's premier opera house, one of the world's great operatic citadels.

Notwithstanding the temptation, he finally declined. The impetus for Pavarotti's decision came from his agent Alessandro Ziliani who had forged a very substantial career as an international tenor in his own right before becoming an agent. It was he who advised Pavarotti to decline the offer from La Scala; Ziliani knew that if he sang William Tell at this stage of his development, it would surely ruin his voice. This is the kind of advice that makes all the difference in a career, and that is why it is widely accepted in authoritative circles that whilst natural talent is important it is not of itself sufficient to sustain a long career. Talent must be combined with technique, knowledge, wisdom and a highly developed intuition. The ability to make good decisions based on logic, a cool head and intuition remains indispensable. Good decisions can lead to a change of direction capable of revolutionising careers.

Di Stefano, the young Luciano's hero and later a lifelong friend, had one of the most beautiful and exciting tenor voices of all time. When combined with his undoubted good looks and charismatic stage persona, not to mention his creative genius, originality of interpretation, and a completely modern way of expressing his art, we conclude that he should have had a career on a par with Caruso's. At least this was the conclusion drawn by Rudolf Bing, long time supremo at the Metropolitan Opera.

Very few people appreciate that Di Stefano revolutionised tenor singing every bit as much as Callas revolutionised soprano singing. However, his vocal technique and performance choices which were designed to elicit and heighten audience excitement were so reckless, especially around the *passaggio*, that they ruined his voice. The premature demise of an otherwise unparalleled career was a tremendous loss to the operatic world. The same premature ending attended the Golden Greeks, Maria Callas and Elena Souliotis. Callas' stellar career and creative contribution to our art remains unequalled in the annals of opera. Many predicted that Souliotis would inherit Callas' artistic mantle. However, that turned out to be a disaster, not because their natural gifts were not of the first rank but rather because their technical deficiencies and artistic choices (premature excursions into the dramatic repertoire) led to the early collapse of their respective voices and the demise of their careers.

By contrast, Pavarotti sang gloriously into his late fifties before a slow decline was triggered by time rather than technique. Most vocal authorities understand that this was not an accident. His decisions on vocal technique and intelligent choice of repertoire delivered a number of legendary performances whilst maintaining the freshness of his voice well into his sixties. He achieved this artistic feat, in spite of the fact, that he did not at the beginning possess a perfect technique and his musicianship as opposed to musicality was questionable. In fact, Pavarotti had a number of very serious problems as an advanced student and even in the early years of his professional career. That is what makes the examination of his development and professional journey such an interesting and challenging intellectual and artistic study. His glorious natural voice enabled him to construct an equally splendid career, but what really made him different was his extraordinary intelligence. We will see in this book that one of Pavarotti's defining characteristics was his ability to think both logically and in depth before finally making decisions with great clarity and conviction. Consequently, he surrounded himself with people who knew their business and were right for him: people who helped him obtain an impeccable technique, combined with great artistry which allowed him to build an immense career and a discography that has few equals.

However, when I hear people speak about his wonderful technique, I ask myself which Pavarotti technique are they referring to because, unlike other singers who often have problems acquiring one good technique, Pavarotti in his search for perfection conquered a number of techniques which he deployed with consummate ease and skill. The technique he adopted at any given time was determined by repertoire, musical style, the stage of artistic development, and age. Pavarotti did not just possess a wonderful technique but was a vocal chameleon, altering his technique and vocal colour if not for every role, then certainly for every phase of his career. It was this vocal and technical flexibility that allowed him to deliver a stream of glorious sounds throughout the scale and a seamless legato line interspersed with a flexible and malleable quality allowing him to execute a wide-ranging repertoire ranging from Aria Antiche, Mozart, Rossini, Donizetti, Bellini, Verdi, Puccini and the Verismo repertoire, culminating in an excellent Canio in *I Pagliacci*, and although not a dramatic tenor as required by the role, he still sang a creditable *Otello*. Fortunately for us most of these roles have been committed to tape, allowing us to examine his work at our leisure.

My research suggests that this achievement owes much to Pavarotti's natural talent but also his extraordinary vocal intelligence, his intense motivation to be the best he could be, and his tremendous determination to acquire an impeccable technique and superb artistry.

Bonynge confirms that Pavarotti was always striving to do better.

> We all thought that he sang marvellously from the very start but, like all real singers, Luciano was never satisfied with himself and worked to improve his singing [Bonynge in Wright, 1981: 100].

Leone Magiera confirms that Pavarotti was not only serious but also passionate about getting his singing right. He witnessed first-hand how tremendously competitive Pavarotti really was when he won the silver medal at the Achilli Peri competition in 1960. Silver was simply not good enough, the idea of being the second-best tenor did not sit well with him. He wanted the gold medal, he wanted to be the best [Magiera, 2008:34].

Pavarotti himself attests to his extraordinary appetite to keep developing. He states that,

> No matter how much success I have had, there has never been a time when I was not working on improving my singing. There is always something new to learn, a different way of controlling the breathing managing the vocal cords, attacking a phrase. You cannot think hard about a subject for forty years and not have strong ideas about it. I believe I have learned a lot and understand some of the mystery of the human voice. I would like to pass along some of this knowledge [Pavarotti, 1992: 281].

Richard Bonynge recalls that Luciano was not afraid to ask for help with respect to his singing and he knew intuitively whom to ask. Bonynge continues:

> He was never complacent, everybody thought he was marvellous from the start, but Luciano was never satisfied with himself and worked to improve his singing.
>
> 'Luciano admired Joan's technique enormously'. Every time I'd turn around, there he'd be with his hands on my wife's tummy trying to figure out how she supported her voice, how she breathed. Luciano was dead-serious about singing and worked constantly to get better. He's continued to do so throughout his career [Bonynge in Wright, 1981: 102].

As a result of this constant quest for perfection, Pavarotti's voice became more natural and therefore increasingly unique. Sutherland believes that 'Pavarotti's voice which was always very distinctive has become increasingly so over time, to the point where you could not mistake his voice for anyone else's' [Sutherland, 1981:101].

Richard Bonynge believes that Pavarotti had a great intelligence about the whole thing. He recalls that Pavarotti began his career performing all the high tenor roles which few other tenors could perform such as *La Fille du regiment*, *I Puritani*, *La Sonnambula*, *Rigoletto*, *Lucia*, *La Favorita*, and his perennial favourite *La Boheme*, but gradually moved to the more dramatic repertoire, making that transition without putting a foot wrong.

Bonynge recalls that it was a wonderful voice from the very beginning, This was 'A voice for the ages that comes along once in a century.'

The thing that most impressed Bonynge about Pavarotti was:

> His dedication, his tenacity, his humility, he was never happy with himself. Although by nature a gentle personality, he had great tenacity and willpower which drove him on his quest to master his singing [Bonynge in Wright, 1981: 101].

Sutherland and Bonynge were not the only colleagues to make-reference to Pavarotti's delightful personality. In fact, it is a common theme amongst friends and colleagues. With that type of charismatic, winning personality it was only a question of time before the public at large would discover the true Pavarotti. And this, according to his manager Herbert Breslin, occurred in 1972, the year that Pavarotti sang *La Fille du Regiment* at the Metropolitan in New York. According to Breslin his performance of the aria *'Ah mes ami'* followed by *'Pour mon ame'* created a furore, stopping the show every night.

Mayer (1986) confirms Breslin's statement and writes that Pavarotti and Sutherland performed *La Fille du Regiment* all over America including Boston, Cleveland, Atlanta, Memphis, New Orleans, Minneapolis, and Detroit, all with enormous success [Mayer, 1986:74].

According to his manager Hebert Breslin:

> It was this phenomenon that turned the attention on Pavarotti: The television and newspaper interviews and all the rest of it — the public began to learn that Luciano was also a delightful personality in his own right. The love affair between him and his public began, and it hasn't slowed down since.
>
> Many artists are loved, but with Luciano, it is something different. He projects a niceness and a lack of guile that people sense right away, and they respond strongly to it. I don't know how to explain it. Maybe it's his smile — he has a magnificent smile.
>
> His responses are always natural, unaffected, and personal — one human interacting with others. I think the public picks up on this very quickly — and they love it [Breslin in Wright, 1981: 160].

Pavarotti was a wonderfully natural human being, complete with a spicy humour and natural wit. Breslin recounts a much-told story of Pavarotti doing a televised interview with the journalist Pia Lindstrom. She was 'Ingrid Bergman's daughter and half-sister to Isabella Rosellini, with looks, befitting of her pedigree'. Pia said to Luciano, 'They say that your vocal cords were kissed by God.' To which Luciano replied, 'I think he kissed you all over' [Breslin, 1992: 69-70].

Breslin is adamant that Pavarotti's success and fame were the result of his own enormous gifts and not the product of some imagined public relations and advertising campaign. In fact, Breslin points to the fact that one medium-sized advertisement in the New York times was enough to sell out his Carnegie Hall concerts. None of his other clients came close to that kind of popularity. He contends that Pavarotti had the ability to create a phenomenon wherever he sang. Breslin declares that he had never seen an audience able to resist the Pavarotti magic, a combination of a glorious voice, great technique, and wonderful interpretation, all married to the personal charm and the sunny warmth of an Italian virtuoso. You can't achieve that with a public relations campaign, that only works when you have an authentic and exceptionally gifted artist to promote and a beloved personality that people wish to see on the cover of newspapers or magazines.

In this book I hope to make a compelling argument with respect to Pavarotti's status as the greatest Lyric tenor of the century and probably of all time.

Having said that I must emphasise that this claim is limited to the lyric repertoire and excludes all of the dramatic tenor literature. Pavarotti's excursions into the dramatic repertoire have undoubtedly yielded some excellent results. However, his depictions of these roles, often characterised by some truly beautiful singing, remains essentially lyrical. Pavarotti offers a refreshingly lyrical approach to many pages of *Il Trovatore, I Pagliacci, Aida, Chenier, Don Carlos* and *Otello,* operas that too often have been treated with bombast and a percussive approach by heavier dramatic tenors. Notwithstanding his assumption of these dramatic roles, Pavarotti's voice remains by his own admission a lyrical instrument that does not possess the ideal colour, nor the appropriate harmonic structure for the dramatic repertoire. It is true that both the richness of his harmonics as well as the great use of resonance ensures that the voice carries well over a large orchestra in a big theatre. However, the colour and shape, which became increasingly bright and often unbalanced in terms of the *chiaro/scuro,* do not conform to the requirements of the dramatic repertoire. In fact, in a reversal of the norm, Pavarotti's vocal colour and amplitude were more appropriate for the *spinto* repertoire during his middle period. For instance, when one listens to the 1972 recording of *Turandot* conducted by Zubin Mehta or the 1973 recording of *La Boheme* conducted by Von Karajan as well as his later *Luisa Miller,* and later still *Ernani,* one is amazed at the vocal colour, amplitude and focus that Pavarotti brings to these performances. In fact, there is considerable agreement amongst vocal authorities that these recordings, including *Rigoletto, L'elisir d'amore, Lucia, Ballo in Maschera, La Favorita, I Puritani* and *Maria Stuarda* are as close to perfection as we are likely to hear. Unfortunately, in his mid to late-forties, Pavarotti experienced a psychological crisis. The event was prompted by naturally occurring physiological changes that ensue in every vocal instrument in the mid to late forties. In Pavarotti, these natural physiological changes were exacerbated by two conflicting desires: the first was his desire to undertake the more dramatic repertoire, and the second was to maintain the ability to sing the very high roles of *I Puritani* and *La Fille du Regiment.* Even a cursory examination of these roles reveals that these are conflicting objectives that are fast becoming mutually exclusive. It is very difficult indeed to assume the dramatic repertoire such as *Il Trovatore, Andrea Chenier, I Pagliacci, Aida*, and *Otello* and still maintain the high *tessitura* of *I Puritani, La Fille du Regiment, Rigoletto*, and the vocal line and stylistic grace required for *La Sonnambula*.

As we saw above for the first fifteen or so years of his career Pavarotti concentrated on the lyric high sitting repertoire. Operas such as *La Boheme, Rigoletto, Lucia, La Fille du Regiment, La Sonnambula, I Puritani* and *La Favorita* were the vehicle for his extraordinary international success. He believed that in terms of his own development, *Rigoletto* and *La Sonnambula* contained a lifetime of challenges, but the role that he created a sensation with at Covent Garden was *La Fille du Regiment* in 1966, repeating that success when he sang it at La Scala with Mirella Freni, in 1969. The respected Italian critic Eugenio Gara stated:

> As far as the tenor Pavarotti is concerned, the fact that he knows what he is doing was a known, after the fine performances in *Rigoletto* and *I Capuleti e I Montecchi*, but we still hadn't seen the reason for the great enthusiasm that he stirred at the Covent Garden in London. Now it's all clear, the English were not tricked. Pavarotti truly has a rare voice in terms of timbre and range, easy and educated like few others. All those high Cs 'Nine, if we include the one in the final cadenza,' in the insidious octave jumps on the words Qual destin! Qual favor! We really don't know who else could tackle them with equal confidence and precision today. He is expressive, and what's more, colourful, clear in the words and unconventional in his gestures. If he carries on like this 'and perhaps with an eye on the scales' nobody will be able to contest his place in the first row [Gara, 1969].

In 1972 the Metropolitan Opera in New York was the next citadel to fall under a barrage of the most glorious top Cs heard in generations. The New York Times reported that Luciano Pavarotti burst into superstardom with the particularity and force of a supernova. The Times refers to the show-stopping bravos and huzzas for his Tonio in Donizetti's *La Fille du Regiment* at the Metropolitan Opera. The paper reports that the tenor was accorded twelve prolonged curtain calls. As a result of these sensational performances, he was dubbed the King of the high Cs.

In 1976 he elevated his career to an even higher level of success when he sang a phenomenal series of *I Puritani* with Joan Sutherland at the Metropolitan Opera, New York. *I Puritani* created an even greater sensation than *La Fille du Regiment*. In the same year he created another sensation in the Lirico-spinto repertoire, performing in Verdi's *Il Trovatore* in San Francisco. Sutherland was keen to point out that their success was not limited to the *bel canto* repertoire. She recalls that the first time they sang *Il Trovatore* in San Francisco and 'he was fantastic. His *Di quella pira* was unforgettable' [Sutherland, 1981: 101].

But we are getting ahead of ourselves because the Pavarotti story began many years earlier in Modena (1935). His development was not as straightforward and unimpeded as his legions of fans believe. In fact, that is one of the reasons I am writing this book as there is far too much misinformation about Pavarotti and I want to put the record straight. However, the main reason for writing this book is that we can learn so much by analysing Pavarotti's career as outlined in the following:

- Luciano Pavarotti was the greatest bel canto lyric tenor of the twentieth century (and arguably of all time). I therefore feel comfortable highlighting both his enormous natural gifts, but also sensitively pointing out some of his vocal flaws, purely for the purpose of learning.

- I have been encouraged by the fact that during his lifetime Pavarotti managed honest criticism extraordinarily well, his main interest being to obtain the knowledge required to best serve the art. How can we do less when using his name in the title of a book?

- There has never been another tenor who so consciously and so dramatically altered his vocal technique for each phase of his artistic development as did Pavarotti. Therefore, we can learn more about voice production from Pavarotti than we could from examining any other tenor past or present. Pavarotti was a vocal chameleon and the changes he rang were quite remarkable. I am not talking just about a change of colour but rather a complete change of vocal technique. We are the beneficiaries of his experiments, and a deep analysis reveals why he altered his technique and what physiological changes he made in order to achieve his technical and artistic goals. This type of analysis is designed not only to penetrate Pavarotti's mind retrospectively but also (because his voice was so natural) to simultaneously penetrate the universal mind to discover nature's design and thereby extrapolate some generalities.

- I must convince my readers that having a great voice is a wonderful gift but it is not in itself sufficient to build a really significant career. Much more is required: intelligence; a winning psychology; memory, musicality, and perseverance; a charismatic personality, and the strength of character to push through when things become difficult, as they do for everyone at some point or another.

- To realise that to be an artist is a privilege, not a right. You must take responsibility for the development of your gifts, studying with a renowned teacher and striving to attain the highest standards possible. If you devote yourself to the patient and intelligent work required to reach an appropriate international standard from the beginning, you are more likely to have a consistent and uninterrupted career.

- I hope to convince my readers that they should begin the work with the conviction that they know nothing, partly because it's true, and partly because a lack of prejudice and arrogance are the *sine qua non* for obtaining and processing new knowledge. If on the other hand, you begin with the conviction that you have already arrived, it will be very difficult for you to attain an open, enquiring, and penetrating mind, combined with the requisite humility to learn that which you must know to succeed. There is a time when you need to take charge of your career, not at the beginning of your study (when you are likely to get in your own way) but towards the end of your study.

- If you are lucky enough to be working with an excellent opera producer who has a good knowledge of history and a great sense of place, then I exhort you to listen to him or her and give full-throttled cooperation in your quest to recapture the feel and culture of that period. Please do not bring your twenty-first-century sensibilities to the work because this century has not prepared you for anything resembling the Paris of the eighteenth and early nineteenth centuries. I know it is not fashionable to make such statements as I am about to make in today's world dominated as it is by a culture of discontent, but I will do so anyway. I will tell you what I believe to be the truth and I am sure Pavarotti and Freni, Adua Veroni, and Leone Magiera and most of our heroes to be found in this work would agree with me when I say 'You have no idea how lucky you are to be living at this time of abundance, and you have no idea how horrendous life was in the Paris of the period we are discussing. So please get some help with building your character because the chances of some twenty-first-century young man or woman getting into the skin of a character such as Mimi, Violetta, Butterfly, Tosca, Medea or Norma are practically zero. The same applies to a young tenor understanding Werther, Rodolfo, Cavaradossi, or Otello. Consequently, and for the sake of the art, my advice is to get some help where possible with characterisation because your present lifestyle has not prepared you to play these wonderful, but poor and ever-suffering heroes and heroines.

- This last point is directly out of the Pavarotti playbook, and I thank him for the idea. Pavarotti's idea was that to keep our art form alive and relevant, we don't have to change it or apologise for it, or talk about how relevant it is. Opera is popular amongst the more sensitive souls of our community because it is served by glorious music, very powerful stories and excellent production values that serve both music and drama. According to Pavarotti, the only thing we need to do is to do it justice, touch people's hearts, and keep educating our audiences. They will fall in love with the art form the way we did, and that is irrespective of whether they are serious vocal students or devoted opera lovers. So what I mean to do here is to inspire people not only to love opera and singing but also to think about why they love a particular tone and beyond that to inform people's understanding of how that particular effect is been achieved. Don't just say I love that voice or that timbre, or that is a brilliant quality and that is a round and velvety quality. What I wish to do in these pages is to look beyond the superficial level and ask the big questions such as: Why is Pavarotti making this artistic or technical choice; 'How is Pavarotti achieving these effects?'; What are the critical techniques and physiologic response, necessary for achieving these affects? It isn't enough to say that this is a dull tone, and I don't like it, or this is a brilliant, ringing tone, or a round, mellow tone and I love it. You must educate yourself to understand why Pavarotti is making artistic choices, and then examine the physiological consequences of these choices of different timbres and varying quality of sound. Finally, you should be able to decipher which muscle group, set of organs, or articulators are responsible for a particular sound quality or effect. I know you think I am asking a lot of you, but I am sure Luciano would applaud the notion that we should take this kind of knowledge out of the classroom and into the public arena so that we might educate and inform people about our art form and the difference between a God-given voice and a wonderful technique acquired through blood, sweat and tears. The latter says more about the singer than the earlier. To be born with a great voice is a wonderful gift from God or the Universe but bringing that gift to fruition is much harder. It requires intelligence, creativity and perseverance. What I intend to do in this book is to establish objective criteria by which we may analyse not only Pavarotti's great work, but in essence the work of all the great artists, because whilst the personalities and vocal quality and timbre may change, the vocal paradigm, the physiology and methodology of how the instrument functions remains constant. With that in mind, let us return to the Modena of Luciano's youth; the pre-war Modena of 1935 for what I hope will be a revealing and original account of the well-loved Pavarotti Story.

In those days no-one would have imagined that in 2008 another generation of city fathers would do him the great honour of erecting a bronze statue of Pavarotti in the courtyard of the theatre. Here is the great man, as always bigger than life, in that familiar pose with chest up and out, shoulders squared, arms wide open, standing like a colossus with his enormous chest and arms inviting the audience to join him in a universal embrace. The idea that the Teatro Comunale would one day be renamed the 'Teatro Comunale Luciano Pavarotti' would not have entered his mind.

Finally, we may reiterate that Pavarotti's life was not always rosy, but he was indeed lucky to have the unconditional love of a large and generous family, including his fiancé Adua Veroni. However, long before he had won the respect of his colleagues and the love of a legion of fans, Pavarotti had learned about hardship, injustice, humiliation and war.

For too long critics and fans have extolled the natural attributes of his voice with scant regard for the intelligent and sustained hard work that contributed to his great success.

Pavarotti acknowledged his natural vocal gift and the responsibility to bring it to fruition. However, he remained adamant that perfecting his voice was a laborious process and part of a never-ending quest for artistic and technical perfection.

It should be clear that in large part the intent of this book is to demonstrate how Pavarotti overcame adversity to achieve universal admiration. He was indeed fortunate in the early years to be sustained by a community that loved opera and tenors as much as they loved soccer. This was like a healing balm to the young Pavarotti. It helped to make him resilient, capable of taking risks, and willing to accept the consequences.

Chapter 2

The Pavarotti Familiy During The War Years

Pavarotti was born in Modena, Italy, on October 12, 1935. His father Fernando, an excellent amateur tenor, earned his living as a baker but music was always close to his heart. His mother Adele worked in a cigarette factory alongside her best friend Gianna, Mirella Freni's mother. The two women were very close and their progeny, the two future opera stars Mirella and Luciano, actually shared a wet nurse.

Modena was not yet the prosperous city it has since become and the Pavarotti family were no better off than their neighbours, especially during the war years. Mirella Freni, who was destined to become one of the great divas of the twentieth century and a lifelong friend of the Pavarotti family and Luciano in particular, often referred to him as her brother and declared that:

> We were both from Modena, we were born only a few months apart. Our mothers worked side by side in the tobacco factory. From the time we were born, we grew up together. We lived through a very brutal war. Our fathers were at the war and our mothers had to take care of everything. We were poor, we didn't have much; in fact, we didn't even have enough food to go around. There is no point in denying it and no shame in stating that we were poor. But there was always a great deal of love and affection. We were always trying to help each other. It was very real, a very beautiful relationship and very healthy [Mirella Freni, personal communication].

In an interview with the journalist Candido Bonvicino, Pavarotti neither refutes nor confirms Freni's contention. He just says that he didn't know whether they were rich or poor because he had nothing to compare it to. He recalls this period as follows:

> I never thought of us as rich or poor. We always had enough. We never had a car and we didn't have a radio until after almost all other people had them. My father's little motor bike was the family transportation. I never thought about what we didn't have; I am still that way. All around me I see people making themselves unhappy with such thoughts [Pavarotti in Candido Bonvicino, 1992: 10].

However he subsequently declared that if they were poor then he was happy in his poverty. The horrendous memories that followed him for the rest of his life had nothing to do with poverty, but were rather the result of those brutal years of war when he saw many of his compatriots hung from lamp posts on the streets of Modena. Those horrendous visions never left him. Any material hardship he might have experienced was as nothing to him when compared to the vision of those lifeless bodies laying in the streets of Modena. Sixty years later with the comfort of wealth, success and fame, he would reminisce thus: 'I know what war is; I know what it is to be bombed. War is when they bomb your city not when you bomb the city of the other' [Pavarotti documentary, The Last Tenor].

He recalled vividly that in 1943 the German army marched into Modena in the Emilia Romagna region and established themselves as the dominant force. However they failed to convince the 20,000 tenacious Italian partisans of the righteousness of their cause or the permanency of their campaign. They were determined to defend their city. Over the next two years they engaged in guerrilla warfare, transforming the lives of their enemies into a nightmare. Pavarotti never forgot the interminable sound of machine guns pounding the city and its surrounding districts all night long.

The Pavarotti family managed the difficult circumstances as well as any of their neighbours. Then suddenly one evening war took a very personal turn for the Pavarotti family. As a baker Fernando was declared as an essential worker, and as such he had obtained official papers allowing him to negotiate his way through all the checkpoints of the city. In an undernourished and demoralised nation bread (being the last staple food available) was highly prized. However his protection as an essential services provider came to an abrupt end after the partisans killed five German soldiers. The Germans had decreed that for every soldier killed, ten Italians would lose their lives. Fernando was on his way home when he was arrested. However fate stepped in because the man responsible for choosing the victims recognised Fernando immediately. As a very young man he had migrated from the South and being young, and without support, Pavarotti's grandfather took him into his home and under his wing. Pavarotti continues:

> After settling near Modena, this man went on to become an important Fascist in the area. He remained grateful to my grandfather… Which was fortuitous because now he was involved in the selection of reprisal victims. As soon as he saw my father, he let him go. It was only the day after he had been arrested, but that one night had to be, for all my family, the worst time of the war [Pavarotti/Wright, 1981:10].

It is clear that World War II had left an indelible mark on Pavarotti's psyche. He remembered vividly the bombing and destruction of his city, the scarcity, the going without, the fear, the bodies in the streets, the dislocation, and in particular his father's imprisonment. In an interview with William Wright he recalled the night that his father didn't come home from work and, as the hours passed by, his entire family understood that something was very seriously wrong. They were all highly anxious but his mother in particular was in agony.

Luciano remembered that, although worried about his father, as the hours went by he was equally concerned about his mother. Adele Pavarotti was beside herself, and the young Luciano thought that his mother 'was going to die that night' [William Wright, 1981: 10].

Fortunately it was both propitious and karmic that this young refugee from the South now had the power over life and death. That he used that formidable power to repay the old man's kindness by restoring his son Fernando back to his family says much about both men. It was wonderful to have his father back and the family would be forever grateful. However Fernando could see the writing on the wall; as a result of this traumatic experience it was becoming increasingly obvious that Modena had become a very dangerous place. The young Luciano was sufficiently intelligent and sensitive to sense this danger. The fact that he had already lost track of many of his young friends (whose families had joined the throng leaving Modena in search of safer places) was sufficient evidence of the need to make a move. Many had already moved to the various small villages and farmhouses on the outskirts of Modena. Once there, they scattered all over the countryside; complete families crowded in one room, living in abject poverty, and yet giving thanks for the gift of life and being out of harms way. The Pavarotti family rented an apartment on the fringes of Modena as they had imagined that being at the margins of the city, surrounded by farms, would ensure their safety. However they were wrong as they had miscalculated the importance of Modena as an industrial centre, and therefore a significant target. Pavarotti's emotional recollections inform us that, 'The bombing got so bad that we had to leave the city. I was there, however, the first time the planes struck Modena. It was dreadful...I remember being terribly frightened' [Pavarotti in Wright, 1981:9].

As the bombing intensified Fernando made the decision that the family should leave the city altogether. It was 1943 and they moved onto a farm in the vicinity of Carpi, some 25 km from Modena. To be more precise it was a farm in a tiny village called Gargallo, just outside of Carpi. It was there that they rented a single room from one of the farmers that was meant to accomodate the whole family. In so doing they too had joined the evacuation from Modena by people seeking a safe haven, and if it meant that a whole family had to camp in one room, that was a small price to pay.

Their landlord had four sons as did the farmer next door, the latter also having two daughters. Luciano was not afraid of work and he never had problems making friends. Consequently he quickly became an integral part of what really amounted to a children's workforce. All children were expected to help and Luciano was no exception. He loved this work and like most young children was fascinated to observe how the different animals mated, gaining a most natural education. Later in life he would recall:

> 'Young as I was, I was put to work on the farmer's fields. How I loved that work! It was so free, so healthy. At the age of nine, I became a dedicated farmer. I couldn't imagine doing anything else' [Pavarotti in Wright, 1981: 10].

Notwithstanding the danger posed by the presence of the Germans, it was a good healthy life. The children received an experiential education in survival as they came face to face with the partisans who would often call in seeking food and items of clothing. The children appreciated that survival in those circumstances was not one person's responsibility, so everyone did their best to help as much as they could. Young as they were these children learned the importance of the collective, as well as the meaning and importance of fear as a component of survival. (In later life Pavarotti would say that a little bit of fear is healthy for you.) These children saw first hand how fearful the partisans were of German brutality, knowing that if they were caught it would mean a prompt and vengeful execution for all, sometimes even the children. Pavarotti declares that on many occasions the visits from the partisans and Germans almost overlapped. No sooner had the partisans left than the Germans would arrive, interrogating everyone in a forceful and intimidating manner.

Finally in 1945 the Americans liberated Reggio Emilia and were welcomed with open arms. Italy had been devastated and was still by no means a land of plenty in the post-war years. However, notwithstanding material hardship, the large Pavarotti tribe were happy in each other's company. They compensated for the lack of material abundance with an outpouring of love, and a nurturing environment, emphasising resilience and emotional security.

Many years later Pavarotti still remembered vividly the fear he felt at the sound of the warplanes flying over Modena and surrounding districts, simply because he knew that the bombs would follow. The sound of the planes, the constant artillery fire and screeching sound of the bombs created painful and enduring memories. Decades later he would recall those horrendous times when Modena was constantly bombed by enemy planes.

Years later two of his biographers, Candido Bonvicino and William Wright, both confirmed that Pavarotti became emotional as he described the bodies he saw on the streets and footpaths, not to mention those hanging from trees and lamp posts. Notwithstanding this Pavarotti considered himself very fortunate not to have witnessed the most horrendous event that occurred in the region, which was burned in the memory of every patriot in the Emilia Romagna region. It occurred in the town of Marzabotto, some 25 miles from Modena. Pavarotti recalls that on that tragic day '1830 civilians were rounded up and shot at one time' [Pavarotti in Wright, 1981: 12].

> According to Pavarotti and confirmed by Micaela Magiera, the aftermath of the war was often as horrible as the war itself. Just when all seemed at an end, civil war broke out. Different groups were fighting for supremacy and power over the carcass that

was the inheritance of World War II, and which for some came to represent the nucleus of a new world order.

Freni recalls not only the poverty of the times but also the consolation of family and friends. The Pavarotti family were a little luckier than most because Fernando, being a baker, was able to provide the family with bread and olive oil. Despite the economic hardship the family was happy and from all accounts the young Pavarotti enjoyed his childhood. His mother Adele remembered him as a very happy boy who loved football, music and friends in equal measure. Three separate events remained vivid in her memory. The first recollection was that at the age of three Luciano stood on a stool and announced that his father was a tenor and he therefore was a 'tenorino'. Similarly at the age of six he stood on the family table where he gave an enthusiastic rendition of 'La Donna e Mobile' from Rigoletto, after which he announced that one day he would be a tenor. The third incident was more onerous and placed tremendous pressure on the family's meagre budget. Luciano was playing so much football that he was wearing out a pair of shoes every two weeks. That Luciano was football crazy is beyond doubt, as demonstrated by the following story. Fernando and Adele were summoned to the headmaster's office and were informed that although Luciano was a good boy, he spent too much time playing football with his friends, neglecting his school work. Football, music and friendships remained important to him. Even after he became a really big star he would often telephone his friends in the middle of the night for a chat, completely oblivious of the time difference in their part of the world [Pavarotti in Bonvicino, 1992: 63]. Joseph Volpe, long time manager of the Metropolitan Opera, recounts a typical Pavarotti story which has been corroborated by other friends. Luciano would ring him at two o'clock in the morning with the greeting 'What are you doing Joe?' 'As a matter of fact I was asleep until you rang,' came Joe's reply, hoping in vain that Luciano would get the message and let him go back to sleep. Luciano would simply say, 'Well you are awake now,' he would say, and that was the cue for a prolonged conversation.

However, it must be said that much as he loved football, music was not only pervasive throughout his life but was also a representation of paternal attachment. In short he loved music *per se*, but when this naturally emotional medium was shared with his father it took on an extra dimension that was more than the mere act of singing. His father Fernando, a talented amateur tenor, had the record player ringing out with the voices of the great tenors all the time. Fernando was also a member of the *Corale Rossini*, a beloved institution in Modena that was established in 1887 and had achieved very high artistic standards. However it was much more than a choir: it was an artistic and musical community. Here is a vivid description of the *Corale Rossini* by the conductor and vocal coach Leone Magiera.

> As a boy Luciano, like his father, became a member of the Società Corale Gioachino Rossini, a group of opera lovers and fans of *bel canto* who would use a stop watch to measure the length of a high note or a *filatura*, then hotly discuss the results as if they were comparing sprinters on a sports field [Magiera, 2008: 13].

Like all artistic communities inhabited by passionate characters there was always an element of professional criticism which often turned into unnecessarily harsh judgments. This was the artistic environment that Luciano Pavarotti had to negotiate if he were to progress in the musical life of Modena. Subsequently he penetrated their consciousness in the most unexpected and spontaneous way. The particular event took place during the celebrations for the anniversary of the Corale Rossini. The early part of the evening saw these valiant singers devouring copious amounts of lasagna, tagliatelli, tortellini, chicken and other favourite dishes. The rivers of sparkling red lambrusco that accompanied the meal only served to inflame the already heated discussion on whether Fleta's diminuendo was better than Gigli's or whether Tamagno's *Otello* was better than that of Mario del Monaco.

The disagreements were reaching a crescendo and threatened to get out of control until someone provided a round of Parmesan cheese. This pause served to make the combatants aware that it was nearly time for each singer to compete for the singing laurels of the evening. It was already late into the night but the battle for glory was just beginning and this test of endurance would go on until dawn. Each contestant would sing their favourite party pieces, displaying their strengths and weaknesses in pieces of exaggerated romanticism, often with excessively long high notes.

Soon it was Fernando Pavarotti's turn and, although gripped by an almost pathological fear of his audience, he remained the possessor of the finest voice in the Corale.

Surrounded by friends and admirers who were already convinced of his outstanding gifts, Fernando was able to control his nerves to an unprecedented degree. His voice filled the night air with a rendition of 'Nessun Dorma' of such beauty and firmness of tone that many were reminded of the great dramatic tenor Galiano Masini. Having crowned the 'Nessun Dorma' with a truly beautiful and full-blooded top B, he was enjoying the adulation of his friends when in an uncharacteristic act of self-deprecation he mumbled:'But my son Luciano can also hit those notes' [Magiera, 2008: 15].

That was the unexpected cue for his friends to turn their attention to the young Pavarotti. Luciano had to sing 'Nessun Dorma' if only to verify his father's claims. Luciano's voice was still underdeveloped but it was fresh and clear, which served to impress everyone present.

His singing did not eclipse his father's that night but it won him a lot of admirers. The Corale Rossini directors listed him with the first tenors, giving him an opportunity to sing on special occasions such as national and international competitions, including the 1955 Llangollen Eisteddfod in Wales. In addition Maestro Bori, who was not only the conductor of the Rossini Corale but also the chorus master of the Teatro Comunale, was able to engage him for the opera chorus. This provided Pavarotti with the opportunity not only to learn a great deal of the operatic repertoire but also consistently hear some of the great singers of the day.

That the Corale achieved such a high standard was a testament to the seriousness and dedication of its members, and to its unassuming conductor Livio Bori. The whole town celebrated when the Corale won first prize at the Llangollen Eisteddfod in Wales in 1955. Adua Pavarotti confirms that Luciano and his father did a lot of work not only with the Corale Rossini but also with the chorus of the Teatro Comunale [Adua Pavarotti, 1992: 22 confirmed at a personal interview]. According to Leone Magiera, the Teatro Comunale was producing performances of a very good standard indeed, engaging all the major stars of the day. He recalls that these were Modena's golden years of opera. The Teatro Comunale, a 19th-century architectural gem, had recently reopened after the war and offered audiences the chance to hear the best voices of the time...artists of the calibre of Magda Olivero, Mario Del Monaco, Ferruccio Tagliavini, Giulietta Simionato, and Mario Filipeschi, as well as young talents such as Giuseppe Di Stefano, Renata Tebaldi, Franco Corelli, and Giuseppe Taddei. At the Corale Rossini these performances were subjected to minutely detailed and usually unforgiving critiques [Magiera, 2008: 13]

Notwithstanding the high standards attained by the Teatro Comunale, tickets for the opera were very reasonable in those days. In fact Adua Pavarotti declares that sitting in the gods of the Teatro Comunale was only a little more expensive than going to the cinema. Consequently she and Luciano frequented the opera regularly [Adua Pavarotti, private interview, confirmed in her book [1992: 23].

The Corale Rossini was a hive of activity according to Magiera, its members consisting of opera fanatics who thrived on constantly discussing the strengths and weaknesses of famous opera singers. This was the kind of intense fanaticism that led to success not only at home but also internationally.

When the Corale made a decision to compete at the Royal National Eisteddfod at Llangollen they took with them many experienced singers including Fernando Pavarotti and his son Luciano. Even so the stated objective of Livio was to achieve a top ten placing amongst the twenty-three international competitors. There was certainly no thought of winning the competition outright as it was an international competition with choirs coming from all over the world. As teams were gradually eliminated, it became clear that the Corale Rossini would finish in the top three. They would have been happy with third, and thrilled with second, but you can imagine the scene when they were announced as the winner of the first prize. Livio literally fainted and had to be revived with brandy before he could accept the prize on behalf of the choir [Adua Pavarotti, 1992: 23]. The event became a great triumph for everyone involved, but especially memorable for Pavarotti. It is important to remember that for the young Pavarotti singing was not an intellectual concept but a vigorous and emotional response that connected him not only to his boyhood but also his community, and above all to his father. Bonvicini confirms that even as a young boy Fernando Pavarotti *'would take his nine-year-old son by the hand and the two would sing vespers in the church choir'* [Bonvicini, 1992: 12]. In summary we can say that the musical life of Modena was not only pleasurable but also culturally vital, dynamic and relevant — a prized activity in the community. By the time he had reached his late teens Luciano had grown into a strapping, confident young man, definitely an eye-catching leader amongst his friends.

It was around this time that he met Adua Veroni at a social gathering arranged by a mutual friend. He was seventeen and she was sixteen. They were at school together, but they had not been part of the same circle. On this occasion, however, he sang 'Rondine al Nido' hoping to impress her, but she was none too impressed. She sang an aria from *Rigoletto* in a husky mezzo voice, which is still a characteristic quality of this lovely lady, and he understood that although intelligent, and very attractive, she needed to be rescued from herself. He approached her, and in a flirtatious manner told her that he liked her chequered dress because it reminded him of the tablecloths at the Pizzeria. She immediately saw the humour and they both burst into spontaneous and hearty laughter. At this point she enjoyed his great sense of humour more than his singing. She was also struck by the easy manner with which he stood out from the crowd. There was nothing forced or self conscious about it: it just was.

He asked her out to the pictures and she said yes, but with one caveat — her cousin had to come along as chaperone. Pavarotti accepted the terms but was none too happy with the arrangement. She discovered later that he had tried to bribe her cousin to stay away but was unsuccessful. They began to see each other regularly and seriously, and Adua contends that 'in spite of his obvious appeal Luciano was never the typical Italian lover; he was stable, serious-minded and very mature for his age.' So began a relationship that in spite of its rocky start would last for nearly forty years. According to Adua, 'In the first few months, however, it was punctuated by seemingly irreconcilable rows and separations at least three times a week, some were more serious than others and the separation lasted longer' [Adua Pavarotti, personal interview].

Adua admired the fact that, 'The Pavarotti family were as close as most Italian families of the time, and they knew they could depend on each other for help whenever they needed it' [Adua Pavarotti, 1992: 25]. They were a very big family — Fernando being one of eight brothers and sisters and Adele one of five. Their siblings lived close by with children of their own. Luciano was sustained and buoyed by these close family ties and enjoyed a marvellous relationship with all his family but particularly with his parents and his grandmother Giulia. It was she who virtually reared Luciano because Fernando and Adele were working such long hours. Years later he would recall with nostalgia these formative years. Many members of the family lived in the same apartment building in the outskirts of Modena in the region of Emilia, in north-central Italy. Their apartment building faced an open field with nothing but trees and green fields for as far as the eye could see, a wonderful environment for the rearing of young children. The Pavarotti family shared the building with 16 other families, all of them friends and relatives, including his grandmother and two aunties. They occupied a two-bedroom apartment on the first floor where they managed quite well until Luciano's sister Gabriela came along. Then it became more difficult. Gabriella slept in their parent's room, whilst Luciano slept in a fold-up bed in the kitchen [Pavarotti in Wright, 1981: 4].

His grandmother Giulia was a wonderful woman; Luciano really loved her and she adored him. Luciano believed that in part this was because Nonna Giulia had lost a daughter named Lucia, who passed away not long before he was born. Adele was complicit in the decision to name Luciano after her sister and his grandmother loved him twice as much, not just because he was a gorgeous little boy, but because he filled that horrible void in her heart that had been left by the death of her beloved daughter Lucia. Pavarotti declares that his grandmother was not an educated woman, but she was intelligent and philosophical. When confronted with a wayward husband, she didn't complain, she didn't questions it, she didn't try to prevent him from going out at night; she simply got on with it. Caring for the home as well as looking after her children and grandchildren were the pillars of her life. Pavarotti remembers his grandmother as a strong woman, someone who was highly respected. Everyone listened to her and she had the final say in most issues to do with the family, but for all that she was really well loved. Pavarotti loved her and greatly admired her intelligence and ability to hold the family together. Her husband was a charming man who was rather too fond of the good life, which may have been alright had he not been so irresponsible. Pavarotti continues:

> 'She kept the family together and in her way she was happy — a lot happier, I think, than many liberated women. My grandmother made me feel fantastic. She understood me and was always protecting me' [Pavarotti/Wright, 1981: 4].

Pavarotti recalls that from the earliest days he was engulfed by love and attention. Everyone in his apartment building spoiled him, partly because he was a very affable little boy, but mostly because he was the first boy to be born in that apartment building for ten years. However of all the people who cared for him, his grandmother Giulia held the central place in his heart. Pavarotti confessed to Bonvicini that of all the photo albums and newspaper articles, the album he loved most was that which contained his early photos, stating that 'these pictures take me back in time. These photos document my true roots. This one contains the most intimate pictures and memories of my childhood and early youth, when I was still poor and unknown. To be happy but poor is a wonderful condition' [Pavarotti, in Bonvicini, 1992: 37].

According to Pavarotti, although his artistic life was beautiful:

> It has not changed the substance of my personality and true value. If I had not been so lucky with singing, if I had not become famous, I would still have been Luciano Pavarotti. I would have had the affection of my parents, the respect of my friends, the love of my wife Adua, who married me convinced that I would become a good elementary school teacher. These are the things that matter and I never want to forget it [Pavarotti in Bonvicini, 1992: 75].

Of all these important relationships, none was closer than the one he enjoyed with his father. Their emotional connection was sealed by their mutual love for music and singing, and they built a whole routine based on this. Luciano would regularly visit the bakery where his father worked, and it was there that he learned how to roll the bread, something he valued and enjoyed immensely. After dinner father and son would walk hand in hand to church where they would sing vespers together. A few years later Luciano joined his father at the Corale Rossini and later still the chorus of the Teatro Comunale. When Fernando was not working they would listen to all the great tenors on the radio or Fernando's gramophone. Amongst the many great tenors were Caruso, Martinelli, Schipa, and Gigli, but the latter was definitely the favourite. Imagine then the excitement when at the age of twelve Fernando decided to take him to the Teatro Comunale to hear Gigli sing Edgardo in *Lucia di Lammermoor* by Donizetti, with soprano Margarita Rinaldi in the title role. The critics were unkind to Gigli, who admittedly was almost certainly a little past his prime but still a very great tenor.

Pavarotti went to the theatre and asked when Gigli was going to rehearse next, as he was determined to speak with him. He knew Gigli's remarkable voice very well because his records were played regularly on the radio. In addition Fernando Pavarotti, who believed that Gigli was without doubt the outstanding tenor of his age, played his recordings constantly on the gramophone, pointing out the finer points to his young son.

Luciano, having had the privilege of hearing Gigli in Lucia the previous night, stood outside the theatre listening in wonderment for three quarters of an hour as his hero exercised his voice. He sang loudly and softly, sostenuto and staccato, full voice and falsetto, then practised all his ornaments. A few minutes later, as Gigli was walking out of the theatre. Pavarotti approached him and announced that he too would one day become a tenor. Gigli listened to what the young boy had to say and with as much encouragement as he could muster he said: 'Bravo, bravo *ragazzino*. That is a fine ambition. But you must work hard'. Luciano promptly asked him how long he had studied, to which Gigli answered that he had only just now finished. Years later Pavarotti would recall the significance of that meeting:

> I can't tell you what an impression that made on me. He was world-famous, acknowledged by everyone to be one of the great singers of all time; yet he was still working to improve his artistry, still studying. I think about that even now, and I hope I am the same, that I will always keep the desire to become better [Pavarotti/Wright, 1981:16].

The young Pavarotti had learned a big lesson that day: it wasn't enough to have a marvellous voice, you had to work hard and use your voice intelligently.

As the years went by and Luciano's voice began to mature, he joined his father in the chorus of the Teatro Comunale. Throughout this period his father remained the greatest vocal influence on the young Luciano, but the future great tenor also had a mind of his own. His father loved Gigli and Luciano went along with him until he heard Giuseppe di Stefano on radio. He was awestruck by the beauty of that voice, the clarity of tone and diction, and the thoroughly modern way Di Stefano expressed himself. Consequently Luciano began to question the accepted wisdom: maybe Gigli had been the greatest tenor since Caruso, but this young Di Stefano had something very special. At this point, Luciano had the audacity to tell his father that he had heard a new young tenor on the radio called Di Stefano, and frankly he liked him better than Gigli. It was not just his voice; he also like his diction, his temperament and his power of expression. Fernando thought this conclusion was sacrilegious; he was furious and for the first and only time he slapped his son. However the young Pavarotti stood his ground: he liked Di Stefano better and he would not be persuade otherwise.

In addition to his singing Pavarotti played football with his friends everyday until after sundown. These were his mother's recollection about that period: 'Soccer was a passion that couldn't be controlled. He never ruled out the possibility of one day playing for Juventus, which is still his favourite team' [Bonvicini, 1992:63]. In fact for a short time he seriously considered becoming a professional footballer, but his love of singing finally reasserted itself. Whilst redoubling his efforts at the Corale Rossini and the chorus of the Teatro Comunale, he and his family were becoming painfully aware that Luciano had some important choices to make. According to Adua, Luciano had put his singing above his studies. For instance, his final exams before graduating from the *Instituto Magistrale* were due during the week when Luciano was travelling to Wales for the International competition with the Corale Rossini. He was determined to go on the trip, so he petitioned the board of examiners for permission to sit for his exams earlier. Permission having being granted, he sat all the exams in the space of three days. As Adua recalls, the rush to get finished, combined with the anticipation and sense of excitement, 'it predictably produced mediocre results' [Adua Pavarotti, 1992: 23].

This undoubtedly had an effect on his future. Nonetheless he did have other choices and three possibilities stood out. He could have become a mathematics professor or physical education teacher but both of these choices meant leaving Modena and residing in Rome for four years and three years respectively, something he was not too keen to do. Like most Italians Luciano loved his hometown — this was where his family and all his childhood friends and memories were. Also the family was not wealthy and going away to university would have two deleterious effects. The first was the strain it would place on the family's already scarce resources; the second would have deferred by a number of years the possibility of helping his family. For these reasons, the third option became increasingly attractive. He loved singing and he could keep studying with Arrigo Pola in Modena, and therefore live at home. This would give him the opportunity to work part time and help the family as long as it did not interfere with his studies.

His father advised against a singing career, as he knew how difficult it would be, and he didn't want Pavarotti to be disappointed. However his mother was of the opposite opinion. She had from all accounts a very discerning ear and believed that he had a good chance of success, having said on many occasions that his voice spoke to her, unlike that of his father. These words infuriated Fernando who still regarded himself as the major voice in the family. To prove that it was not just about her son, Signora Adele would say the same thing about Mirella Freni. 'She has a little voice but it speaks to me.' This was long before Freni was the diva she was destined to become. Pavarotti's mother was so certain that Luciano had a big future that she encouraged her son to pursue a singing career. Adele concluded the discussion by saying, 'when you sing, you voice touches me' [Adele Pavarotti in Wright, 1981: 27]. Bonvicini remembers her as a highly intelligent woman who was supremely sensitive to music and had been moved by it ever since she was a little girl. For years she could not attend any of Luciano's premieres, fearing that her nerves would overcome her. Finally she did attend the premiere of *L'Elisir d'Amore* at the Teatro Comunale in Bologna. This passed without incident [Bonvicini, 1992: 64].

Adua Pavarotti remembers this event thus:

> His mother, who has always had an excellent ear for music and instinctively good judgment for vocal technique, decided it should be singing; when he sang his voice moved her, she said. It was agreed that that his parents would continue to support him at home until he was thirty, and if he had had no real success by then he would abandon all thoughts of an operatic career and find something else to do with his life [Adua Pavarotti, 1992: 27].

Adele's argument easily carried the day. However it was well understood that if Luciano were to achieve his dreams the choice of teacher would be critical. He had been having some lessons from Maestro and Signora Dondi who were competent enough teachers. However Luciano was not only ambitious but also intelligent and he knew that if he were to thrust himself into the arena he should give himself the best chance of success. Therefore he would need the very best teaching available to him.

We will presently examine the Modenese operatic scene, but before we do that let us analyse the broader Italian environment after the Second World War.

Pavarotti — Technician and Magician

Chapter 3

The Prevailing Cultural Conditions in Italy in 1954

At the end of the Second World War, Italy was a devastated country. Bombed buildings were still in ruins, food was in short supply, money was a scarce commodity, and the elite who possessed most of the available wealth and resources were reluctant to invest. Conspicuous expenditure was frowned upon, especially when the majority of people were experiencing considerable hardship. Most people were of the opinion that there was something quite indecent about living in luxury when your neighbours were struggling to put bread on the table.

In her excellent 2019 book, *The Girl Under the Table*, Micaela Magiera provides us with a vivid recollection of the period when the Anglo-American forces, through an unprecedented show of force, broke through the Gothic line, which left the German and fascist troops with very little choice but to retreat. Soon Anglo-American tanks were travelling through the streets of Modena and other Northern Italian cities. They were flanked by partisans who had come down from the mountains in order to fill the power vacuum left by the German and fascist troops. The enthusiastic crowd celebrated the end of the war, but the fears and apprehension associated with retaliations were still fresh in everyone's mind. Micaela Magiera recalls that:

A campaign of retaliation and revenge against the losers began within days of liberation. The reaction was particularly violent, ruthless and long drawn out in Emilia Romagna, particularly in the area named 'the Triangle of Death' between Regio Emilia, Modena and Bologna. A dreadful civil war ensued, possibly worse than the horrors of the war, causing an undisclosed number of victims. The 'death squadrons' killed not only the fascists but often targeted those who were considered class enemies, an obstacle to the desired communist revolution. Very often though, personal envy and resentment lurked behind political remonstrance. The other side used equal violence in an atrocious and bloody downward spiral, which the state failed to curtail for a few years [Micaela Magiera, 2019: 41].

Magiera asserts that much of the city centre had been destroyed or damaged by bombs, food was scarce, the fields could not bear sufficient produce, and schools had been damaged, as was the Teatro Comunale [Micaela Magiera, 2019: 42].

Micaela continues:

> Modena was, like the rest of the nation, on its knees. The number of homeless and unemployed was astounding. Food was extremely scarce, and the black market was increasingly resorted to. Many factories had been damaged, and most of the fields could not bear enough food, having been fallow for so long. The recently constituted Italian Republic was faced with a considerable undertaking. Europe as a whole was in ruins after the war and was finding it difficult to recover [Micaela Magiera, 2019: 42].

There was only one commodity available in abundance, and that was a large dose of humanity. Circumstances forced people to band together for the common good in order to survive and overcome their common misery.

The wonderful thing about this was the embodied manifestation of the human spirit's resilience and the Italians' emotional strength.

Where the arts were concerned, the rebuilding of opera houses and museums was prioritised in preparation for Gala openings, which were deemed critical to restoring some sense of normality. The vocal scene was, as always, dominated by famous singers and conductors whose objective was not only to serve the composers but also to excite Italian audiences. This would create a distraction from the misery that had been visited upon them during this long war.

Modena, after the war, was as ravaged as any other city in Italy. The only difference was that the Modenese people were particularly resilient and spirited, with the capability of thinking and acting on a large scale. A wonderful description of the Modenese philosophy and spirit was written by Rocco Mastrobuono, the author of a short biography on Pavarotti simply called 'Vincero'. An excerpt is paraphrased below.

> He believed that the people of Modena knew only too well that theirs was a provincial city and that they must keep expanding their horizons, overcoming inertia and launching themselves into the world. These people understood that in life, one must learn how to sell oneself. The Modenese were not close to an ocean, and they did not have the advantage of a sweet climate and an appealing landscape. They had neither a sense of Baroque self-sufficiency nor the pomp of the two Sicilys. However, they knew how to create the myth of exporting: cars, food, floor tiles, and tenors. These people understood that the more humble you are and the more understanding you have of your place and rank in life, the more possibilities you have to expand the sphere of your potential [Mastrobuono, 2016 :14].

This is a marvellous philosophy, something as simple as playing to your competitive advantage. The unofficial motto of the citizens of Modena was (and, according to Micaela Magiera, remains) as follows:

In adversity, let's roll up our sleeves and get on with it; let's not give it too much thought. [M. Magiera, 1919: 37].

As a result, they punch way above their weight in terms of international achievement. It is a small city that produced not only Pavarotti and Freni but also the engineering feats of Ferrari, Maserati and Ducati. More recently, they produced the Trattoria Franciscana, voted by Michelin several times as the finest restaurant in the world. These are people who are used to quality in every facet of life and won't settle for mediocrity, especially in opera.

The Teatro Comunale, like all the other major theatres in Italy, had been closed during the later years of the war. To understand the importance of its restoration and opening, we must remember that opera for the Modenese was part of the essential fabric of the entire community. Modena was a city where singing was part of everyday life. It was also a place where mothers would lovingly recount the stories of famous operas to their children as a substitute for fairy tales. People would sing arias as they cycled or walked to work. The beggars in the street would play famous arias on their accordions or barrel organs. It was not unusual to hear a person, somewhat under the influence, wrapped in his cloak, singing Celeste Aida on his way home [M. Magiera, 2019:59].

It was a city where great artists were not just celebrated but also venerated.

It is true that most of the numbered seats and boxes were held tightly by many of the wealthier families of Modena, but that only made inexpensive seats in the 'gods' all the more precious. According to Micaela Magiera, on the performance day, these people would assemble before dawn to obtain the inexpensive seats up in the 'gods'. A queue would form snaking back to via Fonteraso, becoming increasingly long in direct correlation to the opening of the box office. Towards the front of the queue stood a very young Mirella Freni with her grandmother Bruna. The young girl was excited at the prospect of hearing her idols, whilst Nonna Bruna became animated at the mere recollections of her younger self. A festive atmosphere gripped the waiting throng as they enjoyed a sense of community warmth, a sense of belonging to a very special tribe. Soon the high spirits combusted into a spontaneous but well-organised street party: out would come the salami sandwiches and the bottles of Lambrusco whilst others busied themselves with starting fires in the street braziers in an effort to ward off the winter cold. They all knew each other, and although their ages varied greatly, they were all connected by their common love for opera. They would talk for hours about the art form and their favourite singers, invariably leading to heated discussions always centred around the merits of the various opera singers. The younger members, barring the odd dissenting comment, would listen in awe at the tales of legendary singers and their greatness in certain roles. Every time someone brought up a singer, everyone took sides: some would argue for their respective merits whilst others would emphasise their flaws. They passionately defended their heroes and barracked for their favourite singers in a fashion that was more reminiscent of a soccer match than an opera house.

Micaela Magiera expressed my feelings and sentiments most elegantly with respect to the beauty of this kind of society and also my lamentations at its imminent fast decline.

> It is difficult to imagine the atmosphere of the time since very little of that enthusiasm is left over. Nowadays, melodrama sparks an excited response all over the world, yet it has inexplicably become a distant, dusty memory for most Italians, though we actually fathered it, a phenomenon for a privileged elite. Possibly the urge for renewal led us to throw out our best traditions along with the bad moments [Micaela Magiera, 2019: 59].

Here Micaela is referring to the sad reality that an increasing number of Italians prefer listening to pop music and attending popular concerts. This style of music is more representative of American and English culture than their own. Consequently, we conclude that there has been a tremendous cultural transformation from the time when opera was the primary vehicle for mass Italian cultural expression to one in which it has been relegated to the Italian cultural elite.

In her excellent book published in 1992, Adua Veroni Pavarotti takes up a similar theme. She confirms Micaela Magiera's recollections and recalls that in those days, tickets to the opera were almost on a par with going to the cinema, provided that you were prepared to sit in the gods, of course. She recalls that she and Luciano attended every new production staged at the Teatro Comunale. Luciano and his father, Fernando were heavily involved with the whole music scene in Modena. They both sang in the church choir, in the Corale Rossini and in the opera chorus of the Teatro Comunale. Singing and music-making were very important in their lives. It was just as well that Luciano had a solid foundation with respect to his family and his music because he certainly had not achieved it in his relationship with Adua.

She confirmed that for a long time, their relationship was very tumultuous, characterised by frequent arguments and separations. One particularly heated argument led to a twelve-month separation. It was during this separation that she had time to think about their relationship, and young as she was, she had the wisdom to question whether she had subconsciously imbued Luciano with some of the qualities she so admired. Then she would see him during the *passata* around the Piazza Grande, and she was immediately reminded that she had not exaggerated his qualities — they were there for all the world to see. He was still very striking, vibrant and confident but not at all mannered.

The following are her impressions in her own words:

> He was charismatic and confident, the one his friends seemed automatically to look to as the leader of the pack, and during the evening passeggiata, when the population of Modena turns out to stroll around the Piazza Grand and along the arcaded streets, he always stood out from the crowd. He and some of the boys he knew liked to congregate on the corner outside the Café Molinari and watch the girls go by, but in spite of his obvious appeal Luciano was never the typical Italian lover; he was stable, serious-minded and mature for his age — 'molto uomo' (very much a man). We soon realised that we wanted our relationship to mean more than a casual flirtation, and in June 1954, we became engaged [Adua Pavarotti, 1992: 22, confirmed in personal interview].

It would appear that in this particular case, the old adage that absence makes the heart grow fonder was very true because once they were reunited, they made the decision to stay together. They saw each other all the time in and out of school. As I intimated above, Modena was still not the very prosperous centre it would become, but there were a lot of activities for youngsters, such as dancing, ice skating, going to the movies, and attending sporting events such as soccer and volleyball matches. On a summer evening, they often went for walks along the river Secchia, which weaved all the way to the Po. They would ride off on a picnic when they could borrow bicycles for the afternoon.

Modena was a very different place back then; it was not yet the vibrant, prosperous city it was destined to become, but it had a special spirit about it. The following are Adua Pavarotti's recollections of postwar Modena:

Modena was still a quiet place; people slept with their front doors open, there were no drug problems, and we were a great deal freer than the younger generation is today. We had none of their concerns about philosophical issues — ours were more fundamental and immediate because the war had made the future so uncertain- and there were not the same opportunities for spending money even if we had had it [Adua Pavarotti, 1992: 22].

These, in many respects, were Luciano and Adua's halcyon days: they were young, in love, full of dreams and hopes, and the biggest gift of all was to be poor and yet happy.

Pavarotti — Technician and Magician

Chapter 4

Italian Vocal Technique During Pavarotti's Youth and Beyond

Vocal education at the beginning of Pavarotti's career in the later fifties, sixties and beyond was dominated by famous singers who, at the end of a splendid career, turned to this noble profession ostensibly to help young singers. History testifies to a type of vocal pedagogy in which the empirical model was most prevalent. This style of pedagogy was personal, subjective and uncertain, and the fees these famous singers charged these poor souls suggested that they were more focused on helping themselves rather than the students. I hasten to add that Pavarotti was not amongst these unconscionable singers. Later in his career, when he made the decision to help some gifted young singers, he did so without fanfare and without charging a cent. He was aware of how generous the gods of song had been to him, and he was eager to give something back.

At any rate, this was about forty-five years later than the period I was referring to as Pavarotti's developmental era. As we saw above, the scene during his student days was dominated by empirical pedagogy driven by singers turned to teaching. There were two problems with that: the first was that the school was not based on objective physiological knowledge, a style of scientific teaching that was still some forty years in the future for the Italians. The second problem was that in the fifties and sixties too many of the former singers were not even teaching the traditional Italian School but were teaching their own personal method. This was as removed from the traditional Italian school as it was from vocal science. It is true that the traditional empirical school had its roots in the distant past, but the school had been founded on a reliable, systematic body of knowledge with established precepts and rules that had proven effective over the centuries.

Personal methods were a moveable feast at the discretion of the particular teacher, implying a great deal of guesswork based on trial and error and a considerable amount of imitation. In many respects it was a derivative experiential method combined with ideas generated by their own teachers in the previous generation. The advice invariably was to 'sing as I did because it is a proven method, and it took me a long way. At any rate, this is how my teacher taught me and she was legendary, so you really can't go wrong'. The application of this advice, ignoring the traditional Italian school as well as contemporary physiological and scientific knowledge, made many Italian teachers, including Arrigo Pola, rile against the personal method outlined above.

Pola was not the only major teacher to rile against these personal methods. Rachele Maragliano Mori, the doyenne of Italian singing during Pavarotti's developmental period, described the contemporary Italian scene of the fifties and sixties in her excellent book *Coscienza della Voce (1970)*. In this book, Maragliano Mori states that Italian singing teachers of the 1950s and 1960s had traditionally been reluctant to change their pedagogy. This was a reluctance that manifested itself through the neglect of new discoveries and the refusal of new scientific knowledge. Frankly, they treated many of the new discoveries with suspicion until they were convinced that they had accomplished what they said they would do. There were many reasons for this suspicion of new knowledge, but the most compelling was without doubt the fact that the traditional Italian School was still producing the world's greatest and most successful singers in the world. When you're on a winning formula, they argued, there should be no urgency or rush to change.

It did not help that many vocal scientists made exaggerated claims with respect to singing and science whilst denigrating empirical knowledge and intuitive teaching, thus fuelling resentment amongst voice practitioners. Consequently, in Italy more than most other places, the empirical system is not only highly prized but also positively cherished. Rachel Maragliano Mori asserts that 'The prevalent pedagogical paradigm dominating our century is one that is linked to its glorious past from which it cannot, and should not be separated' [Mori, 1970: 10].

In addition, Nanda Mari (1975) and Sanchez Carbone (2005), along with Antonio Juvarra, make compelling arguments for the need to differentiate and decouple the relative value of the great artist from that of the great teacher, as the two are not synonymous.

Nanda Mari (1975) adds her considerable voice to Juvarra's and suggests that:

> It is not always necessary to have had a great career in order to attain the experience that very often benefits others when we succeed in transmitting it to them. On the contrary, those who have had the good fortune of being above all nature's students have found, as a second part of good fortune, a teacher who has not been able to ruin that which nature has bestowed upon them. Often, they experience few problems, and at the very least, certainly not the problems of those who have constructed their voices with intuition and patience, overcoming the doubts and uncertainties of a technique that, although very natural, remains essentially unknowable [Mari, 1975: 16].

Sanchez Carbone affirms Nanda Mari and also makes a compelling argument that:

> Being a famous artist and esteemed interpreter is not sufficient to guarantee the required results, that is, the synthesis and transmission of the multiple and composite respiratory combinations, muscular, physical, psychological, mental and also intuitive. All these operational functions should converge not only in the intent of emitting sound but also in that of creating a resonant voice of particular beauty and power, born of optimum articulation for the purpose of making the voice the most harmonious of all instruments, simply because it is the only instrument capable of uniting text and music [Sanchez Carbone, 2005: 14].

I agree with both Nanda Mari and Sanchez Carbone that it is not necessary to be a famous singer in order to teach an excellent vocal technique capable of transforming the voice into a most harmonious instrument. Certainly, Manuel Garcia Fils, Francesco Lamperti, Giovanni Battista Lamperti, Mathilde Marchesi and even Salvatore Marchesi were not famous singers, and yet history is lavish with praise for what they accomplished as teachers. Mari makes a compelling argument when she declares that those endowed with great natural gifts who have had no major obstacles or serious difficulties to overcome are most fortunate, but they are unlikely to have attained the detailed knowledge of the instrument and the skill to transmit their method to anyone else. Truth to tell, one can only hope that fortune keeps smiling on these extraordinarily gifted singers, firstly because they are capable of giving so much pleasure to so many people, and secondly, history informs us that when something goes seriously wrong, they never quite recover, so they resort to teaching a vocal technique that they themselves had never totally conquered.

I also subscribe to Sanchez Carbone's idea that the time has come to confront the problems emerging during the process of building a voice with a body of physiological and scientific knowledge. Supported by a great majority of serious authors, Sanchez Carbone urges her colleagues to dispense with the lingering suspicions surrounding the scientific paradigm and its effectiveness and end the love affair with the legend of the great artist as a singing teacher. She exhorts her colleagues to end the prevailing chaos at both the conceptual and terminological levels by engaging with vocal science.

Having argued for more objective and scientific knowledge to be integrated into the empirical method of teaching, I am conscious that it will elevate the temperature and create enormous resistance. Pola himself, one of the more successful teachers of his generation, was sceptical where vocal science was concerned. In fact, even in the nineties, some forty years after he began teaching, Pola was still deprecating science. Here is what he had to say about it:

> I'm afraid that one day someone will pop up and say that you can teach with computers, and it's already hard enough to make a living in a world where everything is upside down. Supposedly, there are two thousand new methods of teaching. But the true teacher is still the vocalist, someone who can teach what the diaphragm is and who can shape the voice properly. You have to fully understand that the voice can neither be photographed nor written. You have to know how to listen to it, trust your intuition, and then apply singing techniques according to the authentic nature of every single voice [Pola in Bonvicini, 1992: 42].

Pola does not reserve his criticism for singing teachers and vocal scientists alone but also denounces the Italian operatic scene in general, including agents and, bureaucrats and even teachers who have accomplished nothing more than singing in the chorus. He doesn't believe that their experience is sufficient qualification to warrant them setting up a studio. Arrigo Pola seems to be equally sceptical of the developing scientific method as he is of the underqualified empirical teacher. Having said that, I feel compelled to declare that he was not the only Italian singing teacher in the 1950s to be sceptical of vocal science. Let us be completely honest: I think that science can facilitate our work, but the fact remains that most of the historical singers of renown have not been trained through the scientific method. I am thinking of Garcia, Mario De Rezske, Caruso, Pasta, Patti, Lind, Lehmann, Tetrazzini, Melba, Sutherland, Ponselle, Tebaldi, Callas, Gigli, Bjiorling, Di Stefano, Pavarotti, Domingo, Carreras, Caballe, Scotto, Freni, La Blache, Bastianini, Cotogni, Delle Sedie, De Luca, Scotti, Cappuccilli, Milnes, Bruson, Chaliapan, Ghiaurov, Christof, and this list could be extended by 500% without missing a beat. What I am saying is that vocal science can enlighten our path tremendously, and I would never underestimate its benefits, but vocal scientists need to be careful about the evaluation of their predecessors. Some of the disdain I have heard levelled at people who produced the great singers of the past without the advantages of the technology and science that we enjoy today has been nothing short of disgraceful. If you think that a little increase in knowledge can be offset against the wholesale loss of wisdom and degradation of our humanity, not only are you sadly mistaken, but you will also richly deserve the consequences of such stupidity.

Notwithstanding this type of scepticism, the merits of vocal science would not be ignored. What may not have been obvious to Pola in the 1950s and 1960s was the fact that time was on the march and change was inevitable. Today vocal science and objective knowledge are very well established and valued by most singing teachers as they can no longer ignore such knowledge if they wish to be taken seriously. Consequently, many teachers who began looking to vocal science as a sceptical exercise learned enough about its undeniable benefits in terms of describing and understanding the vocal instrument, not to mention finding solutions to vocal problems.

Over the last fifty years the proliferation of vocal science has been quite unprecedented. Consequently, we can say that contemporary singing teachers are much more open to the acceptance and utilisation of vocal science and have therefore obtained a new level of objective knowledge, resulting in a more precise, more nuanced and more refined level of teaching. Although many teachers still seem to be incapable of producing a large, ringing, exciting operatic sound, there is agreement amongst authorities that the overall standard of teaching has improved. However, the standard of elite singing has seriously declined.

Nanda Mari believes that the best singing teachers are those who combine erudition and science with a high level of intuition. That is, the kind of intuitive personality for whom teaching appears to be an improvisation involving a sense of creativity [Mari, 1975: 18].

Sanchez Carbone makes a compelling argument that a good singing teacher is of critical importance in the process of voice production, and really, we need to expand our appreciation and understanding of the complexities involved in developing the human voice. Her ideas are well thought out and well argued, so it is no wonder that they are well supported by Mori (1970), Mari (1975), Juvarra (1987), and Bruno and Paperi (2001). Sanchez Carbone extolls the virtues of fine teachers, declaring that their unique gifts and knowledge are superior and even more highly valued than those of a good singer.

Sanchez Carbone argues cogently that it is wonderful to have lovely natural voices, but they are in abundance and typically only a few are brought to fruition. Those who succeed as singers can give a great deal of pleasure. However, those who succeed as teachers can disseminate objective knowledge that influences generations, producing hundreds of lovely singers and giving much pleasure to millions of people. In short, being a great singing teacher is even more rare than being a great singer. I agree with her unless the singer in question happens to be in that rarefied league of Pavarotti, Freni, Sutherland, Callas, Corelli, or Domingo.

Sanchez Carbone prioritises the solution to physiological and psychological problems. Her particular emphasis is on the importance of individual physiology. In line with most other Italian authors, myself included, Sanchez Carbone urges the unconditional embrace of vocal science.

The Prevailing Vocal Environment In Pavarotti's Youth

I have argued in these pages that Italy was a country renowned for producing the greatest singers in the world, and it did so with the empirical system of vocal pedagogy. Consequently, the case for changing the empirical system to a more scientific paradigm has been marred by the school's own extraordinary success, as well as a fear of change and the unknown. Given the success of the Italian school, it should not come as a surprise that some teachers have resisted change. I do not advocate this resistance, but I try to understand it.

Mori has described the interactive aspects of the empirical method in a most insightful and colourful manner. She presents a portrait of the vibrant Italian scene at the juncture where empiricism meets scientific research. She refers in particular to the voice conferences arranged by scientists, which included singing teachers and other voice professionals in a beneficial exchange of information. Mori depicts these events as 'nothing less than a contest of ideas from which all singers, young and old, would gain enlightenment and encouragement' [Mori, 1970:7].

Mori continues:

> We would discuss openly and in a lively manner topics such as modes of respiration, the direction to give to resonance (the sound waves in the resonating cavity or '*impostazione*' or placement), pronunciation, articulation, as well as interpretation. These dialogues would sustain the interest of artists, teachers and amateurs alike, all of whom addressed the question of vocal technique that eventually would become the mortar that tied together the various practices of the interpreters, the teachers, and voice devotees [Mori, 1970:7].

Mori's description resonates because it informs us that singing in Italy is not just the domain of the vocal scientist and the professional singer but also that of the amateur singer, opera lover and voice devotee. It is not just about the singing. It's about the romance of singing. I really can understand why so many people remain nostalgic about the traditional Italian singing school. Too often when we speak of the Italian School we look at it through the prism of the great singing teachers and the even more famous artists they produced. We very rarely meditate on the fact that the true greatness of the Italian school was the strength it obtained through its deep communal foundation. It was all about the people who simply loved music and singing, such as the farmers whose lives were enriched and whose talents were validated by a beautiful singing voice. It was about the fruit pickers and the men and women who harvested the wheat, the olives, and the wine grapes, all of them singing as they worked side by side picking their crops. It was all about the truck drivers, the muleteers and the women in the fields, singing as they went about their work. It was all about the choral societies where, from a very young age, children were regaled with opera choruses such as *Va Pensiero,* from *Nabucco* and the *Anvil Chorus* from *Il Trovatore*. The Italians sang because they loved singing; they never thought of opera as high art because, for them, it was the people's art. In fact they thought of *Va Pensiero* as their national anthem. They sang it in the streets because they identified with the plight of the Hebrew slaves and because they loved the music and what it expressed. It was an emotional response that was elicited not only by the music but also by the real-life historical events dominating Italian life and culture. Sociologically, I would be remiss if I did not remind my reader that in a society where there are very few opportunities to differentiate yourself, a beautiful voice and a lovely demeanour can go a long way towards earning great esteem and even affection from your fellow citizens. If you were lucky enough to have the kind of graceful nature that allows you to accept compliments and laurels without it going to your head, your chances of success in that society increased tenfold. If you were a handsome young man with a beautiful voice worthy of serenading the most sought-after beauty in town, your chances of success also increased greatly.

It is also important to remember that at the time Verdi was writing his early operas such as *Nabucco* (1841), *I Lombardi* (1843), *Ernani* (1844) and *Giovanna D'Arco* (1845) and even his middle period masterpieces such as *Rigoletto* (1851), *Il Trovatore* (1852), *La Traviata* (1853), Italy as a nation existed purely as a beautiful idea. It had no substance and did not exist in any material or concrete sense. In fact, Italy was non-existent as a national entity. The many states that would eventually constitute the Italian nation were all under the yoke of foreign powers, and the Italian Risorgimento became an intoxicating idea, nurtured and given substance by the seminal and patriotic music of Giuseppe Verdi. Following the collapse of the 1848 republican revolutions, Giuseppe Mazzini created an association called 'Young Italy', which had its roots in a literary movement. Acting as a catalyst for the renewal of a national consciousness, Mazzini's movement became another motivating force towards the Risorgimento and unification of Italy. The ideals of 'Young Italy' were espoused in the writing of Benedetto Croce, whose great contribution included the philosophy known as the 'Triumph of Liberalism'.

However, not everyone adhered to their program or shared their views. The Carbonare for instance regarded 'Young Italy' as an aristocratic and bourgeois revolution that largely ignored the average Italian, resulting in a forceful backlash and opposition to the program. The Carbonare were a secret society comprising members of the nobility, membership being contingent on an elaborate initiation not too dissimilar to the one practised by the Freemasons. Their domain was mainly in central and southern Italy but particularly strong in Naples, where Ferdinand I bestowed major concessions on the movement. Their quest was of a nationalistic nature, which necessarily demanded liberation from the Austrian oppressors.

It is important to recall that the seminal force for change had its origins in the reforms introduced by Napoleon Bonaparte after his conquest of Italy at the end of the eighteenth century. Napoleon had granted the Italian people greater freedom and increased participation in the political process, as a result of which the middle class in particular grew not only in numbers but also in influence. Unfortunately, when Napoleon lost the war in 1815, these Italian states were returned to the conservative rule of the Austrians. However, having had a taste of freedom and liberalism, the Italian people were now prepared to go to great and creative lengths to oppose the oppressive Austrian regime.

Italy was eventually unified under the extraordinary statesmanship of Count Camillo Cavour and King Vittorio Emmanuelle II. However in the end it was Giuseppe Garibaldi who fought the final decisive battles which eventually unified all Italians. His victories were hard won because a number of Italian states were determined to resist unification. One might say that there were simply too many vested interests among the stakeholders.

Giuseppe Mazzini's movement 'Young Italy' continued its agitation for democracy and a Republic. Their quest ensured that the locus of political action and intrigue shifted to Turin, the capital of Piedmont. It was from Turin that in 1859 Camillo Cavour was successful in enlisting the support of the French in their effort to defeat the Austrians.

Having defeated the Austrians, they were able to unite most of Italy under Piedmont's rule in 1861. Later, in 1866, they brought Venice into the Federation and the Papal States in 1870, the latter conquest signalling the final step in the process of unification. Twenty years earlier Verdi had vividly depicted the heartbreaking lamentations of an oppressed people in the famous and moving chorus *Va Pensiero* from Nabucco. This chorus became an anthem representing the yearning and sacrifice of the Italian people to gain their own unified homeland.

This was the prevailing culture in Italy in the interwar years, and it was, to a large degree, sustained even after the Second World War.

In her excellent book *The Girl Under the Piano* (2019), Mirella Freni's daughter Micaela Magiera confirms much of her mother's nostalgia. In fact she gives a wonderful description of amateur singing in Italy being the people's art, recalling that it was not at all unusual to see people singing as they cycled or walked to their jobs. All day long, the streets of Modena rang with favourite arias that were sung, played on the accordion or ground out on a barrel organ, and even inebriated men would stagger home singing one Verdi aria or another. Thus Modena became one of many Italian cities displaying an extraordinarily vibrant musical life.

Mirella Freni, Luciano's childhood friend, is quite nostalgic about her youth in Modena. These are some of her recollections:

> I remember that it was normal for people to sing in the streets. We just sang, even when riding a bicycle in the streets or going about their work. It was an entirely different life, very different. Frankly, it didn't have much in common with life as we

know it today. There was an assured simplicity, but not only simplicity. We were also very human and very close [Mirella Freni, personal communication].

Describing an event that occurred in Lecce during this same period, the great baritone Tito Gobbi reinforces Freni's recollections. In his memorable 1979 biography, he relates a very vivid encounter with a local young tenor. Gobbi, Gigli and the soprano Maria Caniglia were in Lecce for a performance of Verdi's *Ballo in Maschera*. The performance finished late, as was often the case in those provincial cities, but one restaurant always stayed open to provide a long and relaxing supper.

> Having finished their supper, the three artists were walking back to their hotel just as dawn was breaking. Suddenly a glorious tenor voice filled the dawn sky, followed by a great vignette of Italian provincial life worth recalling. A fruit vendor, pushing his wheelbarrow filled to the brim with fresh vegetables, was singing 'Amor ti vieta' from Giordano's *La Fedora* at the top of his voice with the most glorious tenor sound. Gigli was instantly captivated and lavishly complimented the young tenor on his beautiful voice. He volunteered to arrange lessons for him if he wished to study, but the fruit vendor turned him down. He told Gigli that he was perfectly happy gracing the streets of Lecce with his voice and had no desire to complicate his life by becoming a professional opera singer. Gigli protested, saying that he had a great voice and could have a very good career. 'To what end', asked the young fruit vendor, to which Gigli responded: 'You would travel the world, and make a lot of money and be very happy'. Whilst expressing his gratitude and not at all lacking in grace, the young man unexpectedly asked Gigli whether he was happy. Somewhat taken aback, Gigli answered: 'Yes, I think I am. Yes, certainly, I think I am.' 'Signor Gigli,' came the reply, 'you think you are – I know I am. Thank you, but I will sell my vegetables.' With that, the young man pushed his barrow into the night, leaving everyone to ponder what may have been [Gobbi, 1979: 111].

There were countless such stories in post-war Italy, many of which are the stuff of legends and all of them inspirational tales, stirring the next generation of great singers, including Luciano Pavarotti and Mirella Freni.

Speaking of Gigli, Pavarotti first met him in Modena in late 1947 when Luciano was 12 years old, and the great tenor was 57, a defining moment for the young Pavarotti. His father had taken him to see *Lucia di Lammermoor* with Margherita Rinaldi as Lucia and Gigli singing Edgardo. Pavarotti enjoyed the opera and thought that Gigli was excellent but was not overawed by his performance. However when the opera was over, Gigli had the piano wheeled onto the stage and began giving his audience a spontaneous concert. We are not talking about two or three encores but about sixteen or seventeen major operatic arias. To make things even more interesting, he began taking requests from the audience. Someone would call out 'E lucevan le stelle', and Gigli would sing it. Someone else would request *'Che gelida manina'* and he would nod to his accompanist. The house erupted as he began the first notes of Nessun

Dorma, followed by 'Una furtiva lagrima,' 'Recondite armonia,' 'La donna e mobile' and so on. According to Pavarotti, it was incredible.

By the end of the night, the audience was totally conquered, and Luciano had experienced greatness in action. It is true that at the age of fifty-seven, Gigli was a little past his prime, but what remained of that wonderful voice was still glorious. In addition his generosity of spirit and his emotional connection with his audience were something to behold. Now the young Pavarotti understood why Gigli was feted everywhere as the greatest tenor of his generation. He had learned the magical art of transporting his audience into another dimension in which the firm emotional connection became an indestructible bond between the artist and his audience.

The next day, Luciano was determined to meet his hero. He went to the *Teatro Municipale* where he could hear Gigli doing his scales, alternating forte with piano singing, agility with sostenuto, the high register with the low. Pavarotti was amazed. Forty-five minutes later, when Gigli came out of the theatre, Luciano steeled himself and, with just enough courage, approached the great tenor. In an attempt to prolong the conversation Luciano announced, as he had when he was only three, that one day he too would be a tenor. Gigli took it all in his stride, actually encouraging the young boy and adding that he would be required to work hard, enduring a prolonged course of study. Luciano was not daunted by this and promptly asked Gigli how long he had studied. Gigli's reply made such an indelible impression on Luciano that he would remember it for the rest of his life. He simply said, 'I just finished five minutes ago. Didn't you hear me doing my scales?' Luciano was struck by Gigli's perseverance and constant dedication to the art, immediately connecting Gigli's unrelenting discipline with his artistic achievement. He had learned, in a two-minute conversation with the great tenor, what it takes to be prodigious. Later in life, when he was asked to espouse his philosophy for success, he gave a very simple but compelling response. He would say: 'If your opposition practises something 10 times to be good, you do it 100 times to be excellent…if they practice 100 times, you must do it 1000 times. Very simple.'

Modena may have been a pastoral regional city, with less sophisticated people than in major centres, but they were mentally sharp, hardworking and enterprising with a natural instinct for what was important in life. In short they were able to see the truth of things in an intuitive way, which more sophisticated and complicated societies could not. They understood the value of honest hard work as an indispensable component of success.

Many years later in an interview with Peter Ustinov, Pavarotti confessed that he liked the people of his region because 'they are suspicious of excessive progress'. Theirs was not a sophisticated and complicated society but one that continued to retain its wholesome simplicity with an emphasis on family, love, food, football and opera.

Artistically and technically there was a very strong connection between Pavarotti and Freni's formation as Modenese artists. They both sprang from Luigi Bertazzoni's school, studied with Campogalliani and coached with Leone Magiera. Mirelli Freni is again most eloquent when she elaborates on how interwoven their artistic journey had been. She recalls that:

> Luciano and I followed a similar course of study: Luciano's first vocal teacher was the Modenese tenor Arrigo Pola, who had been a student of my first teacher, Luigi Bertazzoni, and his young nephew Leone Magiera, who worked as a repetiteur in his uncle's school.
>
> Our friendship, which began at kindergarten, became even more intense after I married Leone, and my early success under my husband's guidance persuaded Luciano to join us in our quest for perfection. Leone advised us with respect to repertoire and prepared us musically; he even persuaded us to attend lessons for a couple of years with the prestigious teacher Maestro Campogalliani in Mantova. He was a highly respected musician and teacher with a modern concept of interpretation.
>
> We would spend entire afternoons together comparing the effect of different respiratory strategies on vocal emission and arguing over the best way to express a certain phrase. We would compare certain passages and help each other, and the experience of each would enrich the other. They were wonderful times; we were young and full of enthusiasm, and our common love of the music conditioned our attitude toward hard work [Mirella Freni, personal communication].

What I find particularly appealing about the Italian School relative to others is its richness of its humanity, its warmth, its holistic approach, and its emphasis on singing as a mode of expressing emotions. The Italians know only too well that you cannot turn back the clock and that the Italy of their youth has long since vanished. However, artists like Pavarotti still manage a more holistic expressive approach, moulding a number of intangibles into a whole that is very tangible. The other issue was one of being alive to musical emotions. Leone Magiera, Freni and Adua Veroni, Pavarotti's first wife, all spoke about the importance of expressing emotions through music and text.

With this human approach the Italians were better able to balance vocal science with historical empiricism by combining the physical with the mental, the physiological with the psychological, the intellectual with the emotional, and the profane with the divine. Above all, Italians only have to walk through the streets of Rome, Florence, Milan, Naples, and a number of other cities to be reminded that the world did not begin yesterday. The truth is that there were giants in Italy long before this present generation, and Italians are aware of the privilege of walking in their footsteps.

Chapter 5

The International Italian School and the Modenese Chapter

In order to understand the present situation in Italy and appreciate how the Italian school evolved, we need to know a little about its history. The guiding principle of the Old Italian Masters was embodied in Gaspare Pacchierotti's dictum *Chi sa respirare e pronunciare sa cantare (He who knows how to breathe and pronounce knows how to sing)*. This simple dictum would over time emerge as the most sophisticated and complete vocal paradigm known in the history of singing. In the following pages we will elaborate on this and other important principles of the old school. The model includes such elements as posture, respiration, register blending, vocal onset and release, and a deep study of articulation, resonation, and *messa di voce* and well as ornamentation. Richard Miller suggests two other organising principles of the old school, namely *Si canta come is parla* and *Raccogliere la bocca*. We will deal with these principles in more detail in later pages of this book. For now suffice to say that over time this paradigm gained such legitimacy and universality that it was transferred down from one generation to the next with more or less skill and various degrees of authenticity. Some modifications were necessary to accommodate the evolving musical styles as well as the singer's voice and temperament. In addition the increasing size of operatic theatres, rising orchestral pitch, and the constant march of emerging scientific knowledge demanded flexibility of thought, creative solutions, and where necessary modification and adaptation of technique. These are the criteria, the characteristics and principles by which we will judge Pavarotti's vocal and artistic success.

The Modenese Operatic Scene

In a city such as Modena with its rich musical tapestry there are always several teachers with the appropriate knowledge and experience to develop a young singer. However realistically only a couple of teachers had the qualifications and the track record to bring a gifted young man such as Pavarotti to fruition. Indeed this proved to be the case in 1954 Modena. The artist who stood out most by virtue of his professional success both as a singer and teacher was Luigi

Bertazzoni, a well known and highly regarded baritone in the early part of the twentieth century.

Bertazzoni had enjoyed a distinguished career, having sung with all the major artists of his generation. These included Lina Bruna Rasa, Celestina Boninsegna, Elena Rakowska, Carlo Galeffi, Titta Ruffo, Beniamino Gigli and most important of all, Enrico Caruso. By nature a Bohemian personality, Bertazzoni loved women, good food and music in equal measure. He came back to Modena in the 1940s where, after living as a *bon vivant* for a time, he decided to establish a school of singing.

According to Leone Magiera whenever the old maestro was asked to describe Caruso's voice his expression would become quite serene and dreamy:

> 'Indescribable my dear, indescribable!' he would say. 'It was velvet, yes, the velvet of that voice was indescribable...' And Bertazzoni, usually such a talkative and expansive man, would suddenly be speechless, his eyes misty with emotion. Soon however he would regain his fighting spirit. To make us forget the emotional moment he would invariably tell how Caruso had solved the problem of breathing support (every singer's nightmare and delight) by pushing exactly as you do when seated on the lavatory! [Leone Magiera, 2008: 21].

There is no denying that Bertazzoni had enjoyed an excellent career but as we argued above, it is not necessary to have had a great career as an artist in order to become a great teacher. However in Bertazzoni's case this was irrelevant because in addition to having a proven track record in producing excellent singers, he had enjoyed a great career in the theatre. Amongst his most successful students we remember Arrigo Pola who was enjoying an excellent international career at that time, and Mirella Freni who was at the beginning of what would become a legendary one. The only problem with this highly regarded teacher was that as a result of his advanced years he would sometimes be caught napping at the piano, a fact that would have weighed heavily on Pavarotti's decision.

Therefore in 1954 when Pavarotti was eighteen Fernando arranged an audition for his son with his old friend Arrigo Pola. Fernando and Arrigo had studied singing under the same teacher in their youth, Maestra Mercedes Aicardi. Whereas Fernando failed to pursue an operatic career, Arrigo Pola continued advanced studies with Bertazzoni and went on to achieve great success as a tenor of considerable stature. He sang in all the major Italian and international theatres including La Scala.

Originally Pola was studying trumpet at the Modena Conservatorium. However someone discovered that he had a fine voice and persuaded him to major in singing. In 1940 he won the Italian Opera competition alongside the great bass Cesare Siepi and the mezzo-soprano Fedora Barbieri. However when his career was ready to take flight he was drafted into the army, delaying his success. He made his debut as Mario Cavaradossi in *Tosca* at the Teatro Comunale in 1945 and returned many times over the years in various roles such as Pinkerton in *Madame Butterfly* with Mafalda Favero, Alfredo in *La Traviata* with Margherita Carosio, and the Duke in *Rigoletto* with Tito Gobbi. Other major debuts followed at the Teatro dell'Opera in Rome, La Fenice in Venice, San Carlo in Naples, the Liceu in Barcelona, the Teatro Colon in Buenos Aires, and La Monnaie in Brussels where he was much admired as des Grieux in Massenet's *Manon*.

La Scala followed in 1947 where he sang a memorable *Faust* with Renata Tebaldi. Then, in what he believed would be the thrill of his career, he was engaged to partner Maria Callas in *La Traviata* at the Teatro Regio di Parma. Unfortunately disaster followed simply because Callas and Meneghini took a dislike to him, an unfortunate fact that created a negative impact on his career. Consequently when the President of the Philippines invited him to become principal tenor for the Manila Opera as well as offering him a position on the Voice Faculty of the Conservatory, it was an offer worth considering.

The conversation took place at the reception following a performance of *La Gioconda* at the Caracalla Baths. The President so admired Pola's portrayal of Enzo Grimaldi that he was moved to bring him to Manila. After consulting his family Pola accepted. This was the beginning of the next chapter of his artistic activities which would now be mainly centred around the Philippines and Japan. In fact he had just returned from Japan where he had completed a season in which he had sung thirty-nine performances of Don Jose in *Carmen*. By the time he returned to Modena he was very tired and the last thing he wanted to do was to audition some unknown young tenor. He tried to defer it for another day but Fernando was insistent and agreed to wait until the Maestro had rested. Out of respect for his boyhood friend Pola decided to hear the young man but he had no expectations. Pola was also aware that his relationship with the Modenese public was a little ambivalent. They were proud of his success but they thought he had become arrogant. Had he refused to audition Fernando's son, it would have confirmed the already prejudiced Modenese that he was indeed an arrogant so and so. In fact the relationship between Pola and Modena was an interesting phenomenon. Leone Magiera elaborates:

> The people of Modena felt ambivalent towards Pola. They could hardly fail to admire the unique and almost angelic tone-quality of this tenor's voice in *Faust* at La Scala, or his *Traviata* with Callas at the Teatro Regio di Parma. On the other-hand his fellow citizens disliked his rather proud demeanour, which could easily be construed as arrogance. In fact, this brilliant singer put on his bravado as a means of concealing his anxiety and insecurity in the face of such eminent colleagues as Beniamino Gigli, Ferruccio Tagliavini and Giuseppe di Stefano [Magiera, 2008: 19].

At any rate and for whatever reason, Pola dismissed his tiredness and jet lag and invited the young Luciano to the piano. It didn't take long before Pola, an astute judge of voice, realised that he was in the presence of a very major talent. Magiera is again informative when he suggests that soon 'Pola's fatigue gave way to a state of excitement and euphoria' [Magiera, 2008:19].

In fact many years later Pola would recall that Luciano's voice 'was a present from God,' although he admitted to the fact that at the beginning 'his voice was a beautiful, sweet, supple sound but rather small'. However Pola had faith in his own ability to develop and enlarge the voice; he also sensed that this strapping, athletic young man was prepared to use his enormous natural gifts (voice, intelligence and willpower) to accomplish the necessary work [Bonvicini, 1992: 37].

Pola had already warned Luciano that without willpower it was all a waste of time. However, after listening to him for a few minutes, he realised that he need not have worried. He understood immediately that he was not only 'dealing with a phenomenal voice' but also with an intelligent young man who was not only serious about the craft, but also very determined to succeed. Sensing Luciano's special gifts, Arrigo Pola immediately accepted Luciano as a student. He taught him every day, and the more they worked together, the more amazed he was with Luciano's wonderful gifts, not least, his capacity for concentrated and detailed work [Pola in Bonvicini, 1992: 36].

In a 1992 interview with Bonvicini, Pola enumerated Luciano's many qualities:

> Luciano had rhythm, artistic intelligence, musical memory and perfect pitch. As a consequence of this conviction he undertook his vocal and artistic development very seriously indeed, teaching Luciano every day for three years, some Sundays included. Pola 'realised that together (they) could complete the circle' [Pola, in Bonvicini, 1992: 39-40].

Many years later, when Luciano was already a superstar, Pola would recall:

> When he came to me he was already pretty determined. I realised right away that I was dealing with a phenomenal voice. The above notwithstanding, Pola did have some reservations about his vowels and arpeggios, but in essence the voice was in very good order and there was little to rectify. 'I was able to build his technique almost from scratch. In any case, I found him a wonderful pupil. He worked hard and with great intelligence. After the voice itself, his intelligence is the most important attribute as a singer. If I would tell him something or demonstrate a way of producing a tone, he would pick it up right away... From the start, I never doubted that Luciano would one day be a very great tenor. It wasn't only the voice, it was his approach to the work — he was dedicated, mature, alert. He wasn't dabbling, he was totally serious about perfecting his voice [Pola, 1981: 39-41].

This was Pola's rationale behind his method. He explains it as follows:

> I felt it was essential that he learn very well at that age correct vocal technique — correct placement of the voice, correct breathing — which underlies all singing.

For a long time Pola and Luciano just worked on enunciation and vocalisation, to ensure good pronunciation and correct technique became automatic through repetition.

In 1981 Pavarotti confirmed that when he first started serious study with Pola, he did nothing but vocalise. He declares that for six months 'we did elaborate exercises with vowels for the purpose of opening up the jaws, making the voice bigger, and of course, making clear, exaggerated pronunciation of vowels automatic. Then we vocalised — hour after hour, day after day — not music, just scales and exercises' [Pavarotti in Wright, 1981: 29].

> Day after day I would be singing [ay], [ee], [oh], [eye], [oo]. It is not a very interesting way to spend six months, but my teacher Arrigo Pola, believed it was essential. And he convinced me. Over the years I have become even more convinced of the importance of this. Anyone who wants to be an opera singer must learn not only to manage the voice but also sing words.
>
> With my kind of music, the words carry the drama; the music is the words. If from the very beginning you learn to sing notes rather than words, you will get into trouble later [Pavarotti/Wright, 1992: 282].

Adua Pavarotti confirms this ritual. Pola worked very hard with Luciano in those days.

> Every day Pola subjected Luciano to an unrelenting routine of scales, solfeggi, breathing exercises, exercises for stretching the facial muscles, exercises to produce clear and rounded vowel sounds and above all exercises to cover the voice at the *passaggio*, ensuring a seamless transition between middle and head register [Adua Pavarotti, 1992: 28].

The Passaggio

The term *passaggio* refers to the point in an ascending scale at which the singer leaves the chest or mixed register and moves into the realm of the head voice. To achieve this, the singer must prepare his physical posture as well as his mental and breath energy, which he must combine with the flexible modification of the vocal folds in order to attain a seamless register transition. These variable vocal fold gestures are responsible for the production and blending of registers. According to Mori (1970) a thick and round vocal fold shape corresponds to the thick or heavy register, often referred to as chest register. On the other hand the thin or head register is represented by a vocal fold that is stretched, thinned and tensed by the antagonistic action between the CT and the TA. Further adduction of the vocal folds remains the responsibility of the LCA which enhances the firm adduction of the glottis. As the sound proceeds towards the high register the vocal folds undergo various alterations in posture and a constantly changing interrelationship between the thyro-arytenoid (internal tensor) and cricothyroid muscles (external tensors) which serves to increase the action of the adductor muscles such as LCA, IA, VOC. Finally in the extreme high range only the anterior portion of the folds maintains its vibrating stance whilst the posterior occluded part (posterior occlusion) remains silent and is therefore inoperative. In this part of the high range the vocal folds are not only characterised by a marked posterior occlusion, but also the disappearance of the vertical phase [Mori, 1970: 77].

To avoid any sense of antagonism at the *passaggio* between one register and another the singer must never reach the limits of that particular register but rather prepare the *passaggio* by slightly lightening the emission and mildly modifying the vowel just prior to arriving at the *nota di passaggio*. It is important to understand that the actual nota di *passaggio* varies with each individual but also with the different vowels. The singer must not become fixated on the idea that the F sharp must be his nota di *passaggio* because it may not be and even if it were it is still the *arrotondimento* of the E natural and the F before finally turning into head voice that makes all the difference.

This so called *arrotondimento* or rounding of the mouth cavity, especially the anterior portion of the resonator (also referred to as covering the vowel), protects the pharynx from the progressive but natural reduction of the pharyngeal space, which naturally occurs in an ascending passage. This type of sound is often referred to as '*voce chiusa*'. Richard Miller describes it as 'a voice that selects vowel formations that migrate towards front-vowel resonances, and avoids open, dull, vowel sounds. The resulting timbre has been subjectively described as pursuing the 'high side' rather than the 'open side' of the vowel' [Miller, 2004: 67].

It is important to recall that vocal authorities regard the *copertura* technique that is involved in negotiating the *passaggio* as critical to the seamless *passaggio* from one register to the next. There is also good agreement that the conquest of this critical *copertura* technique (covering the passaggio) is very difficult to attain. The *passaggio does not* function automatically but rather it is a mechanism that requires prolonged, difficult and patient work. According to Juvarra (1987) this covering mechanism (characterised by an artificial sensation) allows the singer to experience sensations that are generally not part of the normal consciousness of vocal emission (typically a more instinctive production). This is how Pavarotti describes this mechanism to William Wright in 1992:

> Probably the most difficult thing to learn for the beginning voice students is the importance of the *passaggio*. Everyone has two voices, the lower and upper registers. If you start singing from a low note and go up the scale, you will hear a place where

you switch from the lower to the upper register. The sound becomes different, and in order to make the transition, you switch to a different part of your throat.

The professional singer must learn to manage this transition without any sign. It must all appear to be one voice, a voice without seams. You must not let anyone hear you change gears, but rather you must learn to sing like an automatic transmission of a Cadillac. Learning to do this correctly is one of the most difficult things a young singer must do…The voice must be trained to pass from one register to the other, not as two instruments, but as one. Although the human voice is a unique musical instrument, it must be trained to be as consistent and versatile as any other musical instrument such as a violin or clarinet.

Learning to control the passaggio is very difficult and takes much time and work.… For the student, it can get very discouraging, because it is one of those things you work and work on without seeing any progress. But one day it happens, and you are the master of your passaggio [Pavarotti, 1992: 282-83].

This is as accurate a description of the *copertura* mechanism, which affects the *passaggio*, as you are likely to read. Its detail clearly demonstrates that Pavarotti has studied this particular aspect of voice production very intensely over a long period of time. He knows exactly what needs to be done and why. He speaks about its importance and its desired outcome. What he does not say is that these changes are determined by the antagonistic alterations of tensions between the vocalis and cricothyroid muscles.

We will discuss breathing, vocal onset, registration, resonation and many other techniques in the following pages. For now however it is sufficient to say that the routine was relentless and while most nineteen year olds would have buckled under the pressure Pavarotti thrived on it. He was naturally inquisitive and absolutely fascinated by vocal technique. The more demands Pola made on him, the more intrigued Pavarotti became with different vocal techniques and the effect they had on his vocal sound. In a conversation with William Wright, Pavarotti recalled that:

> This work may have been a bit tedious for any red-blooded eighteen year-old such as Luciano, but that was not Luciano's nature. Once he got really involved with singing mechanics, he really wanted to know how it works. He recalled this aspect of his study with great enthusiasm. He believed himself fortunate to be able to develop a curiosity about whatever he happened to be studying at the time. In this case of course it was singing [Adua Pavarotti, personal interview].

In an interview with Wright in 1981 Pavarotti recalled that,

> While studying with Pola, I became fascinated by the voice and how it responded to different vocal techniques. Many people find studying voice — *solfeggio*, the endless vocalising, the exercises, — very boring. I didn't. I became intrigued with the entire process. I was interested from the detached point of view of an experimenter as well as the point of view of one who stood to profit from the lessons' progress [Pavarotti in Wright, 1981: 29].

This was the kind of attitude that would not only make Pavarotti a great tenor, but also endear him to all his teachers and colleagues. It actually helped the young tenor and his teacher to forge a tremendous bond, Pola developing quite a paternalistic relationship with the young Pavarotti. Pola's reward would come in the form of an enduring gratitude and genuine affection on the part of his student. In fact in an interview with Wright in 1992 at the age of 57 Pavarotti would emphasise the importance of this particular lesson. Here are his 1992 comments:

> Pavarotti had hardly changed his stance with respect to vocalising. If anything, he now took more responsibility for the technical aspects of his singing than he had done previously. Whereas, earlier he would say my teacher convinced me, he now declared that 'over the years I have become even more convinced of the importance of vocalising on pure vowels. [Wright in 1992: 282]

By the end of his life Pola had good reason to be proud of what he and Luciano had achieved together. He worked hard to help him understand the importance of 'correct vocal technique, correct placement of the voice, and correct breathing, which underlies all singing' [Pola in Wright, 1981: 30]. Pola continues his analysis:

> Today he is the complete master of his voice. No one can fault his technique, his breathing, his pronunciation, his phrasing. It was also a big help that Luciano was born musical. [Pola in Wright, 1981: 39-41].

Chapter 6

The Three Amigos, Pavarotti, Freni and Magiera

It was around this time that Luciano Pavarotti had a rather fateful encounter, the benefits of which would persist for the rest of his life. It was 1955 and Luciano was nineteen. Leone Magiera was a child prodigy on the piano who had already graduated from the Parma Conservatorium of Music. By the time Pavarotti came to call on him he had been working as an operatic repetiteur for many years and was capable of playing a number of important operatic scores from memory. More recently he had married the soprano Mirella Freni who had been Pavarotti's 'milk sibling'.

On this particular evening the couple were preparing to watch a new television show on RAI Television (Italian National Television Network), an experimental telecast. Such programs were designed to do two things. The first was to test and stimulate the use of television for musical entertainment, an idea that was still in its infancy. The second was to discover and promote new talent by providing a platform that would eventually lead to great exposure. Although at this time there were only a couple of dozens television sets in existence in Modena, Mirella and Leone Magiera owned one of them.

Ironically they too had been invited to take part in this very program but they refused on the grounds that they were already established artists and couldn't possibly participate in an amateur television show. However that did not take into account that young artists especially are always interested in what other artists are doing. So the Magiera family settled in front of the television to watch any potential new discovery that may impact their own careers. Mirella was trying to explain her sisterly relationship to the young Luciano as he was the son of Adele Pavarotti, her mother's best friend. By this time Leone had lost interest in the whole story until the host announced that the nineteen-year old Pavarotti would sing 'Nessun Dorma' from *Turandot* by Giacomo Puccini. At this point Magiera pricked up his ears. He recalls the event as follows:

> A tenor with a very youthful, smiling face attacked the opening phrase with great aplomb. It was of course somewhat light for the piece, but it rang out as bright and clear as silver. At the point where it's melody begins its hazardous climb up the rungs of the stave, his voice, rather than straining, acquired a greater tone, reaching

59

and sustaining the last high note with effortless ease. My torpor gave way to excitement — the kind that one feels when witnessing an extraordinary event without being fully aware of it…I found it very hard to get to sleep that night. That voice, so clear and natural, had given me a rush of adrenalin that took several hours to disperse [Magiera, 2008: 23-4; confirmed in a private interview].

This was a similar reaction elicited from Arrigo Pola when he first heard Pavarotti around the same time. Since then Pola and Luciano had been working assiduously on establishing his singing technique.

As stated above, every day they would repeat the same exercises on A, E, I, O, U. He would recall that this routine was not a very interesting way to spend six months, but Pola believed it was essential [Pavarotti, 1992: 282]. Although the repetition may not have been very exciting, it seems to have been effective. Pavarotti was building a good technique, but Pola knew that the voice was only one important element of an operatic career; other necessary elements nominated were memory, musicianship, clarity of diction. In later life when Pavarotti was established as one of the greatest tenors of all time, he would say that now more than ever he was convinced that Pola had been right to emphasise those fundamental requisites so vehemently.

According to Bonvicini it was no surprise to find that after his television debut it was Luciano's mother Adele who rang Leone Magiera. She asked him whether he had seen Luciano on television, to which he replied in the affirmative. She then asked a second question, 'Would you be willing to hear him? Naturally Magiera accepted' [Bonvicini, 1992:44]. The appointment having being arranged, 'Luciano presented himself at Via Rua Muro, 68, one of the oldest and most beautiful streets in Modena's historic centre' [Magiera, 1992: 24].

When the doorbell rang, Mirella thought it prudent to absent herself from the audition; she would catch up with her old friend afterwards. Consequently, Leone was sent to open the door. He immediately found himself in front of a big, strapping, charismatic young man with a great smile on his face and two penetrating eyes that elicited an immediate familial feeling. Without preamble Pavarotti asked, 'Do you remember me?' 'Of course, I remember you; we used to play football together' answered Leone. 'You were very good'; he proffered, 'I was less so. I was too concerned about injuring one of my hands or breaking a finger. Imagine a pianist with a broken hand. Anyway, I don't think I was much of a loss to the football world'.

Both laughed uninhibitedly, then Luciano got straight to the point. Luciano made it clear that he was here for an honest assessment of his artistic prospects because he had not yet determined whether he should be an elementary school teacher or a singer. Luciano said:

Listen Magiera, I know how well esteemed you are in musical circles, and I know how much you have helped Mirella, so I want your honest opinion on whether you believe I could make a successful career as a tenor. I won't lie to you, becoming a tenor would be a dream come true for me, but I am engaged to be married and we want to have a family and I don't want to abandon myself to flights of fancy [Private Interview with Micaela Magiera, 2019].

The more he spoke, the more Magiera found himself being totally disarmed by what he referred to as 'Luciano's uninhibited and open-hearted manner' [Magiera, 2008: 24]. By the time they made their way to the piano and Luciano started to sing 'Tombe degli avi miei' from *Lucia di Lammermoor*, all preconceived ideas as to whether his voice had been enhanced by microphones for television had been dispelled. Magiera recalls:

> As I listened to the opening bars of the recitative, delivered with such clean, smooth phrasing, I realised with pleasure that his voice sounded even better live than on television. True, there was the odd musical or rhythmic inaccuracy; but wasn't this precisely why he had come to me? His performance of that difficult aria, in the original key (many tenors, even famous ones, regularly take the entire final act of Lucia a semitone lower) confirmed my impression that this was someone out of the ordinary. I expressed my admiration unreservedly, which pleased Luciano. However, I also stressed his need for more serious, in-depth musical studies. He replied enthusiastically, 'Let's start right away, I want to prepare for some singing competitions, and I don't want to miss a single day of study'. We worked strenuously for many months [Magiera, 2008:24].

It was the beginning of a very productive artistic collaboration that would in time see Freni and Pavarotti grace the great opera stages of the world, often on the same bill, with Magiera in the orchestra pit. Above all, however, it developed into a very close and beautiful friendship that was able to withstand many heated artistic arguments. The passionate discussions on vocal technique and musical interpretation would in the long run help to shape all three artists. As a repetiteur Magiera was in touch with all of the singing teachers around Modena and was therefore able to decipher not only what technique they were teaching, but also even more importantly the results they were achieving with these varying techniques. We may recall that Arrigo Pola complained about the number of teachers who developed their own method which was consequently untested. Each method was personal, and based on sensations all claiming to have been derived from empirical sources. Every teacher believed their ideas were terrific, but without an objective or scientific framework to evaluate these ideas, it was difficult to ascertain who was right and who was wrong. Consequently, many young students were ruined by the proliferation of half-baked ideas that originated with incompetent teachers.

At least our triumvirate was learning from reputable artists and teachers with proven track records. Having made her debut as Micaela in Carmen in

February 1955 Freni was already a well-established *prima donna*, sharing the stage with Elizabeth Schwarzkopf, Sesto Bruscantini, Geraint Evans, Luigi Alva and others. Magiera was also very well qualified. Having graduated *cum laudum* in his diploma as a concert pianist he then repeated the effort to achieve a similar qualification in voice and singing. As a result he was in a position to discuss in detail the various techniques and the many ideas provided by Freni. These were derived from observations and discussions with her more famous colleagues. Consequently the three of them would discuss vocal issues and argue into the night [Interview with Magiera, 2019]. The corollary to this was that in the years that followed Magiera would often be a source of fun for Luciano. It is perhaps not very well known that in the early years the only way that Pavarotti could learn his roles was with Magiera singing difficult phrases to him and often repeating the phrase several times until Pavarotti sang it correctly. In the process he would quite often crack on certain difficult notes which Luciano thought was hilarious. He would burst into spontaneous laughter, leaving Magiera to explain that he was meant to be the pianist not the singer, and even when he sang he was a baritone not a high tenor. Luciano would have none of it and would use the episode as an excuse to raid the fridge. Magiera didn't mind about the food but his elderly father who was rather an old fashioned gentleman took a dim view of the whole scenario. This was not good manners: 'You don't go to other people's houses and raid their fridge'. It just isn't done. For Leone and Luciano these events marked the early days of a relationship which either generated a great deal of laughter, or else led to heated musical arguments that nearly came to blows. It was nothing serious, only disagreements over how to attack a phrase or how to interpret a certain passage [Personal interview with Leone Magiera, 2019].

We can see from the above that Modena enjoyed a vibrant musical life which was further enlivened by certain personalities. The most colourful of these was without doubt that wonderful and by now old Bohemian Luigi Bertazzoni. That he was a *bon vivant* who loved women and music in equal measure was well known, and it must be said nobody cared very much about it. In fact it was almost expected from a personality such as Bertazzoni. Europeans in general were and remain much more realistic about these things than the English speaking world, resulting in a generally much happier people.

Certainly in Bertazzoni's case the dinner invitations to the great houses of Modena never ceased. Anyone who was anybody wanted the honour of having Bertazzoni at table. After all he was the legendary artist who had shared the stage with such luminaries as Caruso, Gigli and Ruffo. In fact his was a well-established archetype: the gifted and creative artist who almost gets away with everything short of murder as a consequence of enormous gifts, an uncommon level of charm and an affable sense of fun. Truth to tell most people didn't care about his escapades simply because he was involved with ladies not only of consequence but also of independent means. Like Bertazzoni they felt entitled and had the means to live their lives as they chose to. This attitude was exemplified by the epithet coined by a well-known Italian actress who declared that: 'It is my carriage and I alone will decide whom I wish to take for a ride'. It was clear at this time that there were many ladies who were very happy to take Bertazzoni's for a ride on their carriage. He was indeed a very gifted man.

For quite a long time he did nothing more than grace the dining rooms of the most elite homes in Modena, but at some point the invitations were less frequent so he decided to open a music school in Modena. Having enjoyed an illustrious career as artist and teacher, Bertazzoni's next foray was to enter the fray as an opera impresario.

It all began when he received a phone call from the Teatro Duse in Bologna. They wanted his student Mirella Freni to substitute for the ailing Vittoria de los Angeles as Mimi in La Boheme. At first the public, expecting an international star, were a little disappointed to be presented with a relatively inexperienced soprano but as the performance progressed they warmed to the beauty of tone, the freshness of approach and the simplicity of interpretation of this gifted young singer. By the end of the night audience members were referring to Freni as a revelation, an ideal Mimi. The next day the phone was ringing off the hook with congratulations and several new offers to sing Mimi and Micaela.

Leone and Mirella were delighted with the success, and Bertazzoni in a singular act of generosity invited them for supper at one of the better Trattorias. He immediately saw the opportunity to make some real money as an impresario, as he had an excellent Modenese cast at his disposal. Mirella was a wonderful Mimi, Arrigo Pola an excellent Rodolfo, and Gianna Gallo a lovely Musetta. Why not stage a production of La Boheme at the Teatro Comunale? The management at the Comunale embraced the proposal with great enthusiasm and rehearsals began forthwith.

On the evening of the performance there was a real buzz in the air. According to Micaela Magiera by the end of the first act the audience erupted into what seemed to be endless applause. At this point there was no reason to believe that the whole evening would be soured by an incredible act of bastardy. Micaela Magiera is once again eloquent in this matter when she recalls that at that time it was customary to pay the artists between the first and second act, after which the opera would continue to its natural conclusions. On this occasion, however:

> Everyone was waiting for Bertazzoni to show up, but he was nowhere to be seen. The orchestra and chorus were threatening not to resume the performance unless they were paid. The audience was already seated when a slight delay was announced, in the hope that Bertazzoni had simply been held up but an hour later reality set in and

it became obvious that he had disappeared with the evening's takings [Magiera, 2008: 125-6].

The audience was becoming increasingly hostile, threatening to trash the theatre. They had paid for their tickets and they expected to see the opera. However the orchestra and chorus were refusing to take their place in the pit and stage respectively. The tension was so palpable that it became evident that a riot was imminent.

In the circumstances the chief of police was obliged to step in, demanding that the opera be brought to its conclusion for the sake of public order. News of the debacle spread like wildfire within the music world. 'From that day on, Mirella refused to meet with Bertazzoni and decided to study with Leone alone' [Micaela Magiera, 2019: 126].

However the sober-minded Leone had reservations about that. Even though he had a double major in pianoforte and voice, he was disinclined to take over his wife's total vocal education. He felt she should have a more experienced and established teacher to give her the polish that she required for an international career.

Chapter 7

To Mantova and Ettore Campogalliani

For some time now Leone had been engaged as the official accompanist for a number of international singing contests, during which he noted that Ettore Campogalliani's students were winning more than their fair share of the prizes. They were very musical, very cultured and very polished, not to mention a thoroughly modern interpretation. He himself was a renowned concert pianist, but his real passion was the quest to reproduce on the piano the colour and emotional intensity of the composer's orchestration. It was not always possible to produce the exact colour of an orchestral instrument on the piano but he maintained that if you could hear the orchestration in your minds eye as you played, you were more likely to attain a closer proximity. He was an extremely cultured man who never resorted to affectation.

Leone had met the Maestro at the Conservatorium in Parma and decided to call him to discuss the possibility of Mirella joining his celebrated classes. Campogalliani was unexpectedly congenial and offered to audition her with a view to accepting her as a student.

Micaela Magiera, Freni's and Magiera's daughter, confirms that the audition went very well and Campogalliani appreciated Mirella's enormous gifts but was also specific about what needed to be done. He told her that she

> Had a rare style of phrasing, but you must give every word the right hue, every facet of the character the right colour. You must also improve your diction because your inflection from Emilia is too strong. If you follow my advice, things will surely improve enormously, you'll see [Micaela Magiera, 2018: 128].

Mirella began her lessons with Campogalliani and her progress was spectacular, so much so that a few months later he suggested that she should enter the prestigious Viotti competition in Vercelli. Mirella refused to even consider it, but Leone knew better. He arranged the entry form and sent it off without telling her until it was a *fait accompli*.

Leone and Mirella prepared most diligently in the hope that a first prize might replenish their extremely depleted personal finances. However they knew this aspiration was difficult to convert into a reality as for a number of years the judges had refused to give a first prize. They believed that the standard was insufficiently high for them to allocate a first prize. Be that as it

65

may, a few weeks later Mirella Freni won first prize, propelling her career to an altogether higher level.

When in 1957 Pola left Italy to become artistic director of the Fuiwara Opera Company, he introduced Pavarotti to Ettore Campogalliani.

With Bertazzoni out of contention and Arrigo Pola migrating to Japan, Modena lost its two best singing teachers. It therefore seemed that the time was propitious for the artistic epicentre to move from Modena to Mantova.

Pola contends that there were a number of teachers who could teach an operatic score to a young artist, but Campogalliani differed in that he really knew the voice. Although his background had been as a concert pianist with an enviable knowledge of orchestration, he was serious enough to go back to university at a mature age to qualify in voice. In an Italian system where anybody who had a reasonable career felt qualified to teach, Campogalliani took the teaching of singing very seriously. He understood in a way that most of his contemporaries did not that a little bit of knowledge could be dangerous. He was well qualified to teach singing but he lacked the finite physiological and technical knowledge required to teach it in a scientific manner, which was the trademark of his American contemporary William Vennard, Marilyn Horne's teacher and author of *Singing: The Mechanism and the Technic* (1964). Campogalliani also lacked Richard Miller's ability to combine the cumulative knowledge of the Italian Historical School with the available contemporary scientific knowledge. Even though their respective students had almost parallel careers, the method could not have been more different. Campogalliani understood this and preferred to approach the whole thing obliquely by stimulating the emotional, psychological and artistic aspects of the art rather than concentrating on the technical and physiological aspects. He achieved outstanding results, inducing the instrument to respond in a particular manner through an impulsive response based on emotional and psychological aspects of the character.

Much of Campogalliani's philosophy was based on the Stanislavski method later refined in the United States by Lee Strasberg and simply called *The Method*.

Campogalliani's philosophy could only work in the setting of a finishing school for people who possessed enormous gifts and had already established a good vocal technique, having learned the importance of physiology and hard work. Within his sphere of operation Campogalliani achieved majestic results, being very demanding of the students, not only within the confines of the studio but also in the wider artistic sense. His approach may not have been technical but it was certainly intellectual. He recommended that his students visit art galleries, attend symphonic concerts, listen to instrumental recitals, study art songs including German Lieder and French melody.

Magiera refers to Campogalliani's philosophy as one of doing nothing, allowing nature to take its course and the emotions to show you the method. Magiera refers to this as 'his idiosyncratic and very effective technique, of no technique' [Magiera, 2008: 29].

There is no denying that Campogalliani's idiosyncratic method produced some excellent results and I agree that as far as interpretation goes there is no better way to elicit certain preconceived (unconscious) responses. However there is a train of thought within vocal pedagogy which is shared by most of the great teachers and which I happen to share. This theory refers to the belief that the art of singing, or any art for that matter, has two aspects to it. The first is the attainment of a good, reliable and reproducible technique; the second is to place the technical aspects at the service of art.

I am of the opinion that a combination of physiological knowledge and technological know-how, in conjunction with psychological and emotional responses, provide the artist with a most complete and effective technique, with impressive artistic results.

Within his sphere of operation Campogalliani achieved majestic results, being very demanding of the students. Magiera refers to Campogalliani's philosophy as one of doing nothing, allowing nature to take its course and the emotions to show you the method. Magiera refers to this as 'his idiosyncratic and very effective technique, of no technique' [Magiera, 2008: 29].

The lack of objective and scientific knowledge at this time remains a real concern. For instance, even at the beginning of Pavarotti's career, Italian authors believed that the all-important technique of respiration was a voluntary act and that a good breathing technique could be acquired through physiological knowledge of the instrument. It therefore should be taught consciously and voluntarily. We also know that Pola spent many months teaching Pavarotti proper annunciation of vowels and worked on solfeggi and *vocalizzi* to integrate this knowledge with consonants. Had a more objective and physiological body of knowledge been applied, it would have undoubtedly saved Pavarotti a great deal of grief in those early but important years. In a protracted and generous interview, Adua Veroni Pavarotti was able to confirm that after his encounter with Joan Sutherland and the *appoggio* system of breath management, Luciano never had any problems with his breathing and by extension his voice again [Interview with Adua Pavarotti].

For instance, even at the beginning of Pavarotti's career, Italian authors believed that the all-important technique of respiration was a voluntary act and that a good breathing technique could be acquired through physiological knowledge of the instrument. It therefore should be taught consciously and voluntarily. We also know that Pola spent many months teaching Pavarotti proper annunciation of vowels and worked on solfeggi and *vocalizzi* to integrate this knowledge with consonants. Had a more objective and physiological body of knowledge been applied, it would undoubtedly have saved Pavarotti a great deal of grief in those early years.

With respect to this issue I refer my reader to my great predecessor, Richard Miller. As always Miller is perspicacious when he suggests:

> Obviously, with regard to time and professional commitment, it is easier for a teacher of singing to ignore the extensive body of information on vocal function and to invent an idiosyncratic system. Reading and digesting the body of available material requires more discipline than most teachers of singing can muster. Much of the insistence on 'simplicity' has its source in pedagogical laziness. It takes less ingenuity and factual information to 'coach' the singer in musical concepts than to 'build' the voice.
>
> As a rule, persons who downgrade information on the function of the vocal instrument, or who distance themselves from systematic vocal technique, consider themselves best qualified to teach the high performance level student, not the beginner. Such high-level teaching involves musical phrasing, style, ornamentation, linguistic accuracy, communication, and stage deportment... But those factors cannot be accomplished until the achievement of a unified vocal instrument makes artistic response possible. It is clear that unless the voice is able to operate as a well-functioning instrument there will be no realisation of musical or imaginative insights [Miller, 1996: 44-45].

I agree with Richard Miller wholeheartedly, but in fairness I have to say that this very important concept did not begin with him. In fact Richard Miller was following in the footsteps of luminaries such as Porpora, Garcia, Lamperti, Marchesi, Cotogni and more recently Vennard, all of whom drew the same conclusions. Nonetheless there was much to admire in the teaching of Campogalliani, not least the fact that he aimed at an organic and holistic education by asking his students to visit art galleries and attend orchestral symphonic concerts so that it was not just about vocal music. According to Magiera, Campogalliani also acted as a manager for some of his students and his advice would invariable prove to be not only correct but also astute. He seemed to have a talent for synchronicity, that is, knowing when the time was right to give a journalist a story about a rising talent in his studio or a critique of a young singer.

With respect to accompanying singers on the piano, Campogalliani would ask Magiera to play for his wife Mirella Freni as well as Luciano during their lessons. He went to great pains to teach his philosophy in order to recapture the colour and feel of the orchestration of each piece. As a result Magiera never again sat at the piano without knowing in detail the orchestration of each individual aria, a knowledge that allowed him to duplicate the mood and colour of the piece with great precision. It was this type of discipline that would eventually catapult Magiera into the realm of fine operatic conductors and without doubt Italy's leading accompanist.

Fifty years later Magiera still remembered Campogalliani with great admiration and gratitude, recollecting the following:

> He maintained that the piano accompanist, having to act as a substitute for a large orchestra, needed to produce the same tone and colour as an orchestra. He expected me, therefore, to have perfect knowledge of the instrumentation of every piece I played, and if I played an oboe solo too forcefully, or a horn solo too fast, he would reprimand me indignantly.
>
> Consequently I got into the habit of studying both the vocal and orchestral scores of the pieces Mirella and Luciano were performing. This habit has stayed with me, and I strongly recommend it to young pianists who intend to devote themselves to the art of accompaniment [Magiera, 2008: 28].

In summary, Campogalliani believed that the mood created by trying to duplicate orchestral colours combined with a deep understanding of the text and empathy for the character would automatically elicit not only the right sound but also induce correct vocal production. Consequently we can say that his whole philosophy was based on the principle of doing nothing but feeling everything. The student was supposed to just feel it, getting out of the way so that the right natural sound would emerge. This method seemed to work well enough with singers endowed with great natural gifts and a well-established technique such as Renata Tebaldi, Aldo Protti and Piero Cappuccilli.

However it did little for the likes of the young Carlo Bergonzi who relaxed his instrument to such a degree that he unconsciously emphasised the lower harmonics of his voice. This had the effect of enriching the darker tinges of his timbre to the point where both he and Campogalliani believed he was a baritone. It was only sometime later, after having debuted as a baritone, that he accidentally discovered he was a tenor, a discovery that rewarded him with one of the most illustrious careers of his generation. Certainly there were few to equal him in the Verdi repertoire. This prodigious result, however, was due to his personal tenacity rather than Campogalliani's technical skill. At this point it is important to recall Witherspoon's compelling maxim, which refutes the idea of complete relaxation:

> 'For we do nothing, physically, with complete relaxation, except die....Correct singing is not directly the result of relaxation, but of correct physical action' [Witherspoon, 1925: 16].

Singing therefore requires muscular contraction, especially the tension imposed on the respiratory muscles, which can be voluntarily controlled. This muscular tension is reflected at the level of the vocal folds in order that they not only shorten to maintain a thick and rounded posture (chest register), but also stretch, thereby lengthening, thinning and tensing the vocal folds in the process of moving into head register. This *passaggio* from chest to head voice (often referred to in the literature as thick or thin register) is determined by the interplay between the thyroarytenoid muscles and the cricothyroid muscles respectively. When the thyroarytenoid muscles dominate, the voice remains in chest register; on the other hand when the cricothyroids dominate, the voice moves into head register, with mixed voice being a more balanced adjustment between these two polarities.

In this lower or thick register the vocal folds remain thick, short, and rounded. The excursion from the midline is wider and therefore occupies a much greater length of the vocal cycle. When the vocal folds do finally meet at the midline the closure is much firmer and remains closed for a longer portion of the cycle. The opposite is true of the so-called thin register, the equivalent of the head register. In this register the vocal vibratory cycle is much shorter, meaning that there are more complete cycles per second. This is the result of a less rounded fold stretched to a greater length, creating greater tension on the much-reduced vocal fold mass. Consequently the vocal folds are apt to move rather faster than the thicker, shorter, less tense vocal fold mass employed for the lower register. That is why Bergonzi was considered a baritone, not because his natural register was baritonal but rather because he produced the voice with an unbalanced glottal setting, a setting that was rounder, shorter and thicker than usual. This was the result of an overly tense vocalis muscle (chest voice) which in turn was determined by overly relaxed cricothyroid muscles, the pull of which failed to balance the isometric tension of the vocals muscle. This vocal fold setting created an imbalance between the stretching muscles and isometric tensing of the vocalis muscle. Concomitantly Bergonzi also employed an overly relaxed breathing strategy which failed to create sufficient glottal resistance. He combined this with a lowered larynx that enriched the first formant and combined this with protruding lips, especially for the darker [o] and [u] vowels. This had the effect of lengthening the vocal tract, lowering all the formants enhancing the obscure aspects of the sound at the expense of the upper harmonics (chiaro aspects of the sound). In addition he added a pharyngeal wall that was insufficiently firm — a setting that emphasised further the lower harmonics at the expense of the higher ones. For his transformation into a Verdian tenor Bergonzi had to consistently utilise a greater level of breath pressure and an increased amount of vocal fold tension. This led to a longer, thinner and more tensed glottal adjustment which he combined with a shorter vocal tract and a much firmer setting of the pharyngeal wall.

Having said that, Campogalliani took the responsibility of guiding his students very seriously. However Pavarotti always credited Pola with the development of the individual characteristics of his voice — clarity of diction, a constantly vibrant and sonorous tone, a smooth legato and seamless register transition.

Despite the type of pedagogical environment prevalent in Italy at the time, Pavarotti did not negotiate the transition from boy wonder to *bona fide* international tenor as well as the public was led to believe in later years. The first thing to understand is that Pavarotti mentally comprehended the magnitude of the enterprise he was undertaking, and he appreciated that it would take several years to arrive at his goal. In fact he had given himself until the age of thirty to become a successful tenor. However on an emotional level he had hoped that somebody would recognise his considerable gifts after only two or three years of study. Unfortunately this did not happen. As the years passed friends were settling down and getting married which was exactly what he and Adua wished to do. There is no question therefore that the situation created a great deal of tension for Pavarotti although neither his parents nor Adua put any pressure on him. Adua in particular seems to have been a tower of strength, understanding perfectly the tensions that gripped Luciano and maintaining her unshakeable faith in his enormous gifts and personality.

I mention the circumstances only to explain that this kind of persistent and systematic pressure often promotes an emotional environment that leads to vocal problems. However these problems always have their roots in some form of technical deficiency.

It was during this time that Pavarotti started to experience some issues in the form of hoarseness during his lessons with Campogalliani and some of his coaching sessions with Magiera. According to Leone Magiera this phenomenon manifested itself only during his lessons, and was restored to its former glory within the hour of cessation. Since the problem was never exhibited in public, nobody outside the inner circle was privy to it.

However it was around this time that Luciano realised that to build a successful career you need more than talent. It is also necessary to make many intelligent decisions and surround yourself with people that you can really trust. With that in mind he began to look for a manager who could guide him along the road to a successful career. According to Magiera there were a lot of agents, but only a handful of really good ones. Amongst these were Ansalini, Barose, Finzi, and Laudino Bonardi, the latter being the most powerful agent in Milan, known to everyone as Laudino.

Mirella Freni had recently signed on with Ada Finzi (perhaps the most intellectual and refined of this group) who had been Laudino's secretary before deciding to establish her own agency. She did not want to go directly into competition with her former mentor so she decided to limit her operation to a number of prestigious festivals. These included Aix-en-Provence, Glyndebourne and the Holland Festival. Finzi was therefore the right manager for the young Mirella Freni, the latter destined to take over much of the festival repertoire from the ageing Graziella Sciutti. As Freni was very happy with Finzi she was eager to have her childhood friend join the same agency, and Finzi would have been delighted to take him on. However Luciano was not yet ready to make that commitment, as he was just becoming more aware of his possibilities and prospects. He had noted that over time his voice had developed into a substantial instrument that was better suited for lyrical grand opera repertoire such as *La Boheme, Rigoletto, La Traviata* and *Lucia* rather than Mozart and other elite works traditionally staged by opera Festivals. Consequently he concluded that the operas he was interested in and better suited for were organised by Liduino not Finzi, concluding that Liduino was a better fit for him. It is important to inform my reader that even as a young man Pavarotti thought things through very carefully, but once he made up his mind he was not easily moved from that position. He was not stubborn but he was resolute and his decision in this instance was that he should audition for Liduino.

After due consideration he asked his former teacher Arrigo Polo to arrange the audition with Liduino Bonardi. That was not as easy as it sounds because Liduino was a top impresario and was not one to waste time on any young tenor who could not make him money. Consequently Pola described Pavarotti as a tenor in command of not only the top C but also a C♯ and D natural. Pavarotti began with 'Che Gelida Manina' and according to Magiera when Luciano sang a glorious B flat on the *'Chi son'* phrase, Liduino's eyes lit up at the prospective 'tinkling of the coins'. Liduino began to think that Pola's extravagant words were well founded'[Magiera, 2008:31].

The following is Leone Magiera's recollection of the event:

> The performance continued 'ever more fluent and touching'. Suddenly, disaster: the A flat in *Talor del mio forziere* stuck in his throat, producing an unexpected and jarring false note. Pola's face went white and he gripped the arms of his chair. Liduino reacted violently: he shot up and left, slamming the door and muttering that he had no need of short tenors and time-wasters. Luciano, more shocked than humiliated, found words of comfort and encouragement from Alessandro Ziliani, a tenor famous in the first half of the century, who was soon to take over the agency [Magiera, 2008: 31].

According to Magiera (2008), Luciano took himself off to a health spa in a town near Sassuolo. The treatment proved successful because the problem occurred less frequently, disappearing completely over the next years.

In 1960 Pavarotti decided to take part in the Achilli Peri competition. He had been rehearsing his competition arias with Magiera almost daily and his problems seemed to have disappeared. During the elimination rounds his voice sounded perfect and he performed resolutely and with confidence.

From all accounts, barring any unforeseen circumstances, Pavarotti was set to win. In the final, he chose to sing '*Ah! Fuyez douce image*' from Manon by Massenet. He began the difficulty aria with great 'intensity and pathos'. The following is Leone Magiera's recollection of the event from his vantage point at the piano:

> The performance seemed to be going beautifully. We were approaching the first of the two vocal pitfalls: in both cases the melodic line finds its way up to some B flats which are difficult because of the preceding *tessitura* (of repeated Gs and A flats) and the tense and agonising drama of the song.
>
> Suddenly I noticed a chink in Luciano's vocal armour: apparently the old problem was back, at the worst possible moment, playing havoc with the first series of B flats, which sounded tight and dull. I felt icy beads of sweat running down the sides of my body, and, throwing a quick glance, I could see his distress. Nevertheless, he carried on bravely. The low, middle and passing registers did not seem to be compromised, and Luciano still had a chance to redeem himself with the repeat of the difficult phrase. But the second time, as though in a nightmare, the high register just refused to function, and the climb up to those horrifying B flats seemed as steep as a sheer rock face [Magiera, 2008: 33-34].

As a consequence of these humiliating events, first prize was awarded to the American tenor John Allen who had earlier given a convincing rendition of 'Nessun dorma'.

Magiera continues his recollection:

> Mafalda Favero went out on stage to hand out the prizes, and I realised then, from the furious expression on Luciano's face as he received his silver medal, what kind of man he was: second place was not for him [Magiera, 2008: 33-34].

Pavarotti's failure to win the Achilli Peri competition in 1960, as well his disastrous audition for Liduino, left him quite traumatised. The situation was made worse by the fact that Mirella Freni's agent, Ada Finzi (a woman of great culture and refinement who had lately been courting Luciano) suddenly went quiet. He assumed that he was seen to be not only out of work but also perceived as an inadequate tenor.

The whole affair was devastating for Luciano and he literally withdrew from society. Neither Campogalliani, Freni nor Magiera could induce him to emerge from what the latter called the 'crisis of discouragement that had gripped him' [Magiera, 2008: 35]. His disappointment was palpable. The only person he would see was his fiancée Adua.

According to Magiera all his friends did their best to support him and encourage him to return to his singing, but to no avail. Cracking on a B flat in the final of a major competition with a voice like Pavarotti's just shouldn't happen. It made him question his talent, nervous constitution and technique.

Chapter 8

Family and Friends Rally in a Crisis

Through sheer tenacity Pavarotti's friends brought him back to singing, helping to arrange a series of concerts with piano accompaniment. According to Magiera when Luciano made his come back in a provincial concert series he was supported not only by Magiera at the piano but also by Freni who insisted on sharing the stage with him. She was already a well-established singer performing in major theatres and could have supported Luciano by just being there. However she did more than that, insisting on sharing the stage with him, especially for the first concert.

Many years later Freni would recall that in a world characterised by jealousy and envy, she and Luciano had developed a mutually supportive relationship that was more akin to a relationship between siblings rather than friends. In a private communication she elaborated on their relationship:

> There was never any jealousy between us and envy was not a word in our vocabulary. In difficult moments, and there were quite a few of those, we always helped and supported each other. Luciano was a brother to me and I was a sister to him [Freni, personal communication].

This theme of familial solidarity was taken up by Freni's daughter Micaela in *La Bambina Sotto il Pianoforte* (The Girl Under the Piano).

Micaela Magiera declares that:

> The solidarity between my father and Luciano signals the birth of a particular alliance that I like to define as 'the Family Freni-Magiera-Pavarotti,' simply because the years spent at Rua de Muro refers to a period in which the particular climate of collaboration and exchange, typical of familial relationships, developed between the three protagonists. Perhaps this was one of the components that facilitated the manifestation of a quiet singular phenomenon, the birth in the same city and the same ambiance and ultimately in the same studio of two of the greatest singers of the last century.
>
> I had the good fortune to observe from very close up their preparation: I use to always play under the piano and, even though I was young, or perhaps because of it, I was very attentive and instinctively sensitive to people's character and reactions.
>
> My memories of Luciano are always as someone who was a part of the family, a type of uncle, someone with whom one shares everything.
>
> Whilst the world of the theatre abounds with jealousies, rivalries and the will to come first, in our home experiences were generously shared for the common good and in the service of future artistic perfection and success.

> My mother had begun singing before Luciano and anticipated his debut on the major international stages, alongside the most prestigious names in opera by about six years.
>
> If my mother spoke of the astonishing vocal technique of Schwarzkopf, he would respond by discussing Sutherland's breathing technique, and they tried to adapt the secrets of the greats singers to their own instrument.
>
> I remember the hours they spent on sfumature (shading of the tone), emission, breathing, cadenze, all under my father's extremely severe and rigorous guidance.
>
> We cannot deny the existence of a certain rivalry between these to singers from Modena, but it was a healthy rivalry; that small dose of emulsion which served to keep them improving; it was never hidden, but accepted in a playful manner as would happen amongst brothers.
>
> Even at that stage the notable character differences between Luciano and Mirella were in evidence. My mother, who was beginning to feel the weight of her success, was developing an immovable meticulousness in her preparation and in her lifestyle; she was like an athlete: diet, regular hours, not a hint of self-indulgence, few deviations, totally concentrated on singing.
>
> Luciano was quite different: for him studying was a sacrifice that he confronted because of his great passion and the determination to get there; nonetheless, he felt as if he were being dragged along by the iron will and discipline of his two friends; consequently, he would come to our house for a two-hour daily lesson [Micaela Magiera, 2018: 118-122].

Further, in a private interview:

> Micaela Magiera declared that Luciano loved eating excessively, loved playing football and tennis, loved women and did not deride certain types of fun. In fact, he enjoyed life in all its aspects. She wondered whether his love for life (*joie de vivre*) was the result of a youthful misadventure. She reminded me that,
>
> As a child of twelve he was miraculously resurrected from a mysterious coma which for many days had threatened to take his life. The priest was called and having given him the last rites, Luciano overheard him telling his parents that the child was ready to go off with the angels. His inexplicable recovery left him with an insatiable lust to live life to its fullest. He felt that he had been spared for some rational reason which he did not yet understand, but which brought him great joy and gave vent to his exuberance. This combination was always going to cause complications, and it did. Mirella was often reproachful, lecturing him on his intemperate conduct' [Interview with Micaela Magiera, 2019].

In these circumstances Leone became the mediating force between Mirella and Luciano. Although Leone's pedagogical style was more in line with Mirella's more disciplined and rigorous philosophy, Leone willingly allowed himself to be led astray by Luciano's pleasure-seeking personality. Nonetheless Leone used all his powers of persuasion to inculcate the notes and solfeggi into Luciano's mind. He often made him repeat certain musical phrases ad infinitum, sometimes scolding him. On rare occasions, when the work was progressing slowly and his frustrations got the better of him, Leone would roar his instructions at Luciano. It all sounded worse than it really was because at the end of the lesson they would both head for the kitchen where Luciano would extract everything edible out of the fridge and begin devouring it. Leone would soon join him but always in a more constrained way, that's who he was, but not so when it came at making fun of Arceri's students across the road. Every time a student cracked on a top note or sang out of tune, they thought it was hilarious and they couldn't helping laughing. Micaela recalls that Nonno Ubaldo was quite disturbed by this daily invasion of his home, but more importantly he was even more disturbed by his son's behaviour under Luciano's influence. Leone was normally a serious young man with a lot of poise, but now he was under the spell of this giant who ate everything he could get his hands on and led his son astray. Micaela recalls that her Nonno would often say to her, 'Be careful not to stand too close to him because he is so big and ample that if he falls, he will squash you' [Micaela Magiera, 1918: 122].

However Micaela confesses to the fact that she ignored her Nonno's advice as she'd discovered that she really liked Luciano very much and was unable to stay away from him. She had very fond memories of Luciano and her father driving her to the vineyards where they eventually bought their wine, but not before taking advantage of the wine-tasting ritual, preferably whilst consuming slices of bread and salami. Some sixty years later Micaela was still moved by those memories of a time long since passed, but that was still capable of invading her inner thoughts and dreams. She recalled that:

> Luciano had brought a playful and irreverent attitude to our family; he was the only one who could permit himself to make fun of my mother for some of her rigidities without her getting cross and I liked this sacrilegious spirit very much [Micaela Magiera personal interview and book, 2018: 122].

Following that most revealing but heart felt recollections by Micaela Magiera, let us return to Pavarotti's vocal rehabilitation. As time went by, Luciano began to emerge from his self imposed exile, and to a large degree it was his recollections of the audience's enthusiastic response that finally served to restore his faith in his own enormous gifts. It made him even more determined to win the Gold Medal at the 1961 Peri competition; he determined that this would be the year that he would begin to show the world what he could really do. It wasn't wishful thinking. He had understood that many of the vocal problems he had experienced in the past could be traced back to problems with his breathing. Whilst he was very respectful of Campogalliani's 'do nothing' philosophy he had decided that there was too much at stake and began to experiment to see how he might improve his technique. Pavarotti realised that neither he nor his teachers had been paying sufficient attention to acquiring a reliable breathing technique that could withstand the rigours of an important career.

I feel obliged to remind my reader that a singer can survive an imperfect technique as long as the voice is not placed under considerable pressure, simply because the demands made on the instrument are relatively inconsequential. It is only when you apply great pressure to the vocal instrument that the system begins to exhibit its strengths and yes, weaknesses. If it is a good technique it will hold under pressure; if not the deficiencies will be amplified. Mind you an artist who knows the difference between a tone that is *bene appoggiato* and one that is not can discern the tonal quality immediately, simply because the difference is enormous, and yet it is amazing to me that so many teachers can't recognise it. The truth is that theoretically most teachers understand the importance of breathing, but in practice very few know how to teach it. They do not comprehend how much muscular effort and energy is required to properly execute respiration. They do not understand that it takes time to strengthen and conquer the muscle tonus that eventually leads to a balanced appoggio.

They don't understand that in the process of finding a balance you may over do things and create temporary tension in the throat, or you may under do it and let the larynx do all the work but that is not the last word. I personally prefer a pupil who takes time to develop a balanced breathing technique, but given that we live in an age where everything is expected to happen yesterday, then my second preference is someone who is prepared to run with the bulls. Simply because it is easier to ask a student to pull it back a little than it is to ask for an increase in pressure.

This leads me to a citation by one of the leading critics of the nineteenth century and incidentally a long time Garcia student, Hermann Klein.

I am now going to give you three quotes that will give you an idea of the importance of breathing. The first comes from Hermann Klein who studied with Garcia. He contends that breathing is of such import that if you can't teach it but still profess to teach singing, you are nothing more than a charlatan. The second comes from Bernard Shaw who informs us that singing is one of the most vigorous physical activities that man can accomplish. The third is from Witherspoon who declares 'that the only thing we do in life without effort is to die'.

Therefore if you can't teach breathing, swallow your pride and admit that you don't know as much as you thought you did. Learn something from your betters or leave the field to people who can deliver the goods. Too many teachers in the twenty-first century are contributing to mediocrity, unfortunately a statement that is no longer politically correct. The consequences of this dumbing down of our scholarly, intellectual and artistic life will at some point come home to roost. At this point one becomes nostalgic for the good old days when Hermann Klein could openly say if you can't teach breathing and you persevere with teaching singing, you are nothing more than a charlatan. I also like Ceasare's 1936 contention that there are over two thousand singing teachers in Milan and two thousand of them are assassins. In 1987 Antonio Juvarra was sufficiently moved to call many of his colleagues charlatans; a similar conclusion was drawn by Professore Acceri in the forward to Maria Sanchez Carbone's book in 2005. We can't do that in the English speaking world because it has become so sanitised that we can no longer speak the truth to each other, but that does not mean that we don't have our share of charlatans.

More importantly it goes to credibility, would you really believe someone who tells you what you want to hear all the time (Ask King Lear how well it worked out for him), or would you rather listen to someone who tells you the uncomfortable truth so that you can plan and develop your career on objective knowledge?

Let us return to Pavarotti's development.

In a private interview Leone Magiera confided that over a period of time Pavarotti became convinced that the Old Italian masters were right when they proposed that, 'The art of singing is the art of breathing'. He was sufficiently intuitive to know that he had not conquered this most important element of singing. Consequently he began on a quest to overcome this deficiency.

He discovered that if he actively used the breathing muscles to squeeze out as much breath as possible at the end of a phrase preceding the climax to an aria, he would then automatically take a deeper breath in preparation for the climax. This technique would ensure an abundance of *appoggio* for the difficult top C of '*La Speranza*', the climax to the tenor aria in La Boheme. The supported tone possessed a more natural and penetrating ring and was altogether more voluminous and more consistently opulent [Leone Magiera, private interview].

Many years later in 'My Own Story' (the first of two books written in collaboration with William Wright) Pavarotti points to the problems associated with the teaching of singing. The first is that there are as many theories as there are teachers. Having said that Pavarotti continues:

> Beyond that, each voice is a little different-like a signature or a fingerprint-and presents the teacher with special problems. But some things are fundamental to all voices. First among the basics is the support and the breathing. I knew this in theory for many years but I didn't master it or learn how essential it was to an important career of constant singing until I made the tour of Australia with Joan Sutherland in 1965... The support from a strong torso is so important because it takes the strain from the vocal cords, which are small sensitive membranes, and distributes it to the diaphragm, which is a large muscle development and, if you develop it

> correctly, a strong one. If you support the voice correctly from below, you can sing far longer-in one evening and in one life-without signs of strain…
>
> The sound comes from the stomach area — the lungs, really — and not from the throat. It is so simple and so true, yet how many singers forget this. You must work and exercise until there is a natural reflex of support from the diaphragm [Pavarotti/in Wright, 1981: 129].

Pavarotti also reminds us that the physical attributes of a singer are very important. As he puts it, it is unlikely that a really important voice would come out of a tiny body.

He talks about Joan Sutherland and Franco Corelli as two singers who have the physique to support their talent. Here are his ideas on Joan Sutherland:

> For me, Joan Sutherland is a dream singer because she has such a strong build. She has a large body, and it is well-distributed and well-constructed. Another singer who has the physical requirement is Franco Corelli. He is not skinny, but a full-sized man. These two people possess incredible voices and incredible diaphragms for support. A violin can't be a little tiny thing and produce a great sound. Important voices usually go with the important body [Pavarotti/Wright, 1981: 129].

We know that Pola appreciated the physiological aspects of singing. However he also left us in no doubt that Pavarotti had the intelligence, the musicality, the memory, the determination and the temperament to become a great artist. Let us address each of these in more detail, beginning with intelligence.

We recall that Pola himself declared that after the voice itself, which he described as phenomenal, Pavarotti's greatest gift was his intelligence. Pola was again in the mainstream of singing opinion because most Italian teachers of standing over the last fifty years agree with the need to combine an excellent voice with a high level of intelligence.

Mori (1970), Mari (1975), Juvarra (1987), and Fussi and Magnani (1994) all agree with the proposition that apart from the student's voice, he/she needs the intelligence to combine the teacher's wisdom and educated ear into a synergistic and cohesive whole. In addition they all agree that it is no longer sustainable for Italian vocal pedagogy to remain anchored solely in the empiricism of the past. These are propositions with which I fully concur. However I am also conscious of the fact that some of the physiological and scientific knowledge may be more difficult to implement but this should not deter us from proceeding towards this pedagogical objective. Vocal pedagogy needs to move towards a more objective, physiological and scientific method.

As far back as 1970 Rachelle Marigliano Mori highlights the issues of intelligence and concentration, as well as mental agility and acuity, by placing them at the forefront of her vocal pedagogy. Mori believes that:

Singers who do not exercise their intelligence or make an extra effort to acquire a gradual and deeper understanding of how the instrument works, will invariably lack the concentration required for the deep study of music, voice or singing. A successful study of these elements demands great mental agility as well as the ability to reflect logically and to apply oneself intelligently to daily practice. This regimen should establish the conditioned reflex responsible for the development of the voice in both the physical and artistic aspects [Mori, 1970: 8].

Rachelle Maragliano Mori (1970), Nanda Mari (1975), and Sanchez Carbone (2005) all agree that it is wonderful to have a voice, but unless that voice is accompanied by a high level of intelligence, mental agility, and great determination the student is destined to make little progress. Mari specifically declares that: 'Voice, Voice and Voice is all very well, but a voice without intelligence will be nothing more than noise either pleasant or unpleasant, depending on the case in point' [Mari, 1975: 26].

Maria Sanchez Carbone joins her predecessors when she denotes physical and mental agility combined with flexibility as critical elements of successful vocal pedagogy [Sanchez Carbone, 2005: 15].

It is clear from the above that there has been a collective realisation that a naturally beautiful voice is insufficient to guarantee success in the present cultural climate and that musicality, intelligence and mental dexterity are indispensable to the art of singing.

These are conclusions that most teachers would agree with. However I would be remiss if I did not add my voice to my illustrious colleagues. I believe that there is no substitute for a combination of intelligence, application, deep and protracted concentration on the work, and a healthy dose of arrogance and humility. This may appear like a paradox but in fact it is not. You need to have some arrogance because you need to know you are a good artist, but you need to remain sufficiently humble to keep learning.

Chapter 9

The Sostegno System of Breath Management

Pola understood the importance of working assiduously on Pavarotti's vowels, vocalizzi, breathing and diction. In her excellent book (1992) Adua Veroni Pavarotti recalls that 'Pola subjected Luciano to an unrelenting routine of scales, solfeggi and breathing exercises' [Adua Pavarotti, 1992: 22].

The second element they worked on was respiration. Pola taught him the *sostegno* technique because that was the system he himself had been taught by Bertazzone and utilised throughout his very considerable career. Let us examine the strengths and weaknesses of the *sostegno* system (often referred to as the up and in system) of breath management.

Respiration

The second element designated by Pola as being critical to voice production is breathing technique, the foundation of all singing. I concur and would add that if a singer does not work diligently to acquire an excellent and reliable breathing strategy, he/she is destined to be forever second rate, no matter the natural merits of the voice, or even the good work achieved on interpretation and diction. The truth is that nothing can be well executed without an unshakable control over the respiratory musculature which takes years to master. There is wide agreement that the art of singing consists of two broad aspects with many subdivisions supporting each of these. The two aspects of which I speak are the conquest of the technical elements, followed by the development of artistic creativity.

The Garcias, Lampertis, Marchesis, Vennard, Miller and other giants of our art and industry are all in accord with the notion that there can be no vocal art without first achieving a solid and reliable technique, of which breathing is the foundation. The perceptive teacher can hear, and through hearing visualise the physiological function. However they cannot materially manifest it because the singer's vocal technique is too limited.

I believe that you must first accept that the whole vocal system is an interwoven system of cartilage, ligaments and muscles which one must learn to control before one can manage the breath.

Consequently my own position with respect to breath management mirrors the Louis Mandl and Francesco Lamperti system of *appoggio* based on the *lotta vocale* (vocal struggle), also advocated by Hermann Klein, William Shakespeare, and Jean de Reszke. In his excellent book *The Structure of Singing* (1996) Richard Miller expressed my sentiments perfectly when he declared: 'Most vocal problems can be traced back to an inefficient respiratory strategy' [Miller, 1986:24]. This is a proposition with which I strongly agree.

In this book we will elaborate on the various breathing strategies available to singers, with particular emphasis on the old school *sostegno* and later the more scientific strategy of *appoggio*. Since Pavarotti had not at this stage been introduced to *appoggio*, we will proceed to study the *sostegno* system first, the method he was using in the early stages of his development and for a number of years afterwards.

Arrigo Pola's Method of Respiration

Pola argues correctly that respiration is the vocal element that forms the foundation of good singing. In practice he seems to have been less sanguine about breathing than he was about *articulations, resonation, copertura* and the *passaggio*. To the degree that he did speak about breathing, his technique was based on the *sostegno* (up and in, or pear shaped up) system of breath management rather than the *appoggio* system (down and out or pear shaped down).

In a private conversation Leone Magiera confessed that in the early years Pavarotti did not discuss breathing very much at all. To the extent that he did, it was in the context of the *sostegno system,* an 'up and in' strategy as opposed to *appoggio* which is the 'down and out' strategy he would later learn from Joan Sutherland. Rodolfo Celletti argues cogently that the *sostegno* system of breath management was developed by Antonio Bernacchi (co-founder of the Bolognese School) but was later embraced almost universally by all the great castrati of both the Bolognese and Neapolitan Schools.

In an attempt to clarify the difference between the systems of breath management systems, Rachele Maragliano Mori described and contrasted the two systems in her excellent book, *'Coscienza della Voce'*. Mori differentiated between the subjective and objective *appoggio*. The former is the site where the proprioceptive sympathetic vibrations are concentrated most intensely. The latter is diaphragmatic objective *appoggio*. The objective system offers a real and antagonistic vocal support system which is consciously controlled (*lotta vocale*) and does not rely on sensations.

The *sostegno* system of breath management demands 'the retraction of the abdomen whilst dilating the base of the thorax'. Mori suggests that this represents:

> 'The model posited by Garcia, Bonnier and Lehmann, which they define as the *appoggio* system of breath management, based mainly on low costal breathing. This breathing system involves the moderate rising of the chest, the dilation of the lower thorax, and the lowering of the trachea; significantly, these are typically physiological responses that favour the opening of the lower pharyngeal resonance cavity' [Mori, 1970: 70].

Bernacchi's *sostegno* system was used by the bel canto singers of the past, which they aptly described as the *sostegno del petto* or sustaining the chest. This was characterised by maintaining a moderately high chest position which they subsequently used as a prop to support not only the chest but also the larynx, albeit more indirectly. The *sostegno* system was the classical school's most treasured support system, and was taught in the very best schools of the era.

Having described the elements of this system Mori then elaborates on a number of the subjective focal points beginning with two polar opposites. The first focal point is:

> The *appoggio nella nuca* (on the nape of the neck) which produces a sound characterised by vibratory sensations and a series of harmonics that have a distinctly backward orientation, perceived to impinge on the back wall of the pharynx. The second focal point is referred to as *appoggio in maschera*, in which the emission of the sound is directed towards the cavity of the head or the mouth, sometimes known as *appoggio facciale* (appoggio on the mask or face). There are other focal points such as *appoggio sui denti* (on the teeth), *appoggio palatale* (on the palate), *appoggio nel velo del palato* (on the soft palate) and appoggio in testa (in the head). Mori urges the singer to use the most appropriate focal point depending on the style of singing and the type of sound he wishes to produce. In general however, Mori believes that the *appoggio in maschera* is probably the most effective [Mori, 1970: 70].

Note that Mori not only differentiates between the objective system of *sostegno*, but also addresses its interrelationship with the subjective *appoggio*, the latter emphasising the concentration of sympathetic vibrations within the vocal tract.

Historically a great deal has been written on the *sostegno* respiratory strategy. The castrato Gianbattista Mancini was by far the most eminent and representative author of that fabled golden era. He was later joined by the tenor Bernardo Mengozzi who explored the *sostegno* system in his influential *Method du Chant* for the Paris conservatoire (1803). Other authors such as the legendary bass Luigi Lablache, Manuel Garcia Pere and Fils, as well as the castrati, advocated the *sostegno* system.

I have argued at length in my previous books *A History of Vocal Pedagogy, Vocal Science for Elite Singers,* and *Italian Bel Canto in the Age of Vocal Science* that *sostegno* is a perfectly legitimate strategy for coloratura singing, but is also very effective for *fioritura,* agility and ornamentation. However it is insufficient for the more dramatic, more sustained Puccini and Verdi repertoire. For the more open throated sound required for this repertoire the singer needs considerable command over the *appoggio* system of breath management as the lowered diaphragm, lateral and posterior expansion all contribute to a concomitant lowering of the larynx and elevation of the soft palate.

Pavarotti and the Sostegno Technique of Breath Management

Leone Magiera reports that the strategy used by Arrigo Pola was originally theorised by Luigi Bertazzoni and later taught by Pola to Luciano Pavarotti. According to Leone Magiera 'The strategy favoured by Pola consisted of a slow emission of air (furnished) by contracting the abdominal muscles and subsequently compressing the abdomen' [Magiera, 2008: 212].

This strategy was characterised by an 'up and in' orientation which meant that the connection between the vertical position of the larynx and the diaphragm was both higher and more tenuous. Effectively a singer who lost partial control of his/her breath would automatically allow the larynx to rise indiscriminately in sympathy with rising frequency. These conditions often lead to a loss of control over laryngeal and diaphragmatic position, which has the effect of constricting the larynx with calamitous consequences for the sound produced.

Pavarotti became convinced that his breathing technique was inefficient, and in order to make the necessary progress he would need to alter his breathing strategy. He began to experiment, testing his discoveries in his classes and later in concert performances. Over time, through trial and error, this strategy began to yield very good results. Consequently he was determined to implement them in the 1961 Achilli Peri competition. However this marginal tinkering did nothing to resolve the overarching problem, which was that Pavarotti was using the *sostegno* system of breath management when he really needed to explore and conquer the *appoggio* respiratory strategy. Further, had the young Pavarotti conquered the *sostegno* strategy, brought to perfection by the castrati, he would have attained greater control over his breathing than he had hitherto managed to do.

The truth is that whilst most teachers agree as to the importance of breathing, they simply don't know how to teach it. His teachers had simply failed to sufficiently emphasise the importance of a solid breathing technique, and they clearly could not furnish him with a well thought out *sostegno* strategy. They simply did not know how to teach it. Teaching breathing is not as easy as it looks; it is very difficult and if not conquered, it can become the single most fertile source of functional atrophy and vocal problems.

I like Luisa Tetrazzini's description of the *sostegno del petto* technique very much. She declares that when she breathes she scarcely draws in her diaphragm but she still feels her upper ribs expand and the air fills her lungs. She continues:

> In singing I always feel as if I were forcing my breath against my chest. and, as in the exercises you find the chest leads in all physical movements, so in singing you should feel this firm support of the chest for the highest as well as the lowest notes…A singer should stand freely and easily and should feel as if the chest were leading, but should not feel constrained or stiff in any part of the ribs or lungs.
>
> From the minute the singer starts to emit the tone the supply of breath must be emitted steadily from the chamber of air in the lungs…It must never be held back once… This feeling of singing against the chest with the weight of air pressing up against it is known as 'breath support,' and in Italian we have even a better word, 'appoggio,' which is breath prop [Tetrazzini, 1909: 14-15].

Tetrazzini gives an excellent description of the *sostegno del petto* strategy (which she mistakingly calls *appoggio*) with its emphasis on posture, freedom and ease, and leading physically with the forward movement off the upper chest.

Conclusions

This *sostegno* system of breath management was favoured by the bel canto singers of the past, which they appropriately described as the *sostegno del petto* or sustaining the chest. This was characterised by maintaining a moderately high chest position which they subsequently used as a prop to support not only the chest but also the whole breathing apparatus. However they were also careful to advocate for a lowered larynx and opened lower pharynx, all of which should be accomplished without either hardening the chest or exerting undue pressure. The *sostegno* was the classical school's system of support as well as a characteristic of the Pistocchi/Bernacchi Bolognese school and Porpora's Neapolitan school.

Chapter 10

Arrigo Pola's Belief in *Si Canta Come si Parla*

The first thing to say is that Pola's vocal philosophy was based entirely on the Old Italian School. His pedagogical model was purely empirical, without a trace of either scientific or objective knowledge. To the extent that Pola mentions vocal science, he does so in a dismissive and disdainful fashion. He doesn't speak about the 'source/filter theory' or the 'myoelestic/aerodynamic theory', and he ignores the concepts of formants, harmonic partials or even sub-glottal pressure. Pola emphasises the sculpturing of the resonating cavity through the manipulation of the articulators which finally shape the formants. These formants may best be defined as concentrations of acoustic energy within specific regions of the vocal tract. The first and second formants are responsible for creating the various vowels, the first (created in the pharyngeal cavity) representing the *oscuro* (dark) element of the vowel and the second (created in the mouth cavity) representing the *chiaro* elements. Consequently I can say that the clearer and crisper the vowels are, the closer the matching of the source harmonics to the vocal tract formants. The corollary to that equation is that the closer the matching of formants to the harmonics partials, the more naturally resonant the voice, the greater the vocal clarity, and the completeness of the *chiaroscuro* tone.

We have already heard from both Pola and Pavarotti confirming that they spent the first six months working on nothing but the five cardinal vowels. The second phase was characterised by repeated execution of vocalizzi and solfeggi, an essential part of Pola's teaching displaying a great deal of patience and dedication from both student and teacher.

As we saw above Arrigo Pola taught the empirical method which was nonetheless built on very sound foundations and in keeping with the dictates of the Classical Italian School. Pola was a man of his time which was dominated by the empirical system of vocal pedagogy. He undoubtedly taught Pavarotti what he had learned from Luigi Bertazzoni, his former teacher and more recently Mirella Freni's teacher. Pola informs us with some pride that he would regularly demonstrate technical aspects of singing and Pavarotti was very apt at repeating what he had just demonstrated. He emphasised the word and the text in order to create the right physiological and articulatory configuration, enhancing the clarity of the text and the resonance of the sound.

Pola confirms that his vocal philosophy is in line with the dictum of the Old Italian school — *si canta come si parla (we sing as we would speak)*:

> One should arrive at a way of singing similar to the way of speaking. When Luciano speaks, you understand every word. It is the same with his singing. He enunciates with great clarity and this is very important to the public…I worked on him to develop a technique that was pure, natural, spontaneous - I think that is what you hear today [Pola/Wright, 1981: 39].

Si Canta Come si Parla and its Limitations

Si canta come si parla refers to an old tenet of the traditional Italian school, a maxim that has been tested by time and vocal science, especially in the lower and medium part of the voice. It would seem that physiologically we use the same instrument whether we are speaking or singing. Consequently we can say that subject to the absence of linguistic distortions (as the Italian language lends itself towards a purity of tone), one can mount a strong case for the Italian vocal adage *si canta come si parla*. When combined with Pacchierotti's dictum *Chi sa respirare e pronunciare sa cantare* becomes quite a substantial vocal paradigm, the essence of which was used by Pola as the foundation of his pedagogy. It is therefore the paradigm cited above which will be used to analyse Pavarotti's singing.

First of all the above paradigm is one of the most powerful concepts of the traditional Italian school. On the other hand it must be mediated with some clarification. The most important of these caveats to *si canta come si parla* are listed below:

- In its purest form this axiom is applicable only to a limited vocal range; it is generally confined to the lower half of the singing range, with the singer experiencing a surge of breath energy and slight modification of the vowel around the first *passaggio*.

- The second caveat refers to the fact that the demands of the singing voice far exceed those of the speaking voice. Singing is not just sustained speech maintained over a wider range. It actually makes more demands on breath energy, acoustic precision, clarity of diction and *aggiustamento* or *arrotondimento* which is critical to negotiating the *secondo passaggio*. Nonetheless when these adjustments lead to the desired seamless blending of the voice between the mixed register and head register, the results can be majestic.

- The third is that in addition to an extended vocal range, the singing voice also demands a greater dynamic range, increased intensity, and a more sustained tone (duration). More often than not this is combined with alterations in sub-glottal pressure below the glottis and a reconfiguration of the articulators above it.

- The fourth difference is an understanding that duration is very different between speech and singing. Speech consists of a number of rapidly produced sounds that constitute a whole intelligible sentence or message. Singing on the other hand demands that the singer sustains a particular vowel for several seconds at the behest of the composer. Depending on pitch and intensity, both the breath and the articulators need to be adjusted and the vowels need an *aggiustamento*. In particular the jaw must be judicially lowered and the sub-glottal pressure must be increased for both rising pitch and increased intensity.

The theoretical and scientific paradigm that validates much of the celebrated maxim is called the source/filter theory of speech production originally posited by Gunnar Fant in 1960. The theory states that the harmonic partials issuing from the larynx must be filtered through the vocal tract. In so doing we match the source harmonics with their relative formants, that is, formants with the same frequency to the harmonics arising from the primary source. The frequency of the harmonics is determined by the tension, length and mass of the vocal folds. On the other hand the formant frequencies are a function of the total configurations of the articulators. The major articulators are the tongue, lips, jaw, soft palate and velum.

The Resonator and its Articulators

As stated above the pharynx and mouth represent the most important resonators in the human body. By virtue of its location, the pharynx is accorded the primary opportunity to modify and amplify the vocal product issuing from the larynx. As Meano suggests 'it is the first area to contain the sound waves produced in the larynx during their projection and amplification, and contributes to the formation of timbre, or quality' [Meano 1967: 35]. The pharyngeal space emphasises the lower harmonics. It also furnishes the tone with the typical characteristics of the 'oscuro' sound, which is full and round combined with mellowness and warmth. Consequently the pharynx remains the resonator *par excellence* with respect to the foundational partial of any harmonic series built upon this load-bearing base. However the mouth resonator, with its extremely elastic and mobile walls, also enjoys considerable influence on the quality of the tone, forming a natural amplifier through which the tone is projected to the external environment. As always, Meano remains eloquent with respect to the mouth resonator. He agrees that this amplifier takes the shape of a megaphone 'which gathers the sonorous vibrations and amplifies them during their outward projection' [Meano, 1967: 36].

From the above we conclude that with some articulatory flexibility, and within the limited frequency range already delineated, it is possible to maintain the resonator in a given but flexible position. This is typically associated with a particular vowel formation represented by a combination of the first and second formants which also safeguard the integrity of the vowel. When we add the third formant to the equation we can easily see that this configuration conforms with the chiaroscuro of the traditional Italian School.

The situation changes when, on an ascending scale, the voice is raised beyond a comfortable singing range. Exploration of the higher register automatically demands an increase in breath energy and expansion of the resonating cavity, designed to accommodate rising frequency and increased intensity. These adjustments to breath energy and resonator are typically implemented in a manner that will maintain consistency of vocal timbre and sonorous vibrancy. The adjustments are generally determined by minor alterations of the articulators, especially jaw and tongue.

From the above we conclude that it is only when we extend the range in either direction (but especially when entering the high head register) that the *si canta come si parla* paradigm breaks down. It is at the *zona di passaggio* that we must increase breath energy and slightly lower the jaw to accommodate rising pitch and intensity, whilst also covering the tone at the *passaggio*. In the male voice formants three, four and five are responsible for the singer's formant or '*squillo*'. The singer's formant is a function of a moderately lower larynx, an expanded pharynx, open ventricular folds and wide pyriform sinuses, all supported by just the right measure of objective and subjective *appoggio*, breath pressure and sympathetic vibrations.

Vertical Laryngeal Position

Sundberg (1987) postulates that altering the vertical position of the larynx alters the length of the vocal tract. Consequently we conclude that changing laryngeal height alters all of the formant frequencies within the vocal tract. More specifically raising the larynx shortens the vocal tract and elevates all the formant frequencies. Lowering the larynx elongates the vocal tract, thereby lowering all the formant frequencies.

Sundberg also believes that it is inappropriate to elevate the larynx in sympathy with rising frequency and I agree with him whole heartedly. However my own ideas are more in line with those espoused by Richard Miller. He argues (and my own experience confirms his contention) that a slight alteration of the lips resulting in a hint of a smile will in most cases sufficiently shorten the vocal tract, allowing the singer to match the formant frequencies to those of the harmonic partials issuing from the glottis. Sundberg further states that laryngeal position has an impact not only on resonance but also the voice source. He continues thus:

> Lowering the larynx is associated with the act of inhalation, a gesture that induces glottal widening. If we adhere to the scenario in which lowering the larynx is closely connected to glottal abduction (widening the glottis). Then it is logical to conclude that lowering the larynx causes the opening of the glottis and therefore has the potential to transform the tone from pressed phonation to flow phonation. Consequently, we conclude that lowering the larynx aids flow phonation which naturally emphasises the fundamental [Sundberg, 1987: 133].

At this point it is important to recall that both firmness and duration of glottal closure are a function of the interaction between the vocal fold tissue and sub-glottal pressure. The coordination between these critical elements of voice production causes the abrupt cessation of breath flow, a process that not only creates the complete harmonic series but also excites the upper harmonics which lend 'squillo' to the voice. If the correct relationship is not established between the lower and upper harmonics, you cannot expect to create a balanced and harmonious *chiaroscuro* tone. If you do not achieve this balance at the point of inception, it hardly matters what you do with the resonator after the partials traverse the glottis. Let me be very clear, the resonator is extremely important, but for all its significance it cannot make a weak harmonic strong and it cannot change the relative strength of the partials within the harmonic series which is ultimately responsible for vocal timbre. That is another way of saying that you cannot change the sound wave once it has been fed into the vocal resonator. This is not in anyway aa denial of the need for a fully integrated and coordinated instrument, it is just a recognition of the limits of particular parts of the instrument. People are spending an awful lot of time on baubles of questionable values without understanding that you must keep coming back to first principals. Keep it simple stupid!

Nanda Mari (1975) produces an excellent description of the interior space of the vocal tract. She explains that the vocal tract, that is the combination of the mouth and pharyngeal resonator, resemble a temple or a theatre constituted of arches, vaults and a concave ceiling. Mari makes the point that sometimes it only takes one defective screen, hanging, or curtain to shatter the acoustic perfection of the whole theatre.

The human resonator contains such a defect in the form of the soft palate which is located in the posterior part of the vocal tract. We become aware of this kind of structural deformation through an analysis of the sound. According to Mari:

> The tone that emerges is flat and dull; the vocal colour is opaque, deformed and nasal: that disagreeable nasal tone that permanently disturbs both he who produces it and he who listens to it. This defect which emanates from the resonating cavity rarely influences the vocal folds but manifests itself in the singer's low and medium register [Nanda Mari, 1975: 60-61].

Nanda Mari indicates that there is no easy remedy for this type of problem. However, she believes that the beginning of a yawn or the simple gesture of pretending to smell a flower can bring immediate if not definitive relief. She confirms that generally an elevation of the soft palate has the effect of closing the nasal port, and relieving the tone of these unpleasant characteristic.

Since the soft palate and the larynx tend to work in opposite directions, creating the effect of an open fan within the posterior faucial arches of the resonator, it may be better to simultaneously lower the diaphragm which lowers the larynx and encourages the natural elevation of the soft palate. Richard Miller agrees with Mari and suggests that opening the throat and lowering the larynx with the consequent rising of the soft palate can be achieved through the gesture of smelling a flower. This is a wonderful and natural device which allows the singer to achieve the desired results without exaggeration or contrivance.

We saw above that the vocal tract is constituted by a combination of the pharyngeal and buccal cavity, with the tongue separating and shaping the space for each of these cavities continuously.

The most important muscles and organs within the vocal tract are the already examined nasopharynx as well as the tongue, jaw, lips and larynx. Let us elaborate briefly on the action of each.

> **The Jaw.** As with the tongue, the position of the jaw is nowhere near as important as a relaxed Tempora Mandibular Joint, ensuring that the jaw remains free from all tension. Barbara Doscher reports that research suggests most problems issuing in the TMJ emanate from ill-advised orthodontic procedures. The effect of TMJ dysfunction can be particularly severe on posture and the laryngeal musculature, but absolutely devastating on the vocal tract articulators, such as the tongue, jaw and lips. Very often tightness in the jaw is caused by other functional tensions, but it doesn't matter which deficiency, the results are the same as it undermines all attempts at finding a functional equilibrium [Doscher, 1994: 122].

> **The Lips.** The position of the lips depends upon the vowel being formed and the frequency being sung. Individual physical characteristics vary and

the shape of the mouth and lips is determined by the configuration that produces optimum resonance. Some singers use a puckered-lips embouchure very successfully. For others the diameter of this embouchure proves to be too narrow, resulting in an excessively damp and overly dark sound which is often muffled. The opposite is also true: a lateral position can produce a metallic tone which, if carried too far, can be really piercing. There is no perfect position for any of the articulators, mainly because every singer's physiognomy is different. According to Doscher the only unbreakable rule is that these articulators must shape the vocal tract so that the resonating space can vibrate sympathetically with the sound waves coming from the vocal folds. Ideally these adjustments should be made with a minimum of effort and a maximum of efficiency to avoid counterproductive tensions [Doscher, 1994: 124-25].

The Tongue. In normal circumstances the apex of the tongue lies against the gum ridge just below the teeth. Apart from the central vowels such as the [a] for which the tongue lies reasonably flat in the buccal cavity, all other vowels are determined by the position of the hump of the tongue which separates the pharyngeal resonator and the buccal resonator. Generally the pharynx and mouth enjoy a collaborative relationship with the hump of the tongue separating them. For instance when the hump of the tongue is elevated and leaning forward almost against the hard palate, the space in the pharynx is increased and that of the mouth is decreased. This creates the overall position for the bright vowels such as [i], [I] and [e]. On the other hand when the tongue hump rises and moves back almost against the soft palate, the space is larger in the mouth and smaller in the pharynx. This articulatory configuration represents the darker, round vowels such as [o] and [u].

In addition we must remember that the position of the larynx plays a major role in the quality of the sound produced, as do the state and condition of the pharyngeal walls and the spacial interrelationship between the pharyngeal and mouth resonator.

The position of the larynx is generally determined by the antagonistic action of the suprahyoid (elevating muscles) and infrahyoid (lowering muscles). When the infrahyoid muscles combine with the tracheal pull off the diaphragm to lower the larynx, some really important developments occur.

First is that there is a sensation similar to that of inhalation, accompanied by a moderate lowering of the larynx, an elongation of the vocal tract (which lowers all the formants of the vocal tract), an instinctive abduction of the vocal folds and a tone that is round, velvety, mellow and generally lovely.

The singer must guard against being over zealous with the lowering of the larynx. Too low a laryngeal position can lead to an exaggeratedly dark and guttural sound, as well as a spreading of the pharynx, which is inimical to good articulation and can lead to serious vocal problems. James McKinney offers the following remedy:

The chief cause of sounds which are too dark is in placing too much emphasis on the pharyngeal resonator. There are several factors which can cause this to occur: (1) Overuse of the 'yawning muscles, with resulting spread throat and/or depressed larynx;(2) Lack of oral space due to lip, jaw or tongue position; (3) wrong tonal models: (4).flabby surfaces of pharyngeal wall (not enough muscle tonus to give any character to the sound); (5) tongue pulled back into the pharynx (retroflex tongue).

Darkness in a sound can come from too much or too little tension, so it is important to try to identify the specific causes before starting corrective action [McKinney, 1994: 141].

On the other hand, if the larynx is riding too high it will shorten the vocal tract, rise all the formants and tense the lower posterior wall of the pharynx. When combined with the contraction of the constrictor muscles, the above manoeuvre reduces and shapes the space of the vocal tract whilst simultaneously hardening the walls of the pharynx. This muscular and articulator configuration hardens the pharyngeal wall and renders the sound metallic, thin, and too bright. McKinney singled out the contraction of the constrictor muscles as one of the major sources of bad singing. He does so because he believes that tensing the constrictor muscles hardens the resonator walls, reducing much needed space, and creating tension in the primary vibrator, the vocal folds. This contributes to a tight, hard, pressed sound [McKinney, 1994: 131] As always McKinney is not only informative but also cogent. He believes that:

> The tonal preference of most teachers seems to lie in a balanced sound-one which has both highs and lows present (both 'tweeters' and 'wolfers'). If the lows are cut out of the sound, the result is a too white or too bright tone quality; if the highs are cut out, the sound becomes too dark or too dull (often referred too as a 'tubby' sound)....Most listeners like to have both ends of the harmonic spectrum present in a sound, but differ as to the desirable amount of each. The point of this discussion is to say that there is plenty of room in the broad middle ground of tonal preference for persons who like brighter or darker sounds [McKinney, 1994: 138]

However, if we encounter a sound which is too metallic, too bright and too pungent, then he recommends that we enact the following remedy:

> Sounds which are too bright are often associated with a high laryngeal posture. Some singers, particularly those with low voices, start with the larynx comparatively

low and then raise it progressively as the pitch ascends, somewhat like an elevator (lift) moving from floor to floor in a department store. Other singers, chiefly those with higher voices, tend to elevate the larynx as soon as sounds begins and force it even high for the higher pitches. There is nothing in the laryngeal mechanism which requires that the larynx raises as pitch ascends, with the possible exceptions of the extremes of range and of minor higher adjustments associated with different vowels. Research has revealed that there is little laryngeal movement in many well-trained singers [McKinney, 1994: 140-141].

Laryngeal Position

Mori addresses Laryngeal position as another important element in the technique for blending registers. According to her, there are authors such as Wicart who believe that the larynx should be maintained in an elevated position, whilst others recommend a lowered and stable laryngeal position. These positions are related to an idealised sound world which has its foundation on the *chiaroscuro* paradigm of the Italian School [Mori, 1970: 79].

Generally the high laryngeal position corresponds with the forward, brighter vowels such as [i] and [e] whilst the lowered larynx is associated with the darker and rounder [o] and [u] vowels. Mori regards the [a] vowel as having a perfectly balanced mediated position which creates flexibility and dynamism, depending on frequency and register.

Consequently she concludes that the laryngeal position is lower for the darker and more intense sounds, and higher in the clearer, brighter, sweet sounds. It is important however to understand how to achieve this variation in vertical laryngeal position and when to do so. The velocity, fluidity and delicacy of movement of the vocal organ during vocal and musical production make it difficult and dangerous for the instrument to find a definitive absolute position. In this sense the bel canto aphorism 'descending whilst rising' signals the utilisation of the antagonistic opposition to the natural, progressive resistance of the vocal organ in ascending the scale [Mori, 1970: 80].

Chapter 11

Mori on Vocal Registers and Passaggio

There is no better example in the Italian literature of the deference and affection for the historical Italian School (combined with a forward looking scientific orientation) than that which we find in Mori's work. There is no better analysis in the Italian literature of the interrelationship between registers, timbre, resonance, laryngeal posture and vocal fold configuration than that found in her treatment of registers. It is worth recalling that Mori had written a thesis addressing the many issues and principles pertaining to the Old Italian School before she wrote her now famous book.

By the time she published *Coscienza della Voce* in 1970, Pavarotti was heading towards the peak of his career. It is significant that close examination of her text reveals that many of the principle issues she grapples with are the same as those nominated by Arrigo Pola who was in fact her contemporary. Is it any wonder then that they eventually reached many of the same conclusions, although they approached the issues from an entirely different and almost opposite direction? Pola arrived at those conclusions from the vantage point of a practising artist and teacher: Mori tackled the issue from an intellectual, scientific and much more academic stance, although she too was a practitioner. Let us now examine Mori's treatment of registers.

Mori's Registers

Mori begins her work on registers by declaring that the word 'register' must have had its origins in the terminology of the organ. The register of the latter serves to alter the timbre of the notes of that instrument. We can therefore state that a change in vocal timbre is commensurate with a change in vocal register. With respect to her definition of registers, Mori is in line with the great Manuel Garcia. Below find her definition of registers:

> In the didactic of the singing voice the term register refers to a series of sounds equal in timbre, produced by the same mechanism of the larynx, in an equilibrated relationship with the articulatory gestures produced by the resonance cavity [Mori, 1970: 75].

In addition Mori believes that every generation in every era in one way or another has signalled the presence of registers. Medieval singers cite voices of the head and those of the throat, and singers of the classical period such as

Caccini, Tosi and Mancini also mention two registers: chest and falsetto. For these singers however, falsetto was synonymous with head register. These singers believed that falsetto and chest registers referred to a preponderance of one of the two resonance cavities, and not to the exclusive dominion of one over the other [Mori, 1970: 76].

According to Mori it would appear that the theoreticians of the sixteenth century had an altogether more limited view of registers. However this only serves to reflect the fact that at the beginning of the sixteenth century composers explored a very small range. It was just a little more than the spoken range, hence the soubriquet *'si canta come si parla'*. This limitation was designed to achieve the effect of *recitar cantando*, the ideal vocal style of the period. In addition Giulio Caccini and his contemporaries offered an elegant solution: they recommended the transposition of their songs to the key that most naturally suited the singer's voice, thereby eliminating the need to resort to *'voce finta'*.

In the eighteenth century with the development of *'stile fiorito'* vocal emission was set on a level of such lightness and fluidity that the registers were comprised almost entirely of their own mechanism, which combined the different timbres of the vocal range.

Mori reminds us of the controversy surrounding the whole question of registers. Mori contends that it is important to acknowledge that there is little agreement with respect to registers. There are some who even question the existence of registers, let alone agree with respect to the number and nature of them. Indeed, Mori suggests that there are many who would prefer to forget the existence of the problem altogether, simply because some singers are so naturally talented and intuitive that they manage to blend their registers anyway [Mori, 1970: 76-7].

Vocal Registers: Long, Medium and Short Cord

Mori recalls García's Three Registers Paradigm and register blending strategy:

> The three-register mechanism (long, medium and short cord), enables the vocal folds to produce an extended series of sounds. Consequently we conclude that singers have used Garcia's three-register mechanism to learn how to simultaneously increase the range of the voice, whilst also producing an infinite variety of colours.

According to Mori it was not until García invented the laryngoscope that the nature of this diverse mechanisms was revealed to us. Before García, we knew the effect of these registers but not the cause [Mori, 1970: 78].

García's observations taught us that we must not change our vocal technique to accommodate the subtle alterations we sense in the mechanism as we ascend the scale. Instead he suggests that the solution to the problem is connected to the principal of equalisation. The singer must seek uniformity of respiration, a steady and moderate laryngeal position and constant resonance. Mori believes that the latter is perhaps the most important, enabling the voice to be reflected in its definitive anterior position and maintained there by the airflow which is pressed out by the interaction of the abdominal girdle and the diaphragm. It is only then that the vocal folds begin to enjoy that elasticity and calmness, essential to the free modification of their movement even during sudden changes or register breaks, so characteristic of inferior singers [Mori, 1970: 78].

In passing from one register to another the vocal folds are activated by a subtle and antagonistic interrelationship of tensions that are regulated by the internal tensors (thyroarytenoids) and external tensors (cricothyroids).

Mori contends that depending on whichever mechanism dominates at a certain point determines the nature of the register, which generally is referred to as chest register or the head register. As we progressively ascend the scale the medium register is characterised by the gradual diminution of the internal tensor (vocalis) and a concomitant increase in tension on the external tensor (cricothyroid). The tension is regulated by the contractible fibres of the vocal folds; these fibres alter the shape of the vocal folds, but not the overall volume. This is another way of saying that the mass is simply reshaped [Mori, 1970: 79].

Conclusions

We should recall that Mori (in line with her great predecessors ranging from García and Lamperti to Marchesi and Stockhausen) adheres to the three-register model. This model is characterised by a thicker and more rounded chest register, a bright and brilliant head register, and a mixed register that separates these two and is much more difficult to balance. She contends that there are teachers who still don't acknowledge the middle register in the male voice. In fact she reminds us that the ancient teachers didn't even mention it. She acknowledges that the mixed register has neither the colour of the chest register nor the penetration of the head register, being a mixed colour and easy on the voice. For this reason many of the great schools of the past paid particular attention to the mixed register, referring to it 'as the homeland of the voice' [Mori, 1970: 83].

Mori describes the medium register as one in which the tensions of the vocal folds (internal tensors: vocalis) gradually diminish and are substituted by the steadily increased tension of the external tensors (cricothyroid). This is generally called the mixed register or half chest register (mezzo petto) [Mori, 1970: 83].

With the development of the *stile fiorito* (florid style) in the eighteenth century, vocal emission evolved to such a level of lightness and fluidity that all register problems seemed to have vanished quite naturally. However during the romantic period and even more so during the later verismo style, singers became increasingly conscious of vocal registers and of the onerous demands these new styles of singing made on them and consequently on the vocal folds. (Previously Garcia confirmed that registers are an essentially glottal phenomenon). This configuration not only validates the existence of vocal registers but also highlights the importance of the *passaggio* and the necessity to modify the vowels (*arrotondimento*) in order to facilitate the process of register blending [Mori, 1970: 77-78].

Covering or Copertura

According to Juvarra we cannot overstate the importance of covering the voice at the *passaggio*. This simple technique has many benefits which we have delineated below:

- Protects the vocal folds
- Facilitates access to the high notes
- Modulates the vocal musculature in a manner that allows the singer to develop the full extension of his vocal range. This can only be achieved when there is a deep understanding that at a certain frequency (the point at which we become aware of tension between the registers) the singer must deploy the register blending mechanism referred to as *covering the passaggio*. Conquering the *covering* technique is amongst the most important elements of singing technique.

The Italians refer to this technique by various names such as *'copertura della voce'* (covering the voice), *'girari i suoni'* (turning the voice) and *'passare in testa'* (passing into head voice). Each suggests that it is based on a particular subjective perception.

Whilst this covering technique originated in Italy it was exported at the beginning of the eighteenth century. Consequently Raul Husson, working at the Sorbonne in Paris in the early 1960s, decided to study the *passaggio* mechanism in considerable depth. In so doing he was able to clarify both its action and its function. Antonio Juvarra credits Husson for discovering that the *copertura* mechanism is 'a fundamental element of laryngeal protection. This technique is designed to stabilise the larynx, offering a level of technical and vocal security' [Juvarra, 1987: 43].

Let us continue with Antonio Juvarra who also believes that the importance of *copertura* cannot be underestimated simply because the benefits are so consequential:

- It is a fact that *copertura* protects the vocal folds
- It also facilitates the entry into the head register
- It modulates the musculature in such a way as to allow the singer to develop the full extension of the voice
- It creates an extreme facility, fluidity of emission and vocal power.

These are the benefits bestowed by a covered voice or *voce coperta*. However I must stress that none of these benefits are obtainable without a proficient *appoggio technique* (appoggio is here defined as the coordinated interaction between the breathing strategy and *l'imposto in maschera*) [Juvarra, 2015: 60].

At this point Juvarra suggests that it is even more important to know the internal modifications upon which this mechanism is built. Following in Husson's footsteps he believes that the most significant features are:

- The contraction of the cricothyroid muscle which inclines the thyroid cartilage forward and down;
- The lengthening of the vocal folds through the relaxation of the vocalis muscle, tending to relax the larynx as a whole, allowing for an increase in amplitude of vibrations at the glottal level;
- The lowering of the larynx reflected in a lowered and opened pharynx with considerable expansion of pharyngeal space;
- The dorsum of the tongue moves forward;
- The soft palate slightly lowered.

These modifications increase the intensity of certain harmonics. In fact it is appropriate to remind my reader that the description provided by Husson is particularly reminiscent of Sundberg's description of the physical configurations associated with the singer's formant, particularly with respect to the upper harmonics. It is also true that the expansion of the pharyngeal space reinforces the fundamental. The different modes of emission (open and closed tone) should therefore be a point of departure from the normal [Juvarra, 2015: 61].

At this juncture we are ready to begin the work of equalising the two registers by managing the break at the *passaggio* [Juvarra, 1987: 44-5].

Having studied this mechanism we are now able to understand the various elements that constitute it. We should add that the contraction of the cricothyroid muscle does not pertain to a voluntary action even though it intervenes automatically during the execution of the [i] vowel which provides most exercise for these muscles on the high notes. We do however experience some acoustic and visible signs, alerting us not just to the *passaggio* notes but also to what Miller refers to as a broader setting called the *zona di passaggio*.

According to Juvarra the realisation that it is impossible to sing with an open vowel beyond the *passaggio* can be most disorienting to singers who are not fully aware of the problems confronting them. This is simply because their limited experience has taught them that in an ascending scale the vowel must be gradually opened in order to lighten and brighten the sound (allowing the larynx to rise). Consequently we can say that ascending exercises are counter indicated in terms of developing the *passaggio* technique of *copertura*.

The teacher must do everything possible to ease the difficulties confronting the student, whilst at the same time ensuring that he/she does not eschew the difficulties involved in smoothing the *passaggio* by reinforcing the need to collect the vowel. In fact in this type of exercise the most important requirement is that of uniformity of emission and melodic legato. In the case of an ascending scale it is possible that a preoccupation with maintaining evenness and agility of tone leads to an open emission which mentally conditions the student, thereby retarding his progress to a covered tone. It is therefore desirable that before ascending a scale the student is taught to ascend the notes of the *passaggio* in isolation, training himself to alternate between a closed last note and an open first one [Juvarra, 1987: 45-6].

Vocal Onset

There is considerable agreement that there are three types of onset, sometimes called attack. Titze, Sundberg, Colton and Caspar, Doscher and Miller all agree with this proposition and list the simultaneous or coordinated attack, the breathy attack and the hard attack as the major forms of onset. However there is an increasing number of teachers, myself included, who believe that the hard attack can be divided into two subdivisions: one form of the hard attack which should be eschewed at all costs; the other which is most desirable because it produces a particularly ringing tone with an abundance of rich harmonics (especially in the higher register) and which refers to the firm onset. We will deal with these presently but for now let us content ourselves with examining the three traditional types of onset.

Simultaneous Onset or Attack

In simultaneous attack we coordinate adduction of the vocal folds with the onset of breath flow so that the two meet simultaneously at the midline of the glottis. According to Seikel et al., in this type of onset the vocal folds reach their critical level of adduction at the same time as the sub-glottal pressure is sufficient to initiate sound.

Ingo Titze believes that coordinated or simultaneous vocal attack and its corresponding normal mode of vibration lie somewhere on the continuum between breathy and pressed voice. He suggests that the coordinated vocal onset 'is the result of a small separation of the vocal processes that allows an optimal pattern of vibration to be maintained.' This mode of vibration gives a moderately large airflow, large amplitude, and rather little air turbulence and vibration interference.

Miller also considers the coordinated or simultaneous onset as the ideal vocal attack. He agrees with Titze that in the coordinated onset glottal closure is modified to incorporate a narrow slit before phonation, similar to Titze's separation of the vocal processes. He believes that in the absence of this narrow slit in the glottis before phonation, the buildup of sub-glottal pressure would result in a glottal plosive — a sound similar to a light cough.

Miller links the simultaneous attack with full abduction of the vocal folds just prior to inhalation. He does so because he believes as I do that a full abduction induces a clean and precise adduction. A full abduction can only be secured by a deeper than normal breath and a comfortably low larynx.

The coordinated onset is characterised by a complete closure of the glottis resulting in a spectrum with substantial peaks denoting a tone rich in higher harmonic partials. In terms of the continuum between breathy and pressed phonation, this type of phonation is a little firmer than the so-called flow phonation, but less firm than pressed.

Physiologically Hirosi and Gay found that in soft or simultaneous attack, activity of the abductor muscle PCA (Posticus) decreases gradually during the pre-phonatory period. At the same time the activity of the adductors (VOC, LCA, INT) and the CT increases gradually, reaching a peak after vocal onset. This represents a departure from Hirano who found that in soft onset the muscle activity reaches the maximal level around vocal onset.

Other forms of Vocal Attack

There are two other forms of onset, the first being the breathy vocal attack, and the second the hard vocal attack. The first occurs when significant airflow is activated prior to the adduction of the vocal folds; the second occurs when the vocal folds are adducted prior to airflow being activated. The first form results in a breathy vocal attack while the second results in a glottal attack [Seikel et al., 1997: 225].

Breathy Onset

Breathy onset represents a failure to coordinate air flow or sub-glottic pressure with the adduction of the vocal folds resulting in excessive air pressure, and preventing the vocal folds from coming together as required to produce a clean sound. This results in a source spectrum that is rather round without the peaks that characterise a tone rich in high harmonic partials. In terms of the continuum of phonation between breathy and pressed, this configuration represents breathy phonation, a very round spectrum.

Physiologically this type of onset is characterised by a small but persistent opening of the vocal processes which remain separated by a fraction of a millimetre due to PCA activity. Even though it is a small separation it is nonetheless sufficient for a small amount of air to escape, thus preventing the sudden interruption of airflow at the end of the cycle. The abrupt decline in airflow is a necessary condition for the excitation of the higher harmonics in the source spectrum, the absence of which tends to tilt the spectrum towards the lower frequencies. Consequently the tonal quality (characterised by a noisy, breathy, flute-like quality) emphasises the fundamental and lower harmonics at the expense of the upper harmonics.

Hard Onset

Seikel and associates conclude that there are two types of hard attack, and that it is only the extreme one that is really harmful to the vocal mechanism. According to these authors this hard onset becomes inimical to vocal health and artistic singing only in its extreme condition, known as the hard attack, glottal shock, or glottal stop. This is the result of the complete closure of the vocal folds before phonation, causing air pressure from the lungs to build up and eventually burst the folds open with an audible click at the onset of sound. Apart from producing an unpleasant sound represented by a type of pressed phonation, this type of violent attack creates unnecessary friction and harms the vocal folds through excessive tissue collision. I think it is safe to say that this is not the attack that Garcia was referring to with his *coup de la glotte*.

Colton and Caspar also found that there are two types of hard attack. They too have a separation of the two types of hard attack, the corollary of which is that they also maintain that the first of these is safe whilst the second and more extreme one is to be eschewed at all costs. The following description makes the reason self-evident.

In the first type of onset, medial compression of the vocal folds is observed almost to be simultaneous with the onset of phonation.

However in the second type of hard attack the sound is characterised by pre-phonatory laryngeal constriction in which the ventricular folds approach each other, as do the arytenoids and the epiglottis, obscuring vision of the true vocal folds. As phonation is initiated, there is a reduction in the forced adduction and a sudden springing open of the larynx as the true vocal folds become visible [Colton/Caspar, 1996: 80].

The Myoelastic Aerodynamic Theory

In an effort to explain not only vocal fold vibrations but also the mechanism through which we may control or modify them, vocal scientists have developed a number of theories. These various theories seem to converge into an overwhelming support for the myoelastic/aerodynamic theory. The myoelastic component of this theory combines the muscular and elastic forces associated with the characteristic structure of the vocal folds and their muscular function. This tends not only to adduct the vocal folds but also coordinates them with the sub-glottal pressure which is the base of the rhythmic movement of the vocal fold cover, often called the free border of the mucous membrane.

On the other hand the aerodynamic aspects of the theory are determined by the pulmonary bellows which, in the expiratory phase, provide the sub-glottal pressure required to overcome the resistance of the vocal folds in their closed phase. This interaction results in varying degrees of glottal opening. As a result of the escaping trans-glottal airflow there is a rapid reduction of sub-glottal pressure and an increase in kinetic energy, with a consequent increase in the myoelastic adduction of the vocal folds. The airflow across the subtle fissure of the glottis determines the expiration that gives origin to the glottal mucosal wave. The latter is propagated from the inferior phase of the vocal folds right up to the ventricles, whilst simultaneously contributing to the closure of the vocal folds.

Fundamental frequency is determined by the speed of the sound waves which depends on the tension, shape and mass of the vibrating portion of the vocal folds through the modulation of length, thickness, and elastic tension of the vocal folds. Every increase in this elastic tension results in an acceleration of the vibratory cycle.

Generally the posture of the vocal folds and the action of the laryngeal muscles combine to reduce glottal area, an action that contributes greatly to glottal resistance. As a rule the smaller the glottal area is, the greater the resistance. As a consequence we can say that the number of times the expiratory air current opens and closes the glottis in a given period corresponds to the fundamental frequency. The number of cycles per second is determined by the mass, length, and tension of the vocal folds. The thicker, the rounder and the shorter the vocal folds the slower they vibrate and lower the frequency. On the other hand the longer, thinner and tenser the vocal fold mass, the faster the vibrations and the higher the frequency.

Generally speaking these elements constitute the criteria by which we are going to be judging Pavarotti's development. Clearly, in our analysis we will go into greater detail and we will be more focused on the relevant issues rather than generalise, but the overall elements will remain the core.

Chapter 12

Success at the Achille Peri Competition, 1961

Following this critical diversion, let us return to Pavarotti's defining moment. The 1961 Peri competition had a significant amendment to previous years, as the prizes included the opportunity to participate in a fully staged opera production. It was rumoured that the opera chosen for that year would most likely be Puccini's *La Boheme*. Pavarotti loved this opera and had his heart set on singing the role of Rodolfo, the poet. As it was, he nearly failed to compete because a month before the competition, he developed a nodule on his vocal folds, for which his doctor recommended silence for three months. Pavarotti was mute for fifteen days, and then on the day of the competition, as he began *'Che gelida manina,'* a torrent of sound came pouring out in all its pristine freshness.

Pavarotti believed (and I agree with him) that the role of Rodolfo in *La Boheme* was one of the great creations for the lyric tenor voice in general and especially well-suited to his particular voice in particular. Leone Magiera was engaged to be the official accompanist and was bracing himself to play literally hundreds of arias in a very concentrated period of time, namely three days. Leone and Luciano travelled together every morning and, on the way home, discussed the performance of every contestant appearing on that day. It was all part of their education.

In line with Campogalliani's pedagogical philosophy, Pavarotti didn't miss a single moment of the competition. Leone was playing so constantly every day that he hardly had time for lunch, so it was left to Luciano to bring sustenance to his friend in the form of bread rolls and drinks. Luciano himself enjoyed every moment of the competition, comparing his perceptions and ideas with those of the adjudicators:

> He was persuaded that careful listening to over one hundred young colleagues was an opportunity for professional development that shouldn't be missed. As the various auditions ended, he would share with me his astute observations on the singers who impressed him most. The judges' opinions invariably coincided with his' [Leone Magiera, 2008: 36].

When Pavarotti's turn came to compete, he only needed to sing one aria to secure his place in the final. According to Magiera, he was first in the provisional rankings, just as he had been the year before. Consequently, we can say that barring any unforeseen disasters, the prized role of Rodolfo was well within his grasp.

On the evening of the final, the theatre was packed, and many audience members were already Pavarotti fans. Some had seen him in provincial concerts around their region; others had heard him in the previous year's Peri competition, and, notwithstanding his unfortunate mishap in the final, they had noted and valued the gold in his voice.

Now came the moment of truth. It would be impossible for him not to be haunted by the previous year's disaster, and it was, therefore, more a question of how he would handle the adversity that all artists are confronted with. Artists need to learn to treat both glory and disaster with the same indifference — not an easy task.

According to Leone Magiera Pavarotti decided to sing Rodolfo's aria *'Che gelida manina'* in the final. The following is Leone Magiera's recollection of the event:

> He started the performance of this very challenging aria with just the right emotion in his voice, gradually becoming warmer and more passionate. Then, on the phrase preceding the top C, which begins with '*Poiche, poiche ha preso stanza,*' he was conscious of pressing the air out with the sound, creating the condition for the rebounding muscles to produce a significant expansion of the chest and a deep lowering of the diaphragm. Having created this under pressure in the lungs, the new breath came rushing into his lungs automatically. Therefore, when he arrived at the phrase '*La speranza*' with a full breath and in optimum condition, he emitted a pure, clear and strong top C5 such as he had never done before. Magiera recalls that it was an unforgettable performance with just the right emotion in his voice, gradually becoming warmer and more passionate during the performance. The whole culminating in a pure and clear, powerful top C. 'Audience members could hardly contain their enthusiasm, erupting into wild applause before the aria had even finished. The Judges were in no doubt. Within minutes, Mafalda Favero was on stage, holding the winner's gold medal in her hand. Moved, she held Luciano in a long embrace' [Magiera, 2008: 36].

In a personal interview, Magiera reminisced about that evening with genuine delight for his friend, student and colleague. Luciano had finally put his demons behind him and was ready to take on the world. It was a glorious evening, concluding with an equally memorable dinner. Following this, Leone sat at the piano and accompanied the great Mariano Stabile in two excerpts from his signature role, Falstaff. According to Magiera, Stabile sang in full voice and with excellent refinement despite his very advanced age.

Just as Pavarotti had hoped, he was assigned the role of Rodolfo as part of the winner's prize. Rodolfo was his dream role, but even he could not have imagined that it would become his calling card — his signature debut role in all the major opera houses of the world.

However, we are getting a little ahead of ourselves. Firstly, Pavarotti had to learn the role, which is challenging both vocally and musically. Rodolfo is a significant role, but it has a number of inherent difficulties not only in set pieces such as *'Che Gelida Manina'* and *'Mi Chiamano Mimi,'* or even *'O Soave Fanciulla,'* but also in ensembles. The opera is intrinsically an ensemble piece with hundreds of interjections and individual entries for all the singers. Each entry requires precision to avoid impacting the other characters as the entire opera moves like quicksilver. Luciano had already been spending much time at the Magiera's home preparing for the Peri competition. However, now that he was studying the entire role of Rodolfo, he was virtually camped there, constantly going through the score with a tremendously punctilious Leone. They had developed a wonderful friendship, and although Leone could be, and often was, a challenging taskmaster, once the work was over, they returned to being just a couple of young friends. Luciano was more of a larrikin, and not only did he regularly raid the fridge, but, according to Mirella Freni, he was also a bad influence on Leone. She was often annoyed with her husband for allowing himself to be unduly influenced by Luciano.

On the other hand, Nonno Ubaldo would show his exasperation by donning his hat and coat and leaving the house. On his way out, he would often retard his exit for a moment, then observing these crazy young men, would shake his head and murmur, 'What is it with this Pavarotti? Doesn't he have a home to go to [Micaela Magiera, 2019: 147].

Pavarotti was to sing three performances of *La Boheme*, two in Reggio Emilia conducted by Molinari Pradelli, and one in Modena to be undertaken by Magiera, who had recently made his conducting debut in Parma in Puccini's *Suor Angelica*. The Modena performance would also mark Leone's debut in *La Boheme*. Magiera made sure that Luciano was very well prepared because he knew that Molinari Pradelli had a reputation for being obstinate and inflexible.

Mafalda Favero had been assigned the task of producing *La Boheme*. She had been a marvellous singer, but this was her directorial debut, and consequently, she compensated for her lack of experience by rehearsing certain scenes repeatedly. Nonetheless, the end product achieved an excellent standard, and Luciano enjoyed working with her.

Molinari Pradelli arrived a few days before the dress rehearsal and quickly knocked the orchestra into shape, threatening to sack some of the musicians who were not up to the task. Fortunately, he took a somewhat more lenient attitude with the young singers.

Pavarotti recalls the rehearsal period with great nostalgia. The cast was booked into a one-star hotel with all the men on one side of the corridor and the ladies on the other. Everyone used the communal showers at the end of the hall, and the ambience was not too dissimilar to the one depicted onstage by the Bohemians.

According to Magiera, Luciano sang Che Gelida Manina at the dress rehearsal with great beauty and conviction. Molinari Pradelli, who was renowned for putting the fear of God into singers, stopped the orchestra and, in a moment of uncharacteristic generosity, said, 'Young man, if you sing like that before the audience, you will be triumphant' [Magiera, 2008:36].

Finally, on 29 April 1961, Pavarotti was ready to make his operatic debut. One can only wonder what he may have been thinking as he was waiting for the curtain to go up at the Teatro Comunale in Reggio Emilia. He certainly couldn't help but feel the buzz emanating from the audience as they anticipated the possible discovery of a significant new talent. Magiera, looking up to see a theatre filled to the rafters, became somewhat nervous for Luciano, although he would never admit to it. Almost unconsciously, his eyes continued to peruse the audience with a certain sense of wonderment until he came upon a well-known face. Alessandro Ziliani, the leading Italian agent and a former tenor of the first rank, was in the house. Ziliani had enjoyed a fine career as a leading tenor of the previous generation, and following his retirement from the stage, he began working with Arduino in Milan. Liduino Bonardi was a complex personality, but he knew his business. He ran the biggest and most successful opera agency in the country, of which Ziliani was now an entrenched part. Magiera recalled that Luciano had auditioned for Liduino at his agency in Milan; the latter heard something in Luciano's voice that really excited him. However, later in the aria, when Pavarotti cracked on one of his high notes, Liduino walked out of the audition, slamming the door and calling out that he didn't have any patience for time wasters.

Since that audition, Liduino had passed away, and Ziliani had assumed the management of the agency. From his offices in Via Santa Radegonda in Milan, he provided the talent (singers, conductors, directors, and designers) for all the major theatres of Europe. Rumour quickly spread that Ziliani was there to support Mafalda Favero, who was making her directorial debut. It was well known that in their youth, the couple had been very much in love. However, later in the evening, it was revealed that the invitation had not come from Favero but from the novelist Vladimir Nabokov, the literary critic and famous author of Lolita. Nabokov was there to support his son Dimitri, who was debuting as the philosopher Colline.

Finally, the curtain went up, and Leone Magiera recalls the evening vividly:

> Luciano embarked on a memorable performance from its opening lines: '*Nei cieli bigi, vedo fumar da mille comignoli Parigi,*' showing that his voice had matured nicely. Until now, certain critics had claimed, with some justification, that it lacked volume and intensity of tone. That evening, he proved them wrong, utterly and conclusively.

From beginning to end, the assurance and ease of his marvellous tenor timbre reminded me of other great voices of the past: the captivating lustre of Jussi Bjorling and Mario Filipeschi's unforgettable high notes. The C5 in Speranza, the B natural of the *concertato* in the second act, and the B flat in the third act were all moments of delight for the audience. They awarded him triumphal honours with the most indescribable pandemonium when the opera ended. Some people were crying; some were waving their handkerchiefs like flags; others were shouting his name. Luciano, happy as a child, was thanking them with sweeping gestures and was moved to tears — he certainly wasn't expecting such a frenzy [Leone Magiera, 2008: 38]. (These facts were confirmed in personal interviews with Leone Magiera and Adua Veroni, his fiancé at the time, later Signora Adua Pavarotti.)

Having witnessed Pavarotti's sensational success, Pradelli immediately regretted the compliments he had paid the young tenor at the dress rehearsal. Pavarotti's triumph took nothing away from his conducting, but it was common to experience professional jealousy and envy in the theatre. The conductor's reaction marred an otherwise glorious debut for the young Pavarotti.

As we remember from Magiera's recollections, at the end of the performance, the theatre erupted, causing pandemonium. According to Magiera, Luciano was thanking his audience with sweeping gestures of his arms, and at one point, he was so touched by this outpouring of love that he burst into tears of joy. He had not expected such a rapturous reception from his audience [Magiera, 2008: 38]. It was as if the collective unconscious had recognised that here was the birth of an Italian icon, someone who would embody the best of Italian culture. Pavarotti reminded Italians that, although they were no longer part of the Roman Empire that had dominated the world for more than a thousand years, nor the zenith of the humanistic Florentine Renaissance, they still had something unique to offer. He reminded the world not only of their humanity but also in the tradition of Neoplatonism embraced by all great artists; he demonstrated that human beings, especially artists, do indeed possess a touch of the divine.

It was no wonder then that Ziliani was shocked as he saw Leone Magiera attempting to create a pathway for him to Luciano's dressing room through the hordes of new Pavarotti fans. According to Magiera, Ziliani was following him backstage in a hypnotic state; he just kept repeating Jussi Bjorling, Jussi Bjorling, all the way to the dressing room. He could not believe what he had heard.

Arriving at the dressing room, Ziliani complimented Luciano for his superb depiction of Rodolfo. Then, with a gesture worthy of a great soul, he declared Luciano the world's greatest tenor. In 1961, this declaration may have been interpreted as an exaggeration, but time would prove that Ziliani's assessment was perspicacious rather than rash [Magiera, 2008:38]. As

Pavarotti was reminiscing many years later, he admitted to William Wright that he was surprised he had made any sense out of his conversation with Ziliani. He declared that by nature, he was 'an exuberant person, but a part of me always knows what's going on'. He remembers that Ziliani asked about his plans, and Luciano was honest enough to admit that Rodolfo in *La Boheme* was the only role he knew really well. However, he intended to work hard over the next six months with a view to conquering another two or three roles before looking for work. Ziliani was impressed with Luciano's seriousness, inviting him to get in touch when he felt ready to begin his career, and he would do what he could.

Fortunately, we have a recording of that evening's performance, so let us examine the reasons why Ziliani became so excited.

Chapter 13

Pavarotti's Debut as Rodolfo in La Boheme, 1961

Pavarotti's debut in the role of Rodolfo in Puccini's *La Boheme* took place on 29 April 1961 at the Teatro Comunale in Reggio Emilia. The recording is pretty straightforward and, in terms of this analysis, absolutely priceless. However, it is still an amateur recording of a young tenor making his operatic debut. In these circumstances, the commentary should err on being temperate. This principle is particularly true when dealing with a beloved artist such as Pavarotti, who has earned our respect and consideration.

The problem with this kind of detailed forensic critique is that the investigation can be misconstrued as a personal attack as opposed to a constructive evaluation designed to help the next generation and, hopefully, the one after that to understand what constitutes excellent singing and the evolving indispensable techniques necessary to facilitate it. In this respect, I identify with Jurgen Kesting when he suggests that: 'because of the emphasis on mistakes and weaknesses, what follows may seem excessively critical, but it is not meant to be so by any means' [Kesting, 1996:121]. Kesting expresses my thoughts precisely concerning the analysis of our mutual subject, Luciano Pavarotti. In my case, it is even more so because this analysis is inherently more detailed and technically more explicit. Consequently, I feel compelled to declare that I regard Pavarotti as the greatest lyric tenor of the modern era and arguably of all time, which is in large part the reason I have chosen to investigate his vocal technique. The other reason is that Pavarotti is a vocal chameleon, and his development from his debut in 1961, which we are about to examine, to the late seventies to the mid-eighties remains an impressive artistic achievement by any standards.

However, it remains a fact that very few genuinely great artists begin their careers with the level of technical and artistic perfection they seem to achieve in the mature phase of their creative lives; Pavarotti was no exception. This book is dedicated to tracing Pavarotti's spectacular journey from a gifted young man to one of the greatest tenors of all time, a journey that hopefully will reveal not only the man behind the image and the artistry but also the vocal technique that made the artistry possible. As mentioned previously in this work, it is well-accepted amongst elite singing teachers that singers who do not conquer the technical aspects of their art rarely go on to become great artists, and those few who manage to do something special do so because of their natural endowment and generally have very short careers.

A Technical Critique of Pavarotti's Debut Role

Consequently, one of the issues we will discuss at length in this book is that a good vocal technique is not only indispensable but also very difficult to obtain. The mere quest of it is often sufficient to temporarily derail us simply because a great deal of it is experimental, as each voice is different, as is every student. Unfortunately, that difference is not limited to physiological aspects but also psychological and emotional factors. Acquiring a balanced technique requires an open mind, determination and perseverance, simply because with almost every adjustment, the vocal instrument tends to overshoot in the opposite direction and can, in the beginning, be quite discouraging. This is the typical trajectory for most young singers, and this study reveals that even singers as gifted as Pavarotti can't escape the process, which is part of the journey towards enlightenment. With this in mind, I remain convinced that if one is going to learn anything about a great technique and the characteristics of becoming an influential artist, then the prominent place to start is by analysing the journey and achievement of a great artist: Pavarotti is such an artist.

Returning to Pavarotti and Rodolfo, I believe that even this early amateur recording has general principles that can be inferred from Pavarotti's approach to vocal technique. These extrapolations can be helpful in terms of following his progress over a long career, and we are lucky to have several later and excellent performances of this great tenor in the role of Rodolfo. Initially, this was his signature role, remaining so for many decades. Consequently, it is reasonable and desirable to analyse specific strategic passages, noting differences and similarities over time.

In general, right from the beginning of the performance, we are aware of being in the presence of a phenomenal talent. The voice is a beautiful lyric tenor of the first rank. In terms of quality, it is not only an individual sound (although not as unique as it would later become) but also, notwithstanding the technical limitations, by nature, equal to the remarkable voices of the Golden Age of Singing.

Its production suggests a forward ringing tone resulting from a moderately high laryngeal position and a firm and relatively long closed phase of the glottic cycle, especially in the high register. (I say relatively long because the overall length of the process is exponentially shorter in the high record simply because with increased frequency comes an increase in the number of cycles per second.) This formula provides the tone with rich upper harmonics and sound waves guided without force towards the subjective *appoggio* (proprioceptive sensations) on the zygomatic arch. This allows sufficient space for the development of the upper harmonics, which, when matched with formants of the vocal tract with a corresponding frequency, furnishes the voice with brilliance and ring (the *squillo* associated with the singer's formant). These were the precise sound qualities that Pavarotti was aiming for — consistency in tone due to a variable level of energy; this was particularly so in the bigger moments of the opera, allowing him to achieve a vibrant and resonant tone. Pavarotti had created a voice that, in the acute (high) register, was particularly rich in high partials, often at the expense of a balanced *chiaroscuro*. Nonetheless, it rendered the overall timbre both luminous and fascinating, especially around the *passaggio*, which had clearly been well-developed with his teacher, Arrigo Pola.

Unfortunately, this brilliance in the higher extension came at the expense of the vibrancy associated with a well-developed lower and medium register. The latter lacked firmness, buoyancy and focus, often allowing the sound to remain lodged too far back in the pharynx for the round vowels (throaty tone) and a letterbox aperture for the lateral vowels. The latter was particularly evident at the *passaggio,* the result of an unbalanced *chiaroscuro* strategy and an inferior respiratory strategy, preventing Pavarotti from raising sufficient sub-glottal breath pressure to enact a firm attack of the tone. As importantly, he could not sustain a firm glottal closure and the mental follow-through action to engage the buccal cavity, which would tap into the higher formants and balance that with the lower ones emanating from the pharynx (*chiaroscuro*).

Consequently, Pavarotti was vocally inconsistent, often unnecessarily using the hard attack to begin a phrase and, on other occasions, issuing forth with a breathy tone or onset and a vocal release that seemed to gather force instead of tapering off into a price release. In this recording, the lack of abundant sub-glottal breath pressure ensured that the tone in the lower and middle voice was often sagging, falling back into the throat and creating a darkish and frequently unsteady tone, issuing into an uneven vibrato. This had the effect of unbalancing the *chiaroscuro* aspects of the tone, particularly in the low register.

Having been critical of this youthful performance, let us introduce some balance into the discussion. It is important to note that young as he was at the time of his debut, Pavarotti had attained a high level of proficiency in clarity of diction, in the execution of the high register, in covering (*copertura*) of the *passaggio* to the higher register and a great feeling for the character. These elements provided him with an unambiguously beautiful tone, which he combined with a very personal timbre and sense of drama.

On the other hand, when speaking about the higher register, we conclude that the balance between *chiaroscuro* (especially at the *passaggio*) and head register often demonstrates excessive brightness or open timbre. However, as previously stated, the lower register tends to sag and is frequently too dark and too back. Similarly, the balance between breath pressure and breath flow errs on the side of flow phonation, meaning that there is insufficient sub-glottal pressure and a concomitant lack of glottal resistance, which is important in the process of creating a firm onset and abrupt cessation of airflow with its attendant jagged spectrum and brilliant tone. Consequently, we can say that the voice has not yet *been applied* (well-supported and appropriately focused). With respect to the all-important laryngeal position, James McKinney theorises, and I happen to agree with him:

> That a raised larynx only produces a tight, edgy sound. On the other hand, an overly lowered larynx, as in one which is produced by a total yawn, can result in a depressed larynx. The repercussions on vocal quality relating to vertical laryngeal position are enormous. McKinney informs us that the laryngeal position significantly influences the size of the pharynx and the tension of the pharyngeal walls. When the larynx is high, the length of the pharynx is diminished, its walls are made harder, and its horizontal dimensions are decreased by the actions of the constrictor muscles. All of these actions tend to restrict the resonation capabilities of the pharynx [McKinney, 2007, 130].

Having discussed the resonator and laryngeal position, let us return to our argument on respiration. We recall from our earlier discussion that '*appoggio*' or support may be defined as the antagonistic vocal struggle or *lotta vocale*, often resulting in what is better known as singing on the gesture of inspiration. More recently, scientists have referred to this manoeuvre as 'checking,' meaning that even though the internal and external muscles act in opposition to each other, they still strive for coordination and equilibrium. This is nature's attempt to pursue peace through the simultaneous contraction of the inner and outer muscles on the one hand and the antagonistic action of the abdominals and the diaphragm on the other (*Lotta vocal*). Any deficiency in the *appoggio* system is reflected in the failure to affect both a firm and consistent glottal resistance and stabilise the larynx through the respiratory muscles. Both the old and new masters hate this scenario. The authoritative masters of singing recommend that the larynx be maintained in a moderately low position, anchored by the cricopharyngeous, the sternothyroid, a lowered diaphragm and a relatively high chest. The diaphragm should not be allowed to rise indiscriminately with increasing frequency. Although counterintuitive, maintaining the relatively high chest contributes to preserving the lowered diaphragm position. It is also impossible to sustain a beautiful legato line when the respiratory and laryngeal muscles remain primarily unstable. This was the state of Pavarotti's breathing strategy at the beginning of his career.

Consequently, a well-supported voice leads to an easy *passaggio* into the head voice and is generally associated with a moderately low and stable laryngeal position. It should neither be too low (creating a dark and hollow sound) nor too high (producing a white, overly bright sound or excessively open one). Suppose this passage is followed by a beautifully sustained head voice (voce piena in testa). In that case, it serves to tune the instrument, preparing it for the rather tricky *tessitura* that comes later in the first act and then again in the third act of *La Boheme*. It may be propitious to recall that Sundberg et al. found a direct correlation between lowering the diaphragm and vertical laryngeal position, meaning that often excessively dark or bright sounds can be traced back to some deficiency within the breathing strategy. Reducing the diaphragm impacts the laryngeal position and, indirectly, the tongue position through its attachment to the hyoid bone. This is confirmed by Meribeth Bunch, who reminds us that the tongue is attached to the hyoid bone from which the larynx is suspended [Bunch, 1996: 63].

According to McKinney, the essential element pertains to phonemic integrity:

> The critical element is that the phonemic integrity of the vowel is maintained — that an [I] vowel, for example, will still retain its basic [i]-ness and its phonemic identity despite all the variations it may undergo. Only when it crosses the border of a neighbouring phoneme will it lose its identity and integrity? Research seems to reveal that when a singer tries to reach the goal of a consistently produced voice (giving the illusion of uniform tone quality from top to bottom), he makes a lot of compromises with 'vowel purity,' choosing versions of phonemes that make it easier to move smoothly from one vowel to another without any drastic changes in vocal technique. Conversely, the more one concentrates on singing each vowel only one way, the more likely problems will develop because of this inflexibility.... In other words, they tend to become more central or neutral in character. The front vowels migrate back towards the central ones, and the back vowels move forward to the central ones. One evidence of this is the fact that the two extremes of tongue positions — [i] and [u] — can be sung with a much wider mouth opening in the upper voice, the type of mouth position which is required by an [a] vowel.... Singers who resist this tendency of the vowels to migrate and insist on singing 'pure vowels' in the upper voice are likely to encounter vocal problems such as loss of quality, tight phonation, elevated larynx, and vocal strain [McKinney, 1994: 158-159].

The above commentary gives us a glimpse into the reasons why Pavarotti had been experiencing vocal difficulties in the two years leading up to the final of the Achilli Peri competition. These difficulties culminated in the growth of a nodule on his vocal folds that prevented him from winning the competition in 1960.

Effect of Winning the Achilli Peri Competition

Before we begin our examination of La Boheme, let's say a word about how winning this competition affected the young Pavarotti. First of all, it confirmed his belief in his vocal talent. The sight of Ziliani running towards his dressing room, making a comparison with Jussi Bjorling, was more than even Pavarotti had hoped for. He had made a lot of friends and gained many fans during this competition. Ziliani offered to represent him, and Mafalda Favero was another influential artist predisposed to help. She would be directing the production of *La Boheme* to be staged in Reggio Emilia, which was part of the prize for winning the competition. Favero would be very nurturing and very helpful in developing his stagecraft. Rarely after this would he have as much rehearsal time with a producer, and undoubtedly, the Bohemian conditions that this competition spawned would never be recaptured again. The difference was that these young artists were all starting their careers together. There were no stars at this stage. They had nearly two months of rehearsals and were all booked into a three-star hotel, with the men's rooms on one side of the hall and the ladies on the other, with a common bathroom at the end of the hall. For two months, they lived the Bohemian life just like the characters they depicted on stage. At this point, there was no hint of the opulent accommodation, luxurious limousines or pop star perks for Pavarotti and his entourage, which would become the norm later in his career. All he wanted in 1961 was to learn his craft and make his debut. It is interesting to recall that at that time, the only cast member already driving a red Ferrari was the Russian bass, Dimitri Nabokov.

I agree with Pavarotti that Puccini's *La Boheme* is one of the greatest artistic creations ever accomplished for the tenor voice. Consequently, we should say a few words about Puccini's opera in general, the music of which is wondrous. There are moments when it moves like quicksilver, with the characters disrupting the action and interrupting each other with tiny fragments of *quasi-parlando* and innovative melodic phrases. These fragments are musically and dramatically meaningful; miraculously, they fuse into a seamless whole. However, the most memorable aspect of this opera is the sustained and open-throated melodic line that soars over a dense orchestration. I remember one of my excellent teachers, Afro Poli, who sang the Marcello in the complete recording of La Boheme with Gigli and Albanese, saying to me that he believed that this open-throated sound was not confined to Puccini but is extended to other leading Tuscan composers, including Mascagni and Catalani, all of whom demand an open-throated generosity. *La Boheme* was characterised by high originality, creativity in orchestration, and its romantic and inventive melodic structure. The other element often underestimated and overlooked in La Boheme is the compact structure of the libretto, which revealed vivid, sensitive characters who were also well-delineated, differentiated, compassionate, sensual and perspicacious. Illica and Giocosa recreated an authentic Parisian lifestyle, presenting a very human and vivid depiction of Paris in the 1840s. Here, we experience the brutality and harshness of life as portrayed in original and dramatic situations, skilfully juxtaposed with the heart-breaking beauty of the poetry by Luigi Illica and Giuseppe Giocosa. Their dramatic structure is so tight that it leaves the audience with nowhere to go except on the journey with our ill-fated heroes. The libretto's dramatic construction combines with the poetry's beauty and fluidity to ensure a majestic artistic tapestry at the level of drama. Puccini's task 'therefore' is to take this excellent libretto and bestow upon it what can only be described as a jewel of a musical score: a score of such passion and power that the richness of its humanity resonates directly with the emotional life of each succeeding generation.

La Boheme

La Boheme is set in the Latin Quarter of Paris on a freezing Christmas Eve circa 1835. This particular winter was an extraordinarily cold one and Paris was freezing. Diseases such as pneumonia and tuberculosis were rampant, and life was brutish and short.

When the curtain rises, we are introduced to our two leading male characters, the poet Rodolfo and the painter Marcello.

The two young men are so cold that they sacrifice their art for a few minutes of warmth. Marcello surrenders his painting of the Red Sea, but Rodolfo rejects it because he can't stand the stench of burning paint. Instead, he offers his melodrama as a sacrificial lamb to the fire: anything for a bit of warmth. However, they soon discover that not even the most ardent love scenes in Rodolfo's play will keep them warm for any length of time. As if things were not bad enough, Colline the philosopher appears. He is in a lousy mood and adds to the misery by complaining that you can't even pawn your books on Christmas Eve. Fortunately, Schaunard makes a grand entrance laden with food, wine and all manner of goodies, thus raising the temperature and the spirit of the occasion. The provenance of his good fortune, he tells them, was an unfortunate English Lord who hired Schaunard to play music for his very sick cockatoo: for three days he played nonstop, until the bird passed away. By now the other Bohemians are so busy setting the table and being tantalised by the promise of a good feast that they are no longer listening to his story.

Suddenly Benoit the landlord appears at the door demanding his rent. The Bohemians concoct a scene in which they appeal to Benoit's manly ego, thereby inducing him to brag about his adventures with the ladies. At this point, the Bohemians feign outrage at his adultery and throw him out of the attic without paying him a penny. Having won that particular round against Benoit, they now decide that no-one should stay home on Christmas Eve. Schaunard still has a few francs left so they choose to assemble at the Caffe Momus for supper. The streets are already teeming with life and vitality and our heroes mean to join the celebrating throng on their way to Momus. However, Rodolfo remains in the garret to complete an article for his journal before joining them.

No sooner is he seated at his desk than he realises that he is not in the mood to write anything. Fortunately, there is a knock at the door, providing a genuine distraction and reason enough for not finishing his article. It is their neighbour Mimi, a seamstress whose candle has been extinguished by the wind and asks for help to relight it. During the exchange that follows, it becomes clear that Rodolfo is smitten by her and she by him. Having relit her candle, he reluctantly ushers her to the door. She stands in the doorway bidding him farewell for a moment, but a gust of wind blows out her candle again. Rodolfo takes the opportunity to ask her inside again, where she conveniently loses her key. While both are on the floor looking for it, Rodolfo finds it and, hiding the key, takes her hand. He might have found the key but would soon lose his heart to this beautiful, humble, and unassuming young woman. In the glorious tenor aria *'Che gelida manina,'* Rodolfo shares his hopes and dreams with Mimi. His reply comes in the exquisite narrative aria, *'Si, mi chiamano Mimi'*. The act ends with the inspirational love duet 'O soave fancifully. Puccini imbues the scene from Mimi's entrance to the end of the first act with gloriously inspired music. Still, the location itself, as depicted by Illica and Giocosa, gives him much scope.

Opening Night Performance, April 1961

Let us examine the first scene of Pavarotti's opening night recording of his Reggio Emilia *La Bohéme*. Significantly few people realise how important and challenging the first few minutes of the opera are for Rodolfo. On the surface these simple exchanges between two young men in an attic in the Latin Quarter of Paris appear to be inconsequential — an economical way of introducing the characters and setting the scene. However, there is much more to these exchanges than meets the eye, both dramatically and musically. Dramatically we are introduced to Marcello, the painter and Rodolfo, the poet. Through their dialogue, we see that they have a witty but dry sense of humour, allowing them to laugh at their present hardships. We discover that Paris is a harsh place to live in throughout the 1830s and 40s, with little food, less sanitation and virtually no medications for those souls seriously ill. As if these conditions were not sufficiently depressing, we later discover that tuberculosis is running rampant, especially, in the poorer parts of Paris such as the Latin Quarter. In this exchange, we also learn that our heroes are cold and hungry without immediate relief in sight. In fact, it would be more accurate to say that life in Paris in this period was dangerous, brutal and short. Musically almost every interjection requires Rodolfo to sing around the *passaggio*, the notes around F4, F and G4. This is the most challenging part of the tenor voice, especially early in the performance when still warming up if these passages are combined with a couple of other signposts, such as the [A] natural on the exclamation *Eureka!* And the B flat on the [a] vowel that completes the phrase *'l'idea vampi infiamma'* we have a fair idea of how the evening is going to turn out. If these passages are *bene appoggiate* with just the right measure of vowel modification and ease of entry into the head register, we will most likely experience an excellent performance and a great night at the theatre.

Consequently, we can see that the connection between diaphragmatic and laryngeal position also impacts the resonating cavity and articulators, not just the tongue, which is the most critical articulator, but also the soft palate and, therefore the length of the vocal tract, which influences the frequency of all the formants of the vocal tract.

The tenor must sing these first pages of *La Boheme* with a firm but lyrical tone and a high sitting centre, producing a boyish quality. The technique must be a balanced, firm sound in which the *chiaroscuro* of the Italian school prevails. The manner in which the tenor sings these early pages of *La Boheme* has an impact not only on *'Che gelida manina'* but also on the success of the whole performance.

Having established the criteria by which we will analyse this and other Pavarotti performances that follow in these pages, let us see how the young Pavarotti managed these obstacles inherent in the role of Rodolfo.

As stated previously, from the opening bars, we are aware of being in the presence of a truly remarkable voice. We also understand that we are still in the fact of a great singer. The Pavarotti that we grow to love and applaud is still in the future; this is the embryonic stage. Now and then, we experience a fascinating glimpse of the great tenor still in the making.

Nei Cieli Bigi

The curtain goes up to reveal two young men in a Parisian attic on a cold winter night, Christmas Eve, in the 1830s.

We are in the Latin Quarter of the capital: one of our young heroes is sitting at a desk attempting to write a play, and the other stands before an easel painting his depiction of the Red Sea.

At the beginning of the performance Pavarotti starts with 'Nei cieli bigi guardo fumar dai mille comignoli Parigi. E penso a quell poltrone d'un vecchio caminetto ingannatore, che vive in ozio come un gran signor.' This translates into the following:

> 'I am just admiring the thousands of chimneys smoking all over the rooftops of Paris and wondering why that good-for-nothing fireplace makes no effort to earn its keep'.

Pavarotti opens the scene '*Nei cieli bigi*' with a hard attack on the [e] vowel instead of a simultaneous or coordinated onset traditionally employed by great singers, especially when they are still warming up. In addition, all the bright, lateral [I] and [e] vowels within the opening scenes are too narrow, brilliant, and throaty. The onset of these forward, lateral vowels is constricted, beginning too far back in the throat and remaining there for the duration. This is simply

because the sound, although quite lovely in its harmonic structure, is still tight and throaty (guttural tone). Further, the *appoggio* is ineffective, especially at an objective level (breath support), and the larynx remains insufficiently stabilised by the sternothyroid and sternocleidomastoids. The hump of the tongue does not rise to the required level for the bright, lateral vowels, nor is the hump sufficiently forward to approach the hard palate as it should for these lateral vowels. The lips are protruding as if he were preparing (pre phonatory tuning) to sing a [u] vowel rather than the [i] vowel. The first formant's frequency is around 340 cps for the brightest and darkest vowels. However, the frequency of the vowel-defining second formant for the [i] vowel, which is about 2750 cps, is decidedly higher than it is for the [u] vowel, which comes in at about 1100 cps.

I will say no more for the moment, but it must be evident to anyone with a vocal sensibility that there is still a great deal to be done before this voice is ready for an elite international career. Let me proceed with our analysis of Pavarotti's performance and, in so doing, utilise the same technique as did our great predecessors for hundreds of years, namely by relinquishing all available technology and reverting to the power of the well-trained human ear: that is, hear the sound and visualise the corresponding muscular action. By utilising this aural technic, we diagnose vocal problems, muscular deficiency, or a perfectly vibrating vocal engine: we eliminate the discordant sounds and concentrate on the natural timbre of the voice.

Let us follow Pavarotti's early development:

On the phrase '*che vive in ozio come Un gran signor!*' the [a] vowel on '*gran*' on the G4 is too open, the larynx is too high, and the tone is too white. This may best be described as '*voce aperta*' or Garcia's '*voce chiara*'. It sounds as if Pavarotti is maintaining a lateral position of the mouth, jaw and tongue in a part of the voice that requires *copertura* (covering). The remedy here pertains to laryngeal function and pharyngeal space, including the soft palate and *appoggio*, which will be elaborated below. Richard Miller confirms that:

> Holding the mouth in an unmodified lateral position while singing in the upper range will forfeit the first formant, produce an overly bright, thin tone, and destroy diction. Conversely, too large a buccal opening will create disequilibrium amongst overtones [Miller, 2004: 75].

It is now well established that a natural mouth opening with mounting frequency maintains the first formant while enriching the higher formants.

The remedy is to raise the soft palate and moderately lower the larynx from below through the simultaneous contraction of the sternothyroid muscle and the diaphragm whilst also modifying the vowel towards the [o] and adding more roundness and depth to the *oscuro* aspects of the voice. This will also retain the integrity of the vowel [Lamperti (c 1883)]. On the other hand, the [o] on the F4 '*signor*' is too narrow, a trifle tight, and throaty. This throatiness results from all the harmonics being crushed and compressed by the severe contraction of the vocal tract and suppressed by the subsequent mismatch between harmonics and formant frequencies.

I like Brown's conclusions in this respect, especially as it concurs with mine. He believes, as I do, 'A larger resonating cavity is needed to accommodate the high frequencies and intensities in the sound waves of higher and louder tones' [Brown, 1996:109].

Consequently, the [o] vowel is too narrow and tight. It needs to be modified towards the [aw] vowel, providing greater resonating space, which allows the upper harmonics to vibrate freely, enhancing the ring and resonance of the voice. Let us recall that it is not about purity of vowels but rather about vowel integrity and vocal comfort. One of the casualties of this quest for vowel purity is a cavalier disregard for the vocal blending mechanism, making the phrases more homogenous. The successful execution of these remedies can only occur when they are coordinated with the objective *appoggio* (breath management) and subjective *appoggio* (sympathetic vibrations-facial focus) with just the right measure of energy.

In addition to creating more space, the whole phrase needs to be energised with a greater level of *appoggio*, resulting in increased glottal resistance and a much firmer and longer glottal closure, all of which elicits an abrupt cessation of breath flow and a sharp, jagged spectrum yielding a firm and harmonically rich tone: brilliant it is only when the voice is given over to the breath (instead of being placed and poked) that the breath pressure is assured and constant. The breath guides the tone into the correct position (Vennard's idea of the illusion of placement) and what the Italians call *impostazione. On the other hand, scientists* refer to it as the location upon which the proprioceptive or sympathetic vibrations impinge with the greatest concentration of energy. Even though Campogalliani had taught Pavarotti not to place the voice, it would be years before he finally understood the limitations of this principle and accepted that doing nothing is not an option. Years later, he admitted that: 'every sound starts back in the throat, but it is the breath pressure that sends it forward and keeps it there' [Pavarotti, 1976: 5]. Even so, this is not a sufficient explanation: the truth is that the process is more complicated than that.

For a start, the ideal vowel is determined by pitch and intensity and must be allowed to find its most natural shape and space within the vocal tract. The articulators determine the length, area and shape, including the tongue, the lips, the mandible, the pharynx and the larynx, which configuration determines the formants and helps to track the modification of vowels. However, it is essential to recall that only the first and second formants are responsible for the formation of the vowels, whilst the singer's formant (a cluster of formants 3, 4, and 5 which are combined with a sizeable pharyngeal space and small laryngeal space) is responsible for the *squillo* or the resonance of the higher partials.

Finally, the singer may guide the sound waves towards a predetermined sympathetic focal point, especially at the *passaggio*, but never physically intervene. However, he cannot direct them there as it is only the impression of placement. The free movement of the articulators creates the right shape and space for a balanced *chiaroscuro* tone.

The G4 on '*Che lieto baglior*' is as brittle and vulnerable as short; it is also too open, resembling a [a] vowel rather than a collected [o]. The same may be said of the phrase 'ardent mio dramma ci scaldi.', in which the [a] vowel in '*scaldi*' is also far too open for a G4. The notes around the passaggio must be more collected (*voce chiusa and coperta*) if Pavarotti is going to affect a more covered tone (*suono coperto*) throughout the performance. The main problems derive

from the larynx, which is generally sitting too high (creating a disconnect between the breath and the vocal source), and a placement (*l'imposto*) which is the too indistinct and lacking definition. The *appoggio* is fragile at respiratory and proprioceptive levels (breath support and sympathetic vibrations, respectively).

The same remedy applies to the G4 of '*L'amor é un caminetto che sciupa troppo*'. The [o] in '*l'amor*' requires a deeper and steadier respiratory foundation: a type of respiration that typically lowers the larynx, abducts the glottis, and enhances the *oscuro* aspects of the tone to balance the brightness of the *chiaro*.

The remedy for the above problems lies in the ability to entice the stabilisation of the lowered larynx, which can only be achieved through the simultaneous contraction of the laryngeal strap muscles, mainly (sternothyroid, combined with the stabilising force of the sternocleidomastoid and respiratory muscles). This laryngeal posture can only succeed when combined with the contraction of the fibres surrounding the central tendon of the diaphragm in conjunction with the quadratus lamborum muscles, which lower and anchor the diaphragm posteriorly. These manoeuvres maintain the larynx in a moderately low position, creating the condition for the vocal tract to shape the source harmonics into a foundational tone (complete with depth, roundness and colour) but also creating the requirements for the singer's formant (squills).

Considering McKinney's principles — the differentiation between vowel purity and vowel integrity and the consequent need to modify the vowels without losing integrity — let us continue our analysis of his 1961 debut.

The phrase rising to the B4♭ on the [a] vowel in '*L'idea vampi in fiamma*,' is again too open, the laryngeal position too high, and the lower harmonics need more significant excitation so that it may gain in roundness, fullness and velvet — a more *oscuro* quality. Even phrases in the middle voice (such as '*zitto si da il mio dramma*' and '*in quell'azzurro guizzo languente sfuma un'ardente scena d'amor*') are too choppy and bumpy. There is no legato to speak of (the breath pressure is too inconsistent), and the follow-through (the breath and mental energy required to merge one vowel into the next) remains ineffective.

Finally, all the passaggio notes (F4s and G4s) in the early part of this performance display an uncertain and inefficient emission; this is a vocal production requiring greater firmness, precision and definition. On the other hand, much of this inefficiency is well-disguised by an easy and naturally beautiful voice. There are some inspiring sounds, especially in the high register, not to mention the *passaggio* notes when properly executed. It also helps that

the high-spirited, skylarking mood of the scene is one in which the audience is caught up in the fun and not expecting every note to be perfect.

That said, the [e] vowel on the A4 on the exclamation *Eureka!* is a more solid sound but still relatively narrow and constricted, lacking the amplitude that would make it an exciting top A. The [i] vowel on the '*si*' starts more forward, and one can hear that Pavarotti's intention is instinctively right simply because he attacks the [i] vowel solidly and with a forward thrust. However, this is marked by inefficient lowering of the diaphragm and, therefore, the larynx, insufficient breath pressure to maintain laryngeal position and the forward thrust of the sound wave, and inadequate vocal tract space to fulfil the singer's intentions. Consequently, I contend that the lack of subglottal pressure allows the trajectory of the sound waves to falter before finally falling back into the throat. Apart from a deficiency of *appoggio*, the configuration of space within the oropharyngeal cavity fails to honour the vowel. Concerning space, it remains a fact that for the lateral vowels [i] and [e], the apex of the tongue rests against the lower gum ridge, whilst the hump of the tongue arches forward against the hard palate. In so doing, it diminishes the space in the oral cavity and increases the area in the pharyngeal cavity. The opposite is valid with the darker round vowels such as the [o] and [u]. The latter mainly induces the curve of the tongue to arch back and up towards the soft palate, resulting in an expanded resonating space in the oral cavity and a diminished area in the pharyngeal cavity. These physiological and acoustic facts cannot be contravened without producing considerable tonal distortions.

The larynx must retain a flexible but moderately low position, which whilst not fixed, still prevents it from bopping up and down like a cork in deep water. This laryngeal stability is achieved by the combined action of the infrahyoid muscles (sternothyroid) whose contraction lowers the larynx, and the sternocleidomastoids that stabilise it. However, all of these suggestions need to be accompanied by the antagonistic contraction of the respiratory muscles, which provide the whole framework with a stable but flexible and dynamic foundation, in which constant adjustments are determined by both frequency and intensity.

Che Gelida Manina

The beginning of the famous aria reveals a young Pavarotti who still needs excellent control over his instrument. As I argued above, most of his problems can be traced back to an inadequate breathing strategy and consequent laryngeal constriction. Contrary to the techniques espoused above, Pavarotti too often allows the larynx to rise in alignment and sympathy with the fundamental frequency, especially on some lateral vowels requiring the tongue to arch up and forward against the hard palate. This tongue manoeuvre elevates the hyoid bone and the larynx attached to it, a gesture that impacts vowel integrity, prevailing timbre, and the legato line. This lack of respiratory and laryngeal stability contributes to an unsteady vibrato and an ensuing lack of clarity, firmness and tonal focus (*imposto*). In these circumstances, any serious attempt at interpretation and vocal colouring would seem chimerical and unlikely to succeed. Throughout this aria, we are reminded of the potential glory of the Pavarotti voice. However, we are also confronted with the fact that we are at the embryonic stages of his career, and nothing in this singing would suggest any more than the prospect of an outstanding job. Indeed, it would have been a brave prognostication to indicate that this was the beginning of a legendary career that would harken back to the great Caruso. Today, with the weight of history behind us, it is hard to imagine that Pavarotti's career may have been short and inconsequential. Yet, that scenario was a definite possibility at this stage of his development.

Let us proceed with forensic examination of this famous and very demanding aria. Right from the beginning, the phrase '*Che gelida manina! Se la lasci scalar,*' the voice is tremulous, lacking clarity, firmness and legato. The vocal line is uneven, with a variable vibrato that is quite unpredictable. On the interval of a fifth in the phrase '*Se la lasci riscaldar*' [A♭ to E♭], the larynx rises indiscriminately with pitch. In an accomplished singer, including the future

Pavarotti, the larynx remains moderately low, allowing only minor but controlled variations mainly driven by tongue position to accommodate the various vowels. It is important to remember that alterations in pitch are a function of the isometric tensions of the vocalis (intrinsic tensor) and the antagonistic action of the cricothyroid (stretcher). The intrinsic muscles of the larynx are responsible for frequency, firmness of tone and vocal quality (harmonic series), whilst laryngeal position is the responsibility of the extrinsic laryngeal muscles (suprahyoid and infrahyoid). These have consequences for matching the source harmonics with the formants of the vocal tract and considerable influence on resonance and vocal quality, but not, however, any direct influence on frequency.

Pavarotti deploys a sudden surge of energy for the difficult phrase '*cercar che giova?*', providing an excellent example of negotiating the *passaggio* notes and entry into head voice (*copertura*). However, by his later admission, he had not yet recognised that the consistent and balanced management of breath pressure is the glue that binds the different vowels together irrespective of the interval, frequency and intensity. With that in mind, the excursion between the syllables [o] in '*gio*' and the [a] '*Va*' in '*giova*' needs more mental energy and continuous respiratory follow-through. This concept is a powerful mental construct that subconsciously activates a more consistent sub-glottal pressure and promotes legato, ensuring that one vowel blooms naturally and seamlessly into the next. The foundation of this mechanism is a firm, constant, stable, but flexible breath pressure (flexible does not mean slack sub-glottal pressure).

On the other hand, Pavarotti had been working diligently on his *copertura* technique throughout the passaggio notes. In general, the *passaggio* phrases seem well rehearsed and confident; it is not until he reaches the descending phrase after the *passaggio* that he allows the energy level to drop. Campogalliani had warned him about the drop in energy and its effect on the sound, but Luciano followed his instincts. In this instance, Campogalliani was right.

In the phrase, '*e qui la luna l'abbiamo vicina,*' the [u] vowel on '*luna*' is distorted and deficient in objective *appoggio* (breath support). Let me hasten to add that making a minor aggiornamento on the [u] vowel on an A4 is not unusual. However, the *aggiustamento* generally maintains a greater vowel integrity level than Pavarotti in this passage. In addition, the tone should maintain its ring and forward posture (with the sensations from the subjective *appoggio* being felt on the masque), a sensation that this tone fails to achieve here.

The second '*chi son?*' on the B flat is generally excellent but could benefit from a slightly lower larynx. The latter manoeuvre would furnish the tone with more excellent roundness and fullness (*oscuro* aspects of tone), all under

the conscious control of the objective *appoggio*. Nonetheless, the ease of execution and the ringing quality of the tone offer an insight into where this marvellous voice is heading over the next few years. Unfortunately, the pursuant vocal performance is still uneven and inconsistent. For instance, '*e che faccio?*' is not *ben appoggiata*. The tone lacks sufficient mental energy and respiratory follow-through to ensure a lovely legato line between the *faccio* (see the music passage below).

On the glorious phrase '*Talor dal mio forziere*', the Pavarotti voice is again under energised on the A4♭ and not sufficiently *appoggiata*, resulting in a more uneven tone than we would typically expect from such a gifted voice. This lack of *appoggio* is evident in the under-energised A4♭, and in the [e] vowel last syllable of 'forziere' the voice becomes a little hoarse, always a sign that it is under pressure.

The phrase '*ventrar con voi pur ora*' should be an entirely different colour; it is still passionate, but in this instance, it should have a lilt in the tone and employ a more languid tone. The phrase that follows, '*E I bei sogni miei, tostosi di leguar*', reveals his dream world and his unconscious longing, represented by a globe of tempestuous and conflicting desires.

The first phrase of '*E I bei sogni miei*' should be more intense and expansive, and the phrase *tostosi di leguar* should be contrasted with a softer and more languid tone.

In these two contrasting passages, let us examine what is happening at the laryngeal level.

In the more intense phrase, '*E I bei sogni miei,*' the aryepiglottic folds (laryngeal collar) and ventricle bands are both narrowed, and the epiglottis is lowered over the supraglottic orifice. On the other hand, in the softer singing, the aryepiglottic folds and the ventricle bands are more relaxed and, therefore, opened wider, whilst the epiglottis is raised [Doscher, 1994: 141]. Subglottal pressure is greater for the more intense singing than moderately soft singing.

These contrasting phrases suggests a world of colliding emotions, almost as if Rodolfo is uncertain as to which emotion is dominating his subconscious at this very moment. These contrasts represent Rodolfo at his authentic best, displaying a great deal of passion and temperament as well as imbuing every phrase with a more nuanced emotional expression. Mimi should have the sense that Rodolfo has dreams that would change the world. He may be just another struggling young poet right now, but the plans he dares to dream are for the ages.

Finally, in the phrase '*Ma il furto non m'accora*' Rodolfo recognises that Mimi has invaded his senses and stolen his dreams but concedes that he does not regret the theft. Unfortunately, in this instance Pavarotti's singing does not always reflect Rodolfo's noble emotions. The phrase should be more elegant, more passionate, with greater abandonment and control.

Vocally there are some difficult moments for Pavarotti. For instance, on the phrase '*tortoise dileguar!*' his voice almost disappears; and on the phrase '*Ma il furto non m'accora,*' he is trying to save his voice for the top C. This is about the worst thing a tenor can do, because the [u] vowel in '*furto*' lacks both *appoggio*, breath pressure, sympathetic vibrations and facial focus. This allows for a surge of energy on the phrase '*poiche, poiche vi ha preso stanza,*' just before an excellent top $C5$ on the [e] vowel of the *Speranza*.

The C5 on '*la speranza*' is a beautiful sound and the B♭ that follows is its equal. Although we hear a more accentuated abandonment in later Pavarotti performances, this is an excellent debut, representing what Pavarotti is all about at this point of his career. He is young, ambitious, and determined to play to his strength, which was his top register at this time.

The phrase '*Or che mi conoscete, parlate voi*' should be an entirely different colour and intensity from that which preceded it and that which follows. However, Pavarotti sings each of these phrases with the same colour, the same timbre and similar intensity, and whilst it is a beautiful sound, it remains lacks imagination. Each of these four phrases should differ, ranging from uncertainty to a more assertive sound on the martellato phrase, and a more pleading sound on the last phrase, 'Vi piaccia dir', which should fade to double *pp*.

In the final phrase, '*Vi piaccia dir*,' Rodolfo invites Mimi to tell him her story. He has made his play for her affections, and now comes the moment of truth. Has he said too much, too little or just enough? Does she believe him, and is the description of his inner world sufficiently fascinating and enticing for her to accept the invitation?

In her wonderful narrative *'Mi chiamano Mimi'*, she seems to like him well enough to tell him her own story.

'Yes,' she says, 'I will tell you.' 'They call me Mimi, but my real name is Lucia. My story is a brief one, not much to tell. I spend my time embroidering, but my life is serene. In fact, you could even say that I am happy. I like the simple things of life, those that speak of love, like the perfume of a flower. I live alone; I don't go to church much, but I pray a lot.' 'Ah,' she declares, 'but what I love most is when spring breaks through the winter freeze: that first ray of sunshine is mine; that first kiss of April is mine.' Then she repeats softly and even more sensually, 'The first kiss is mine'. By the time Mimi finishes her aria Rodolfo has been completely conquered by her simplicity, her authenticity, her disarming candour.

O Soave Fanciulla

The scene is now set for one of the most powerful and passionate love duets in all opera. Rodolfo is at the window talking to his friends; he tells Marcello that he is not coming alone and asks him to hold two seats for him at Café Momus instead of one. When Marcello discovers that Rodolfo is bringing someone to dinner he understands perfectly; and calls out to the other Bohemians that Rodolfo has found his inspiration. At this point, Rodolfo turns around and catches a glimpse of Mimi bathed in moonlight. She is simply the most beautiful, most angelic sight he has ever seen. Being his romantic soul, he already imagines what life would be like with this divine creature. Moved by this unexpected surge of emotion he begins — *'O Soave Fanciulla'* — O lovely maid in the moonlight.

In this performance, beginning with *'O Soave Fanciulla,'* the whole phrase is uneven, but the [u] vowel on the G3♯ of 'fanciulla' and the [a] vowel at the end of 'fanciulla' are particularly throaty (*voce ingolata*). This is because this particular [a] vowel is distorted, resulting in a sound that is not only under-energised but also too heavy and plummy. In the lower range, Pavarotti's [a] vowels are much closer to the [o] rather than the [a]. He has over-modified the vowel, using the lips instead of the breath to focus the tone. However, in the process he has lost the integrity of the vowel and elongated the vocal tract, lowering all the formants.

In the phrase *'O dolce viso di mite circonfuse alba lunar,'* the [i] vowel in *'viso'* is too throaty, caused by a retroflex tongue. The [a] vowel in 'lunar' is also unsteady because it is under energised.

The phrase *'In te ravviso'* reveals a much better tone because it is in the zona di passagio, sung in mixed register, allowing the voice to find a better position (importation) and eliciting a firmer appoggio.

In the phrase '*il sogno ch'io vorrei sempre sognar*', Pavarotti is making more of an effort to infuse the tone with a surge of breath energy by adhering to the climax of the phrase. The sustained [e] vowel on the G # in vorrei is once again too narrow, a little constricted and throaty. In fact, not only does the [e] lack the *oscuro* aspects of the tone (as it needs more fundamental), but it also lacks the width associated with a lateral vowel. This duet confirms our earlier assessment of Pavarotti's singing. There are too many [i] and [e] vowels beginning with a faulty and throaty onset, in which the sound starts in the throat, attempts to come forward, only to drop back in the throat again. Even when he attempts to begin the tone forward on the mask, it soon loses focus and falls back because it is under energised.

The idea of singing the phrase '*fremon gia nell'anima, dolcezze estreme*' on the E4♭ in a suspended more ethereal vocal quality is excellent, but breath management remains problematic. For instance, the [a] vowel in '*anima*' is not

appoggiata, causing the larynx to rise, rendering the sound tremulous and uncontrolled. In the repeat '*dolcezze estreme, fremon dolcezze estreme, nel bacio fremon amor*' Pavarotti is trying to sing softly and produce a floating, more suspended tone. This is an excellent artistic choice, yielding a better position (*impostazione*). Still, unfortunately it is creating a different set of problems, as the sound itself is now unsteady and lacks legato. This is particularly so at the end of the phrase '*Nel bacio freme amor*' in which he loses control of the breath, and therefore the tone, and the vibrato. The remedy for this problem is a much-improved breath management strategy which would allow Pavarotti to control the *appoggio* and anchor the larynx in a moderately low position. Both strategies are designed to steady the tone and enhance the legato line.

The following phrase in which he sings '*Sei mia*' on the F4♯ is very aggressive.

Quite apart from the fact that it is not very poetic, he cuts the passage short, in particular the [i] vowel in *mia*. Even the final [a] vowel is short, uncertain and distorted. The phrase '*Gia mi mandi via*' reveals a contrived, manufactured sound: the [i] in '*mi*' is particularly throaty (*ingolato*).

In the following phrase Mimi hints that she would like to propose something, but she dare not; Pavarotti aggressively orders his Mimi to elaborate when a graceful invitation would be so much better. The '*di*' is a command rather than an invitation and particularly aggressive at that.

Mimi's rejoinder that she could perhaps join him for dinner is both endearing and provocative. Rodolfo responds with the phrase '*sarebbe cosi dolce restar qui, c'e freddo fuori*'. The sentiment is suitably boyish, but the sound is shallow, choppy, colourless, and lacking legato. We don't get the sense of the quick wit that marks Rodolfo's character when he suggests '*that it would be lovely to stay here; it's so cold out there*'. This is a sound that again lacks firmness, legato, incisiveness, and definition. It doesn't sound at all seductive. This suggestion is loaded with intimate subtext, which is missed in this particular depiction, because it is all played at a surface level, with the real emotions remaining largely unexplored. In this instance, there is not even a hint of the future Pavarotti.

The phrase '*Dammi il braccio mia piccina*' again displays a tremulous, uncertain tone, utterly devoid of subtext. I believe that most of Pavarotti's problems stem from technical difficulties that can be traced directly back to his breathing strategy and, to a lesser degree, to his vocal emission and pronunciation. The latter displays a greater level of overall accomplishment but still manifests specific problems with the [i], [e], and [o] vowels in particular. This is the result of not only a deficient breathing strategy but also an incorrect laryngeal position and an equally bad articulatory configuration, especially the retracted tongue on the [i] and [e] vowels. At this point of his development, Pavarotti's technique was inadequate for many of the demands made by Rodolfo's music as it prevented him from attaining an elegant legato line, a well-focused tone and a high level of sophisticated expression. The breathing strategy prevented him from stabilising the larynx and steadying the vibrato and overall sound.

Although Pavarotti tried to maintain a forward ringing sound, the inadequate breath pressure strategy and a vocal tract which too often remains in an ideal fixated position, ensures an inherently inflexible vocal tract and a tone that is too far back and too throaty. This imbued the sound with a lovely velvety hue, but more was needed for clarity of diction, and incisiveness of tone.

It would be nearly fifteen years before Pavarotti could express his understanding of the connection between breath and voice source, and when he did, this was the outcome:

> One must never forget, in my opinion, that the voice is formed in the throat, and 'throaty singing' is caused by the diaphragm not being able to push the voice out of the throat. All sounds originate in the same way, but it is the diaphragm that succeeds in pushing enough air through the vocal cords making them vibrate intensely (as in a wind instrument). When this does not come about, there is an insufficient vibration of the cords and the sound becomes throaty [Pavarotti, 1976: 5].

Pavarotti is right about the insufficient breath energy being a problem, but we also need to consider laryngeal position, vocal onset, and the connection and coordination between the breath pressure and the glottis. Any of these and other malfunctions can result in a throaty tone. In fact, throatiness is often the result of a cluster of these defects.

Now, let us return to our examination of the 1961 La Boheme. Instead of petitioning Mimi to love him as would be expected from a poet singing the phrase '*che m'ami di,*' he aggressively orders her to tell him of her love. He sings the [i] on '*di*' more like a French [ü] than an Italian [i], which is not necessarily a bad thing in a more skilful tenor, but it doesn't work here. In this depiction, the '*amor, amor*' at the end of the scene is nothing more than an opportunity to sing a glorious top C5, and all power to him for that. However, in years to come, he would understand that the phrase is meant to be an ode to romantic love, the first consciousness of a seminal feeling between two young people susceptible to love. They hope to nurture this immediate attraction, resulting in a deeper emotional attachment.

I am not going to go on at length about this analysis. I want to make four points:

1. even though Pavarotti had a magnificent voice, his instrument at the time of his debut was not in optimal technical condition.

2. Even though Pavarotti was the possessor of a great voice, he would not have become a truly great tenor had he persisted with his original technique.

3. Pavarotti worked very diligently to transform an inferior vocal technique into one of the most complete and cohesive techniques in operatic history.

4. It does this great tenor a disservice to attribute his success only to his undoubted natural talent without acknowledging the role played by his tremendous determination, his vocal intelligence, and his strong desire to develop his artistic education, honing his technical skills for future greatness.

Many years later, Pavarotti himself concluded that,

> I always have faith in a well-educated voice, great technique, and facility in the high register. This is not because a high note in itself is of great importance but because easy high notes denote a technique, as I said before, already well developed in the covering of the transitional notes, which are the actual stumbling block [Pavarotti, 1976: 5].

According to Bonynge, Pavarotti showed great intelligence in who to ask for help and how to ask. He has a sixth sense about who was best equipped to assist him with a particular problem at a specific time.

Act II

In act two, a couple of exchanges point to the future, the first being the phrase *Chi guardi?* This [ee] on 'chi' is again far too aggressive, taking on a menacing tone and making Rodolfo a less sympathetic and attractive character. This phrase shows more hurt than aggression, the exchange taking on a very different manner. Rodolfo is literally asking, 'What are you doing, you are supposed to be with me?' Mimi's retort, '*Sei geloso?*' should be both teasing and playful. A good Mimi takes every opportunity to make her character as multi-dimensional as possible. That is why the exchanges in the second act are so crucial for both characters, especially Mimi. She never gets another chance to be just a coy, young girl in the process of falling in love. This is her last chance to demonstrate her wit, sense of fun, and capacity to love. Rodolfo's response is also most revealing of his character when he declares, '*All'uom felice sta il sospetto accanto*' (a happy man should always be suspicious), showing another aspect of his humanity — his philosophy. He is not taking anything for granted. These are the thoughts of a sensitive young soul who understands that happiness is fleeting and that humans are not as much in control as they would like to think they are. So, when Mimi asks him if he is happy (*Sei felice?*) He responds with an emotional outburst on an A *flat*, '*Ah, si, tanto!*' (Ah, *you have no idea.*)

This scene is consolidated after Rodolfo introduces Mimi to the Bohemians (his friends) with the most poetic and memorable introductions in all opera. '*Questa e Mimi, gaia fioraia. Il suo venir completa la bella compagnia, perche, perche son io il poeta, essa la poesi. Dal mio cervel sbocciano I canti, dalle sue dita sbocciano I fior; dall'anime esultanti sboccia l'amor, sboccia l'amor*'. 'My mind creates the poetry, she is my inspiration, and from our exultant souls blooms our love'.

This scene suits Pavarotti very well; he handles it vocally and temperamentally with aplomb. Vocally, he is much better in these exchanges, maintaining a more lyrical approach. Although some unsteadiness of tone creeps into the phrase, he manages well. It is significant that at the climax on the top A4 in the phrase '*sboccia l'amor,*' Pavarotti allows the larynx to rise, creating a disconnect between the breath and the voice source, with a concomitant moment of uncertainty. The significance lies in the fact that he still manages to produce a more than acceptable climax, whereas a lesser voice would not have managed it. This passage could be more complex, much more than one would think by looking at the score.

Act III

In this performance, Rodolfo's opening to the third act, '*Marcello finalmente qui niun ci senti*' is marred by a late musical entry. In the phrase '*io voglio separami da Mimi,*' the [i] vowel on *Mimi* is too bright and too forced because the tone is not cushioned by the breath. In this instance it is not the type of pushing that comes from aggression. On the contrary it is a type of vocal wildness that comes from the instrument not being harnessed by the *appoggio* as experienced in Lamperti's *lotta vocale* (antagonistic action of the breathing muscles). In the next passage '*ma di quegli'occhi azure allo splendor, esso e risorto*' Pavarotti has found an excellent *impostazione* (Vennard's illusion of placement). Unfortunately, his attack on the [o] vowel in the phrase '*Ora il tedio lassa!*' is not equal. He creeps into the note instead of attacking it directly with the mind as well as *appoggio*. This results in an unsteady and opaque tone, momentarily finding the correct position only to then fall back into the throat. The remedy for these faults is to enact a simultaneous onset, allow the '*ora*' to migrate towards a more open [aw] vowel, slightly drop the jaw and increase the level of breath *appoggio*. The objective should be to unify the instrument by creating a coordinated, solid connection between the larynx (voice source), the breathing system, and the resonator. Once having connected the instrument, the singer should get out of the way and allow the voice to utilise its inherent intelligence and natural freedom to produce the sound initiated by the mind.

The following phrase begins on the G4 [a] vowel — '*amo Mimi, sovra ogni cosa al mondo Io l'amo*'. The '*amo*' is launched with the breath as a nicely modified [o] vowel. However, it soon loses the connection between the breath and the tone on the B♭ on the word '*mondo*,' creating a disconnect that persists for the rest of the phrase on '*Io l'amo*'.

In general, the problems with the deficiency of breath energy and *appoggio* lead to an unsteady sound. The uneasy vibrato persists, as does the emission of the [i] vowel which is consistently throaty (*ingolato*). The [e] vowel is either *ingolato* or alternatively very bright, especially on the *passaggio* notes and those above the stave. Pavarotti handles the big moments very well even though the sound is not yet the full-blooded, harmonically rich Pavarotti tone that it would later become. He also manages the diminutive, more lyrical moments very well, including the moving phrase '*ma ho paura, ma ho paura*'. Having tried to convince himself that he no longer loves Mimi, Rodolfo is finally left with his fear and acceptance of the truth. With the phrase '*Mimi e tanto malate,*' we begin the sad exposition of this romantic tragedy. Young as she is, Mimi is dying of consumption. Artistically, Pavarotti captures the gravity and tragedy of the scene very well, but vocally, he still has problems with the emission of certain vowels, especially both of the [i] vowels in *Mimi* and some of the [e] vowels are still constricted and throaty.

Overall Pavarotti manages this music very well. He has a definite feel for the character, even if not yet sufficiently accomplished to depict the heartache that the imminent separation from Mimi demands. This is particularly true of the passages in which he is forced to acknowledge the seriousness of Mimi's illness. Once Marcello is able to break down the veneer and bravado, we see the extent of Rodolfo's distress as he is forced to realise that Mimi is dying — '*La povera piccina è condannata,*' *(the poor girl is condemned)*. This music combined with the force of the dramatic situation demands raw emotions.

A fine example is to be found in the phrase '*una terribil tosse les'il petto le scuote, già le smunte gote, di sangue rosse*', which describes her terrible plight. The tenor melody weaves its way up to a glorious and heart wrenching B♭ on the [a] vowel in the phrase '*sangue rosse*'. Pavarotti sings this music very well, and although lacking poise, and not yet able to furnish the requisite emotional depth, he knows how this piece should sound.

Dunque è Propio Finita and Quartet

Following Mimi's *Addio senza rancor* (Farewell, I wish you well), Pavarotti begins the duet, which eventually becomes a quartet with the phrase '*dunque e propio finita, te ne vai, te ne vai La mia piccina, addio sogni d'amor*'. Here he laments her imminent departure, farewelling not only Mimi but also their dreams of love. Unfortunately, the Pavarotti tone is all very bright and displays none of the genuine emotional depth and pathos that one would expect from a poet being vanquished by the end of a passionate love affair. The same could be said of the touching phrase '*addio sognante vita, che un tuo sorriso aqueta*'. This is followed by a tender farewell to a life of dreams, suspicions, and kisses:

'*Addio sospetti, baci,* and '*ch'io da vero poeta rimavo con carezze*' (as an authentic poet rhymed with caresses). Once again, Pavarotti knows how this piece should be sung, but he does not yet possess the technique to execute the necessary nuances.

There is no sense of caressing the notes, no sense of devastation during the phrase '*addio sogno d'amor*' (farewell to dreams of love). Nor is there a sense of lilting lightness on '*chiacchieran le fontane*' (the chattering of the fountains-see music excerpt below).

These are the kind of demands and nuances that the future and great Pavarotti will have no problems fulfilling but right now, he is still at the required point of development.

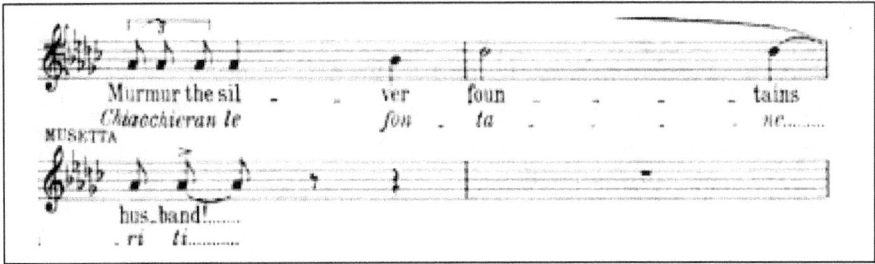

Pavarotti ends the act with a lovely B♭ and a most touching descending passage, '*Ci lascerem alla stagion dei fior,*' (They will separate in spring; being alone in winter is far too depressing). The lovers determine to postpone their parting until spring, when the roses are in bloom. It should be a little more bearable when the sun is shining, and the flowers are blooming (see the music excerpt below). Pavarotti gives a fine vocal rendition in this act; even if he is yet to mature into the role both vocally and emotionally, the material is just splendid.

Act IV

In the fourth act, Puccini brings his Bohemians back to the attic where we first met them in act one. However, the contrast between the good-natured hilarity of the first act and the depressed atmosphere of the fourth act couldn't be starker: it is tinged with loneliness and longing. The duet between Marcello and Rodolfo reveals the earnest longing and nostalgia they both feel for the halcyon days when they shared this very attic with Mimi and Musetta.

In the final act of the opera, Pavarotti has overcome his nerves and the voice is well warmed up, flowing very comfortably for the stage of technical accomplishment he has achieved at this time. He still has some problems with the attack (onset) and release of the sound. For instance, in the opening phrase 'con pariglie e livré' the 'livré' bursts out with an uncontrolled blast of air which effects not only the sound but also the line. However, the overall sound in this duet is really quite lyric, lean and bright, and a fresh sounding tone possessed of a lovely bloom. The first phrase of the duet '*Oh Mimi tu più non torni*' is not only light but also a little shallow. This is a sound that requires more fundamental (*oscuro*), as well as the roundness and depth that traditionally come with such an adjustment (*chiaroscuro*).

Nonetheless, it is a charming sound, although often displaying a weak first formant which unbalances the *chiaro/scuro*. When the G4 on '*giorni belli*' finds its focus, it is further evidence of an excellent and easily accessible head register. The same applies to the G4 on '*collo di neve*,' which is beautifully poised notwithstanding the presence of a low level of laryngeal rigidity in its formation (Please see music below).

Some of the singing in the second half of the duet displays a fast vibrato which, when combined with a stentorian delivery of the text, mars not only the legato line but also the inherently melancholic and nostalgic mood of the piece. The act continues with some exciting interjections, many of them promising but, at this stage rather light-voiced, mainly due to an inefficient *appoggio*. This produces a tone that is often constricted and an interpretation that is a little strident, lacking depth of characterisation and roundness of fashion. This notwithstanding, it would be bloody-minded in the extreme not to recognise that we are in the presence of a major talent possessing a genuinely phenomenal voice and considerable interpretative potential.

Overall Pavarotti's debut performance was very promising and there were many moments during which he did himself proud, allowing the audience to glimpse the future great tenor. However, recognising the extent of his nervousness, he performed with such concentration that he was barely aware of what was happening around him.

Pavarotti later declared that on that night, he was afraid of the conductor, fearful of the audience, afraid of everything until '*Che gelida manina,*' after which he knew that the audience appreciated him, thus releasing most of the tension.

People came backstage, and the feedback was overwhelmingly positive. However, his father Fernando was the exception. He pulled Luciano aside and said,

> 'That was very nice Luciano, very nice. But you still don't sound like Gigli and Schipa. You must work some more' [Pavarotti in Wright, 1981: 59].

When the Nova Gazette di Reggio Emilia came out the following day, the critique was more generous and more favourable than his father's judgement. The paper reported that,

> The tenor Luciano Pavarotti sang with estimable good taste and vivid musicality, displaying vocal equipment both penetrating and flexible. He was liked perhaps more than his colleagues [Pavarotti in Wright, 1981: 59].

For the purpose of learning and furthering our knowledge of vocal technique, I have perhaps been more critical of Pavarotti's youthful technique than I had intended. Overall, I believe that the general praise and encouragement elicited by his debut was fair and abundantly justified. One could not help but hear and encourage the potential, and yet those of us who have studied the art form for over fifty years know that potential is highly fragile. When not accompanied by a solid technique, intelligent decision making and smart choices, it can prove rather fleeting. I am happy to say that Pavarotti's future career would be characterised by very intelligent decision making and a number of wise choices, not to mention a great deal of instinct.

Years later, in a contemplative mood, Pavarotti believed that you need certain events that recharge your batteries and enthusiasm. He felt that an artist is primarily sustained by self-belief and the worthiness of his mission and that if you believe in something, it can be of enormous help. He continued:

> I had worked hard for six years without earning a penny. But it is much easier to keep that faith when it is being recharged by someone from the outside who knows

the profession you are trying for...I suppose the so-called belief in ourselves is the foundation of our talent, but I am sure these encouragements are the mortar that holds it together. In the case of Ziliani liking my voice, it was more than just support for my morale, of course. He was a man in a position to get me jobs in opera houses throughout Europe [Pavarotti in Wright, 1981: 60-61].

I would now like to address the issue of saving the voice before the top notes, which problem I believe is all in Pavarotti's mind. If you have the right voice for the role, which he had in abundance, you don't have to worry about saving your voice. The real problem was that Pavarotti had not yet acquired a reliable and systematic technique that would allow his voice to do what it was meant to do consistently. Most of his problems can be traced back to a lack of objective *appoggio*. Harsh though this may sound, his early vocal issues must be explained so that the reader may understand the immensity of his later achievement. Pavarotti, like his great predecessors Enrico Caruso and Beniamino Gigli, had some severe problems to resolve before greatness would be bestowed upon him. That he proved lavishly equal to the task is now the stuff of legend and the real story here. Pavarotti in fact requires historical honesty, authenticity, perspective and truth. He was constantly talking about truthful and authentic performances and that is what this book strives to achieve.

Pavarotti travelled a long way from his humble beginnings in Modena, but he always remained humble and grateful for his good fortune (There are many people today who would benefit by adopting Luciano's humility and gratitude).

The problem is that often the lateral vowels have too much point and are essentially too narrow, because Pavarotti seems to focus the tone with the lips on the [i] and [e] in a similar position to the [u], instead of using the energy of the great to focus. I believe this event is not just about focusing the tone, but rather a quest for singing a modified vowel that would take the edge of what would typically be a very metallic and edgy tone.

These problems are the result of protruding lips, a constricted throat, a sagging zygomatic fascia, an elongated vocal tract that lowers all the formants, combined with an inadequate appoggio. Too often Pavarotti attacks the note without appropriate prephonatory-tuning, so that the attack is not coordinated with the breath, and the resonator is not ready to either enhance or suppress the product emanating from the vocal folds, resulting in a throaty, constricted tone. Consequently, we can say that the remedy to these problems is the complete reversal of these vocal faults. The singer must have clarity of thought and respiratory preparation before even opening their mouth thus preparing the instrument to achieve his vocal intentions. Do not underestimate the power of the mind in singing.

The reversal of these faults requires the acquisition of the noble posture, a highly developed awareness of the appoggio system, the elevation of the zygomatic arch which also raises the soft palate, a pleasant countenance and a hint of a smile. Additional requirements include a lowering of the larynx and widening of the pharynx, a withdrawal of the protruding lips, a moderate lowering of the jaw and freedom of the tongue to make the necessary phonetic adjustment even as we sing. All of this has to be built upon the foundations of an excellent objective and subjective *appoggio* strategy.

We saw earlier that McKinney (1994) informed our argument by suggesting that we can sing the [i] and [u] vowels with a slightly opened mouth which creates space, relieves the constriction in the throat and maintains vowel integrity. The [i] and [u] vowels are formed with the extreme and opposite position of the tongue, the hump of which is fronted towards the hard palate for the [i] vowel and backed towards the soft palate for the [u] vowel). This produces a very bright tone for the earlier clear lateral vowel and a dark tone for the round vowel. When the vocal tone becomes too shrill or too dark the vowel must migrate towards its closest relative vowel, generally in a more central position. Many young singers aim for an extremely brilliant sound or a distinctively dark velvety tone depending on their voice culture and voice type. Pavarotti aimed for the earlier quality for most of his career and Caruso for the latter category. Concerning particular tonal affinities, I urge young tenors against exaggerated brilliance and baritones against exaggerating darkness. A balanced *chiaro scuro* is the mantra of the day. The answer, I believe, is for young tenors not to attempt what is unnatural to their particular voice quality nor to overemphasise what may come naturally to them. Extremes are always dangerous. In this regard, I like Richard Miller's treatment of this subject very much. He states:

> Tenors should not be admonished to produce brighter sound by increasing the intensity of upper harmonic partials…the *chiaroscuro* (light/dark) timbre of the classical international school demands balance among the prominent areas of acoustic strength, the fundamental and the first, third, fourth, and fifth formants. Every vocal instrument has its own individual quality, but all timbres must adhere to the chiaroscuro principle [Miller, 2004: 83].

It is important to recall that in the historical Italian school, the designation 'chiaroscuro' is used universally as a vocal pedagogy term. Miller continues:

> 'Chiaroscuro' means much the same thing in voice timbre as it does in the visual arts: the balancing of bright and dark aspects of colour, and degrees of shading. In vocalism, '*chiaroscuro*' refers specifically to the equilibrium of acoustic strength manifested by an ideal distribution of lower and upper harmonic partials (overtones) clustered in formants. Modern spectral analysis has verified the chiaroscuro (clear/dark timbre) concept, a balance of force among the formants that represent acoustic peaks in voiced phonation [Miller, 2004: 63-64].

The above principles are joined to the technical framework espoused earlier in these pages, and which we are going to utilise to examine Pavarotti's future development.

Richard Miller addresses this issue very well, when he contends that: 'holding the mouth in unmodified lateral position while singing in upper range will forfeit the first formant, produce an overly bright, thin tone and destroy diction. Conversely, too large a buccal opening will create disequilibrium among overtones [Miller, 2004: 75].

At this point, we can begin to draw certain conclusions about Pavarotti's technique,

- The first is that Pavarotti's respiratory technique is a long way from being a good foundational technique.

- The second is that his focus or subjective *appoggio* needs to be more consistent.

- Pavarotti is so determined to maintain the purity of vowels at the *passaggio,* and beyond that, his tone manifests considerable constriction and loss of quality. I like the explanation offered by James McKinney below:

> The critical element is that the phonemic integrity of the vowel be maintained — that an [i] vowel, for example will still retain its basic [i]-ness and its phonemic identity despite all the variations it may undergo. Only when it crosses the border of a neighbouring phoneme will it lose its identity and integrity. Research seems to reveal that when a singer tries to reach the goal of a consistently produced voice (giving the illusion of uniform tone quality from top to bottom), he makes a lot of compromises with 'vowel purity' [McKinney, 1994: 158-159].

Preparing the Future

In the glow of his marvellous success, Pavarotti and Magiera settled down to a routine of coaching lessons so that Pavarotti could secure a repertoire that would allow him to begin his operatic career. Years later, in a contemplative mood, Pavarotti recounted the story of his debut in La Boheme, the type of evening that recharges an artist's enthusiasm. He recalled:

> You always hear about struggling artists having faith in themselves. Well, I had confidence in myself. I had worked hard for six years without earning a penny. But it is much easier to keep up the faith when it gets recharged by someone from the outside who knows the profession you are trying for...I suppose the so-called faith in ourselves is the foundation of our talent, but I am sure these encouragements are the mortar that holds it together. In the case of Ziliani liking my voice, it was more than just support for my morale, of course. He was a man in a position to get me jobs in opera houses throughout Europe [Pavarotti in Wright, 1981: 60-61].

Over the next six months Magiera and Pavarotti worked on the role of the Duke in *Rigoletto*, Alfredo in *La Traviata*, Edgardo in *Lucia* and Pinkerton in *Butterfly*. They worked assiduously and meticulously, and a page at the time, Pavarotti began to conquer these roles. The Duke in *Rigoletto* is a particularly difficult role because the *tessitura* is consistently high, and there is an abundance of notes around the *passaggio*. Even La Donna è Mobile, which is often underestimated because of its popularity, contains some very difficult moments. This is especially so with the sustained F before rising to the final cadenza and the interval of a fourth rising to the to B4 on the last *'pensier'*. Even more challenging is the aria *'Parmi veder le lagrime'*, which contains the most significant number of differentiated obstacles than anything else in the score. However, the duet with Gilda and the famous last act quartet are not as easy as they appear on the page.

Perhaps the authoritative word on the duke should be given to Pavarotti: he declares that the duke is:

> One of the most challenging tenor roles for me is the Duke in Rigoletto. It is difficult because Verdi has asked the tenor to sing in so many different styles - lyric, spent, leggier. All these styles are required at one moment or another [Pavarotti, 1981: 144].

It was during this heady time that Luciano and Adua made the decision to marry. Finally, after so many years of hoping and waiting, they began to feel confident in the future. Adua, in particular had a good feeling about Luciano's prospects. They married on 30 September 1961, some five months after Pavarotti's successful debut. They had been engaged for about eight years, and their relationship had not always been easy, resembling in the early days a roller coaster ride. However, the time had come and somehow that big decision was easy. They travelled to Tuscany in Luciano's pride and joy, an ancient little Fiat. From Tuscany, they drove to the Italian Riviera for a two-week honeymoon.

Having returned from their honeymoon, the couple moved into a two-room apartment provided by Adua's father. The apartment was directly across the hall from his own, and Adua was happy to be near her father. Her mother having passed when Adua was only six, he had been not only the material provider, but also the constant source of emotional security and domestic stability for both Adua and her sister Giovanna. The sisters were also very close. In fact, up until the wedding, Adua and Giovanna, lived with their father. Later Giovanna's husband and their baby also lived together in their father's apartment.

Having established their living arrangements, Adua secured a new position at the office of the Agricultural Association of Modena and soon resigned from her teaching position. Luciano's engagements were still sporadic and consequently, her relatively meagre but consistent salary became critical to the Pavarotti's well-being.

Meanwhile Luciano had been in contact with Ziliani. The man was as good as his word and began to represent Luciano in the most assiduous manner. Ziliani was not a great salesman; in fact, he was rather understated, but it was for this reason that opera managers took him seriously. When he told a particular manager that Pavarotti was a fine young tenor nobody questioned his judgement. I would not wish to convey the impression that promoting Pavarotti was an easy task for Ziliani; introducing an unknown tenor to opera impresarios who are risk averse is never easy.

Pavarotti experienced the perennial problem that all young singers at the beginning of their careers experience. You may be talented; you may even be gifted but you're nobody until someone in a position of power gives you the opportunity to earn your stripes. Most managements and impresarios are uneasy with an unknown quantity, and conductors also find comfort in working with established artists who can follow the baton. At the very least they knew what their leading man or lady was going to deliver, and most established artists brought their own kudos and as well as their own following with them.

Another problem that confronted Pavarotti and Ziliani was the fact that after the war many of the smaller provincial theatres that had served as grass roots opera companies as well as nurturers of young talent, failed to reopen. Previously these theatres had served as a combination of opera school, *consevatorio* and community opera house, so their failure to reopen ensured that this middle step somewhere between amateur theatre and the great opera houses had disappeared. Consequently, young singers began their careers alongside fully fledged opera stars in major houses whose mandate was staging quality productions of opera rather than nurturing of new talent. This was a catastrophic event at the time and its echoes can still be heard today.

Nonetheless Ziliani believed in his young charge and worked tirelessly to help establish his career. Only once did he have to resort to accepting a blind booking for Pavarotti just to keep him working. A blind booking describes a situation in which an impresario demands a world-renowned singer from an agent such as Ziliani for his opera. The latter agrees to arrange this booking on the condition that the impresario also employ a young and highly talented singer such as Pavarotti. Ziliani did not have to do that again for two reasons. Firstly, word was getting around that Pavarotti was indeed a very gifted young tenor. Secondly, Ziliani himself had a reputation for having integrity and if anything, he was entirely reserved about his clients. When the management of the Teatro del Giglio in Lucca (Puccini's hometown) was looking for a tenor to sing Rodolfo in *La Boheme,* Ziliani strongly recommended Pavarotti and he was given the role. During rehearsals the conductor confessed to Pavarotti that he had never known Ziliani to praise anyone as he had the young tenor from Modena, so he knew before he even opened his mouth that Pavarotti must be a very good tenor indeed.

Even so *La Boheme* at the Teatro del Giglio proved to be a disappointment for Pavarotti. Rosanna Cartieri who was singing Mimi was no longer in her prime, and having heard her leading man singing *Che gelida manina* she became very insecure, turning the production into a nightmare especially for Pavarotti. Consequently, even though he sang well he felt that the voice could have been more secure. From the very beginning of his career Pavarotti was his own harshest critic. He believed that he could have attained greater freedom in this performance, especially in the high register.

In the early days Adua used to travel with him as often as she could, leaving their baby Lorenza with her sister Giovanna. Adua confirms that the first two or three years were not glorious for Luciano, simply because there were so many fine established tenors to choose from. We are talking about a plethora of established international tenors such as Di Stefano, Corelli, Bergonzi, Del Monaco, Raimondi, Tagliavini, Krauss, Gedda, Aragall and Tucker.

The second problem was that Pavarotti only knew one complete role — that of Rodolfo - and consequently the work he was able to obtain was not of the first rank and the fees were reflected in the stature of the work.

In the next few months, Luciano conquered the role of the Duke in *Rigoletto,* Alfredo in *La Traviata* and later still, Pinkerton in *Butterfly* and Edgardo in *Lucia.* Ziliani managed to secure some interesting engagements for him. As well as *La Boheme,* Pavarotti was now ready to perform the Duke in *Rigoletto,* whose debut took place in Carpi on the 1st of November 1961. Pavarotti recalls that Carpi, although not a large town, had a really beautiful opera house and the young Pavarotti's voice was ideally suited to the duke's music. The tessitura of the role sat high, and much of it was centred around the passaggio and high register. The role requires a brilliant voice with a great deal of squillo and an indefatigable head register, qualities that Pavarotti exhibited in abundance at this stage of his career. Consequently, in what was a homecoming for Luciano, Rigoletto proved a tremendous personal success. During the rehearsals for *Rigoletto,* Ziliani heard that the Teatro Massimo in Palermo was looking for a tenor to sing the duke under the baton of the great Tullio Serafin. Ziliani was able to secure an audition for Luciano.

Meanwhile, in January 1962, he sang two performances of *La Boheme* in Reggio Emilia and then another two performances of the same production for his long-awaited debut in his hometown of Modena.

He followed *La Boheme* with a series of great successes as the Duke in *Rigoletto*. These performances took places in Brescia, Rovigo and Genoa.

Pavarotti — Technician and Magician

Chapter 14

Rigoletto and Serafin, Teatro Massimo Palermo 1962

Meanwhile, Pavarotti and Leone Magiera were busy preparing other roles: Alfredo in La Traviata, Pinkerton in Butterfly and Edgardo in Lucia were all roles that proved effective in the not-too-distant future. Notwithstanding some problems of professional jealousy emanating from his ageing leading lady, the performances of *La Boheme* in Lucca were a great success. Buoyed by this continuing success Ziliani was emboldened to send Pavarotti to audition for Serafin in Rome. Serafin was to conduct a production of *Rigoletto* in Palermo and was looking for a tenor to sing the duke. Serafin was eighty-three years old at the time and revered throughout the operatic world, not just as a great conductor but also as the man who had turned Maria Callas, Rosa Ponselle and Joan Sutherland into superstars. What is not often remembered today is that he made a bountiful contribution towards Sutherland's early stardom. It has become *de riguer* to give all the credit to Richard Bonynge, Sutherland's husband, who deserves a great deal of it. There was an incredible youthful arrogance about him in those early years and an unshakeable belief in his wife's enormous gifts. However, Serafin led the team, including Bonynge and Zeffirelli, to international success.

He did so not only in *Lucia* but also in *I Puritani, Sonnambula* and *Alcina* in Venice.

We also need to remember that, had it not been for Serafin, *Lucia* would have been staged in English, endowing the production with a tinge of provincialism before it even opened. It was Serafin's insistence that *Lucia* should be staged in the original language that changed the complexion of the production, allowing him to invite Zeffirelli to Covent Garden. With Serafin at the helm and Zeffirelli in charge of production and costume design, the door was entirely open for Sutherland to create a sensational *Lucia* and she did. However, it is appropriate to recall that it was Serafin's reputation that raised the interest in the gifted Zeffirelli to come to London. All of a sudden, this Lucia took on a different complexion. It is doubtful that Sutherland alone singing Lucia in English would have commanded sufficient prestige to grant the production international status. Certainly, the international press would not have come to London, and neither would celebrities such as Maria Callas,

Swarzkopf and others. It was Serafin who turned what was destined to be a provincial Lucia into an international event.

Lord Harwood contends that, in some respects, Serafin was a more versatile conductor than Toscanini. In addition to doing virtually all the repertoire that Toscanini performed, he also conducted Rossini, Bellini and Donizetti. He had been artistic director at the Rome Opera and later at La Scala and had conducted all over the world, including the Metropolitan and Covent Garden, Teatro Colon and so on. Therefore, Pavarotti was in awe of his reputation but eager to sing for him.

Consequently, he arrived for the audition at Serafin's home far too early. Given that he couldn't go in, he had a mineral water in a nearby bar and then walked the streets for over an hour before ringing Serafin's doorbell. The maid Rosina showed Luciano to the lounge and in due course the great man joined him. From the outset, it was clear that Serafin was a man of very few words. Pavarotti declined an offer of water, but Serafin insisted, saying, 'You may not need it now, but by the time we are finished, you will need it' [Pavarotti in Wright, 1981: 65].

Pavarotti had expected to audition with a couple of arias and maybe the quartet, but Serafin wanted to hear the whole role. Fortunately, Pavarotti had recently performed the part of the duke in the lovely provincial theatre in Carpi, the very town in which he had spent a great deal of time during the war. Those years on a farm had been a real education, now; the town fathers honoured him by giving him an opportunity to debut in this beautiful role.

Serafin was no fool, and he quickly assessed that he was in the presence of a great talent, but he was determined to test him. By the end of the audition, Pavarotti was undoubtedly glad that Rosina had left the water on the piano. Then Serafin, being a man of few words, closed the score and said, 'When you come to Palermo, I want you to sing the quartet with exaggeration, just like Caruso' [Pavarotti, 1981: 65]

Pavarotti's career was definitely moving in the right direction, providing Adua and Luciano with sufficient confidence to take the big step they had long been contemplating.

Pavarotti performed his second operatic role, the Duke in Verdi's Rigoletto in Palermo in November 1962. As discussed above, his voice suited the duke's *tessitura* and character. The opening scene of the opera takes place in the great hall of the duke's palace, and Pavarotti displays not only vigour but also a great deal of personal ardour and swagger. His rendition of *'Questa o Quella'* establishes not only his character as a lothario but also his considerable vocal credentials. By the time he ends this aria, the audience knows clearly that they are in for an excellent night at the theatre. Unfortunately, the great baritone Ettore Bastianini was not in good voice and was inclined to take it out on his colleagues who became quite resentful. Pavarotti gave an excellent depiction of the role, even if his vocal performance was not as yet perfect.

Regrettably, we do not have a recording of the 1962 performances in Palermo under Tullio Serafin. However, his 1964 studio recording displays a number of deficiencies that we can learn from. In our quest to assess Pavarotti's development, we will use this 1964 recording of the Duke of Mantua.

The first thing to understand about Rigoletto is that Verdi is breaking new ground with this opera. The three central male characters in Victor Hugo's play *Le Roi s'amuse* are truly horrible personalities. For the first time in operatic history Verdi placed not only a physically deformed character — a hunchback — centre stage, but also an emotionally and psychologically damaged character. Rigoletto displays no redeeming features that would endear him to anyone. His jokes are cruel and indiscriminate, and he doesn't care whom he has to betray or destroy in order to maintain his influence at court. He is the perfect ambassador and mouthpiece for his womanising master the duke. Unfortunately for him this lifestyle comes at a price as Rigoletto has made a lot of enemies. For instance, when Count Monterone, comes to the palace to reclaim his daughter (who has been dishonoured by the duke) he is confronted with Rigoletto's laughter and derision. Disgusted with his malicious lack of humanity Monterone, responds by cursing Rigoletto for making fun of a father's sacred pain. This is too close to home for Rigoletto, and Monterone's curse sends a chill down his spine. Nonetheless. he returns to his work and urges the duke to seduce Contessa Ceprano, preferably in the presence of her husband, thus ensuring that he is a witness to the seduction. Rigoletto ridicules Count Ceprano, putting himself in further danger.

The philandering Duke is no less a break with operatic tradition than Rigoletto. The duke is an awful character, and his behaviour is appalling, especially for the period in which the opera was composed. There was an unwritten law that men should not defile decent girls like Gilda, making both Rigoletto and the Duke exceedingly destructive characters. Therefore, it does not come as a surprise when one of these men turns to the assassin Sparafucile to eliminate the other. Verdi made the audacious decision to adopt Rigoletto and the Duke as his central characters although both are morally bankrupt, acting with awareness in a wilful and damaging manner. As if his two main characters are not enough, Verdi enlists Sparafucile (a paid assassin) and his sister Maddalena (who is no more than a courtesan) as his two secondary characters. All I can say is thank God for Gilda. Her innocence, sincerity and commitment remind us that decent and occasionally even wonderful human beings do exist. Let us be honest, the duke makes Don Giovanni look like a boy playing at a man's game. Whereas in Don Giovanni, our lead character fails to make one single conquest during a long opera, the duke makes a clean sweep, beginning with the off-stage seduction of Monterone's daughter, followed by Contessa Ceprano, the innocent Gilda and later still the courtesan Maddalena. The most exciting aspect is the way in which Verdi manages to change the duke's musical style for each of these liaisons: the first encounter with Contessa Ceprano is at court, the music here reflecting the lady's sophistication through the exquisite melodic beauty and formal elegance of a courtly minuet. The second encounter is the one in which the duke seduces Gilda with his music. The first part of this duet is designed to speak to a more ethereal innocent love, '*E il suol dell'anima la vita e amore*' being a perfect example of this style. The duke, however, is not satisfied with winning Gilda's heart; his desire demands her physical conquest.

Consequently, the second part of the duet dispenses with the hearts and flowers and appeals directly to the passionate ardour required to conquer her innocence. Finally, we see the duke in action with Maddalena. Here, the musical content is very different. He dispenses immediately with the stately formality of the court and the heart-felt love proposal he makes to the young Gilda. Instead, he is depicted as the lusty young man whose first phrase reveals his desires: '*Un di se ben rammemori O bella t'incontrai…Or sappi che dall'ora quest'alma a te adora*'. This sensuous little duet merges into the quartet '*Bella figlia dell'amore,*' the whole of which is an overt sexual play as the duke finally beds Maddalena. Thus, the quartet is a fantastic study of the delineation of each of the characters through musical characterisation. Furthermore, it is achieved with such consummate ease, creativity and skill that it makes the whole feel organic and natural.

Let us return to the close examination of the duke's character. The difficulty here is that he is often portrayed simply as a mere rogue when he is a much more complex character, full of contradictions. He is a man who has been given the best of everything, including a natural sense of style and refinement and a noble title and chooses to live a roguish lifestyle. However very rarely are these contradictions and complexities clearly depicted in performance.

We will now examine the ways in which Pavarotti manages these complexities. Before beginning with *Questa o Quella*, let us record our first impressions. We will follow this with a deep examination of the various issues and offer some remedies. Firstly, it must be stated that Pavarotti possesses just the right voice for the role at this stage of his career. The overall quality is noble, velvety, and yet brilliant. In this particular performance, the connection between the antagonistic action of the respiratory muscles (*lotta vocale* and *appoggio*), and the voice source (larynx) is often tenuous, and consequently, the instrument is chronically under-energised, significantly above the *primo passaggio*.

The lateral vowels are too narrow and constricted, and the round vowels are too dark and opaque. There are some notes in which the tone lacks overtones and often sounds flat. The tone needs not only more *squillo* but also a more balanced *chiaroscuro*.

The remedy for this is a hint of a smile which helps to raise the zygomatic arch and the soft palate all founded on a simultaneous surge of breath energy. The lateral vowels beyond the *primo passaggio* all require the treatment suggested above. However, they also need an elevation and forward movement of the hump of the tongue whilst the apex of the tongue remains against the edge of the lower gums. The lips should not protrude, nor should there be any attempt to cover the upper teeth with the upper lips.

Concerning the rounded vowels, on the other hand, we know scientifically that the vowel-defining areas of the spectra alter as we move from the lateral vowels to the rounded ones. However, the singer's formant, which comprises the third, fourth and fifth formant, should remain constant at around 3000 HZ (3K) irrespective of the vowel or *tessitura* being sung. According to Richard Miller:

> With male singers, the acoustic strength of the 3000 Kz (3K) region can be lost, particularly in the upper range, through excessive modifications of the back vowels formed by mouth shapes inappropriate to vowel tracking. What is popularly termed 'ring,' 'ping,' or 'focus' is lost.... Proper vowel modification requires that while the mouth opens more for the rounded vowels, the zygomatic muscles do not drop from their slightly raised posture. Preference given to the mouth as a resonator (as in back or rounded vowels) increases the acoustic strength of the lower harmonic partials. Preference given to the pharynx as a resonator (as in front or lateral vowels) encourages greater acoustic power in the higher formants contributing to the 3000 Hz factor in the male voice.... [Miller, 2004: 73-74].

In Pavarotti's case, all the upper harmonics need better focus and more intensity. The way to achieve this is to ensure the integrity of the vowels whilst pointing the slightly raised zygomatic arch and providing the foundation of the whole edifice with a sustained surge of breath energy, which is responsible for a longer and firmer closing rate. If the voice is energised, it is easy to excite the upper harmonics.

Continuing with our analysis — the first octave of the voice requires an elevated level of buoyancy and greater breath energy, which comes from a sense of excitement and energy, rather than more breath pressure. The sound requires a steadier and faster vibrato. The legato line needs to improve, and this can only be achieved through the application of a steady and constant *appoggio*, breath pressure. In addition, Pavarotti doesn't negotiate the ornaments at all well: the acciaccaturas are hardly sounded and in Parmi veder le lagrime he doesn't manage the chromatic passages. In fact, he is pretty inaccurate, a condition that persists in the final run of *La Donna e Mobile*.

Questa o Quella

The duke's first act aria, '*Questa o quella*' establishes his character immediately. In this performance Pavarotti produces a lovely warm, velvety sound. However, it is generally too far back, a little too open in certain areas and too narrow in others. The sound is under energised, with a slightly loose vibrato which, fortunately is limited mainly to the first octave. Pavarotti struggles with the low notes in the phrase '*a quant'altre d'intorno mi vedo*,' the low E3 on '*tant'altre*' being throaty and opaque, requiring more depth and more of the *oscuro* aspects of the balanced tone (scientists would call it fundamental).

These lower notes, which would hardly be heard over an orchestra in the theatre, are neither exciting nor thrilling. In the phrase '*del mio core l'impero non cedo*' the A4♭ on the [o] vowel should be modified towards [aw] which is a more open vowel.

The A4♭ on the [a] vowel on the '*infiora*' is also a little under the note and the *impostazione* (placement) is too far back; the tone is under-energised and lacks buoyancy. These conditions typically dampen the upper harmonics, suggesting a detrimental effect on the *squillo* of the voice.

Consequently, we can say that this performance lacks energy, legato, poise and precision. With few exceptions, the notes from the *passaggio* and beyond are either to narrow and tight (lateral vowels) or too far back (rounded vowels). The focus needs to be sharpened, the vibrato needs to be steadier and the legato more seamless. The remedy for this is a greater level of objective breath *appoggio* with a more definite focus (subjective *appoggio*), a rising of the zygomatic fascia, and a greater proportion of *oscuro* aspects of the tone (more fundamental), creating a more balanced chiaroscuro tone. The above recommendations can only be achieved when they are accompanied by a simultaneous increase in breath energy and a sense of buoyancy.

The *con brio* section that follows should be more buoyant and bounced off the breath. Also, Vennard's 'bouncing epigastric' strategy could be employed.

The next A4♭ on the [a] vowel in the phrase '*forse un'altra forse un'altra doman lo sara, un'altra, doman lo Sara*'; the [o] is too closed, too far back in the throat, and a little flat in pitch. Pavarotti then stops to replenish his breath and in so doing changes position, so that when he attacks the next *forse un'altra* on the G4 he does so from a lower position.

Francesco Lamperti exhorts singers to remain in the position of singing even as they replenish their breath energy.

The remedy for this is a more authentic [a] vowel with minor modification, a more lateral posture of the vocal tract, raising the zygomatic fascia, and a more energetic *appoggio*.

On the other hand, the A4♭ that follows on the [e] vowel of '*fedele*' is in tune, but the vowel is so narrow that the resonator dampens the upper harmonics. This, I believe, is because Pavarotti is physically pre-tuning the shape of the A♭ on the [e] vowel as a substitute for visualising the timbrel quality he envisions, heading the mind and body towards his imaginary sound and then allowing the vocal instrument to make the more fined adjustments. I like Richard Miller's description of why this should be so. Miller suggests that:

> No matter the language, clean vowel definition results from vocal-tract shapes that correspond to what the larynx is 'saying'…The filtering process of the supra-glottal resonators of the vocal mechanism depends on constant alteration of relationships among vocal-tract spaces. To hold the jaw or mouth in a single shape while attempting to define vowels is contrary to the expected, uncontrived vocal tract response to the laryngeally generated tone. It is in direct conflict with the adage of the historic international school, '*Le parole sempre sulle labra*' (the words always upon the lips) …. The changing posture of the lips, the tongue, the jaw, the fascia of the zygomatic region, the velum, and the larynx determine flexible articulation.

If, as the mouth opens naturally with rising pitch and amplitude, the integrity of the vowel is retained, the first formant will grow in strength and there will be no loss of upper harmonic partials ('ring,' 'ping'). Resonance will pertain throughout the scale [Miller, 2004: 66-67 & 75].

On the other hand, the [e] vowel on the word '*smanie*' A4♭ is good, pointing towards the future and a more skilled and refined Pavarotti. The final B4♭ is perfectly in tune but it is still constricted at the throat. This is the result of an [a] vowel which is being over-modified towards the [o]. This in combination with a collapsed zygomatic arch which effects the soft palate and is underpinned by an inefficient respiratory strategy. The remedy here is to reverse these inefficiencies by increasing breath energy, raising the zygomatic arch and soft palate and aiming for more authentic vowels. This causes an abrupt cessation of the breath flow by closing the glottis firmly and for a more extended period of the glottal cycle. All of which skews and excites the high harmonics and redefines the focus. The [a] vowel demands that the tongue lies comfortably in the mouth, slightly arching back towards the soft palate, imitating the position of an open [aw] vowel. These elements generally combine to provide the voice with more excellent definition and brilliance.

There is no reason to believe that because we are singing a rounded or back vowel, we should forfeit the singer's formant or the (*squillo*) of the tone. When the singer learns to preserve the formant in all of the vowel sounds, there will be no substantive difference between the forward or lateral vowels and the rounded, back vowels. (We note that Pavarotti achieves this objective over the next few years with the most exciting and thrilling results).

The [e] syllable on the word '*beltá*' on the lower A3♭ is sagging, lacking in buoyancy and energy. It is not what one expects from a great tenor singing a notorious character such as the hedonistic and thoughtless Duke. This character lacks a moral compass; he is devastatingly charming and leads a reckless lifestyle that wreaks havoc and heartache for everyone who becomes involved with him. Everywhere he goes he leaves a trail of destruction, and yet nothing seems to touch him, nothing seems to disturb his peace of mind or alter his thinking. His attitude is simple: 'Poor Gilda, what a pity, she was a lovely girl…Well, nothing to be done'.

In this recording Pavarotti needs to make a genuine effort at sounding the acciaccatura on the B flat. In fact, he totally ignores all ornamentation. In the phrase marked *con brio* (see sample below) he appears to totally disregard the markings.

These [e] vowels are so narrow and tight that Pavarotti's vocal tract seems to dampen some overtones, resulting in inconsistent pitch. Pavarotti's voice is glorious, but his instrument is too fixed, too inflexible, and the objective *appoggio* (breath) is constantly under-energised. I like Miller's explanation of the consequences of a fixed and rigid vocal tract or buccopharyngeal cavity. Below, finds his take on this problem:

> Holding the mouth in an unmodified lateral position while singing in the upper range will forfeit the first formant, produce an overly bright, thin tone, and destroy diction. Conversely, too large a buccal opening will produce disequilibrium among overtones [Miller, 2004: 75].

At this stage of his career, Pavarotti does not yet possess the vocal freedom to allow the articulators to readjust quickly as required by the varying formant frequencies, which are to be matched with the frequencies of the harmonics emanating from the primary source, vocal folds. This matching of formants to the source harmonics is the *sine qua non*e of great singing, and Pavarotti is too often just missing the mark. In the final cadenza on the phrase '*se mi punge*,' the '*se*' on the A♭ rising to B♭ is virtually a [i] vowel, starting low in the throat and remaining lodged there. The final expressive [e] on the A, which is not written in the score, is piercing in quality and just a little under the note. He seems to be to open the vowel and support the sound, but he miscues the degree of effort and opening required.

It is important to remember that a lack of coherence between the harmonics issuing from the vocal folds and the formants established by the vocal tract can lead not only to less than optimum resonance but also faulty pitch. Pavarotti did a great deal of mistuning in the early part of his career.

In conclusion, too many of the [a] vowels are overly modified and muffled, bordering on becoming an open [o] sound. Also, too many of the [e] vowels are inserted into a predetermined space rather than creating the correct vowel and allowing the area to evolve naturally. Consequently, some of the [e] vowels are too broad and back in the throat, and others are too narrow and much closer to an [i] vowel, especially in the higher register. Too often, Pavarotti lengthens the vocal tract even in the lateral vowels by simply using the lips as if singing an umlaut, dropping the zygomatic arch and allowing the tongue to retract and rise towards the soft palate in the position of [u]. All of, this manipulation is simply unnecessary. By virtue of the tongue's elevated and fronted position, the vibrations of the [e] vowel naturally tend to impinge on the hard palate and zygomatic arch. It is, therefore, not necessary to attempt to direct them forward by protruding the lips and lowering the zygomatic angle, manoeuvres that lengthen and lower all the formants of the vocal tract.

Parmi Veder Le Lagrime

The aria *Parmi veder le lagrime* begins with a good attempt at collecting the complex opening G♭ at the *passaggio*. However, it is all too loud and too forceful, while the tone remains too covered and overly hooded. We don't get the sense that seeing a tear running down Gilda's face, the face of the woman he professes to love, has moved the duke's emotions; his expression here is all very matter of fact. He approaches the syllable '*giglio*' from below the note, where it remains, just a little under the pitch throughout the sostenuto and the phrase that follows — '*dubio e l'ansia*'. An even more severe pitch problem is found in the word '*del subito periglio*'. The problem occurs in part with the [u] vowel, which is too open and far back. The focus needs to be sharper, as do the boundaries around that [u] vowel and the appoggio needs to be firmer and more responsive. The whole instrument seems a little muscle-bound; it lacks flexibility and elasticity and is stifled by stiffness and rigidity. The chromatic passage in '*dell'amor nostro memore*' is musically inaccurate.

The phrase '*vorria dell'anima, farti quaggiu beata,*' is also under the note, as is the first phrase of '*le sfere agli'angeli*'. However, Pavarotti seems to rally for the climax to the aria, finding a surge of breath energy for the phrases beginning with '*ei che le sfere, le sfere agl'angeli, per te, per te, le sfere agl'angeli*'. However, even with this burst of energy, he is not able to sustain the open throated [a] vowel on the B♭, resulting in a throaty and unfocused tone.

The last cadenza, which is sung on the phrase '*non invidio per te,*' is also out of tune.

The previously mentioned notes were all flat in pitch because they were approached from below with insufficient buoyancy and breath pressure to create the necessary resistance at the vocal folds. Nor was there sufficient glottal tension at the vocal fold level to create the abrupt cessation of breath flow, which is required to excite the higher harmonics. Had Pavarotti been taught a more efficient breath management strategy such as appoggio, he would have been able to raise sub-glottal pressure and make the necessary adjustments to raise the pitch. On the other hand, the passage that rises to a climax '*ei che le sfere, le sfere agl'angeli per te, per te le sfere agl'angeli*' has a substantial reserve of breath energy. In fact, it possesses sufficient sub-glottal pressure and breath energy to accommodate both the [e] vowel on the A4♭ and the [a] vowel on the B♭. The problem here is not the breath, but rather the supra-glottal space created by the laryngeal height and the configuration of the articulators that render the supra-glottal mechanism too narrow, too rigid and too constricted. This tightness of the articulators distorts the space created for the [a] vowel on the B♭ in the agl'angeli, preventing the necessary adjustments required to fine-tune the formant frequencies designed to match the harmonic frequencies issuing from the vocal folds. Pavarotti is not sufficiently sensitive to this delicate and precise process (known as formant tuning) which represents tuning the formant frequencies of the vocal tract to match the frequencies of the source harmonics.

This is partly because the vertical laryngeal position is too high (which results in the mistuning of the fundamental), and partly because there is insufficient flexibility on the part of the articulators and the often inefficient breath pressure to keep the sound buoyant and forward.

I like Nanda Mari's observations concerning the adjustments required for the high register. She states that:

> In the process of emitting the high register, the larynx rises as does the epiglottis, whilst the walls of the pharynx narrow, and the base of the tongue contracts and rises lightly. The soft palate is raised towards the back, the pharyngeal pillars narrow the fauces: even the cheeks participate by contracting and coming together [Mari, 1975: 115-16].

Pavarotti displays five significant defects in this area at this point. Let us remember, however, that he is not yet the tenor he will become, so it shouldn't come as a surprise that he still has certain defects to overcome, which is the whole point of this book — to trace his progress. The following are his main problems:

1. He has a particularly rigid jaw.
2. He allows the zygomatic arch to sag when it should remain raised.
3. He possesses a flabby and inflexible tongue; tongue exercises are indicated.
4. He has a propensity to overuse the protruding lips technique not only for the round and dark vowels, but also where it is counter indicated: such as the lateral vowels.

He possesses a chronically under activated and irresponsive respiratory system.

5. These defects are emphasised by difficulties which make it impossible to attain an elegant legato line, clarity and definition of tone, emotional expression, and a more mature and sensitive interpretation.

The whole instrument needs to be innervated to a much higher level of performance if Pavarotti is to attain his goal of becoming a great tenor.

La Donna è Mobile

In general, Pavarotti's singing in this aria is much better quality, resulting in a warmer and more fluid tone. However, it comes at the expense of clarity of tone and sound production, a lack of legato being another deficiency, as well as a throaty tonal orientation. This performance needs to be better. As part of the remedy, the tone needs greater buoyancy, a firmer sub-glottal pressure and a raising the zygomatic arch, which would help raise the soft palate and lift the sound out of the throat and towards the masque (the area around the zygomatic arch).

The overall performance is better with virtually no out-of-tune singing (apart from a couple of notes which are under energised and therefore a little out of focus). Both the diction and the legato line are better, but the overall performance still needs to improve in temperament, precision and more imaginative expression.

The accents and the acciaccaturas need to be better realised. In fact, much of the lower register lacks ring, and even though some of the notes in the higher mixed register display a lovely tone and adequate *squillo*, some of the [e] vowels are still too narrow. For instance, the A4♯ at the end of the run lacks amplitude and remains a little under the pitch, while the final ornamental run to the sustained B4 contains a couple of extraneous notes that simply disrupt the flow. The final B4 seems to stick in the throat and, although Pavarotti reaches the note well enough, it doesn't seem to have sufficient sub-glottal pressure to take the sound waves into the right focal point (*impostazione*), which sympathetic vibrations for the [e] vowel should be felt most vividly around the zygomatic arch.

In general, we can say that there are several problems with Pavarotti's singing at this point in time.

1. There were problems with pitch, problems with vocal onset, a lack of legato, and a sound that remains uneven. In fact, it may best be characterised as primitive, lacking the finesse associated with a *tenore di grazia*, not to mention that the ornamentation is consciously eschewed.

2. The second issue refers to the fact that Pavarotti doesn't seem to be able to raise sufficient sub-glottal pressure to induce appropriate glottal resistance to firmly adduct the vocal folds and create an abrupt cessation of airflow.

3. The combined deficiency in sub-glottal pressure and firm glottal closure leads to flow phonation at best and breathy phonation at worst, but never to firm phonation, which is what is required here.

4. Flow or breathy phonation rarely adducts the vocal folds sufficiently to affect the collision of the tissue. This alone creates the abrupt cessation of breath flow which in turn skews the spectrum and excites the high overtones of the harmonic series. In so doing, they strengthen the acoustic power of these upper harmonics.

5. In Pavarotti's case, even though he is capable of creating particularly rich upper harmonics at the glottal level, he doesn't seem to have the capacity to accommodate them within the constricted and fixed vocal tract. It remains a fact that for an ideal resonant voice to occur the harmonics

issuing from the vocal folds need to be matched by the formant frequencies created by the articulators of the vocal tract. For this to happen, the articulators need to remain flexible, agile, and capable of fluid readjustment for the various vowels. In Pavarotti's case, the vocal tract and the position of the articulators are predetermined and far too fixed, deterring the possibility of fluent vowel tracking, or as it is often called, formant tuning. Rigid muscular conditions interfere with the process of acoustic matching between the harmonics of the vocal folds with the formants of the vocal tract.

Richard Miller, whose work I admire greatly, suggests:

> In singing the very lowest pitches that lie beneath fundamentals of the normal speech-inflection range, additional buccal opening is generally desirable. Uniform vocal timbre throughout the scale is not achieved by maintaining one set buccal posture, or even something close to it, because vowel definition results from acoustic positions that alter with the changing shapes of vowels, pitch and dynamic levels. Any 'unification' of the vocal scale that avoids flexibility of vowel definition causes a common quality of distortion throughout the scale. Most transition sound is caused by inappropriate attempts to maintain a distended mouth posture or to preserve a fixated narrow buccal aperture (the opposite error). Brightness of timbre, clarity of diction, and legato line are all inevitably diverted [Miller, 1992: 49-50].

I agree with Miller wholeheartedly.

Chapter 15

Comparison of the 1967 RAI and the 1971 Decca Rigoletto

Before proceeding to a detailed analysis of the 1971 Decca recording of Rigoletto, which I believe is Pavarotti's finest depiction of the duke, we should review a RAI live recording from 1967. The singing here is much firmer and more masterful than the 1965 Decca offering, but not yet as complete vocally or artistically as the forthcoming 1971 recording.

In this 1967 recording, the voice has attained an easy-flowing sound which, although sitting a little lower and further back than one would ideally desire, lends the tone a lovely velvety colour. Unfortunately, this often comes at the expense of vowel integrity or vowel definition, and *squillo* or brilliance. However, this only applies to the medium register; once the voice reaches the first passaggio, or high mixed register, it really starts to ring. This active and often exaggerated search for *squillo* leads the young Pavarotti into some out-of-tune singing, especially on the [i] and [e] vowels sung in head-register. These notes are not only out of tune but also display a sharp quality verging on harshness. Not only is the tone a bit too biting, but it loses the roundness and balance associated with the *chiaroscuro* tone.

On the other hand, the lower notes, which were a problem in the 1965 recording, are much improved in this 1967 performance. I am referring to such notes as the E3♭ on the phrase '*a quant'altro dintorno mi vedo*,' and to its equivalent in the second verse of *Questa o quella* beginning with the words '*qual morbo, qual morbo credele*,' also on the E3♭. The higher sub-glottal pressure, which induces greater resistance at the vocal fold level, is managed much better. This lends the sound increased firmness, definition, and ring.

The middle register is also firmer and more in tune than the earlier recording, especially in the '*Parmi veder le lagrime*'. However, even the middle register is still not immune to the occasional out-of-tune note. For instance, the phrase '*subito periglio*' is still a little under the note, as is the '*farti qua giù beata*'. The wrong notes in the chromatic passages such as '*ma ne avro vendetta*,' and '*dell'amor nostro memore*', '*dell'amor nostro memore, il suo Gualtier chiamo*,' are still persistently just out of tune or at the very least lacking focus. (He should have been working on chromatic passages from the beginning of his study. Pavarotti was neither the first nor the last singer to have problems with chromatic passages: practice makes perfect).

The legato line is also better in this 1967 rendition, but still a long way from what it would become. Here again, we find Pavarotti lifting up to the higher note of a considerable interval rather than delivering it with poise from above the note and a smooth legato where the upper interval just naturally blooms into position (*imposto*). Although some of the acciaccaturas are much improved, many other ornaments, such as the mordents, are all aspirated, needing more clarity and definition.

This performance is very much improved, and we are privileged to hear some really lovely singing throughout the vocal range. However, it has yet to be as refined and accomplished as it would later become. Nonetheless it is an essential document in terms of tracing Pavarotti's development in general and more specifically his depiction of the duke. This character along with Rodolfo in *La Bohème* and Edgardo in *Lucia di Lammermoor* (later to be joined by Donizetti's *La Fille du Regiment, L'Elisir D'amore, La Favorita,* and Bellini's *I Puritani, Ballo in Maschera,* and *Il Trovatore*) would become one of his signature roles. There were three other roles that he sang often and very well early in his career, but he dropped them as quickly as was advisable to do so. These were *La Sonnambula, La Traviata,* and *Madame Butterfly. La Sonnambula* is a very difficult role for the tenor and my personal opinion is that it was never meant for such a substantial voice as Pavarotti's. Also, it is a vehicle for an accomplished soprano rather than a tenor. The other two operas, *La Traviata* and *Madame Butterfly* are ungrateful roles. They were well suited to his lyrical voice, especially in the early years, but the truth is that the tenor sings complex music all night long knowing that the soprano is going to walk away with the laurels. This was an untenable situation for a big star like Pavarotti who was being paid top fees for his services. There has been some criticism (from people who should know better) of his refusal to assume certain roles such as *Attila* and *Giovanna D'Arco* which is ridiculous. Attila is a great opera, but Foresto, the tenor role comes in fourth after Attila, Odabella, and Ezio. With respect to *Giovanna D'Arco*, it is one of Verdi's lesser operas, and again, the tenor is overshadowed by Giovanna and Giacomo. Do you really think that management would pay the fees that Pavarotti was commanding just to have him singing a secondary role? Better still, do you think Pavarotti should have sung operas that knowingly facilitated someone else starring at his expense? I don't think so. Having said that I personally would have loved to hear him singing Gabriele Adorno's music in *Simone Boccanegra*. The other opera he would have been glorious in was Verdi's *I Due Foscari*: his 1968 recording of Jacopo Foscari's aria is the finest rendition of that work I have heard from any tenor, as is his McDuff in the Solti recording of Macbeth.

Pavarotti managed his career extraordinarily well. He knew exactly what he was doing, and he had marvellous advisors at his disposal, people he believed in.

Let us return to the three roles under original discussion. Pavarotti recorded all three of these roles for Decca, but the *La Sonnambula* and *La Traviata* came too late.

I feel that the best rendition of the duet from La Sonnambula 'Prendi l'anel ti dono' came in the 1976 duets recording with Joan Sutherland. This is a beautiful rendition of this duet: it is characterised by a firm but flowing tone, '*voce chiusa,*' produced with a firm appoggio, firm attack and '*bocca raccolta,*' issuing into a warm, flexible, velvety tone.

Pavarotti applies this firm but flowing '*voce chiusa*' tone to the duets from La Traviata also on this recording and in my view these duets are considerably better than the complete recordings.

The *Butterfly* recording with Von Karajan and Freni came at the right time, but he needed to be in better voice. Freni on the other hand was in a glorious voice, thus presenting a touching and convincing Butterfly. More about this later, but for now, let us return to our main story.

Chapter 16

Comparison of La Bohème, London 1963 and Modena 1967

In February 1963 Pavarotti made his Vienna debut in *La Bohème* which was so successful that he was offered *Rigoletto* in April of the same year. In September 1963 he made his Covent Garden debut in rather dramatic circumstances. His boyhood idol Giuseppe di Stefano cancelled halfway through a performance of *La Bohème* at the last minute and Pavarotti took over the performance as the official understudy. The story behind this dramatic event is a very interesting one and has since become the stuff of legends.

In the early 1960s Joan Ingpen was working at Covent Garden as the controller of opera planning, which meant that she was responsible for casting the repertoire. This was a role that she would later fulfil at the Paris Opera and later still at the Metropolitan Opera, New York. At any rate in 1963 she was at Covent Garden and was more than a little concerned about their production of *La Bohème* with *di Stefano*. She knew that at his best he was a genuinely great Rodolfo; however, more recently he had gained a reputation for cancelling at the last minute. Given that their house tenor was on vacation, Ingpen was intent on protecting their production. She asked Sir David Webster if she could search 'for a young Italian tenor — someone of Covent Garden standard but unknown enough that he would be willing to come to London just to cover, without any assurance that he would get an opportunity to sing the role'. Having attained David Webster's approval Ingpen set out to find her tenor. She remembered that the Dublin Grand Opera Society was mounting a production of *Rigoletto* at the Gaity Theatre as part of their spring season, and they generally assembled a company of ad hoc Italian singers.

Being Irish, Ingpen enjoyed returning home occasionally, but this year, she had a particular objective in mind — finding a tenor who could sing Rodolfo. She arrived at the theatre full of hope, but also a little circumspect. She knew that it wouldn't be easy to find a young tenor with the right qualities to sing Rodolfo at Covent Garden. Fortunately, she didn't have long to wait, because, by the time Pavarotti had sung the opening aria *Questa o quella*, she was totally conquered. Here she was in front of a large young man named Luciano Pavarotti (not as large as he would later become) 'very inept on the stage, singing a bit to the gallery, and hanging on to the top notes' a little too long, 'but my God what vocal material' [Ingpen in Wright, 1981: 70].

Ingpen continues:

> Luciano was so unknown; he was delighted to come to London for a modest fee. To make it more attractive for him, we promised that if he would cover Di Stefano for all the performances, he would definitely be singing the last performance of the season. He came a little early so that we could give him some extra stage coaching before the regular rehearsals began. The result of all this was, if I recall correctly, that Di Stefano sang one and a half performances, cancelled, and Luciano sang the rest — and with enormous success. He made such a hit at Covent Garden that we asked him back immediately [Ingpen, 1981: 70].

Pavarotti's Rodolfo was a revelation, and the review in the London Times announced, 'the discovery of great new Italian tenor'. Following his spectacular introduction to English audiences, Pavarotti began to enjoy spending time with his many new friends. According to Adua Pavarotti everybody took to Luciano because he was so attractive and fun to be with. Let's be honest — taking over from Di Stefano halfway through a performance of *La Bohème* at Covent Garden should by any measure have earned you both respect and admiration.

Che Gelida Manina 1964

We do not have the 1963 performance from Covent Garden, but we do have a studio recording of a 1964 *'Che geli manina'* conducted by Edward Downes.

The opening line 'Che gelida manina' is throaty; the [a] vowel in *'riscaldar'* is under energised (insufficiently *appoggiata*) whilst the [o] in *'giova'* lacks vibrancy. The phrase *'Chi son'* rising to the B♭ also lacks vibrancy and therefore affects the *'e che faccio',* which starts off more like an [o] than an [e] on the A4♭ but is eventually transformed into an authentic [e] vowel. Many of the [o] vowels are also lacking vibrancy. The phrase *'In povertà mia lieta, scialo da gran signore'* is pedestrian and lacking in sensitivity. This privileging of the [o] colour is a very English not an Italian approach.

Pavarotti doesn't seem to have a deep understanding of what he is saying: *'even in poverty, he enjoys the life style of a lord'.* The phrase *'Rimi ed inni d'amore, e per castell'in aria'* (rhymes and hymns of love and castles in the air) should be more spontaneous and more explosive. In this performance, Pavarotti lacks exuberance and temperament, and it's all a little tame, except for the 'talor del mio forziere' and the magnificent top C. This aria reveals the inner thoughts of our young poet who has a lovely soul and is not afraid to dream. This is largely why Mimi falls in love with him; she too has dreams and possesses a poetic soul! She is very religious and loves beauty, particularly in nature. She longs for spring to thaw the cold winter freeze and deliver the first ray of sunshine. *'The first kiss of spring is mine,'* she sings.

Rodolfo uses all his creative powers to persuade Mimi to fall in love with him, his poetry, and indeed his vision of the world — one which two people who are genuinely in love can create together.

Rodolfo is a romantic soul who remains spontaneous and authentic throughout; he is passionate, creative and fiery which makes him such a compelling personality.

Nonetheless, this recording provides us with a realistic idea of the nature of Pavarotti's performance the previous year at Covent Garden. Pavarotti made many friends that year, one of his favourites (and perhaps most impressive) being Sir George Solti's assistant Enid Blech. This lady was by any standard extraordinarily accomplished: she spoke seven languages, flew her own plane and made sure that things ran like clockwork for the artistic director. If that were not enough, she was genuinely delightful and was to become a very dear friend of the Pavarottis.

A few days later Pavarotti was invited to Enid Blech's cottage in Alfriston East Sussex.

On that particular Sunday afternoon, Luciano went out riding with friends for quite a long while, and on the way home, he became aware that his muscles were sore and was looking forward, therefore to a long bath.

When he was in sight of the cottage, Luciano saw his friends running towards him, but he couldn't understand why they were gesticulating like crazy people. Before he could dismount, Enid said, 'You must go to the television station. Di Stefano cancelled his appearance on *Sunday night at the Palladium*, and they want you to substitute for him.' They quickly explained that *Sunday night at the Palladium* was England's most popular television show, and Luciano immediately understood the significance. 'Let me have a quick bath, and then we will go,' he said. Enid replied, 'You don't have time for a bath, we must go now'.

The die was cast for Pavarotti, creating a sensation to the extent that even taxi drivers were talking about him the next day. In that single performance, he reached more people in Britain than he could have in a lifetime of singing on the stage. The British had taken Pavarotti into their hearts, and he loved them back.

Following this phenomenal success, Covent Garden invited him back for the 1964/65 season to sing Alfredo in *La Traviata* with Renata Scotto and *La Sonnambula* with Joan Sutherland.

La Boheme, Pavarotti, Freni, 1967

Let us continue with our analysis of Pavarotti in the defining role of Rodolfo. We meet him next as Rodolfo in a live recording from the Teatro Comunale in Modena in 1967. This performance, which was conducted by Leone Magiera, confirms that the respiratory muscles are much more robust and as a result, the larynx is more anchored and the vertical laryngeal position steadier and more conducive to good vocalising than previous performances. This breathing strategy, which was greatly influenced by Sutherland during their Australia tour, not only improved his breathing but also impacted the vertical laryngeal position ensuring that both breath strategy and laryngeal position were much more cohesive and appropriate for the demands made by this beautiful score. However, it must be said that six years after his debut, and with a well-established international career behind him, I had expected Pavarotti to have conquered many more of his problems than is the case in this performance. The notes at the *passaggio* F and G4s that we identified as having been problematic at the beginning of the 1961 production are now much improved, but we can still hear some uncertainty and wavering of the tone in its effort to maintain the original focus. Nonetheless, his technique overall is much more controlled despite the fact that the larynx is still a little high, and both onset and release are not as clean and crisp as one would have expected. For instance, for the G4s on '*un gran signore*' the larynx is still too high and too rigid, and the same can be said of the '*si*' after *trovasti*' as well as the B♭ on *L'idea avvampi infiamma*'.

These notes would be much better if he relaxed the larynx, allowing it to find a more natural position instead of artificially maintaining a high one. A more natural and less rigid laryngeal position would promote a better and more synergistic coordination between the larynx and respiratory mechanism while resulting in a more flexible adjustment of the articulators.

Concerning an analysis of '*Che gelida manina*,' this performance is a semitone down, a practice widely accepted in significant houses, but which does not serve our purpose because it is not an equivalent comparison.

Whilst I am a little indifferent to the C5 in '*Che gelida manina*' having been transposed down to a B4, I object greatly to the second part of '*O soave fanciulla*' (beginning with '*dammi il braccio mia piccina*') being transposed down a semitone. I heard Jose Carreras and Katia Ricciarelli commit the same sacrilege in a concert in Milan a decade later and it was terrible. This is a totally unacceptable practice. For the record the top C at the end of the love duet is not so complex that it needs to be transposed down. As far as top Cs go, it is one of the easier ones for the tenor.

However, let us continue our analysis. We can say that because '*Che Gelida Manina*' is transposed down a semitone, it is generally more secure and more even in tone. However, whilst some phrases are more comfortable, such as the '*Talor dal mio forziere*' (which is much firmer and possesses a more significant proportion of the *oscuro* colour, displaying better legato with a much more exciting tone) there are many fragments that are neither as good nor as exciting. For instance, the top A on '*chi son*' is nowhere near as exciting as the B flat in his earlier performance, and the top B4 on '*speranza*' is but a shadow of the beautiful full C5 he unleashed in his debut performance or even the 1964 recording with Edward Downes. However, I must confess my delight in discovering that much of '*O Soave Fanciulla*' demonstrated greater breath control, a steadier laryngeal position, and greater firmness of tone than the earlier *Boheme*.

On the other hand, I don't believe that artistically Rodolfo's introduction of Mimi to the Bohemians in the second act was as good in this performance as it was in the earlier recording. The tone is clearly firmer but Pavarotti sounds as if he has something better to do, throwing away the early part of the introduction — '*Questa e Mimi, gaia fioraia, il suo venir complete la bella compagnia*'. It is all too fast, shallow and lacking colour. He seems disinterested, which we would not expect from a poet. The A4 on '*sboccia l'amor*' eventually finds its position but this climax is decidedly under energised and the objective *appoggio* (subglottal pressure) is decidedly inadequate.

Act III La Boheme

In the opening phrase, '*Marcello finalmente qui niun ci sente*', Pavarotti is producing a much better sound — a tone characterised by an increased flow level (flow phonation). However, the A natural in the phrase '*Ora il tedio massa!*' seems to stick in the throat, as do many other notes during this performance. I conclude that the sub-glottal pressure or objective *appoggio* is insufficiently energised, and the breath pressure lacks the necessary force to maintain the intended *impostazione*.

This recording makes it patently evident that Pavarotti is consciously raising the larynx in an effort to sit the voice higher, and deliberately aims it towards the masque. Since sound cannot be placed, although Vennard concedes that we can create the illusion of placement, the only way we can achieve this forward ringing tone is to manipulate the articulators combined with an appropriate level of subglottal pressure. In this instance, Pavarotti's effort creates laryngeal rigidity responsible for undermining the link between the voice source and the respiratory mechanism.

The placement that many singers talk about is no more than the proprioceptive sympathetic sensations created by the vibrations within the buccopharyngeal resonator. In this case concentration of proprioceptive sensations takes place in the anterior part of the vocal tract including the masque. With these in mind, Pavarotti directs the [e] vowels forward against the hard palate because that is where he feels the concentration of the sympathetic vibrations. Then, as that focal point feels comfortable, he aims the [a] vowel more towards the position of the [e]. On the other hand, the [o] vowels are modified towards the [aw] vowel. The latter would be acceptable, except that Pavarotti exaggerates the amount of [aw] colour in this vowel, modifying it towards an [a] vowel. These exaggerations make the sound rather white, a tone that Garcia referred to as '*voix blanche*'.

This particular performance is too exaggerated, the emotions are too contrived, and the vocal line lacks a firm legato. His depiction of '*Mimi e tanto malate*' is a perfect example of this exaggeration. In this scene he produces an excessively open and whitish tone bordering on '*canto sguaiato*' *(exaggeratedly open)*. This is an emotionally contrived and melodramatic performance which at times sounds a little uncontrolled, especially the affected phrases such as '*è condannata*' in which he recognises that the A4♭ needs to be sung in head

register and he ensures that it is. However, the subsequent modified vowel is distorted, an indication that the *aggiustamento* is too severe, thereby distorting the vowel. The process of vowel modification suggests that you can add a small percentage of one vowel colour or another, but you should not and cannot lose the integrity of the vowel altogether—just a note of caution at this point. I am reluctant to make too many definitive pronouncements at this stage simply because this particular live recording is rather primitive and, in view of Pavarotti's ongoing experimentation with vocal technique, it may be kinder to give him the benefit of the doubt. At this point in his development, Pavarotti seems to be lurching from one mini-crisis to another. One moment he is arranging the articulators in such a way as to ensure that the larynx remains artificially high, and the next moment he sings a [o] vowel in which the larynx is artificially low. His technique is a moveable feast; it is all just a little too uneven and emotionally contrived. In many respects it mirrors the confusion that was apparent in Italian vocal circles at the time this performance was recorded. Every teacher had a particular technique that they believed in. They thought they were terribly clever by developing little tricks to plug a specific deficiency, only to find that another problem would appear as a result of the original adjustment.

Essentially, Pavarotti has four problems:

1. The emphasis is on a predetermined *impostazione* (placement) and the manipulation of the articulators, including a laryngeal position to achieve his end. This determination comes at the expense of a natural organic tone, a balanced *chiaroscuro*, and the firm link between voice source, respiration and pronunciation.

2. All the [e] vowels at the *passaggio* and in the high register are too narrow and tight. These [e] vowels display enormous brilliance, but really great singers know that brilliance alone is an inadequate measure of good singing. Other characteristics are required if we are to produce a complete and balanced tone.

3. Most of the [o] vowels at the *passaggio* and high register are too tense. This is a tension that comes from creating an essentially vertical vowel such as the [o] and then placing it into the space generally designed for the lateral or brighter vowels such as the [e]. You can modestly modify the [o] vowel to accommodate specific conditions and fulfil artistic objectives. It does mean that you cannot alter the essential nature of a vertical vowel to a horizontal one without incurring stiffness in the jaw and rigidity in the larynx. This is what he appears to be doing here. I understand that Pavarotti started with a 'do nothing technique' which he

inherited from Campogalliani and that he is now eager to gain control over it. In the absence of a great teacher, Pavarotti has no alternative but to experiment, but in this instance, he goes too far.

4. The tension here is that he creates a general horizontal or lateral shape at the beginning of the *primo passaggio*. This would be perfectly permissible were it not for the fact that when he arrives at the *secondo passaggio*, the [a] and darker vowels require more space to cover the tone and facilitate the entry into head register. However, Pavarotti refuses to supply that extra space. The larynx is too high and the lower pharynx too narrow, as are the back and sidewalls of the pharynx which are narrowed through the contraction of the constrictor muscles. The remedy for this problem is to be found in a moderate lowering of the diaphragm, which automatically lowers the larynx and widens the pharynx, combined with a slight opening of the mandible. Pavarotti is at odds with this principle because he is determined to maintain a high laryngeal position by trying to accommodate every vowel into that general space instead of allowing each vowel to create its own individual space. This space is dictated by the requirements of the first and second formants which are responsible for the production of all vowels. Also, with respect to the smooth *passaggio* into head voice the sound needs to be collected (*copertura*), meaning that an *aggiustamento* occurs that automatically alters the formants. This includes the position of the larynx, affecting not only the first formant but also giving access to the laryngeal resonator. This laryngeal collar is an important resonator because it is the first to receive the soundwaves produced by the vocal folds, providing the voice with the singer's formant or what the Italians refer to as *squillo*.

The above notwithstanding, this performance still has some excellent singing; it needs to be more consistent. There are some moments when he uses that perpetually smiling sound, which may be acceptable for the first two acts of La Boheme, but it is not appropriate for the separation scene in Act 3 and Mimi's death scene in Act 4. Fortunately, Pavarotti understands this and banishes the smiling tone for Acts 3 and 4. He produces some of his best singing in the latter part of this performance.

Overall, the problem is that the young Pavarotti makes everything more complicated than it needs to be, a problem shared amongst young singers. In time, we will see that Pavarotti strips things down to the bare essentials, all part of the journey. One of the best descriptions relating to the issue of simplification is the one offered by the legendary Manuel Garcia in an 1894 interview for the *Musical Herald*:

He was very emphatic in his recommendation to avoid all modern theories and stick clearly to nature. He also doesn't believe in teaching by means of sensations of tone. The actual things to do in producing tone are to breathe, to use the vocal cords, and to form the style in the mouth. The singer has nothing to do with anything else. Garcia said that he began with other things, he used to direct the tone into the head, and do peculiar things with breathing, and so on, but as the years passed by, he discarded these things as useless, and now speaks only of actual things, and not mere appearances. He condemned what is much said of nowadays, the directing of the voice forward, back or up. Vibrations come in puffs of air. All control of the breath is lost the moment it is turned into vibrations, and the idea is absurd, he said, that a current of air can be thrown against the hard palate for one kind of tone, the soft palate for another, and reflected hither and thither [Manuel Garcia in the Musical Herald, Root, 1894].

After 55 years of trying to perfect our art, I have drawn the same conclusion that the closer we remain to Garcia's tenet with respect to initiating the three significant essentials — breathing, setting the vocal folds into vibration, and filtering the sound waves through the vocal tract (resonators) — the better and more natural the sound we produce. I know that Pavarotti drew the same conclusions later in life towards the end of his illustrious career. With that in mind let us proceed on our journey.

Chapter 17

Joan Sutherland and Lucia di Lammermoor

Before undertaking her position at Covent Garden, Joan Ingpen had acted as Joan Sutherland's manager. However, that was before Sutherland had become the superstar she was destined to become. Ingpen knew first-hand the problems Sutherland had in finding leading men who looked like her partner rather than her son. Consequently, when she discovered Pavarotti, she was eager to inform Richard Bonynge of her discovery and much as she was excited about his voice, she was just as enthusiastic about his size. Soon she was on the phone detailing the young tenor's enormous gifts, including his size. She praised his incredible voice, which she believed could sing Joan's repertoire. What's more, she added, 'He is a big man, taller than Joan' [Ingpen, in Wright. 1981: 72].

Having arranged an audition, Luciano was to encounter two of the most significant people in the making of his illustrious career, something that he always remembered. The Bonynges loved him, and he loved them back. The event marked the beginning of a beautiful personal connection as well as a musical and vocal relationship that would become not only historical but also for the ages.

Richard Bonynge immediately engaged him for the Sutherland-Williamson Tour of Australia in 1965. This was a fourteen-week tour initiated by Sir Frank Tait who, in partnership with his brother, had been running JC Williamson for many decades. It was meant to be his swan song and so it proved. Having completed the most successful opera season in modern times, Sir Frank covered the deficit that was incurred and passed away within the month. He died believing that making contributing to the art form was worth every penny required to make it happen. Further details of this tour will follow in the next chapter.

What followed was indeed fortuitous for Pavarotti. As luck would have it Renato Cione, who was meant to perform Edgardo in a production of *Lucia* with Joan Sutherland in Miami, made the momentous decision to cancel. He loved singing with Sutherland, but he had been offered the chance to sing Cavaradossi in a production of *Tosca* with Maria Callas. This was the opportunity of a lifetime and Cione did not want to miss it. Sutherland understood the situation and was gracious about it, but then began to fight hard to secure Pavarotti as his replacement. The management was intent on hiring a name tenor, but finally, the artistic director, Arturo de Fillippi (a former tenor, who from all accounts was a lovely man), surrendered to the inevitable. Pavarotti was duly hired for the role.

When he arrived in Miami, he realised that this was a low-budget affair with a relatively short rehearsal period. He was expected to know his role, which was not a problem because he had already sung Edgardo in a production of Lucia in Amsterdam.

What he had not expected was that the director, an Italian/American by the name of Stivanello, would take such umbrage to his acting. However, unlike many directors who belittle artists for their poor acting, Stivanello understood and decided to help Luciano by surreptitiously arranging extra rehearsals. He realised that much of Pavarotti's awkwardness was the result of a lack of confidence in his stage technique. He also understood that in large part this problem was a cultural one. The Italian operatic theatre had been divided into two factions: those who believed that opera was under an obligation to produce believable characters and dramatically fluent storytelling, and those who still gave primacy to the singing and the music. Artists such as Callas, Gobbi, Christoff, Visconti and Zeffirelli were in the vanguard of the former, and essentially the domain of the very significant theatres was theirs, primarily La Scala but also the Rome Opera. Those in the more provincial theatres were less inclined to concern themselves with the acting. At this point in time, Pavarotti definitely belonged to the latter; acting had been an adjunct activity for him, not a core skill. Anthony Stivanello was determined to change the situation, in part because it would benefit this particular production of Lucia, but also because he believed that Luciano was at the beginning of a truly remarkable career, and he should not be hampered by weaknesses. They embarked on a number of excursions to the rooftop of the McAllister Hotel where Luciano was staying, and they literally spent hours and hours developing his acting skills. They worked their way through the entire opera scene by scene and in great detail, by the end of which Pavarotti had made enormous progress. He credits Anthony Stivanello with the improvement in his acting, not just for this production of Lucia but also for all his subsequent work.

Many years later, Pavarotti would declare that he had devoted a great deal of time and effort to his acting over the years, almost as much as he had committed to his singing. Consequently, he believed that he had made good progress in that area.

Lucia in Miami was a great success, Pavarotti recalling: 'Naturally the Miami audiences went crazy for Joan, but they liked me very much too. It is much easier to become enthusiastic about a singer's performance if you have been told in advance that he or she is something special' [Pavarotti/Wight, 1981:112].

Pavarotti was fast becoming a force amongst operatic tenors. However, although he had conquered Miami, he knew he must do the same in San Francisco, Chicago and New York before he could rightly claim to have arrived in America. His debut in San Francisco occurred the following year in an unforgettable production of *La Bohème* with Mirella Freni as his Mimi. He was immediately invited back for a *Lucia di Lammermoor* with Margherita Rinaldi, which was also a great success.

Chapter 18

Lucia Di Lammermoor, Scotto/Pavarotti/Pradelli, 1966

Lucia de Lammermoor, first performed at the San Carlo theatre in September 1835, is without doubt one of the finest and most melodic of Donizetti's Italian Operas. It is in fact a transitional opera, one of the greatest late bel canto operas ever composed, and its dramatic structure, both innovative and emotionally poignant, shows the way forward for the young Verdi.

Lucia is replete with glorious melodies, dramatically convincing situations and vivid characters. Musically it is one highlight after another — 'Regnava nel Silenzio,'the duet, *'Verranno a te,'* the sextet, *'Chi mi Frena'* the mad scene, *'Ardon gli'censi'* and Edgardo's death scene. The latter begins with *Tombe degli avi miei, Fra poco a me ricovero* and the final aria *Tu che addio spiagasti l'ali*. It is one musical treat after another.

The story, based on Sir Walter Scott's The Bride of Lammermoor, is a dramatic retelling of Romeo and Juliet in the Scottish context, which is also driven by religious undertones. Enrico Ashton hates his mortal enemy Edgar of Ravenswood, the last living member of his clan, others including his father having died in the protracted wars which saw the Ravenswood estates confiscated by the Ashtons. In these circumstances, it is clear that Lucia had no intention of falling in love with Edgardo. However, she had never envisaged a situation in which, confronted with a charging bull, Edgardo would be the one to save her life. She is naturally grateful and inexorably drawn to this man who is both saviour and enemy. She tries hard to resist her emotions but finally surrenders to them, despite knowing the consequences of this forbidden love. They begin to see each other, and every morning Edgardo can be seen leaving the castle.

A male chorus begins the next scene in which Normanno, captain of the guard, leads his men in a fruitless search for the intruder. Upon his return, he notices that his master, Enrico Ashton, is perturbed and Normanno decides to confront him in order to learn of his problems. Enrico concedes that he is highly troubled, mainly because his treasure chest has been drained by this recent military campaign involving the King. Consequently, his fortunes have been seriously depleted. The one person with the power, wealth and prestige to restore Enrico's own noble status is Lord Arturo Bucklaw. He is keen to marry Lucia, Enrico's sister but she, knowing his situation, adds insult to injury by refusing to marry Bucklaw, the only man who can restore their fortunes.

Nonetheless, Enrico still believes that Arturo would make an excellent match for Lucia and the Ashton family. At this point, Raimondo (Lucia's tutor and religious advisor) reminds Enrico that his sister is still mourning her recently departed mother. Normanno contradicts him; suggesting that far from being in mourning, Lucia is burning with love for a still unidentified intruder. Enrico demands to know who it is, but Normanno can only suspect that it is his enemy, Edgardo. Outraged at his betrayal Enrico orders his men to find the object of his sister's desire. Normanno and his men leave on a quest to apprehend the culprit whilst Enrico gives vent to his desire for vengeance in his aria *Cruda, funesta smania*. Normanno soon returns and confirms his suspicions that Lucia is in love with Edgardo.

The next scene finds Lucia and her companion Alisa waiting for Edgardo near the fountain in the castle grounds. He is late and Lucia takes this opportunity to tell Alisa the story of the ghost of the fountain in the aria *Regnava nel silenzio*. Apparently, her ancestor, a beautiful young woman like Lucia herself, was in love with the Lord of Ravenswood who in a jealous fit killed her. The ghost prophesied that things would end badly for Lucia and Edgardo also. Alisa is alarmed by the whole episode and begs Lucia to forget about Edgardo and make a new life for herself. She refuses to contemplate life without him, confessing that Edgardo is the light of her life. She continues with the cabaletta *'Quando rapita in estasi'*.

Edgardo visits Lucia at a rather inappropriate hour, asking her to forgive his intrusion and explaining that he had to see her before leaving for France on government business. Further he declares that, notwithstanding the sad history between their two houses, he is prepared to make peace with Enrico and ask for her hand in marriage. Lucia, who is already distressed by the announcement that Edgardo is leaving the country, becomes increasingly distraught at the thought of her brother's temper being unleashed on Edgardo. She begs him to keep their love a secret for a while longer. Edgardo understands perfectly and in an accompanied recitative of great power, he asks: 'What more can he possibly want from me? He murdered my father and kinsmen and destroyed my family home; is that not enough?' What will it take to stop his unrelenting thirst for blood? What else does he want?' The duet that follows — '*Verrano a te sull'aure i miei sospiri ardenti*'— is just incredible and full of juxtaposed emotions. One moment it is passionate and fiery, full of heat and temperament; the next it is languid and sensuous.

Duet: Lucia Perdona

We begin by analysing the 1966 Rai performance of *Lucia di Lammermoor* conducted by Molinari Pradelli with Renata Scotto in the title role and Pavarotti singing Edgardo.

This performance is characterised by what we know as flow phonation, but with an increased level of glottal resistance relative to some of his earlier work. The tone is *appoggiato* more effectively, the laryngeal position is a little higher than it had been previously (especially in the high register), and the articulators are more responsive, more flexible, and more pliable. These glottal and vocal tract settings imbue the tone with warmth, roundness, velvet and ease, especially in the lower and middle registers. However, there is something new happening in the recording of this performance. Pavarotti's voice is still fresh and natural, totally unspoiled in its virginal beauty, but now possessing a newly found firmness as well as a brilliance which seems to radiate through like sunshine on a field of sunflowers. It is also true that the voice is still not consistently *appoggiata* (well supported), nor is it always well focused. The *impostazione* is also inconsistent, giving the impression that the *impostazione* is too far back in the pharynx relative to the forward ringing sound that would later become a compelling characteristic of Pavarotti's singing. Many of the round vowels (mainly the [o] and [u]) maintain a backward pharyngeal concentration which is too dark and too covered; on the other hand, the bright and lateral [i] and [e] vowels tend to emphasise the oral cavity, producing a tone that is too forward and too narrow. However, notwithstanding these reservations his singing is overall in better technical shape than earlier efforts. The voice is *appoggiata* with greater efficiency, the *passaggio* is generally more open and the vocal timbre possesses a brilliant tinge. In part this is because the laryngeal position remains stable, but also more responsive and flexible to the events determined by the vocal tract above, and the *appoggio* strategy below. Overall, the *note di passagio* and the head register are especially *bene appoggiati* and ringing. However, whilst the first octave is also much improved it still requires attention. The *appoggio* system, despite the occasional lapse, is also much better. Vowel tracking difficulties often mar the sonorous legato line and interfere with the ornamentation.

It is also significant that as a result of the inconsistencies in the objective *appoggio*, the sound in the lower and mixed registers is often tremulous, displaying a very fast vibrato. Pavarotti's tone in the mixed register lacks the firmness and direction that is derived from a firmer glottal setting. A more vigorous contraction of the breathing musculature would provide a more consistent level of sub-glottal pressure below and firmer pharyngeal walls above the voice source. Ironically Pavarotti seems to support the head register much better than the medium register, almost bracing himself for the heavier bodywork associated with the big moments of the role. The result is that there is some really lovely singing in this performance, characterised by a beautiful ringing head register and a more open-throated but leaner sound than it would later become.

The larynx is in a moderately low position and the breath is more flowing, although often lacking the firm support of the vocal instrument. Significantly Pavarotti does not allow the larynx to rise to the degree that it would reduce the effectiveness of the laryngeal collar in the production of lower harmonics. Nor does he poke the sound on the mask in an effort to manufacture a forward, ringing, and brilliant tone. He is a far more intelligent singer and a far more natural singer than that. In fact, as time goes by, Pavarotti is one of a handful of great tenors who learns the art of encouraging the vocal tract to allow sufficient space so that the sound waves may affect their continuous cycle of propagation and rarefaction.

Meanwhile, Enrico has become financially impoverished mainly because of his political activities against the king. He is exploring various strategies before he settles on the only one that would recover his family's fortunes. Unfortunately, and unbeknown to his sister, the strategy involves the marriage of Lucia to Lord Aurthur Bucklaw, a wealthy and influential man who is in love with her. Consequently, Enrico becomes entangled in a web of lies and deception and confiscates all the correspondence from Edgardo to his sister, Lucia. In addition, he arranges the falsification of a document accusing Edgardo of abandoning her.

Lucia, already distraught at what she believes to be her lover's betrayal, surrenders to what seems to be the inevitable and against her better judgment agrees to marry Arturo Bucklaw. No sooner has she signed the marriage contract than Edgardo rushes in and claims Lucia as his betrothed.

The role of Edgardo sits beautifully in the lyric tenor voice, and what is true of most lyric tenors is doubly true of Pavarotti. Edgardo is a vital role in the tenor lexicon for two reasons. Firstly, the inspired melodic line makes for a glorious night of singing, and secondly Edgardo's character is dramatically powerful even though it is best described as ill-fated. Consequently, we can say that Donizetti gives the tenor an opportunity to display not just his glorious voice but also his dramatic, creative and interpretative powers. Edgardo doesn't make an entrance until the end of the first act, but when he does, he sings a long and dramatic recitative followed by a taxing duet with Lucia, who has by now already sung 'Regnava nel silenzio'. We will see in our detailed account that this duet powerfully establishes Edgardo's character: he is decisive and strong and knows what he wants. His only problem seems to be the perpetual struggle against his enemy, Enrico Ashton.

Edgardo's entrance provides Pavarotti with the opportunity to bring forth a character of considerable warmth, strength, and with a touch of primordial force. He delivers the recitative in a straightforward but committed manner, demonstrating both a good sense of character and situational awareness which, he depicts with clarity of diction and appropriate colouring of the text. It is an excellent entrance filled with passion, moderation, and warmth without being sentimental. The first flaw we hear comes with the phrase *'Il tradito genitore'* in which the *[i]* vowel is placed too far back and remains throaty.

The phrases 'Dalle patrie sponde,' and 'E la tua destra pegno fra noi di pace, chiedero' and 'che brama ancor quell cor feroce e reo' all share the same vocal flaw — an overemphasis of the aggiustamento or vowel modification making the passaggio notes between the E4 and G4 far too covered, too constricted and often too throaty. In addition, this constriction has the effect of distorting some of the vowels. I will not delineate every example of vowel modification in this score but there is a pattern of overcompensation at the passaggio throughout this particular performance of Lucia, especially on the [o], [a] and [e] vowels.

For a better tone and one that is also *ben appoggiato*, I would ask my reader to listen to the phrases *'pur quel voto non e infranto…io potrei, si, si, si, potrei compirlo ancor.'*

Pavarotti, following in the footsteps of his great predecessors, sings the high B flat on the [a] vowel in the excerpt above. This is an exciting and brilliant sound and the only thing that could improve it is a more relaxed laryngeal position, inducing an even more comfortable *aggiustamento* and rendering a more precise chiaro/scuro balance. These phrases are much more exciting, mainly because the tone is *ben appoggiato*. On the other hand, the coloratura phrases on *'pur quell voto non e infranto io potrei, si, potrei compirlo ancor'* lack focus, the vocal line is tenuous and the delivery a little jerky. Nonetheless, Pavarotti demonstrates a natural vocal flexibility that we would rarely find in his later work.

Let us explore some further excerpts which I believe will prove instructive.

The first is the phrase *'modi e trema,'* in which Pavarotti ascends from the G4 to the A4.

Rather than descending as written below; this is one of those traditions in Italian opera that developed over time and which succeeding generations have maintained, mainly because it works.

The first '*m'odi*' is excellent, both open-throated and ringing. The second one above is less so, being under supported which induces a dark and heavy tone and produces a loose vibrato. The G4 on the [e] vowel is too reliant on the illusion of placement or *impostazione* instead of the objective *appoggio* required for a phrase such as this. The result is that when Pavarotti ascends to the A♭ on the [a] vowel the tone is under energised and therefore unsteady. Therefore, I will stress again that, as important as the subjective *appoggio* may be in singing, it is the objective appoggio that forms the foundation for the singing voice. You cannot build an edifice on rickety foundations. In addition, it is the breath pressure that offers the best chance of pursuing a forward ringing tone.

By comparison, the phrase '*Verranno a te sull'aure I miei sospiri ardenti*' demonstrates a really beautiful lyrical sound with a hint of romantic nostalgia, which fortunately never crosses over into sentimentality. This style of singing comes closest to the type of sound that the very best vocal scientists would refer to as flow phonation.

The second Act is hardly better for Edgardo. Lucia sings her heart out in two wonderful duets: the first with her brother Enrico and the second with her spiritual advisor Raimondo. Both men in very different ways, attempt to convince her for the family's sake to forget Edgardo and marry Arturo. This scene is followed by Arturo's entrance, which allows Lucia a few minutes rest before her reappearance for the signing of the wedding contract and the famous sextet 'Chi mi frena in tal momento'. This is followed by arguably the most excellent mad scene in all opera, 'Ardon gl'incensi,' and a beautifully structured and musically glorious final death scene comprising *'Tombe degli avi miei'.* The opera continues with the discovery of Lucia's demise and the powerful and highly nuanced *'Tu che a Dio spiegasti l'ali'* which ends with Edgardo's death. There is a particular symmetry in the way the act establishes its structure. Lucia sings her glorious mad scene before relinquishing the stage to Edgardo. Depending on how gloriously the soprano manages the mad scene, it becomes either very difficult or almost impossible for Edgardo to conquer the audience. However, most tenors are grateful to at least have this opportunity to demonstrate what they can do with his remarkable recitative and aria, *'Tombe degli avi miei'* and *'Fra poco me ricovero'*. It is unusual for the hero not to have a solo aria until the very last scene of the opera, but that is the structure of *Lucia di Lammermoor*.

Chi mi Frena

The second Act is dominated by the famous sextet 'Chi mi frena in tal momento'. Pavarotti's voice is just right for this music, and throughout this act (not only the sextet but also the malediction scene that follows) he is at his most convincing. However, I will mention the following specifics for the purpose of learning, for instance, the opening phrase of 'chi mi frena in tal momento'. The F4 on the [a] vowel of '*tal*' is not only firmer but also more open, exhibiting greater clarity and ring than the Fs in his previous performances.

On the phrase '*il suo duolo, il suo spavento*' we note the lovely forward ringing [e] vowel Pavarotti produces on the '*spavento*'.

In the phrase '*ma quel rosa inarridita, ella sta fra morte e vita*' the [o] in '*rosa*' is slightly dampened but still an authentic round vowel. The [a] vowel on '*sta;* is still very much in head tone but with a more open [a] vowel than previously displayed on the G♭. The latter could do with elevating the zygomatic fascia and sustaining the last G♭ with more significant subglottic pressure, eliciting more glottal resistance and promoting the upper harmonics.

The following phrase to admire is '*Tamo ingrata, t'amo ingrata, t'amo ancor,*' the first [a] in "*t'amo*' being the type of tone that the Old Italian School referred to as the '*suono di mezza testa*'. It is the most beautiful open-throated, ringing, and genuinely exciting sound you are ever likely to hear — one which makes Pavarotti a unique and exciting tenor.

The tone on the pause on the G♭ of '*t'amo*' is also a very exciting sound. It is a shame that just as we are becoming accustomed to this beautiful sound in the sextet, Pavarotti makes a late entry on '*come rosa inaridita*' which temporarily throws him off for several bars not only musically but also vocally.

However, by the end of the sextet he has recovered very well so that the '*ingrate t'amo ancor*' finishes with the same strong ringing sound with which he began. This is the quality of the tremendously exciting sound that he carries into the malediction scene.

The Malediction Scene

Beginning with the phrase '*Hai tradito il cielo e amor*' Pavarotti produces an exciting, ringing, and virile sound, conveying his message with great force. The actual phrase '*Hai tradito il cielo e amor*' exhibits some breathiness on the E4, suggesting that the vocal folds are not adducted as efficiently as they should be. This loose phonation can be traced back to a deficient level of sub-glottal pressure, or objective *appoggio*. The remarkable thing about this singing is that Pavarotti begins the phrase with a loose, breathy phonation. When he performs the portamento up to the A4 he also manages to squeeze the loose air out of the glottis, creating the condition for firm phonation on the [a] vowel of '*maledetta*'. He produces a lovely tone for the next four bars before launching into the [e] vowel in '*che*' for which he unfortunately uses too hard an attack on the note.

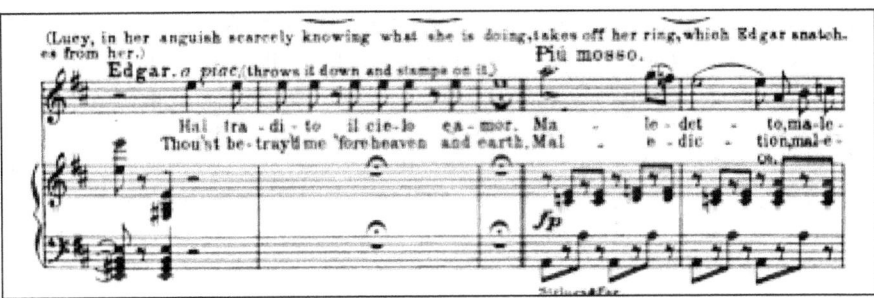

Without the cushioning effect of the breath, you can actually hear the fierce collision of the vocal folds. However, once the tone settles into the sostenuto phrase, it becomes gloriously brilliant, although personally, I prefer less rigidity at the larynx and a higher degree of relaxation of the laryngeal position. This should be combined with a minor release of the mandible and a more controlled lowering of the diaphragm than he is able to achieve here.

The rest of the singing on this page is just marvellous. It is not until Pavarotti arrives at the A4 on the [a] vowel, taking over from Lucia's A4, that we see that this onset (as opposed to an attack) is much softer, and perhaps a little under-energised. This creates a few problems when he develops the crescendo that follows. It is difficult to affect a crescendo when the breathing muscles are not already contracted. It is much easier to increase contraction when the muscles are already activated. Nonetheless, there are some very exciting moments in this performance of Lucia and, whilst the tone is still uneven, overall, he produces an exciting and virile sound throughout the range.

The question, as always is how it could be improved. It is true that the voice, in general, needs a more consistent objective *appoggio* (sub-glottal pressure) as well as a more forward focus and *imposto*, a placement that privileges a balanced tone between the chiaro/scuro of the Old School. The oropharyngeal resonator must be balanced; too often the pharyngeal walls are too soft and flabby, especially for the darker vowels. This has the effect of dampening the higher harmonics, and in contrast privileging and therefore enhancing the lower harmonics. The vocal folds at the glottal level are only sometimes efficiently adducted, resulting in considerable variation of timbre. Too often Pavarotti uses the hard attack which, has the effect of thrusting the tone either too far forward and hardening the sound, or too far back, promoting a hard attack and over darkening the sound. Balance in all things is the name of the game. Pavarotti would eventually find a better balance and achieve more consistent results. However, once accepted, the general *impostazione* (placement) of the tone, one can say that it is a truly beautiful, natural, velvety and tremendously virile sound

Tombe degli'avi miei

The final scene of the opera begins with Edgardo's recitative and aria — 'Tombe degli'avi miei and Fra poco a me ricovero'. Overall, the recitative is beautifully sung. The first flaw we encounter is the [u] vowel in the phrase *'d'una stirpe infelice de raccogliete voi'* and the first [u] on *'tu delle gioie in seno'*. Both are too forward with a much reduced first formant or *oscuro*. In the second phrase *'tu delle gioie in seno'* he sings more loudly with a much more authentic [u] vowel displaying stronger lower harmonics (darker vocal colour). The dramatic phrase *'ingrata donna'* on the G4 is dramatically effective, and vocally shows a good blend of a focused, ringing tone whilst also retaining the natural freedom of the sound. In the big phrase *'Io della morte'* the A4 is excellent, whilst the B♭ that follows required more subglottal pressure to stimulate the upper harmonics. Although Pavarotti does fabulously well in this performance, he is still at the stage of development where he slightly miscalculates the amount of energy required by particular notes, in order to create sufficient tension and resistance at the vocal folds. Please note that a change in pitch is primarily a function of the length, mass and stress of the vocal folds. However, if subglottal pressure is insufficient to maintain the balanced relationship between breath pressure and vocal folds tension, the fundamental frequency inevitably falters. Alternatively, you may allow the tone to flip into falsetto. The latter strategy will maintain pitch but will relinquish most of the tension.

In the aria *'Fra poco a me ricovero'* we encounter a truly beautiful lyric sound which unusually for Pavarotti embodies some of the characteristics of the light lyric tenor. The voice is not small but from the point of view of its production it remains lean and lyrical. It seems to me that Pavarotti consciously accesses a more significant portion of the edges of the vocal fold ligaments at the expense of the vocalis, the body of the folds. This produces some really lovely singing throughout the aria, ending on a truly brilliant but full-blooded B4 that is really exciting to listen too. However, before we arrive at this glorious finale let us see if there is anything else that we can learn from this particular rendition of Edgardo's big aria.

The first thing to note is that, notwithstanding the fact that the tone is not as firm as it could be and the legato line is not yet as smooth and seamless as it would later become, there is already a good sense of what needs to be done. However, the breath management technique has yet to achieve the requisite level of proficiency. The first evidence of this, and indeed the first flaw in the aria, appears when on the phrase *'non scendera su quello'* the *'quello'* is under-energised resulting in a wavering, unsteady tone. As it descends to the F the tone sags further, losing its natural ring and jeopardising pitch. This loss of control of the tone mirrors an incomplete breath management strategy, in the form of an erroneous antagonistic *appoggio* system (the lotta vocale of *appoggio*). Appoggio remains the most economic and efficient strategy for supporting the vocal instrument for an unusually long period of time. In the young Pavarotti, the support or objective *appoggio* is not as even as it should be and the length of time, he is able to maintain this antagonistic relationship between the internal and external muscles (which support the instrument) is underdeveloped.

Amazingly the *impostazione* on the phrase *'del tuo consorte a lato'* and the exclamatory *'Ah'* that follows on the G4 are much more natural and better placed than anything he would achieve in this aria for a long time to come. On the first *'rispetto almen le ceneri'* he needs to better manage the descending passages. On the other hand, when the exact phrase rises to the A4 on the [e] vowel of *'cenere'* he needs to open the vowel. (This narrow focus on the [e] is something that would bother Pavarotti, for some time to come). In the rest of the aria, he produces some really lovely singing, notwithstanding the fact that I would like the sound to be more focused and more efficiently guided by a firmer breath pressure towards the general area of the zygomatic arch, without actually poking it there. A stronger breath pressure would also provide better control over the diminuendo notes and more defined boundaries around some vowels.

Edgardo's Reaction to Lucia's Death

Edgardo's '*giusto cielo, rispondete, rispondete*' and the phrase '*Di chi mai, di chi piangete per pieta*' are breathy, in part because Pavarotti uses it as an emotional affect and in part because he doesn't yet possess the technique to cope with such an emotional situation whilst retaining a pure vocal line. However, once he arrives at the more dramatic moments with an open-throated tone he is on much firmer terrain, although not yet out of the woods. He still needs to focus the tone and support the lower register in a more consistent and precise manner. It is a bit too loose, affecting both vibrato and pitch.

Tu Che a Dio Spiegasti L'ali

This final aria finds Pavarotti producing a beautiful lyric sound which, whilst still retaining some of the already mentioned flaws (such as a lack of focus and a chronic miscalculation of the required sub-glottal pressure) is nonetheless an authentic, truthful and vocally natural performance.

The first phrase is beautiful but lacks the accent that would make the performance more interesting. Pavarotti's diction enjoys a high level of clarity and when he rises to the climax of '*bell'alma innamorata, ne congiunga il Nume in ciel*' the A4 is more open throated than we have previously observed — the result of a moderately lowered larynx.

The phrases '*Morir voglio, morir voglio*' and the '*No, no, no*' are both forceful and virile. The G natural on the phrase '*A te vengo*' is much softer with a more authentic and open [a] vowel whereas he typically sings the [a] vowel with a fair tinge of [o] vowel.

Conclusions

In this early Lucia with Scotto, Pavarotti has gained significantly both in technical proficiency, interpretative authenticity and creativity relative to his previous performances. The voice is more lyrical than it would later become, but it has all the freshness and the bloom that makes it a truly beautiful sound. He still has some problems to solve, but many have already been considerably diminished. He needs to work on vowel integrity, a greater level of breath pressure capacity and greater precision to the target, objective *appoggio* and *lotta vocale*. Accuracy in flexibility and the *passaggio* is also in need of further work.

Chapter 19

La Traviata, Modena, Pavarotti, Freni, Magiera, 1965

La Traviata is based on a play by Alexander Dumas '*La Dame aux Camelias,*' the story of a young woman who comes to Paris in search of the good life and personal success. She soon learns that when the gods want to punish you, they grant you your wishes. Violetta manages to become part of an elite and well-off community, but these riches are part of the *'Parisienne demi monde'.* She later discovers that the good life comes at a much higher price than her youthful enthusiasm would have allowed her to believe. Verdi read the book by Alexandre Dumas fils upon its release in Paris and immediately fell in love with it.

Violetta is a well-known Parisienne courtesan who unfortunately has been seriously ill for some time. With the help of her friend Flora and financial support from her patron Baron Douphol, Violetta marks her return to society hosting a lavish dinner party. The event is well attended by Parisian nobility and gentleman of rank. These men rarely failed to take advantage of these elegant functions which in many respects served them well as they could be accompanied by their respective mistresses. Their wives of course belonged to an entirely different circle.

Amidst the revelry, Gaston introduces Violetta to a young middle-class gentleman, Alfredo Germont. Gaston informs Violetta that his young friend has been in love with her for some time. She begins to laugh at the whole thing until Gaston tells her that he has been coming to enquire after her health every day for the last year. Violetta starts to take it more seriously and coquettishly asks her suitor 'Is it true?'. She finds his candour touching: he has loved her for over a year and has been coming to the house daily. By way of changing the conversation Violetta and Gaston cajole Alfredo into making a toast. After a false start, he finds inspiration and launches into the drinking song whereupon he is joined by Violetta.

As the guests retire to the other rooms, Violetta grows pale and is about to faint when Alfredo comes to her aid. Being alone with her gives him the opportunity to declare his love. She resists, but finally surrenders to the idea when he is honest enough to tell her that no one on earth loves her, except him.

Dawn is just breaking through when the guests finally depart. Reluctantly Alfredo also takes his leave, once alone, Violetta is left to ponder whether having a profound and true love is a possibility for her. In her aria *'Sempre Libera'*, she savours the prospect of such a relationship before concluding that it is not suitable for her. In fact, she believes that a serious love affair would be most unfortunate as an intimate relationship is potentially destructive. She resolves to continue her hedonistic lifestyle.

Act II, Scene 1

Three months later: Alfredo and Violetta are cohabiting in a house in the country.

To everyone's surprise, Violetta and Alfredo are now sharing an idyllic lifestyle in the French countryside. In his aria *'Dei miei bollenti spiriti'* he acknowledges the fire burning in his blood and the ardour in his heart. He just adores Violetta and loves the life they have built together. He is still in his own world of wonderment when he is brought down to earth by their maid, Annina who has just returned home. He asks her where she has been and discovers that she was sent to Paris to sell Violetta's possessions to support their idyllic lifestyle, to which they have both become accustomed. He chastises Annina, for not telling him of their financial difficulties and resolves to go to Paris to raise the necessary funds.

Meanwhile, Violetta has received an invitation from her dear friend Flora, begging her to come to a party that very evening. The invitation brings memories of the trivial and superficial lifestyle that had once been hers. So removed is she from her previous life that she now feels that everything that occurred before she met Alfredo had happened to another woman. She feels ashamed and wants nothing to do with that world or the people who inhabit it.

Violetta is still pondering the foolishness of her previous life when her servant announces a visitor. It is Alfredo's father, Giorgio Germont, who makes an unexpected entrance. He is at once haughty and impersonal, but Violetta maintains her dignity and receives him with respectful grace. However, when she feels that he is becoming disrespectful, Violetta quickly points out that this is her home and she will leave him alone, more for his sake than hers. Her dignity, her manner and her carriage immediately alert Germont Père to the fact that this is not the typical former courtesan that he had expected to encounter. Violetta has definitely struck a chord. That notwithstanding Germont demands that she leave his son, not just for Alfredo's sake but for the sake of his daughter, Alfredo's sister. The latter is about to marry into an old and respected family but now that her fiancé's parents have learned of Alfredo's relationship with a courtesan, they have threatened to cancel the wedding. If Alfredo were to continue with this relationship, he would surely ruin himself and his sister. He swears that he has nothing against Violetta herself but is merely trying to protect his family, more specifically his daughter.

Violetta suggests a compromise, saying that she will leave Alfredo until after the wedding and resume the relationship when Germont's daughter is settled in a happy marriage. Germont can't accept this sacrifice; it is not enough. It would not only create a scandal but also severe problems of trust and honour for his daughter after the wedding.

Violetta confesses her love for Alfredo and does not believe that she can leave him. Even if she mastered the courage to leave, he wouldn't let her go. Germont however remains unrelenting until she finally breaks down and agrees to the sacrifice he demands, but on condition that he tell his daughter of Violetta's sacrifice (*dite alla Govan*). Violetta asks Germont to embrace her as his daughter, which he does. Then in the most beautiful duet she asks Germont to tell the young woman that the victim of this drama has sacrificed the only thing she has ever loved so that she may be happy, and her victim may die.

This duet is conceived on a grand scale both for its emotional power as well as its sheer diversity and magnitude. By the time Germont finally bids Violetta farewell, he is almost as devastated as she is. He came with the intent of intimidating her into submission but leaves believing her to be the consoling angel of his family. He had not expected to find her so strong yet so vulnerable, so beautiful, so intelligent and yet so human, so passionate and ardent and yet so compassionate. He could not help but wonder what may have happened to this magnificent woman in a set of different circumstances. That she loved his son was beyond doubt; that his son loved her was now perfectly understandable. Winning his point was indeed a hollow victory and he felt wretched.

As Violetta sits at her desk writing a farewell note to Alfredo, her lover returns unexpectedly and asks her to whom she is writing. She is flustered and appears confused, leading him to believe that all is not well. Frantically she asks Alfredo if he loves her. He confirms his deep love for her, yet even this does nothing to calm her fears. Her passionate and anguished entreaty to her lover, '*Amami Alfredo*' is one of the most desperate and emotional cries in all opera. Alfredo leaves and Violetta instructs Annina to ensure that he does not read her letter until after she has gone. When Alfredo reads it, he is devastated and inconsolable. Germont Père tries to soothe his son without success. In the aria '*Di provenza il mar e il sol*' he depicts a beautiful portrait of a simple and innocent lifestyle where the ocean and the sun emphasise Provence's natural beauty. Germont Père begs his son to come home with him, but it is all to no avail. The end of this scene finds Alfredo rushing back to Paris determined to find Violetta.

Scene 2 Paris, that same night

When Alfredo arrives at Flora's home the party is in full swing, and her guests are being entertained by groups of masked gypsies and bullfighters. Alfredo arrives alone and is burning with jealousy as he observes Violetta on the arm of her former lover, Baron Douphol. The two men join a card game during which the tension rises as they aggressively project their hostility towards each other. Finally, Alfredo declares that his luck at cards would explain his misfortune in love. The dangerous undercurrent continues until Violetta manages to speak with Alfredo, begging him to leave the party as she and the Baron love each other, and she will not return with him. However, she does not want to see either of them die in a duel. The more she says the more furious Alfredo becomes until he can stand it no longer. He summons the guests to him: '*Do you know this woman?*' he asks. '*Of course,*' they answer. '*Do you know what she did?*' '*Yes*', they say. '*Well, I want you all to witness that I have repaid my debt to her.*' As Alfredo viciously throws money at Violetta, Germont Père arrives and scolds his son for this shameful and unjust outburst. Realising the extent of his viciousness towards a woman whose only sin was to have loved him, Alfredo is jolted back to his senses and is most remorseful. A glorious Verdian concertato follows, combining a touching dramatic situation with a superb melody and text designed to touch the human heart.

Act III Violetta's bedroom a few months later

The doctor visits Violetta and then delivers the bad news to Annina: her mistress's condition has deteriorated, and she is near death. Annina is devastated but hides her feelings when Violetta asks her to give what little money they have left to the poor. She then begins to re-read a letter from Germont Père, informing her of the fact that Alfredo has been made aware of her sacrifice and is returning to beg her forgiveness. She understands her situation and realises that it is too late for them to be reunited. In '*Addio del passato*', she bids farewell to all her former hopes and dreams and prays to be released from this suffering. Verdi juxtaposes the sound of innocent children downstairs enjoying a street carnival with the pain and suffering felt by the dying Violetta. Then to her amazement and elation, Alfredo enters. He embraces her passionately and promises that his love will be the tonic for her recovery.

Together, they will leave their beloved Paris, returning triumphantly to their rural and idyllic lifestyle as expressed in 'Parigi o Cara'. Finally, a remorseful Germont arrives and offers his blessing, which just for a moment allows Violetta to believe in miracles. Unfortunately, her hopes are dashed by the same cruel fate that extinguishes her life.

Along with Mimi, Gilda, Butterfly, and Norma, Violetta is one of the most touching heroines in all opera. The fate of Violetta and Mimi is particularly moving as their everyday life wears them down and they are not responsible for their ultimate demise. Unlike Gilda who chooses to protect her lover by substituting her life for his, or Butterfly, who commits suicide as part of her Japanese code of honour, Mimi and Violetta make no such decision. Their mortal foe is not human but rather the cruelty of nature in the form of tuberculosis, an unrelenting, untreatable disease sweeping through Paris at that time. The old Paris was cold, dirty, ill-nourished, crowded, and inadequately serviced in terms of sewerage and running water. All of this meant that conditions were rife for the spread of the disease, not only in Paris but throughout Europe. Verdi was drawn to this subject in the first place due to his affinity with Violetta's story and her unforgiving and deadly environment. He viewed death as an insuperable force which cruelly took those you loved most from you.

Soon after graduating from his studies in Milan, Verdi married his childhood sweetheart Margherita Barezzi. The educated opinion about Ghita was that she was intelligent, sweet tempered, and the most understanding and supportive of wives. That Ghita loved Verdi goes without saying, and, as a result of her musical background and understanding, she believed in and nurtured his enormous gifts. After the birth of a beautiful little daughter Virginia, the family moved to Milan, allowing Verdi to pursue his dream of having his operas presented at La Scala, the premier international opera house of the era. Soon, they were blessed with a son, Icilio, who completed their family. Whilst her husband pursued his career Ghita kept the family running like clockwork. When they ran out of money, she didn't bother Verdi, instead pawning her jewellery to pay the rent and keep the family going. Finally, his opera *Oberto* was scheduled to be performed at La Scala that November; it would seem that all their dreams were about to be realised.

Then suddenly, disaster struck. Their little daughter Virginia died in October 1838, their son Icilio in 1839, followed by Ghita in June 1840. None of the deaths could be explained, all three succumbing to an unspecified disease. Verdi was absolutely devastated and inconsolable: nothing mattered to him, certainly not his music. If not for the latter, they would have stayed in Busetto where his family would have been safer. His devastated father-in-law Antonio Barezzi took Verdi back to Busetto, where they could share their enormous grief.

After a long period of time, Verdi returned to something resembling normality and when he did, he was in great demand. He began a tentative friendship with the soprano Giuseppina Strepponi. At first hesitantly, then more willingly, he allowed Strepponi to win his heart, becoming his life's companion and later still his second wife. She was a wonderful woman, sophisticated and charming with a penetrating intellect that allowed her to become a trusted advisor to Verdi at a time when his career was in the ascendancy.

However, Strepponi had a major secret which in the mid-nineteenth century served to marginalise her socially. As a young artist, she became involved with her leading man, the tenor Napoleone Moriani, who was married and made it clear that he wouldn't leave his wife. However, his relationship with Strepponi was strong, and over a period of time, they had two children., When Strepponi was thirty-four, her father died, and she inherited the burden of being the family's breadwinner, responsible for providing not only for her mother but also her four siblings. Fortunately, Giuseppina had the talent and the business acumen to provide well for her family, and she did. She was an excellent musician, showing exceptional vocal promise and winning the *Bel Canto* prize at the Milan Conservatorium in 1834.

As a result, I suggest that Verdi was uniquely qualified to set Duma's play *A Dame aux Camelias*. He understood very well the complications and nuances of Violetta's life and the European mindset. He knew about premature death, having suffered the loss of his family. Consequently, Verdi's *La Traviata* is a product of first-hand experience, an empathetic spirit, and an outpouring of humanity by an artist at the peak of his creative powers, resulting in a heartfelt and emotionally moving score.

Critique of La Traviata, Modena — 7 February 1965, Pavarotti/ Freni/Magiera

On February 7, 1965 (only six weeks before performing *La Traviata* at Covent Garden and four months before singing it again in Australia), Pavarotti sang Alfredo at the Teatro Comunale in his hometown of Modena. Fortunately, the performance was recorded for posterity, and whilst the quality of the recording is not as straightforward as one would like, it does allow us to draw certain conclusions about Pavarotti's progress. This recording is particularly important because it was a few months before he sang '*Lucia di Lammermoor*' with Sutherland in Miami and immediately before he reprised *La Traviata* with Renata Scotto at Covent Garden. It also coincided with '*La Sonnambula*' at Covent Garden with Sutherland which was later repeated on their Australian tour. The importance of this recording can't be overstated. It allows us to compare the young Pavarotti before his Australian Tour (when he was still employing the *Sostegno* system of breath management) and after this tour when he began adopting the *Appoggio* system of breath management which Joan Sutherland taught him.

The *'sostegno'* system of breath management was the polar opposite of the *appoggio* system employed by Sutherland. This old school *sostegno* strategy could best be described as 'up and in', as opposed to Sutherland's *appoggio* strategy which was defiantly "down and out", i.e., in the anterior posterior direction and laterally. I like the life buoy analogy used by William Vennard to describe this *appoggio* strategy. Nonetheless, if you have a voice like Pavarotti, you can still sound marvellous under any system, but the educated ear can easily detect the difference.

Under the *sostegno* system, the sound is natural, lyrically lean, and fresh, with a lovely velvety bloom. It also has a round and flexible tone that is very responsive to subtle dynamic change and vocal colour. This is precisely how Pavarotti sounds in the February 7 performance: fresh-voiced, youthful, brilliant and ringing but still with a lovely velvety bloom. There are occasions when the vibrato is a little fast, but overall, it is a beautiful, flexible and accessible sound.

Alfredo's *tessitura* in 'La Traviata' is generally a little lower than many of Pavarotti's *bel canto* roles, allowing him to maintain a comfortably lower laryngeal position. The latter part resembles a more moderate version of that generally employed in the *copertura* strategy. This *copertura* or covering technique provides the singer with easier access to the high register, and it does so in a more natural and less contrived manner. At this stage of his career, the role of Alfredo suits Pavarotti's velvety, lyrical tenor very well, and he takes full advantage of his excellent natural gifts. Nonetheless, there are moments when the tone is quite uneven, either too far back and plummy, or too far forward and metallic. Too often, the sound is either constricted or forced. However, these moments never overshadow the natural glory of his voice.

However, at this stage Pavarotti is yet to achieve the consistency of sub-glottal pressure (breath pressure) and the ability to make the necessary and precise pressure adjustments coinciding with alterations in pitch and intensity. The tone often lacks the consistency of colour and brilliance and timbral quality that is the product of a firm glottal closure. This strong closure is produced by a longer closed phase which is also responsible for skewing the spectrum and exciting the upper harmonics. When this is combined with a concomitant shortening of the vocal tract it further serves to strengthen the upper harmonic partials which enhance the brilliance of the tone. At any rate Pavarotti's tone still requires a higher level of focus, concentration and definition (Vennard's illusion of placement). The soft singing, in particular, becomes too disembodied and airy, lacking a foundation and precision. Vowels such as the [e] and the [o] are often too narrow but not as severely limited as we have heard in other recordings. Once or twice, the upper register is a little uncertain — something that the *appoggio* system of breath management will surely rectify. Concerning the resonator, there are moments when the articulators are not as active and flexible as they should be. The tongue is sometimes incorrectly retracted; the mandible does not open naturally; the zygomatic arch tends to drop a little, the latter defect having a considerable influence on the soft palate. Finally, the volume and shape of the pharynx and the firmness of the pharyngeal walls naturally mirror what is happening at the respiratory and laryngeal levels. This means that all inconsistencies and functional inefficiencies in any part of the vocal instrument are always reflected in other elements of the vocal apparatus. The whole device is much more interactive than people imagine.

Notwithstanding some of the reservations expressed above, Pavarotti is on the right track. His voice sounds youthful and bright, as befits a young man depicting an even younger hero, Alfredo. The voice is thrilling and brilliant but still retains a beautiful natural bloom. His interpretation, like his tone, is honest and straightforward, yet rudimentary and sometimes musically tentative.

La Traviata, Covent Garden – 19 March 1965: Pavarotti, Scotto, Carlo Felice Cillario

Fortunately, we do have a recording of the Covent Garden performance of 'La Traviata' with Renata Scotto, Pavarotti and Peter Glossop.

Violetta's story in *La Traviata* is tremendously tragic, and Verdi understood this better than most. Consequently, he managed to Squeeze every bit of emotion from the catastrophe. In large part, this was because Verdi had a natural predisposition towards this kind of emotional ringing out, and in large part, it was because his own devastating life had prepared him exceptionally well for this moment and this material. It would have been impossible for him to compose such touching and emotionally charged music for the last act of La Traviata, especially Violetta's death scene, without recalling the premature death of his beautiful young wife, Ghita (Margherita Barezzi).

How could Verdi compose such heart-breaking music for the second act scene between Germont Pere and Violetta, in which Germont demands her sacrifice to save her daughter's marriage and happiness, without recalling Barezzi's ominous warning about the disastrous consequences of Verdi's relationship with Giuseppina? He could not help but connect Violetta's alienation from mainstream society and Giuseppina's social isolation in Busetto.

In an exchange of letters between Francesco Piave, the librettist for La Traviata and his friend and colleague Luzzio, this very topic came up for discussion:

> In this opera, Luzzio has suggested a possible reflection, or sublimation, of the intimate drama of Verdi's personal relationship with Giuseppina Strepponi and Antonio Barezzi. Violetta's redemption through love and the elder Germont final

recognition of her worth had, indeed, parallels in real life, not long before the opera was written. Giuseppina escaped Violetta's tragic end, it is true, but her health was anything but good, and some of her letters exhale a melancholy, sick-room atmosphere not unlike that of the last act of La Traviata [Walker, 1972: 207].

How could he help but recall Giuseppina's grace, poise, compassion, and rich humanity when composing the third act scene for Violetta? Indeed, that glorious, heartfelt lamentation '*Alfredo, Alfredo di quest core*' was not an accident. How could such a wonderful woman with a brilliant mind and a beautiful artistic soul be marginalised by society? And yet, this was Giuseppina's fate, a fate she was destined to share with Violetta. Fortunately for her, she was lucky enough to have Verdi in her life, and he could shield her from the full brunt of the repudiation she would typically have been subjected to. That notwithstanding, even Verdi was obliged, for the sake of decency to keep Giuseppina in the background for many years before they were married.

La Traviata opens with an atmospheric intro which is dominated by the higher strings, introducing an atmosphere of impending doom. Verdi juxtaposed this premonitory prelude with the somewhat frenzied atmosphere that is so characteristic of Flora's party at the beginning of the opera.

He knew the world they lived in and how unforgiving it could be towards a fallen woman. In such a world, people like Giuseppina and Violetta would find it difficult to redeem themselves. Since the loss of his family, Verdi had lived with a premonition of impending doom, but in the opening scene of *La Traviata*, he wants none of it. The curtain rises to reveal a magnificent party, wherein Verdi introduces all his main characters with one exception, Germont Pere. But he like the great puppet master that he was, seems to be saying to his audience: 'You are right! I know this affair is going to end badly, but just for tonight, I don't want to know about it'.

Covent Garden Traviata Analysis

Concerning the Covent Garden's performance of *La Traviata*, the first thing I would like to say is that Pavarotti's voice is too heavy and leaden, and it is hardly recognisable. It is a great deal more serious, more voluminous, much too dark and more dramatic than the Modena performances in February of that year. It hardly sounds like Pavarotti.

He opens the drinking song '*Libiamo new lieti Calici*' with relatively soft onset and proceeds to a mezzo forte tone. The latter is a little breathy and throaty but develops into a lovely, suspended sound on the [a] vowel on '*calici*,' an F natural. However, the very following phrase, '*che la bellezza infiora*,' is meant to be sung softly and Pavarotti follows the instruction. However, his soft singing lacks core, brilliance and squillo; it is also a little breathy, flabby and lacking in focus. This type of singing, a style that lacks substance and focus, often impacts the pitch; consequently, Pavarotti has a couple of tricky and muffled moments to deal with. In the following phrase, the vowel [a] on the phrase, '*E la fuggeva, fuggeva lore* displays a hard attack, mainly because it is not cushioned by the breath, but also because in his attempt to increase vocal intensity, he fails to raise the breath pressure. Consequently, this failure to increase respiratory pressure makes it impossible for the air accumulating below the larynx (subglottal pressure) to sustain the necessary buoyancy, allowing the whole edifice to collapse indiscriminately under the force of a hard attack. Pavarotti either forgot or was never taught that there is a direct relationship between an increase in intensity and subglottal pressure. There is a line of thought in the Old Italian School suggesting that if you properly prepare the tone, the breath will follow. In this instance Pavarotti seems to believe that if you sing louder, the breath energy will follow which occasionally it does but mostly does not. Consequently, the breath related to the objective appoggio must be prepared first. Then, thought may be given to the subjective appoggio, which is all about proprioceptive sensations (Vennard illusion of placement).

When Pavarotti combines this vocal deficiency with an exaggeratedly low larynx, it results in an overly dark and throaty sound. The soft singing that follows on '*fuggeva, fuggeva l'ora sinebrie a volutta*' is meant to be sung softly, but Pavarotti's sound is disembodied and lacking a foundation in breath energy.

We recall that one of Lamperti's laws related to singing piano:

> *The piano* should in all respects, with the exception of intensity, resemble the *forte*: it should possess the same depth, character, and feeling; it should be supported by an equal quantity of breath, and should have the same quality of tone so that even when reduced to pianissimo it can be heard at as great a distance as the forte [Lamperti: c. 1983: 19].

To remedy this vocal problem, the first thing to recall is that the onset of your tone is critical because once you have launched the tone you cannot alter it. The simultaneous onset will do in most cases, but if you want a particularly brilliant and focused manner you should aim for a firm vocal beginning. This, as the name suggests, closes the vocal folds particularly firmly and creates a great deal of resistance at the glottal level. This resistance indicates that there must be an accompanying firm attack on the breath and a simultaneous onset of sound. Tight glottal closure and the consequent subglottal pressure must be maintained throughout the phrase. Too often, singers begin the passage firmly only to slacken the tension at the glottal and subglottal level in the latter part of the phrase.

Having dealt with the softer and less focused singing, we should now examine Pavarotti's loud singing in this performance. Pavarotti produces a delicate and powerful operatic sound in this role, especially when singing loudly. The only problem is that too often, the larynx is set too low. Consequently, we can say that the tone is too back, too dark, too voluminous and altogether too demanding for Pavarotti's technique at this stage.

The *impostazione* (the subjective *appoggio*) is too far back, and the pharyngeal walls are too soft, creating a muffled, dark, flabby tone that lacks focus and brilliance.

I have rarely heard Pavarotti make as dark and voluminous a sound as he does here. It is not an ugly sound; one could describe it as quite lovely with its velvety youthful bloom. The bright lateral vowel sounds are not as biting or piercing as they would later become, so my objection is not as much about aesthetics as it is about healthy singing, which is not. The tone is too big, heavy, and dark to be healthy. In addition, the tone lacks both objective *appoggio* (breath pressure) and subjective *appoggio* (the illusion of forward placement). The resulting tone is not compatible with Pavarotti's technique at this time, nor is it sustainable.

The remedy I recommend for this type of overly dark tone is the one suggested by James McKinney. He contends that the leading cause of extremely dark sounds is the overemphasis of the pharyngeal resonator.

According to McKinney, several factors can cause this, including:

> (1) overuse of the yawning muscles, with resulting spread throat and depressed larynx; (2) lack of oral space due to lip, jaw, or tongue position; (3) wrong tonal models; (4) floppy surfaces of pharyngeal walls (not enough muscle tones to give any character to the sound); (5) tongue pulled back into the pharynx (retroflex tongue). Darkness in the sound can come from too much or too little tension, so it is essential to identify the specific causes before starting corrective procedures. Look first for lack of activity in the articulators, such as failure to move the lips or make any significant mouth opening; this can darken and muffle the sound even when no other faults are present. Such lack of movement is usually easily corrected by calling the student's attention to it and requiring him to practice in front of a mirror.
>
> If this is not the problem, listen to the student's sound to see if it is breathy in addition to being dark. If so, it is best to first work on the breathy sound, since it is a phonatory problem. Often, the darkness will disappear when the breathiness is eliminated [Mckinney, 1994: 141].

There is a great deal of wisdom in the above suggestions.

The ideal for every student is not to just read it and then forget about it. It would be best if you studied it until these strategies become part of your vocal armoury. These strategies need to become second nature if they are to be helpful.

Chapter 20

Sutherland and Pavarotti, Australia 1965

The Joan Sutherland story began in Sydney in 1926 when she was born into a comfortable middle-class family. Her father was president of the Master Tailors Association and a leader within the Scottish community. Her mother, Muriel Alston, was William's second wife and came from an upper-middle-class family. Muriel was an attractive woman with a strong personality and a beautiful singing voice. Her compelling mezzo-soprano had been well-schooled, and her training could be traced back to the great Manuel Garcia via Mathilde Marchesi. For years, she maintained an impressive regimen of daily scales and exercises.

The Sutherland house resonated with Muriel's beautiful voice and the sounds of great artists emanating from the gramophone. Joan's favourites were Galli Curci, Enrico Caruso, John McCormack and above all, Nellie Melba. She particularly loved Melba's performance of 'Home Sweet Home'.

When she wasn't listening to music Joan loved swimming with her sister Barbara on the beach at the bottom of their property. This was an inspirational ambiance for young Joan, and she thrived on it.

Although Joan loved singing, Muriel discouraged formal training until the age of eighteen. However, she gave Joan some breathing exercises to expand the chest and train the muscles around the diaphragm. These exercises, combined with the beautiful sound of Muriel's singing and the gramophone, provided Joan with a firm foundation for her later career. It was an idyllic world for the young Joan but, as fate would have it, the idyll would not last. William Sutherland died of a heart attack on Joan's sixth birthday, shattering her world and fracturing the family beyond repair. He died intestate, and the house had to be sold.

Joan was far too young for such a bitter lesson, but there was no alternative. She learned that, notwithstanding personal tragedies, life somehow goes on. As a consequence, her singing began to take on a new meaning.

She was enrolled at St Catherine's Sydney, where she studied piano and music theory. She was removed from the choir for a time because her voice was too big and drowned out the other girls.

Joan was eighteen when she saw a notice in the Sydney Morning Herald that John and Ida Dickens were offering a coveted two-year scholarship to a talented young singer. Winning this prize was very important to her as it was the first public recognition of her gift. More prestigious awards would follow.

Soon Ida Dickens became convinced that Joan was not a mezzo like her mother Muriel but a dramatic soprano, her range developing from a G to an insecure top C.

Muriel didn't like the idea, but Joan, who loved Kirsten Flagstad's voice, thought it would be great to sing the Wagnerian repertoire, and began competing in local Eisteddfods with considerable success. At this time, she met a young pianist named Richard Bonynge, who was studying with Lindley Evans, Melba's last accompanist. Evans nurtured in Richard the love of the early nineteenth-century *bel canto* repertoire, which would later play such a big part in Joan's development. Meanwhile, Joan's singing was progressing very well. She won the Sydney Sun Aria in 1949 and competed in the 1950 Mobil Quest. There were nearly two thousand entrants, but she reached the Grand Final, singing 'Mother you know the Story' from *'Cavalleria Rusticana'*. As an added incentive, her uncle John promised to complement her winnings with another thousand pounds, thus giving her the impetus to leave for England in pursuit of her quest to sing principal roles at Covent Garden.

In London she studied with Clive Carey and with his help, enrolled at the Royal College of Music Opera School. She also caught up with Richard Bonynge, an encounter signalling a flurry of activity as he eagerly introduced her to the joys of London's cultural and musical life. Richard's love of *Bel Canto* had intensified under the spell of Maria Callas. In particular, Callas's recording of Bellini's *'Qui la Voce'* from *I Puritani* had conquered him completely.

Joan auditioned three times for Covent Garden. At first, they could see the talent but needed to figure out how to utilise it. Finally, they saw her performing Giorgietta in Puccini's *Il Tabarro* in the end-of-year production at the Opera School. They knew she could sing, but they now recognised her potential as a stage performer. It was enough to secure her a Covent Garden contract for ten pounds a week, and she made her debut as the First Lady in Mozart's *'The Magic Flute'*. Antonia followed this in *The Tales of Hoffman*, Eva in *'Die Meistersingers,'* the countess in *'The Marriage of Figaro,'* Amelia in *'Masked Ball'* and Desdemona in *'Otello'*. Her biggest thrill in those early years was reserved for her appearance as Clotilde, Norma's maid to Maria Callas's legendary Norma. This changed her life as night after night she marvelled at Callas's capacity to completely transform herself into Norma and enslave her audience. Joan had never experienced anything like it.

Between music making, learning new roles and career development, Joan and Richard found time to get married on 16 October 1954, and their son Adam was born in February 1956. Muriel was aghast when she heard the news of their wedding.

Every day, Richard worked away in the background, teaching her the *Bel canto* repertoire, extending her vocal range and developing her agility. He would trick her by starting her scales a third higher when she resisted, which she did regularly. She believed she was singing a top C when she was singing an E natural above the ultimate C. Richard did everything in his power to entice, persuade and even deceive her into believing she could sing the coloratura repertoire.

By the time she took *'Qui la Voce'* to a lesson with Clive Carey, Richard had won the argument but not yet the war. Joan's initial doubts and insecurities were nothing compared to Muriel's resistance to the direction her daughter's career was taking. She was convinced Joan should be singing Wagner and accused Richard of ruining her voice. Richard thought Muriel lacked musical knowledge and she responded by taking out the music to 'O Don Fatale' from *Don Carlos*, waving it at him and saying: 'If you can play it, I can sing it'. He knew he could play it but did not expect that she, looking every inch the diva, would deliver this most difficult mezzo aria with such panache as to leave him breathless. He would never again question her qualifications to discuss singing.

Richard Bonynge was a powerful force in Sutherland's artistic development. He was more than her mentor: he envisioned, structured, and championed her career. When the Covent Garden power brokers wanted her to study Sieglinde, Chrysothemis and the Marschallin, it was Bonynge who stood up to them, defending her right to refuse that repertoire, which he regarded as inimical to her artistic interest. He was unrelenting in his pursuit of their goal — the conquest of the bel canto repertoire and international glory. His Australian irreverence was not always appreciated, and many considered him a pest, but his assessment of her splendid gifts was correct. His contribution to her development was both immense and undeniable.

It was around this time that Bonynge talked Covent Garden into letting Sutherland sing the role of the doll in *Tales of Hoffman*. This role made people sit up and listen, and her performance stopped the show. Soon, she was singing in the Tales of *Hoffman* and another remarkable performance in Handel's *Alcina*.

Armed with fantastic reviews for the Doll in *Hoffman, Alcina*, and Gilda in *Rigoletto*, Bonynge began agitating for Joan to be given the title role of *Lucia di Lammermoor*. David Webster, head of Covent Garden, was essentially in Joan's corner anyway, but Richard's unflagging faith stiffened his resolve. Having decided to entrust Joan with *Lucia di Lammermoor*, Webster enlisted the great conductor Tullio Serafin to take charge of the production. Serafin agreed, but only if the opera was sung in Italian and not in English as planned. It was a momentous decision that propelled Sutherland's career from a mainly British affair into an international one.

Bonynge was delighted with Serafin's involvement. Finally, here was a man that he could not only respect but also learn from. In fact, according to Zeffirelli, Sutherland and Bonynge were eager to have Serafin nurture her career. They knew that he would develop her talent and protect and advise her as he had done with Maria Callas, Rosa Ponselle, Tito Gobbi and others.

In the interim, Sutherland sang a breath-taking Gilda, which left the critics searching for superlatives.

In 1959, Serafin was nearly 81 and, by any measure, the doyen of Italian opera, having had a splendid international career. For ten years, he had held the post of artistic director of the Metropolitan Opera, New York and a further decade as the uncompromising director of the Rome Opera. Singers just loved working with him. Rosa Ponselle referred to his divinely inspired gift, while Tito Gobbi, believed him to have '*an infallible instinct for voice...and to be the most complete man of the theatre in our time*'. Maria Callas simply revered him and, now in his eighties, Joan Sutherland found him an inspirational artist.

The last word on Serafin should go to Lord Harwood:

> Very few conductors had a more distinguished career than Tullio Serafin and perhaps none apart from Toscanini had more influence. He conducted almost everything in the Italian repertoire; a lot of Wagner, but in Italian opera, he was a sovereign authority. He knew...much more than Toscanini did about it. Toscanini never did in a big way the Rossini, Donizetti Bellini, repertoire; he did some, of course, but not in a big way. Serafin knew them all... He had a great sense of the past and of the future. Above all Serafin was a singer's conductor [Lord Harwood's interview with Maria Callas].

This was the man that Sutherland and Bonynge were sent to visit in Venice. According to Norma Major, they worked together on Lucia and *me Puritani, Sonnambula* and *Norma*. Serafin complimented Sutherland on her vocal technique and expressiveness, and congratulated Bonynge on his work with Joan, specifically his ornamentation for *Lucia*. He suggested that she should keep working with her husband, and he would see them both in London.

When Serafin began rehearsals in London, he loved Sutherland's vocalising, but it was clear that she needed some work on her stagecraft if she were to have a complete success. Serafin summoned Zeffirelli to London and, as a man of few words, stated: 'We are doing Lucia with an Australian girl, marvellous voice but she needs your help.'

Zeffirelli arrived to take up the combined challenge of designer and producer for Lucia. He recalls his first meeting with Joan: 'She was a stout, awkward, badly dressed woman, with a cold. My heart sank!' Serafin, sensing Zeffirelli's reservations, invited Sutherland to the piano. She hadn't made an excellent first impression, but when she began singing, Zeffirelli's reservations vanished.

A protégé of Count Luchino Visconti, Zeffirelli was an ambitious young man with an eye to the main chance and Serafin made sure he knew the importance of this Lucia. He said: '*You have done enough to deserve this.*' Zeffirelli understood that Lucia would catapult Sutherland to international stardom and give his already considerable career another burst of brilliance.

As he approached Joan, he could feel her recoil. This made things very difficult because as he explained, '*I am an Italian, a tactile person; I have to touch people, to feel their physical presence as a person.*' She took a big breath and gave him a big hug. It was a professional embrace that would transform Sutherland from a great singer into a complete artist [Zeffirelli, 1986: 147].

February 17th, 1959, was a typical winter's day in London, cold and miserable. That evening the premier of *Lucia* was no better, but Sutherland was comforted by a sold-out theatre and her impeccable preparation.

From the beginning, there was a sense of great expectancy and occasion, and by the time Sutherland completed her first act aria '*Regnava nel Silenzio,*' the house erupted.

The audience was delighted with expectation before the Mad Scene, and when Sutherland appeared at the top of the stairs with a knife in hand and blood-stained dress, she created a furore. She combined Zeffirelli's inventive choreography with Bonynge's ornamentation and cadenzas, culminating in a glorious E flat. The effect was electric, and the audience was mesmerised.

The critics struggled to find the appropriate superlatives to describe Sutherland's performance and offers started pouring in from all over the world. The transformation was complete, and life would never be the same for this unassuming but brilliant new star.

She may have been unassuming, but she was among the brightest in the opera firmament.

Sutherland was now in a position to help Luciano, which she did with incredible generosity. He had developed tremendously well since his April 1961 debut in *La Boheme*, with significant successes in Amsterdam, Dublin, London, Vienna, Paris, Rome, Miami, Milan, and finally Sydney, Melbourne, Brisbane and Adelaide. However, he was about to learn from Sutherland that his vocal education was incomplete.

With great success, Sutherland and Pavarotti had just sung *Lucia di Lammermoor* in Miami and *La Sonnambula* at Covent Garden. Sutherland believed Pavarotti was technically in good shape even then. However, time would prove that Pavarotti still had to learn the most important lesson from Sutherland. After his season of *La Sonnambula* and *La Traviata* at Covent Garden, they both began preparing for their four-month tour of Australia. As discussed above, Sutherland had already arrived in Melbourne, and Pavarotti was soon to follow, rushing immediately into rehearsals.

Moffatt Oxenbould, long-time artistic director of Opera Australia but at this time one of the stage managers, stated:

> Luciano Pavarotti, who was virtually unknown at the time and yet to make his first significant recording, began to rehearse *L'Elisir d'amore*, and from this ever-smiling young man with a slightly awkward, rolling gait came forth a sound so unique in timbre and colour, and so mellifluous, that everybody in the room beamed. Luciano's eyes danced with delight as he realised the effect his singing was having on his new colleagues [Oxenbould, 2005: 106].

The Sutherland-Williamson Grand Opera Company opened their season in Melbourne and then toured other capital cities for fourteen weeks. Pavarotti sang thirty-nine performances of *L'Elisir D'Amore*, *La Traviata*, *La Sonnambula*, and *Lucia di Lammermoor*.

Sutherland opened with *Lucia* and brought the house down. A few nights later, when Pavarotti made his Australian debut in Donizetti's *L'Elisir d'amore*, audiences knew immediately that they were in the presence of something special. He created a sensation, and the tumultuous applause following the last act aria *'Una furtiva lagrima'*, ensured an encore, which was received even more enthusiastically.

Here is my Analysis of Pavarotti's rendition of the arias *'Quanto e bella, quanta e cara'* and *'Una Furtiva Lagrima'*.

Quanto e Bella Quanto e Cara

The first thing that strikes the ear in this rendition of *'Quanto e Bella'* and then the *'Una Furtiva Lagrima'* that follows is the beauty and freshness not just of the tone but also the interpretative approach. This is a voice in its first bloom — flexible, malleable, brilliant, and with excellent carrying power.

The style is generally more forward and ringing than in the early 1965 Traviata he sang in Dublin and Covent Garden. The next issue that reveals itself in this performance is the fact that the [a] vowel has more width than previously, often resulting in a slightly more backward pharyngeal tone than it should be. Nonetheless, the discerning ear can hear where this voice will be heading over the next few years.

Some of the [o] vowels are still unnecessarily narrow and tight — one can hear the lips protruding, and in some notes, even the cheeks are involved in this narrow funnelling of the tone and elongation of the vocal tract. On the other hand, many of the lateral vowels which had been problematic previously are now a lovely forward, ringing sound, less harsh than the earlier performances.

The final issue to contend with in the 1965 *L'Elisir D'amore* is the fact that Pavarotti too often interpolates the nasal continuant [n] not so much as to complete or even compliment the text, but rather as a pilot note to find the proper placement. However, he is not sufficiently subtle to carry this off. The [n] is too intrusive, its duration is too long, and its execution is too glaring and lacks grace.

Una Furtiva Lagrima

The overall vocal qualities described above for the *Quanto e Bella Quanto e Cara* also apply to '*Una Furtiva Lagrima*'. This is a truly beautiful tone endowed with all the glorious bloom of youth — a beautiful blend of brilliance and velvet. He really is boyish and apparently lacking in sophistication, but not intelligence.

Critique of Una Furtiva Lagrima, Australia 1965

Pavarotti opens the aria with a beautiful soft [u] vowel on the F 4 on '*una*'. We can say that to a varying degree all the [a] vowels that follow are all too broad and privilege width above roundness. The principle here is that when you open on a lovely note you should follow through to the next note whilst retaining the mental connection and influence of the foundation note of the phrase. The singer generally has two choices: the first is to emphasise the difference between vowels, pitch and intensity, and the second is to highlight the similarities and have one note merging into the next in a seamless legato.

The onset (attack) on the [e] vowel G flat in the phrase '*Negli occhi suoi spunto*' cannot be so retarded as it creates a hiatus between notes, mars the legato and allows time for a buildup of sub-glottal pressure which invariably leads to a plosive attack.

This problem of a hiatus between notes is repeated in the phrase '*Festose e giovani*'.

Pavarotti must learn to attack the sound more directly and with greater firmness, following through mentally and with the breath between one note and another or, even better, between one phrase and another.

The [o] vowel in Giovani, moving from E natural to F, is just slightly under the pitch.

Pavarotti modifies the [e] vowels in '*che*' towards the French [oe] as in '*cour*'. This is a very interesting mixed vowel, which according to Miller, combines both back and front aspects of vowels. The tongue is in the position of the closed [e], and the mouth and jaw are in the position of the [aw] [Miller, 2004:78].

The soft singing at the beginning of the second verse is just lovely, so much so that I find myself thinking that he should have sung the [i] vowel in '*sospir*' softly also.

As it is, it needs more pharyngeal space. This is best obtained by taking a deep breath which lowers the diaphragm and the larynx and raises the soft palate, especially when combined with a gentle rise of the zygomatic arch.

The run in the phrase '*di piu non chiedo*' has several wrong notes in it, especially in the chromatic passages. The final cadenza is uninteresting because it is too much the same. Here is an opportunity to do something more imaginative with a little crescendo here and a soft note there, or even a '*messa di voce,*' especially on the last sustained F natural. However, the young Pavarotti misses it. Nonetheless, the promise and beauty of that voice are unmistakable. At age 29, the only tenor to compare with Pavarotti was Jussi Bjorling, and even he could not fashion such a brilliant and ringing high register. His manager had predicted this on that propitious opening night of La Boheme in April 1961, when he ran to the dressing room calling out Jussi Bjorling's name as a comparison.

In the context of the Australian tour Pavarotti and Sutherland had yet to appear on stage together, although they had both experienced tremendous success in their respective roles. Now, the time had come for Australian audiences to hear two of the greatest voices of all time in Verdi's *La Traviata*. The results were majestic. Writing in a national newspaper, 'The Australian,' Kenneth Hince captured the mood in the theatre very well:

> I have never heard a pair of voices like these, soprano and tenor, on the Australian stage... There is an inevitable temptation to speak *ex cathedra* and say that we will never hear this evenly matched excellence again. Perhaps we may: but it will be one chance in tens of thousands.

The performance of La Traviata we are about to examine occurs some four months later during his Australian Tour of 1965. This is not a perfect performance either, but it is a vast improvement on the previous Covent Garden performance as Pavarotti has adopted a much healthier technique. Consequently, he displays not only a firmer glottal setting but also a greater level of sub-glottal pressure. The voice is more focused and more concentrated in the oral cavity. The pharyngeal walls, as constituted by the three constrictor muscles, are all so much firmer relative to the previous performance. I feel that this firmer, more focused, more forward and brilliant tone is the result of his discussions about breathing with Sutherland, which led to his transformation from a high respiratory strategy (the *sostegno* system) to a lower and more complete strategy (the *appoggio* system). The tone is much more natural, forward and flowing, resulting in a greater level of artistic expression and more nuanced singing. There is greater firmness and purpose in this tone, but it is juxtaposed with increased malleability and more flexibility. Hence the interpretation is not only more nuanced but also light years ahead of his previous effort.

Chapter 21

La Sonnambula, Sutherland and Pavarotti, Sydney 1965

La Sonnambula is set in a small mountain village in Switzerland where the villagers have gathered to celebrate the betrothal of Elvino (a young landowner) to the village sweetheart, the orphaned Amina. After her mother's early death Amina is adopted by Teresa, owner of the local mill. In large part these experiences shaped Amina's personality as a young adult. Her mother's tragic death and the subsequent love bestowed upon her by Teresa (not to mention the kindness demonstrated by the villagers) have left an indelible mark.

Everyone is happy to be celebrating this famous couple, the only exception being Lisa, the inn keeper. She was previously engaged to Elvino and has never accepted the end of their relationship. Alessio, a young man in love with Lisa, makes every effort to support her but to no avail.

Amina joins the revellers and expresses her happiness and gratitude to all, especially to Teresa who lovingly brought her up *'Come per me sereno'*. Elvino is a little late but finely rushes in with an apology and a bouquet of violets for Amina. He explains that he has been to visit his mother's grave to seek her blessing for this union. They sign the contract and with characteristic warmth he gives Amina the ring that once belonged to his mother The duet: *'Prendi, l'anel ti dono'* is followed by what really amounts to a cabaletta in the form of a duet —*'Tutto, ah tutto in quest'istante'*.

No sooner has the ritual ended than they become aware of a carriage racing down the dusty pathway. An elegant stranger arrives and alights from the carriage, followed by his manservant. He is tired and declares that it was a dreary trip. He asks how far it is from the village to the count's palace, to which Lisa responds that it is three miles away and the road steep and uncomfortable. Lisa suggests that he should stay at her inn for the night, the sight of which seems to trigger a stream of remembrances for the stranger. He speaks nostalgically of the inn, the mill and the farm next to them (appearing to know the village well) and is immediately enchanted by his surroundings, expressing his affection for the village in his aria *'Vi ravviso o luogui ameni'*. Suddenly, he becomes aware that he has interrupted some festivity. Asking about the occasion, he discovers that it is Amina's betrothal ceremony to Elvino. He is struck not only by her beauty and simplicity but also by her resemblance to a great love of his youth. As night falls, the villagers become apprehensive, and Teresa explains that a ghost haunts the town. Amused, the stranger says this is something that he would like to see and departs for the inn, followed by the villagers. A quarrel ensues between Elvino and Amina concerning not only the Count's flirtations but more importantly, her joyous acceptance of his attentions. Elvino is confronted with his boyish insecurities and jealousy, apologising for his reaction in the duet, 'Son geloso del zeffiro errante'.

Back at the inn Rodolfo confesses that he is not at all sorry to have remained in the village, with its beautiful ambience and friendly people, in particular Amina and Lisa. The latter reveals that the mayor has confirmed what many of the villagers suspected - Rodolfo is the lost heir of the former count. Count Rodolfo then begins a flirtation with Lisa which is reciprocated. However, they are soon interrupted by a noise which forces Lisa to hide, in the process of which she drops her handkerchief. Amina enters the room, walking in her sleep and Rodolfo rightly concludes that she must be the infamous village 'ghost.' Lisa however is happy to assume that Amina is coming to meet Rodolfo for a romantic tryst, slipping away to alert Elvino and the town folks to the scandal. Meanwhile Rodolfo is moved by Amina's unconscious expressions of love for Elvino, and respecting her innocence, he leaves her to sleep on his bed. Unfortunately, with Lisa's encouragement, the ever-inquisitive villagers choose this very moment to wish the count goodnight. Lisa appears with Elvino and Teresa, and everyone is predictably shocked to find Amina in the count's bed. The commotion created by the villagers soon awakens Amina who protests her innocence ('D'un pensiero e d'un accento'). The entire village is devastated as it appears that Amina has betrayed her vows to Elvino. His sense of loss and treachery turns to anger and as he calls off the wedding ('Non più nozze') the villagers turn on Amina. Only Teresa stands firm, pleading with the townspeople to consider Amina's protestations of innocence. In the ensuing chaos Teresa picks up Lisa's handkerchief.

Act II

Following their immediate shock and anger, many of the townspeople feel remorse at their readiness to believe the worst about Amina. Consequently, they make their way to Count Rodolfo's castle to ask him why Amina was found asleep in his bed, explaining that she was welcomed and honoured in every villa. They ask him to defend her honour if she is innocent and help her if she has fallen from grace. Teresa and Amina enter and overhear Elvino's lamentations ('Tutto è sciolto'). When he sees Amina, he reproaches her and takes his ring from her. The villagers protest his cruelty and inform him that Count Rodolfo has confirmed Amina's innocence and will arrive shortly. Elvino refuses to believe it and leaves in despair as Teresa leads Amina away.

As Elvino has decided to marry Lisa after all, he enters the scene to lead her to church. However, they are interrupted by the arrival of Rodolfo, who again proclaims Amina's innocence, explaining to the incredulous crowd that she was only sleepwalking. Teresa appears and asks for quiet as Amina finally falls asleep from exhaustion. She is shocked to see that Lisa is about to marry Elvino, who replies that Lisa was not found in another man's room. Teresa immediately produces Lisa's handkerchief, which she retrieved from the Count's room at the inn. Elvino has no option but to accept that Lisa has lied to him.

He is processing all his recent disappointments when Amina suddenly appears, sleepwalking above the fast-moving wheel of the mill. Careful not to wake her, the villagers watch and pray as she slowly makes her way to safety, still distraught about her separation from Elvino. Amina remembers better times, such as the bouquet of violets he gave her that has since faded and the gift of his mother's wedding ring ('*Ah! non-credea mirarti*'). Convinced of her innocence and disturbed by her suffering, Elvino returns her engagement ring. Amina's sadness immediately turns to joy as she realises that her dream of love is coming true.

Critique of the 1965 *La Sonnambula* with Sutherland

The voice in this performance is endowed with all the vitality, buoyancy and naturalness of youth. The overall setting of the voice is higher than it would later become, emphasising the cover mechanism rather than the body of the vocal folds. This type of voice production is much more in line with the easy, velvety tone he produces in the legendary performance of *La Fille du Regiment* which he sang at Covent Garden the following year (1966), recording it for Decca shortly after.

This is the beginning of a Golden Era for Pavarotti's singing in particular and the history of opera. The next few years would be the halcyon days of bel canto. This is simply because Pavarotti was rising to his full powers as a singer and an artist, and Sutherland was in her prime. As far as bel canto singing is concerned, one cannot overestimate the glory of this period. I know that every generation produces its geniuses, but I think the period under discussion would be difficult to improve by every objective measure.

Critique of *La Sonnambula* and comparison between the 1965 performance and the 1982 recording.

In the 1965 performance, the voice still needs to be entirely anchored by the respiratory muscles (appoggio), nor is it as focused, brilliant and full-bodied as it would later become. However, Pavarotti more than compensates for these perceived deficiencies with a glorious dose of youthful bloom and a tone that is naturally fresh, elastic and more flexible than would be the case in later performances.

The first caveat about this performance is that whilst I am grateful to have it, it is, at best, of variable quality and often not very good at all. However, it is a beautiful opportunity to hear Pavarotti in one of the essential and exciting roles of his early career — a role that, judging by this performance, he discontinued too early. I understand why he did so, but it is a real loss to the history of vocal pedagogy.

Let me state that Elvino is a particularly difficult role, far more so than it looks on paper. My objective in this book has been to compare Pavarotti with Pavarotti to track his development. In addition, I have compared his performances to many of the other great exponents of these roles to draw conclusions about his ranking within a particular role. I have consciously remained mute concerning other tenors in the role because I do not wish to turn this book into an Eisteddfod, giving out first, second and third prizes. However, I have not spared myself the pleasure of listening to other contenders for best artist in a particular role. With respect to *La Sonnambula*, it wasn't easy to find an utterly unsurpassable performance, including Pavarotti. There are several reasons for the lack of great Elvinos, the most prevalent of which are listed below.

- This is a genuine bel canto role: the legato line is everything and needs to be impeccable, and the *passaggi* and ornamentation need to be woven into the overall fabric and interpretation of the work, not to mention the legato line.

- The *tessitura* is generally high, and much of it sits around the *passaggio*.

- These roles were not composed for the full-throated high register utilised by all significant contemporary tenors. It was written for voices that may have been reasonably full in the middle register, but the high register was predominantly sung in a supported falsetto.

- Further, these operas were composed for orchestras pitched about half a tone lower than they are today, which made a great deal of difference by the end of a long night's singing.

- These operas were composed in an era when the sound was more natural and diffused. Voices were undoubtedly not as firmly produced and focused as they are today. That is one of the reasons why, notwithstanding the size of his voice, Pavarotti emerges relatively unscathed. The 1965 performances are excellent by any standards.

Notwithstanding these considerable differences and some reservations, there is much to learn from a detailed study of this role as outlined below.

Prendi l'anel ti dono: Duet — Pavarotti/Sutherland, Sydney 1965

Pavarotti opens this duet with a beautiful lyrical tone and a fresh, poised, but flowing vocal line. He completes this beautiful flowing line with excellent execution of the ornaments in the passage '*recava allara*' and then in the passage '*il nostro amor,*' in which he is just a little behind the beat, meaning that he has to rush the next beat, thus giving the impression of not being entirely correct.

In addition, the [o] vowel on the G natural on the word '*sacro*' is too closed, too collected. Pavarotti has not yet understood that there is no need to overly modify the vowels in this kind of lyrical music. The remedy for this is not difficult, just requiring that the [o] be modified a little more towards the [aw] and the jaw be dropped slightly. I want to emphasise that in good singing, small increases or decreases in various vectors can make tremendous differences. It is only when we negotiate great leaps in frequency or significant increases in intensity that breath pressure, glottal tension and oropharyngeal space are required to make substantial shifts in space and energy. Let us continue with our analysis.

The phrase '*sia dei tuoi voti*' is beautifully executed, sufficiently collected, but without exaggeration. In the phrase '*cara, nel sen ti posi questa gentil viola*', all the F naturals on the [e] vowel are nicely executed, already in head voice but not overly so. This is equally true of the [o] vowel on the G flat of '*posi*'. The three G naturals that follow on the [e] vowels of the consecutive '*Ei mi rammente a te, ei mi rammente a te*' display a lovely, easy head tone with a particularly mellifluous sound, liquid gold.

The reprise is just a lovely suspended, easy-flowing sound. In the following phrase, '*I nostri cori Iddio,*' the [o] of '*cori*' is too restrained, overly collected and throaty. This is the kind of constriction that alters the relationship between harmonics. Once again, this is a phrase that should be floated, suspended even just using the edge (cover) of the vocal folds, engaging a minimum of vocal fold body. This style is not just bel canto; it is romantic bel canto, a style that demands an ethereal tone capable of expressing emotion and otherworldliness.

In the phrase '*con te rimase*', the two F naturals on the [e] vowels and [a] vowels, respectively, are a much better quality, more naturally collected (*arrotondimento*). I do not feel that Pavarotti is imposing his will on the voice here. The duet Cabaletta that follows is an example of absolutely fantastic singing.

The tone beginning with the phrase '*Tutto, ah tutto in quest'istante*' is buoyant, with a beautiful lilt and an incredible and exciting outpouring of sound.

Son Geloso del Zefiro Errante, Sydney 1965

Pavarotti begins this duet with a beautiful diminuendo on the F natural on the [o] vowel of '*perdona*'. Although the discerning ear can perceive a moment of uncertainty as Pavarotti moves from the closed [o] vowel towards a more open [aw] vowel.

The coloratura on the [e] vowel of '*Zeffiro*' would be smoother and more deliberate if the tempo were just marginally slower. However, if the postural and breathing muscles were a little contracted, they would serve to steady the larynx and redirect and steady the tone.

The same is true of the [i] vowel on the word '*mira*'. The coloratura is too fast and jerky, suggesting a lack of control at the diaphragmatic and laryngeal levels.

More unusual still is the [i] vowel on the A natural on the phrase '*Fin del rivo,*' in which Pavarotti protrudes the lips forward thereby elongating the vocal tract and lowering all of the formants, whilst at the same time flattening the tongue which occupies the position of [aw] rather than [i]. This unusual technique furnishes the tone with a lovely warm and velvety quality. This from a singer who traditionally sang the lateral vowels with a great deal of brilliance, penetration and often a constricted and narrow tone. In this instance his modulation is just right, at least for Pavarotti.

The coloratura on the [e] vowel of the phrase '*specchio ti fa*' is far too jerky and tentative. On the other hand, the [a] vowel on the F natural of the '*Ah perdona, il sospetto*' is a really lovely, opened tone that in Pavarotti's voice produces a natural sense of excitement. The only thing I would alter would be to modify the closed [o] vowel of '*perdona*' towards a more open [aw] which would track and more naturally match the formant structure of the [a] vowel on the preceding F natural.

Much of the singing that follows is just glorious. Consequently, we can say that is all the more reason to be disappointed with the throatiness exhibited on the [i] vowel at the F natural on the word '*si*'. This tone is too constricted and throaty and in large part it is so because Pavarotti has envisioned the tone he wants to produce and prepared his instrument for it, but then instead of shaping the vocal tract in a gross manner and allowing the breath and articulators to make the fine adjustments, he continues to control the fine adjustment of the vocal tract to the detriment of the ensuing tone.

This pattern persists, albeit to a lesser extent, in the following phrases '*Si per sempre, ti prometto, mai piu dubbi*'. The [i] vowel in 'is' and 'ti' and the [a] vowel in 'mai' are all a little constricted and throaty. On the other hand, the [o] in '*timore*' is a beautifully collected tone and an excellent execution of the copertura at the *passaggio*. The first note then seems to stick because the larynx suddenly rises, causing the sound to be out of focus in this passage '*Non posse odiarti*' is the [a] vowel on the G natural.

The reviews for Bellini's *La Sonnambula* were just as stunning, with John Cargher predicting that Pavarotti would join the ranks of the great tenors of the past. Critics described his singing as sensational and Sutherland's as superb: the sustained applause at the end of each performance was unprecedented.

Australian audiences came to see the local girl who had made good, and they were not disappointed. In fact, they were stunned by the beauty and glory of a voice that had catapulted her to international fame. Unfortunately, that meant that the performances she did not appear in were not very well attended. Fortunately, Pavarotti shared most of his performances with Sutherland and even though audiences came to hear her, they were not only struck by the quality of his voice, but also his easy charm. Soon however Pavarotti had developed his own following. During the fourteen-week season, Australian audiences rightly learned to love Joan Sutherland, but they also took the young Pavarotti into their hearts.

In short, I can confirm that according to Adua Pavarotti, Luciano's sojourn to Australia was not just a remarkable success, but also a great deal of fun. He sang thirty-nine performances of four operas: *Lucia di Lammermoor, L'elisir d'amore, La Traviata* and *La Sonnambula* in fourteen weeks in four different states, all with great success. The above notwithstanding, the most important element of his Australian tour was what he learned from Sutherland, from whom he acquired the fundamental knowledge of the *appoggio* system of breath management: it changed his life and with it the course of international operatic singing.

Chapter 22

The Appoggio System of Breath Management

Pavarotti was now a formidable tenor but always eager to learn. From the early days with Arrigo Pola, Leone Magiera, Mirella Freni, and later Ettore Campogalliani, he had made a point to surround himself with the very best people. He was very clever about knowing how to ask for help and from whom. Having done so, he was not precious about taking instruction and remained forever grateful. Throughout, he remained humble and generous in his acknowledgement of Arrigo Pola and Dame Joan Sutherland. He would later say:

> What I learned from Joan was that when my voice was tired it was because I did not control the diaphragm [Pavarotti/Wright, 1981: 114].

Now he was fortunate enough to be in the company of Sutherland every day for four months and he began to observe that this lady, who often sat knitting during rehearsals, enjoyed an inexhaustible reserve of vocal energy. One day they were rehearsing *La Sonnambula* in the afternoon and that evening she gave an impeccable performance of Violetta in *La Traviata*. Pavarotti would later recall, 'I saw that lady sing both in full voice and at the end she was not tired' [Pavarotti, 1981: 114-15]. He soon realised that she must have a unique way of producing the sound because she was creating vocal feats and acrobatics with a consistency that left not only Pavarotti but also the rest of the cast open-mouthed. He wondered how she could be so amazingly consistent, and what he had to do to arrive at the same level of consistency. Not that he didn't give some great performances, he did. But he knew that the difference between his very best and his lesser performance was much too wide. He approached Sutherland who frankly told him he was not supporting his voice as well as he should. She began to reveal the secrets of her own breath control. During rehearsals, Pavarotti would ask permission to examine her breathing and to feel her abdominal muscles whilst she was singing. He was tenacious as always, and before long he developed a natural feel for this breathing technique. She gave him breathing exercises to control the excursion of the diaphragm and strengthen his rib cage; he showed his gratitude by practising them with the enthusiasm of a young boy and not that of a tenor who had already triumphed in many of the world's great theatres.

The Appoggio Strategy

As discussed above, the *appoggio* system of breath management is characterised by a 'down and out' strategy, whilst still retaining a moderately high chest position. The diaphragm is lowered until it meets the resistance from the abdominal girdle, that is, the internal and external oblique and the tranversus abdominus. The exterior and internal intercostals are responsible for the raising and lowering of the thorax respectively, but they also act in an antagonistic manner. Thus, the *appoggio* support system consists of two separate but intertwined adversarial relationships. The first relates to the antagonistic action of the internal and external muscles (the external and internal intercostals and the external and internal obliques combined with the transversus abdominus), which antagonistic posture induces a balance that keeps each protagonist in check. The second antagonistic relationship is between the diaphragm and the lower abdominals. In this scenario, the contraction of the muscle fibres around the edge of the central tendon of the diaphragm lowers the diaphragm onto the abdominals. As the air in the lungs is utilised and the lungs release the air in the millions of alveoli, the abdominal girdle upon which the diaphragm is resting, contracts and in so doing pushes the central tendon of the diaphragm back into the thorax.

It is important to recall that either of these antagonistic support systems can prove effective; however, the most effective system is the simultaneous utilisation of both.

The last element relating to the *appoggio* is maintaining the inspiratory position for as long as possible. Joan Sutherland describes the *appoggio* breathing strategy most eloquently to Opera News:

> You have to make some muscular effort to control the compressed air, but you still have to control the issue of that air…You don't sing with breath, but rather on the breath, and you let as little escape as possible to project the sound [Sutherland, Opera News, Nov. 1998:20].

The big difference here is that Sutherland, in line with Francesco and Giovanni Lamperti, is more interested in compressed air which of necessity requires muscle contraction, as opposed to air flow which is based on the liberal release of the antagonistic muscular contraction and hence allowing the breath to flow freely. On the other hand, the *appoggio* strategy as described by Sutherland to Pavarotti, demands that we allow 'as little air to escape as possible'. This can only mean that the antagonistic contraction between the internal and external muscles must be maintained for an unusually long period of time. Hence,

Francesco Lamperti's exhortation to keep the inspiratory position for as long as possible:

> To sustain a given note the air should be expelled slowly; to attain this end, the respiratory (inspiratory) muscles, by continuing their action, strive to retain the air in the lungs, and oppose their action to those of the expiratory forces, which, at the same time, drive it out for the production of the note. There is thus established a balance of power between these two agents, which is called the *lutte vocale* or vocal struggle. On the retention of this equilibrium, depends on the just emission of the voice, and by means of it alone can true expression be given to the sound produced [Lamperti, c 1883: 25].

This therefore is the basis of the famous *Lotta vocale* [of the Mandl/Lamperti school [Lamperti, c.1883:25].

Definition of Appoggio

An elegant definition of the 'appoggio system' of breath management is to be found in the *'Enciclopidia Garzanti della Musica'* (1974). This definition confirms that the Italian view of the *'appoggio system'* is much broader and more holistic than is sometimes understood. Specifically, there are two conflated but different levels of 'appoggio'. The first deals with respiration; its focal points are concentrated around the abdominal, lumber, thoracic and diaphragmatic muscles. The second refers to subjective focal points concentrated around the proprioceptive sensations impinging on the face, the teeth, the neck and other focal points. The Italians refer to these as the objective *appoggio* and subjective *appoggio,* respectively. The following is my translation of the definition obtained from 'Enciclopidia Garzanti':

> In the terminology of vocal technique, we refer to the region in which we experience maximal muscular tension during singing as the point of *'appoggio'*: this may occur in the abdominal /diaphragmatic or thoracic area (that is, *'appoggio'* at the abdomen, diaphragm, thorax, or chest), or in that part of the facial cavity where the cervical resonances of the sound are perceived (*appoggio* at the teeth; *'appoggio'* at the palate; *'appoggio'* at the nape of the neck, and so forth). The point of *'appoggio'* varies depending on the type of emission we adopt [Enciclopidia Garzanti, 1974: 35].

The only Italian author between Mori in 1970 and the excellent contemporary authors who address the appoggio system of breath management was Antonio Juvarra (1987) who posits that breathing is the engine of the singing voice. Juvarra postulates that the *'appoggio'* system of breath management is associated with specific physiological postures and antagonistic muscular configurations. He goes as far as to declare that the *appoggio* can be regarded as the engine of the voice, which muscular activity is mainly concentrated around the abdominal lumbar girdle [Juvarra, 1987: 31].

Sanchez Carbone's contribution is particularly memorable concerning the outcome of this vocal strategy. She confirms that:

> The emission 'on the breath' is also the foundation of that particular technique of producing the sound that acts upon the intention of amplitude, which naturally amplifies the sound, equalises the vocal line, and the emission of the voice in all its extension, all the while displaying the qualities required for good singing, such as ring, smoothness, and brilliance of the sound. It activates an action that safeguards the health and integrity of the phonatory organ [Sanchez Carbone, 2005: 102].

In line with Juvarra (1987), Fussi and Magnani (1996) and Bruno and Paperi (2001), I also believe in the co-contraction of the respiratory muscles. There is hardly an author of stature who does not believe in co-contraction of the internal and external intercostal muscles. The only controversy was over the co-contraction between the central tendon of the diaphragm and the abdominal muscles, the argument being that the central tendon does not possess contractile fibres and therefore cannot be controlled. This proposition is correct but needs to be completed. It does not allow for the possibility of educating the muscle fibres surrounding the edge of the diaphragm, which can be contracted and offer an antagonistic force against the abdominals. More and more authors today, including Sundberg and Von Euler, James Stark, Juvarra, Bruno and Paperi and Sanchez Carbone, are convinced that diaphragmatic/abdominal co-contraction takes place. My own opinion coincides with these authors. Below, finds their narrative, which I cite at length:

Bruno and Paperi concur with Sanchez Carbone concerning the principle of co-contraction and the *'lotta vocale'*. They too believe that:

> The primary function of the diaphragm, particularly in the inspiratory phase, is to expand and lower itself, pressing down anteriorly against the abdomen and laterally against the lower costal ribs all the way back to the spine, where it transfers the daily emotional function to that of interpretative expressive energy, especially with the respect to the big sentiments associated with certain styles.

Bruno and Paperi elaborate on the physiology of the diaphragm and its educational capabilities. They contend that:

> In reality, the diaphragm, which is inserted to the sternum and vertebral column, is not ordinarily controllable during phonation; however, by implementing a considerable training regime of the surrounding muscles of the central tendon, the diaphragm can be educated to assume the role of dosing the airflow [Bruno & Paperi, 2003: 89].

The views expressed by Bruno and Paperi correspond to those of the most authoritative Italian authors. The latter adhere to the notion that although the central tendon does not possess extensible and contractile fibres, the surrounding muscles do, and these muscles can be educated to maintain a lowered and antagonistic position not only against the abdominal viscera but also against the lateral/lumbar region [Bruno & Paperi 2001: 89-90],

The inspiratory muscles then act as a 'brake' by maintaining the inspiratory position for a considerable time. These muscles should not become rigid and in fact, they de-contract (relax) slowly and gradually during the act of expiration. The rate of de-contraction of the inspiratory muscles is dependent on the artistic requirements of the piece, with the air leaving the body slowly and by the gradual squeezing of the thoracic cavity. The 'inspiratory brake' can therefore be either costal or diaphragmatic. The first is constituted by the muscles that dilate the thoracic cage and, by maintaining their contraction during the expiratory cycle, impede the exceedingly rapid collapse of the thorax. The second is constituted by the diaphragm which by contracting even during expiration, maintains its lowered position, impeding the abdominal viscera, which are compressed by the abdominal girdle, and which generally prevents it from pushing into the thoracic cavity either too rapidly or too violently [Sanchez Carbone, 2005: 105].

Sanchez Carbone rightly contends that the more tenaciously the singer clings to the inspiratory position (the expanded thoracic cavity and lowered diaphragm), the slower and more gradual the relaxation of the diaphragm and the expiratory costal muscles transpires, inducing a more significant contraction of the thoracic/abdominal girdle which creates the expiratory force required [Sanchez Carbone, 2005: 105].

Sanchez Carbone concludes from the above that:

> Every expiratory emission partakes of the 'lotta vocale,' the struggle between the inspiratory and expiratory muscles: that is, the first aims to keep the thorax dilated and operates as a 'brake' to the airflow; whilst the second constricts the thorax and 'accelerates' the airflow. The expiratory tension must be in perfect equilibrium with the inspiratory pressure during vocal emission. Such equilibrium allows for a precise vocal onset, that is, an instantaneous emission of a vocal sound that is of well-defined intensity, and of good quality that would otherwise be impossible. Any impurity, such as breathiness or turbulence in the emission will be eliminated instantaneously. And it is as the result of this voluntary and conscious muscular antagonism that the expiratory current is formed, incessantly controlled, modelled, forged and elaborated for the purpose of acquiring all the gradations of intensity and duration, corresponding to the demands of the art of singing [Sanchez Carbone. 2005: 106].

Sanchez Carbone is absolutely correct! She is also well supported by the other Italian sources cited above. There is no question that these antagonistic forces were precisely what both Mandl and Lamperti were referring to when they established *'la lotta vocale'* (Vocal Struggle). Just as a matter of interest, the designation was initially assigned to the co-contraction between the diaphragm and abdominal musculature. It was only later that Lamperti realised that even though this vertical model was a considerable advance on the 'clavicular' breathing that preceded appoggio, the paradigm remained incomplete. It was at this point that he decided to balance it by adding the lateral movement of the lower floating ribs to the equation. This strategy involved the contraction of the internal and external obliques, the transversus, and rectus abdominus. Notwithstanding my historical elaboration above, Sanchez Carbone has provided us with a compelling description of the 'lotta vocale'. She describes not only the antagonistic 'vocal struggle' and its effect on a steady stream of 'subglottal pressure', but also its effect on vocal quality through firmness of tone, and its benefits to glottal onset, and purity and quality of tone.

Pavarotti on Sutherland's Appoggio

The following are Pavarotti's recollections of this momentous event in 1965. The occasion was a discussion about vocal technique with his biographer William Wright, who at the time was collaborating with Pavarotti on their second book, *Pavarotti My World* (1992). In this book he nominates breathing, articulation, diction, registers and the mastery of the *passaggio* in order to blend registers as the most critical elements in singing. With respect to breathing, he states that one of the most essential elements of technique for the beginner student is to learn to give full support from the diaphragm.

This was the strategy that Sutherland taught and advocated for Pavarotti. These are well-known facts, but what needs to be better known is the important caveat that Sutherland attached to this strategy. She warned him not to try what she was doing unless his thoracic and abdominal musculature had developed sufficiently to carry out the physical work. Pavarotti recalls that:

> Essential to her method was the support she gave her voice from the diaphragm. Joan was a big woman and very strong. Her torso muscles work hard when she is singing. She seems just naturally strong and doesn't appear to work at it, but she knows others are not so lucky; they must first develop the muscles needed for support.
>
> If your body is not in shape to sing this way, she told me, you will push and push but keep falling back on your throat to make the sound. This will ruin your voice. That is why you shouldn't try it, unless you are in the right physical shape [Pavarotti in Wright, 1981: 114].

Pavarotti and Appoggio

Having discussed the theoretical aspects of *Appoggio*, let us glance at Pavarotti's practical experience with *appoggio*. First let me say that time would prove that it was not until he discovered, and then began to practise, the *appoggio* system of breath management that most of his problems were finally resolved.

The *appoggio* strategy is characterised by a down-and-out action. The diaphragm is lowered until it meets the resistance from the abdominal girdle — the internal and external oblique and the transverses and rectus abdominus. The external and internal intercostals are responsible for the raising and lowering of the thorax respectively. Thus the '*Appoggio*' system consists of two separates but intertwined antagonistic relationships. The first relates to the antagonistic action of the internal and external muscles (the external and internal intercostals and the external and internal obliques combined with the transversus and rectus abdominus). This antagonistic posture induces a balance that keeps each protagonist in check. The second antagonistic relationship is between the diaphragm and the lower abdominals. In this scenario, the contraction of the muscle fibres that surround the edge of the central tendon of the diaphragm contract, lowering the diaphragm onto the abdominals. As the air in the lungs is utilised and the lungs release the air contained in the millions of alveoli, the abdominal girdle upon which the diaphragm is resting contracts. In so doing it pushes the central tendon of the diaphragm back into the thorax.

It is important to recall that either of these antagonistic support systems can prove fairly effective. However, the most assured, the most balanced, and therefore the most effective system is the simultaneous utilisation of both.

The last element relating to the *appoggio* is the maintenance of the inspiratory position for as long as possible.

Diaphragmatic Co-contraction

From the above narration we may conclude that in the very best schools (those dedicated to the management of the various firm but flexible levels of co-contraction), the diaphragm remains active, retarding the rise of the abdominal muscles and the collapse of the chest whilst never blocking its upward trajectory. Juvarra reminds us that this manoeuvre also involves not only the diaphragm but also the lumbar/abdominal region and the costals, all of which correspond with the breathing adopted by the classic masters of singing. He is also very clear on the need for co-contraction and has considerable support in this, not only from Sundberg and Von Euler who proved conclusively that co-contraction occurs regularly. They have been confirmed by many other prominent Italian authors such as Mori (1970), Fussi and Magnani (1996), Bruno and Paperi (2001) and Sanchez Carbone (2005).

The mechanism for achieving this balanced equilibrium is represented by the retention of the inspiratory phase for an unusually long period of time. This relates to the equilibrium established between the double support mechanism, constituted vertically by the diaphragm and the abdominal girdle, and laterally by the external and internal intercostals and internal and external obliques. The mechanism for the application of the 'appoggio' strategy is primarily constituted by the 'noble posture' as represented by the double support system and preserved for an indefinite period of time. The combination of the double support system and the retention of the inspiratory position for an extended period of time remains the significant characteristic of *'appoggio'*.

This was the strategy that Sutherland taught and advocated for Pavarotti on his tour of Australia. We will elaborate further upon this eventful tour in the following pages but for now let us focus on the *appoggio* system of breath management. These facts are well known because Pavarotti has been talking about them for years. What could be better known is the important caveat that Sutherland attached to this strategy. She warned him not to try what she was doing unless his body was ready and in proper physical condition and this was and remains very sound advice.

Pavarotti never ceased to credit Sutherland, in the most generous and heartfelt way, for explaining the *appoggio* technique to him. This system of breath management and vocal support effectively revolutionised his singing.

Joan Sutherland describes the difference in breathing strategy not only most eloquently but also correctly. Her system of *appoggio* had its foundations in considerable muscular antagonism. Let us recall her own words:

> 'You have to make some muscular effort to control the compressed air…You don't sing with breath, but rather on the breath' [Sutherland, Opera News, Nov. 1998:20].

Pavarotti also wrote:

> Learn to give full support from the diaphragm. People think you sing from the throat, but you actually sing from the throat and the diaphragm working together. I was already a few years into my career before I understood how extremely important this was [Pavarotti in Wright, 1981: 129].

Let us recall from above that the *appoggio* strategy is characterised by a 'down-and-out' action: that is, the diaphragm is lowered until it meets the resistance from the abdominal girdle, combined with the antagonistic activity of the internal and external muscles. So, the *'appoggio'* system consists of two separate but intertwined antagonistic relationships.

It is important to remind ourselves that either of these antagonistic support systems can prove effective; however, the most effective system is the simultaneous utilisation of both. The implementation of the appoggio breath management strategy and maintaining the inspiratory position for as long as possible changed everything for Pavarotti. This was the knowledge that altered the trajectory of his life and career. He remained forever grateful to Joan Sutherland and Richard Bonynge for their guidance.

In fact, it is not an exaggeration to say that one of the most endearing qualities about Pavarotti was his great and generous soul. He has an innate old-fashioned wisdom by which he understands not only his own inner self but also, by projecting his own rich humanity onto the other, he illuminates and understands them better. There is room for everyone in his vision of paradise. With all his human frailties Pavarotti lived an authentic and truthful life, giving credit where credit was due whilst accepting responsibility for his own shortcomings and human flaws.

In a personal interview his first wife Adua Veroni Pavarotti, who came on the Australian tour with him, declared that Luciano really enjoyed Australia and always remembered it with great affection. The tour was also technically and artistically very rewarding, mainly since he learned so much from Sutherland, whom he credited with having completed his technical education. It was she who introduced him to the *appoggio* system of breath management and support that would transform his singing. It was also during his Australian Tour that he sang his first Nemorino in the *L'elisir d'Amore*, a role destined to remain amongst his favourites for the rest of his life [Personal interview, Adua Veroni Pavarotti].

According to Adua Pavarotti, Luciano would never have problems with his breathing again, and with that the last piece of his vocal jigsaw puzzle was in place. He had developed a precise and sonorous sound with Arrigo Pola who had also taught him the *passaggio* and how to access the head voice. He had learned the importance of an impeccable legato from Gigli, and he had been influenced by Caruso's deep expressivity. He had intuitively understood that Giuseppe di Stefano possessed the interpretative genius of a great creative artist, but he was shrewd enough to avoid his technical faults. Then from Sutherland he learned the power of the breath, which allowed him to mould all these varying elements into one of the most complete vocal instruments in history.

Chapter 23

I Capuletti E Montecchi, 1966

Pavarotti went from his Australian tour directly to a triumphant four-month season at La Scala where he sang two productions of *La Bohème*, the first with von Karajan (with whom he also sang the Duke in *Rigoletto*) and then Bellini's rarely performed opera *I Capuletti e i Montecchi* conducted by Claudio Abbado. This last production toured Amsterdam, Rotterdam, Utrecht, Rome, Edinburgh, Montreal and then the following year back to La Scala.

Two essential elements occurred immediately after the Australian tour. The first was the international tour of *I Capuletti e I Montecchi*, the story of Romeo and Juliet set to music by Vincenzo Bellini with a libretto by Felice Romano. Claudio Abbado cast the pants role of Romeo with a tenor, Giacomo Aragall — a stroke of genius. With Bellini's glorious score, Giacomo Aragall as Romeo, Renata Scotto as Giulietta and Luciano Pavarotti as Tebaldo, audiences everywhere swooned at the quality of these performances. I must say that you would be hard to please if you didn't fall in love with those artists. Unfortunately, we do not have a studio recording of *I Capuletti e I Montecchi*. However, we do have two live recordings: the first is a 1966 performance with Aragall and Margherita Rinaldi, and the second is a 1968 performance with Aragall, Pavarotti and Scotto. I must say that with respect to the latter recording, I don't believe that I have ever heard Tebaldo's music sung better than Pavarotti's rendition in this live performance.

More of the performance critique later but for now let us speak a little about the opera itself, *I Capuletti e I Montecchi*.

Bellini composed the opera in six weeks, far too little time for his perfectionist nature. He only achieved the deadline set by the impresario Lanari if he plundered his previous compositions for suitable material. His treasure chest was to be found mainly in his opera *Zaire* and, to a lesser degree, in *Adelson* and *Salvini*.

His librettist Felice Romani also resorted to plagiarising his own work, mainly in the form of a libretto of 'Giulietta e Romeo' which had previously been adapted by Nicola Vaccai. Romani had based his book on a play by Luigi Scevola and not Shakespeare.

Act I

The curtain rises on a hall in the Capulet Palace where Capello and his followers have gathered to consider a proposal from their archenemies, the Montecchi. Against the advice of Lorenzo, the family physician, Capello and his men have decided to reject the offer of peace without waiting to hear the proposal.

Disguised as an emissary, Romeo makes his entrance at the meeting and begins to relay the peace offering from the Montecchi, only to be met with a decisive 'No!'.

Undaunted the emissary continues to plead his master's cause, saying that Romeo sends Capello greetings and wants him to know that he has regretted the death of the latter's beloved son ever since that fatal day when the two met in mortal combat. It all happened in the heat of battle, and it could just as easily have gone the other way.

Unfortunately, what happens in war is ugly and totally unpredictable, which is why his master believes that this enmity between their families must end and peace must prevail. To demonstrate the seriousness of his offer he proposes that this act of peace should be sealed by the marriage between his beloved daughter Giulietta and Romeo Montecchi. Further he pledges to honour his daughter and act as a son to Capello, not to replace his dead son but rather to make amends for their unfortunate misadventure.

Capello refuses the offer defiantly, announcing instead that Giulietta will marry Tebaldo who has already proven to be like a son to him.

Defeated, Romeo has no alternative but to leave the premises. However, as he makes his way out with Lorenzo, he can hear Giulietta's voice in the beautiful aria *'O Quante Volte Quante'*. In which she sings of her secret longing for the man she loves, Romeo Montecchi. It is clear that just the mention of his name sets her on fire. So strong is the desire burning in her breast that she fears it will envelop and destroy her.

Tenacious as always Romeo asks Lorenzo to arrange a meeting with Giulietta, which he promises to do. When Romeo meets his beloved, they can hardly keep their hands off each other and Romeo begs Giulietta to elope with him, as it is their only chance. Her response is devastating. There is nothing that she desires more; however, she can't betray her father. The notion that she would elope behind her father's back with the man who killed her brother is just too much to contemplate.

This fuels Romeo's anger, and he precipitously runs out into the street challenging Tebaldo to a duel. As his followers take over the city square Romeo declares himself Tebaldo's rival for Giulietta's affections.

Act II

Giulietta begs for Lorenzo's help in extricating herself from this unhappy betrothal with Tebaldo in order to marry Romeo. He demurs for a moment but finally believes he has found the solution to her problem. His plan involves a very powerful sleeping draft, which he will provide for Giulietta and which, for all intents and purposes, will render her lifeless for some time. Believing her dead, the family has no alternative but to bury her in the family mausoleum. Lorenzo and Romeo will greet her when she wakes and at that point, and with everyone believing her dead, she can elope with the man she loves and wants to spend her life with.

Giulietta resists the plan until she hears her father walking up the stairs to her room. She has no alternative but to take the draught, which soon overcomes her. Capellio, by now suspicious of Lorenzo, has the poor man clapped in irons. He enters Giulietta's room only to find the poor girl lifeless. He now believes that perhaps Lorenzo was right; it is possible that Giulietta's fever had been more severe than everyone thought.

After her body is taken to the family vault Romeo comes to her. He laments her death and, unaware of Lorenzo's intrigue, decides to take poison. Soon, Giulietta awakes to find her lover waiting for her and believes that all has worked out as predicted. Discovering that Romeo is really dying, she decides to die with him. When her father and his entourage are escorted into the vault, he finds the lovers dead in a warm embrace that still speaks to us of love through the centuries.

Critique of I Capuletti e I Montecchi 1965

In general, we can say that in his first act aria *'E serbata, e serbata a quest'acciaro'* the sound is firm, the *appoggio* is much improved and the attack is cleaner. He typically employs a simultaneous attack but now it is more precise and firmer than previously, facilitating a superior balance between chiaro/scuro and allowing for a more lavish display of temperament. The voice still displays a lot of velvet, but it is now balanced by the richness of the higher harmonics. Because the objective *appoggio* is greatly improved, it automatically enhances the legato line and the quality of expression. In addition, the improved connection between the breath and vocal folds has created a firmer and longer closing phase, a formula that issues into the excitation of the higher harmonics resulting in a more brilliant and better-carrying tone. This recording is a significant step forward relative to his previous efforts and it is clear that what he learned from Sutherland is helping his singing. However, that knowledge is not yet totally assimilated and refined. For instance, the opening phrase is quite lovely, demonstrating a subtle *aggiustamento* at the *secondo passaggio*, especially the [a] vowel on the E4 of '*E serbato*'.

On the other hand, the attack on the first note of this aria ([e] vowel on the C4) displays an unnecessarily burdensome onset. The [a] vowel in the word '*acciaro*' ([a] on the F4) is beautifully modified but the double [cc] consonants are glossed over and insufficiently emphasised. On the other hand, some of the [a] vowels below the first passaggio (contained in the words *serbata* and *vendetta*) have been invaded by the [o] vowel, suggesting insufficient breath pressure to open the vowel towards a genuine [a]. This is something that Pavarotti would rectify shortly. In fact, the purity of his vowels would become a feature of his best singing. The [a] vowel on (G4) in the phrase '*il ciel lo sa*' is subtly but well modified as is the [e] vowel on the G4 in the phrase '*solo affretta*'. In between the two full-blooded G4s Pavarotti produces some lovely soft singing in the phrase '*Tu d'un nodo a me si caro,*' before approaching another excellent G4 on the [a] vowel of '*il consorte adempira*'. In the latter passage, the G4 is approached from below the note, creating a slight vacuum between the dotted E4 and the G4 thus disrupting the vocal line. However, once Pavarotti reaches the G4 in head register it is quite a lovely sound. Finally, Pavarotti crowns the aria with a glorious and easy sound on the B4 of the cadenza.

The *caballetta* that follows needs to be better negotiated and needs to be energised with a greater sense of springy *appoggio*. The basis of this results in increased antagonism between the internal and external muscles as well as the collision of the abdominals and the diaphragm (This mechanism has been defined and explained under the section on *appoggio* in this book).

It is this lack of antagonism that creates the *lotta vocale* (vocal struggle) resulting in a weak and anaemic tone at the beginning of the phrase '*L'amo tanto, e me si cara*'. In particular, the [a] vowel on the accented E4 demonstrates a loose vibrato as does the phrase '*e viva in lei*'. On the other hand, the reprise on the phrase '*ah piu tosto io sceglirei*' should all be bounced off the breath. For this to be successful the singer needs to ensure that there is sufficient flexibility in the respiratory apparatus. This allows the muscles to spring back into action quickly and with full vigour, not with a half-baked excuse for what really needs to feel like a trampoline. A very good exercise to remedy this type of mechanistic deficiency is to perform a number of staccato exercises, very judiciously to begin with but increasing exponentially in both number and length as the muscles grow in strength, vigour and response.

We can also learn from the phrase '*mille giorni, mille giorni di dolor*' in which the [i] vowel on the G4 on the word '*mille*' lacks clarity. The vowel has been modified towards the mixed [ir] vowel, in which according to Miller the tongue assumes the position of a lateral vowel whilst the mouth and the jaw assume the position of a round [o] vowel.

Consequently, some of the acoustic strength of both back and front vowels is incorporated within the acoustic power of this mixed vowel [Miller, 2004: 78].

Artistically I like what Pavarotti is doing here. He is an exciting artist always looking to incorporate different sounds and colours in his voice. Technically speaking, what Pavarotti is trying to avoid here is the tight, cutting and edgy sound associated with a closed [i] vowel. In this instance, it may have been better and more economical just to think of the [i] and maintain that tongue position and slightly drop the jaw, allowing a small percentage of [e] to invade the [i] position. This manoeuvre achieves greater freedom, increased intelligibility, and a more acceptable timbre with the [i] vowel.

Chapter 24

Beatrice di Tenda, Sutherland, Pavarotti, Decca 1966

We need to examine the following important event: Pavarotti's studio recording of *Beatrice di Tenda*, an opera composed by Vincenzo Bellini to a libretto by Felice Romano. The opera was commissioned by Lanari, the impresario at La Fenice and was written for the diva Giuditta Pasta. So committed was Bellini to the idea of pleasing his prima donna that he neglected his relationship with his librettist, Felice Romano. Theirs was a problematic relationship anyway, mainly because Bellini was not easy to deal with, but the total emphasis on Pasta at the expense of Romano was the last straw. *Beatrice di Tenda* premiered at La Fenice in Venice (1831).

Based on historical events, the opera recounts the story of Filippo Maria Visconti and his marriage to *Beatrice di Tenda*, the widow of General Facino. Before the curtain goes up, we learn that Filippo Visconti had lost both his brother and his father, Gian Galeazzo Visconti, Duke of Milan. As a result, he has inherited not only his father's titles and estates but also a continuing war and social unrest. To restore some semblance of order, Visconti joined forces with General Facino. When the latter was killed in action, Filippo Visconti wooed and wed his widow Beatrice (Historian Lauro Martines suggests that Facino himself, whilst lying dying, urged Beatrice to marry Filippo Maria).

The curtain goes up on a lavish party where it becomes clear that Filippo Maria has become bored with Beatrice and has begun a relationship with Agnese di Maino.

Beatrice too has learned to regret the early passion that led her to Filippo's bed and delivered her people into his cruel and tyrannical hands. Orombello, Lord of Ventimiglia, is not only a great admirer of Beatrice but also appreciates how badly this lady has been treated and how far she has fallen as a result of her marriage to Filippo Visconti.

Outraged, Orombello offers to lead Beatrice's people in a revolt against Visconti. Beatrice is grateful for the support but rejects the offer. Aware of the accusations of infidelity generated by Agnese di Maino, she is determined not to give her any ammunition. She believes that collaborating with Orombello against her husband would only lend credence to those vile rumours emanating from Agnese.

It is during one of these discussions that Filippo Visconti becomes suspicious of their close and intimate relationship, which he takes to be confirmation of Agnese's accusations. Urged by Agnese, he sends both Beatrice and Orombello to prison.

Act II

When the curtain goes up on act two, we discover Orombello being tortured to the degree where, under pain of death, he wavers, thus compromising Beatrice. However, she remains both exemplary and steadfast. When the judge orders further torture for Beatrice and Orombello, neither moves from their position, at which point both Filippo and Agnese realise that they have gone too far. Filippo Maria determines to set them free, but then the unthinkable happens; the castle is surrounded by the populace demanding Beatrice's release. Angered by such a sign of defiance and disloyalty, Filippo Visconti signs the death sentence.

Critique of Beatrice di Tenda

Let me say from the outset that Orombello is not the kind of role that tenors would kill for. However, it does contain some excellent music, and Pavarotti takes full advantage of what really remains a minor role, using it to demonstrate his considerable talent.

His easy tone, however, remains low-slung, a little too far back, too velvety, too relaxed and finally too heavy. In fact, physiologically, the whole instrument remains overly relaxed: subglottal pressure is deficient, with concomitant consequences for the firmness of adduction, closure time at the glottal level, and inadequate firmness and tension in the walls of the vocal tract. The tone is quite attractive, accessible and velvety, and therein lies the problem: a voice needs all of those qualities, but it also needs to be balanced with metal, ping brilliance and a little bit of edge. In the present state of development, resonation of the Pavarotti voice is mainly concentrated in the pharyngeal cavity, which strengthens the fundamental but does so at the expense of the singer's formant: that is, the brilliance, the ping, and focus associated with the singer's formant has been diminished greatly. In this instance, the lowered larynx and protruding lips have lengthened the vocal tract and lowered all the formants, producing an overly dark and inordinately round and velvety tone.

I like the remedy offered by James McKinney concerning over-emphasising the pharyngeal resonator, which issues a velvety and dark tone. He suggests that several factors can cause this to occur:

- Overuse of the yawning muscles, resulting in a spread throat and depressed larynx.
- Lack of oral space due to lip, jaw and tongue position.
- Wrong tonal models.
- Flabby surfaces of pharyngeal walls (not enough muscle tones to give character to the sound).
- The tongue pulled back into the pharynx.

McKinney believes that darkness in a sound can be the result of either too much or too little tension. So, the first thing to do is to look at the student's use of the articulators; inadequate use of the lips or insufficient mouth opening can produce a dark and muffled sound. If this is the problem, it can be easily rectified. He next suggests listening for phonatory issues, such as breathiness in the tone:

> This, too, can produce a dark, round and muffled tone. If the student is aware of this problem, we should begin work on developing a new sound world that emphasises a more balanced, more forward and vibrant sound that privileges the zygomatic arch and hard palate as a balancing focal point to the dominance of pharyngeal cavity [McKinney, 2005: 141-42].

Chapter 25

La Fille du Regiment, Pavarotti, Sutherland, July 1967

Having gained complete control over his technique as well as enormous confidence in his powers of communication and expression, Pavarotti now knew that he was on his way to becoming a truly great tenor. Everywhere he sang, he created a sensation. However, his father was still a barometer. He would say to Luciano that his singing was great but not as good as Gigli and Schipa; another time, it would be that he was great but not as good as Di Stefano or Caruso.

He accepted all this with grace but knew that he had to do something extraordinary. Pavarotti felt he was great in *La Bohème, Rigoletto,* and *Lucia di Lammermoor* but there were other tenors who also sang these roles very well (although in my view not quite as well as Pavarotti). He needed a position that no other tenor in living memory could have performed as well. Tonio in *La Fille du Régiment* was that role, and its great aria *Ah! Mes Ami*, with its nine glorious top Cs, was his vehicle for vocal distinction.

Pavarotti first sang the opera at Covent Garden with Sutherland and Bonynge in 1966, then repeated that success at La Scala in 1969 with Freni. However, the really transformational experience came in 1972 when he sang *La Fille du Regiment* at the Metropolitan Opera with Sutherland where he created a sensation. His reputation as the king of the high Cs was now totally consolidated.

La Fille du Regiment

This is a marvellous and joyous work written by Gaetano Donizetti for the 1840 season at the Opera Comique in Paris. It was presented in February 1840, and although unfairly criticised by a professionally jealous Hector Berlioz, others praised it for its *joie de vivre* and its idiomatic French style emanating from the pen of a gifted Italian composer.

The curtain rises on a Tyrolean village where a group of women is praying in front of the statue of our Lady. Sitting inconspicuously at the end of this group we find the Marquise of Brekenfield who is attended by her steward Hortensius. The cannon fire heard from a distance has made everyone fearful, especially the Marquise. Consequently, they pray fervently to the Madonna for protection and a resolute victory that will deliver them from their enemies. Finally, one of the villagers announces that the soldiers have retreated — they have been spared. The Marquise, now a little more relaxed, has reverted to her imposing and grand personality. She complains that in war not even her rank and station quarantine a lady from these disrespectful peasants. She sends Hortensius off to check that the carriage is in good order and that nothing has been stolen before resuming their journey.

The next scene introduces Marie, a girl abandoned as a very young child and brought up by the soldiers of the Twenty-First Regiment of the French Army. These soldiers are best described as a little rough and ready, but this does not do them justice, as they really do have hearts of gold. Eventually, and to the delight of Marie (who has grown tremendously fond of all her protective fathers), they decide to adopt her as their daughter.

Sulpice, sergeant of the twenty-first regiment, makes an entrance and hears a voice singing a lovely cadenza. He feigns indifference, but his face lights up at the sound of her voice. In expectation of her entry, he asks who is singing. As she joins him on stage, he blurts out, 'Oh, it's Marie, the pride and honour of our regiment'. Sulpice is delighted with the way things have turned out for the lovely little girl who was abandoned at the army barracks so many years ago.

Despite some disconcerting soldierly mannerisms, Marie has developed into a beautiful young woman, not to mention that she is also regarded as the official mascot of the regiment. Sulpice however is concerned that she has not been her usual carefree self of late. Marie confesses that she has developed certain feelings for Tonio, a handsome young Tyrolean peasant who recently saved her life. Asked to elaborate, Marie recounts her adventure. She was out collecting flowers when she saw a particularly beautiful one, but as she reached out for it, she lost her footing and was about to plunge into the precipice. Tonio, who had been hanging about in the hope of catching a glimpse of her, saves her life. At first, Marie is merely polite but then develops genuine feelings for him and longs to see him. Presently, Tonio is caught lurking around the encampment, hoping to catch a glimpse of Marie, who has been mistaken for a spy, captured and brought back to camp. Predictably, Marie comes to his defence, claiming him to be her personal prisoner. In the ensuing duet '*De cet aveu si tendre*' they reveal their true feelings for each other.

Tonio brings up the question of marriage only to discover that as a *vivandiere* Marie is obliged to marry a member of her regiment. Tonio wastes no time in announcing that he wishes to enlist in the army, which news is greeted with cheers and celebrations by members of the twenty-first regiment. They call on Marie to sing the regimental song (*Chacun le sait, chacun le dit!*).

In the next scene we find the traumatised Marquise in deep conversation with Sulpice, who is concerned about documents belonging to the captain that mentioned Berkenfield castle. The Marquise confesses that her sister was involved with the captain, and they had a little girl. Unfortunately, both parents were killed, and the little girl disappeared. Despite an extensive search, she was never found. When Sulpice reveals that he has a letter from the captain that he has never even read, it becomes evident that the missing little girl is none other than Marie, the mascot of the regiment. The Marquise claims Marie as her niece and demands that she come to live in her castle, where she will have the future that her parents always wanted for her. Tonio returns in uniform to claim his bride, only to find that Marie is living in the castle, a more appropriate environment for a young woman of her rank and class.

Act I

Act 2 finds Marie suffering as she endures the constrained life in the castle. She is bored with all the formalities, the etiquette, the singing lessons, and minuets, rituals that are so far removed from the simple and practical life she enjoyed with her Regiment. All this respectability and trivial lifestyle prevents her from finding any meaning in this lifeless existence. Nor does it help that Sulpice is in residence at the Chateau — a constant reminder of the regimental life she so misses. To make things worse she fails every attempt to forget Tonio even though she is betrothed to the duke. In an effort to reclaim Marie, Tonio arrives at the castle determined to prevent her from marrying the duke. He does so in one of the most moving arias in a very rich score — *'Pour me rapprocher de Marie'.*

Critique of La Fille du Regiment

In general, we can say without fear of contradiction that Pavarotti's depiction of Tonio in *La Fille du Regiment* is a majestic achievement by an august tenor at the peak of his powers. Pavarotti captures the mood of Donizetti's hero in a meticulously judged performance, managing to balance the most exuberant moments of the score, such as '*Ah mes Amis* and *Pour mon Aimé*,' with the passionate but poignant last act aria, 'Pour me rapprocher de Marie'.

Pavarotti's performance *of 'La Fille du Regiment'* represents a depiction for the ages. This is a portrayal of Tonio that has, over the last fifty-five years, garnered legions of admirers and is now widely recognised in the annals of opera as a genuinely legendary vocal performance. Pavarotti's voice is in magnificent and pristine condition, displaying roundness, a delicate balance of velvet and metal, an excellent colour, and an instantly recognised rich timbre. The tone is even throughout the scale, and the top of the voice is glorious. There has never been a tenor with the volume, amplitude, beauty and richness of tone that has been able to throw off nine open-throated top Cs with such ease, consistency, beauty and abandon. Pavarotti delivers this performance without ever losing ease of emission, vocal power (penetration), or timbral quality. It really is in every way a monumental performance. Moreover, analysing later performances, such as the 1972 Metropolitan performances with Sutherland, only serves to remind us that Pavarotti was a supreme artist who was consistently seeking to develop his enormous gifts long after he was a household name. I only mention this to demonstrate that as great as the Covent Garden season was, Pavarotti's singing in the New York season of 1972 was even better.

However, much as I totally subscribe to the above, the objective of this book is to disseminate vocal knowledge, so I cannot in good conscience leave it at that. No one is going to learn anything from a statement such as: 'This is a monumental performance, the likes of which we will never hear again'.

So, I will begin by saying that, whilst, in general, I stand by all my comments on the 1968 Decca performance, the particulars indicate some issues that could, if amended, deliver an even greater level of perfection. For instance, we can say that, notwithstanding the beauty of the tone and the overall emission, the voice remains too far back and a little throaty, mainly because the articulators (the base of the tongue, the zygomatic arch, and the soft palate) demonstrate a propensity for remaining in a lower position than they ideally should be. This results in the elongation of the vocal track, a configuration that lowers all the formants, thereby privileging the fundamental at the expense of the upper harmonics. This mode of vibration is inefficient in terms of exciting the upper harmonics responsible for providing the voice with its customary ring (squillo).

The Old Italian teachers would say that in terms of the *chiaro/scuro* model, Pavarotti's vocal production at this stage of his career favours the o*scuro* aspects of the tone, especially in the first tenth of the scale. On the other hand, when he moves into the head register, he seems to find an articulatory configuration and a level of breath energy that, without exceptions more amply excites the upper harmonics. This is a configuration that maintains the warmth and colour of the lower formants whilst developing a more energetic, more brilliant, and more balanced tone.

He does not, however, totally abandon his predilection towards the *oscuro* aspects of the tone. The top, however, is generally more energetic and more brilliant. In part this is a natural physical reaction from the singer to the psychological preparation for the physical demands required to secure the top C.

The improvement to the quality of tone, therefore, is a by-product of the conscious and subconscious muscular effort required to ensure the attainment of the note. For the sake of learning, I will point out a few exceptions to make the reader more aware of the difference in tonal quality.

Detailed Critique of La Fille du Regiment, London: July 1967

First Act Duet Between Tonio and Marie

We first notice how tentative the recitatives introducing the first act duet really are. I am going directly to the opening phrase *si je vous aime.*

In this sequence, the whole instrument is lacking coordination, and the larynx moves indiscriminately instead of being harnessed by the breathing apparatus in a steady and moderately low position. This has the effect of influencing not only the already precarious French text, including authenticity and clarity of vowels, but also vocal timbre and quality. For instance, the syllable 'Aime' on the [G] natural is marked with an accent in the score, but Pavarotti seems incapable of following this instruction simply because his breathing is still too high (more sostegno than appoggio) and not sufficiently anchored by the antagonistic respiratory muscles. Consequently, the respiration is insufficiently responsive, and in a rising interval the larynx follows pitch instead of being independent of it. In elite singing the larynx should remain stable and moderately low, irrespective of pitch and vowel.

To achieve this accent, Pavarotti would have needed to produce greater firmness of tone by lowering the diaphragm, with a concomitant expansion of the lateral floating ribs and the lumbar region. This has the effect of not only controlling respiration but also lowering and stabilising the larynx. This balanced and flexible firmness of support allows the respiratory muscles to do the work whilst encouraging the singer to relax the organs of the vocal tract, including the jaw and the tongue, preventing the latter from arching up indiscriminately, as it does in this passage. In this passage Pavarotti is captive to the worst aspects of the French tradition — that of allowing the larynx to follow the frequency in an ascending passage. This is a tradition in the French School that was advocated by Jean Antoine Berard as far back as 1754.

The phrase '*ecoutez et jugez vous meme*' is much better. The sound within the phrase is much more controlled and the tone is not only velvety but also more even, especially the interval from the F natural to the E♭ on the phrase '*vous même*'. However, whilst the control is much improved, the overall tone is still too far back and down towards the throat. The vowel has migrated away from its original [E] and is now sounding more like a French [Ü].

In the excerpt above we find that the [A] vowels in *'l'instant'* and *'où, dans mes bras, je vous reçus toute tremblante'* lack definition and clarity. The tone is too far back, insufficiently focused, and therefore throaty and lacking ring (*squillo*). In fact, the base of the tongue has assumed a mildly retroflex position, altering the space within the vocal tract and forcing the vowel sound to migrate towards the [O] vowel, hence losing the integrity of the [A] vowel. This kind of severe vowel modification is not only unnecessary but also undesirable and inappropriate, especially for the low middle register. This is the part of the voice typically characterised by the dictum *'Si canta come si parla'.*

The [ç] consonant in *reçus* lacks precision and projection, as well as lacking the *slancio* generally associated with a phrase that incorporates both a crescendo and rising frequency. Consequently, this type of phrase is accompanied by a gradual crescendo culminating in a climax on the first beat of the next bar (the [çu] in *reçus*), the latter remaining too far back. In this instance the tone dissipates rather than developing into a ringing tone accompanied by a moderate crescendo. The remedy is to sing this vowel with the tip of the tongue against the ridge of the lower teeth and the dorsum of the tongue arching further forward, almost approximating the hard palate. It is therefore much closer to the [i] position rather than the [u] position in which the tongue arches further back towards the velum.

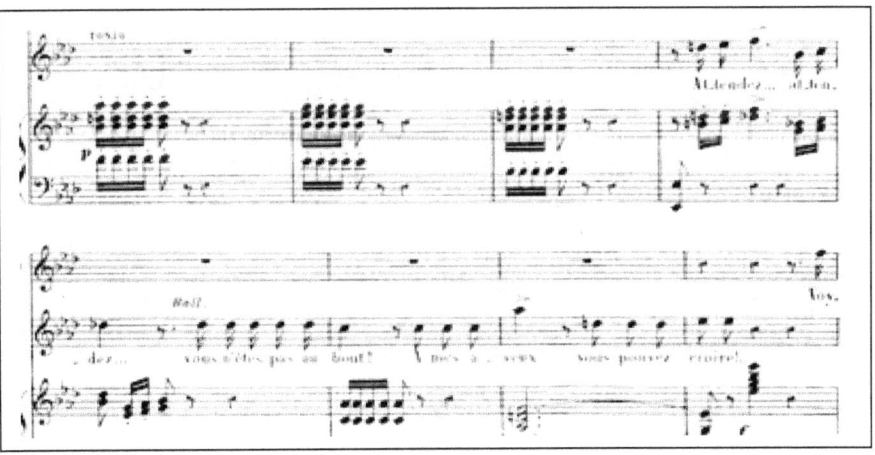

The word *attendez* is too insipid and lacks articulatory precision. At this point of Pavarotti's vocal development, the emission retains a lovely, round, velvety tone, but it is also too generalised. The configuration of the articulators is not sufficiently defined to focus the sound vibrations towards, a particular point (the mask).

The A♭ on the *aveux* is an indistinct sound: it is not an [e], nor is it an [er]. What we can say is that the vowel is too open, insufficiently focused, and inadequately supported. Consequently, the vibrations emanating from the source remain back in the throat.

We then come to the second verse of this duet, beginning with '*Le beau pays de mon enfance*'. The main feature of the second verse is its similarity to the first and therefore what was said about the first applies equally to the second. This performance is characterised by the lower notes such as '*le beau pays*' and '*Ah! pour vous*' being positioned too far back in the throat, and the notes above the secondo passaggio such as '*Les amis*' and '*sans peine je le quitterais*' are all too narrow and constricted, preventing the sound-waves from bloom.

On the other hand, the notes above the stave, such as the affrettando passage above beginning with 'Et puis enfin de votre absence', are more accessible, and the emission is more forward and decidedly more energised. However, whilst the sound overall remains very beautiful, the tone is still contained, lean and relatively small.

The phrases '*Epuis enfin de votre absence*' and '*ne pauvant vaincre le tourment*' are quite revealing. The [i] vowel on *puis* has a good ring about it,

but the [e] on the F natural is not only collected but, in an effort to change register into the head voice, the vowel is too closed and therefore lacks a ring. On the other hand, the sequence of [a] vowels in '*absence, peuvant,* and *tourment*' are all sung on lovely open [a] vowels and, although not as open as they would later become, they have a pleasingly warm and lyrical tone.

The passage on the repeated G naturals '*J'ai bravé dans ce camp*' is a good ringing sound but is lean and tight. This passage requires a greater sense of abandon and generosity with a more overt display of emotion — a passionate outburst that occasionally expresses itself in an open-throated roar of the human spirit. In the 1967 performance this passage is too tame and controlled. The lower register has a lovely warm sound, but it lacks drive and height, the notes between the first and *secondo passaggio* being quite dull because Pavarotti is too concerned with changing registers. Consequently, he moves into head register too early and dampens the notes around the *passaggio*. Once he moves into head voice the sound becomes considerably more brilliant, but it is still too studied, too collected and too contained to be a really exciting sound.

Analysis of the 1967/8 Performance

We can state that overall, Pavarotti's voice in the low and mixed register needs more buoyancy, a sense of lightness, and a feeling that the tone naturally impinges on the mask without ever being forced there. This sense of buzzing vibrations on the mask is the result of sympathetic vibrations, the memory of which allows us to give the tone greater focus, definition, and ring (*squillo*). In this performance, the notes between the first and second *passaggio* are often dull and under-energised. On the other hand, the notes above the stave are forward and ringing but with a small aperture, until the B flats, Bs and Cs which are fantastic. However overall, the voice is not as forward as it would later become. The vowels typically need to be more incisive with a harder edge at their boundaries whilst simultaneously increasing sub-glottal pressure, ensuring a greater velocity of airflow. Singing is not just a physical act but also an act of will, possessing a mental and emotional element. Consequently, we can state that the greater the level of mental energy and intensity of sub-glottal pressure the more significant the acoustic energy, thus rectifying most of the problems outlined above.

In this recording Pavarotti is inclined to use a simultaneous onset followed by what would best be described as the type of emission somewhere between flow and firm phonation, supported by a less-than-firm sub-glottal pressure, engendering a less-than-firm glottal adduction combined with a shorter closure phase and a broad, round spectrum as opposed to a spiky one which provides the tone with ping and brilliance.

With the exception of the very highest notes of the head register, the voice tends to be a little static, and the vibrations too diffused, needing greater focus and follow-through as well as direction and breath velocity. The whole instrument needs to be more energised and more dynamic if it is to create a sense of focused direction, as well as the excitement that comes from enhanced upper harmonics. I don't mean just within the phrase but also within a given note. Every note should have its own ideal vibrancy that is both continuous and consistent and which eventually merges into the next note. The vibrations that constitute the sound waves need both breath pressure (sub-glottal pressure) and mental energy. This minimises the return that is associated with the part of the soundwave that collides with the zygomatic arch and then bounces back towards the glottis.

If we increase sub-glottal pressure whilst remaining flexible and facilitating a quicker response time, we will elicit a greater resistance from the vocal folds, creating a sharper cessation of breath flow at closure. This delivers the spectrum with a steeper and sharper curve resulting in greater excitation of the upper harmonics which provide the voice with *squillo*. This is the type of production that induces the proprioceptive sensations (vibrations) that the singer comes to feel on the zygomatic arch *(impostazione)*. This is the right *impostazione* for such concentration of vibrancy as demanded by a role such as Tonio. Many years later Donald Miller came to believe that he tuned the singer's formant to the second harmonic. Pavarotti does not totally achieve this more exciting mode of vibration in the 1967 performance simply because his vowels are too generalised. They lack clarity and definition, qualities that sharpen the edges forming the boundary lines of such vowels, which lines in this performance are a little vague, requiring greater articulation and enhanced definition.

The Remedy

The remedy for these perceived deficiencies remains simple in theory but difficult to achieve in practice. Pavarotti needs to raise the zygomatic arch, combined with simultaneously raising the soft palate and moderately lowering the larynx, whilst creating a larger space in the pharynx. This is particularly important in effecting the singer's formant.

The tip of the tongue needs to come forward where it finds its resting position at the posterior aspect of the lower teeth or, as James McKinney calls it, 'The dental ridge of the lower teeth'. The base of the tongue should be raised marginally, allowing the body of the tongue to be elevated, moving forward against the upper palate and alveolar ridge for the lateral [i] and [e] vowels and arching up and back towards the soft palate for the round vowels, [u] and [o]. The body of the tongue remains flat within the oral cavity for the [a] vowel. The apex of the tongue remains forward on the lower teeth for all vowels, and the base should be slightly elevated.

The breath should remain flexible but firm, providing each note and therefore each vocal manoeuvre with the appropriate breath support.

In this performance the vocal tract is too long, simply because the larynx is too low. In addition, the lips are protruding, and the zygomatic arch is down, all of which elongates the vocal tract and lowers all the formants. This configuration is reflected in a slightly lowered soft palate and relaxed pharyngeal walls, sometimes verging on flabbiness, a configuration that privileges the lower harmonics at the expense of the higher ones. The pharyngeal walls should be firmer, stretched and tensed — a condition that promotes the higher harmonics in the harmonic series thus creating the ring of the voice (*squillo*).

The sub-glottal pressure is insufficient to elicit a firm closure of the vocal folds and excite the upper harmonics. We can say that Pavarotti has not as yet found the right balance between the *chiaro/scuro* of the old school or, as contemporary scientists refer to it, the fundamental and upper harmonics of the scientific school. If anything, he errs on the side of too strong a fundamental at the expense of the upper harmonics in all but the highest notes of the scale. It is in the highest notes of his range (in which Pavarotti has to make more of an effort to generate greater breath energy by utilising greater sub-glottal pressure) that we hear a more balanced *chiaro/scuro* sound. In general, the high Cs and even some of the B flats are more forward and open-throated, consequently producing a more ringing sound (*squillo*) than both the mixed voice and the *passaggio*. Many of these problems could be rectified by bringing the tip of the tongue against the lower teeth and promoting a slight elevation and more forward thrust in the body of the tongue, thereby preventing the retroflex tongue position which often occurs in these early recordings.

The worst offenders are *Beatrice di Tenda*, the early *Traviatas L'amico Fritz*, and parts of *La Fille du Regiment*. If the above recommendations regarding the articulators were to be combined with a more lateral rather than vertical approach to the vowels (using a hint of a smile, less lip protrusion, raising the zygomatic arch and, by extension, the soft palate, and increasing sub-glottal breath pressure), I am sure that these elements would enhance an already excellent performance.

Chapter 26

L'Amico Fritz, Mascagni, Pavarotti, Freni, Gavazzeni, 1968

Having discussed at length the 1967 performance of the *La fille du Regiment*, let us turn briefly to his 1968 offering, Mascagni's *L'amico Fritz*. As with *'Beatrice di Tenda,'* Pavarotti never performed *'L'amico Fritz'* on stage. However, many connoisseurs and authorities believe that this opera, not Beatrice, represents his best and most consistent singing in his early recordings. Nonetheless this is not one of the defining operas for Pavarotti. In fact, aside from the Cherry duet (which he recorded at least three times and sang in a couple of concerts), I don't believe he sang any other part of this opera again. Therefore, it is not an opera like *La Boheme, Rigoletto, Tosca, Lucia* or even *La fille du Regiment* and *I Puritani*, all of which made Pavarotti's reputation. I will therefore treat it respectfully but in less detail.

One of the positive aspects of this recording is the excellent rapport he developed with Gianandrea Gavazzeni. He didn't always see eye to eye with the conductor, but in this instance, Gavazzeni was able to elicit a beautiful performance from Pavarotti. Certainly, it was the most assured interpretation, with greater depth than anything he had performed to this point. However, their first meeting at the Teatro Donizetti in Bergamo did not fare so well.

According to Leone Magiera, following a less than propitious audition for the artistic director of La Scala — the legendary Francesco Siciliani — Pavarotti decided that he would no longer audition for anyone. His career was going very well, and if they wanted to hear him, they could come to one of his performances or send an emissary. Siciliani was an incredible musician and a remarkable diplomat, excellent gifts for an artistic director of a theatre where Renata Tebaldi and Maria Callas were competing for supremacy. He came to La Scala with a tremendous reputation which was based on his enormous success as artistic director of the Maggio Musicale in Florence. According to Leone Magiera, during his tenure at La Scala Siciliani would quite regularly sit at the piano and sight-read complex scores (such as *Doktor Faustus* by Ferruccio Busoni and *Pelleas et Melisande* by Claude Debussy) with such virtuosity that it would have been the envy of many conductors not only at La Scala but also other major theatres. It was Siciliani who offered Pavarotti either Arturo in *I Puritani* or Arnold in *Guglielmo Tell*, which Pavarotti, of necessity, had to turn down for fear of ruining his voice at that early stage of his career. It was Siciliani who suggested auditioning for Gavazzeni simply because he was the designated conductor for the Verdi and Puccini repertoire at La Scala, the repertoire that Pavarotti wanted to sing.

Pavarotti was ready to decline the offer, but Ziliani, his manager, talked him into making an exception just for Gavazzeni. He reminded Pavarotti that Gavazzeni had earned a formidable reputation over a period of forty years at La Scala. Pavarotti finally agreed.

As the journey from Modena to Bergamo was long, Magiera and Pavarotti had a great deal of time to discuss Gavazzeni's reputation, musical gifts and taste. They had enormous respect for Gavazzeni, both as a man and a musician, as well as conductor and composer. However, it did not escape Pavarotti's attention that Gavazzeni was very good friends with Di Stefano, whom they all admired but who sang the passaggio notes in a completely different style from Pavarotti's. Whereas Pavarotti was very disciplined in covering the *passaggio* notes, Di Stefano went with nature — a more open, spontaneous, and very exciting sound but one that affected the top notes and ultimately proved ruinous.

At any rate here he was in Bergamo's Teatro Donizetti, preparing to sing 'Che gelida manina' for Gavazzeni with Leone Magiera at the piano. He sang the aria superbly and was therefore most surprised by the thundering silence from the stalls. However, in the face of such indifference, Pavarotti nodded to Magiera, who immediately began the introduction to 'Tombe degli avi miei' from Donizetti's 'Lucia di Lammermoor'. This was a most propitious choice given that they were in the Donizetti theatre in Bergamo. However, his glorious singing was again met with silence; undaunted, Pavarotti ventured forth, asking, 'Maestro is that enough?'. 'Carry on' came the authoritarian reply from the stalls. Pavarotti nodded yet again to Magiera, who began the accompaniment to the third aria, 'Ah dispar vision' from Massenet's *Manon*. Yet again there was no comment from Gavazzeni at which point Pavarotti was ready to walk out. Traditionally in an audition no more than two arias were required but Gavazzeni was not yet satisfied. He asked for two more arias from *Tosca* —- 'Recondite Armonie' and 'E Lucevan le Stelle'. Pavarotti responded, saying that he had no more music, at which point Gavazzeni's white hair emerged from the protective darkness of the stalls. 'I am sorry, but I absolutely must hear other pieces', he insisted. Unfortunately, the library was closed that day, but Gavazzeni knew about Magiera's prodigious memory and decided that he could play all the arias he requested from memory. He then asked for the three arias from *Rigoletto*, followed by the two arias from *Elisir d'amore*, and two more arias from *La Favorita*. What began as a test for Luciano turned into a nightmare for Magiera as well because, by the time he finished testing his memory for all those arias, he was dripping with perspiration from head to toe. According to Magiera: 'Gavazzeni, at the end of this tour de force, dismissed Luciano with a few formal compliments, telling him, essentially, that he did not think he was good enough yet to sing at La Scala under his baton' [Magiera, 2008: 53]. Pavarotti never found out what it was about his audition that Gavazzeni didn't like, but he suspected that the Maestro had found his *passaggio* too covered and perhaps a little unnatural. Nevertheless, here they were, recording Mascagni's minor masterpiece together.

L'amico Fritz

Act I

The curtain goes up on a dining room in Fritz Kobus' home. Fritz is a wealthy landowner whose only stimulation, aside from overseeing his lands, is the protracted discussions with the local rabbi David, an old friend. We also discover early in the act that Fritz has a particular disdain for marriage. His friends join him to celebrate his birthday. Suzel, the daughter of one of his tenant farmers, presents him with a bouquet for his birthday, together with a charming little aria, '*Son pochi fiori*', in which she displays a disarming innocence and simplicity. She is invited to join the celebration and is moved when the gypsy Beppe enters, playing his violin. Following Suzel's departure, David pointedly comments that she will make a good wife for someone and that he intends to find her a husband. Fritz protests that she is too young, but David disagrees. The disagreement evolves into a general discussion on the positive and negative aspects of marriage. Fritz is eventually lured by David into a wager based on the proposition that he, Fritz, will never marry.

Act II

The farmers are walking to the fields where they are about to harvest the cherries. Suzel is among them, but she is momentarily retained by Fritz. The encounter develops into the beautiful Cherry Duet (one of the highlights of the opera), during which they sing about the enchantment of spring, flowers and nature. However, when Fritz's friends arrive, he is suddenly back in the real world, excusing himself as he leaves to carry out his duties as overlord of his farms. David stays behind to talk to Suzel and to her embarrassment he suggests that someday she will make a lovely bride. She leaves just before Fritz returns. When David announces that he has found the right husband for Suzel, Fritz becomes visibly irritated. The mere thought of the girl marrying someone else makes him realise that he has fallen in love with her.

Act III

Thoughts of Suzel have totally invaded Fritz's mind. Beppe enters and attempts to raise his spirits with a song, but it has the opposite effect, causing Fritz to become even more morose. David arrives and tells Fritz that Suzel is about to become engaged to a fine young man, and her father will soon ask for his blessing. Fritz is saddened and outraged in equal measure at the thought of her being with someone else. He is tempted to refuse her father's request, but he knows that no good will come from it. Suzel enters, and in spite of David's assurances that everything will be all right, she is overcome by a sense of sadness. Left alone she voices her love for Fritz and her despair at the thought of marrying someone else. Fritz enters and in the ensuing conversation, he realises that she does not love her fiancé. Fritz finally reveals his love for her, and they embrace the new reality. David declares that he has won his wager with Fritz but announces that his winnings, Fritz's vineyard, are going to be his gift to Suzel as a wedding present.

Critique of L'amico Fritz

Gavazzeni's conducting and interpretation of this opera are just fantastic, which should not come as a surprise as he had been very good friends with Mascagni and knew exactly how the composer wanted his opera performed.

There is no question that he elicits a remarkable performance from both Freni and in particular Pavarotti, whose performance as Fritz is a quantum leap from *'Beatrice di Tenda' (1966)* and *La Fille du Regiment* (1967). He is much more in control of his respiratory mechanism although not all of his singing is connected to the breath. In fact, some notes are quite off the breath but not as severely as previously. The same may be said of the passaggio which is undoubtedly more open, more natural, far less contrived and with more complex and more defined boundaries around the edges of the vowels. Consequently, with the exception of one or two [o] vowels, his diction has more clarity and greater definition, while the colouring of the text is more refined, nuanced and convincing. The sound retains a lovely velvety quality, but it is less exaggerated, transforming the prevailing rate into a more forward, ringing tone, one that conveys greater clarity of intent. The high register is still accessible, but the soft singing is much better and even more so than his previous performance in *La Fille du Regiment*. He is making a genuine effort to sing '*mezza voce*' in order to create a more diverse and nuanced tone. However, the vocal tract is still too long, affecting all the formants but not as severely as in previous recordings. He has not yet learned to shorten the vocal tract, especially for the darker vowels and, even worse, from the point of view of voice production, there are occasions when he lengthens the vocal tract even for the lateral vowels. The shortening of the vocal tract requires mild elevation of the larynx, a raising of the zygomatic arch, and a slight rounding of the lips rather than their protrusion for the dark vowels, with only a hint of a smile for the lateral bright vowels. *L'amico Fritz* is also characterised by a slightly higher larynx, a shorter resonator cavity (vocal tract), all of which results in and a more forward tone than he previously emitted. The vocal folds are still insufficiently occluded, suggesting that the correlation with the breath pressure is still to be perfected. The breath needs to be firmer, not only to harness the vertical laryngeal position but also to more firmly occlude the glottis, creating more resistance and greater tension at the vocal fold level, resulting in a sharper, spikier spectrum.

It is this firmer glottal setting that is responsible for the longer closure time, the firmer collision of the tissue and the resultant skewing of the spectrum that excites the upper harmonics, giving the voice its natural *squillo*. Pavarotti is much better in this recording as he is in glorious voice and, apart from a few notes, he has found mostly the right blend of *chiaro/scuro*. I say almost the right combination because the Pavarotti sound could still do with more brilliance and *squillo* and a more forward ringing tone. His diction and artistic expression are not only significantly improved but of a very high calibre, with the beauty of tone, diction, characterisation and overall expressivity producing an excellent performance. My only reservations refer to the technical aspects still to be achieved which include a firmer connection between the respiratory muscles and the vocal folds (voice source) and greater control over onset and release. Firmer glottal settings are required, as well as the shortening of the vocal tract through the judicious raising of the larynx, elevation of the zygomatic arch and a retreat of the previously protruding lips into a hint of a smile. Nonetheless, within the paradigm of his present level of development, his performance is wonderful.

I give the last word to Leone Magiera, who prepared both Pavarotti and Freni for this recording and stated: 'In *L'amico Fritz*, released in 1968, which we prepared for at length with Mirella Freni, he is almost perfect. The conductor was Gianandrea Gavazzeni, who imbued the opera with a deeply sympathetic understanding of Mascagni which makes this recording extremely interesting and novel, even today' [Magiera, 2008: 93].

Having discussed how Pavarotti might improve an already legendary performance, let us apply this knowledge to specific phrases within the opera.

According to Adua Pavarotti, by 1968, Luciano's career had gained a momentum of its own. Consequently, she decided not to return to work after the birth of their third daughter but instead began taking care of Luciano's business. She undertook the task of responding to his ever-increasing fan mail, kept his diary and maintained a number of other administrative duties.

Having made his mark in the major opera houses of Britain and Europe, Luciano was now ready to conquer the final citadel: the Metropolitan Opera. Following a successful debut in La Boheme in San Francisco in November 1967, he was invited to make his Met debut as Rodolfo in La Boheme in November 1968.

Aware of his great success in this role, not only all over Europe but also at Covent Garden and San Francisco, he had no reason to believe that the Metropolitan Opera would long remain unconquered.

There were several legitimate reasons why Pavarotti was a little nervous about his Met debut. It certainly would be the last citadel to fall, which would bestow upon him a truly international career. He was also aware that the acerbic New York critics were not easily swayed, not to mention that the house had a capacity of 4200 discerning patrons on any particular night. That is a very large house to fill and a very large crowd to please.

His philosophy up to this point had always been, 'Cometh the hour cometh the man'. Unfortunately, according to Adua Veroni Pavarotti, on this occasion Luciano came down with a devastating dose of the Hong Kong Flue. He couldn't bear to cancel the whole season so he and the management devised a plan that would allow him a week to recover before embarking on his debut. The following week, he sang Rodolfo the poet as scheduled and performed the role well. He even won some good reviews, but he knew he had not done himself justice. Nonetheless, the critic for the New York Times, Peter G. Davis, an excellent and well-deserved critique: Mr. Davis asserted,

> 'Mr Pavarotti triumphed principally through the natural beauty of his voice — a bright, open instrument with a nice metallic ping up top that warms into an even, burnished lustre in midrange. Any tenor who can toss off high Cs with such abandon, successfully negotiate delicate diminuendo effects, and attack Puccinian phrases so fervently is going to win over any *La Boheme* audience. And Mr Pavarotti had them eating out of his hand' [Peter G Davis, *New York Times*, 1968].

This was a great review by any standards. The problem was that whereas he had expected to do even better in his next performance on December 5, he sang the first two acts and was forced to cancel. This was devastating for a gifted and ambitious man like Pavarotti. After cancelling not only *La Boheme* but equally disappointing also his performances of *La Sonnambula*, Pavarotti was soon on a plane back to Modena. Pavarotti was so devastated by these events that he failed to phone Adua to let her know he was coming home. When she opened the door, he looked so pale and distraught that she immediately thought he had been booed off the stage.

Notwithstanding Adua's dedicated attention towards his recovery, it still took him three months to recover from this horrible flu; however, shortly after, he was back singing and giving even more spectacular performances than he had ever sung before.

The closest Boheme we have on record to Pavarotti's Metropolitan debut is the Boheme he recorded in Rome with Freni and Schippers in July 1969, and this is the production we will analyse next.

Chapter 27

La Bohème, Pavarotti, Freni, Schippers RAI, July 1969

A far better live performance of *La Bohème* is the broadcast by RAI in 1969, conducted by Thomas Schippers, and beautifully sung by Pavarotti and his friend Mirella Freni.

All the sustained G4s that were troublesome in the 1961 and 1967 performances, in such phrases as '*che vive in ozzio come un gran signor*' and '*L'amor è un caminetto*,' not to mention '*l'ardente mio dramma ci scaldi*' are now solidly connected to the breath and have attained a much higher level of balanced chiaro/scuro. This effectively means that the respiratory muscles perform most of the hard work, resulting in greater freedom around the neck and flexibility around the mouth, jaw, tongue and other articulators.

The 1969 performance is a very different proposition as Pavarotti sings everything in the original key with a lovely, natural and lyrical tone. The whole performance is characterised by great sincerity and spontaneity. The voice production owes a great deal to what we recognise as flow phonation. This is marked by the fact that vocal fold adduction is firmer than the 1967 performance but less firmly adducted than the 1972 von Karajan performance. In the latter, Pavarotti emphasises firm phonation combined with increased sub-glottal pressure and a moderately lowered laryngeal position. This type of production privileges the excitation of the higher harmonic at the expense of the lower.

On the other hand, in the 1967 performance, which is the one under discussion, the voice is characterised by a lovely relaxed vocal style with a velvety colour that enhances the lower harmonics at the expense of higher harmonics. The result is that in the 1967 recording, the vocal folds offer less resistance to the sub-glottal pressure created by the contraction of the respiratory muscles. Consequently, the voice is warm but has a ringing, fresh-sounding tone, which is the product of a reasonably firm glottal setting and a well-harnessed laryngeal position that is stabilised by the respiratory muscles. This is particularly evident in the beautifully balanced Act 1 G4s that were troublesome and much discussed in the earlier performances on the words '*Come un gran signor*', *and L'amor è un caminetto*,' and '*L'ardene mio drama ci scaldi*'. Combined with a beautifully poised B flat in the phrase 'Vampi in fiamma', we immediately understand that this is a very different and much better performance than his earlier effort.

Pavarotti had by now been on the international circuit for eight years, with his Rodolfo being his calling card at Covent Garden, the Vienna Staatsoper, San Francisco, La Scala and The Metropolitan Opera to name but a few major centres. Consequently, many technical and interpretative concerns from the earlier 1961 performance are a thing of the past. This performance is generally an excellent balance between naturalness and spontaneity on the one hand and solid technical achievement on the other. Artistically it is more buoyant, more refined, more spontaneous, more natural, and more graceful than anything he had produced so far.

Technically, there is a much stronger connection between the respiratory muscles and the voice source (larynx), preventing the larynx from rising pitch. This allows Pavarotti to make the necessary *aggiustamento* by adding just the right amount of vowel modulation, allowing the [a] in the words '*gran*' and '*scaldi*' to be modified towards the [o] vowel. This process slightly lowers the larynx, modifies the vowel and blends the modified vowel into a ringing but still mellifluous sound. The same applies to the [A] natural on '*Eureka*', which remains a little tight although ben *appoggiata* (supported), unlike the♭ on '*l'idea vampi in fiamma*', which displays greater freedom. At this stage of his development, the Pavarotti sound is still very narrow on the [i] vowel and the [e] in the head register. The remedy to this would be a slight lowering of the jaw from the temporal-mandibular joint, which would also release the larynx, providing the sound vibrations with more resonating space.

Mimi's Entrance and Che Gelida Manina

Pavarotti manages Mimi's entrance in a lyrical but simultaneously sophisticated and spontaneous manner. The singing is quite exquisite, and '*Che gelida manina*' is beautifully sung, notwithstanding the fact that both the B♭ on '*Chi son*' and the top C5 on '*La Speranza*' could do with a little more consistency in breath pressure. The problem is that the majority of the vowels start too far back, and there is insufficient sub-glottal pressure to bring them forward. In addition, Pavarotti occasionally allows himself to be distracted by feeling that he has to collect the F natural before launching into the A♭ preceding the top C5. This is the type of nonsense that takes concentration away from the breath at the very time when the singer should depend only on the *appoggio*. This alone is a good argument for the intervention of vocal science in Italy to counter many of these old wives' tales. My experience was that I spent many years trying to collect the sound the way Pavarotti did and for the same reason, in order to guard against the possibility of being too open like

Giuseppe di Stefano. We all loved and admired di Stefano back then, and his immense influence was evident, not only in Pavarotti's expression but also in the singing of the young Jose Carreras. However, much as we admired him, we were also wary because none of us wanted to lose our voices by the age of thirty-five, which is what happened to di Stefano. It took me years before I realised that you didn't have to be as open as di Stefano nor as closed as Pavarotti. If you create a strong connection between the breath and the voice source, the respiratory muscles, especially the diaphragm, will bring the larynx down into a naturally lower point facilitating the modification of the [a] vowel in '*La Esperanza* giving it a hint of an [o]. This will result in just the right amount of laryngeal descent and just the right amount of vowel modification or *aggiustamento*, often referred to as formant tracking. Best of all, this will happen naturally and automatically whilst the singer is still concentrating on breathing.

This is because too often, Pavarotti allowed poor production to spoil what should have been a colossal performance. He did the same thing ten years later in 1979 (but with worse results) in the live performance from the Metropolitan with Renata Scotto and James Levine. This was eighteen years after his debut, and he should have known better by then. Everything issues from good breath management and most vocal problems can be traced back to an erroneous breathing strategy. Time and experience have convinced me of the wisdom of Manuel Garcia's pronouncement cited above. We recall that Garcia informed Root: 'I used to think about many things but as time passed, I realised the best way is not to complicate it. Just get on the breath, make a clean attack and get out of the way' (Root, as quoted in James Stark's work '*Bel canto*' 1999).

O Soave Fanciulla

The *O soave fanciulla* brings forth a lovely round, warm sound, which is appropriate for this glorious love duet. From a technical point of view, Pavarotti might have wanted to sing a more authentic [A] vowel in the word '*soave*' such as the one he sings on the '*circonfuso alba lunar*'. The '*sognar*' on the F *sharp* is a little hooked into the mask, which does not allow it to find its natural place and interferes with the resonance on the '*fremon gia nell'anima*'. The placement of the phrase '*fremon nell'anima, dolcezze estreme, fremon dolcezze estreme*' is excellent, but the vibrato is too fast because the respiratory muscles are not providing sufficient pressure.

Act II

The second act takes place in the Café Momus in the Latin Quarter of Paris. Rodolfo buys a bonnet for Mimi before meeting his friends, the Bohemians. Mimi's introduction to the Bohemians is really well handled by Pavarotti in this performance. The tempo set by Schippers is less frantic, enabling Pavarotti and allowing the music time to breathe. The phrase '*Quest'è Mimi gaia fiorai, il suo venir completa la bella compagnia*' is quite lovely, as is the passage '*dal mio cervello sbocciano i canti, dalle sue dita sbocciano i fior, dall'anime esultante sboccia l'amor, sboccia l'amor*'. One feels that Pavarotti is coming to terms with the subtext of this piece. He still has problems with the proper support at the end of phrases, and his release is not always good. Still, in this scene, his primary problem is his inability to bounce off the *acciaccatura* at the end of '*sboccia l'amor*'. This is not as insignificant as it would seem because these ornaments — *acciaccature*, *appoggiature* and *mordents* — are intrinsic to Puccini's work. Pavarotti either ignores them or does not execute them well.

Act III

The third act is particularly sensitive, passionate, poetic and stylish. Were it not for the Pavarotti, Freni, Von Karajan offering of La Bohème on the Decca label, this would be the finest depiction of Rodolfo in the history of the opera. It is a beautiful, sincere and boyish representation of the role. The only thing that would have made it even better would have been the application of more breath pressure to forge a firmer glottal closure, ensuring the stimulation of the higher harmonics and thereby creating a more brilliant ringing tone (more *squillo*). Pavarotti's onset and release of the sound have improved, but it is still a slight weakness. Too often, there is a surge of energy at the end of phrases, releasing a rush of breath on the final note. Although this is a less sophisticated interpretation of the role, it makes up for it with boyish charm and sincerity relative to von Karajan's offering.

Marcello Finalmente

Rodolfo's opening in the third act occurs after the enormous duet between Marcello and Mimi, beginning with the announcement that Rodolfo wants to separate from Mimi. Whereas in the earlier version, his cry '*Voglio separarmi da Mimi*' lacked line and control, his 1969 performance displays a good legato line, a better understanding of the text, and greater control over the problematic intervals and vowels such as the [i] in '*separate da Mimi*'. Pavarotti's 1969 performance of Rodolfo is still boyish, spontaneous, unaffected, and fresh-voiced. Still, relative to the 1961 and 1967 performances, the sound is now imbued with a new subtlety and depth of emotion. In the phrase such as *'Già un'altra volta credea morto il mio cor,'* both Schippers and Karajan move the tempo a great deal more than Molinari Pradelli and then follow it with an effective *rit.* on *'In van, in van nascondo la mia vera torture'.* This allows Pavarotti to feign a sense of exaggerated nonchalance before responding to Marcello's retort, *'I must say that you don't sound very sincere,'* to which Rodolfo responds, 'Ok, you are right, I am not. In vain, I hide my true sorrow. I love Mimi more than anything on earth, but I am so afraid. 'Mimi is very ill, every day she is declining'.

The quartet that begins with the phrase *'addio sognante vita che un tuo sorriso acqueta'* is beautifully sung and full of genuine anguish. The G♭ is beautifully collected. The B♭ in such phrases as *'mentre a primavera ci e compangno il suol'* and *'vuoi che aspettiam la primavera ancor';* these heart-breaking utterances are beautifully sung as is the A♭ in phrases such as are the [e] vowels and the [o] vowels in the phrases *'rimavo con carezze'* and *'ci lascierem alla stagion dei fior'.* The first phrase is as close to being caressed as any 'caress' on disc, and the second A♭ on *'ci lascerem alla stagion dei fior'* (we will part when the flowers are in bloom) produces a beautiful diminuendo at the very end. On the whole, this is one of Pavarotti's most successful efforts at soft singing on record, something which has not always been his forte. Even smaller moments such as *'ch'io da vero poeta'* and *'si parla coi gigli e le rose'* and *'chiacchiaren le fontane'* could easily have fallen into sentimentality but they do not. Finally, he ends the act with a beautiful B♭ in *'ci lascierem alla stagion dei fior'* before fading to a gorgeous soft cadenza.

Act IV

The final act brings the Bohemians back to the garret where we initially met them in the first act. Now, however, both Mimi and Musetta have departed, leaving Rodolfo and Marcello lonely and bereft of love. The girl's painful absence is felt everywhere. So much has changed, not only in their everyday lives but also within their souls. The two men are working on their respective projects, but things are not going well. In the first act, they are deprived of physical warmth and material well-being; in the last act, they seem to be materially better off but emotionally empty. Rodolfo is happy to report that he has seen Musetta, and she definitely does not miss Marcello. In fact, when he asked her, 'How's your heart, Musetta?' She answered that she couldn't feel it because of the thickness of the velvet she was wearing. In a move designed to counter Rodolfo's smugness, Marcello taunts him. 'I saw Mimi riding in a carriage dressed like a queen.' 'I am glad that she is still alive' is Rodolfo's retort.

It soon becomes evident that both of them are miserable as they retrieve memorabilia left behind by their sweethearts. In the beautiful and nostalgic duet '*O Mimì tu più non torni*' Rodolfo caresses Mimi's bonnet while Marcello kisses the ribbons left by Musetta. This duet is both introverted and nostalgic and more contained and thoughtful. At the start of the duet '*O Mimì tu più non torni, o giorni belli, piccole mani odorosi capelli,*' Rodolfo reminisces about their glory days of love when Mimi's tiny hands and the odour of her hair were enough to invade his senses and set his heart skipping a beat. Pavarotti sings very long phrases before taking a breath; the *passaggio* notes and head voice are rather wonderfully poised. This is singing of a very high calibre and a quantum leap from his previous efforts.

Chapter 28

L'elisir d'amore, Pavarotti, Sutherland: January–June, 1970

Nemorino, a young man from the village, is desperately in love with the beautiful but capricious Adina. She comes from a family of landowners, but he is just another peasant boy who falls in love with someone way beyond his status. Nonetheless, she cannot prevent him from loving her, and consequently, he spends a great deal of his time hanging around admiring her. His admiration evolves into his first aria, *'Quanto è bella, quanto è cara,'* in which he expresses his great affection for her beauty and her constant quest for knowledge: she is always reading, studying, and learning.

During a break from work, Adina recounts the story of Tristan and Isolde to the peasant workers who gather around her. The relevance to our story becomes even more apparent as she recalls how Tristan drank a magic potion in his quest to win Isolde's heart. This of course foreshadows the next scene in which Nemorino buys a love potion from Dulcamara.

Meanwhile, Sergeant Belcore arrives in the city square ahead of his regiment. He has a high opinion of himself and wastes no time attempting to charm Adina with his aria *'Come paride vezzoso'*. He soon asks her to marry him and cannot imagine a refusal. Adina is gracious in her response to the proposal but makes it clear that she is in no hurry to marry.

Everyone clears the square except for Nemorino and Adina. Left alone, she confesses that she really cares for him and has no desire to lead him on by giving him false hope. She suggests that he would be better off spending his time looking after his sick uncle rather than hanging around her in the hope of winning her affection. He responds, stating that his uncle's illness is nothing compared to his own pain. In the duet *'Chiede all'aura lusinghiera,'* she lightens the atmosphere by suggesting that he too should adopt her attitude and change the object of his affections every day. Nemorino replies that you may as well ask the river why it weaves its way towards the sea that beckons it.

They leave the stage only to return moments later as the ruckus from the villagers builds to a crescendo.

Suddenly, we have a grand entrance from a very colourful character who is really nothing more than a loveable rogue. In this instance, he presents as a travelling confidence man who goes by the name of Dr. Dulcamara. His patter aria *'Udite, Udite o rustiche'* is a little gem of the genre. It must be said that he is not at all a doctor, but he is very confident in the capacity of his elixirs to cure anything, and he is very happy to tell the world about it. Nonetheless, even he is initially taken aback when Nemorino asks if he sells the elixir of love consumed by Tristan to win Princess Isolde's heart. Dulcamara's reaction is, 'What?' However, he recovers quickly and exclaims, 'Of course, I have just the elixir for you.'

Nemorino is apologetic because he only has two ducats, but Dulcamara assures him that the sum will do nicely. He gives him a bottle of Bordeaux and explains that it takes 24 hours for the love potion to take effect. This should provide Dulcamara plenty of time to sell his wares and leave the village before his false claims are discovered. Nemorino drinks it immediately, and although the elixir is nothing more than a placebo, he convinces himself that he is already feeling the effect of the 'potion'. In the duet that follows *'Obligato, obligato, son felice son content,'* he sings of his happiness and his belief that tomorrow Adina will find him irresistible. Assuming an air of indifference towards Adina, he manages to irritate her, and as punishment for his obnoxious attitude, Adina begins flirting with Belcore, going as far as agreeing to marry him.

The plot backfires when the sergeant arrives brandishing an order commanding Belcore to return to his garrison immediately. He asks Adina to bring the wedding forward and she agrees to marry him that very evening. Shocked and saddened, Nemorino begs her to wait until tomorrow, but she carelessly dismisses his entreaties, inviting the entire village to the wedding. Nemorino is genuinely devastated at the thought of losing Adina forever.

Act II

At the wedding feast Adina and Dulcamara entertain the guests with a beautiful little duet, *'Io son ricco tu sei bella'.* Adina appears to be having a good time, but she is very much aware that Nemorino is missing. She is still cross with him and refuses to sign the marriage contract until he arrives, as she intends to make him suffer the pangs of unrequited love.

Meanwhile Nemorino is convinced that he needs another bottle of the elixir of love and as he has no more money, he is reduced to begging Dulcamara for it. The doctor refuses to give him the love potion without the money, but he agrees to provide Nemorino with more time to borrow the payment. Meanwhile Belcore needs help understanding why Adina keeps postponing the wedding.

When Nemorino tells him that he needs money right away, the sergeant persuades him to enlist in the army, and he will receive *'Venti scudi'.* This is a beautiful duet in which Belcore is delighted that he finally has his rival where he wants him, whilst Nemorino dramatises the possibilities of going to war. The truth is that he is glad to have the money to buy another bottle of elixir from Dulcamara. No sooner has he finished the drink than Giannetta and a group of village girls surround him. He naturally assumes that the mixture has finally taken effect, and they are all over him. These women really cannot help themselves! In fact, his newly found popularity has nothing to do with the elixir of love but, instead, everything to do with his altered status. We recall that in the first act, Adina made reference to his sick uncle, who apparently died and left Nemorino a considerable fortune, transforming him from a peasant boy to an eligible bachelor overnight.

Adina is saddened for causing Nemorino to enlist in the army, so she buys back his contract with Belcore. However, her nascent affections evaporate very quickly when she sees him with Giannetta and the other village girls. Dulcamara takes advantage of the situation by making exaggerated claims about the power of his elixir. He attempts to sell a bottle to Adina who rebuffs him, taking the opportunity to let him know that she is aware of his trickery.

Adina has been deeply affected by Nemorino's flirtations with the village girls. He now notices a tear running down her cheek and realises that finally his feelings are reciprocated. Nemorino reflects on these developments in 'Una furtive lagrima,' one of the most beautiful tenor arias ever written.

Adina breaks off her engagement with Sergeant Belcore but not before buying back Nemorino's army contract. She returns to the city square and announces to Nemorino in the aria 'Prendi per me sei libero' that he is free. She displays a genuine affection for him, but when he still feigns indifference, she is forced to confess her love to him, and he reaffirms his love for Adina. Returning to the city square, Belcore finds the couple embracing and consequently redirects his affections towards Giannetta, declaring that thousands of women await him elsewhere. Dulcamara on the other hand takes advantage of the new developments to exaggerate the efficacy of his miraculous elixir of love.

Critique of L'elisir d'amore (1970)

We begin the examination of this beautiful work with Nemorino's first act aria, '*Quanto è bella, quanto è cara*'. Pavarotti presents us with an excellent rendition of this beautiful aria, opening with a really lovely, warm, velvety tone. The Pavarotti voice really is an exquisite sound — natural and easy with a beautiful bloom — as well as sounding youthful, fresh, malleable and flexible. However, the voice is also a little heavy, too far back, and lacking in buoyancy. This is not because Pavarotti is trying to make it dramatic or unnecessarily dark but simply because his vertical laryngeal position is too low. In addition, the root of the tongue weighs heavily on the hyoid bone and epiglottis, often inducing a retroflex tongue, especially at the *passaggio*. The *appoggio* system is still inadequately activated.

Soon, it becomes evident that whilst the quality of the natural voice is splendid, some technical concerns, although better, persist. There are issues of insufficient follow-through, an onset and release that often need more firmness and precision, and an uneven sound at the *passaggio*. For instance, F4 is excessively heavy (eclipsing all the upper harmonics to the point where it's almost out of tune) which then requires the G4 to be lightened in order to access the head register. Also, the melismatic passages are uneven.

Does it matter? Yes, because it mattered to Pavarotti, who spent his whole life experimenting and working on perfecting the art.

The first issue that emerges from this examination is that Pavarotti is still thinking in terms of notes rather than thinking of singing through the phrase. Consequently, we hear that he still allows the larynx to rise and fall with the melody. For example, listening to the semitone between the E and F natural in the phrase '*più la vedo e più mi piace*', rather than mildly increasing sub-glottal pressure and singing through the words, he actually goes up to the F4.

Although this is easily fixed Pavarotti fails to do it because his teachers, good as they were, were not able to instil scientific knowledge. This knowledge arrives at the heart of the matter in a very simple manner which is easy to understand and manage. Too many teachers need to distil and synthesise knowledge by explaining it plainly and objectively, which would remove the mystery and uncertainty of training the voice.

The distillation of objective knowledge for the student is critical to the whole enterprise of teaching singing. Keep it simple, and don't complicate issues.

Technique

Let us analyse one of these defects and explain it in a scientific manner. If Pavarotti's teachers had taught him that there is little connection between the vertical position of the larynx and fundamental frequency, it would have saved him much time, experimentation and heartache. He should have been taught that fundamental frequency is a function of the tension, the length, the thickness and the general shape of the vocal folds (short or long, thick or thin, round and sharp, tense or relaxed).

The longer, thinner and more tense the vocal folds are, the higher the fundamental frequency issuing forth. A shorter, rounder and thicker vocalis would lower the frequency. The abduction of the vocal folds is also essential, but adduction is more of a determinant of quality of sound and not so much of frequency. A loose glottal adduction will issue into a breathy, veiled and dull sound. This is especially true in falsetto singing, during which the vocal folds fail to adduct completely.

On the other hand, a firm adduction issues into a brilliant, healthy tone that enjoys excellent carrying power and breath economy. This is because the vocal folds (glottis) adduct firmly and for a more extended closing phase, ensuring a perfect energy conversion and preventing air leakage. However, if you adduct the glottis to a still higher level of occlusion, you will most likely induce what is best known as pressed phonation. This could be better technically (too much glottal resistance) or aesthetically because the tone is too tight and pressurised. It is also the reason why we as singers must strive for complete dominance of our respiratory or *appoggio* system. This is simply because the elements discussed are a combined function of sub-glottal pressure and glottal resistance.

The teacher should explain what we know with respect to high laryngeal position. It shortens the vocal tract, aiding the resonator into taking the shape and size that is most conducive for the lateral vowels, as well as enhancing the higher formant frequencies which give the voice its brilliance.

The larynx lowers for the darker, round vowels and rises for the lateral, brilliant ones, with the [a] vowel being the most neutral. The tongue tip remains on the lower gum ridge, but the body of the tongue is raised and forward towards the hard palate for the lateral vowels and raised and back towards the soft palate for the rounder, darker vowels. The raising of the larynx for the very highest frequencies is designed to ensure correspondence between the vibrations emanating from the voice source and the formants of the vocal tract. In general, the higher the frequency, the shorter the vocal tract resonator is required for compatibility between the two elements of the source filter theory. Raising the larynx is not the only way to shorten the vocal tract. Miller (2000) reminds us that there is another way (in my view, a better one) of shortening the vocal tract, which is to use the hint of a smile, which will also serve to shorten the vocal tract. This was a strategy genuinely beloved by the old masters (please see my History of Vocal Pedagogy 2017)).

Consequently, it is not necessary to sing with a high larynx, especially when you consider the advantages accruing from a lowered larynx and a widened pharynx with respect to resonance. More specifically I refer to the resonatory benefits generated by the singer's formant, which requires a lowered larynx, widened pharynx, ventricles and pyriform sinuses. These conditions favour the singer's formant as espoused by Sundberg [Sundberg, 1974 & 1977].

With respect to the follow-through, the technique has more to do with unrelenting effort of distributing sub-glottal pressure and breath flow as required by each individual phrase and then mentally willing the sound waves through the vocal tract to the audience. So, it is not just about legato or mentally singing a little more forward or a little further back. It is about ensuring a consistent but variable pressure through the vocal folds and mentally following the soundwaves issued by the vocal folds as they are processed by the vocal tract and delivered to the audience. The singer's work is not complete until the last note, whether it be sung loudly or softly, is projected to the audience in the last row of the gods. I don't say that the act of thinking is not essential. In the end there is no substitute for a well-educated mind capable of planning the performance and remaining alert throughout, always ready to make the necessary adjustments during the performance. So, let me make it clear that I realise the importance of applied intelligence, for which there is no substitute. However, thinking in and of itself is not sufficient. There must be a physical reaction to the thinking, invariably involving sub-glottal pressure and just the right amount of breath energy. The latter provides a very strong theoretical framework capable of guiding the singer through the production and delivery process. This type of breath energy heightens the artistic aspects of singing.

What I have noticed here is that by the time Pavarotti ends the first phrase, he is unable to maintain the breath pressure on the last syllable [a] in *'quanto e cara'*. This is simply because the antagonistic action of the appoggio (internal and external intercostal muscles and the antagonistic action of the diaphragm and abdominals) has virtually been erased.

The same lack of follow-through is evident on the [a] vowel of *'Piu la vedo e piu mi piace'.* The G4 on the [o] vowel of *'son'* is too narrow, too constricted and too throaty.

At the end of the next phrase, the word *'inspirar'* needs more breath energy and a greater level of singing through the phrase, especially since the E4 on the [a] vowel is in the *'zona di passaggio,'* as well as falling on the first beat of the bar.

'Essa legge studia e impara' is all fine; the open F4 on the [a] vowel on *'impara'* is particularly well produced. The two G4s on the [o] vowels *'io son sempre un idiota, io non so che sospirar'* are too far back and too constricted, although the second [o] is marginally better than the first. The [a] vowel on the F4 just before the return to *'quanto e bella, quanto e cara'* is just an expression and should not be manufactured, but Pavarotti surrenders to the indiscriminate modification of the [o] vowel, which makes it too constricted. I like what James McKinney has to say about vowel integrity and identity [1994:159-160].

Consequently, and because the voice lacks adequate appoggio, it is too heavy, too dark, and too throaty. It remains true that a moderate vowel modulation can be very effective, not only for the rounding of the vowel and tone but also for the preparation for head register, especially on the F4 and F4 . The modulated vowel however should never migrate totally into the [o] vowel domain. In fact, vowel modification is at its best when it is subtle and temperate. In this case the vowel modification is too severe; the tone should begin more forward and not be allowed to undermine the overall beauty of the voice through a constricted throatiness. Returning to the theme, 'Quanto e bella' Pavarotti makes virtually the same errors in strategy. For instance, the accent on the 'quanto e cara' is once again ignored and under-energised. The same applies to the lack of energised follow-through on the semitone intervals, such as the [a] vowel on the word piace on the interval D4 to the E4. The same defect may be attributed to the accented G4 on the 'pa' syllable of 'non son capace'. This requires only a tiny adjustment of the mandible to transform it into a great sound. The remedy here is just a minor opening of the mandible and a slight lowering of the larynx with a concomitant adjustment of the appoggio.

In these passages Pavarotti should trust the breath and sing through the phrases rather than concern himself with individual notes. The following section is well managed mainly because these phrases are lively, bouncy and accented, sharing a natural vitality. However, the sustained G4 on the word 'd'inspirar' should display a more authentic [i] vowel. Ideally, it should also be less constricted and more forward, and both the tone and vowel should be more natural. In the cadenza, the chromatic passage on the G, F and F natural is uneven, especially the F . The sustained A4 sung on the [a] vowel in the final cadenza is a little throaty, and the vibrato is irregular. This is due to the under-energised breath supply (subglottal pressure) which at its best energises the whole instrument.

Chapter 29

La Traviata at the Metropolitan Opera, 1970

The next time we meet Pavarotti in the role of Alfredo is at the Metropolitan in 1970, where he shared the stage with Joan Sutherland, with Bonynge conducting. Pavarotti is certainly on more assured ground in this production. The voice is generally *ben appoggiata* and more secure. It is also more resonant, and the upper harmonics are greatly excited, providing the tone with a more forward and ringing quality.

Pavarotti employs a firm attack and a firm adduction (closure) of the vocal folds; the closure phase is maintained for a more extended period than it was in earlier recordings. However, some of the vowels are still too narrow; some of the *passaggio* notes are too collected and marginally under energised, creating a slightly unsteady vibrato.

Overall, this performance is more assured, more refined and, for a live performance, more consistently fulfilling. It is better than the 1979 studio recording issued by Decca, which I find pretty troubling in spots, purely because Pavarotti is falling into the trap of emulating Sutherland. His voice is too dark, placed too far back in the throat, and the tone is unusually opaque. In the 1979 rendition of '*La Traviata*', Pavarotti's voice sags and lacks buoyancy, causing the lovely translucent chiaro/scuro quality he displayed in his earlier recordings to suddenly vanish. He doesn't seem to be able to excite the upper harmonics, which add to the brilliance and vitality of the voice. This is the result of a loose respiratory strategy, which fails to induce sufficient glottal resistance and abrupt cessation of the breath flow, which alone can skew the glottal *glottogram* and excite the upper harmonics. When these settings are combined with a reasonably soft vocal tract wall, we can see why this results in flow phonation. This is the type of phonation that emphasises the excitation of the lower harmonics at the expense of the higher ones, which would generally furnish the tone with *squillo* or brilliance.

So, we are dealing with a hollow, dark type of sound which is neither *ben appoggiato* in the traditional sense of breath support nor focused forward against the zygomatic arch as may be expected from a tenor who was constantly seeking a forward production. In this instance, I agree with Jurgen

Kesting (1997) that Pavarotti was not in excellent form in this recording. It is well known in private circles that Pavarotti was going through a difficult emotional period, which unfortunately negatively impacted his vocal prowess during the late seventies. Kesting is correct when he suggests that Pavarotti's vocal physiognomy had changed, indicating that he had outgrown the role of Alfredo [Kesting, 1996: 171]. This theory makes perfect sense to me. By this time, Pavarotti had been singing *Un Ballo in Maschera, Il Trovatore, La Gioconda,* and *Turandot* on stage. He had already recorded *Cavalleria Rusticana* and *I Pagliacci* and *Tosca,* as well as other more dramatic roles. It would have been miraculous had this type of work not impacted on his lyrical singing.

La Traviata, 1992: Levine and Studer

However, in 1992 Pavarotti released another recording of *La Traviata* under Levine's direction in which his performance is of a much better level. Although no longer a young man — indeed he was fifty-seven at the time — the voice is *appogiata,* not only in terms of breath support but also in terms of leaning the sympathetic vibrations issuing from the sound wave against the zygomatic area. In this recording the tone is more forward because the vowels are formed more forward in the buccopharyngo cavity. The vocal folds are more firmly adducted, and the closed phase is longer in duration relative to the earlier recording. This configuration produces a spiky spectrum, stimulates the upper harmonics, and produces a more balanced chiaro/scuro tone. Amazingly, in this rendition of *La Traviata,* which was recorded some twelve years after the Sutherland Bonynge recording, the voice sounds not only more even and more secure but also more youthful. It is so gratifying to hear Pavarotti come through what must undoubtedly have been a very difficult mental and emotional struggle to regain his best form and reclaim his dominance in the realm of the *lirico spinto* repertoire.

Chapter 30

La Bohème, Pavarotti, Freni, Karajan, 1973

In this performance, Pavarotti's voice is, for the first time, imbued with that unique and non-characteristic Italian/Germanic sound. This collaboration between Pavarotti and Von Karajan yielded the most excellent depiction of this most popular of operas ever recorded. Von Karajan had a unique vision of this opera; it's almost Lieder-like in its sensibilities and pointing of the words, whilst Pavarotti brings that unbridled boyishness and Italian spontaneity that is infectious. He fulfils and compliments Von Karajan's vision in the most eloquent and creative manner. This truly is a synergistic meeting of minds and creativity. In this instance, the demands superimposed by Von Karajan on Pavarotti and this version of *La Boheme* have resulted in the most unique and glorious representation of this opera on record. The larynx is anchored by a combination of the sternothyroid, sternomastoid muscles and the laryngeally lowering action of the diaphragm. This is the result of a particularly strong *appoggio* due to the antagonistic action of the respiratory muscles (lotta vocale), resulting in a firmer, darker and more focused sound and steadier vibrato. In addition, Pavarotti utilises a firmer attack (onset), a lowered larynx and increased subglottal pressure (breath pressure) as well as glottal resistance to transfer the quality of the onset onto the sostenuto. The lowered larynx, the widened pharynx, combined with greater subglottal pressure forge a firmer connection between the larynx and the respiratory apparatus, yielding a better and more resonant tone with greater freedom of the articulators and evenness of fashion.

This performance of La Bohème is not only a more individual reading from the Schippers' account of the score but also a very different vocal production from Pavarotti. If we characterised the 1969 performance as flow phonation, the 1973 performance under Karajan demonstrates a much firmer phonation, the name of which comes from the tight glottal settings that offer a much greater level of glottal resistance to the subglottal pressure generated by the respiratory muscles. This type of production is generally characterised by an abrupt cessation of breath, a sharp and jagged spectrum that excites the upper harmonics at the expense of the lower, resulting in a harmonically rich sound that emphasises the brilliance, clarity and *squillo* of the voice rather than the velvety colour we highlighted in the Schippers' recording. Mind you, the very best singers manage to keep a little velvet in the *chiaro/scuro* sound, and Pavarotti does this very well. This recording confirms that he is undoubtedly one of the very greatest singers of all time. The *appoggio* system is not only more intense and emotional but also, as predicted by Lamperti, produces an aesthetically more appealing tone.

Consequently, diction, clarity and firmness of tone, as well as *impostazione*, all benefit from this newly found naturalness and freedom. The overall sound is broader, warmer, more voluminous and more incisive. The legato remains seamless and flowing, and the pronunciation has more clarity and definition. The larynx no longer rises with frequency (pitch) as it did in the 1961 recording, nor is it in a fixed high position as it was in the 1967 performance. However, it is not as consistently laryngeally relaxed (emphasising the lower harmonics) as it was in the 1969 RAI performance. In fact, the larynx assumes a consistently and moderately lower position. This position is maintained throughout with only minor and controlled variations, which are directly related to vowel differentiation and *aggiustamento* rather than alterations in pitch.

There is a strong connection between the breathing muscles and the vocal source, which, when complemented by inertial reactance, prevents the larynx from bobbing up and down with rising pitch. It also allows Pavarotti to make the necessary *aggiustamento*, adding just the right amount of [o] vowel to the [a], which slightly lowers the larynx, modifies the vowel and blends the two vowel colours into a ringing but still mellifluous sound. The same applies to the A natural on '*Eureka*'. Although supported, it is still a bit tight, unlike the B♭ on '*l'idea vampi in fiamma*' which displays much more freedom and generosity. This type of singing is what we call *canto appoggiato*, which in Italian means not only leaning the sound on the breath but also finding the correct focal point against which the sound waves impinge proprioceptively as the sound waves are directed out to the audience. According to Rachele Maragliano Mori, the Italian school advocates several focal points, but the most common is in the area framed by the zygomatic arch.

The following is a detailed analysis of arguably the finest rendition of *La Bohème* ever recorded. Von Karajan conducts an incredibly original and imaginative depiction of Puccini's masterpiece, and his creativity seems to have infected all of his artists who reward him with a performance of extraordinary quality. This *Bohème* is just fantastic, and Mirella Freni's Mimì is particularly memorable. Overall, however, it is Pavarotti's boyish, poetic and sincere representation of Rodolfo, not to mention his monumental vocal performance, that makes this *Bohème* quite irresistible.

The Opening of Act I

The opening scene begins with:

> 'Nei cieli bigi guardo fumar dai mille comignoli Parigi, e penso a quell poltrone d'un vecchio caminetto ingannatore, che vive in ozzio come un gran signor'.

All of these open phrases should have more presence, which would come about as the result of more follow through and breath energy. The [a] vowel on '*un gran signor*' is too closed and needs to be freer and more forward. The phrase '*Ed io Marcello non ti nascondo che non credo al sudor della fronte*' is sung with a high larynx, displaying laryngeal rigidity.

The phrase '*L'amor è un caminetto che sciupa troppo*' is all too narrow and too tight. This should have been sung with an open-throated balanced *chiaro/scuro* sound produced with a moderately lowered larynx, followed by a diminuendo. In the phrase '*L'ardente mia dramma ci scaldi*' the G4 on '*scaldi*' is much better, although still not my favourite sound. The phrases '*Zitto si dà il mio drama*' and '*fuoco ci vuole*' are tight and rigid.

Act II

The second act is set at the café Momus in the Latin Quarter of Paris. Having bought Mimì a lovely bonnet, Rodolfo tells her about his wealthy uncle with a promise to buy her more beautiful things. Rodolfo accompanies her to Momus, where his friends are waiting for them. His introduction of Mimì to the Bohemians is, as we have already stated, one of the most beautiful and poetic in all opera.

Pavarotti is absolutely fantastic in von Karajan's depiction of the work, with a sound that is warm and burnished with a velvety colour while maintaining the metal and brilliance of the voice. The tone is lovely and more *lirico spinto* than anything he has sung before. His introduction of Mimì ('*Dal mio cervello sbocciano i canti, dalle suoi dite sbocciano i fior, dall'anime esultante sboccia l'amor*'), is just marvellous. Not only is the singing powerful, balanced, and ringing, but also warm, emotional, and expressive.

Act III, The Barriere d'Enfier

In this performance, we begin to understand Rodolfo's misguided attempt to escape from the pain inflicted by his ill-fated relationship. With the phrases '*Amo Mimì sovra ogni cosa al mondo, io l'amo,*' followed by '*ma ho paura, ma ho paura*' and '*Mimì è tanto malata*' Rodolfo expresses his great love for her as well as the heart-wrenching situation of her fatal illness. However, as good as this performance is, the 1972 Karajan depiction is even more vivid, emotional, and heartfelt. Rodolfo's farewell following Mimi's '*Addio Senza Rancor*' is not only poetic and heartfelt but also restrained. Vocally this is an extraordinary performance: the sound is much firmer, with a much higher level of subglottal pressure than any performance hitherto. Pavarotti sings '*dunque e proprio finita, te ne vai, te ne vai la mia piccina, addio sogni d'amor*' not only softly but also with great emotional intensity. There is great tension between an emotional breathiness (consciously produced) and a generally firmer tone. Usually, I don't approve of a breathy tone, but in this instance, it constitutes a genuine effort to depict intense emotion, as expressed by the phrase '*she takes my breath away*'.

The quartet that begins with the phrase '*Addio sognante vita che un tuo sorriso acqueta*' is not only beautifully sung but also full of intense feeling bordering on anguish. The G♭s are beautifully collected, facilitating an easy entry into head register. The B flats in such phrases as '*mentre a primavera ci e compangno il suol*' and '*vuoi che aspettiam la primavera ancor*' are beautifully sung, as are the A♭s in phrases such as '*rimavo con carezze*' A delicately controlled phrase ('*ci lascierem alla stagion dei fior*') is supported by a beautifully poised sound. It is soft but extremely *appoggiata* so that the upper harmonics are strongly excited, embuing his *piano* singing with a really rich timbre. The first phrase is as close to being caressed as any on disc, and the second A♭ sung on '*alla stagion dei fior*' ('we will part when the flowers are in bloom' emphasises the loss of their love with a nostalgic diminuendo. Only at the very end does Pavarotti constrict the throat a little, but on the whole, this is one of his superior efforts at soft singing.

Even smaller moments such as '*ch'io da vero poeta,*' and '*si parla coi gigli e le rose*' and '*chiacchiaren le fontane*' avoid sentimentality and are a delight to listen to. These phrases are characterised by a lovely, firm tone, rich in harmonics but also flexible, playful and poignant. Finally, Pavarotti ends the act with a beautiful B♭ in '*ci lascierem alla stagion dei fior*'.

Act IV, Back to the Attic

The scene established for Act 4 of La Bohème, developed by Puccini in conjunction with Illica (librettist) and Giocosa (the poet), is a stroke of genius. Six hundred years earlier, Dante wrote that there are no more poignant moments in life than recalling happy times during a period of greatest despair. By bringing Rodolfo and Marcello back to the attic where they had lived happily with Mimi and Musetta, it only serves to highlight the absence of the two girls. Returning Rodolfo and Marcello to the garret, where we originally met them in happier times, is an inspirational move and an extraordinary piece of theatre. I sometimes feel that we do not sufficiently appreciate the marvellous structure and touching poetry in *La Bohème* - a most critical element in the astonishing success of this evergreen opera.

Having established the scene, we are reintroduced to Rodolfo and Marcello as they attempt to fulfil their artistic intentions. In the first act they are cold and hungry, but happy. In the last act they are simply miserable.

Rodolfo breaks the silence by announcing that he has seen Musetta, and she is not missing Marcello at all. In fact, when Rodolfo asks about her heart, she says *'I can't feel it for the thickness of the velvet I am wearing'.* Marcello counters that he too has seen someone. 'Musetta?' asks Rodolfo. 'No, Mimi' comes the reply, to which Rodolfo responds: 'Really, I am glad she is still alive.' It soon becomes evident that the two friends are both miserable without their lovers. In the expressive duet *'O Mimì tu più non torni'*, Rodolfo caresses Mimi's bonnet whilst Marcello surreptitiously kisses Musetta's ribbons.

This duet is far more contemplative and filled with inner longing in the Karajan version than any of Pavarotti's previous or later performances. The opening phrase *'O Mimì tu più non torni, o giorni belli, piccolo mani odorosi capelli'* (*'O Mimi, I know you will never return: gone are our golden days, the feel of your tiny hands, and exquisite scent of your hair'*), is full of genuine longing. Pavarotti's performance is characterised by long phrases and a natural ascent from the *passaggio* into head register. The voice is rather wonderfully poised, retaining a beautiful mixture of velvet and metallic edge. This is singing at a very high level and is a quantum leap from his previous efforts.

Comparison and Conclusion

Both performances demonstrate a poetic Rodolfo, but whereas in the 1969 performance, Pavarotti's voice is boyish, bright, spontaneous, and more homogenous in colour and expression, the 1973 performance is more mature, more sophisticated and imaginative in its presentation and sound world. The von Karajan performance is more introverted and thoughtful but also more controlled and less boisterous, with Pavarotti displaying a more excellent range of expression, colour, and dynamics. Karajan's concept is much more intellectual, original, controlled, creative and tempered, showing a greater variety of colours and depicting more complex and rounded characters. He was able to successfully convey this concept to Pavarotti with majestic results. In fact, one could argue that he uses not only Pavarotti but also Freni and Panerai to recreate Puccini's *La Bohème* in his own image. By the end, one feels that Karajan has transcended the role of interpreter and entered the domain of creator. It is so original, so different, so interesting, and so gloriously realised that you are at once grateful to have it committed to disc whilst at the same time lamenting the fact that we will never hear the likes of this again. This representation of *La Bohème* in general, and Pavarotti's depiction of Rodolfo in particular, is so close to perfection that one can only listen in wonderment.

Chapter 31

La Fille du Regiment, 1972/73

Set in the Austrian Alps, *La Fille du Régiment* is a an *opéra comique* in two Acts by Donizetti. It tells the story of Marie, an intrepid young orphan raised by a regiment of French soldiers. When the man of her dreams turns out to be a rebel fighting against the French family she has always known, Marie overcomes war, fatherly disapproval, and even the discovery of her own noble birth to achieve a happy-ever-after ending. Pavarotti's performance in the opera alongside Joan Sutherland at the Met in 1972 is considered by many as his breakthrough to stardom.

A Critique of La Fille du Régiment

At this stage of Pavarotti's career his lower register is still a lovely, warm sound but he has created a more balanced mixture of velvet and metal. The lower record is more forward and generally impinges on the zygomatic arch. This applies to the A4 on *instant* and *bras*. The main characteristic of this sound is that it has a great deal more drive than the earlier studio recording, with the upper harmonics exhibiting a greatly enriched timbre and *squillo*. The notes between the first and *secondo passaggio* (such as *sans peine je le quitterais*) are much more open-throated, exhibiting greater amplitude and ring. Pavarotti is no longer as concerned with changing registers, mainly because his new lower laryngeal position and firmer sub-glottal pressure have facilitated a more natural *passaggio* into head voice.

Pavarotti has discovered that lowering the larynx and widening the pharynx, combined with an increase in sub-glottal pressure, automatically facilitates the switch into the head register (*copertura*) whilst at the same time fulfilling the primary conditions for establishing the singer's formant. Consequently, he changes register whilst maintaining a more open and more natural tone on the *note di passaggio*. Having moved into head voice, the tone expands into a more ample, brilliant, and exciting sound.

On the other hand, the notes above the stave (such as the *affrettando* passage that begins with '*Epuis enfin de votre absence*') are emitted to a more forward position and are decidedly more energised. However, whilst the sound overall remains very beautiful, the tone is still contained, lean and quite small.

The phrases *'Epuis enfin de votre absence, ne pauvant vaincre le tourment'* are quite revealing. The [i] vowel on *puis* has a good ring about it, but the [e] on the F4 is not only collected but, in an effort to change register and move into head voice, Pavarotti closes the vowel too far, resulting in a lack of ring. On the other hand, the sequence of [a] vowels on the *'absence, peuvant',* and *tourment'* are all sung on a lovely open [a] vowel, which also incorporates a

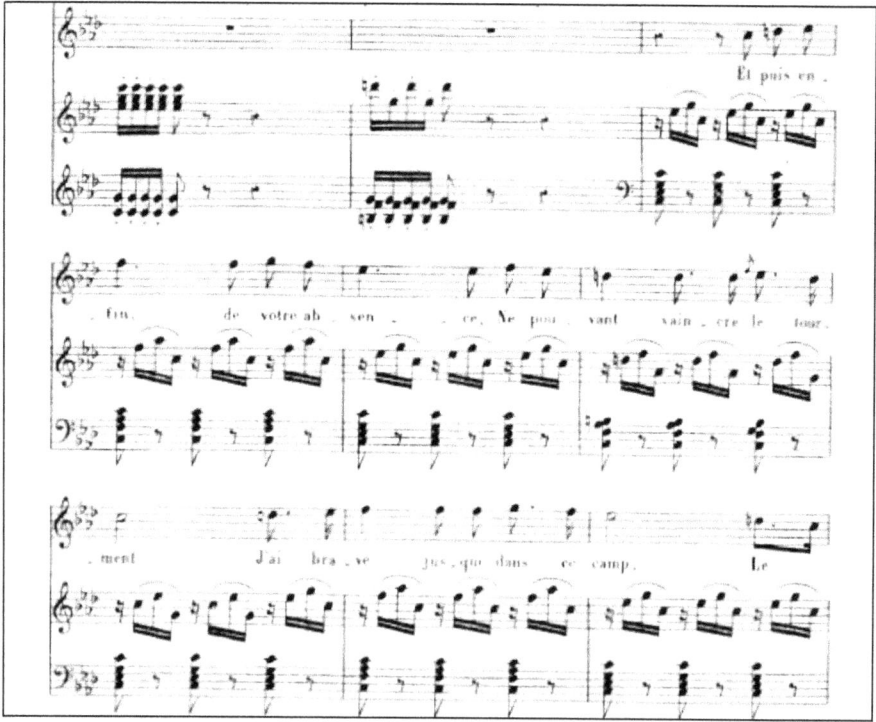

moderately lower larynx, a widened pharynx and an increase in breath pressure.

The phrase '*Je brave jusque dans ce camp*' is all a little more open and energised.

The passage on the repeated G naturals '*J'ai brave dans ce camp le coup d'une balle enemie*' is not only an excellent ringing tone but, in this 1973 performance, much more open-throated. More importantly, it is what we would refer to as '*voce appogiata*'. This is not only a far more generous and open-throated sound but also healthy vocalising. It has a newly found sense of both security and abandonment that was lacking in the 1967 performance. This passage displays a greater understanding of abandonment and a more overt display of emotion. It is the type of passion that expresses itself in an open-throated roar of the human spirit, which delighted his audience on opening night at the Met in February 1972 and was later celebrated all over America.

Having discussed the two performances in a general way, let us be more specific. The criteria by which we are going to judge the two performances are as follows.

Relative to the 1967 performance already discussed, the 1972/3 performances provide us with:

- A faster and firmer onset.

- An increased level of sub-glottal pressure and a higher level of breath energy.
- On the continuum from breathy to pressed phonation, this performance demonstrates a firm phonation, somewhere between loose and pressed.
- Glottal settings also display a firm closure and a longer closing time, especially at the top of the voice.
- Vocal tract configuration suggests that the zygomatic arch is high, as is the velum. The base of the tongue is higher in the pharynx, and therefore, the epiglottis is up, ensuring an unimpeded passage of the sound waves emanating from the source.
- The tip of the tongue is leaning against the gum ridge of the lower teeth for all vowels, whilst the dorsum of the tongue is more relaxed in its movement, arching up with a greater level of freedom.
- All vowels have more definition and greater clarity than they did in the 1967 performance.
- The passaggio, which had previously been implemented too carefully and rigidly, is now more open and relaxed in its execution. While in the 1967 performance, all the Fs at the passaggio were covered irrespective of vowels, in the 1972 performances, they remained not only open but also more ample and open-throated.
- The sound itself has gained in freedom, fullness, naturalness and ring.

The following passages contain specific comments designed to mark Pavarotti's progress.

Firstly, in the 1972 performance, the tone is much firmer, more nuanced and enjoys a greater sense of buoyancy and freedom. A greater variety of colours and dynamics are in evidence, and the tone is more open-throated and more natural around the *passaggio*. By 1972, Pavarotti was sufficiently relaxed to throw caution to the wind, releasing a freer, less studied, and deliberate tone than that which was evidenced in the 1967 recording. The second issue (revealed by repeated listening to the 1972 performance of *La Fille du Regiment* at the Metropolitan Opera) is that we can hear a vastly different tone issuing from Pavarotti's throat. I know that some people say that his voice did not alter much over the years, but that assertion is simply not true. Pavarotti's tone improved immensely over the next thirty years before entering a period of slow vocal decline. This was the natural consequence of an ageing musculature and ill-health.

1992 Version of the Duet Depuis L'istant

The best rendition I have heard of this duet by Pavarotti occurred in the Pavarotti Plus concert in 1992 at the Lincoln Centre with June Anderson. Anderson is absolutely charming and fresh-voiced in this duet, if somewhat uneven on an ascending scale. However, the performance that really captures one's attention is Pavarotti's *Tonio*. The voice is opulent, firm, and ringing, so even in its impeccable legato and so secure in the coordination between the antagonistic action of the respiratory muscles, the voice source and vocal tract (resonance) that it is difficult not to be in awe of the manner in which he has fulfilled the promise of his earlier performances. As well as being more even and secure, the performance is also more idiomatic, the attack being not only firmer but also more energetic and cushioned by the breath. It is therefore more even and controlled, the tone having evolved from flow phonation in 1967 to firm phonation in this performance. The *appoggio* is more emphatic both in the management of the respiratory support system and the resonance focal points which, through the skilled arrangement of the articulators, naturally aim the sound vibrations towards the zygomatic arch, but without ever forcing them there. This is just marvellous singing — Pavarotti at his best. The only possible reservation might have been related to the fact that he sounds more like Radames than Tonio. However, by then he was fifty-seven years of age and had been singing everything from Donizetti to Verdi's *Luisa Miller*, *Aida* and *Otello*. Let us be honest; no one can turn back the clock.

Fifty years in the theatre have taught me the truth of Francesco Lamperti's theory that the sounds that carry best over an orchestra in a large theatre are the more vibrant, forward-ringing sounds possessing a great deal of *squillo*. This type of sound is generally associated with the lateral vowels such as [e], [i], and the central vowel [a] rather than the rounded vowels such as [o] and [u]. These more brilliant sounds are enhanced by an excitation of the upper harmonics that induces the singing formant. This formant is comprised, according to Sundberg, of a combination of formats 3, 4, and 5 which are the result of a lowered larynx, a widened pharynx, open ventricles and pyriform sinuses. The singing formant is designed to give the voice its ring that will allow it to sail over the orchestra and carry to the back of the hall. It is all very good to enjoy a lovely velvety sound in the recording studio, but in the theatre, you need more *squillo*. Pavarotti knew this, and that is why, over the next few years, he worked relentlessly to bring the voice forward and away from the throat by manipulation of the articulators of the vocal tract and the development of a better *appoggio* strategy. By this I mean not only a superior *appoggio* of the breath but also a concomitant greater glottal resistance, as well as a manipulation of the articulators, in order to lean the sound waves forward against the upper palate. This is what real *appoggio* is about, and the concept should not be confined to the application of sub-glottal pressure. By these means alone can the resonating vocal tract be prepared: it involves raising the zygomatic arch and bringing the apex of the tongue forward against the surface of the lower gums, providing a free passage for the sound waves processed by the vocal tract and released into the theatre.

'Ah! mes amis' and 'A Mon Ame'

Pavarotti's depiction of this famous but extraordinarily difficult scene is a veritable tour de force, undoubtedly one of the most incredible displays of bravura singing on record. Consequently, I have concluded that rather than perform a detailed analysis of this scene, which may be interpreted as either lacking in generosity or being petty, it would be better to discuss this performance in general terms. Therefore, I have decided to give an example or two of the issues that may be of concern before proceeding to a comparison with the 1969 La Scala performance with Mirella Freni and the 1972 Metropolitan Opera performance with Sutherland.

With respect to the 1967 performance, I will start by saying that the sound in this scene may best be described as a lovely, warm, round tone that is both lyrical and flexible. The sound production may be characterised as a flow phonation with a medium glottal setting, a medium length, a closing phase and a sub-optimum sub-glottal pressure. The vocal tract length is too long in the lower register, mainly because the lips are protruding, the larynx is lowered, and the zygomatic arch is insufficiently raised. In the mixed and head register, however, the zygomatic arch rises, and the lips retreat to the hint of a smile. Overall, the sound maintains a youthful energy, a lyrical buoyancy, and a lightness of touch that culminates in a lovely legato line.

The first thing we notice about the 1967 performance is that Pavarotti is obsessed with the *passaggio*. He inevitably turns into head voice on the F4 independent of the vowel being sung, which is too early for a lyric tenor singing a lyrical role. Pavarotti's type and size of tenor voice generally turns on the F♯, especially in a lyrical role such as *La Fille du Regiment*. Even allowing that there is the occasion when passing into head register on the F4 may be more appropriate, Pavarotti's rigidity suggests that he is not thinking about the individual passage and the particular vowel. Leone Magiera emphasised that Luciano was quite manic about the *passaggio* and moving into head voice as soon as possible, and I find this to be an accurate assessment.

Consequently, we may state that too many of Pavarotti's F4 in this performance are dull, lacking clarity and definition. In the case of the [e] vowel on the F4, the aperture is tiny and frequently afflicted with a slightly retroflex tongue, resulting in a sound that lacks clarity, generosity and naturalness. My readers may assess the value of this appraisal by following the scene for themselves with the score below.

Our first realisation is that, beginning with the utterance '*drapeaux*' and its repetition on the next page, we are presented with a prototype of his *note di passaggio* F, F♯ and G at this point of his development. Following the score, we note that almost all the Fs are sung in a dull, veiled and slightly throaty head voice which is too constricted and too far back.

The second '*Je vais marcher sous vos drapeaux*,' which is sung on the E♭, F, F♯ and G, is much more ringing. However, the instrument could still do with more muscular support and a more collected [A] vowel on the F♯, so that the G on '*drapeaux*' would just evolve from the F♯, rather than accentuating the difference in the [A] and [O] vowels.

The idea of blending registers at the *passaggio* is to also blend the vowels. In this instance, the [A] F♯ should be more collected, and the [O] on the G4 should be lightly modified towards the [aw]. I think Pavarotti would have done even better had he concentrated on acoustic imperatives rather than the authenticity of the vowels. It remains a fact that if the F♯ is sufficiently collected (thus facilitating the *passaggio* into head register), then opening the G4 a little more will maintain the head voice but take on the characteristics of a more open and ringing sound with enhanced overtones.

Pavarotti produces a beautiful warm legato line on the phrase '*L'amour qui m'a tourne la tete*'. However, on the '*désormais*' of the following phrase he uses a hard attack at the onset of the sound. This causes the F natural on the [e] vowel to become percussive, followed by a tone that is too narrow, too far back, and too constricted. This is a defect that he repeats over and over on the F4 with most vowels, but in particular, the [o] and [e] vowels.

As an example, see the [o] on '*drapeaux*,' the [o] on '*écoutez moi*,' and the [e] on '*eh bien*'.

In the staccato phrase above Pavarotti loses the coordination between breath and larynx on the last bar G4 and A♭. This has the effect of allowing the larynx to rise indiscriminately with a concomitant deleterious impact on the sound.

The phrase above beginning with '*Oui, celle pour qui je respire. A me voeux a daigné sourire*' is a really lovely sound. However, the '*Et ce doux espoir*' he uses a hard attack resulting in a percussive tone.

On the other hand, the onset of the [a] vowel on the high B♭ that follows is insufficiently firm, allowing both the larynx and the tone to rise indiscriminately. Notably, in this instance, it remains a fact that just when the voice requires the tone to be launched with a *coup de glotte*, Pavarotti settles for an insipid onset (somewhere between breathy and simultaneous) in which the sound is initiated, and then the breath follows. This is the opposite of Garcia's *coup de glotte*. The resulting sound suggests that he would have been better off using a firm onset.

The '*Messieurs son pere, écoutez moi*' and '*Car je sais qu'il dépend de vous*' are just lovely phrases, and only towards the end of the last word does Pavarotti allow the external muscles to give way to the internals, allowing the diaphragm to rise. I hasten to add that this is a perfectly natural manoeuvre, but what we don't need is for the audience to hear it.

On the other hand, the next B♭ on the [e] vowel pertaining to the *m'aime* is a much firmer onset, resulting in a firmer tone that is more forward and ringing.

Pour Mon Ame

In the aria 'Pour mon ame' Pavarotti displays a wonderful sound, simultaneously warm, lean and brilliant. It has a lovely, easy, and lyrical tone, and Pavarotti refuses to get carried away with it. If anything, he is still a little careful until he arrives at the legendary 9 high C5s, and then he lets go. For instance, the opening pour on the G4 is quite slim and lyrical, as is the [e] '*in the 'quel destin*'. The [e] vowel on the G4 in the phrase '*J'ai sa flamme*' is a little tight and too narrow, which comment also applies to the je on the A4 that follows.

All of the [e] vowels above are too narrow and systematically tight, especially the [e] vowel on '*quell destin*' on the portamento up to the A♭. The A4 that follows on the [e] vowel in '*J'ai sa flame et j'ai sa main*' is not only too narrow, but Pavarotti approaches it from below. Whilst it is in tune, the narrowness of the vowel dampens the ring on the higher harmonics, giving the tone a sense of being flat as opposed to getting above it. To remedy this problem, which is widespread at this point in his career, Pavarotti would have to summon greater breath energy and build a sense of internal excitement about these passages, thus energising the tone. From a mechanical point of view, Pavarotti should raise the zygomatic arch and the velum, then arch the body of the tongue forward towards the hard palate, with the tip of the tongue resting against the gum ridge of the lower teeth. Even this will not suffice unless it is supported by a surge of breath energy, not only physical but also a mental and emotional response to the phrase.

La Fille du Regiment, Atlanta, May 1972, Pavarotti, Sutherland, Bonynge

In general, this depiction of Tonio is a much cleaner and more nuanced performance. The Pavarotti sound is characterised by greater amplitude and ring, the tone being much more forward, and the soundwaves aimed, but not pressed, towards the raised zygomatic arch.

The attack (onset) is much faster and incisive; the sostenuto sound that follows displays a more full-blooded, open-throated, and exciting *squillo*.

The tone production is no longer flow phonation as it was in the 1967 version but rather firm phonation, the result of an increased sub-glottal pressure inducing greater glottal resistance, firmer closure, and a longer than usual glottal-closing-time (i.e. the closed phase of vibratory cycle is longer than the open phase).

In order to accommodate the much richer harmonics emanating from the source, Pavarotti needs to reconfigure the articulators within the vocal tract in such a manner as to satisfy the more open-throated, ample and brilliant tone. More specifically, by 1972, in the lower register, the larynx had found a moderately higher vertical position, allowing the base of the tongue to find not only a more elevated position but also a more forward one, thereby alleviating downward pressure on the epiglottis, generally associated with a retroflex tongue.

At the same time, the tongue tip is leaning more consistently against the lower gum ridge, and the previously protruding lips have retreated into a gentle hint of a smile (please do not resort to grinning like a Cheshire cat). This configuration has the effect of shortening the vocal tract and raising all the formants, thereby enhancing the higher source partials and the natural brilliance of the voice. This muscular configuration is very different to the one adopted for the voice production on the 1967 recording.

Even this would not be enough to warrant such improvement relevant to the earlier Covent Garden performances had Pavarotti not also learned to increase sub-glottal pressure through a superior use of the antagonistic action of the internal and external respiratory muscles, thereby ensuring a firmer glottal adduction and a longer closure time. The ensuing spectrum is spiky in nature and skewing to the right. This type of glottal setting is cohesive with the higher laryngeal setting and shorter vocal tract discussed above.

In this performance, all of the articulators have been configured in such a way as to ensure that all the vowels have a greater level of definition, incisiveness and clarity. The articulators no longer exhibit the rigidity of the earlier performances, producing a freer sound with greater naturalness and ring (*squillo*).

Chapter 32

A Change of Direction

As always, having achieved this level of singing, Pavarotti went looking for another challenge. Sensing that he could not do much more to exhibit his high register, he decided to go in the opposite direction and judiciously darken his voice to incorporate heavier roles. Riccardo in *A Masked Ball* filled every requirement — darker than his high-sitting lyric roles but still in the realm of the darker full lyric tenor.

The city of choice for this role debut was San Francisco. Pavarotti had developed a very special relationship with the city and its artistic director Kurt Herbert Adler. He had made his debut there as Rodolfo in 1967 and his relationship with Adler had developed into a close friendship, not to mention that he really loved San Francisco and its opera company. It was a symbiotic artistic relationship; he felt really comfortable there and they loved him. Consequently, he decided to offer the city several role premiers.

It was about this time in 1973 that Pavarotti embarked on his unique concert career. His manager Herbert Breslin urged him to try it, the catalyst being an invitation from the city of Liberty in Missouri. At first, Pavarotti resisted, but Breslin rightly insisted as the venture was a major success. That same year, Pavarotti appeared at Carnegie Hall to great acclaim, followed by further concerts in Hyde Park London and Central Park New York, not to mention the phenomenon at Caracalla.

However, Pavarotti remained loyal to his operatic audiences with many performances scheduled every season, whilst at the same time bringing opera to the masses and in the process making a fortune.

The following year, he was back in San Francisco to perform his first Manrico in *Il Trovatore*. Truth to tell, he was now launching himself into the lirico-spinto repertoire. Needless to say, Pavarotti was too intelligent not to remain true to his voice, but in so doing, there were moments when his voice was too lyrical and light in colour to be totally convincing as Manrico. However, the sound was gorgeous and the beautiful legato in the cantabile of *'Ah si ben mio,'* which was readily contrasted with the more stentorian aspects of the *'Di Quella Pira,'* combined with a glorious top C5 at the end of the scene to ensure that Pavarotti triumphed over all obstacles.

Pavarotti's response to the criticism as to the appropriateness of his vocal colour for Trovatore was simple. His voice resembled that of Jussi Bjorling, who was a terrific Manrico, arguably the best.

At this point it is tempting to continue with the narrative of our hero Luciano Pavarotti, his story which being so compelling. However, the value of this book is not in the retelling of this beautiful story but rather the technical deviations that allow us to appreciate the vocal art so much more. In this type of book, I have a responsibility to analyse the technical aspects of singing. Consequently, I hope to ask and answer the questions about one of the better Italian schools of vocal pedagogy that nearly robbed the world of two genuinely great tenors, Carlo Bergonzi and Luciano Pavarotti. Bergonzi was singing in the wrong register as a baritone, meaning that he never had to put his voice under pressure. Pavarotti was so discouraged as a result of repeated vocal problems that he seriously considered giving up singing altogether.

Having reached his mid-forties, Pavarotti began to embrace a number of lirico spinto roles such as *Il Trovatore, Luisa Miller, I Pagliacci, La Gioconda* and *Aida*. They demanded a darker and more ample voice, particularly in the middle register, creating difficulties in the high register. He describes the process thus:

> With the natural darkening of the voice, I am moving more towards operas like *Un Ballo in Maschera, Luisa Miller, Tosca* and one day I would like to do Don Jose in *Carmen* [Pavarotti in Wright/1981: 138].

This is a natural progression for the tenor voice, and Pavarotti was no exception. The big difference was that, unlike most tenors, Pavarotti had constructed a spectacular international career founded on his high register and was widely known as king of the high Cs. Consequently, the idea of being unable to execute that fabled high note had the effect of creating an emotional dislocation in the form of a temporary but real psychological uncertainty. For a time, Pavarotti tried to manage both the high lyric repertoire and the more heroic *lirico spinto* repertoire, but he knew that this needed to be more sustainable. He would eventually conclude that in performing the more dramatic roles, you may have to say goodbye to *I Puritani*, but you may have said goodbye to *I Puritani* anyway [Pavarotti, in Wright, 1992: 291].

> His friend Dr Boeri, during a discussion with Pavarotti, declared that 'the voice is like a sheet of rubber; if you pull it one way, it loses something in the other dimension' [Wright/Pavarotti, 1981:136].

At first glance, this makes perfect sense, and Pavarotti certainly took it to heart, lightening all the first octave and a half of his range and concentrating on the power of the voice in his high register. This was an unfortunate development because it reduced not only the amplitude and intensity of his '*voce mista*' (mixed voice) but also the roundness and warmth of his vocal quality. To make things worse, it was all to no avail because the premise, whilst making sense generally, did not stand up to deep scrutiny.

We recall that Garcia defined a register as a series of notes produced with the same mechanism and issued in the same quality or timbre', a definition that is correct. However, this does not consider the fine mechanical adjustments required on almost every note within the series of notes that constitute a register. The truth is that each note of the scale is determined by a minutely different glottal setting, yielding an optimum sound for that particular tone in the scale. In that respect, every note could legitimately be seen as a mini but separate register, which deserves to be treated slightly differently from the notes that precede and follow it. This being the case, the idea of lightening a whole register to benefit the other is unnecessary, and it defeats the purpose of achieving an easy and seamless *passaggio*, thus cheating the audience. There are two ways of achieving this type of *passaggio*, the first being to lighten off the tone of the last two semitones just before the *passaggio* note to facilitate the *passaggio* into the head register. The second way is to cover the sound by lowering the larynx and collecting the tone for the two notes just before the *passaggio* note. This is not easy to achieve, and for a long time, Pavarotti could not find the right balance. He confessed to William Wright that:

> Over the years, the quality of the sound has changed little, thank heavens. It has, however, grown more prominent, more secure, more from the diaphragm. In the early years, my voice was a little more flying (not sitting on the breath) — it was too much in my throat and not under complete control. I think I have tamed it now [Pavarotti /Wright, 1981: 137].

It is to his everlasting credit that he eventually found that balance and he did so to a level that was unequal in the annals of singing.

Having found this balance he realised that he didn't have to put up with a sound that was throaty and not under complete control; a sound that was under-supported, lacking the breath energy to project the originating sound passed the throat, and to excite the higher harmonics. Nor did he have to put up with that lean, tightly focused sound that he produced in the second phase of his development.

His struggle to attain the optimum sound with the proper glottal settings, a beautifully balanced *appoggio* strategy as well as a refined sense of articulation and diction (which contribute to resonance balance and optimisation) represent the journey we are planning to undertake in this book.

Notwithstanding these observations, Pavarotti confessed to the fact that:

> Occasionally, I worry that my voice is not 'brown' and rich enough for the dramatic repertoire. It is not my desire to have a brown, dramatic sound. I want to have a clear

voice with a strong metallic sound, but not like a castrato [Wright/Pavarotti, 1981:137].

The result was a lightening of the middle voice in an effort to concentrate on the *squillo* of the head register, that is, the ring, brilliance, clarity and strength of the high register. To achieve this objective, he was obliged to raise the vertical laryngeal position as well as the zygomatic arch and reduce the forward projection of the lips, all of which had the effect of shortening the vocal tract and firming up the texture of the pharyngeal wall. This also had the effect of raising all the formants, but in particular, it enhanced the higher harmonics issuing from the vocal folds as they are swept through the formants in the resonator.

At a glottal level he induced a firmer onset followed by a firm and longer glottal closure time. This reduced the contraction of the vocalis muscle which allows the smooth contraction of the cricothyroids to stretch, lengthen, and tense the vocal folds, having the effect of reducing the mass and roundness.

He also altered the respiratory strategy to reflect the quest for a new artistic paradigm and a new aesthetic. We may recall that he originally altered his breathing strategy from *sostegno* to *appoggio* under Joan Sutherland's influence. This effectively meant that he went from an 'up and in' system to a 'down and out' strategy.

In terms of the resonator, he activated the zygomatic muscles and raised the zygomatic arch, which had previously been allowed to sag. This had the effect of not only emphasising his tremendous smile and raising the soft palate but also firming the internal texture of the pharyngeal wall. This had the effect of producing a less velvety, more metallic, brilliant sound that possessed greater carrying power and provided Pavarotti with that ultimate vocal distinctiveness — a bright, sunny sound.

This *appoggio* breath management strategy, combined with a firm glottal setting and highly flexible resonator (but one that resulted in a firm pharyngeal wall), yielded terrific results. In fact, one could argue that his very best recordings, such as *La Bohème, Turandot, Lucia, Rigoletto, La Fille du Regiment* and *I Puritani*, were all recorded under the *appoggio* system of breath management. Then, in an attempt to lighten the voice, he modified it again. He went from a really firm lower diaphragmatic/abdominal *appoggio* system of breath management (involving the transversus and internal and external obliques as well as the *quadratus lamborum* posteriorly) to a strategy that became a mixture of *appoggio* and *sostegno*. This saw the diaphragm and the abdominals meet at a higher level within the thoracic cavity in compliance with the higher laryngeal position already mentioned above. We should recall that there is a correlation between the vertical laryngeal position and the lowering of the diaphragm, which affects the laryngeal position through the tracheal pull. This higher diaphragmatic and laryngeal position is generally associated with the *sostegno* system of breath management. The latter emphasises not only a higher diaphragmatic position but also relies more on the internal and external intercostals for its lateral expansion. This occurs at the expense of the obliques and transversus abdominals and the lowered diaphragm, which are traditionally involved with the *appoggio* system. In addition, the *quadratus lamborum* muscles anchoring the posterior aspects of the diaphragm reduce their contraction, releasing the stable anchoring effect on the larynx, impeding the legato line and increasing the stentorian qualities of the sound. So, this quest for brilliance and *squillo* comes at a price, mainly the loss of the full-bodied sound. Using sufficient *vocalis* muscle and a moderately low larynx (combined with a firmer and more stable connection between the laryngeal and respiratory apparatus) has the effect of cushioning the larynx with a higher level of sub-glottal pressure. This enhances the intensity and stimulates both the upper partials of the tone and its emotional content.

For a time, Pavarotti went in the opposite direction, and consequently, his voice lost some of its lower harmonics, colour, roundness, and emotional intensity. It also diminished the connection between the respiratory and suspensory muscles of the larynx. This muscular configuration created not only a more percussive style of sound production but also contributed to a considerable loss of colour, fullness and amplitude. The resulting lyric voice was far too light and bright for the *spinto* repertoire. Ironically, this came at a time when he began recording and performing the more *Lirico Spinto* repertoire, such as *Tosca, I Pagliacci, La Gioconda, Il Trovatore, Aida,* and *Andrea Chenier* — roles that require more body and greater vocal amplitude. This deficiency in the lower harmonics contributed to the less-than-spectacular critical success of his dramatic depiction in these roles. My hypothesis is not confined to the roles above but rather to the entire dramatic repertoire that requires an open-throated middle register and a trumpet-like head voice, the absence of which would ensure that these roles would be out of his reach. At this time, a mutual friend of ours, Stefano Gottin (during a personal interview), was listening to Pavarotti rehearse in the studio of his beach home in Pesaro. He suggested that: 'although Luciano's singing was glorious, if he were to give a little more body and colour to the middle voice, it would be even more spectacular.' Pavarotti's reply was interesting:

> You are right, Stefano, but you know the voice is very elastic. If I put more weight in the middle register, it will affect the high register. Given that people pay a lot of money to hear my high notes, it would not be brilliant to do anything that will reduce the freedom, the brilliance, the ease of my high register [Interview, Stefano Gottin: 2019].

Giuseppe di Stefano also thought that Luciano's singing was too narrow. Pavarotti was inclined to listen to him, and he even made minor alterations designed to achieve a more open-throated sound. Overall, however, he was very cautious. He believed that di Stefano's sound was too open and therefore too dangerous, and he told him so, adding that for him Gianni Raimondi was a better model. Raimondi's voice was more compact and more focused, resulting in a much more reliable and consistent execution of the *passaggio* into the head register. Consequently, Pavarotti regarded Raimondi's collected technique as a much better model for him to emulate [Di Stefano in Wright, 1981:269].

This was a fact confirmed by Stefano Gottin, who, in his *everyday* visit with Pavarotti and also in a personal interview with me, informed us that:

> Pavarotti never copied anyone because he had an excellent teacher who was very good at resolving his problems. Nonetheless, he borrowed from everyone with admirable qualities. For instance, he borrowed the collected sound from Gianni Raimondi, the open sound from Di Stefano and the middle voice from Bergonzi [personal interview with Stefano Gottin].

The above notwithstanding, Pavarotti had more success with the spinto repertoire later in life due to yet another transformation in his production. This allowed the diaphragm and the larynx to find a lower position, bringing back some of the earlier colour, roundness and amplitude. At the same time, he maintained a raised zygomatic arch with a more natural forward position, sharper diction, and a harmonically richer forward sound, emphasising the second formant. He adopted a moderately low laryngeal position relative to the high one he had adopted in the late seventies and early eighties, and he returned to the *appoggio* system of breath management. In addition, he kept the high position of the zygomatic arch, which he adopted in the late sixties but which was missing in the early years of his career. The combination finally clicked, and the results were majestic.

Just as a matter of interest, the tenor who possessed the open-throated sound in the middle register and the trumpet-like head voice attributable to the dramatic tenor was Enrico Caruso. It is now widely accepted that whilst Caruso owned the first part of the twentieth century, especially in the dramatic repertoire, Pavarotti was the dominant tenor of the second part of the twentieth century. We will discuss these issues at length in this detailed study of Pavarotti's singing as it applies to different periods of his career.

Therefore, Pavarotti's outstanding achievement is confined to the lyric repertoire. His achievement within the Donizetti, Bellini, and the more lyric Verdi and Puccini roles (the Duke in *Rigoletto* and Rodolfo in *La Boheme*) was outstanding. Consequently, in this book, we seek the answers to these questions:

- What did Pavarotti achieve, and how did he achieve it?

- How did he overcome some of the problems that plagued him in his early years (many of which are still in evidence at the beginning of his recording career)?

Let us first deal with the characteristics that allowed him to achieve so much.

Herbert Breslin believed that when Pavarotti began his collaboration with Sutherland and Bonynge, Joan was the more significant star. However, as time went on, Luciano surpassed Joan; he was a more brilliant star than she was; he had all the power, popularity and notoriety that being a big star entailed. Unfortunately, the relationship with the Bonynges had not changed to reflect this new reality. Consequently, Pavarotti believed that he was not given the respect he deserved and became a little resentful.

Herbert Breslin recalls that Pavarotti was a straight arrow; he had integrity, and when he made a social contract with anybody, he delivered on it. His thirty-six-year relationship with Herbert Breslin was very instructive: they never agreed, the whole relationship being based on a handshake. Breslin recalls those early days with genuine affection:

> Luciano was still so young, fresh, and eager that everybody loved him. He was the most pleasant person in the world. I loved the guy. He was like an eager puppy. He was so excited about everything that was going to happen to him and so willing to do what everyone told him that you couldn't help but like him. And the voice, what I had heard of it, sent goose pimples up your arms. We hit it off right away. And I signed him up. Actually, signing up is the wrong term. In all our years together, I never had a contract with Luciano Pavarotti…But Luciano was a straight arrow: contract, or no, he was a man of his word. As was I. And Adua, his wife, who looked after their financial affairs, ran a tight ship. Still, I was shocked to find, between the first and fifth of the month, every month, that there was a bank transfer from Italy into my account for $250, which is what I charged for publicity back then. Usually, getting money out of an artist is like pulling teeth [Breslin, 2004: 46-7].

We gather from Breslin's commentary that the young Pavarotti possessed much more than a great voice. He had great integrity and disarming humility, and he knew where he stood in the pecking order. Even more importantly, he knew what he had yet to learn and where to seek help, which is a natural gift. These are tremendous qualities, but they also point to the seeds of future problems that could have and perhaps should have been anticipated. For instance, it would not have been too difficult to predict that anyone with his gifts and attitude would at some point become a master in his own right, which is precisely what happened. Then they would demand the space to take flight, which is also what transpired. Pavarotti remained loyal and grateful to all who helped him along the way, but it would be too much to ask that he should stay that young man who was so eager to please everyone he worked with. He also remembered where he came from and how far he had come.

Many years later, when Pavarotti was a superstar earning unbelievable fees, he still remembered vividly the fear he felt at the sound of the warplanes flying over Modena. He knew what was coming — the bombs that devastated his city, creating enduring and painfully raw memories.

He would recall:

> 'I know what war is; I know what it is to be bombed. War is when they bomb your city, not when you bomb the city of the other.'

The aftermath of war is often just as horrible as the war itself. Just when it appeared to have ended, the civil war started. Different groups were fighting for supremacy and power over the carcass left by World War II, which came to represent the new world order.

These horrendous wartime experiences, combined with the fact that at the age of twelve, he very nearly died, taught him something about the randomness of life and the vagaries of destiny. The wheel of fortune is always turning, and we never really know where it is going to stop. In Pavarotti's case, it was not a good place. They had actually called the parish priest to give him the last rites, but fortunately, through some kind of miracle, he survived. From then on, he felt that he had been saved for a reason, as life must, after all, have a purpose, some meaning. He gained a deepened enthusiasm for life and a genuine gratitude for everyday blessings, which translated into a strangely optimistic philosophy. He was eager to extend his knowledge, and for this purpose, he enlisted the help of many people from whom he thought he could learn. I believe his enthusiasm was genuine; I don't think he was trying to ingratiate himself to anyone. He was ambitious, gifted, and disposed to big dreams, and he knew that to achieve those dreams he had to develop his enormous natural talent.

The problem was that although he graciously acknowledged everyone who helped him along the way, his mentors missed his puppy-like eagerness, as well as his enthusiasm and his keenness to hang on to their every word. However, that expectation could have been more realistic. It is only natural that as an artist develops, they formulate their own ideas, especially in the case of an extraordinary pupil who surpasses the teacher. You cannot expect anybody as accomplished as Pavarotti to mature into one of the greatest tenors of all time and remain the same eager young boy he was at the beginning of his career. That would be highly unusual. As it was, he remained a perfectly grounded and humble human being.

Chapter 32 — A Change of Direction

I think it is a remarkable achievement by any standards that a provincial city of about 130,000 people at the time (many of whom were as poor as church mice during and after the war) could produce two immense international stars such as Luciano Pavarotti and Mirella Freni, at the same time, and literally from the same studio on Via Rua Mura 68, Modena. It is essential to mention here that I am not writing another biography but a critical review of Pavarotti's artistic and technical achievement, any criticism being part of a case study dedicated to the understanding and development of our art form and designed to save future generations the trouble of reinventing the wheel. In fact, I am hoping to explore not only the vocal but also the personal, psychological, and technical qualities that contributed to Pavarotti's enormous artistic achievement.

From the above, we learn that Pavarotti was enormously gifted, very intelligent, extremely determined, very hard working and humble enough to ask for help but astute enough to seek advice from the right people. We have also learned that Pavarotti knew how to honour his word and how to honour his teachers and parents. Separate from his glorious voice, Pavarotti comes across as a perfectly decent man with a well-developed philosophy who attained wisdom through adversity. This is the reason he never allowed his glorious success to undermine the richness of his humanity. He also accepted responsibility for developing and maintaining his extraordinary gift.

Later in life, you hear some critics murmuring about his work ethic. Shame on them! Pavarotti was not lazy when enthusiasm and hard work were required, especially in the first twenty years of his career. His wife, Adua Veroni, suggested that his attitude towards learning new works changed in later years; he had no such reluctance when they were young; he was very passionate and threw himself into projects with great gusto. Leone Magiera may hold the key as to why Pavarotti was reluctant to take on significant new projects in later years. Magiera coached Pavarotti in the title role of Verdi's *Don Carlo*, and for the first time, he became concerned about Pavarotti's memory. He told me that during the coaching sessions, pages that he would have pulverised very quickly just a few years earlier were now much more challenging to recall.

Consequently, he required a more extended period of time and much more repetition than previously in order to make the role second nature. Quite often, he would forget specific passages that they had conquered during their previous coaching session. It has been my experience that many of my colleagues began having memory problems when learning new work as they approached their mid to late fifties. This dilemma only applied to roles that they had performed a few times, especially in their youth. I am not making excuses for Pavarotti, but we should modify our expectations of artists as they age. Finally, it must be said that he no longer needed to work that hard. Whilst there was a time when he had known poverty and what it felt like to go without, fortunately that was long behind him. Most people understand that going without is a great motivator.

It must be said that his teachers, Arrigo Pola, Ettore Campogalliani, and Leone Magiera, always found him active and focused. The first twenty years of his career witnessed his persistent hard work and diligent nature. He not only debuted different roles in the major musical centres of the world but also produced a discography that is second to none and the envy of many. For years, he did everything that was asked of him. If, at some point, he then decided that he needed a better work/life balance, and if, in the process of realigning his life, he erred on the side of fun, good luck to him. Even his great rival Placido Domingo stated that Luciano's personality is deceptive: he appears to joke around and want to have fun, but underneath there is a lot more going on. He is a very deep thinker. Artists are not robots but human beings with a heightened sense of their own humanity, and generally, they do everything passionately, including working hard and, at different times, playing very hard. The other major flaw in Pavarotti's personality was the fact that he really needed friends around him all the time. It was not unusual for him to call a friend at 3 a.m. for a protracted conversation. This was especially so when he was in various parts of the world with different time zones. Joseph Volpe, long-time general manager of the Metropolitan, recounts an instant where Luciano rang him at two o'clock in the morning. Volpe answered the phone, and Luciano said, 'Joe, what are you doing,' to which the latter responded, 'As a matter of fact, I was asleep; it's two in the morning,' half expecting an apology and a 'please go back to sleep'. What he got was a long conversation because Luciano felt like talking.

In this chapter, I will give the last word to his Australian mentors, Joan Sutherland and Richard Bonynge. The latter, having hired Pavarotti for an Australian tour at the beginning of his career, confirmed his enthusiasm for learning about the voice. Bonynge would recall that: 'The voice was already first rate. It is the kind of great natural voice that comes along once in a century [Bonynge in Wright, 1981: 97].

Bonynge also affirms that Pavarotti has been very clever about managing his career. For many years he sang the high roles that other people couldn't sing and that essentially made his reputation. More recently, as his voice matured, he started gradually and carefully undertaking roles in the dramatic repertoire. According to Bonynge, 'He doesn't do anything without first giving it a great deal of thought. So far, he hasn't put a foot wrong. He's brought off *Gioconda*, *Turandot*, and *Trovatore*. These are all very tough roles.

Sutherland contends that his old singing teachers, Arrigo Pola and Ettore Campogalliani, enormously influenced how he cared for his voice. That is true, but Bonynge's rejoinder is even more interesting:

> Luciano himself has tremendous intelligence about the entire thing. He knows how far he can push people; he knows what he can get from people; he plays with his audience — I mean, in a good way. He enjoys his career. He's terribly career-oriented. He loves singing and the response he gets back from his audience. He loves the financial rewards; he loves everything about it. Why shouldn't he? [Sutherland/Bonynge in Wright, 1981: 100-102]

I think this is not only informative but also significant because it tells us that Pavarotti was prepared to take charge of his career.

Chapter 33

L'elisir d'amore, The Metropolitan Opera, Rescigno, 1981

This is a live performance from the Metropolitan Opera New York featuring Judith Blegen as Adina and conducted by Nicola Rescigno. It is very different from the Sutherland and Bonynge performance, mainly due to Pavarotti's own depiction of this, one of his favourite roles. The voice is much more even and under control than in 1971, as Pavarotti has rectified many of the issues that I criticised in his previous depiction of the role. For a start, Pavarotti has struck a much better balance between sub-glottal pressure, the voice source, and the resonator. Secondly, many of his vowels, especially the lateral vowels [i] and [e] and even the [a] and the [o], are substantially more authentic, with greater clarity and a cleaner onset than the 1971 edition. Thirdly, the voice is much more forward and ringing, and therefore, it is less throaty. This is mainly because the larynx has adopted a higher vertical position, helping to thin the vocal folds by eliminating some of the vocalis (vocal fold body) and utilising more of the cover. This adjustment at the glottal level, combined with more sub-glottal pressure, has induced greater glottal resistance and a longer closing phase. The resulting vocal fold shape, combined with a higher sitting resonator, was more conducive to a brilliant, brighter, and more flexible vocal tone.

Pavarotti took advantage of this new laryngeal and pharyngeal condition, combining it with greater control over respiration in order to sing the melismatic passages of the score not only more correctly but also more fluently and with greater fluidity. I declared earlier that coloratura singing was not Pavarotti's forte, but I am happy to confess that repeated listening convinced me of his competence in the coloratura passages — better than almost all other tenors attempting this role.

In this performance he also demonstrates a deeper understanding of the character, imbuing it with a spontaneous and refreshing sense of humour while retaining the human sensibilities. Due to substantial slimming, Pavarotti also looked the part, presenting a credible Nemorino, a considerable achievement by any standard. So why should I be more enthusiastic when he has amended many of the issues that I brought to your attention? The answer is that everything comes at a cost, and every singer must be astute as to whether the cost is worth the benefit. In this case, even though Pavarotti has undoubtedly attained a higher level of technical proficiency, his characterisation has lost its innocence and spontaneity, that wonderful *'joi de vivre'*: that youthful enthusiasm that compensated for an element of uncertainty. The tone quality has also lost something: it has become too constantly bright and metallic and has yielded the variety of colours we admired in the 1971 performance. It is all homogeneously bright, and the velvet that previously disguised the metallic quality at the core of the tone is gone. With respect to the chiaroscuro paradigm, we can say that the tone needs to find a better balance, this time by adding a small degree of *'colore oscuro'.* A vocal scientist would say it needs more first formant, giving the tone greater depth and roundness as well as a velvety quality whilst at the same time maintaining its forward ringing quality provided by the second formant.

Let us be more specific about this 1981 performance. Concerning the opening phrase, the tone is *'piu appoggiato'* — better supported, more balanced, more forward and ringing. However, a little more velvet was required in some phrases. If we are to achieve the seamless legato recommended by the great masters of the past, Pavarotti needs to follow through the vocal line even more. However, it must be said that the line is infinitely better in this edition than it was in the 1971 performance. However, the tone still needs a greater level of roundness and continuity within the *'zona di passaggio'*. As previously stated, the breath is more skilfully controlled in this performance, and it is demonstrably more flexible and responsive. This is especially evident in the execution of accents, ornamentation, and coloratura passages.

If I were to make another suggestion (I refer you to the excerpt above), it would be to attack the [a] vowel on the very first note in '*quanto e Bella, quanto e cara*' with greater firmness while at the same time aiming for a more lateral and more forward and leaner [a] vowel. Physiologically this requires a raising of the zygomatic arch and the hint of a smile as espoused by the ancient masters. As it is now the [a] vowel is too open for a low E3, creating too large a resonating space to correspond with the vibrations issuing from the larynx. Consequently, the tone remains back in the throat simply because, at this frequency, it is too difficult to raise breath power (energy) without pushing the tone. The remedy is to aim for a more lateral [a] vowel, combined with an excellent level of *appoggio* and more fantastic follow-through of the sound. It is important to sing through the vowel for the duration of the note and not allow the consonants to interfere with the vocal line. It is also important to remember that we sing on the vowels, not the consonants, although the continuants can be helpful. If you can manage to do this, you will eventually be able to sing through a seamless and continuous vocal line, not just in phrases but in pages of vocal music. Bettine McCaughan, one of my excellent teachers, constantly reminded me, 'The breath is the mortar that holds the vocal line together, and that vocal line should pour out of your mouth like liquid gold'. I know this citation is not very scientific, but it was effective, nonetheless. Much of the vocal pedagogy Arrigo Pola advocated to Pavarotti was not very scientific either, but I know no one who would argue against its efficacy.

With the above in mind, let us return to our analysis. In this instance, it would have helped if Pavarotti aimed the breath pressure towards the upper palate, followed through the rest of the phrase, remaining as close as possible to the original respiratory and articulatory position.

This is especially important when singing large intervals such as the sixth from the G3 to E4 on the syllables '*be*' and '*lla*' of '*Bella*,' followed by singing through the [a] vowel '*quanto e cara*' on the word '*quanto*'.

Pavarotti achieves these ideals to a much larger degree in this performance than in the 1971 presentation. So, what is he doing that is different? He is not mentally going up to the E4 but remains in position, raising the zygomatic arch and lowering the mandible. However above all he is reinforcing the *appoggio*. The results are in every way superior to the 1971 recording.

Furthermore, a close examination of this excerpt reveals that, in contrast, in the 1971 performance, Pavarotti was intent on emphasising the distinguishing features of each vowel; in the 1981 performance, he continued to differentiate the vowels. When he arrives at the mixed register (*zona di passaggio*), he switches his intentions towards moderate vowel modification, which yields greater unity of tone and continuity of line from the *passaggio* well into head register. This benefits the legato line because the follow-through emphasises the similarities in the vowels rather than the differences. Pavarotti achieves this really well, especially in the first 8 bars. It is in the last bar of the first part that I have something to contribute.

There are three suggestions that I would like to make, which I believe would improve an already outstanding performance:

1. In the first *'non-son capace'* excerpt above I like the accented G4 on the [o] vowel on the *'son'*. However, by the time he arrives at the end of the phrase on C4 on the [e] vowel, the voice quivers. This is because Pavarotti takes tiny breaths designed to get him through to the end of term, and by pressing the breath out of the lungs, he achieves two objectives. The first is to convert as much of the breath into acoustic energy and evacuate the lungs, preparing them for a deeper inspiration. In theory this is an excellent idea because it complies with the axiom, 'the release becomes the breath renewal'. However, the timing has to be just right. In this instance, Pavarotti miscalculates and finds himself short of breath.

2. He repeats the mistake on the [a] vowel, E4, at the end of *'inspirar'*. He is short of breath, and the vowel remains too open simply because he cannot collect it or focus it without adequate breath pressure. Consequently, the tone loses its roundness, colour and focus, becoming tremulous and white. This is similar to Garcia's *Voix Blanche*, which is determined by a high larynx and lowered velum.

3. To improve the performance further, Pavarotti needs to open the lateral vowels just a little and collect the back vowels, but above all, he needs to lower the diaphragm and take a deeper and bigger breath. The advice from the old masters was to take only as much breath as you need to sing the phrase to not overcrowd the lungs. This, however, is nothing more than an old wives' tale. There is no evidence that taking a bigger breath leads to overcrowding the lungs or that it leads to any harm. Think about the issues and do not blindly accept anyone's wisdom as absolute.

The old masters are worthy of respect because they have earned it. Look at what they managed to produce with the minimum of scientific and physiological knowledge. It is nothing short of miraculous. In this instance, their advice doesn't make sense. Think about this: even if you took the most enormous breath, and I am not suggesting that we are talking about beginning a note or a phrase with a capacity somewhere between 75% and 85%, nobody is advocating a straining of the lungs or 100% capacity every time you open your mouth. Furthermore, if you take a rather large breath, once you start singing, which generally is immediately after breath renewal, you begin pressing the breath out and converting it into acoustic energy, a process that immediately begins to release the pressure on the lungs. So, what possible harm can you do that would justify using an inferior technique that leaves you breathless?

Giovanni Battista Lamperti asks us to inhale sufficiently to satisfy the lungs but not to overcrowd them. On the other hand, his father, Francesco Lamperti, encourages his students to stay within their breath. He declares that care 'should be taken to finish the sound before the air in the lungs is completely exhausted' [Lamperti, c1883: 12]. Enrico Caruso informs us that in order to sustain the sound correctly, 'The lungs, in the first place, must be thoroughly filled. A tone begun with only half-filled lungs loses half of its authority and is very apt to be false in pitch' [Caruso, 1909: 53]. My position is definitely in the Francesco Lamperti and Enrico Caruso camp, which is supported by science (vocal scientists recommend a breath capacity of about 80% before the onset of sound).

Although Pavarotti sounds much better in the phrase '*ma non son capace,*' relative to the throaty tone he produced in the 1971 recording, he still does not totally understand that the [a] vowel on '*ra*' is too open and inadequately supported (*appoggiata*) for an E4 which is contiguous to the *secondo passaggio*. On an ascending scale, when the tenor reaches E4, the [a] vowel should be tinged with a small percentage of the [o], the larynx should be moderately low, and the *appoggio* must be firm but flexible. Breath capacity should ensure sufficient reserves not just to sing on but also to create an air cushion for the tone and stabilise the larynx. For an easy emission of the sound, Lamperti recommends that,

The pupil should breathe in as large a quantity of air as the lungs can contain, avoiding noises and all movements of the figure, significantly raising the shoulders, and striving to give consistently to his singing a semblance of ease and elegance. To attain this end, the mouth should retain a smiling expression [Lamperti, c1883: 13].

On the other hand, and as I stated above, today's scientific research suggests that taking a comfortable breath, somewhere between 75% to 85% of breath capacity, is not only sustainable but also manageable respiration.

Vocal science also recognises a direct correlation between diaphragmatic and laryngeal position — the lower the diaphragm, the lower the vertical position of the larynx. It follows from the above that a substantial inspiration automatically lowers the diaphragm unless interfered with and subsequently reduces the larynx. It is difficult to cushion the laryngeal mechanism with half-empty lungs, which leads to instability of both the respiratory and laryngeal mechanisms. Let us be clear: you need to inspire a specific minimum capacity of breath to build an air cushion and stabilise the vocal instrument.

In order to achieve this, you need a concomitant level of antagonistic muscular tension and tonicity of the respiratory muscles.

You cannot control the laryngeal position, the shape of the vocal folds, the onset and release of the voice, or the tension, length, thickness, and adduction of the vocal folds consciously or directly. However, you can achieve all this and more through the art of respiration and its concomitant laryngeal position. These also influence the configuration of the vocal folds and the articulators, especially the retroflex tongue. The latter is apt to push back on the hyoid bone and the epiglottis, an action that covers the laryngeal tube and impedes the sound waves from flowing directly into the vocal tract. Sub-glottic pressure is responsible for singing through the resonating vowels and following through on long phrases. When you lose control of the diaphragm, the previously raised chest begins to collapse. This leads not only to loss of control over respiration but also laryngeal position as well as the intrinsic and extrinsic muscles of the larynx, all of which influence the size and shape of the vocal tract.

In fact, if Pavarotti were to follow through the line with more significant breath pressure, the [a] vowel would be automatically modified towards the [o] whilst also fulfilling the requirements of legato singing and preparation for the *passaggio*, all under the dominion of sub-glottal pressure.

Let us return to our examination of 'Quanto e bella'.

On the phrase '*essa legge, studia, impara*', we find that the [a] vowel of '*impara*' on the F natural is an excellent sound, well rounded and well-grounded, with just the right shade of modification.

However, there are three G naturals on the extract above, none of which I like. They are all the product of a high larynx that is not at all mediated by a lowered diaphragm as this type of throw-away G sometimes is. Consequently, they are all too narrow, too constricted and off the breath, displaying a disconnect between the breath and the voice source.

On the other hand, the [ah] on the F4 natural that takes us back to the reprise of '*Quanto e bella, quanto e cara*', is unnecessarily sung as an [o] vowel.

This egregious distortion is caused by the protrusion of the lips which elongates the vocal tract and lowers all of the formants of the vocal tract. Ironically if Pavarotti had modified the vowel with a moderate degree of the [aw] sound, all of his problems would have been eliminated.

The G natural on the phrase '*non son capace*' (which, in my critique of the 1971 recording, I suggested should be more open) has, in fact, been rectified in the 1981 performance. Similarly, the G4 on the [a] vowel in the phrase '*In quel cor non son capace lieve affetto ad inspirar*' is a passage that I suggested should come more forward to take advantage of greater appoggio. It pleases me to say that all of the final cadenza in this performance is far superior to the previous one.

Chiede al Rio

The first thing we need to know about Nemorino is that he has a good heart and a compelling innocence. At the start of his journey, he is depicted as a lovesick peasant boy who later becomes a wealthy and more assertive character, thus making him a very attractive man.

The second issue we need to discuss is that the *tessitura* is nowhere near as onerous as many of Pavarotti's previous roles examined in these pages. Consequently, Pavarotti makes easy work of this role, bringing a beautifully modulated full lyric voice to the part. He is much more-full blooded as Nemorino, the voice is more robust, more open throated and more *appoggiata*. The improvement from *La Fille du Regiment* is quite spectacular.

I like the recitative very much as it displays a beautifully modulated tone with marvellous clarity of diction — altogether a wonderfully nuanced performance. The above notwithstanding, I often find myself yearning for a greater level of *piano* singing.

As I have said, the recitative is really well sung. There are however several minor issues that can teach us specific lessons. We encounter the first one in the recitative and duet analysed below.

We note that in the phrases '*Il suo mal none niente appresso al mio. Partirmi non possio, mille volte tentai*'. Pavarotti breaks with his usual forward, ringing tone. He instead takes the sound back, creating what the Italians call '*voce intubata*', which, as the name suggests, is a voice that remains intubated within the vocal tract. While I do not like this type of production in general, there is nothing wrong with it when utilised as an expressive tool as it is here. However, I do think there are other ways of expressing this kind of sentiment that do not require Nemorino to sound like a petulant child as he does here — having said that, it is an excellent contrast to the phrase '*E che m'importa*', which he sings in a contrasting heroic, slightly annoyed, or even angry tone. A further contrast comes in the phrase '*O di fame o d'amor, per me e tutto uno,*' sung with a beautiful piano tone. So, we can say that within these few short phrases before the duet proper, Pavarotti has unleashed a rich vein of contrasting but beautifully expressive tones that display great imagination and vocal intent.

The following excerpt I would like to examine is the coloratura at the beginning of his reprise of the central theme in the duet — '*Chiede al Rio perche geminate*'. I highlight this passage not so much to critique Pavarotti (because we know that coloratura singing was not his forte) but rather to learn something about the principles of tenor coloratura singing. However, Pavarotti is not the only great tenor to struggle with this, as other tenors with smaller and leaner voices than his, which should be more responsive and flexible to also fail the test. You would have noticed that I have been very careful in this volume not to compare Pavarotti to other singers, let alone any of his contemporaries (as tempting as that may be), simply because I am determined to examine Pavarotti's own development, which had nothing to do with other singers. This is especially true when we consider that no matter how great your achievement is, there is always something that even a lesser gifted singer can do better than you, simply because they have a more natural aptitude for it. So, the following paragraphs are not so much a criticism of Pavarotti but rather a lesson in how it should be done.

In order to achieve this criticism, we must first set up a critical framework from which we can assess achievement or failure.

The first significant element of agility and coloratura singing is, as with all singing, an appropriate breathing strategy. The correct breathing strategy for agility singing is, as has been argued above, the *sostegno* breath management strategy. In our previous discussion on breathing strategy, I have made it clear that while I subscribe to the *appoggio* system in general for sustained singing and maximum vocal output, I adhere to the principle that with respect to agility singing, the *sostegno* strategy is considerably more appropriate. We recall that whereas *appoggio* is a down-and-out strategy, *sostegno* is an up-and-in process. The *sostegno* model has been discussed extensively in these pages and will therefore be referred to rather than addressed in detail.

Another comment I would like to make concerning breathing and agility is that advocated by Francesco Lamperti. He gives us four distinct and appropriate strategies for coloratura or agility singing:

1. All agility should be studied slowly.
2. The breath should be held steady as we pass from one note to another.
3. These notes should be produced clearly and with a shock of the glottis.
4. Moderation in the study of agility is vital.

Practice should also be moderated simply because the voice is apt to become weak and tremulous through excessively rapid and prolonged use of agility, transforming what would have been a most beautiful embellishment into a most serious defect [Lamperti, 1983: 15].

The definition of the principle of holding is that the breath should be held steadily in the passage from one note to the other. This can only be achieved when the antagonistic action of the diaphragm and abdominals, combined with that of the internal and external intercostal muscles, check each other and enable the singer to maintain that position for as long as possible.

Lamperti also addresses the complicated and sometimes controversial issue of vocal onset. He states, 'It should be a neat, clean and precise attack on the note without any sliding or portamento, with the emphasis on releasing the breath upon which the agility can take buoyant flight' [Lamperti, 1883: 11].

The other element that requires discussion is the vertical laryngeal position. I agree with James McKinney, who encapsulates my own thoughts and experience of over fifty years in the theatre and forty years of teaching. McKinney states:

> Sounds that are too bright are often associated with a high laryngeal posture. Some singers, particularly ones with lower voices, start with the larynx comparatively low and then raise it progressively as pitch ascends, like an elevator moving from floor to floor in a department store. Other singers, chiefly ones with higher voices, tend to elevate the larynx as soon as phonation begins and force it even higher for the upper pitches. There is nothing in the laryngeal mechanism which requires that the larynx raise as pitch ascends or lowers as pitch descends, with the possible exception of the extremes of range and minor height adjustments associated with different vowels. Research has revealed that 'there is little laryngeal movement in many well-trained singers' [McKinney, 1994: 140-41].

We begin by analysing the above excerpt. This will allow us to learn some essential lessons about tenoreal agility and ornamentation, an area of singing that needs to be more frequently addressed by tenors, especially those of the full lyric to *lirico spinto* persuasion. We hear Pavarotti singing the repeated *'perche'* on the F natural and immediately realise that the voice has gained in brilliance, roundness and definition relative to the previous Donizetti recording *La Fille du regiment*. The voice is now much more focused, much richer in harmonics, much more balanced and more generous than his previous endeavours.

Duet — Chiedi al Rio 1981

Pavarotti should begin the phrase *'chiedi al rio'* with a greater degree of sub-glottal breath pressure, which would anchor the larynx in a moderately low position. More importantly, this position can be maintained without allowing the larynx to rise on the fourth between the [b] ♭ and [e] ♭ [per]. Once the singer breaks the nexus between the breath and the voice source, the larynx rises indiscriminately. This creates vocal conditions in which it is very difficult to execute both the turn or mordent on the [e] vowel of *che*, as well as the melismatic passage on the [e] vowel of *'gemente,'* with any authority and control.

Each note of the run on the [i] vowel of *vita* requires a definite articulation of the glottis, with a firm and precise coup de glotte, supported by the lateral expansion of the lower floating ribs. Please see the excerpt above for ease of following the analysis.

The next passage we are going to examine is the phrase *'e nel mar sen va a morir.'*

In the excerpt above, the [a] vowel of *'mar'* on the G4 is marked with an accent and should be sung with a more open-throated tone. If one is to execute the accent through an impulse from the brain that activates the breath, then it is imperative that we remind ourselves that sub-glottal pressure is the motivating force not only for opening the glottis but also for setting the vocal folds into vibration. The lowering of the diaphragm remains the optimum mechanism for lowering the larynx, opening the throat and maintaining a sostenuto tone with an open throat. Absent a relatively high sub-glottal pressure, the throat will close down and extinguish the natural tone and all emotional expression. Let us recall that singing is undoubtedly a physiological and athletic activity, but it is much more than that. It is about expressing excitement and emotions such as delight, melancholy and anger, qualities that are not determined by brute force.

We continue by stating that in the triplets on *'sen va a morir',* the voice should be more *appoggiata*, recalling that *appoggio* in the Italian school is not just breath. It also relates to focusing the tone in a particular area within the vocal tract that familiarity has taught us possesses the greatest concentration of proprioceptive sympathetic sensation to impinge in the vocal tract, which has become associated with the *appoggio* of certain vowels and frequencies. Ideally, the foundation note of each triplet should be guided in a generalised way to lean towards the mask, while the higher note of the triplet should be guided by the compressed breath pressure towards the same position. However, the sound waves should not be pushed towards the mask but also guided, remembering that in order to reverberate in the same position of the vocal tract, it is necessary to increase breath pressure. The great gift that Pavarotti shares with Caruso is the gift of moderation and patience, not pushing the sound forward but instead allowing the sound waves sufficient space to affect their compressions and rarefactions, which develop optimum resonance and great power and brilliance. Caruso recognised early that:

> In attacking a note, the breath must be directed to the focusing point on the palate, which lies just at the critical spot, and is different for every tone. In attacking a note, however, there must be no pressure on this place, because if there are the overtones will not be unable to soar and sound with the tone [Caruso, 1909: 26].

The next syllable for examination is the [i] vowel on *'trascina'.* Pavarotti sings this [i] vowel very well, but it would be even better if he resisted the temptation to place the [i] vowel, which stiffens the larynx. He should trust the breath a little more thus creating just the right space and finding a greater level of freedom.

People speak about trusting the breath, but I must say that after 50 years in the theatre and over forty years of teaching singing, I have concluded that the majority of teachers don't really know what that phrase signifies. It means that in specific strategic phrases, we make the decision to give the responsibility for the finer adjustments of the instrument over to the respiratory muscles. In this strategy the singer is exhorted to consciously guide the instrument into making the necessary adjustments on a macro level.

The micro or finer adjustments to the antagonistic reaction of the respiratory muscles, which constitute the *appoggio* system, have an influence not only on the adjustment of the vocal fold but also on the size and shape of the resonating cavity.

We achieve this by going back to first principles, understanding that the foundation of all singing is sub-glottal breath pressure. By engendering greater breath pressure and stilling the conscious mind, we prevent it from interfering with the sound. This allows the unconscious mind to collaborate with the natural wisdom embedded in the vocal instrument to guide it towards its natural course. This will prevent the singer from contriving the sound which must always remain natural.

The following phrase we will examine is '*un poter che non sa dir, un poter che non sa dir*.' Pavarotti modifies the [i] vowel of '*dir*' towards the [ir] vowel, a perfectly legitimate colouring strategy for the tenor on the G4. However, in this instance, there is a minor constriction in the throat, which is the product of inadequate breath pressure influencing the *appoggio* system. We recall that *appoggio* is described as '*la lotta vocale*', which is a reference to the antagonistic action of the internal and external intercostals or respiratory muscles, as well as the antagonists' posture between the diaphragm and the abdominals. The latter is significant in the *appoggio* system but also in the creation of the supra-glottal resonating space.

The problem is that too often, singers become very conscious of the details of their performance — an excellent artistic trait, but not when it comes at the expense of expressive freedom, fluidity, performance eloquence, and a wholistic approach. Nonetheless, I do concede that this attention to detail depicts the characteristic of a very good mind, capable of great imagination, creativity, and even planning. However, problems arise when we engage the conscious mind exclusively instead of finding a balance between conscious activity and the embedded wisdom within the instrument itself. The latter must be allowed to play its part in a balanced and wholistic performance. We should reiterate that respiration is the only element of the singing instrument over which we have conscious control, which is why, for many great teachers of the past, the art of singing was synonymous with the art of breathing.

Notwithstanding the plethora of scientific knowledge readily available, it remains a fact that the respiratory mechanism is still the only part of the instrument that we can influence directly. We certainly cannot consciously direct the adjustment of the vocal folds. Fortunately, there is a direct correlation between the lowering of the diaphragm and the vertical position of the larynx, and through that mechanism, we can influence both glottal adjustments and the shape of the resonator. Consequently, we can say that vowels can migrate too far from their authentic counterpart. In this instance,

Pavarotti encourages the [i] vowel to migrate towards the [ir], resulting in a final product that is a little throaty. I am sure that he modified the [i] vowel in order to be more seamlessly cohesive with the [u] vowel that follows. However, it was not necessary because for all the differences between these two vowels, especially with respect to the second formant, the lower formant or fundamental in both vowels is virtually identical, 340 cps.

The next lesson we should learn from this duet concerns style rather than a vocal defect. There is a breathy attack on the E4 [a] vowel just before the reprise of 'A te sola Io vedo Io sento'. However, the phrases that follow are quite lovely. I particularly like the diminuendo on the G4 on the word 'son' even though there is a moment when an increase in breath pressure would have led to a more even diminuendo. Let us look at the meaning of a breathy sound in more detail. The three issues to mention about a breathy tone are:

1. It does not carry very well in the theatre.

2. Breathy tone does not comply with breath economy as breath consumption is increased, whilst its conversion into acoustic power is diminished.

3. The vocal folds are not sufficiently adducted for optimal acoustic energy conversion simply because sub-glottal pressure is too low to coordinate the closure of the glottis.

We should keep in mind that Pavarotti was barely 35 when he recorded *L'elisir d'amore*, but he is already an excellent singer. Although the voice is sensational and one of the greatest tenor voices ever, we can hear that there is still work to be done. The breath is not as responsive as it should be. However, a tell-tale phrase occurs in the last bar.

We hear that the first G4 on 'amor' is not glorious but more than passable. However, the second G4 on the [a] vowel of 'ma' is marked with a diminuendo, but neither the diminuendo nor the authenticity of the [a] vowel is faithfully represented by this singer. The dark vowels such as [o] and [u] are all formed too far back in the throat, thus impacting on the placement of the [a] vowel of 'amor', which is also formed too far back. The truth is that the [a] vowel should be more forward relative to the [o] vowel simply because the larynx remains in a naturally higher position, and the tongue does not arch at the back of the pharynx as it does for the [u] and the [o] vowels. Consequently, the tongue remains flat in the mouth with the tip leaning on the lower teeth, and the lips do not participate in the formation of the [a] vowel as they do in the [o]. This prevents the protrusion of the lips and elongates the vocal tract, a configuration that lowers all the formants of the vocal tract and darkens the timbre of the voice.

Consequently, we can say that the [a] vowel in the *'ma'* should be formed more forward, and the diminuendo should be sung with a more authentic [a] vowel, but its success relies on the greater application of sub-glottal pressure (breath pressure) to support the transition from loud to soft singing, whilst also paying attention to the articulators, including the tongue, mandible, lips, and laryngeal position.

The 1981 Performance of L'Elisir, The Met, Pavarotti/Blegen/Rescigno

Pavarotti sings the introductory recitative to the duet with excellent diction and great clarity of tone. He understands not only the text but also the subtext, and he knows how to point out its meaning and colour its mood. Ironically enough, in this performance, he does not use the variety of colours nor display the vivid imagination he did in the 1970 recording. Nonetheless, I am pleased to report that many of the technical issues I critiqued in the 1971 performance have been rectified in the 1981 edition. In particular, I refer my reader to the following matters:

- The phrase '*Cara Adina non possio*' is much more open-throated and yet more forward and focused, simply because the *appoggio* is much more dynamic and active. Let us recall that a firm *appoggio* has the effect of opening the throat and energising the sound.

- The repeated '*perche, perche*' just before the '*chiede al Rio*' has much greater articulation and focus; the sound is more forward and more '*ringing*' yet possesses a balanced *chiaro/scuro*. Please observe that at the end of the second '*perche*', Pavarotti slightly protrudes the lips. The result is obvious and immediately audible. All the formants of the vocal tract are lowered, and as theorised by Sundberg, the sound becomes darker [Sundberg, 1977].

- The beginning of the aria '*Chiedi al Rio*' is firmer, more transparent and better focused than the 1971 production. Pavarotti executes the mordent on the '*perche*' very well, and the '*gemente*' is also well executed, except for the very end of the passage in which Pavarotti seems to run short of breath. This results in a somewhat unfocused tone that lacks a foundation. I believe the problem has its genesis at the beginning of the phrase when Pavarotti misses the entry to the first phrase. It would seem that he was temporarily thrown musically, causing him to take a shallow breath before entering. This may also be why he allows the first note on the [e] vowel of '*chiede*' to be formed a little back, although it is not throaty. The big lesson from the beginning of this duet is very simple: please do not produce any sound before taking a substantially deep breath. Remember Caruso's dictum:

- Once the tone is launched, one must think about how it may be properly sustained, and this is where the art of breathing is most concerned. The lungs, in the first place, should be thoroughly filled. A tone begun with only half-filled lungs less half its authority and is very apt to be false in pitch. 'A phrase began with half a breath loses half of its authority before it begins' [Caruso, 1909: 53]. Please see the musical excerpt below.

- The melismatic passage on the [i] vowel in the word *'vita'* is also greatly improved relative to the 1971 recording, but ideally, it could do with more glottal articulation.

- In the phrase *'e nel mar sen va a morir'*, the [a] vowel in the syllable *'mar'* is also much improved compared to the previous edition. The sound is more forward, more brilliant, and more focused. Can we still improve it, you might ask? Yes, by simply moderately lowering the laryngeal position and implementing greater *appoggio*. The same formula applies to the sequence of triplets in the thirds that follow the sustained [a] vowel on the G4. However, the larynx should not be lowered indiscriminately but rather begin in a moderately low position. It should remain in this lowered position for the third above the tonic while increasing sub-glottal pressure for the third above.

- The [i] vowel on the second syllable of '*strascina*' is too constricted a tone, the vowel is too narrow, the larynx is too high, and the vocal quality has lost much of the lower formant or *oscuro* component. It is a passage that Pavarotti has problems with a number of different performances, and yet the remedy is quite simple. Pavarotti should recall that in a difficult passage you must first still the mind, then consciously brace the appoggio musculature, which antagonistic action constitutes Lamperti's 'lotta vocale'. This muscular bracing is a really critical element of freeing the muscles of the throat, the neck, the temporal mandibular, and all the articulators. It is only when the respiratory musculature takes over the difficult work involved in supporting the instrument that we are able to sufficiently free the laryngeal and articulatory musculature to implement the physiological and muscular changes. The remedy here is a more dynamic and flexible *appoggio*, which encourages the diaphragm to lower, with a concomitant lowering of the larynx. This requires that the breathing muscles take over the heavy work, promoting an unparalleled degree of freedom for the articulators. Having achieved this newfound freedom, we are then able to make small adjustments to the opening of the mouth by dropping the jaw and placing the mouth and lips in a half smile position, placing the tip of the tongue on the lower teeth, and allowing the *appoggio* to take control. The results can be quite majestic.

- The diminuendo on the [a] vowel on the sustained E♭ is much better than 1971, but it reveals the persistence of a minor problem. As Pavarotti diminishes the tone from forte to piano without sufficiently reinforcing the sub-glottal pressure, it becomes evident that the tone quivers because the *appoggio* is still not totally under control. Francesco Lamperti is again eloquent when he suggests that: 'breath pressure should not be diminished as the singer transitions from forte to piano.... piano singing requires every bit as much appoggio as forte singing' [Lamperti, c1883: 19].

- The G natural on the [o] vowel in '*notte*' in the phrase '*giorno e notte in ogni ogetto*' is a good sound.

- Pavarotti sings the phrase '*Col cambiarse qual tu fai*' far too loudly:, it is completely out of character for Nemorino and out of line with bel canto singing. One of the major stylistic elements of bel canto is that you generally take over the melodic line from your singing partner with a sound of a similar timbre, unless the character and situation demands something different. Nemorino is not the kind of character that would shout at Adina.

- In the following phrase, '*puo cambiarsi un'altro amor, ma non puo, non puo gia mai il primiero fuggir dal cor*' I suggested previously that the [a] vowel in '*mai*' should be more forward and more open relative to the [o] that precedes it. Pavarotti is to be congratulated! He has undoubtedly rectified the problems underlined in the previous performance, if anything going a little too far in the opposite direction.

Adina Credimi

This is a very brief aria for Nemorino, and yet it makes a great impression on the audience due to the sincerity, depth of emotion and pathos it conveys. So far, we have seen different aspects of Nemorino's personality, mainly portrayed as the murmurings of a country bumpkin. Now, we become aware that he has much more depth and a richer vein of humanity than we had been led to believe.

Pavarotti's voice in this aria is absolutely wondrous. I just love the roundness, the power, and the slightly suppressed brilliance. However, despite the subtleties — a glorious legato line and a beautifully managed *passaggio* — the audience senses the hidden power within the velvet glove.

The opening phrases '*Adina credimi, te ne scongiuro. Non puoi sposarlo te ne oscuro*' are sung to perfection. Pavarotti has a great sense not only of the vocal line but also of the emotional stream necessary to do the aria not justice, both emotionally and musically. Just wonderful!

The first note that I would execute differently is the G♭ on the [a] vowel on the word '*aspetta*'. The voice may best be described as '*bene appoggiata*', which is the equivalent of a well-supported instrument that elicits a well-focused vocal tone. This is a consequence of the increased lowering of the diaphragm combined with a moderately high chest, lateral and posterior expansion at the level of the lower floating ribs, and a concomitant lowering of the larynx.

With regard to the phrase '*Un breve istante*', I really like the mixed register that Pavarotti is producing here. It is the result of a well-supported laryngeal position, allowing the singer to turn into pure head voice with ease and comfort. The '*io so perche*' is also a lovely tone. However, the [e] vowel in '*perche*' needs more follow-through with breath pressure, providing the tone with a sense of direction, which is the cornerstone of singing '*appoggiato*'.

The acciaccatura on the [a] vowel of '*domani*' should be bounced off the respiratory muscles and not the throat. This phrase is followed by the word '*cara*" to be sung on a pure [a] vowel. Ironically, Pavarotti, generally such a stickler for good diction, in this instance, allows the [a] to migrate too far towards the [o] vowel. This is deleterious not just to the diction but also to the following phrase, which ends with such an anaemic sound that it fails to provide guidance for the subsequent phrase. It does not allow the singer to renew the breath and return to an already favourable position.

According to Lamperti, the best way to proceed in these circumstances is to sing a beautifully placed and *appogiata* note at the end of the phrase, then release the tone through the clean abduction of the vocal folds, holding this position whilst renewing the breath. This breath renewal merges into the onset of the next phrase in the same position with the same tonal quality. It's a beautiful process, a seamless sequence of actions beneficial to both the vocal instrument and the legato line. If we do this as described above, we will see that the coloratura in the next phrase '*ne avreste pena*' just runs off the tongue smoothly and without changing position.

The other issue I would like to underline for very positive reasons is how well Pavarotti executes the *passaggio* in the next phrase, '*Domani forse,*' in which he opens the E4 on the [o] vowel of *forse* and then collects the F4, allowing it to go into head voice. This is vastly better than his earlier performances when he worked very hard but too rigidly to ensure that the *passaggio* into head register occurred on specific preordained notes. He is now much more relaxed about it, and consequently, the tone is more natural.

Adina Credimi (1981) Pavarotti/Blegen/Rescigno

The overall tone in this aria is more forward, brighter, and metallic than it was in the first rendition, but what it lacks is even more telling. The tone lacks warmth, velvet, a distinguishing individuality and, as a result, emotional poignancy. The greatness of Pavarotti's voice is not its sunny disposition or darkish velvety colour but rather that it has both aspects. In addition, there is a definite and solid edge around the boundaries of the tone as well as amplitude and shape. Therefore, at its best, it is one of the most complete voices of all time. However, in this particular aria, the voice lacks the burnished velvety colour to do it justice. Let us examine a few specific excerpts:

- The first important issue we notice in this rendition is how very different the onset on the G♭ on the [a] vowel is in the phrase '*aspetta ancora, un giorno solo*' relative to the 1971 performance. In my critique of the latter, I suggested that the G on '*aspetta*' should be attacked in head voice rather than medium voice. Pavarotti must have heard me because here it is more collected and a little headier, although I must confess that I would have wished to hear even more head voice than is displayed.

- The repeated G♭ on the [u] vowel in the phrase '*un giorno solo*' automatically goes into head voice.

- The phrase '*Te ne dorresti al par di me*' has an acciaccatura and an accent, both of which should be bounced off the air cushion and not the throat. To enable this, the breath should be buoyant and the larynx sufficiently free to lower for the purpose of combining with the appoggio. At this point it is essential to remain in the same position for the next phrase, '*al par di me*', which is an ornamental coloratura passage. Pavarotti is inclined to rise up to this passage.

- The lesson in this case concerns the smoothness of the *passaggio*. In the phrase '*domani forse*', the [o] vowel in the syllable '*for*' on the E4 is an open tone but sufficiently collected to facilitate the entry into head register on the [e] vowel of the syllable '*se*' on the F4.

Una Furtiva Lagrima is one of the most beautiful bel canto arias ever written, and Pavarotti does its justice. He begins very well, the opening F4 being beautifully poised with a wonderful tone.

Unfortunately, the [a] vowel on the C natural that ends the first phrase is a little anaemic, and in the opening of the second phrase, '*negli occhi suoi spunto,*' the G♭ onset on the [e] vowel is not only a little tight but soon migrates towards the [ir] vowel. The tone begins too far back and remains throaty, while the vowel is quite distorted. Let me be clear: for any other tenor, this sound would be a dream, but Pavarotti is not any other tenor, and he has just sung a ravishing phrase beginning on the F4.

However, in comparison with the first phrase, the G♭ is not a good sound.

Often, Pavarotti ends phrases in either an under-energised manner, which often distorts the vowel, or else with an abrupt release, which is either too explosive or too breathy. Either way, the release of the tone is not always good. This indicates a loss of antagonistic muscular contraction, which signifies that the inspiratory muscles surrender their antagonistic action to the expiratory muscles, thereby dismantling the traditional Italian *appoggio* system. This means that whilst still perfectly capable of singing in tune, the tone lacks authority, firmness, presence and vocal focus. These are the elements that generally infuse the sound with a distinguishing and very personal vocal quality. Caruso informs us that a tone begun with half a breath loses half its authority and is very apt to be false in pitch [Caruso, 1909: 53]. The remedy is furnished by Francesco Lamperti, who exhorts us to continue the *appoggio* beyond the end of the note we are singing rather than release the breath before we complete the tone [Lamperti, c1883].

An excellent example of this is the [a] vowel at the end of the first phrase in U*na furtiva lagrima*. The appoggio surrenders before the end of the phrase, leaving the final syllable, 'ma', to linger on in an under-energised fashion.

The second phrase, '*negli'occhi suoi spunto*', begins with a tight sound which is more an [ir] vowel than an [e], but I understand that Pavarotti believes this type of sound is more conducive to executing the *passaggio* in head voice. The truth is that Pavarotti has fixed the muscles of the throat and of all the articulators, including larynx, tongue, lips, jaw, and pharynx well before he starts singing. In so doing, he prevents the unconscious mind from making the final and finer adjustments of the articulators designed to ensure naturalness and spontaneity. The rest of the phrase is fine.

The attack on '*quelle festose e giovani*' should be cleaner, more forward and firmer; the tone should be more natural; the vowel should be a more authentic [e] and not so much an [ir]. Pavarotti is not covering the vocal tone in the traditional sense of covering; he is producing a throaty tone. Once again, Pavarotti created the vocal tract space he believed was correct for that vowel, and he then forced the vowel to resonate as best it could in the space he predetermined for it. But he is so firm and fixed in his ideas that there is insufficient room for finer adjustments. On the other hand, by the time he reaches the A♭ on the [o] vowel of '*festos*' the tone is much better.

The tone in the next phrase, '*Che piu cercando io vo*', is much better, but the [a] vowel on '*m'ama*,' while marked forte, is too explosive. The whole thing is unbalanced, and you don't have to sing loudly in order to attain greater clarity of tone. However, I will admit that it is easier not to have to concern yourself with dynamics in the early stages of development. There is no question that singing softly whilst remaining attached to the respiratory apparatus is too difficult a task for most beginners. However, there is no escaping the fact that ultimately a singer will be required to produce all shades, colours and dynamics of tone whether singing loudly or softly, high or low. Pavarotti demonstrates in other aspects of the role that he can indeed sing softly, so I can only assume that this lapse in artistic taste is for an effect.

In the next phrase the sustained [o] vowel on the F4 is too narrow and should be modified towards the [aw], especially when performing a crescendo as designated by the composer. Opening the [o] vowel towards the

[aw] would create greater freedom and facilitate a far smoother transition into the [a] vowel of 'mama'. However, Pavarotti explodes on this note with a pure [a] vowel, causing the larynx to rise. F4 in the tenor voice requires a minute modification towards the [o] vowel. This is another way of saying that the larynx should be delicately lowered, and even more so on '*si mama*' on the A. The diminuendo that follows on '*lo vedo*' starts too far in the throat, and the resonatory space is also too narrow, a position from which it never quite recovers.

In the second verse Pavarotti repeats many of the same mistakes but also accomplishes some very beautiful effects, especially with the later cadenzas.

From the beginning, the onset on the F4 on the first phrase '*un solo istante i palpiti*' is really quite lovely, but the attack on the G flat that follows in the phrase '*del suo bel cor sentir*' is once again too premeditated, too contrived and constricted.

The phrase '*I miei sospir confondere*' is again too predetermined, the resonating cavity is consciously too narrow, and the breath is under-energised. If you generate sufficient breath pressure through the *lotta vocale*, the antagonistic action of the respiratory muscles will provide you with the *appoggio* required to release any tension in the jaw, tongue and lips in order to make the necessary adjustments to the resonating cavity. The ensuing *appoggio*' will allow the singer to utilise the breath energy, freeing the tone from the throat. The [i] vowel in particular is apt to stick a little if the sub-glottal pressure applied for the task is inadequate. In this instance the problem is further complicated by the fact that the [i] vowel in *sospiri* has an accent.

On the other hand, Pavarotti overemphasises the accents in the phrase '*I palpiti, I palpiti sentir, confondere i miei co' suoi sospir*'. The accent should be determined by the vocal line, with the accented note remaining within the scope of that. This applies particularly to *bel canto* music, this aria being the epitome of that style. Pavarotti is on much surer ground in the cadenza finale where he sings two lovely top A4s in a glorious open throated sound.

Chapter 34

Un Ballo in Maschera, Pavarotti, Tebaldi, Bartoletti, 1970

The plot of *Un Ballo in Maschera* is driven by responsibilities and duties of state on one hand, conflicting human passions of unrequited and forbidden love on the other. How do you love and respect your best friend whilst lusting after his wife? Given that you are king who is used to getting what he wants, can you honour both parties and remain in a state of grace?

The action begins at the court of Gustavo II of Sweden, and the opening chorus establishes the dynamics of the court. Most of the king's subjects sing his praises and wish him well, while a dissenting group led by Tom and Samuel plans his demise. Gustavo is shown the guest list for an official gathering when he spots Amelia's name, and immediately, we are struck by his emotional response. He reveals his love for her in the beautiful aria, 'La rivedrò nell'estasi'. From the outset, Pavarotti displays a free, forward, ringing, and virile sound. The placement (*l'ipostazione*) of the sound is higher and much more forward than previous efforts. Let us be clear: Pavarotti is not forcing the sound high and forward like so many of his contemporaries; he is simply rearranging the articulators of the vocal tract to achieve this outcome. He begins with a moderate degree of elevation of the larynx, the soft palate and the zygomatic arch so that the sound waves experience a higher trajectory' and the vocal vibrations impinge in a higher position as they ring out in a forward position.

Pavarotti's voice is, as always, beautiful and fresh, with a great vocal ring interwoven with a light velvet bloom. The tone is best characterised as firm phonation, which occasionally becomes breathy and too often remains unstable. The tone is lyrical and lean but lacks both the depth and width to be a really great Riccardo. The legato is not always of a high standard, and many of the high notes are too narrow and have a pharyngeal orientation. They require more space as well as an increase in breath energy to bring the sound waves forward and maintain their position. Let us analyse this opening aria in more detail.

The opening phrase '*La rivedra nell'estasi raggianti di pallor*' requires a slight lowering of the larynx and widening of the pharynx in conjunction with increased but variable breath pressure. This strategy would relax the larynx and result in a more focused tone, facilitating greater mastery of the legato line. The [A] vowel on '*rivedra*' on the F4 needs a slight modification of the vowel or a slight lowering of the larynx, which would have the same effect provided that the diaphragm is also lowered sufficiently to harness the laryngeal position. With respect to focus, we are not talking about a tight focus that forces the sound forward against the zygomatic arch, but rather a focus in which intent guides and sub-glottal pressure sustains the well-defined but free resonance of the vocal tract. The vocal tract wall must remain firm', but the pharyngeal wall must not be spread, a condition that destroys flexibility and responsiveness.

This argument applies equally to the phrase '*raggiante di pallor,*' especially the last note on the [o] vowel in '*pallor*' which sags as a result of insufficient breath buoyancy sustained by breath pressure. Based on the auditory evidence it is not difficult to detect the existence of technical deficiencies and inadequate muscular response.

The phrase '*sonar d'amor*' requires more space on the top G♯ and more sub-glottal pressure to compensate for the greater amplitude. Revision of the resonatory and breath strategies would imbue the sound with a sense of generosity and excitement that is still lacking in this Pavarotti performance. The acciaccatura on '*sonar d'amore*' sounds laboured and lacking in energy and buoyancy, as does the breathy G♯ that follows.

The ascending phrase beginning with '*O dolce notte*' is all too careful and narrow, with none of the abandonment that is required to express these sentiments. This is a phrase that is built on a crescendo. As such, it should always be accompanied by an increase in sub-glottal pressure, with a moderate lowering of the larynx, raising the zygomatic arch and soft palate, and a small opening of the mouth and vowel, especially the F♯ and G♯ on the [o] and [e] vowels respectively. The [Ah] on the chromatic passage is a little uncertain and clumsy, as Pavarotti doesn't seem to know what he wants to express with it. He approaches the G♯ from below on the phrase '*Ma! La mia stella equesta*' while keeping the [e] vowel on '*Stella*' and '*questa*' far too narrow and excessively closed. Phrases such as these really need to be better supported with an increasing level of breath pressure on the ascending passage and a more open-throated tone, which can be achieved by lowering the larynx and widening the pharynx. Caruso believed as I do that, you can open the throat with the power of the breath without a wide opening of the mouth. There is a certain amount of space required in the larynx, the pyriform sinuses, and the oropharynx to ensure that the fundamental frequency issuing from the vocal folds is matched by the formant frequency of the optimum resonating space. This will have the effect of accessing the singing formant that provides the sound with a constant buzz (*squillo*) irrespective of pitch or the vowel being sung.

Pavarotti also approaches the phrases on '*sonar d'amor*' from below and hardly differentiates between the first time, in which the F♯ is not accentuated, and the second, which is not only accentuated but with proper management, can give the effect of syncopation.

The final A♯ is also found wanting, mainly because it lacks the breath management technique that would ensure sufficient subglottal pressure to maintain an open throat whilst also anchoring the larynx and cushioning the tone with a healthy reservoir of breath.

Di Tu Sei Fedele

The next aria I have selected for analysis is the barcarole '*Di tu sei fedele*,' a deceptively difficult and complex piece. Despite Pavarotti's enormous vocal gifts, we understand from the first phrase that he still had a great deal to learn about his physical instrument as well as the importance and power of nuanced interpretation, as opposed to general archetypal expression.

The opening phrase, '*Di tu sei fedele il flutto maspetta,*' tells us much about Pavarotti's state of mind and the state of his vocal technique at this point in time. From the opening bar we find that he raises the larynx in sympathy with rising frequency in order to negotiate the octave interval on the E♭ between the '*di*' and the '*tu*' on the E♭ an octave higher. He seems not to understand that the rise in pitch is primarily a function of increased vocal fold tension through the stretching, lengthening and thinning effect of the folds. This increase in vocal fold tension creates a firmer glottal resistance, which can only be overcome by an increase in breath pressure. An octave interval requires an increase in fundamental frequency, which can only be attained with a substantial increase of tension, requiring a commensurate sub-glottal pressure to counter the increased resistance. Sundberg (1987) estimates that a doubling of breath pressure is required for every octave interval.

Pavarotti fails to understand this principle, and as a result, we have a feeble, tremulous, unsteady [u] vowel on the E♭ that lacks both vowel definition and steady focus. If Pavarotti were to add a more constant albeit variable breath pressure, he would ensure a greater level of legato, more open vowels and an increased level of pitch and quality control. The larynx need not rise except for the very highest range, and then only lightly.

Loose phonation (production), such as we observe here, can lead to a mild nasality, as in the phrase '*il flutto maspetta,*' or throatiness, such as we observe in the phrases '*la donna diletta*' on the low E♭ and '*l'amor mio*' on the C♭. The latter lacks both sufficient breath-energy (pressure) and mental and physical follow through the note.

The problem of inadequate breath management also impacts accents and the ability to open vowels. It is the cause of rigidity in the articulators and the inability to tune vocal tract formants to the frequency of the partials issuing from the voice source (vocal folds). As an example,' I offer the phrase '*Con lacere vele e l'alma in tempesta i solchi so franger dell'onda funesta.*' The accent on the '*lacere*' is good, but there is no follow-through on the exact same accented notes on lacere *vele e l'alma in tempesta*'. In the phrase '*I solchi so frangere*' the vowel [o] is too closed, as is the A♭ on the [a] vowel in the phrase '*laverno ed il cielo irati sfidar*' which is crying out for a more open-throated sound. Pavarotti has not yet comprehended that open vowels cannot be sung to their full potential without a concomitant opening of the throat, which cannot happen unless the breath is in support of the instrument. Nor can the tone bloom in the high register as it is meant to do (such as the A♭ on the syllable '*irati sfidar*' if the throat is not sufficiently opened and the breath pressure is inadequate, which is the case here.

The next problem we encounter in this aria is the chromatic passage on the phrase '*Sollecita esplora, divina gli eventi; non possono i fulmini la rabbia dei venti, la morte, l'amore sviarmi dal mar.*' This is a really interesting passage, firstly because singing chromatic passages had not been Pavarotti's forte. To make this effective, one has to perform a crescendo on the apex of the ascending phrase on the words '*divana gli eventi*' and '*la rabbia dei venti,*' with a decrescendo to the lower notes of the respective musical phrases. Pavarotti's pitch, although better than previous efforts, is still occasionally questionable in these chromatic passages. However, his primary problem is that he keeps the notes at the *passaggio* all too narrow and too rigid, making it impossible for the upper harmonics to bloom acoustically. In the phrase that follows the repeated '*No, no, no*', the acciaccaturas are all heavy-handed. The acoustic energy in the phrase '*La morte, l'amor sviarmi dal mar*' is also very uneven.

The first phrases in the second verse are generally better, although some such as '*magita in grembo*' are quite throaty. The more important element to address is the incessant percussive tone occasioned by the octave jumps in this piece. Pavarotti seems unable to use the breath energy evenly or as required. He seems to find great energy for the first part of the phrase, and then it drops off tremendously, allowing the latter part of the phrase to sag and become throaty, lacking definition and buoyancy.

The phrase beginning with the words '*Ripeto fra tuoni ripeto fra tuoni*' requires a firmer focus. The phrase that follows- '*le dolci canzoni*'- is calling out for a more authentic [o] vowel, which would give the tone much more definition and imbue it with a more vibrant resonance. The repeat passage on '*le dolci canzoni del tetto natio, che I baci ricordo dell'ultimo addio*' is marked '*dolcissimo*', and in order for the piece to come to life, it requires a certain temperament and '*slancio*' towards the accented notes. Finally, it demands an efficient execution of the accented notes by bouncing them off the breath, with a certain lightness of touch rather than the heavy-handed approach adopted here. Pavarotti, although displaying a beautiful and honeyed tone, doesn't manage any of these ornaments well.

The A flat climax on the phrase '*e tutte raccendon le forze del cor*' is much better than in the previous passage. This is mainly due to the fact that the [o] vowel in '*cor*' is more sculpted and consequently has more definition, brilliance and completeness than many A♭ he delivers at this time. However, it could still do with a little more opening of the vowel and an increase in subglottal pressure, which would lower the larynx and produce an open throat. However, it has to be said that Caruso felt that you could open the throat without doing very much with the mouth and jaw at all. Caruso believed that: 'It must not be imagined that to open the mouth wide will do the same for the throat. If one is well versed in the art, one can open the throat perfectly without a perceptible opening of the mouth, merely by the power of respiration' [Caruso, 1909 :53].

The next chromatic passage on the phrase '*Su dunque risuoni la tua profezzia, di cio che puo sorgere dal fato qual sia; nell'anime nostre non entra terror*' is much better. Pavarotti is more secure with the chromatic passages and offers a much more nuanced crescendo/diminuendo passage, attaining greater resonance on the [i] vowel on the G 4.

The final A *sharp* climax on '*Nell'anime nostre non entra terror*' is in a much better position and the larynx is lower. However, the breath pressure is still inadequate for maintaining a buoyant tone, resulting in a forward and ringing sound.

Teco Io Sto

The next excerpt to be analysed is the duet '*Teco io sto*' in which Verdi brings his protagonists together for an intimate encounter — the first and only time in the opera. The audience knows from the start of the opera that Riccardo loves Amelia when he sees her name on the guest list ('*Amelia, e dessa ancor, e dessa ancor, l'anima mia*'). '*La rivedro n'ell'estasi*' follows — an ode to the ecstasy he feels every time he is in her presence. At this stage we believe she is not privy to Riccardo's intimate emotions.

Riccardo discovers Amelia's love for him during the scene in which she asks Ulrica for some herbs to quell the longing for unrequited love. Overhearing the conversation, Ricardo follows her to the burial ground. It is here that he witnesses Amelia's strength and courage as she withstands her fear of this monstrous world in order to do the right thing by her husband and child, as well as by the realm. At the end of her aria, Riccardo steps forward to sing '*Teco io sto*', which heralds the beginning of a gloriously impassioned love duet. Although it is not yet a complete portrayal vocally or dramatically, Pavarotti brings forth a truly beautiful lyric tone to the duet.

He begins with a narrow, lean but also fresh ringing sound on the G naturals, such as '*io lasciarti, no giammai*' and '*pieta chiedi e tremi ancora*'. It has a lovely tone but is a bit poked, lacking both flexibility and generosity. This can only come from an open-throated and enriched sound with a balanced fundamental or first formant. In the old parlance, it is described as an open-throated sound that has a better balance between the *chiaro/scuro* than Pavarotti manages in this performance.

The next section — '*Ah crudele in me rammemori*' — is a little self-indulgent for a mature sovereign but still has a lovely feel about it, and the tone is absolutely beautiful. It is followed by '*Non sai tu che di te resteria se cessassi di battere il cor*', which displays not only a lovely tone but also a more restrained and authentic portrayal of sovereign power.

Pavarotti presents a youthful, passionate and ardent monarch, thus bringing an authentic character to the stage. Above all this depiction of Riccardo's character is in keeping with Pavarotti's own youthful rise to power, and it is this synchronicity that gives this performance its authenticity.

Generally speaking, Riccardo's character requires a more mature and darker approach, with a more rounded and sustained tone. It also demands a more mature and nuanced character interpretation than Pavarotti is capable of bringing to the role at this stage of his development. I like the tone that he uses in this duet; it is lyrical, natural, energetic and virile whilst still not as driven as some of his later performances. In fact, much of the mixed register is a lovely resonant and warm tone that has its origins in flow phonation. The latter emphasises a flowing type of tone rather than firm phonation, the latter being representative of the next phase of his development, often represented by a mild phase of pressed phonation.

At any rate we are immediately aware that we are in the presence of something rather special. However, a more generous sound in the climaxes such as, '*Quante volte dal cielo implorai, la pieta che to chiedi da me*', would enhance his already excellent performance. This generosity could be easily achieved by judiciously dropping the jaw and moderately lowering the larynx. This would not only enhance the vocal performance but would also elicit sympathy for a character prepared to abandon himself to his emotions. As he pleads with Amelia to tell him she loves him - '*Un sol detto, un sol detto*' - the sound is all too careful, too narrow and not in keeping with the emotional state of the character. It is very difficult to achieve abandonment and authentic emotion when the sound itself shows no signs of yielding, let alone surrendering. Pavarotti's tone is often too direct, too ringing and too metallic, as in his response to Amelia's admission of love. He pleads with her to admit her love, and when she finally says, 'alright, I do love you,' he responds with a thin, brilliant and relatively cold sound on the top A natural on '*M'ami Amelia*'. When this phrase is repeated on the G *sharp* that follows, he shows no flexibility and no variation of colour, resulting in a tone that is not in keeping with the emotional content of the duet. Pavarotti is much better in the more dramatic outbursts — '*Oh sia distrutto il rimorso; l'amicizia nel mio seno: estinto tutto; tutto sia fuorche l'amor, fuorche l'amor*'.

In the passage '*Ah qual soave brivido lacceso petto irrora*' and then again in the '*Ah ch'io t'ascolti ancora rispondermi cosi!*', the medium register is just a lovely warm flowing tone. The first inopportune moment in this section occurs when he attacks the A4 on the phrase '*Astro di queste tenebre*'. He begins the A4 with a relatively low larynx, which is, in fact, where it should be. However, Pavarotti is unduly concerned about keeping the sound forward, releasing the breath, and causing the larynx to rise involuntarily. This has the effect of eliminating the *scuro a*spects of the tone, making the sound a little brighter but also more opaque and less complete. This is a mistake he repeats in the identical phrase two pages later, the A4 on '*Astro*' needing more fundamental. Finally, in the ascending phrase on '*irradiami d'amor, e piu non sorga il di*', we observe a tendency for the larynx to rise in sympathy with rising frequency (pitch). In instances such as these the larynx needs to be anchored and kept in position by the contraction of the respiratory muscles.

Forse La Soglia Attinse, and Ma se Me Forsa Perderti

The opening phrase, '*Forse la soglia attinse,* ' is just lovely singing and has a beautiful tone. However, Pavarotti spoils the next phrase, '*L'onor ed il dover*', by manufacturing the tone. The [o] vowel in '*onor*' is only an E♭, and there is no need for such severe vowel modification. This only serves to unbalance the vocal line long before he arrives at the modified G♭ on the [e] vowel in '*dover*'. This is the only vowel that should be modified in this phrase, but not as severely as Pavarotti modifies it here. The G4 on the [o] vowel in the phrase '*e la sua sposa lo seguira*' should be more open and better supported, as should the *piano* phrase '*e taccia il core*'. The first '*Ah lo segnata*' does not mean anything as it is presented as just a bunch of notes, not to mention the '*Ah*', which is meant to be an expression of sorrow but is also too short. The second '*Ah l'ho segnato*' is much better, but 'il sacrifizio mio' becomes a breathy, meaningless sound again. The phrase '*Ma se me forsa perderti*' is characterised by a beautiful sound with just the right amount of energy, but the onset of the next phrase ', *per sempre, o luce mia*', begins too far back and is approached from below, not to mention that the first note is out of focus. Pavarotti is not yet at the stage where he can strongly envision the sound he is aiming for before he arrives at it.

However, the G4 on the [a] vowel in the phrase '*a te verra il mio palpito*' is much better. The vowel is just a little more authentic and open, allowing the tone to ring freely. However, the [a] vowel on the A♭ in the phrase '*chiusa la tua memoria*' is again too narrow a space, as is the G♭ in '*quasi un desio fatale*'. These vowels need a larger resonator space and greater *appoggio* (support).

Pavarotti approaches the entire phrase '*come se fosse l'ultima*' (marked *dolce*) from below the note and then tries to crank it into focus. The same applies to the climatic phrase '*Come se fosse l'ultima*' which begins below the note and even though it improves it finally remains under the pitch for the duration.

The phrase '*oh qual presagio m'assale*' is generally characterised by a marked pianissimo. However, in this performance, the onset is too hard, the tone is too loud, and the *aggiustamento* too severe. The same applies to the next phrase, '*come se fosse l'ultima ora del nostro amor*'.

From the above, we may deduce that Pavarotti, notwithstanding the glory of his phenomenal voice, had several technical problems that needed to be resolved at this stage. Having said that, let me remind my reader that there are many glorious vocal events in this recording that are undoubtedly the result of previous problems solved. This man is a very harsh critique of his own work and no slouch when it comes to improving his craft.

Let us record the issues that have not yet been resolved:

- The first octave of the voice is sagging because the breath lacks buoyancy and sufficient sub glottal pressure (energy).

- This lack of dynamic buoyancy and sympathetic '*imposto*' tends to diminish efficient focus, allowing the voice to become dark and heavy. I don't have a problem with a multi-timbered voice. In fact, a darkish colour can be great, especially as a contrast to a naturally bright and sunny voice like Pavarotti's, but this requires a strategy, not an indiscriminate action.

- Pavarotti's '*appoggio*' system is inefficient: recall that '*appoggio*' in the Italian school is a combination of breath management, and proprioceptive sensations (focus).

- The majority of [e] vowels in this recording are too squeezed and narrow; they have too much point and too much metal.

- The [o] vowels in the head register are either too squeezed and/or unfocused; consequently, many of the [o] vowels are just under the pitch or have, at the very least, dampened the upper harmonics.
- Finally, the lower end of the voice is very breathy and weak and still in the developmental stage.

In conclusion, in the 1970 recording of '*Un Ballo in Maschera*', Pavarotti is in glorious, natural voice, but his incomplete technique does not yet allow him to maximise his God-given gifts. His vowels need more definition, and if he is to achieve his objective of producing a more brilliant and generous tone, he needs a moderately wider opening of the mouth and a more consistent and generous opening of the throat. The latter should be achieved by creating a more lateral vocal tract space rather than just lowering the larynx further, which will create a depressed larynx and hyoid bone and a spread pharyngeal space. His breath management is also a work in progress, and he is not yet at the stage where the educated ear can feel confident that he has mastered the different aspects of breath management. He seems incapable of producing an even tone on a sustained long phrase. Too often he begins a phrase with enormous energy only to fade towards the end of it. Also, he is, at times, heavy-handed with ornaments and passages that require dynamic flexibility, precision and charm.

To my readers who may think that I am getting heavy-handed with one of the greatest and most beloved artists of all time, I am happy to announce that Pavarotti goes a long way towards rectifying these problems in the 1982 Solti recording. I can't praise his progress if I don't first point to his early deficiencies. I can't leave this book, which is meant to be a learning tool for future generations, without emphasising the dangerous deviations and the ease with which an artist can fall into traps along the artistic journey.

Being confronted by the problems discussed above is fine: this is the process by which most great artists develop. We will know what type of artist Pavarotti really was when we examine his 1982 recording of *Ballo in Maschera* with Solti.

Chapter 35

Rigoletto, Sutherland, Pavarotti, Bonynge, June 1971

This 1971 performance of Verdi's Rigoletto was recorded at London's Kingsway Hall, and introduces the fresh voiced Luciano Pavarotti at the peak of his vocal powers. He is by turn brilliant and heroic, ardent, and passionate. He is often tender, but never less than glorious.

Sutherland too is in glorious voice, but her depiction of Gilda is more questionable, mainly because the voice is by now too dark and matronly to be a convincing ingenue.

In the first act aria, 'Questa o Quella', Pavarotti is clearly concentrating on his legato. He modifies both vowels on the word '*quella*,' colouring both the [E] and the [A] towards the [O] vowel. This was very much in line with Sutherland's technique but totally unnecessary in this part of the tenor voice. The vowel tracking in the middle and upper middle notes of the tenor range should be handled very delicately and with a lightness of touch. Heavy handedness is not only detrimental to the tone but also compromises the clarity of the text.

The lower E♭ in the phrases '*quan'altra dintorno*' and '*detestiamo qual morbo crudele*' is characterised by loose phonation. The notes do not have a foundation because the vocal folds fail to adduct and do not create a platform upon which to lay the first formant of the vowel.

This interferes with the collision of the tissue, which typically generates a firm closure for an unusually long period of time. This manoeuvre generates a rich series of overtones particularly in the lower register. This lack of firm adduction fails to create a firm platform can bounce back from the glottis and into the vocal tract (resonating cavities).

In contrast, the A on the phrase 'l'impero non cedo' is a good solid sound, which would, however, be improved by the opening of the [O] vowel. Pavarotti sings a closed vowel on 'cedo', but the Italian calls for an open one. Had he opened the vowel it would not only be more authentic, but it would also allow the tone to bloom, providing more amplitude and greater excitement. Pavarotti achieves this kind of amplitude on the next A♭ in which the vowel is more open and the sound much more exciting. However, the next set of A (in the phrases 'forse un'altra forse un'altra doman lo sara, un'altra,'...'si senti fedele,' and 'le smanie derido' all need more amplitude. The A s are generally solid enough, but they are narrow and too pointed. These are followed by the final B which is virtually an [I] vowel instead of an [e] in 'se' as designated in the score. Consistent generosity is not one of Pavarotti's great strengths at this point and, wonderful as the general tone is at this stage of his career, there are still traces of the early defects that betray his beginnings.

In the little duet with the countess Ceprano — *'Partite crudele'* following 'Questa o quella' — Pavarotti uses some really interesting and varied colours.

Some of the techniques he displays here are not generally recommended because they are ineffective in the opera house. He uses 'off the breath' singing to display charm and breathy singing to depict ardour. This is followed by the full-blooded and darkly coloured 'head voice' providing an excellent contrast. I generally don't approve of breathy singing, typically caused by insufficient closure of the vocal folds, and a failure to create the necessary resistance to the air being pressed from below the glottis. This type of manoeuvre fails to effectively convert airflow into acoustic energy and acoustic energy into power. It is not a sound that can be relied to carry well over the orchestra in a large theatre. However, this instance (in the controlled environment of the recording studio over a light orchestration of the minuet) is effective in demonstrating the different ploys used by the duke to conquer his quarry.

As already stated, the breathy tone produced in the phrases *'per voi già possente la fiamma d'amore inebria, conquide, distrugge il mio core'* is not a sound I would recommend for regular use in the opera house. However, in this instance, when combined with the full head voice in the phrases that follow, it creates an interesting contrast in a most imaginative manner.

Nonetheless, it is constructive to recall Francesco Lamperti's maxim in which he posits that :

> *Piano* should in all respects, with the exception of intensity, resemble the *forte*; it should possess the same depth, character, and feeling; it should be supported by an equal quantity of breath, and should have the same quality of tone, so that even when reduced to *pianissimo* it may be heard at as great a distance as the *forte* [Lamperti, 1883: 19].

This is absolutely correct. The only caveat would be that instead of an equal quantity of breath, it should read an equal intensity from the *lotta vocale* — the antagonistic tension between the internal and external respiratory muscles, including the antagonism between the abdominals and the diaphragm. Strictly speaking, these muscles do not support the sound as such, but they do support the instrument that produces that sound.

É Sol dell anima

In the duet '*É il sol dell'anima la vita e amore*', Pavarotti displays a near-perfect vocal line and a most interesting and powerful depiction of theatrical characterisation. This begins with the exclamation '*T'amo, t'amo ripetelo*,' revealing Pavarotti's displays of genuine temperament and ardour. He is indeed a very convincing and imaginative seducer.

Technically, it is also an excellent performance apart from a couple of mordents in the phrases '*sua voce é palpito del nostro core*' and '*umane fragile qui cose sono*', which I believe could have been handled more deftly. In addition, the accented phrase beginning with '*d'invidia a gl'umani sara per te*' is a little too jerky, but the overall performance of the duet displays almost perfect singing. Musically the tricky coloratura (ending the first part of the duet just before the '*addio, addio speranze ed anima*') is a little untidy and lacks fluidity. However, Sutherland pulls him through, and the tone is really quite lovely. He ends the second part of the duet (which he sings very passionately and with great temperament) on an excellent D♭, leaving one wondering if there has ever been a better duke in recorded history.

Ella mi fu Rapita

Despite specific timing problems, the first phrase, '*Ella mi fu rapita*,' is sung beautifully and with fine dramatic effect. However, I would prefer a more emotional tone for the narrative of this beautiful innocent who has managed to touch his heart for the first time. While the words are beautifully sung, the pointing of the text and emotional tension in the voice are sometimes misguided. However, the more dramatic outburst is managed with great vigour and conviction. There are a couple of technical problems that are almost not worth mentioning because they relate more to musicianship than they do to vocal issues. For instance, the phrase '*sull'orma corsa*' is not at all well-defined, with both sound quality and pitch being nebulous. The same applies to the phrase '*Ma ne avrò vendetta*'.

Parmi Veder le Lagrime

The [a] vowel in the syllable '*Par*' in '*Parmi veder le lagrime*' is a little too self-conscious. The phrase '*scorrenti da quel ciglio*' is much improved but the tone is still approached from below, remaining just a fraction under the pitch. As a consequence, even the '*quando*' that follows on the G♭4 requires a surge of breath energy, which would generate more overtones and tune the note perfectly. Unfortunately, it is not forthcoming. In the phrase '*del subito periglio*,' the '*subito*' is more in tune than the previous 1967 performance, but the pitch remains suspect. Musical errors persist in '*dell'amor nostro memore*'. Please see the excerpt below to ascertain that Pavarotti does not handle chromatic passages at all well.

Nonetheless, the phrase *'Ne dei potea soccorerti, cara fanciulla amata'* is characterised by really lovely singing, showing a genuine effort to colour the voice in a manner reflective of the text. In the phrase *'Ei che le sfere agl'angeli, ei che le sfere agl'angeli per te non invidio,'* the A♭ on the second *'angeli'* is a little breathy and throaty, suggesting insufficient breath pressure to ensure the necessary resistance at the glottal level.

The phrase *'per te non invidio'* contains incorrect musical notation. Even the top B♭, good as it is, could have been given over to the respiratory muscles a little more. The idea of really trusting the breath would have prevented the slight laryngeal ascent experienced here. This concept of trusting the breath, which comes down to us through the old masters, is intellectually widely accepted and as much in vogue as it is misunderstood. The truth is that very few people understand what trusting the breath really means. I become somewhat frustrated by people making all the right noises, assuming the right gestures, and then failing to take the necessary action. For an elaborate discussion on the subject see my *History of Vocal Pedagogy: Intuition and Science,* and *Vocal Science for Elite Singers.*

Overall, Pavarotti displays some exquisite singing in this incredibly difficult aria, but he never quite conquers it.

La Donna è Mobile

Pavarotti handles the famous aria *'La donna è mobile'* with just the right amount of irrepressible energy and a devil-may-care attitude. He is in excellent voice, allowing him to create not only the devil-may care nature of the Duke, but also his shadow side; the destructive side of his character, turning him into a loveable monster. The audience is confronted with the pressing idea of not one but two of our central characters (the Duke and Rigoletto) deteriorating before our very eyes — a distressing journey for any audience. Especially when the other two characters that populate the last act are an assassin (Sparafucile) and his sister (Maddalena) a prostitute. The only light on the hill is Gilda who is prepared to sacrifice herself to keep her lover alive.

At the beginning of the last act, Pavarotti is still capable of imbuing the duke with some genuine fire and irrepressible charm, but the irresponsible and destructive aspects of his character are yet to be revealed to Maddalena. Consequently, it is not at all surprising that Maddalena, herself no innocent maiden, is sufficiently mesmerised to plead for his life. Having already contracted to deliver the duke's body to Rigoletto, Sparafucile at first resists strenuously this misguided notion, but his sister's persistence erodes his resolve. He finally surrenders on the proviso that they find a substitute to place in Rigoletto's sack. Gilda overhears the conversation and decides to be a substitute for her lover.

Pavarotti's voice is just right for the role of the duke, and he is also well-suited temperamentally. This rendition of the very famous aria (followed by the *duettino* with Maddalena and the quartet) was destined to form a memorable scene, and it does.

I like Pavarotti's singing of *'La donna è Mobile'* in this recording. He seems to have the right measure and feel for the role, and the singing is not only beautiful but also of a very high level of technical proficiency. The only reservation I have about his singing at this time is that the connection between the respiratory muscles, the vocal folds (source) and resonators is not always maximised. In addition, practically all the high notes on the [e] vowel impinge on the position of the [i], making the tone too narrow and tight because the vertical laryngeal position is too high. On the other hand, the laryngeal position of the [er] vowel is too low, affecting the tongue position and making the sound a little throaty. It would be lovely from time to time to hear a generous, open-throated, authentic [e] vowel, but that is not the manner of Pavarotti's singing at this point in time, although the tone remains beautiful. However, I believe that I have provided sufficient constructive criticism in these pages for anyone wanting to learn about Pavarotti's technique.

Chapter 36

Lucia, Sutherland/Pavarotti, June–July 1971

The recording we are analysing next is the 1971 Bonynge, Sutherland and Pavarotti recording of *Lucia di Lammermoor*. This is such a fine performance that one is tempted merely to say that Pavarotti is in great voice, producing marvellous singing and arguably the finest depiction of the role on record, and leave it at that. In my estimation, that assessment would be absolutely correct, but that is not going to teach anybody anything about the role of Edgardo in Lucia. So, let us proceed with the analysis and see what we can learn.

In general, while the overall singing is lovely, there are four problems that Pavarotti should have been attending to. The first is that too often he uses the hard attack to initiate the sound. The second is that the respiratory system lacks agility and resilience, being a bit heavy-handed and muscle-bound. Thirdly, the vowels he is producing are typically passive and lack definition. The fourth issue refers to the fact that his vowels are not sufficiently sculpted by the articulators, a process that would give them more edge and definition. Consequently, too many vowels are too loose, creating a generalised vocal tract space. This gives the sound a predominantly ora-pharyngeal orientation that lacks the balance between it and the nasal pharynx resonators. This suggests that the sound lacks the focal point in the direction of the zygomatic arch. It is not at all clear whether Pavarotti uses his facial muscles and oral articulators in a visually and artistically expressive manner. These muscles are mostly passive, receiving the sound from the vocal folds instead of actively and skilfully adding their incisive and expressive touches while shaping the final product. While the work of the internal articulators goes largely unnoticed, it is also true that the active use of the articulation is usually reflected onto the facial muscles, becoming not only more involved in the production of sound but also visually more expressive of the drama.

Vocally, the first part of the recitative, beginning with '*Lucia perdona se ad ora inusitata io vederti chiedea*', is very well sung. Pavarotti is excellent at the beginning of the duet. It is not until he arrives at '*ma ti vidi e in cor mi naque altro affetto e l'ira taque*' that we realise he should open the [A] vowel in '*naque*' because it is too closed and too far back in the throat. A similar action is required for the [e] vowel in '*taque*', which is also a little distorted and throaty, with a tight sound.

The '*infranto*' on the A♭ of the triplet is little, but the attack on the B flat followed by the '*si, si, si*' is quite lovely, displaying ringing overtones.

The coloratura on '*più quel voto*' is lacking focus, as is the '*Io potrei*' that follows. This has the effect of producing loose singing which also mars the legato line.

The phrase '*Qui di sposa eterna fede, qui mi giura il cielo innante*' is all throaty, heavy and lacking focus and buoyancy, the connection between the respiratory apparatus and voice source being tenuous. The singing in the next section is excellent until we reach the interpolated A4 on the '*sempre cara*'. The note lacks focus, not so much because of faulty emission, but rather because it is under-supported. The upper harmonics need to be strengthened by a sharper cessation of breath flow and a greater skewing of the waveform.

When Pavarotti takes over the melody on '*verranno a te sull'aure*', it is all too loud and not at all in keeping with the mood set by Sutherland, whose style, in this instance, is much more appropriate. In a duet such as this, the two artists need to blend, with Pavarotti aiming for an elegant lyricism characterised by a forward ringing, brilliant and buoyant tone. The heavy-handed approach that we hear from him is far too loud and leaden. Similarly, the phrase '*Ah su questo pegno allor*' should be more agile and more buoyant. The sustained '*ah*' on the F4 should be more lyrical and flowing, ensuring a greater dynamic response from the breath, as well as a more authentic A vowel Rather than the intensely modified [O] vowel. This would give the phrase the buoyancy, lyricism and gentle vitality it requires. Similarly, the phrase '*I miei sospiri ardente*' is heavy and distorted. The acciaccaturas in the finale phrase just before the B♭ are too laboured, lacking agility and buoyancy. These should just be bounced off the diaphragm in a similar manner to a genuine staccato.

Chi Mi Frena

Just prior to the beginning of the sextet, Lucia has been coerced to marry her brother's wealthy ally, Arturo Bucklaw. No sooner has she signed the marriage contract against her better judgment than Edgardo announces himself. It was only a moment ago that Arturo had sought assurances from Enrico that rumours regarding Edgardo's courtship of Lucia were baseless.

At the beginning of the sextet '*Chi mi frena in tal momento*' there is some really lovely singing, although we note that there is a discrepancy between the piano marked in the score and the mezzo forte adopted by the singer. This is commonplace in major world theatres, and it is in fact normal for Pavarotti and Milnes.

The first criticism is the failure to perform the forte piano and the accent on the G♭. When these are followed by a *subito piano* (which also lightens the sound on the descending passage), an absolutely brilliant effect results. Unfortunately, it is not well executed here. In fact, notwithstanding some wonderful singing by Pavarotti, the overall effect is quite anaemic and tame.

The next problem arises on the acciaccatura on the '*T 'amo ingrata, t'amo ingrata, t'amo ancor*'. The first '*ingrata*' lacks precision, whilst the acciaccaturas on the two repeated phrases '*t'amo ingrata*' are very poorly realised, both vocally and dramatically. Pavarotti lacks the dynamic and flexible breath management to throw caution to the wind and spontaneously bounce these phrases off the diaphragm. In addition, there is too much laryngeal rigidity. As much as these acciaccaturas require dynamic breath management, they also require flexibility in order to instantly adjust at the laryngeal vestibule and vocal fold level before adjusting the resonator to reflect what is happening at the vocal fold level. It is only by strengthening the muscle fibres whilst simultaneously cultivating the dynamic flexibility required that Pavarotti may produce the spontaneous dramatic effect these ornaments are capable of. The piano interjections such as '*chi mi frena*' and '*in tal momento*' are quite lovely, but in the ascending passage on '*come rosa inarridita* I quite frankly cannot hear the triplet.

The next problem follows Sutherland's sustained B♭ on the ascending scale, after which the tenor joins her on an accented G♭ for the phrase '*t'amo ancor, si t'amo ancor*'. Pavarotti joins in at the correct time, but his tame approach does nothing to delineate and dramatically depict the pain and torment he should be feeling at this point of the opera. I know that this ensemble requires each of the artists to listen and blend with everyone else, but you can do that and still bring an individual and well-defined character to the stage within the prescribed vocal line.

Edgardo weaves in and out of different emotions, feeling betrayed by Lucia but also sensing that Enrico is the author of this devastating tragedy. Consequently, he moves effortlessly from his own anger and pain to a feeling of outrage and then pity for Lucia, as she too has been betrayed by her own flesh and blood, resulting in her becoming the embodiment of grief and pain. Edgardo turns his anger on himself and, filled with self-loathing, flagellates himself because he can't accept that he loves a member of this abhorrent family — his sworn enemies. He loves Lucia in spite of the fact that, in his eyes, she has just betrayed him. Not until the last exclamations do we sense these conflicting emotions and even then, they seem to lack conviction and energy. This is an excellent vocal performance by Pavarotti, but it is safe singing; even in the malediction scene, when one can do a little more, Pavarotti plays it safe. For instance, the phrase '*H'a tradito il cielo e amor*' (with an effective portamento attached to '*maledetto, maledetto sia l'istante*') is then followed by an accented A 4 [A880] on the phrase '*che di te*'. Here, the larynx rises, thereby lightening the voice and eliminating the *scuro* aspects of the balanced *chiaro/scuro* sound at a time when the composer demands a full-blooded and open-throated sound. This type of reserved singing is unacceptable at this level. In general, this is excellent singing, but it does not contain the creative energy to transform the opera into an original experience. One does not hear the music anew, but Pavarotti does imbue Edgardo with fresh insights. This particular reading does not shed new light on the drama or the character, and yet its unpretentious, traditional approach remains very effective. I can only put this down to the quality of the singing, which in terms of vocalising is absolutely splendid and second to none.

Orrida E Questa Notte

This scene takes place in the Wolf's Crag in Ravenswood, the traditional home of Edgardo's ancestors. However, it is in ruins, following his father's death at the hands of Enrico Ashton who has also adopted his noble title.

The beginning of this scene takes place in the half-ruined great hall on a night in which a horrible storm is raging ('*Orrida e questa notte come il destino mio*'), the whole scene being as close to perfection as you are likely to hear. The singing is just wondrous, and the expression is very effective also. In fact, the singing throughout this scene is marvellous, but our work here is to learn all we can from Pavarotti's development. So, let us see if there is anything we can learn from this duet.

Enrico has left Lucia's wedding feast in order to meet with and torment Edgardo, informing him that Lucia is now married and being bedded by her new husband.

The first point that displays a potential problem is represented by the phrase '*l'ombra inulta*' where the [u] vowel in '*inulta*' is a little distorted. The next minor problem appears on the phrase '*Ne varcai la soglia orrenda*', which is marked piano, but Pavarotti fails to differentiate it from other phrases.

The coloratura on the phrase '*Come un'uom che vivo ascendi*' (marked '*Un poco piu affrettato*') should be more even in quality, more legato, and less jerky. The acciaccaturas on the phrase '*La sua tomba ad albergar*' are all too heavy, lacking flexibility and elegance. The staccato in the next phrase is sluggish as it lacks flexibility and vitality, and it is not being bounced off the breath. The [A] vowel in '*Quando*' is too heavily modified towards the [o] and should be a more authentic [a].

Pavarotti employs a hard attack on the '*Si, si*'. He doesn't understand that if he lowered the larynx and connected the sound to the breath, it would act as a cushion, slightly opening the glottis and making the whole passage so much easier to execute whilst still retaining the spontaneous effect.

The phrase that follows '*Uccidero*' on the A4 is again a problem. Pavarotti allows the larynx to rise, distorting the [o] vowel and reducing the *oscuro* aspects of the tone. In addition, there is only a tenuous connection between the larynx and the breath. The larynx is more in the position of the [a] rather than the [o]; consequently, the vowel cannot be authentic. This happens a lot in this duet where the larynx is too high, creating a variable disconnect between breath and source, distorting vowels and being unable to utilise the power and flexibility that ensues from learning to manage the breath muscles. There is a problem with laryngeal rigidity on such notes as '*Un odio mortal*' and '*il cieco furor,*' which could be eliminated through a stronger connection between breath, laryngeal position and voice source.

Death Scene: Tombe degli avi miei' and 'Fra poco a me ricovero

Pavarotti sings this recitative and aria very well, and his Edgardo is punctuated by some quite lovely singing. We could actually leave it at that, but in terms of finding patterns with respect to technical difficulties, we should follow through with our analysis.

The beginning of the recitative displays some lovely singing. However, on the phrase '*D'una stirpe infelice*' on the G4 we find that the larynx is too high and the connection between the respiratory muscles and the laryngeal muscles is tenuous at best. The phrase beginning with '*Abbandonarmi vo*' has a similar problem. Were it to be executed with a deeper breath, it would automatically ensure a lower larynx and a firmer connection between breath and voice source.

The phrase '*Tu delle gioje in seno*' begins with a beautifully poised, if still a little tight, piano F4. However, the repeat of the phrase on the G4 (which is marked forte, but Pavarotti sings it here mezzo forte) issues forth with a distorted [u] on the '*tu*'. The distortion comes from an attempt to keep the voice forward at all costs so that Pavarotti tries to keep the [u] forward in the position of the [i]. Now, there is undoubtedly a great deal of acoustic formation in common between the [u] and the [i] vowel. However, that similarity has more to do with the almost identical first formant that gives both vowels their colour and roundness (*scuro* aspects) and not in the second formant, which gives the tone its brilliance and *squillo*. Pavarotti reverses this process, resulting in the distorted vowel which we have just observed.

The aria '*Fra poco a me ricovero*' is essentially beautifully sung and one would be in danger of appearing petty to find too much wrong with it. So, I will mention only the things that I believe we should learn from. The first is the [e] vowel on the F# on the phrase '*del tuo consorte a lato*'. This phrase is marked forte, and the sound should be more forward with a more authentic [e] vowel. Pavarotti takes it back into a position that is foreign to the [e] vowel, indicating more of an [ir] than an [e]. The exclamatory [A] that follows is much too close to an [o] vowel to be an authentic expressive cry. Pavarotti begins the note with a relatively closed vowel and piano dynamic and then opens the vowel as he performs a crescendo. The point is that the dynamics and the vowel are a separate issue — you should be able to produce a crescendo on any vowel. Pavarotti however collapses the two issues into one.

I would also like to point out that the [E] vowel on the A4 in '*rispetta a almen le ceneri di chi moria per te*' is too narrow and unnecessarily tight. It would cost him nothing to open it a little, as he was in no danger of falling into too open a sound. Finally, I feel that the B4 in the cadenza could be sung with more abandon, a slightly lower larynx, and a little more colour. As it is, it is a lovely sound but tends towards the brighter aspects of the *chiaro/scuro* equation.

In the final scene, Edgardo, having discovered Lucia's unexpected death as a result of her heartbreak, makes the decision to join her.

The scene begins with the phrase '*Giusto cielo*', which is beautifully sung. In fact, the whole scene is characterised by genuinely wonderful singing. My only comment is that Pavarotti is too cautious with respect to collecting the voice. It is all just a little too careful and should be more spontaneous and self-assured. The result is that whilst the listener still enjoys the glory of the natural voice (and frankly, some very beautiful singing), if the vowel modification were less severe, it would result in a more open-throated and generous sound with greater potential for excitement. I don't disagree that some modification (vowel tracking) is necessary, but the [A] vowel should never migrate towards the [o] vowel, and nor should an [e] vowel morph into an [ir]. In Pavarotti's case he does just that and it is too severe.

Tu che a Dio spiegasti l'ali

As an example, and in addition to what has already been demonstrated, I invite the listener to observe three instances in which the [A] vowel is too close to the [O]. This occurs on the syllable '*mai*' and the exclamatory '*Ah*' just before the moderato, and the [A] vowel in the phrase '*Questo di che sta sorgendo*'. All of these examples would be more authentic and more exciting were they to be sung with a greater proportion of [A] — not that Pavarotti's voice is lacking excitement, but every voice deserves to be maximised. There are many more examples in this scene, but let us proceed to the final scene.

In the [A] in '*spiegasti l'ali*' and the [E] in '*ti rivolgi a me placata, teco ascende, teco ascende al tuo fedel*' the vowels are throaty and distorted towards the [ir] while the acciaccatura on '*il tuo fedel*' is very pedestrian.

The next minor problem occurs in the ascending phrases with mounting tension on the '*bell'alma innamorata, bell'alma innamorata, ne congiunga il nume in ciel*' in which the top A on the [a] vowel is too narrow and tight. Pavarotti should relax the larynx (allowing it to take a naturally lower position), open the vowel and trust the breath. Pavarotti at this point has still not conquered the technique of singing ornamentation because the acciaccatura that follows the A4 on the syllable '*Ne*' lacks conviction.

There are some instances of a hard attack, but these are for a dramatic effect and could easily be eliminated by lowering the larynx and creating a better connection to the breath.

The other spot in this aria that concerns me is to be found in the moderato section where the tenor is required to sing a beautifully poised G4 on the [A] vowel in the phrase '*Ah, te vengo, o bell'alma innamorata*'. Pavarotti spoils the effect a little by singing a heavily modulated [A] vowel, which at the beginning is almost distorted to a [U] vowel. This is unnecessary as this kind of severe vowel migration is never required, especially when singing softly, as the authenticity of the vowel can easily be retained. The phrase that follows, '*il tuo fedel*,' should be sung softly whilst using the dotted rhythms, creating a laboured staccato tone and imbuing the text with a deeper meaning and effect. Pavarotti mistakenly believes that the emotion comes from creating a breathy tone, which he also sings too loudly. This proves to be ineffective in creating the feeling of fatigue required by a man approaching his final breath. The aria ends well enough except for the slight lowering of the [u] vowels on the repeated '*in nume in ciel, in nume in ciel, in nume in ciel*.'

Overall, Pavarotti creates a believable character, and the vocal tone is glorious despite the reservations expressed above. The instrument with which nature has endowed him is just fantastic, and in fairness, he has come a long way since the 1961 Boheme in Reggio Emilia.

Pavarotti — Technician and Magician

Chapter 37

L'Elisir d'amore, Pavarotti/Battle/Levine 1990

Pavarotti does some exciting and quite lovely things in this 1990 edition of '*L'elisir d'amore*'. Pavarotti's singing has its foundations on a much deeper breath in which the diaphragm plays a more significant part in lowering the larynx, and the voice is *piu appoggiata* or better supported than previous versions of the opera. With a few exceptions, the tone is much more even, open-throated, and forward while also deploying a richer, darker colour than previous editions.

There are also some problems which I will address below.

The first thing we notice is that the [a] vowels are consistently too open and too far back, the tone needs more consistent follow-through and greater focus, and the proprioceptive sensations (tone vibrations) should be allowed to impinge in the most natural position.

The second vowel that is very badly placed in Pavarotti's voice is the [i] vowel, especially at the *passagio* which on many occasions is on the brink of cracking, especially on a G4. This is not normal for Pavarotti and not natural for a voice of this stature, so what is happening? The answer may be found in something that Leone Magiera brought to my attention. He put forward the idea that Pavarotti was constantly looking for different ways of doing things in order to keep each performance as fresh as if he were singing it for the first time. In so doing, he often made things difficult for himself and his colleagues [Magiera, 2008: 8]. In this instance, he makes extraordinary efforts to keep his voice forward and in a high position, thereby creating a significant problem for himself.

I recognise that there may be many young singers and some teachers who may have problems recognising the language I have used above, words such as too open, too forward, too high, too narrow, too lean and so on. The reason I am using this language is because it is the vocabulary that Pavarotti's teachers would have used. With few exceptions, teachers in post-war Italy would not have taught the scientific method, so let us look at the science of this lesson. Pavarotti used the abdominals to push the diaphragm up and, in so doing, compressed the air supply against the vocal folds, resulting in the larynx being no longer anchored down by the diaphragm. The [i] vowel automatically raises the tongue, meaning that the larynx will also follow if it does not have a counterforce from the diaphragm. It is not unusual for the larynx to be raised by the root of the tongue via the hyoid bone from which it hangs. This muscular configuration produces a brilliant, ringing tone until the already raised diaphragm rises a little further. At this point, the chest muscles begin to collapse, and without their support, the singer loses control over the respiratory mechanism, breath pressure, and laryngeal position, which affects the resonator. In addition, when you lose control over laryngeal position, you lose control of the tongue and other articulators. This is what happens with Pavarotti in this version of the opera. Having lost control of the breath, larynx and tongue, almost all the lateral vowels, especially the [i] vowel, are somewhat distorted. These lateral vowels, such as the [i] and [e], represent what used to be referred to as a two-chamber system that needed to be balanced.

Una Furtiva Lagrima

- The phrase on '*negli occhi suoi spunto*' is much better than the 1970 edition, as the tone is more natural and more forward. The vowel is more authentic, with more [e] instead of [ir].

- The '*quelle festose e giovani*' is also much improved as the tone is more natural and less preplanned than it had been previously. The sound is also less contrived. For instance, the [o] vowel in the syllable '*sto*' on the A♭ is a considerable improvement on the 1970 performance. Even so, it could still benefit from further modulation towards the [aw] vowel, thereby preventing the complete and indiscriminate lowering of all the vocal tract formants.

- The phrase '*che piu cercando io vo*' is a lovely tone until we arrive at the [o] vowel of 'vo' in which the lips protrude, the tone becomes throaty, and all the formants are lowered, which darkens the overall tone. This merges with the open [a] vowel, which is a dramatic and explosive moment, although a little too open. However, it is an improvement on the 1970 version.

- The repeated '*m'ama*' on the A♭ is also an improvement as the larynx is lower, the tone is more even and secure (being more a*ppoggiata*), and the [a] vowel is slightly modified towards the [aw]. It is all more thoughtful and more subtle.

- The diminuendo on the phrase '*lo vedo*' is much better and more controlled, with greater clarity of tone and consistency.

- Pavarotti begins the second verse of the aria rather softly, producing a lovely effect. The only problem is that instead of creating a gradual crescendo on each phrase, he keeps the *piano* right up until '*I miei sospir confondere*' and then attempts a crescendo on the accented [i] vowel on the A♭ of '*sospir*'. This is very difficult without the appropriate preparation, which requires greater *appoggio*, a judicious lowering of the larynx, and a further opening of the mouth by dropping the jaw. As it is, the larynx rises and is under-energised, while the aperture is too narrow and the tone too constricted.

- In the final cadenza, Pavarotti sings the first A4 on the [o] vowel very well. This is a beautifully poised and sustained tone, in large part due to the modification of the [o] vowel towards the [aw]. This is significant at many levels, not least of all because it is the first time in this role that he makes this concession. It points to the fact that if he can modify the vowel on an A4, he can do the same on the G4 and the F4. Thus the *passaggio* does not have to be as narrow and constricted as Pavarotti has been making it. The face takes on an entirely new shape, with the lip protrusion lengthening the vocal tract and lowering all the formants, thus producing a dark tone. It is often too furry and lacking in brilliance, precision, definition and clarity. However, if the singer modifies the vowel towards the [aw] it provides a more lateral shape and a hint of a smile. Gone is the excessively lowered larynx, which is part of the elongation of the vocal tract. Gone is the overly humped tongue at the back of the pharynx, as the tip of the tongue is now leaning on the lower rim of the gums. Above all, the sound is freer, more brilliant and more comfortable for both listener and singer.

In this recording, the Pavarotti tone is more concentrated, more natural, more authentic, and better supported. It begins with a firmer onset as well as a firmer and longer glottal closure than the tone in *La fille du Regiment* and *Lamico Fritz*.

Pavarotti was an excellent Nemorino, and it is clear that he identifies with this somewhat naive, warm and sincere character. Vocally, the role is tailor-made for his voice, and he takes full advantage of it. One of the revelations on this recording is Pavarotti's sense of fun and comic timing: it is interesting that, like all good comedians, he plays it straight. Thus, the sincerity and sense of fun. Consequently, we can say that the voice is not as forward as it would later become, but he does produce a beautiful velvety sound: a tone that is still in its first bloom and moving quickly towards its glory years. Just wonderful!

Chapter 38

I Puritani, Pavarotti/Sutherland/Bonynge, May–July 1973

The story of *I Puritani* is a recounting of the English Revolution which led to the regicide of King Charles I at the hands of the Puritan leader Oliver Cromwell and his roundheads. The action takes place in the 1650s in Plymouth.

When the curtain rises, the city is under siege by Royalist troops. It is dawn, the soldiers have just woken, and are about to participate in the changing of the guard, but not before singing a rousing chorus, *'Quando la tromba squilla'*.

This idyllic scene is followed by Riccardo's entry. He is the commander of the battalion, and in a recitative (conversation) with his friend Sir Bruno, Riccardo reveals that Elvira's father, Sir Walter, had promised him her hand in marriage. That notwithstanding, he discovers that Elvira loves Arturo Talbo and will not consider marrying anyone else. Nor will Sir Walter force his daughter into a loveless marriage. In his aria, *'Ah! Per sempre io ti perdei,'* Riccardo mourns for what may have been but finally accepts that he has lost Elvira forever. What he can't accept, however, is the fact that she has chosen to marry a Stuart partisan.

As the curtain rises on Act I, Scene Two, we see Elvira through the open windows in conversation with her uncle, Giorgio Walton. The audience immediately understands that this is a filial relationship and that Giorgio would do anything to safeguard her happiness. He informs her that she is to be married today. Elvira concludes that she is to marry Riccardo and immediately rebels. She reminds her uncle that although pure of heart, she nurtures an overwhelming passion burning in her breast. A little amused, Giorgio reassures her that she is to marry her beloved Arturo. With this, her anguish turns to joy, which she expresses in her delightful aria, *'Son vergin vezzosa'.*

A joyous celebratory scene follows in which Elvira sings of her desire to share her charm, grace, and maidenhood with her beloved Arturo. When the occasional shadow of disbelief comes through, her uncle confirms her father's permission to marry her true love, Arturo.

Arturo appears on horseback, galloping his way to the fortified Castle; it is a mark of his universal esteem that although a Royalist, he is hailed as a hero even by his Puritan opponents.

Everyone gathers for the celebrations. They are eager to witness the moment when Arturo meets his bride. He makes a famous entrance in which he expresses his love for Elvira and happiness with his good fortune in his great aria 'A te o cara', which in turn develops into one of the most glorious quartets in all opera.

Meanwhile, Arturo learns that King Charles's widow, Queen Henrietta, is a prisoner in the Castle and is scheduled to be taken to London, where she will almost certainly be condemned to death. He contrives to be alone with the Queen, taking advantage of this meeting to swear his loyalty to the royal cause and vowing to save her even should it cost him his own life. Elvira returns, enchanting in her beauty and radiant in her bridal dress and veil. Unaware that the lady there is Queen Henrietta, she playfully places her veil over her head. This was the inspiration Arturo was seeking; he immediately understood that the veil was the ideal prop to provide the necessary disguise for the Queen's escape from the Castle. Arturo and the Queen affect their escape, but they are soon stopped by Riccardo, Arturo's intractable enemy. He remains determined to destroy his rival for Elvira's hand.

The thought of his beloved Elvira in an eternal embrace with his enemy is too much for Riccardo. He attacks Arturo, and the two duel for their lives. The Queen is determined to separate them but is ultimately forced to reveal her identity if only to prevent the bloodshed. Riccardo is shocked at the sight of the Queen and immediately retreats, part embarrassed, and pat relieved, he allows them to escape. The guests return for the wedding, and Riccardo informs them of Arturo's escape with Henrietta. Soldiers rush off in pursuit. Elvira, believing that she has been jilted, is emotionally distraught. Overcome by grief, she collapses and breaks down.

Act II

Family, retainers and townsfolks all lament Elvira's descent into madness. Her beloved uncle Giorgio attempts to explain her mental disintegration, connecting it directly with Arturo's abandonment of her at the last minute before the wedding. Riccardo arrives and announces that parliament has condemned Arturo to death for his part in the Queen's escape.

Elvira wanders into the hall, moving in and out of lucidity as she seems to be reliving happier days. In her madness, she mistakes Riccardo for Arturo and dreams of her wedding day. Her aria 'Qui la voce' is a tour de force of coloratura singing. At the end of this famous mad scene, both Giorgio and Riccardo persuade the poor girl to return to her quarters. Moved by Elvira's plight and fearing that any further shocks would push her completely over the edge, Giorgio persuades Riccardo to at least try and save Arturo. His instinctive response is an indignant refusal, but finally, Riccardo is moved to Elvira's plight. He will help even if it means saving his enemy. The two men unite in patriotism: if Arturo returns as a friend, he shall live—if as an armed enemy, he shall die.

Act III

In Elvira's Garden, Arturo reveals that his love for her has brought him back to Plymouth. Overhearing her singing their old love song, he is torn between his affection for Elvira and his loyalty to the Stuarts. Finally, she appears, and Arturo reassures her that she is his only love. Soldiers rush in to arrest Arturo, but at the same moment, a diplomat arrives with the news of the Royalists' final defeat and a general amnesty for all offenders. The shock of this news restores Elvira's senses, and all rejoice as Elvira and Arturo embrace their newfound happiness.

A General Critique of Pavarotti in I Puritani

Pavarotti was first offered the opportunity to sing *I Puritani* at La Scala as early as 1963. However, he declined, and time would prove his decision absolutely right. In fact, it points to one of Pavarotti's great gifts: he knew his strengths and weaknesses better than anyone else. In addition, he was blessed with an abundance of intelligence and strength of character: he knew when to say no.

The first recording we have of him as Arturo is the 1969 recording with Mirella Freni as Elvira and Riccardo Muti conducting. This recording validates his earlier decision to decline the role for the 1964 La Scala season simply because there is a compelling argument that even the 1969 recording was premature. There are some lovely, exciting and velvety moments in this recording, and Pavarotti was in superb voice, suggesting that any deficiencies should be attributed to deficiencies of technique and vocal immaturity rather than whether he was in good voice or not. The fact remains that he was not quite ready for Arturo even in 1969; imagine the negative impact it would have had on his career had he agreed to sing I Puritani in Milan in 1964.

A general comparison between the 1969 and 1973 performances suggests that Pavarotti was not in control of his technique. In particular, his notion of *appoggio* was tenuous at best. We recall that for the Italians, *appoggio* was not only about breath support, which they refer to as objective *appoggio* but also to a heightened sense of where the Proprioceptive vibrations are concentrated within the resonator (vocal tract). These typically are felt most intensely against the zygomatic arch or parts of the hard palate. It follows that what happens below the glottis (sub-glottal pressure) and above the larynx (proprioceptive vibrations) invariably influence what happens at the vocal fold level.

The features of Pavarotti's 1969 performance are as follows:

- Pavarotti's *appoggio*, both objective (breath pressure) and subjective (*impostazione*), are insufficiently prepared, and consequently the breath flow follows the onset of the breath, beginning just before the tone (firm onset). This sequencing results in the late arrival of the breath at the glottis, disrupting the coordination between breath and tone. Unfortunately, this is not the only problem, for when the breath finally connects with the glottis, the sub-glottal pressure is often inadequate for the phrase being sung.

- The vibrations of the sound wave need to be travelling forward more, allowing the sound to be a little plummy and altogether too velvety.

- The vertical laryngeal position is too low, and the throat is sometimes too wide and too relaxed, creating a cavernous, dark tone.

- As a result of this loose and relaxed setting, the pharyngeal walls are too relaxed and loose.   The softer the texture of the cavity wall, the more the cavity emphasises the low overtones. The pharyngeal wall therefore is unable to give the tone the brilliance and *squillo* that it is generally capable of.

- At a laryngeal level, the contraction of the LCA muscles is inadequate to keep the vocal folds from swinging too open and creating too much amplitude to the sound. When the glottis is finally adducted, the closure is neither firm enough nor long enough within the vocal cycle, allowing the sound to become too voluptuous, too velvety, and a little too chesty. This setting creates too much vocal fold mass and tension in the mixed register, thus forcing the high register, which often sounds strained and unstable. The tone needs to be more lyrical, more brilliant and leaner.

- Finally, Pavarotti's diction is not as clear or incisive as it is in the 1973 recording with Sutherland and Bonynge. The reason for this is that the articulators, especially the tongue, are still a little slow to react.

In the 1973 performance Pavarotti sounds like an entirely different tenor; this is the Pavarotti we have come to love and admire: it is just great singing! The tone, although lyrical and bright, possesses a beautiful natural bloom; it is forward, brilliant and rock-solid right up to the D6 in full voice and the F6 in a well-supported falsetto. The diction is fantastic: you can literally write the text down as he sings. Honestly, apart from two or three [e] vowels in the head register, which are still too bright and a little hard, it is very difficult to fault this singing. The *appoggio* has improved enormously from the 1969 recording, so has the onset and release, and the overall glottal settings are simply in another league relative to the previous recording. The vertical laryngeal position is higher, as is that of the zygomatic arch, ensuring a shortening of the vocal tract. The configuration of the articulators ensures that the tone is not only more forward and ringing but also has greater clarity and spontaneity, suggesting that the articulators are not only more flexible but also much more responsive. The vocal folds are more tense and stretched, the amplitude in the mixed register is smaller, and the closing rate longer. When these settings are combined with a texture of the pharyngeal wall, which is much firmer, favouring the higher partials, the result is a brilliant, forward ringing tone with a great deal of *squillo*.

I believe that this prudent decision made Pavarotti not only an outstanding tenor, but an even greater artist. Even his great contemporary, Placido Domingo lauds Pavarotti 'for bringing his enormous gifts to fruition with such intelligence and wisdom'. I say Amen to that.

I Puritani, Pavarotti/Freni and Muti 1969

In the 1969 performance Pavarotti uses a more robust straightforward type of sound. It is rounder and endowed with greater depth and velvet, but the velvet has not entirely overwhelmed the brilliant balancing ping and ring. The tone has a natural feel about it and is less contrived than some of his earlier recordings. However, this comes at a price: the tone is a little heavy, the *passaggio* on the dark vowels is more contrived, and the *imposto* is too far back. The worst price of all for a lyric tenor, it has a deleterious effect on the high register. In a role that is graced by and prized for its stratospheric range, this is an unpardonable offence. There is hardly a high note that does not have a minor and often a major crack.

Having said that, I must not give the impression that it is all gloom as there is some really beautiful singing in this performance. Let us analyse the 'A te o cara' to attain a more refined and accurate picture of what is really happening with Pavarotti in 1969.

A Te O Cara

There are several signposts, including a vibrato, which is a little too fast at the beginning of the aria. Although the tone is lower-slung and heavier than some of his recordings, the upside is that he produces a very beautiful, warm and velvety tone. The A naturals in '*fra la gioa, fra la gioia ed esultar*' are excellent, having a lovely warm sound that remains full-blooded whilst displaying extraordinary beauty. Unfortunately, the C# is not its equal: it is a little detached, off the breath and therefore insecure, displaying a loss of control. The interjections in the ensemble are generally excellent, although '*ah mio bene*' and '*Elvira Mia,*' are under-energised and remain too far back in the throat. In contrast, the soft singing is absolutely exquisite. We will discuss a comprehensive remedy later, but for now let us say that this performance needs more buoyancy and a higher *imposto*. The centre frequency is all a little low because it is under-energised, and the attention is all concentrated on the *imposto* instead of the breath. The vocal fold adduction is tenuous, especially in the very high notes, where the adductor muscles (LCA, and IA) don't seem to be strong enough to hold at the midline. The cricopharyngeal muscles fail to anchor the larynx, preventing the CT from stretching and tensing the vocal folds in the extreme head register.

Vieni Fra Queste Braccia

'Vieni fra queste braccia' begins softly and with a high sitting (central frequency) vocal *imposto*. Unfortunately, Pavarotti loses control of the C#, mainly because the connection between breath, thought, and tone becomes tenuous, resulting in a straight tone in which the overtones are either erased or at best diminished. Unfortunately, this type of sound at the most exciting moments mars what is otherwise a very good performance.

Credeasi Misera

This is a magnificent ensemble in which Pavarotti begins well enough. However, by the time he arrives at the F4 on the phoneme '*Da*', the [a] vowel is over-modified, ensuring that the tone remains not only opaque but also a little distorted and too far back in the throat. The [a] vowel on the G♭ in the phrase '*traea sua vita*' has a momentary glitch in it. There is a definite release of breath pressure which allows the sound to become unsteady or even crack, and it can occur anywhere in the scale. It so happens that it is even more evident in the most important and most difficult moments of the opera.

Pavarotti is very expressive on the phrases '*Or sfido I fulmini* and *disprezzo disprezzo il fato*'. He is also very expressive in the next phrase '*Se teco all'ato potro, potro morir*'. Pavarotti produces a very beautiful and expressive tone in these phrases. However, the A♭ that follows needs greater security and steadiness as well as an enrichment of the harmonic series.

Pavarotti's major problem at this point is a disequilibrium between the objective *appoggio* (breath pressure) and subjective *appoggio* (proprioceptive sensations and focal points). Effectively he is more concerned with the *impostazione* of the voice than he is with breath management. This is not surprising since clarity of diction, in combination with the technique for *copertura* at the *passaggio*, were the elements most prized by his teacher, Arrigo Pola. However, it has to be understood that the prioritisation of the resonator came at the expense of breath management.

It must be said that the problem is not confined to these moments cited above. Pavarotti had yet to be taught early in his studies that the breath is the most important element of singing and must be prioritised before we concern ourselves with other details, including the *imposto*. I am not underestimating the importance of what happens above the larynx; I understand that the paradigm is no longer linear and that the feedback system in the form of 'inertial reactance' impacting the laryngeal mechanism is absolutely critical to the equation. However, I contend that breathing is the foundation of singing, and if that critical element is not right, it doesn't matter what else you do. I am of the conviction that the interaction between the breath and glottis creates the raw material for the voice — a complete harmonic series. The air contained in the resonating cavity modifies the harmonic series through a natural selection of harmonics, enhancing some and suppressing others, resulting in an absolutely marvellous effect, resonance. However, I also agree with Martin Rothenberg when he posits that the resonator cannot compensate for a missing harmonic partial nor turn a weak harmonic into a strong one, nor is it able to sustain a single note without breath support. The moment the breath pressure is diminished below a certain minimal level, the tone becomes unsteady and weak, or, worse still, it cracks.

I Puritani 1973, Pavarotti/Sutherland

Unlike the 1969 performance, in this particular performance, Pavarotti makes every effort to set the voice (*imposto*) in a fairly high position and forward on the masque (A higher centre of frequency). He achieves this by maintaining a slightly higher larynx than his previous recording. In addition, the hump of the tongue is elevated for the lateral forward vowels and raised at the base for the rounder and back vowels. The soft palate is also elevated, as is the epiglottis. The constrictor muscles are contracted and the faucial arches (Palatopharyngeus and Palatoglossus) are elevated and brought closer together towards the midline, whilst the *levetor palato* and *tensor palatine* elevate, tense and pull back the soft palate. This is all achieved under the direct influence of the *appoggio* and the conscious mind. In this role, Pavarotti is extremely careful with the management of the *passaggio*, especially as he transitions from the mixed register into the head register, depending on the vowel. The larynx is sitting higher than usual even for Pavarotti, as is the base of the tongue, the zygomatic arch and a concomitant rise of the soft palate (velum). The resulting tone is lighter in texture than usual but clear and ringing. It is characterised by a great deal of penetration and a high level of buoyancy. Every now and then the vibrato becomes a little too fast. Pavarotti's caution in this role leads him to transition into the head voice a little early. He is right to be cautious: Pavarotti once described the experience of singing *I Puritani* as being similar to 'tightrope walking'. Certain of the roles I sing put a severe strain on the vocal cords. I Puritani is one such role. Pavarotti says that almost the whole role is full-voiced singing for the tenor in the upper part of the voice. There are two Ds and an F [Wright, 1981: 138].

This abundance of caution sometimes leads Pavarotti astray. There are occasions when he transitions into the head register on an E4 — too early for a lyric tenor singing the ultimate bel canto role. The E natural should be sung in mixed voice. Failure to do so gives the sound an unsteady, throaty quality, which is too far back and generally contrived. In fact, this tone is atypical for Pavarotti because it is unnaturally light and a little under-energised by the breath. From the beginning, the breath is rather loose, allowing the vibrato to also become a little fast and vulnerable, especially at the beginning and ends of phrases. Such notes as the [a] vowel in 'cara' and "*talor-mi guido furtivo e il pianto*' are all beautifully contoured phrases with a lovely, collected tone — '*voce chiusa*'.

Pavarotti maintains this type of head tone until he descends into medium voice on the F natural for the phrase '*furtivo e il pianto*'. However, this transition should be smoother. In truth, Pavarotti leaves the head register too abruptly, favouring the medium register in the transition rather than transitioning gradually from the head to the mixed register and finally settling on the medium or mixed register. The phrases that follow are all sung with ' *Voce chiusa,' a technique* which is aided by a collected mouth, '*bocca raccolta*,' as well as a greater level of *appoggio*.

The sustained A4 on the [a] vowel of *esultar* is much more secure and focused relative to the 1969 performance with Muti. It is also more lyrical, more penetrating, and more brilliant (*voce appoggiata*). This is the result of a much firmer closure of the glottis and a faster and longer duration of the closure phase, not to mention a more abrupt cessation of airflow. This provides the vocal tract with a much richer harmonic series than previous efforts.

The tone in the 1969 performance was a little too dark, too heavy, and lacking buoyancy. This type of production is characterised by a decidedly pharyngeal orientation which, when lacking the requisite *appoggio*, can create instability in the tone, especially at the *passaggio* and early head register, as well as over modification of the [o] vowel at the *passaggio*.

By comparison the 1973 recording with Sutherland and Bonynge is more lyrical, more focused, more forward and brilliant. The voice has more ring, focus and '*squillo*'. In large part this is the result of superior *appoggio* which sets up a chain reaction between the breath pressure and glottal resistance.

This interaction leads to a longer closed phase, firmer glottal closure, a more abrupt cessation of airflow and a spectrum that is sharp and spiky and leaning to the right. These conditions furnish the voice with a ringing, brilliant quality that is characterised by a greater carrying power.

Physiologically, Pavarotti is easily capable of generating a greater and more flexible level of subglottal pressure, accommodating both higher and lower levels of pressure in a more responsive and flexible manner.

In this 1973 version of *I Puritani* Pavarotti changes register even earlier than usual. In fact, in the excerpt above he moves into head register on the E4 on the [o] vowel in the phrase '*una fonte afflitto e solo*' on the [o] vowel of '*fonte*' and again on the word '*solo*'. Later in the reprise of this melody, he does something similar on the [o] vowels of '*corre*' and '*monte*'.

I must confess that at first, I thought that for such a lyric voice as Pavarotti's in a high sitting role as Arturo, it was unnecessary to move into head register as early as the [e] natural. Since the instrument itself rebels and the tone is quite unsteady, I thought this was a mistaken strategy. In my view, the voice should be allowed to resonate and focus where its nature guides it, but in this instance, I felt it was focused to a point wherein it was not prepared to go.

Pavarotti makes the most of the head voice

A number of repeat hearings have since revealed Pavarotti's strategy. He was not transitioning into head voice on the E4 because he needed to; he was consciously experimenting to see what effect such a strategy would have on the entire high register. In the sequel, it turns out that it had a beneficial effect not only on the *passaggio* but also his entire high range. The head voice in this recording remains beautifully poised and extremely well-focused. Just as importantly, the *passaggio* gained freedom. Just listen to '*Nel mirarti un solo istante*', and notice how, even though each note is a self-contained jewel, it is all joined together in a stream of glorious tone. Each note is poised within its register whilst still forming a complete unit with its vibrato and timbre, inviting the audience to come closer even as the sound rings out to the back row of the gods. There is no pushing or pulling in this singing: it is neither offensively constricted nor overtly open, neither too forward nor too back. The days when Pavarotti used to kick for goal and just miss by centimetres are forever gone. Now, not only does he hit the sweet spot of the note, but he does so with grace and poise, furnishing the tone with an uncommon level of refined elegance. In fact, much of the head register remains suspended in mid-air like a luminous, radiant ball of sunshine. Even the odd note that is not perfect only adds to his humanity and, relative to other tenors, is still glorious!

I must say that Pavarotti's singing in *I Puritani* is always of the highest level and often so wondrous as to leave most of us breathless. It is with reluctance therefore that I will point out one or two issues from which we may learn. The first of these is the attack on the B natural on the word '*d'ogni*' in which the [o] vowel is the culprit.

There are three distinct steps here that I wish to discuss:

1. Pavarotti doesn't seem to be sure about where the proprioceptive focal point is meant to reside and consequently hesitates at the point of attack. This is about the worst thing you can do because it creates uncertainty — a loss of coordinated rhythm between the singer's thought, breath and sound. This coordinated rhythm of this sacred trilogy is the alpha and omega of great singing. The mind conceives, imagines and guides the tone, the breath combines with the source to create the sound waves and a harmonic series, and the tone or sound is monitored by the ear which sends messages to the brain, and the brain messages the body, requesting the necessary alteration to the mind, the body and the tone.

2. When he finally attacks the note, he does so on the '*imposto*' rather than the breath a*ppoggio* (not unusual for Pavarotti). He really needs to trust the breath a bit more.

3. On the attack, Pavarotti seems to be trying to focus the [o] vowel towards the zygomatic arch or, even more specifically, on the upper teeth. This is an incorrect focal point because the [o] is one of the back vowels, and it goes against its nature to aim its proprioceptive focal point around the *imposto* generally associated with the [i] vowel. Pavarotti seems to come to the realisation that this manoeuvre is not going to succeed and allows the sound to fall back. However, this is an unplanned reaction, leading to a loss of vowel integrity and focus *(impostazione)*.

Consequently, for a note such as this B4, the singer needs to have a clear idea of what he is trying to achieve, while a strong imagination and a sense of visualisation are critical to success. Pavarotti needs to learn to pre-tune notes such as these before attacking them decisively and with a great deal of breath energy. He should aim the tone in the general direction of the masque but with flexibility in the resonator shape. This encourages the sound waves to find their own natural *imposto*. It also allows the interrelationship between thought, breath pressure and the articulators in the resonance cavity to shape the vowel whilst allowing the tone to find its own definitive *imposto*.

In the wonderful duet *'Dal di che ti mirai'* which follows, Pavarotti's singing is as glorious as always, and his understated, subtle but sincere emotional expressivity is a revelation. He brings a restrained delicacy of expression and an emotional otherworldliness that is typically associated with the very best sopranos rather than a tenor. Coming from a tenor who has often and justifiably been accused of being too emotionally reserved, even in the Verismo repertoire, this development is significant indeed. His emotional response to the music in the last act of *I Puritani* may well tell us something about the man's emotional makeup. I am not a psychologist, but I do have an opinion, and I give it here for what it's worth. I believe that Pavarotti, along with other great artists, developed a refined, almost feminine aesthetic. This allowed him to express the most intimate and heartfelt emotions in a very sincere but economical way, mainly with small, sensitive and refined gestures. We will see later when we analyse *Cavalleria Rusticana* and *I Pagliacci* that he was not as proficient at depicting the melodrama of life. When comparing his subtle emotional expression in bel canto roles to the verismo operas such as *Cavalleria* and *Pagliacci*, we are immediately struck by the fact that he is not at all comfortable with the big melodramatic outbursts. The intimate miniature gesture of bel canto is much more natural and in line with his personality. It requires a different kind of creativity in which vocal colour, the pointing of the text and the gentle accent of an acciaccatura are most important. Either way, we can say that he mastered a kaleidoscope of expressive sounds, clarity of diction, beauty of tone and a refined expressivity that can only be described as absolutely disarming.

The variety of colours and emotions he produces not only in this duet but throughout the last act of *I Puritani* is just wondrous. Unfortunately, he also threw in one or two acerbic notes into what would otherwise be a near-perfect performance. He does so on the [E] vowel in the phrase *'Dolce e cara me Sara',* which, apart from the [e] vowels, is really quite beautiful. On this particular phoneme, '*me*', the sound is very focused but constricted as it is altogether too metallic and edgy. In the context of the beautiful phrases preceding and succeeding it, this [E] vowel sounds quite shrill. It requires more fundamental and more space for the upper harmonics to bounce around as they search for their relevant and matching formant (*chiaro/scuro*). This is particularly disturbing because the rest of his singing could only be characterised as a lesson in bel canto. Even more frustrating is the fact that the remedy to this acrid note is so simple. All it takes is a minor lowering of the jaw, a small elevation of the zygomatic arch and soft palate, and a simultaneously moderate lowering of the larynx. The above strategy can only be achieved by activating the respiratory and articulatory systems with an increase in subglottal pressure and an awareness of subjective *appoggio*. The other issue to recall is that it is not necessary to create big shifts in the rise and decrease of actions in singing; everything has to be decisive but modest in gesture. In this respect I like what Meribeth Bunch Dayme says on this subject. She believes that:

> Efficient articulation for speech and singing will involve minimal movement of the jaw. Ideally, it will be lightly suspended, flexible and free to respond to the needs of the moment. Any undue tightness, such as clenching the teeth, jamming the jaw downward, or protruding, will affect the shape of the pharynx and soft palate, the movement of the tongue and hyoid bone, and indirectly, the larynx [Bunch Dayme, 2005: 91].

I think Bunch Dayme makes my point very well. In bel canto singing, you should do no more than is absolutely necessary. However, you still have the responsibility to build resilience and endurance into your instrument so that when you need that burst of energy, it will be available and well-managed. You do not have to maximise your tone for the whole performance, but if you can't muster that extra bit of excitement when you need it, you will be destined to have a mediocre career. My experience over a long period of time is that a good-sized voice that is well-educated and used tastefully and stylistically will always be more valuable in opera than a smaller voice with the same education and stylistic qualities.

We now arrive at the rousingly passionate final duet in *I Puritani*.

Vieni, Vieni. Fra Queste Braccia

Pavarotti is fantastic in this duet with Sutherland. The whole range is beautifully executed, but the top of the voice, which rises to a D5, is particularly exciting.

The first part of '*Vieni fra queste braccia*' may best be characterised as a voice that is brilliant and high pitched — a high sitting voice, capable of floated tones and displaying a minor dose of breathiness. This undoubtedly was meant to signify strong emotions, such as passion and fervour: in short, breathlessness.

I must confess that I personally don't much care for a breathy tone (the result of glottal failure to close completely), but I understand why Pavarotti does it, and it seems to work well for him. Having said that, I like his singing much better when he braces himself and firms up his tone in preparation for the first head note on the G4 [a] vowel of '*non mi sarai rapita*'. The [a] vowel in the word '*sarai*' is a beautifully poised head tone, sufficiently open to maintain vowel integrity but still collected to ensure a firmly rooted, strong fundamental and rich harmonics series, providing a brilliant head tone.

I don't like the approach to the top D5, nor do I love the eventual position it lands on. I find that Pavarotti takes too long to activate the breath muscles

and therefore the required pressure under this D5. Consequently, the tone remains a little under-energised (under-supported), a little back in the throat and marginally vulnerable. This particular tone lacks depth and definition simply because he aims the exclaimed [ah] in the traditional position of the [e] vowel. Hence, the vibrations impinge against the hard palate (zygomatic arch), but they fail to ignite the vibrations in the oral cavity. As the breath follows rather than activates the tone, the fundamental remains weak (insufficient *oscuro*) and therefore an incomplete sound. Overall, and notwithstanding the slightly idiosyncratic interpretation of this duet, the singing remains stylistically elegant and vocally glorious.

Credeasi Misera

Pavarotti begins '*Credeasi Misera*' with a much firmer and more languid tone, but one which is also empathetic with respect to character and musical affinity. There is a great deal of pathos in his delivery. Arturo is distressed to see Elvira stuck between two worlds: there are moments when she is completely lucid and others when she inhabits a world of her own reality. He is remorseful because he knows that jilting Elvira on their wedding day without a word of explanation or regret has generated a deep and enduring pain.

The overall voice production for '*Credeasi* m*isera*' is characterised by an effortless vocal quality. The breath pressure is just sufficient to elicit the correct balance between glottal resistance and the shape and tension of vocal fold configuration. The result is a firm production that easily attains a beautiful, ringing but relaxed tone: a tone that represents the full glory of this flowing, effortless and exquisite sound.

Let us perform a more detailed analysis of Pavarotti's singing in this ensemble from *I Puritani*. I will begin by saying that Pavarotti just over-collects the [A] vowel on the F natural on the phrase '*Da me tradita*'. Even though the F4 is a little muted as a result of early *copertura*, the stage is set for the kind of performance this is intended to be: effortless, expressive and sincere.

In the phrase that follows, the [A] vowel on the G flat on the word '*traea*' has a lovely ring, its '*impostazione*' has a more forward orientation, and the tone has a more natural focus on the *passaggio*. Pavarotti uses the text very expressively but very subtly in such phrases as '*Or sfido I fulmini, disprezzo, disprezzo il fato. Se teco allato saprò, saprò morir.*' This is very expressive singing, in part because he does not overdo the histrionics. He gives the audience an unmistakable idea of bel canto style, establishing the general atmosphere and Arturo's response to it. The tone is just exquisite in a restrained sort of way. One gains the impression that Pavarotti enjoys singing in this style, characterised by a glorious line of legato sound and imbued with a great deal of restraint in its expression of deep emotions. Pavarotti does not allow for any interference of the sound just to give way to an unconstrained mode of expression. He seems to have struck a good balance. The top notes later in the ensemble are well executed, especially the D flat, which is soon followed by an excellent top F6 in falsetto. All of this is exciting because, having been restrained throughout this ensemble, Pavarotti now gives himself a moment of unconstrained expression with glorious results. With respect to the falsetto top F, it is important to remember that this is exactly what Bellini was aiming for when he wrote it. Indeed, it is how we understand that Giovanni Rubini would have sung it back in 1835.

Let us recall that the first C5 in full head voice (*Voce piena in testa*) did not take place until April 1837 when Gilbert Louis Duprez sang the top C5 in *Guillaume Tell* in full voice at the Paris Opera.

At a glottal level Pavarotti proves most proficient at stretching and tensing the vocal folds. He expertly increases the passive tension of the cricothyroids whilst the vocalis muscle concomitantly releases its tension. This allows the cricothyroid to stretch the vocal cover and the second layer of ligaments, which is part of the body immediately below. This is a manoeuvre which is executed by the singer's subconscious processes. Pavarotti's instrument must have had a natural predisposition towards the stretching and tensing mechanism that dominates the *passaggio* during register transition and thins out further in the head register. On the other hand, we also know that Arrigo Pola worked on the *passaggio* with Pavarotti for several years. We therefore conclude that this natural predisposition was well nurtured and drilled by Pavarotti until it became seamless and second nature. At any rate, this is the reason for Pavarotti's wondrous top notes. At this point we should recall Van den Berg's research in 1966. He demonstrated that the greater the vocal fold tension, the greater the natural tendency for the vocal folds to abduct, but only until the LCA and IA increase their contraction, resulting in a firmer closure and a longer closed phase.

In this performance the larynx is sitting higher, and the ventricles project towards the midline. However, as Pavarotti ventures towards the high register, the ventricular folds retreat from the midline, and the ventricular sinuses (sinus of Morgagni) increase their spaciousness. The laryngeal collar is contracted, and the base of the tongue rises for the lateral, bright vowels, lowering slightly for the darker back vowels. The latter manoeuvre results in the tongue pushing back against the epiglottis, which is thereby lowered for the darker back vowels, altering the shape and space of the resonating cavity. The velum is raised (especially around the *passaggio*) as well as the ensuing head register, thereby facilitating the higher notes of the head register. The cricopharyngious contracts, anchoring the larynx on the cricoid cartilage and allowing the CT to stretch the vocal fold cover. Finally, the zygomatic arch is lightly elevated and shapes the mouth in a more lateral position with just the hint of a smile. The mandible (jaw) is moderately lowered, and the constrictor muscles are contracted, especially in head register.

As a consequence of this constriction, the faucial arches are brought closer together, restricting the pharyngeal space and funnelling the sound waves towards the anterior space of the oral cavity. This is often referred to as guiding the voice forward simply because the singer senses the buzzing of the sympathetic vibrations against the alveolar ridge. However, this unbalanced and prominent buzz comes at the expense of the pharyngeal resonating space, which is the '*sine qua non*' of a well-balanced, *chiaroscuro* tone. It is also important to remember that you cannot place the sound forward, back or otherwise. The sound waves respond to a particular configuration of the articulators within the vocal track, reacting immediately to the readjusted space. Having said that, the singer cannot place the voice, and we must add that he/she can, to varying degrees, feel the buzz of sympathetic vibrations on the masque. This is the result of a well-produced sound.

The only thing that could improve an already legendary performance would be a judicious lowering of the diaphragm, combined with a slight decrease of the larynx and simultaneous dropping of the jaw in synchronicity with the larynx and diaphragm.

This would give this otherwise very bright, forward and lean tone, a much greater amplitude, as well as a sense of being increasingly anchored and secure. This configuration results in a tone that is concentrated not only on the hard palate (which is what Pavarotti achieves in this performance) but also in the oral cavity. The tone is luminous yet round, velvety yet ringing — one that imbues the tone with great security.

I will have the answers to these and other questions later in this book.

Chapter 39

La Favorita by Donizetti, Pavarotti/Cossotto/Ghiaurov, 1974

It was 1839, and Donizetti had just completed a four-act opera for the Theatre de La Renaissance when the management declared bankruptcy, leaving the composer with a dilemma: what to do with his four-act Opera *L'ange de Nissida*.

Keen to clean up the mess but aware that it would not happen quickly, Donizetti decided to return to Milan to oversee his production of *La Fille du Regiment* at La Scala. The dilemma was soon resolved when Donizetti was recalled back to Paris to stage a new work for the Opera. It was very short notice, and even though Donizetti was renowned for working quickly, he knew that sometimes this facility impacted the quality of his work. He understood immediately that the way to resolve this problem was to recycle much of the music he had composed for *L'ange de Nissida* for his new Opera, which would be renamed *La Favorita*.

It is important to note that, notwithstanding this shortcut, all the major arias *for La Favorita* were composed anew in line with the dramatic situation, with the distinguishing qualities of the character and the vocal characteristics of the singers creating the roles.

Act I

The curtain rises to reveal the interior of the chapel of St. James di Campostella. Fernando, a young novice, is trying to explain to the father superior his decision to leave the monastery. It does not help that Baldassare, who also happens to be Fernado's father, had developed an elaborate plan to have his son follow in his footsteps as father superior of the monastery of St. James di Campostella.

Fernando explains to Baldassare that he has nothing but admiration for his just and temperate leadership and the manner in which he governs the land and the monastery. He has been very proud and happy to be by his side, but more recently he has fallen in love with a beautiful but mysterious young woman whose love has invaded his senses to the extent that he can hardly think of anyone or anything else.

The fact that Fernando does not even know her name and rank, nor where she comes from, does little to persuade Baldassare that Fernando's decision to leave the order has a great deal of merit. Upon further questioning Fernando reveals that he met the young woman in church where she happened to be praying in the pew next to him.

In the famous aria '*Una vergine un angel di Dio*' Fernando tries to explain to Baldassare the complex and conflicting emotions he experienced in being close to her. The situation elicited both hope and terror, desire and fear — complex emotions that filled his heart with joy but destroyed his peace.

Baldassare becomes very angry when he realises that his son is embarking on a journey of discovery that is going to end in disaster. It does not help that every objection from Baldassare elicits the same response from Fernando — he loves her. In the end, Baldassare surrenders to the inevitable, but not before predicting that when the hostile world has dealt with him, Fernando will return to the monastery.

Act I, Scene 2

The scene changes to the delightful Island of St. Leon, where Inez and a number of Spanish maidens, are singing a memorable ode to nature. This soon evolves into a prayer asking for guidance for Fernando and his safe arrival. Soon Fernando's boat puts to shore and after being blindfolded he is led to the main hall of the palace.

Relieved of his blindfold, he asks Inez whether her mistress still persists in withholding her name and rank from him. She indicates that she is not in a position to discuss anything with him. Fernando persists with his inquiries when suddenly the lady in question appears (unbeknownst to him, she is Leonora Guzman, a lady close to the throne). Leonora greets Fernando with genuine warmth and love. She confesses her love for him, thanking heaven for sending him to her but also insisting that nothing can ever come of it. The duet ends with a mutual declaration of love and a shared sense of loss.

Confused, Fernando is begging to know more. However, Leonora is called away, but not before presenting Fernando with an official scroll. Inez is set to follow her mistress when Fernando temporarily detains her. He learns that the man attending her presence is none other than King Alfonso of Castile.

Fernando finally realises that this woman's station is way beyond his reach. He then opens the scroll that she has bestowed upon him and realises that it is a military commission. He understands that she is offering him an opportunity to make himself worthy of her through military valour, and he is determined to distinguish himself in battle and win Leonora's hand. The act ends with Fernando giving vent in what really amounts to a military march, '*Si in un solo accento*'.

Act II

The act opens with Don Gasparo, the King's minister, briefing King Alfonso on the success of the war against the Moors. It becomes clear from this conversation that Fernando has distinguished himself by roundly defeating the moors and wresting the Castle of Alcazar from the enemy.

Having briefed his King, Don Gaspare departs, leaving King Alfonso to give full expression to his love for his mistress Leonora. He does so in the famous aria *'Vien Leonora'.*

At the end of this powerful and passionate declaration of love, Leonora joins her King.

In a poignant narrative that evolves into a duet, she laments the fact that she allowed herself to be deceived by Alfonso. She reminds him that when, as an innocent young girl she left her father's home to be with him in Castile, she had expected to marry him. She is now devastated to be widely and infamously known as the King's mistress.

Alfonso can see that she is unhappy and is about to tell her that he has decided to divorce the Queen and marry her. However they are called to preside over the feast celebrating Fernando's famous victory over the moors.

Leonora is filled with contrasting emotions; she is overjoyed with Fernando's success but apprehensive about meeting him again and keeping her love for Fernando from the King. Soon Don Gaspare returns with a handwritten note meant for Leonora, but confiscated by him from her maid before it can be delivered to her. The King interrogates Leonora who she remains defiant, refusing to reveal the identity of the author, but confirming that it is from someone she adores.

The scene is interrupted by Baldassare's entrance. He has discovered that the King is planning to put aside the Queen in favour of his mistress Leonora, and has arranged a pre-emptive strike. He walks in with a scroll bearing the Papal seal, threatening King Alfonso with excommunication if he does not retreat from this position.

The King responds arrogantly; whilst he has great respect for the holy man (also his father-in-law), Alfonso is still the King, and he needs to respect that. Baldassare responds by giving the King 24 hours to resolve the problem, at which time he will be back with a Papal Bull excommunicating Alfonso.

Act III

Alfonso is apprised of the fact that many at court agree with Baldassare regarding the Queen. Many nobles and courtiers believe that Alfonso has mistreated their legitimate Queen horribly. With few supporters at court and a papal bull over his head, Alfonso decides to surrender to the inevitable, deferring to Baldassare and avoiding the papal malediction. He orders Don Gaspare to arrest Inez and bring Leonora to him. Just as Don Gaspare leaves the scene, Fernando makes his entrance. Alfonso greets him warmly and is very generous with his praise and gratitude for Fernando's courage and valour. In fact, Alfonso openly calls him the saviour of the country and asks him to name his reward.

Fernando tells Alfonso that although he is nothing but a lowly soldier, he has lost his heart to a noble lady, and it is she who has inspired his valour and glory. If the King were to bestow her hand in marriage, he would be forever grateful. Alfonso accedes to Fernando's request — all he has to do is name her and she will be his. As Fernando is about to comply with this, Leonora walks in. He points to her and says: *'There she is, the most beautiful'*. Alfonso is shocked at the unexpected turn of events, but he is not in a position to go back on his word, especially as the passion between the two lovers is obvious for everyone to see. Reluctantly but with magnanimous grace, Alfonso not only consents to the marriage but promises that it will take place within the hour.

Leonora can see that Alfonso is distressed by the unexpected developments, so she approaches him with an explanation. She reminds him that when, as a young and innocent girl she left her father's house, she fully expected to marry the King and not just become his mistress. Alfonso knows the truth about her declaration, and seeing her in so much pain is genuinely remorseful.

Left alone, Leonora vents both her love for Fernando and her fear that the whole thing can evaporate in smoke. She is conscious of the fact that Fernando is still unaware of her being the King's favourite.

Leonora is a person divided, desperately wanting to marry the man she loves but painfully aware that her past does not bode well for future happiness. In the beautiful scene, 'Oh mio Fernando,' she sings of her fervent love and her fear that he might discover her secret anyway. At the end of the scene, she concludes that they can never be truly happy as long as she is withholding such a dark secret from him. Consequently, she sends Inez a message explaining everything to him, giving him the choice to forgive her and marry her or jilt her at the altar. Unfortunately, the letter is confiscated by Don Gaspare and is never delivered to Fernando.

Leonora awaits her groom with trepidation, not at all sure he will join her at the altar. One can only imagine her relief when she sees him walking down the aisle. Unaware that Inez has been arrested and imprisoned, Leonora naturally assumes that her lover has decided to forgive and marry her. Her delight at this outcome is both total and infectious.

As the wedding takes place off stage the courtiers on stage ridicule what they believe is a sham marriage, partly paid for by the honours bestowed on Fernando by the King.

He is, after all, both Count of Zamora and a Marchese of Montreal. At the end of the ceremony, Fernando joins the courtiers and invites them to share his unbelievable happiness and good fortune. However, they are all rather cool as they refer to the importance of honour as a virtue. Fernando responds by wistfully elaborating on the importance of honour in his life from his earliest days. By comparison, all the riches and accolades he has recently won are as nothing to him.

The courtiers continue to taunt him, so he asks for satisfaction. It is at this point that Baldassare walks in and prevents what could be an even greater tragedy. Fernando soon discovers that Leonora is the King's favourite and that he has been dishonoured by marrying her. It soon becomes clear that Fernando knew nothing of this situation, and he feels totally betrayed. He swears vengeance and asks the courtiers to allow him to defend his honour.

Fernando confronts the King, thanking him for all the honours he has bestowed on him but declaring that the price is too high. He takes off the medal from around his neck and throws it on the ground, then unsheathes the sword given to him by the King, breaks it and throws the pieces at the King's feet. The act ends with brilliant ensemble.

Act IV

The curtain rises to reveal Fernando in the familiar surroundings of the cloisters of St James of Caste. He is back where he belongs, and his voice soars over the chorus in fervent prayer. To the delight of his father Baldessare, Fernando finally takes his final vows for his ordination into their order. Left alone, he is lost in a reverie that transports him to another time and another place. His mind is temporarily invaded by human desire; he uses the magnificent aria *'Spirito gentil nei sogni miei'* to express the various conflicting emotions. Fernando recalls his passionate love for Leonora, his shattered dreams, and his acute sense of sadness and loss.

At the end of the aria, Fernando walks out into the cloisters and finds Leonora disguised as a novice. She has come to beg for forgiveness, but Fernando will have none of it, asking her to leave and never return. He orders her to return to the King so that he may adorn her with jewels and infamy, ensuring that her beauty will shine at its best. She begs him to listen and reveals that she sent him a message letting him know of her tragic situation, but the letter was confiscated, and Inez thrown into prison. He doesn't want to hear any of this, but she persists. Finally, he surrenders to the inevitable, confessing his love for her as well as his plan to live together and begin a new life. She is grateful to have received his forgiveness, but they both know that it has come too late. Holding her in his arms as life leaves her body, Fernando is left in despair and hopes that death will also end his pain.

Critique for Donizetti's La Favorita, 1974 Performance

Pavarotti's singing in this 1974 Performance is youthful, lyrical and fresh voiced. Overall, it can be described as wonderful and much improved from that which he displayed in the early performances of *La fille du Regiment.* In the latter the tone sagged a little throughout the lower and mixed registers, only to spring to life in the high register.

In *La Favorita,* the larynx and the base of the tongue are in a much higher position, resulting not only in a higher sitting tone but also in a more focused and forward sound. This was mainly due to a higher vertical laryngeal position than that which he deployed in both *La Fille du Regiment* and *L'elisir d'Amore*. The breath pressure was also a little firmer, as was vocal onset and vocal fold occlusion. The adjustments of the resonator are much more dexterous, agile and varied, while still maintaining a higher laryngeal position. We find that in this role, Pavarotti is much more in control, with wondrous results. The tone is beautifully warm and velvety, but also brilliant, striking a perfect *chiaro/scuro* balance. There is sufficient focus and metal (providing an impressive *squillo*) but also a judicious degree of velvet at the outer margins of the tone, ensuring that it never hardens. Similarly, the tone is forward in the mask but not to the degree that it sounds too edgy, too rigid or too inflexible. Importantly, it does not lack the space to allow the particles of the sound waves to spin and collide as they travel back and forth through the vocal tract from the glottis to the front of the mask and back again.

In this performance Pavarotti employs a much greater variety of tone, which overall is firm, focused, brilliant and velvety. Some of the sounds at the *passaggio* are extraordinarily precise in both space and focus, resulting in a truly beautiful and complete tone. There is a vast improvement overall, but especially at the *passaggio* and the early notes of the head register. There is some breathy singing in the middle register also, but it is dictated by Pavarotti's emotional interpretation.

I would not have expressed the text and these emotions using the *appoggio* system of breath management, as one can obtain every emotion required for the role without resorting to a breathy tone. Having said that it is not a vocal fault to use a breathy tone sparingly and for expressive purposes as Pavarotti does here, adding to the variety of colours in his tone. The voice is beautifully responsive in this role, with great flexibility both in the particular notes and in the vocal line on a larger scale.

Act I

Having raved about Pavarotti's overall performance in this role, I must confess that I found the recitative before the first act aria quite uneven and disappointing. Pavarotti begins reasonably well, but in the phrase '*Un novella m'assalse dolce desio, che di sperar non oso. Corsi al Tempio, alla prece, e volse il core*' the larynx rises too high, the breath becomes shallow and unsteady, and the tone lacks a foundation.

The good news is that this is the only recitative that I didn't like. The others are wonderful, displaying clarity of diction, the right choice of colour for the mood being created and great dynamic variation in the service of the drama as well as the voice. Pavarotti points the texts effectively, colouring them creatively and imaginatively by using a variety of colours and different vocal qualities. However, in producing these various vocal colours and qualities, he too often releases the connection between the respiratory muscles and the voice source. As a consequence, his larynx rises indiscriminately in softer passages and the sound, although still beautiful, becomes airy-fairy.

The Act one aria, *Una vergine un angiol di Dio*, is also a little disappointing. Even in the aria proper, Pavarotti starts the first phrase reasonably firmly, but the second phrase lacks a solid foundation. The problem here is that he has forgotten Lamperti's rule with respect to soft singing — *piano* singing should be in every way the same as *forte* singing except for intensity. It should have the same depth, the same roundness, and the same firm quality, allowing it to carry in a large theatre over a considerable orchestra. It is also worth reiterating that the authoritative opinion widely accepts that it takes just as much breath pressure to sing *piano* as it does to sing *forte*. In my opinion, this over sight mars all of Pavarotti's soft singing, but especially in the first recitative and parts of the aria, '*Una Vergine un angel di Dio*'.

Pavarotti's forte singing in this role is generally wonderful. In fact, in the more dramatic moments of the third and fourth Acts, his singing is stunning, apart from a couple of notes where the resonator has not been perfectly tuned to the vibrations emanating from the vocal folds. Overall, Pavarotti gives a masterful exhibition of negotiating both the tenor *passaggio* and the ensuing head voice, from which any young tenor could learn.

It is all the more regrettable therefore that Pavarotti has simultaneously under-supported and maintained to narrow a pharyngeal space in the [o] vowel on the E4 in the words *Dio* and *desio*, the [o] being too narrow and a little throaty. Although, it must be said that he does better with the second [o] vowel in the phoneme *desio,* which is also sung on the E4.

Unfortunately, he repeats the error when he sings the G♯ on the words '*scese all'alma*'. The [a] vowel here is a little under the note, as is the *gioia* on the E4 in which he attempts an unsuccessful diminuendo. It is a little insipid as the tone is under-supported and lacking in overtones. This is due to the tissue of the vocal folds being insufficiently occluded, not allowing for the necessary level of collision to produce the higher harmonics. Consequently, the tone is also a little under the pitch.

The same applies to the chromatic passage on the words '*allo sguardo*' rising to the A4 on the last line of the above example. This passage occurs twice, the first being under the note, under-supported and lacking a strong mental visualisation resulting in a deficient resonator adjustment. The second one is a little better.

The second verse of the aria is much better as the sound is *bene appoggiaoto*, more open-throated and more opulent. Fortunately for us, the C♯ at the end of '*Una vergine, un angiol di Dio*' is beautifully poised and focused.

It is important to remember that this aria is very difficult, not only because it is characterised by a high *tessitura* but also because it comes at the very beginning of the Opera before the tenor has much of a chance to warm up and settle in. In addition, much of the *tessitura* of this aria centres around the *passaggio* — not every tenor's strong suit.

Following the first act aria the performance moves into another gear, building dramatically and becoming vocally most compelling. In the duet that follows the aria Baldassare tries to talk sense to Fernando, reminding him that he knows nothing about this lady. Where does she come from, what is her name, what does she do? In the absence of any tangible knowledge, Fernando simply replies that he loves her.

Pavarotti uses a honeyed but forward ringing tone, not only beautiful but also fresh and youthful, flexible and pliable.

In Fernando's solo, '*Cara luce soave conforto*', there are moments that are simply superb, but others that can best be described as lacking emotional depth. In this duet, Fernando is tremendously conflicted: he is excited about the prospect of finding love with Leonora; he is conflicted and apprehensive about leaving his religious order; and he is devastated when his father refuses to give him his blessing. This was heavy emotional baggage for an innocent young man to carry, and as a consequence he turns to God. In this duet he is literally praying for the divine light to guide his footsteps towards a safe harbour. The singing is truly beautiful, but it lacks that emotional tension that emanates from conflict. It also lacks intensity, energy and drive, in no small part due to the conducting which is devoid of urgency and emotional depth.

In the this duet Pavarotti demonstrates that he can express true passion and love, provided that he is provided with the right tempo and freedom to express himself.

Chapter 39 — La Favorita by Donizetti, Pavarotti/Cossotto/Ghiaurov, 1974

This quality persists in the second duet between Fernando and Leonora, shown above. It begins with admirable energy and drive from everyone involved, including the conductor, Richard Bonynge. This is so much better both vocally and dramatically.

Unfortunately, the second part of the duet is, in my opinion, a less inspired moment of the score, and finds everyone, including Pavarotti, falling into the trap of deploying a torrent of beautiful sound, which unfortunately lacks urgency and intensity. This results in a tone that has become excessively languid, requiring greater urgency, additional fire, and increased intensity, thriving on the belief that the power of love will overcome all obstacles.

The recitative and aria which follow (which constitute the end of Act 2) are absolutely wonderful.

Pavarotti's singing of the recitatives '*E l'uom che la desia e il Re*' and '*E sciolto il vel*' is very compelling, characterised by clear diction, varied tone and just the right nuance for each mood change. He uses a variety of dynamics, colour and timbre to point the text, create character and tell the story and is particularly fluent and expressive. He proceeds from having the veil lifted from his eyes to the realisation that he is a nobody, whereas Leonora is very close to the apex of high society with no lesser a personality than the King calling upon her. He now believes that Leonora has provided him with the opportunity to distinguish himself as a military officer by displaying unusual valour so that he may become worthy of her.

Let us begin by analysing the recitative '*E l'uom che la desia e il Re*'. I like the approach that Pavarotti brings to this, finding his passion for the articulation of the text and clarity of diction quite infectious. The various vocal colours, the differentiated dynamics, and the situational quality of tone are most interesting and compelling.

The differentiation in tone on almost every phrase is very impressive. For instance, '*Ed io…Chi sono*' is characterised by a forte in both the first part and the second. This pattern is replicated on the '*Sventurato…oscuro*'.

The tone on the G flat in '*Il suo nome, il suo cuor*' is just marvellous, and the *Gran Dio* section of the recitative resembles a little prayer.

The F sharps on the [e] vowels in '*Io ne divenga*' and '*questo onor sublime*' are both lovely and ringing but covered, whilst the F♯ on '*Mi scorge*' is a little tight. On the other hand, the diminuendo on the [e] vowel in the word '*amante*' is splendid. The quality ranges from a little breathy to a really firm, ringing, harmonically rich tone. The diction is also wonderful, as is the pointing and colouring of the text. All of this provides the recitative with stronger contrast and expression, giving it greater poignancy and affective dramatic impetus.

The aria proper — '*Si che un solo accento*' — represents a march to glory, in which the love for his lady becomes the impulse for conquest and heroic deeds.

The singing in this aria is as close to perfection as we are likely to hear. The tone is beautiful, full-blooded, but easy, resonant and flowing. It has a lovely bloom around the core of the tone and a high level of supple malleability. I love the tone Pavarotti uses in this aria; although forward and ringing, he is not artificially placing it against the mask. It is a perfect *chiaro/scuro* balance; the equilibrium between brilliance (*squillo*) and roundness and velvet is beautifully judged. Pavarotti utilises a firm and precise onset (attack) followed by a torrent of firm, harmonically rich and complete tone emitted through a seamless legato line.

As I said above, this and the dramatic betrayal scene from Act 3 (when Fernando discovers that Leonora has been the King's mistress) are beautifully sung and gloriously acted vocally. Having been quite critical throughout this book, I am thrilled to be able to say that this singing is as close to perfection as you are ever likely to hear. I am totally conquered by Pavarotti's singing in this role. Particularly in the scene and aria above, and the *scena* in which he discovers and reacts to his betrayal by both Leonora and King Alfonso. The singing is technically close to perfection; it is musically and interpretatively sensitive and refined, and his technique allows him to display a great deal of temperament whilst remaining controlled and artistic. Having said that, I feel compelled to point out one or two issues that could have been handled better.

The first is the [o] vowel on the E natural on the word '*valor*' which is too narrow, overly collected and, as Pavarotti would say, '*a little choked*'. The truth is that with a lyric voice such as Pavarotti's, when singing Fernando (a high lyric role) there is simply no reason to enter the head voice as early as the E natural. It is far too early.

The second issue is the chromatic passage where he rises from the E4 to F♯, G, G♯ and A natural. He collects the G4 too firmly, covering it in a way that dampens some of the upper harmonics and gives the impression that the tone is a little flat in pitch. He approaches the G♯ from below the note, but eventually, it blooms into a great sound on the second part half of the G♯. This G♯ evolves into an even more exciting tone on the accented A natural that follows. There are a couple of other [o] vowels in which a little migration towards the [aw] vowel would enhance the sound.

Pavarotti attempts to differentiate the second verse from the first verse by adding some ornamentation. This is eminently sensible, especially since the two verses are exactly the same. He begins by singing the early part of the second verse more softly. This is aesthetically pleasing, but his soft singing lacks core, and it is not as firm as it should be. The second mode of differentiation mentioned above is the use of very minor ornamentation. This takes the form of singing a triad up to a glorious B4 on the word *valor*, followed by a C♯ on the phrase '*e noi vivremo insieme,*' and then rising to a glorious B natural in the finale. This is certainly wonderful vocalising. Nonetheless, it is worth mentioning that the C♯ is not as well supported (*appoggiata*) as it should be. Towards the end of the note there is a disconnect between the respiratory muscles and the suspensory muscles of the larynx, resulting in an undistinguished release of the note. Pavarotti releases the tone with the throat muscles as opposed to a clean release with the respiratory muscles, mainly by using the diaphragm to cut off the air supply exactly at the same time as he abducts (opens) the glottis.

The scene illustrated above, *'per me del ciel si dispiega il favor'*, takes place immediately after the wedding between Leonora and Fernando. In a moment of sheer delight Fernando invites the courtiers to join him in celebrating his good fortune and happiness.

Beginning with a sense of elation, Pavarotti expresses these emotions using the most beautiful, round and brilliant tone. However, while it is luminous, radiant and resplendent, the tone also retains a youthful freshness and a gorgeous bloom. This is the type of sound that Jose Carreras is referring to when he declares that Luciano 'has the sun in his voice, nobody else has this sound'. I concur with him, but I go further by suggesting that whilst Pavarotti possesses a most beautiful and translucent 'sunny' sound, he brings much more than that. This quality of sound has been cultivated and is supported by tremendous technique and superb artistry. Above all, Pavarotti has developed the craft of reproducing a variety of vocal timbres at will.

There is hardly a note out of place in this singing: it is well supported (*appoggiato*), with a beautifully neat and firm vocal onset (attack), setting the vocal folds into free vibration. However, there is sufficient vocal fold resistance. The breath is pressed against the vocal fold tissue, which sets it into vibration. This causes the medial aspects of the vocal fold fibres to collide, stimulating the higher harmonics and skewing the spectrum to the right, ensuring an abrupt end to breath flow. This technique produces wonderfully rich overtones whilst the vocal tract is shaped in such a manner as to maximise the resonance on every note. If there is the odd note that is short of perfection, it comes as a consolation to us mere mortals that Pavarotti too is human.

Having dealt with the joyous emotions of a young man in love, let us deal with the bitter disappointment when that dream is shattered in the scene below. The courtiers believe that Fernando has acquired his titles and fortune mainly as a reward for taking Leonora, the King's mistress, to be his wife, an action that they regard not only as reprehensible but also dishonourable.

In this scene, the courtiers refuse Fernando's extended hand of friendship and remind him that in their world there are still such values as respect and honour, both of which must be earned and not bought.

Fernando's Betrayal Scene

In this scene Pavarotti's voice assumes a new quality — fuller and more dramatic, with tremendous brilliance and energy. The richness of the harmonics, especially at the *passaggio*, is truly unique in the annals of singing. Traditionally, in order to gain a greater ring and amplitude at the *passaggio*, the great tenors of the past opened the vowel and lowered the larynx, creating more space in the throat and gaining more volume and amplitude. However, it lost the collected and focused quality that provided the sound with direction and focus, a quality they used in a more flowing *mezzo-forte* tone.

Pavarotti remains unique as he opens the throat by a moderate lowering of the larynx combined with the activation of the *appoggio* system. To his credit he does not fall into the trap of facilitating the creation of excessive pharyngeal space. (This promotes volume through the indiscriminate opening of the throat and mouth, allowing the sound to go back into the throat, creating a hollow sound and distorting the vowel.) Pavarotti's configuration allows him to attain a tremendous ring (*squillo*), focusing the tone whilst still maintaining vowel authenticity, vocal quality and the bloom of the voice.

The above notwithstanding, we are here to learn. Although his singing is close to perfection, there are still lessons to be learned. Let's begin with the opening phrase with its splendid interval of a fourth up to the [o] vowel in the word *l'onor* on the G♭.

Here, the [o] vowel is quite authentic, and the sound is beautifully accented but not forced. It is simultaneously brilliant, forward and ringing while maintaining a certain colour, roundness, and vocal bloom. Having said that, there is still room for improvement in this sequence. This could be achieved by allowing the [o] vowel to migrate a little towards the [aw], an action that would slightly open the vowel and give it a more lateral shape. This would eliminate the overly covered configuration of the vowel (placing a lid on top of the sound), which often prevents the upper harmonics from vibrating freely in sympathy with the resonator.

The rest of that line is excellent, with a particular mention of the [u] vowel on the '*fu sacra*,' also on the G♭. The [u] vowel can be tricky for the tenor, especially on the G♭, but not for Pavarotti, and what follows is a torrent of excellent singing. I will only mention that the larynx starts a little high for the [a] vowel of '*culla*' on the A♭, but quickly lowers itself into its natural position, resulting in a lovely clear and ringing but velvety sound.

Just a reminder that this over-covering of vowels is something that Pavarotti did quite often at the *passaggio* on the [o] vowel and earlier still even on the [e] vowel.

It is to his credit that the defect of the previously over-covered [e] vowel has been completely eliminated, and similarly, the defect of the [o] has improved to the point where it is almost undetectable.

With respect to the [e] vowel I must agree with di Stefano's comments that even though Pavarotti had learned to open his sounds marginally they were still too lean and narrow, especially so with the [e] vowel. However, we must recall that the [e] vowel is naturally a more lateral and forward vowel, yielding a bouquet of rich upper harmonics, which are less prone to damping.

Technically, Pavarotti achieves this type of tone through a moderate lowering of the larynx and a simultaneously minor increase in mouth and vowel opening. This seems to have the effect of channelling the sound waves towards the palate and directing, but not driving, the sound vibrations forward, while still retaining the feeling or the perception of focusing the voice.

In order to complete this scene, I would like to underline Pavarotti's vocal and mental dexterity. The courtiers offend Fernando by refuting his assertion that honour meant more to him than all the titles and social trappings he had acquired. His instinct is to push back, employing an edgy, metallic tone as he demands to know what they said (*Che diceste, che diceste, di questa ingiuria io vo'raggion'*) and suggesting that they better have a good reason for this insult.

Immediately, Pavarotti changes tone for the phrase 'Ma *no, io m'ingannai. Deh! Parlate vi suplico*.' (Ah no, I must have been mistaken. I pray you speak freely.) He captures the instantaneous change of mood perfectly, going from a metallic, edgy, angry sound to a malleable, soothing tone in a split second — a wonderful effort. In a personal interview, Leone Magiera declared that Pavarotti had arrived at a stage in his development where he had agonised over his interpretation. There is considerable evidence of this fact in his interpretation of Fernado's role not only vocally, but also musically and dramatically.

Finally, when his plea falls on deaf ears, and the murmurings still persist, he decides it is time to put an end to it, and he calls the courtiers out. Fortunately, Baldassare appears and brings his son to his senses by revealing that the courtiers are not lying about Leonora. She is, in fact, the King's mistress, which revelation shatters Fernando, who clearly had no inkling of this. Fernando feels totally betrayed by both Leonora and King Alfonso, believing that they have taken advantage of his love for Leonora in order to bring him dishonour. He is heartbroken about losing the woman he loves, but he is even more devastated about being dishonoured. He expresses his feelings of shame and anger and betrayal.

Unexpectedly, the King enters the hall, and Fernado's despair turns to anger: '*Sire, io ti deggio mia fortuna e mia vita*' (Sire, I owe you my life and my fortune). Up to this point, there has not been a note out of place, but now, as he expresses Fernando's anger and despair, Pavarotti becomes a little reckless. For instance, on the phrase '*Di nome il conte*', he indiscriminately opens his mouth and throat, purposely loosens his control over the focus of his tone, allowing the voice to go back and producing a hollow tone. This hollow sound is symbolic of Fernando's feelings about his achievements; they are not what he had hoped for, all his dreams have gone up in smoke, his heart is in turmoil, and the honorific titles of Marchese and Count mean nothing to him. In fact he removes the medals from his neck and throws them to the ground.

Similarly, he takes his sword and addresses the King, stating that these honours came at too high a price. He sings a chromatic passage to a dramatic A4 on the phrase '*Ah si dell'onor mio*'. Dropping down the octave, he repeats '*al prezzo dell'onore*' with tremendous effect, breaking the sword, throwing it on the ground and exiting the scene.

Conclusion to Act III

This brings us to the central scene of the opera, one that embodies every emotion, from tremendous elation to great anger and deep despair. It is the confrontation between Fernando and the courtiers, followed by an even angrier one between Fernando and King Alfonso. This is a truly magnificent scene, and Pavarotti does its justice both dramatically and vocally. He remains undoubtedly the best Fernando on record, producing a glorious sound that varies every few bars to depict his character's emotions — a sense of deep betrayal coupled with desperate feelings of loss, shame, and dishonour. His singing of the constant *passaggio* notes F, F♯ and G4 is simply a masterclass in how to execute the tenor *passaggio* notes seamlessly, with just the right amount of cover and brilliance (*chiaro/scuro*). With the tone embodying the right proportions of metal at its core (producing penetrating edge) and roundness at its margins, this is simply singing at its glorious best.

Our last excerpt from the opera is the wonderful bel canto aria '*Spirto gentil*'. This is a gain a most beautiful aria but very difficult aria, mainly because the general *tessitura* is high, and it lingers excessively at the *passaggio*. In addition, it begins with quite a dramatic recitative before settling into a gloriously suspended line of legato outpouring.

A critique of Spirto gentil

With his heart broken and his dreams of love and glory shattered, Fernando rejects the secular and mundane for the more spiritual world of the cloister.

On the day of his ordination, his voice soars over the choir. It is compelling not only for its beauty but also for its fervent sincerity as he pledges his life to doing God's work.

The ritual is over, and all appears to have gone very well, and yet Fernando has not been able to still the anguish in his heart; nor has he found the much hoped for peace of mind. In his torment he begins to reflect on the reasons for his disquiet and his mind wanders to another time and another world. Leonora reigned supreme over his heart, and he dared to believe that he had found enduring love and happiness. Then it all vanished.

Pavarotti begins this most beautiful aria rather softly. In fact, the first E natural is rather suspended, avoiding the temptation to make an immediate dramatic impact.

Nonetheless, the recitative demands drama and Pavarotti has to find a way to deliver it. His voice is not inherently dramatic or voluminous but has a tremendous ring on record as indeed it had in the theatre. Its major characteristics were its brilliance, its beauty, its sense of ease, and the richness of its harmonic series. He achieves his dramatic effect through strategic accentuation and dramatic edge (not to mention a light snarl to the voice) and finally by using vocal colouring in an intelligent way to serve the drama.

The lessons to be learned in this aria are:

- Pavarotti should be more reliant on breath flexibility, greater resilience and an appropriate respiratory strategy for the execution of dramatic recitative.

- He does not sing sufficiently through the vowels, nor does he follow through the vocal line.

- Following the end of a phrase Pavarotti is not sufficiently assiduous in maintaining the previous position at the beginning of the next phrase.

- He should be reminded of the fact that the old masters developed a dictum suggesting that we should think up for the lower notes and think down for the higher notes.

- Overall, the singing, which is mainly concentrated around the *passaggio* and the head voice is simply glorious.

The tenor has to create the drama whilst still retaining a buoyant position and preventing the voice from getting heavy.

I like the way Pavarotti begins this recitative relatively softly; however, I also believe that the second phrase with the repetition of *Favorita del Re* should be allowed to flow naturally, as holding back the first beat of the bar on the [i] vowel sounds a little contrived, as it requires more direction and

more follow through. This half-baked approach does nothing for his interpretation, not to mention the drama.

Having failed to accent and direct the first beat of the bar, Pavarotti opens the last part of the bar, which is not only counterintuitive but also ineffective. Having said that, I like very much his delivery of the next few phrases: '*qual nero abbisso, qual mia trama infernal, la gloria mia avvolse in un istante*'. Here, Pavarotti uses the drama to create a snarl in the voice and point out the words with a certain dramatic edge. He does this rather well, if somewhat restrained, but it works well in Donizetti. A decade later, in a Verdi recitative, this treatment would be regarded as rather tame and insipid. The last phrase, '*E ogni speme tronco del core amante*', is not only soft but also beautiful.

Pavarotti begins the aria *Spirto gentil* rather softly with a good legato line and a lovely soft head voice on some of the [e] vowels. Having said that I feel that this singing could have been better supported in order to eliminate a sense of fragility or insecurity, replacing it with a sense of firmness and direction, improved legato line, and greater emotional intensity.

The right respiratory strategy for this style of bel canto singing is the *sostegno* system of breath management. This entails the raising and swelling of the chest, the lateral, (outward) movement of the lower floating ribs, and an outward excursion of the lower posterior costal ribs.

One of the best descriptions of the *sostegno* system of breath management is the one espoused by the great international soprano Luisa Tetrazzini. She contends that:

> In singing, I always feel as if I were forcing my breath against my chest, and, just as in the exercises according to Delsarte you will find the chest leads in all physical movements, so in singing you should feel this firm support of the chest on the highest as well as the lowest notes'. The immediate pressure of the air should be felt more against the chest. This feeling of singing against the chest with the weight of air pressing up against it is known as 'breath support,' and in Italian we have even a better word, *appoggio*, which is breath prop [Tetrazzini, 1909: 14-15].

This breathing strategy maintains a certain sense of buoyancy whilst keeping control of the breath flow, which provides us not only with a glorious legato line but also with a constant emotional stream, not to mention the greater control over the release of the sound. The other issue addressed by this breathing strategy refers to the fact maintaining a high chest high combined with a contracted abdomen prevents the diaphragm from settling to low and bringing the larynx too far. These are critical issues in terms of the bel canto style, because if the sound becomes too dark and a little heavy, it will lose the flexibility and lightness of touch required for the high *tessitura* and *passaggio* singing.

The vocal line is the other issue I would like to discuss, as well as the function of breath flow, legato and sostenuto, articulatory configuration, and mental strategising.

Pavarotti does all this and more with the first line of *spirto gentil*, as discussed above.

This first line is all on the E4 '*spirto gentil, nei sogni miei brillasti, un di ma ti perdei*', which descends from the E4 to the D5 and then C5. In a sequence such as this, each descending phrase should as far as possible, resemble the first line in depth, character, and roundness, but importantly also in this register.

Pavarotti, however, whilst maintaining a good legato line, and a lovely quality tone, fails to maintain the head tone on the D5 and then the C5 and then B4. It is possible to sing the D5 and C5 with a greater prevalence of head voice, bringing them more into line with the first phrase. He repeats the pattern in the next phrases — '*Fuggi dal cor, mentite speme, larve d'amore, larve d'amor*'.

At the change '*A te d'accanto del genitore scordava il pianto, la patria, il ciel*' he produces a more full-blooded sound as befits the aria, whilst essentially adhering to the natural lyricism of his vocal instrument. He could have opened the [a] vowel on the G4 on the word *pianto* and the [e] vowel on the '*Ahime*', also on the G4. The descending [e] vowel from G4 to F♯ and F4 is quite lovely but there is a sense of conscious control. It should be more natural and not such hard work.

It then moves back to the *Spirto gentil*, but the second verse is superior to the first until he reaches the top C5, which, by Pavarotti's lofty standards, is not a good one. The note is in the right position, but the breath support is not sufficiently firm and consequently, the sound is a little unsteady. The lack of sub-glottal pressure impacts on the G4 that follows it is far too open and is more reminiscent of Giuseppe di Stefano than it is of Pavarotti. Fortunately for Pavarotti, this proves to be an aberration and aberrations very rarely ruin voices. It is only the systematic abuse of the voice that causes damage.

La Favorita is a breakthrough role for Pavarotti. It is a much higher tessitura than most of his other roles, with the exception of *I Puritani*. Not only does he manage the tessitura extremely well, but he brings a newly found maturity to his interpretation. The tone itself is exquisitely beautiful, but in an entirely different way to the velvety, lush Italianate tone, inspired by Von Karajan's Germanic School, that he used in *La Boheme*, or the lovely Italianate, but English-mediated tone he uses in *Rigoletto*. In *La Favourite*, the tone can best be described as sunny. There is a certain disarming purity and evenness about this tone. It is an easy, penetrating and yet mellifluous tone. It is forward and brilliant, displaying great clarity and definition of vowels; it is ringing and metallic but with a velvety, warm and translucent quality.

Chapter 40

Maria Stuarda, 1975/1976

The tragic opera *Maria Stuarda* deals with the Tudor Period in English history. Betrothed to the Dauphin of France from a very young age, Mary Queen of Scots had been raised at the French court. After a year on the French throne, her husband Francis II died, and Mary was only 18 years of age when she made the fateful decision to reclaim the Scottish throne. She was no stranger to court intrigue but could not even control her protestant nobles. Finally, the Scottish protestant aristocracy rebelled, forcing Mary to seek asylum from her cousin Elizabeth, Queen of England.

Elizabeth's advisors reminded her that her cousin Mary was a direct descendant of the Tudor line and widely regarded as the rightful heir to Henry VIII's crown. At the same time, Elizabeth had been declared an illegitimate bastard. Elizabeth's henchman then established an inquiry into the vicious murder of Mary's decadent second husband Henry, Lord Darnley, with the explicit objective of implicating her in the crime. Although the search failed to prove Mary's complicity, it was sufficient evidence to keep her imprisoned for years.

Maria Stuarda, Pavarotti, Sutherland and Bonynge

The Pavarotti tone in this role is absolutely radiant—forward and ringing with an excellent metallic core, the circumference of which is always enveloped by a truly beautiful rusty colour and velvet border. A bright sunflower colour is used for the lateral forward ringing vowels. This is just a wondrously beautiful tonal quality and in large part, its interest lies in the fact that much of this singing is soft, often gentle, but quite restrained. Consequently, when he does unleash a forte head register it is characterised by a brilliant, sunny sound that makes an even greater impact. I have never heard a more genuinely complete *chiaro/scuro* and glorious tone than Pavarotti in *La Favourite, Maria Stuarda, I Puritani, Lucia, La Boheme, Turandot, Rigoletto* and his early recording of *Ballo in Maschera*. His first act duet with Roger Soyer, '*Ah rimiro il bel sembiante*' followed by his description of Mary Stuart in his duet with Elizabeth '*Era amor l'immaggine*' and later the duet with Mary '*Da tutti abbandonata*' can only be described as spectacular vocalising.

I had written a detailed critique of Pavarotti in the role of Robert Leicester. However, I have deleted most of it simply because this is singing to be lauded, not to be criticised. Consequently, I have decided to generalise my comments where possible, except in one or two places where I felt there might be a new lesson to be learned that we had not previously elaborated upon. Let us begin with our critique.

The attack is clean and firm, and the laryngeal position is generally moderately low but considerably more elevated than it was in his earlier recordings, such as *Beatrice di Tenda, L'Amico Fritz,* and even *La Fille du Regiment,* but not as high as that which is yet to come. A lower laryngeal position characterised all of these early operas, a sagging zygomatic arch and protruding lips which, in general, elongated the vocal tract, lowered all the formants and darkened the sound. This vocal production was the result of flow phonation. This meant that respiration was under low pressure, and the glottis was not as adducted or tensed as it would later become. The general area around the laryngeal collar was more relaxed, as was the area around the pharyngeal wall. It is well understood that his type of production favours the lower harmonics at the expense of the higher ones, providing a round, velvety tone rather than a brilliant, bright one with ping and lots of *squillo*. Pavarotti's voice was sitting back at this point of his development, and the centre frequency was a little low. The tone was also too round and velvety, lacking that brilliance, ring and focus that is an important aspect of the very best sounds. These are the elements that add excitement to the sound throughout the head voice.

In *Maria Stuarda,* as in *La Favorita, Lucia di Lammermoor* and *I Puritani,* the voice is firm, virile and ringing. Physiologically, we find that both the laryngeal position, the zygomatic arch, and the soft palate are generally elevated, as is the base of the tongue and the epiglottis. The pharyngeal walls are firm, except for the inferior part of the pharynx, where the rising pharynx and base of the tongue create a crumpled pharyngeal wall. In general, the tongue tip is pressed lightly against the lower teeth, and there is evidence of just a hint of a smile not only with the lateral vowels but also, unusually for Pavarotti, with some of the rounded vowels. These physiological configurations favour the matching of higher formants of the vocal tract with the more acute harmonics issuing from the vocal folds. Unfortunately, this occurs at the expense of the lower ones. This is the complete opposite of the manner in which he used his vocal instrument in the early apprenticeship period, such as *Beatrice di Tenda,* parts of the *Verdi Requiem* and even the lower middle register of *La Fille du Regiment* and *L'amico Fritz.*

The *appoggio* is firmer and more flexible with a much quicker reflexive responsiveness than earlier efforts, impacting beneficially both on clarity of tone and the vocal line.

The vocal folds are beautifully and cleanly adducted, and the firmness of their action is a reflection of a firm attack, consequently transferred onto the ensuing sostenuto. It is the effect of firm *appoggio* (breath and *importation*), combined with a clean and firm collision of the vocal folds, which promotes the abrupt cessation of breath flow and the skewing of the spectrum, which confers the tone with brilliance, focus and *squillo*.

Concerning respiration, I believe that Pavarotti could generate more breath energy by breathing more deeply, requiring a more significant expansion of the abdominal and lateral walls combined with the posterior of the abdominal wall. This would create more intense conditions for Lamperti's *lotta vocale*, allowing these muscles to remain in an expanded position for an unusual length of time. Finally, there are times when Pavarotti does not take sufficient breath to give the tone that buoyancy, that sense of sitting on an inflated beach ball. You don't take a larger and deeper breath because you can't arrive at the end of the phrase; you take a deeper breath because it improves the quality of the sound: a sound can be substantial and still take flight.

Let us evaluate *Maria Stuarda*, beginning with the scene between Talbot and Leicester. Giorgio Talbot declares that he has been to Fortheringhay to see the unhappy Stuart Queen. Roberto asks him to keep his voice down and then enquires after Mary. 'She is an angel of love, magnanimous and beautiful as always,' responds Giorgio. 'She sent you an image of herself and this letter. I received it from her hand just before she could bathe it with her tears. She spoke your name with great affection'. Robert declares that he can't wait to see her beautiful face again, resolving to either free her or die with her.

In the phrase '*Ah! Piu sommesso*' Pavarotti begins the G4 on the [a] vowel in a slightly low position but almost instantaneously gives the tone a lift and modifies towards the [o] vowel. In so doing, he creates a vocal tract configuration that provides the tone with greater focus, firmer vocal tract constriction, and dampens the upper harmonics. So, whilst the tone remains sonorous and quite brilliant, technically, it requires greater freedom and a more authentic [a] vowel (vowel integrity remaining important in vowel modification). Even more importantly, this informs us that Pavarotti has not totally conquered the concept of visualising or pre-phonatory tuning — the complete tone before giving it material embodiment.

A very similar criticism could be levelled at the [o] vowel on the G4 in the phrase '*Oh troppo indegno*'. Pavarotti not only fails to elevate the zygomatic arch and soft palate (giving the tone sufficient space) but also protrudes the lips, elongating the vocal tract, lowering all the formants and darkening the voice.

With respect to the [u] vowel in the phrase '*parla tel giuro*,' the G4 on the [u] vowel is markedly different from his earlier efforts. He is now opening this vowel considerably whilst at the same time increasing the pharyngeal resonating space. The same applies to other [u] vowels at the *passaggio*, suggesting that he has altered his approach to this vowel, and it is not an accidental modification. This tone is much improved from previous efforts also.

On the other hand, the [e] vowel remains a minor problem. It is a very difficult vowel for Pavarotti as he either creates an overly narrow space or he modifies the [e] too severely towards the [ir] vowel. All he is required to do is just drop the jaw a little whilst increasing sub-glottal pressure and the vowel modification will take care of itself.

However, that is not Pavarotti at this point in time; this was too simple for him, too straightforward. I like how Miller treats this topic when he suggests that If, as the mouth opens naturally with rising pitch and amplitude, the integrity of the vowel is retained, the first formant frequency will grow in strength, and there will be no loss of upper harmonic partials ('ring,' 'ping'). Resonance will pertain throughout the scale [Miller, 2004: 75].

Pavarotti does arrive at this type of simplicity, but much later in his career. For now, he is looking to introduce more colour to the sometimes penetrating [e]. So, he adapts a mixed sound, one in which the tongue remains in the lateral position of a lateral vowel whilst his jaw and mouth assume the position of a round vowel. This definitely endows the tone with more colour, but it also compromises vowel integrity.

The duet properly begins with the phrase '*Ah! rimiro il bel sembiante*' is glorious. This is a beautiful flowing torrent of sound with an abundance of legato, as well as a great mixture of ring, brilliance and burnished velvet. He adds to the glory of his performance by singing a number of passages either on piano or with considerable restraint, which not only contrasts with the loud singing but also intensifies the emotional and passionate state of Robert's love for Mary. Glorious as this singing is, however, we must remember that whilst Pavarotti is closer to perfection than 99.9 per cent of singers, he is still not perfect. The question then remains, 'What can we learn from his minor imperfections'?

The first thing to learn is that if you do not take a deep breath, you are likely to run short of breath energy — a condition that Lamperti (1883), believes is inimical to good vocal hygiene. According to Titze, when the breath is pressed through the vocal folds, it acts as a shock absorber, creating a firm glottal adduction whilst safeguarding the tissue from a severe collision through a slight fissure in the glottis. The absence of such a shock absorber can and does accentuate the collision of the vocal folds within each vibratory cycle, thereby increasing its potentially harmful effect. The above is a condition that is often revealed in Pavarotti's singing, albeit in a minor way. For instance, in the phrase beginning with '*adorato, vagheggiato,*' he fails to take a deep breath, resulting in an onset of tone that begins too far back. He also fails to observe the *imposto* or subjective *appoggio* (sensation of a focal point for the sympathetic Proprioceptive vibrations). Consequently, the tone not only starts back in the throat but actually remains there. The next issue to learn from this is that the attack or onset has to be neat and precise. This will give the impression that the thought, breath and tone collaborate to produce a forward, focused, ringing tone through a vowel that is clear, well defined and sonorous. Finally, the singer must follow through the tone not just with the mind, which is important, but also with the breath. The latter gives our thinking and pre-phonatory tuning plans a physical basis to materially produce the tone we envisage and desire.

A tone that should be followed through with both breath and thought.

The G4 on the [u] in '*spunta languido*' is a good sound, but it is still a little manufactured. This [u] vowel could be and should be more spontaneous, more thrown away rather than contrived.

Once the singer has conquered this technique, you will find that the attack and *appoggio* will assist you in following through on the phrases. In Pavarotti's case this begins

with the '*adorato*' and '*vagheggiato*' which will be smooth and seamless. On the phrase '*Ah memorie*' the onset should be sharper and cleaner, establishing a firmly defined vowel.

Following on to the next series of repeated and accented G4s in the phrase '*io per lei sfidar sapro, sfidar sapro, sfidar sapro,*' these [a] vowels should be more collected and more forward.

The second theme in this duet begins with the phrase 'Se fida tanto colei m'amo, and Da gl'occhi il pianto le tergero.'

This theme is marked piano by the composer, and Pavarotti does its full justice. Not only does he sing it softly, but he also elevates the larynx and lightens the sound into a truly beautiful lyrical tone. It is just glorious singing through to the end of this duet. Purely in the spirit of scholarly endeavour, I would do four things that I believe would improve this performance.

1. The first is that I would sing the staccato notes a little shorter and sharper concentrating on bouncing the staccato notes of a more buoyant breath.

2. The second would be to open the [e] vowels a little; they are presently too narrow, and a small dropping of the jaw will accomplish his intent.

3. The third issue relates to being a little more cautious about allowing the larynx to rise indiscriminately with increasing frequency.

4. The fourth issue I would address is the issue of not allowing the breath to explode in most of the end notes at the end of phrases. The release of the end notes should be clean, precise, instantaneous and silent.

This second theme in the duet with Queen Elizabeth is marked *piano* and *dolcissimo*, and Pavarotti does the composer's intentions complete justice. This is just wonderful singing, and it is, overall, amongst the best singing I have heard from this truly remarkable singer. However, the question for us remains as always — is there a way to improve even such glorious singing, and if so, what needs to be done? The answer is yes, we can do even better, and the first thing we should do is to analyse the phrase '*Era d'amore l'immagine*'. This begins gloriously, but the second F sharp on the [o] vowel of '*d'amor*' is too collected, too constricted and too narrow. In this case, we could and should open the vowel towards the [aw] vowel, a modification that would prevent the lips from protruding and the larynx from lowering too far.

The combined action of diminished lip protrusion and encouraging the larynx and the base of the tongue to sit a little higher should automatically shorten the vocal tract and privileges the higher harmonics (the ping, the ring and focus of the tone). To a large degree this would happen automatically as result of modulating from a closed [o] to a more open [aw]. However, on this particular [o] vowel, Pavarotti protrudes the lips on the F sharp, elongating the vocal tract, lowering all the formants and darkening the tone. It is worth remembering that in soft singing, one can generally open the vowels a little more than loud singing with impunity.

The following G♯ on the [a] vowel on '*immagine*' requires more space. Dropping the jaw a little, raising the zygomatic arch, and lifting the soft palate whilst increasing breath pressure would be a good place to start. For this to succeed Pavarotti needs to trust the breath a bit more and throw off the consonants with greater disdain and spontaneity; he is too careful.

I think I should say a few words about this phrase, not to be critical but, as always, to learn from it. I note that Pavarotti sings first on the [l] and then the nasal continuant [m] rather than singing through the consonants and arriving at the vowels quickly.

It is possible to sing on the [n] and [m] and [gn] continuants of course but not on other consonants. The next phrase is excellent, but then we arrive at the F♯ followed by the G♯ on the phrase '*sembianza avea*' where both the F♯ and the G♯ should be '*bene appoggiate*' and the vowels should be more open. You achieve this by increasing subglottal pressure, marginally dropping the mandible, and raising the zygomatic arch, which also raises the soft palate.

We then arrive at the B4 on the [a] vowel on the word (*l'anima*). This begins a little under the note because it is insufficiently *appoggiata*, but soon arrives at the bull's eye focus that is required. In large part this is due to a greatly improved *appoggio system*. Above all, Pavarotti should be bouncing that top B of the breath in a similar fashion to the strategy recommended by William Vennard in his 'bouncing epigastric' simile.

As previously, in this duet, Pavarotti makes some wonderful sounds.

The things to watch for are in the phrase '*no, diffidar non dei*', where the E4 on the [e] vowel displays a little movement in the vibrato. This is simply because the vocal instrument is insufficiently *appoggiata* (coordinated) to maintain stability in the larynx and steady the vibrato. The exact same problem reoccurs on the same note in the phrase '*Restava il cor di lei*' on the E4 and again it is the [e] vowel. The good thing is that Pavarotti maintains the position, whereas an inferior singer would tend to poke the tone in the mask as a means of steadying the vibrato.

The remedy here is not just improved objective *appoggio* (breath support), but also the aiming of the sympathetic vibrations (subjective *appoggio*) more purposefully towards the mask.

Pavarotti knows this, but he is trying not to put too much pressure on these preparatory *passaggio* notes so that the various muscle groups are in a position to respond more effectively and with greater endurance when he finally makes greater demands on the instrument. The demands come in the form of increasing muscular contraction, especially at the *passaggio*. This is intelligent singing but not a good strategy for making art: in art, you can't rob Peter to pay Paul. What he doesn't realise, is that with a little more energy he can achieve both.

Overall, this is a felicitous performance. Pavarotti creates a wonderous, easy-flowing tone, but with sufficient breath flow and the necessary glottal resistance to create a sharp-tilting and sharp spectrum, lending the voice a sunny disposition combined with a beautifully balanced degree of brilliance and velvet (chiaro/scuro). Many of these qualities can be attributed to Pavarotti's wonderful instrument, but that does him a great injustice because the way he balances these elements demonstrates a great deal of skill, intelligence and aesthetic judgment.

Pavarotti was at the peak of his vocal and creative powers and by the time he sang in that now legendary production of *I Puritani* at the Met in March 1976 he was the most famous and most beloved opera star in the world. Pavarotti was the man with the Midas touch. Yet, having arrived at a place in his art that is as close to perfection as it is humanly possible to achieve, Pavarotti was now unexpectedly confronted with a very different but equally serious challenge: a mental health problem.

Chapter 41

Pavarotti's Struggle with Depression

In 1981, whilst researching his book *Pavarotti My Own Story*, the great man confessed to his co-author William Wright that in the mid-seventies, something terrible happened to him. For some unknown reason, he said: 'I went into a depression; I am not sure what caused it.'

There is one thing for sure, Pavarotti was at the zenith of his career; he was singing the roles he always wanted to sing in the principal opera houses of the world for the highest fees attainable. He knew that with all that good fortune he had no right to feel depressed, but he couldn't help himself.

'I completely lost my zest for everything!', he would recall. Not even the audience's applause and adulation, which in the past had served as a panacea for all, seemed to work anymore: 'Everything had lost its point'.

A few years later, when Pavarotti was in a much better state of mind and in discussions with William Wright, the tenor advanced several reasons for his inexplicable lapse into a state of depression.

He believed that the first and perhaps the most powerful reason was that after so many years of struggling to improve his vocal technique, working diligently on his dramatic craft, and building a career by overcoming one obstacle at a time, Pavarotti had finally arrived at his destination. However, the journey had been so intense, so unrelenting that by the time he achieved fame and fortune at such a lofty height, he didn't have any unfulfilled goals. He had no more obstacles to overcome, no more dragons to kill, no material goal to aim for. He no longer had a *raison d'être*. For the first time in his life, he didn't have any plans and didn't know what came next. For the first time in his life, he asked himself whether what was coming was worthwhile.

The second reason was that once the New York critics and influential members of the public began to refer to him as the world's greatest tenor, it only added to the immense pressure to perform at your very best every time you step onto a stage. Pavarotti rightly concluded that being number one does not make you superhuman; if anything, it actually makes you more human and more vulnerable. Pavarotti posited that 'You are still a mortal man who can catch a sore throat, be out of form, or make a mistake' [Wright, 1981: 276]. In his depressed state of mind, Pavarotti inverted everything. He now felt that he was trapped by his own voice. There was always another Boheme, another Tosca, another L'Elisir to sing. On and on until you sang so badly that no one wanted to hear you anymore.

The other issue that plagued Pavarotti was the question of his weight. He set very high standards for himself and took pride in doing everything he attempted really well, or else give it up. He hated being overweight, mainly because the Pavarotti he had become had now vanquished the Luciano he had known all his life. In addition, he felt that it was hurting his career. Directors were ignoring him: they gave up on his acting ability before they even started. Pavarotti recalls that:

> I sensed that they were paying little attention to my dramatic performances, either because they didn't think I could do it or they felt that my weight would spoil whatever effect they attempted. This hurt me very much. [Wright, 1981: 277]

Quite apart from what this was doing to his career, on a human and emotional level, being overweight had a tremendously depressing effect on him. Pavarotti had always believed that a vigorous and well-thought-out characterisation would go a long way towards overcoming what he referred to as his handicap. Now, it seemed that he was alone in this belief, and that was a very lonely place to be.

Feeling defeated, he grew increasingly listless, lacking energy and interest in anything much. Unfortunately, he had arrived at a place where he found it difficult to get off the couch. Worse still, there were days when he didn't care whether he lived or died.

Then on the 22nd of December, 1975, he boarded a flight from New York to Milan and then on to Modena to be with the family. He would be home for Christmas! That thought gave him a moment of temporary relief.

He travelled as he always did, tourist class. Simply because he liked the people he met in tourist class better. He also felt safer because he was near the emergency exit.

The flight was uneventful until it started to prepare for landing at Malpensa International Airport. It was a dark, foggy December night, and visibility was not good, but it was not unusual for Milan, especially for that time of year. When the plane finally touched down, it became clear that everything was not going well. The plane barrelled down the runway at almost flying speed, veered off the runway and broke into two pieces. It was horrible — people were screaming and fighting to get out of their seats. Everyone was in shock but also concerned about an explosion. They finally got out.

When Luciano saw his friend, who had driven from Modena to pick him up, he felt immediate relief:

> When I arrived home, safe, with my family all around me, I realised what an idiot I had been in the past month. I saw how lucky I was; how much love I had, what a privilege it was to have a gift hat made over happy. I also saw how good life was and

how much there was about it that I enjoyed. I saw that I had allowed myself to drown in self-pity over things that matter. I knew that all my talk about not caring whether I lived or died was just talk. I was nowhere near ready to die. Since that accident, I have been optimistic and happy, perhaps more so than ever. Because of the terrible things I saw during the war, because of that near-fatal illness as a boy, and then the crash at the Milan airport, I think I know death. I also know life - I know as well as anyone how precious and beautiful it is. The entire plane crash experience was as though God had grabbed me by the neck and said, 'You are so indifferent about life? Here, take a look at death and tell me how you like that!' If that was his plan, it worked [Pavarotti/Wright, 1981: 278/280].

Pavarotti laments that some element in the human condition prevents us from appreciating what we have and being grateful for the wonderful things we have in our lives. It is not until they come face to face with some sort of disaster, a war, a plane crash, or something of that magnitude, that humans begin to understand how fortunate their lives are. According to Pavarotti, this is a common but undesirable trait. He is painfully aware that people are always looking to find problems in every sphere of life. Whether it is to discover yet another issue to complain about or another cause to fight for or against is irrelevant. What is relevant is:

> That complaining is common today because young people have known real trouble. In Italy, today's young people have never experienced war. Few of them have ever known the kind of poverty that leaves you without enough to eat. Everything has been comfortable for them. They will not live in a truly philosophical way, I believe, until they know some disaster. An absolute disaster, not just too little money for a film or a record. It is sad. I wish no one a disaster, but it is necessary.
>
> I have a very good friend, Mazzoli, who was in a German prison camp for two years. He almost starved and weighed eighty-two pounds when he got out, nearly a skeleton. Today he doesn't have all that much, but he is one of the happiest men I know. He is happy to live without problems and does not go looking for them [Pavarotti/Wright, 1981: 280].

Pavarotti was an intelligent artist with a genuine philosophical bent that influenced not only his view of the world but also how he lived his life. In many respects, he was a forward-looking modern man who managed to build an immense career and one of the largest fan bases for an artist at any time in history. That he was able to translate the whole business into a billion-dollar enterprise without missing a beat speaks volumes. These are different from the qualities of someone who is out of touch with the dominant culture of his times.

Indeed Pavarotti knew very well how contemporary society worked and how fragmented its culture and politics had become, and his intelligence and moral compass told him that this was not going to end well. When he compared these divided, troubled societies to his own relatively innocent childhood and youth, he concluded that the value system that was inculcated into him during the Great War and its aftermath was better. The rules, the value system, and the lifestyle were all simpler and more straightforward and, above all, kinder. These people detested shortcuts to success; they abhorred get-rich schemes and refused to worship at the altar of capitalism: making money was good, but making money at any cost was not. There was nothing wrong with making big money either; he certainly didn't undersell himself; he just believed you had to earn it. He became convinced that working hard for what you wanted was important, that serving your apprenticeship and becoming a master of your craft was a better recipe for a good and productive life than looking for quick fixes and good fortune. Indeed, you were more likely to retain the respect of the community.

There were other aspects of Pavarotti's personality that were different to most of his contemporaries and colleagues. For instance, there would not be many artists of his stature flying tourist class because they liked talking to those people better than the ones you meet in first class.

In fact, there would not be many people of his stature who would want to converse with anybody on a plane at all.

The other aspect of this wonderfully gifted and wise personality was the fact that he was listed in the phone book in Modena. You just looked up his phone number in the book and rang him at home. Can you imagine that? To make things worse, his wife Adua told me that there was another Luciano Pavarotti in Modena. This other Luciano Pavarotti was a tradesman, and people would often call the Pavarottis to ask Luciano to come over and do maintenance work on their home.

One young soprano with a bit of spunk rang him on a particular Sunday and asked him for an audition to which he replied yes, but it will have to be tomorrow because today we are having family and friends for lunch. "Oh, Maestro," came the reply, "It will have to be today because we are driving back home this afternoon." She arrived with her husband and another young man!

Pavarotti deferred his lunch with family and friends to hear and advise a perfect stranger. He told her the truth, which was that her voice was not sufficiently developed for him to decide what voice type it was and where it was likely to settle once adequately schooled.

One other aspect of his personality that made him very different from many of his friends and colleagues was his ability to accommodate the number of people who were drawn to him. Most of the time, it began with a love for his singing and then turned into a friendship, but some friendships started as a result of his interest in horses and soccer. Above all, people were drawn to him because he possessed a very rich humanity.

His friends constantly warned him about being too open, too trusting, and too willing to believe that they want what is best for you. Pavarotti, however, was not naive. He knew the ways of the world but refused to live in a state of constant distrust. He believed that it is better to enjoy hundreds of friendships with good people rather than sacrifice those friendships just because you know that a couple of people are not as genuine as they pretend to be. Pavarotti stated that he enjoyed his friends too much.

Following this interesting diversion, I suggest that we return to the central theme of this book, an analysis of Pavarotti's art and technique.

Pavarotti — Technician and Magician

Chapter 42

Cavalleria Rusticana, Mascagni, 1976

This opera is based on a novel by Giovanni Verga (1840–1922) and takes place in Vizzini, a Sicilian village, towards the end of the nineteenth century. It is dawn on Easter Sunday, and from a distance, Turiddu is serenading Lola with a glorious melody, which is underscored by a text that is seething with passion. The last repeated phrase is particularly telling, as Turiddu declares, 'If I should die and be sent to paradise, I would refuse to enter unless I saw you there.'

Turiddu and Lola became lovers before he left to join the army, but by the time he returned, she had married Alfio. Devastated by Lola's failure to wait for him, Turiddu seduces Santuzza. However he discovers that his relationship with Lola is not yet exhausted and their affair is soon rekindled. Turiddu abandons Santuzza in favour of Lola, who does everything she can to lord her victory over Santuzza. Later that morning, in desperation, Santuzza approaches Mamma Lucia, Turiddu's mother. Mamma Lucia tries to be compassionate, but finally she tells Santuzza that Turiddu has gone to Francofonte to buy wine for the tavern. Santuzza disputes that version of events, informing Mamma Lucia that people have seen hanging around the village near Lola's house in the early hours of the morning.

Alfio arrives with a group of men, boasting of the power of his horses and of the constancy of Lola's affection. He asks Mamma Lucia if she has any more of her excellent wine. When she says that Turiddu has gone to get more, Alfio replies that he saw him near his house that same morning. Lucia is surprised, but Santuzza tells her to keep quiet. As the villagers follow the procession to church, Santuzza stays behind and pours out her grief about Turiddu to Mamma Lucia who expresses her pity, then also leaves for Mass. Turiddu arrives in the piazza, where Santuzza confronts him about his affair with Lola. He denies her accusations and reminds her that if she keeps accusing him of such misdeeds he will be killed. Lola walks by on her way to church and, knowing Santuzza's desperate state, takes the opportunity to mock her. Turiddu follows Lola into church where Santuzza implores him not to abandon her, but he refuses to listen. Santuzza then hurls one of opera's most chilling maledictions at him. Arrives '*A te la male Pasqua*' she curses, wishing him an unhappy Easter. His response is equal to her curse: *'Dell'ira tua non mi curo'* — *your anger means nothing to me.*

Just as Santuzza is trying to compose herself, Compare Alfio arrives. He is late for Mass, but Santuzza's anger knows no boundaries, and she asks him to stay and listen to what she has to say. She reveals that she is pregnant with Turiddu's child but that he has now abandoned her for Lola, Alfio's wife and Turiddu's old flame. In an attempt to remain calm whilst making sense of this latest infamy, Alfio begs Santa not to spread her accusations as the consequences will be grave. She assures Alfio that she loves Turridu and that she is having his child. Convinced of the betrayal, Alfio swears that he will get revenge. He rushes off, leaving behind the now conscience-stricken Santuzza.

Returning from the church the villagers gather at Mamma Lucia's tavern. Turiddu leads them in a drinking song — *'Viva il, vino sfumegiente'* — a brilliant and effervescent piece, raising everyone's spirits. However, the atmosphere changes immediately when the brooding Alfio enters the tavern, becoming even more tense when he refuses to drink with Turiddu. Turiddu challenges Alfio to a duel, but not before admitting his guilt. The two men agree to meet outside the village, and Turridu, alone with his mother, asks for her blessing as she did on that day he joined the army. He then begs her to take care of Santuzza, should he not return, and rushes off to meet his fate. As Mamma Lucia waits anxiously, shouts are heard in the distance. A woman runs in, screaming that Turiddu has been killed.

These two operas are very interesting choices for Pavarotti. Turiddu is suitable for him vocally, but he needs the physic du role. For Canio, in *I Pagliacci* he has the right physique, but the part could be too dramatic for his lyrical voice, lacking that trumpet-like *squillo*, an essential characteristic of this role. Let me hasten to add that I do not mean he should never sing Canio, but it is too heavy at this stage of his development.

As Turiddu, Pavarotti makes some lovely sounds. He definitely has the suitable vocal characteristics for the role, but even more importantly, he knows how to unleash a torrent of glorious sound. Forty years of age and at the peak of his powers, Pavarotti sounds young, vibrant, macho, sensuous and intelligent. In short, he makes us believe that he possesses the necessary qualities to cause two beautiful women to fight over him. The voice maintains its youthful bloom, adorned with a lovely velvety quality whilst also retaining ring and brilliance: an almost perfect balance of *chiaro/scuro*.

However, it remains a fact that we are discussing one of the greatest Verismo operas ever composed, one of the most essential characteristics of this style being its adherence to verisimilitude. Therefore, I understand why a man of Pavarotti's intelligence and artistic integrity never performed this role on stage: by the time he was ready to sing the part, he no longer possessed the physical attributes for the role. Having spoken about Pavarotti's vocal endowment and the physical requirements for the role, let us now discuss the manner in which he deployed these gifts in the service of the composer.

The first issue in the opening aria is purely a technical one, relating to the wisdom of boosting the sound and recording the *Siciliana* so far forward on the stage. This first aria is traditionally sung from the wings behind the curtain, giving the audience the impression of distance both from the action and the singing. In terms of diction, one is left with the belief that Pavarotti has worked hard on mastering the Sicilian dialect for this aria. However, as assiduous as he may have been, the idiom doesn't seem to come naturally to him. The first sign of a problem comes when Pavarotti sings *'biato a cui ti da lu primo vasu'*. Pavarotti tends to squeeze the [a] vowel in the phrase 'biato', and because the ensuing resonating space is too narrow, he diminishes the upper harmonics on the A flat. This is a very important issue and one that Pavarotti does throughout his career, although to a much lesser degree.

Vowel integrity is very important, and in order to achieve it, the singer must ensure that the vowel-determining formants, that is, formants one and two, are very finely tuned and capable of being tracked. If for some reason we can't follow them, then we cannot make the necessary *aggiustamento* at the first *passaggio* and then modify the vowels in accordance with pitch at the second *passaggio* and beyond. It remains a fact that whilst vowel integrity is a function of the first two formants, which are constantly changing in the process of forming the different vowels, the singer's formant (combination of formants 3–4 and 5) must remain constant throughout the scale irrespective of vowel and pitch being sung. If we can't achieve that, we will not be able to maintain the ping, ring and focus of the sound. The inability to achieve vowel integrity (formants 1 and 2) and a constant ping, buzz, or focus in the tone (formants 3,4,5) can only mean that there is a malfunction either at the level of articulatory configuration or at the level of breath management. Oren Brown is even more succinct when he states that: 'A larger resonating space is needed to accommodate the high frequencies and high intensities contained in the sound waves of high and loud notes' [Brown, 1996: 107].

If, as the mouth opens naturally with rising pitch and amplitude, the integrity of the vowel is retained, the first formant will grow in strength, and there will be no loss of upper harmonic partials ('ring,' 'ping'). Resonance balance will pertain throughout the scale [Miller, 2994: 75].

In this instance Pavarotti is guilty of the first mentioned: he produces a narrow mouth opening and a laterally unmodified mouth position, which diminish the *'oscuro'* aspects of the tone whilst over-emphasising the *'chiaro'* aspects. Consequently, losing definition and strength on the first formant produces an overly bright sound.

In the very following phrase — *'Ntra la porta tua lu sangue e sparsu'* — during which Pavarotti shows a moment of insecurity by forgetting and stumbling over the first part of the Sicilian text and demonstrating that he is not at all as comfortable as he ought to be with it.

A further musical problem occurs when he holds the last note of the sustained passages right up to the end of the bar and then rushes the breath when he should be starting the new phrase. He should have cut these phrases a little short, creating an appropriate space between the end of a phrase and the beginning of the next to breathe, allowing him to begin the next phrase on time. The present strategy is not conducive to a sense of composure and a seamless flow of glorious tone, but make no mistake — this singing is nothing short of glorious.

The core of *Cavalleria Rusticana* takes place in the city square just outside the church on Easter Sunday morning. Santuzza attempts in vain to detain Turiddu for a long overdue discussion. However, he refuses, making it clear that this would be most inappropriate on Easter Sunday. Santuzza is understandably upset about his failure to respond but refuses to be a slave to her jealousy. When she persists, he calls her out: *'Do you want to have me killed then? Is this the way you repay the love that I bear you?'*

She insists that it was compare Alfio who saw Turridu near his place. This is an essential exchange as the audience learns that Santuzza knows the consequences of her revelations to Alfio in the next scene, and she goes ahead anyway. Alfio may have been able to manage Santuzza a little better had Lola not walked across the square, making it evident that she has been sleeping with Turiddu, describing him as the most beautiful man that she has ever come across.

This exchange has the effect of riling Santuzza even further, becoming even more intent on having that conversation with Turiddu. When all else fails she resorts to pleading with him.

When that also fails, she warns him not to anger her, to which Turiddu that her anger means nothing to him. She has the last word when she curses him: 'May your Easter be ill-fated.' He turns around and runs into church, no doubt in pursuit of Lola. Alfio then arrives at this most inopportune moment; Santuzza is still shattered by her encounter with Lola and Turiddu and has not had a chance to compose herself. She now reveals what she knows to Alfio, which spiteful act results in a tragedy of seismic proportions for everyone involved.

Pavarotti's attitude to this duet results in some very beautiful singing, but often not true to life in terms of the different emotional responses. It is a little too bland emotionally, and vocally too much the same bright colour. This duet requires a more earthy approach, a more full-throated tone and a much darker colour.

Pavarotti's approach to the role of Turiddu is very lyrical but it seems to work quite well for *Cavalleria Rusticana*, mainly because Turiddu is a brash young man about town. His biggest problem seems to be that he does not want to choose between two beautiful women, both of whom love him. He isn't the first man to be involved with two women, but he is so cocksure of himself that he tends to overplay his hand. He knows he has to choose Santuzza and leave Lola with Alfio, but he fails to act on it. Consequently, the situation blows up in his face. Only when he confesses to Alfio do we begin to see the other Turiddu. Only in his touching farewell to Mamma Lucia (in which he asks for her blessing) do we see a glimpse of the decent man he may have become had he lived. His repeated pleadings to Mamma Lucia to take care of Santuzza and to pray for him (should some unfortunate accident befall him) are very touching.

This suggests an acceptance of responsibility for his actions, which is a sign of maturity and perhaps the beginning of wisdom.

Consequently, when we hear the terrifying screams from backstage announcing '*hanno ammazatu Cumpari Turiddu*' (they have murdered Cumpari Turiddu), we still have some sympathy for the character. Despite his thoughtless and reckless actions, he is not a bad person but is overcome by his own passions and desires.

It is important to realise that the village folk are not at all divided: they know the difference between right and wrong. They like Turiddu, but they respect and understand that Alfio did what had to be done to reclaim his honour: you don't seduce a man's wife and expect to get away with it. There is a good chance that Alfio will end up in prison, and if Lola has the courage to show her face in the city square, the village women will call her a '*puttana*' to her face as her actions have ruined so many lives. Mamma Lucia has lost her son, and Santuzza will have to bring up Turiddu's child as a single mother. There are no winners in this story.

Chapter 43

I Pagliacci: Pavarotti/Freni 1977

Pagliacci premiered at the Teatro Dal Verme in Milan on 21 May 1892 and remains a popular opera. In the Prologue, Tonio the clown announces that the audience is about to see a true story on the stage, the actors having the same joys and sorrows as other people.

Act I

The curtain rises on a Calabrian village where a visiting theatrical company is being welcomed to the village by the townsfolk. Canio, the head of this travelling troupe, begins to advertise that night's performance to the crowd, but one of the villagers provocatively suggests that Tonio is secretly courting Canio's young wife, Nedda. None too pleased with that suggestion, Canio warns that he will not tolerate any misbehaving offstage: after all, life and the stage are very different things. However, he makes it clear that if Nedda were to misbehave in this manner, he would know how to deal with her. Left alone, Nedda is highly disturbed by her husband's threatening jealousy. Looking up to the sky, she begins her aria 'Stridano lassu' in which she expresses her desire to be as free as the birds. If only she could fly away just like them. Tonio appears and tries to force himself on Nedda, but she whips him, and he swears to have his revenge. No sooner has Nedda dealt with Tonio than her lover Silvio appears, a young peasant with whom she has been having an affair. In a duet of great beauty and deep sensuality the two express their love for each other, after which Silvio persuades Nedda to elope with him that very night. Tonio overhears the end of their conversation and alerts Canio. Fortunately, Silvio manages to escape before Canio recognises him, leaving Nedda to deal with Canio's crazed temper, which threatens to overwhelm him. Nedda refuses to reveal her lover's name and Beppe, another member of the troupe, restrains Canio. Tonio advises the latter to wait until the evening's performance to catch the culprit. Alone, Canio gives in to his despair — he must play the clown even though his heart is breaking.

Act II

That evening the villagers assemble to watch the performance, Silvio among them. Beppe plays Harlequin and serenades Columbine played by Nedda. He dismisses her buffoonish servant Taddeo (played by Tonio), and over dinner, the two sweethearts plot to poison Columbine's husband Pagliaccio, played by Canio. When Pagliaccio unexpectedly appears, Harlequin slips away as Taddeo maliciously assures Pagliaccio of his wife's innocence. This only serves to reignite Canio's jealousy, and forgetting his role and the play, he demands that Nedda reveal her lover's name. She remains defiant and attempts to continue with the performance, albeit by introducing a greater level of realism than ever before. Canio warns her that she is underestimating his determination to have her lover's name and then avenge himself. Her continued defiance forces him to lose his mind, and in a rage, he stabs Nedda. Horrified, Silvio attempts to come to her aid. As he rushes towards Nedda, Canio grabs him and runs him through with his blade. Turning to the terrified crowd, he announces, '*La Commedia e finita*' (the comedy is over).

Critique for I Pagliacci

Cavalleria Rusticana (June 1976), I Pagliacci (April 1977) and *Il Trovatore* (1976) are of extraordinary importance in the development of Pavarotti's career simply because they mark his initiation into the *lirico spinto* repertoire. Up to that point, he had worked assiduously to consolidate the most spectacular vocal technique that had been heard over the previous century. However, this technique was designed to sustain the lyric tenor repertoire, which he had achieved handsomely. I maintain that in the lyric repertoire, there is not a tenor in living memory that comes even close to his Rodolfo, in *La Boheme*. The same can be said for his Duke in *Rigoletto*, Tonio in *La Fille du Regiment*, Edgardo in *Lucia*, Arturo in *I Puritani*, Fernando in *La Favorita* and Leicester in *Maria Stuarda*, not to mention Riccardo in *Ballo in Maschera* and even *Turandot*. The tone that he deploys in these roles is genuinely glorious.

However, now he was embarking on a new journey, that of the dramatic and *lirico spinto* repertoire — an entirely different story. Consequently, we can say that the jury is out as to the extent of his success in this new repertoire. Clearly Pavarotti would never sing anything badly, so it is more a question of how successfully he would adapt his essentially lyric instrument to the more *lirico spinto* repertoire.

Having discussed *Cavalleria Rusticana* above, let us proceed with an analysis of *I Pagliacci*. This is a *Verismo* opera, and the requirements are very different from the lyric operas in which Pavarotti had made his reputation and great career thus far. *I Pagliacci* requires a darker, more open-throated and penetrating sound. In addition, the approach should be less cautious and more physical and energetic, with a more significant emotional commitment than anything Pavarotti has produced so far.

On the other hand, Canio in *I Pagliacci* is a much older man who could only dream of having the same problems as Turiddu. For Canio, life seems to have been very difficult. None of his dreams seem to have been realised, but he has almost come to grips with his lonely and loveless existence. Then he meets Nedda, who lights up his life. In his final aria, '*No Pagliaccio non son*', he reminds both Nedda and the audience that he is no clown but rather the man who saved her from her destitute life, providing her with a home, a name and a love fuelled by desire that was nothing less than folly. It was this love that betrayed him, and his desire that prevented him from seeing the real Nedda. She showed no remorse for the misery she caused as she shattered all his hopes and dreams.

As always, when tackling a new role, Pavarotti brings a somewhat cautious attitude to this role, approaching it lyrically and refusing to put his voice under pressure. Consequently, the voice goes back and is a little floated at times when it is meant to find another supercharged gear, providing the tone with more focus, a more metallic timbre and greater penetration. However, he certainly does not produce an insipid sound, but one that lacks the dramatic *slancio* that one expects in this role. Consequently, the vocal tone per se, although very beautiful and flowing with considerable velvet, lacks a consistent metallic edge. It requires a firm attack and glottal setting, combined with an increased level of objective *appoggio*(breath pressure) and a more refined subjective *appoggio* (sympathetic vibrations). In addition, this tone does not possess the open-throated sound required in the *pre-passaggio* level of the scale from the E flat to the F4. What Pavarotti does is wonderful, but were he to lower the larynx, widen the pharynx and increase the *appoggio* (breath pressure), he would fulfil all the conditions for producing the singer's formant. This *vocal strategy* prepares the instrument for a more full-blooded and ringing high register. Consequently, we can say that whilst Pavarotti produces a lovely tone, it is not the type of sound that will promote an authentic representation of Canio's dramatic character.

Critique of the 1977, I Pagliacci

The opening scene for Canio — '*Un grande spettacolo a ventitré ore*' — is really splendid. The G4 is a lovely ringing, brilliant tone, conveying a genuine sense of excitement about the grand spectacle his troupe is preparing to present that night. I raise the zygomatic arch a little, modify the [o] towards the [aw] and aim for a more dynamic breath energy in the long sustained [o] vowels. The first such vowel is on the D natural on the word '*ore*' and the second is on the A natural of '*servitore*'.

The G4 on the [i] vowel of '*Venite*' is a little too edgy and metallic for the beginning of the opera. Overall, however, the singing in the more lyrical part of the opera is really lovely.

In his first aria proper — '*Un tal gioco credetemi*'— all the [a] vowels in words such as '*cari,*' and '*Parlo,*' and '*Teatro*' are formed too far back, giving the feeling of a spread pharynx and remaining a little too open. This suggests that the base of the tongue is sitting too low, lacking forward focus and *appoggio,* and spreading the pharyngeal wall. The remedy is to raise the base of the tongue for the [a] vowel, contract the constrictor muscles (which reduce the size of the pharyngeal space), raise the base of the tongue, and contract the oropharyngeal pillars. In so doing this reshapes the entire vocal tract to redirect and focus off the tone towards the zygomatic arch.

In the phrase '*Il teatro e la vita non son la stessa cosa*' the [a] in '*teatro*' on the D5 is formed too far back and remains too open. The [i] vowel on G4 is very bright and edgy, resulting in extreme contrast between the [a] and the [i] within the same phrase. Further, the [o] vowel F natural on '*cosa*' should be more collected (even if not yet entirely *voce coperta*) as it is too open and overly bright. Moreover, when Pavarotti repeats the phrase '*La stessa cosa*' he creates a breathy tone which I understand is purely for an effect. Consequently, I have no problems with this, beyond questioning the strategy of using a breathy tone in *Verismo* opera.

In the middle section, '*E se lassu Pagliaccio sorprende la sua sposa,*' the staccato notes should be sharper and bounced off the breath, or as Vennard refers to it, the 'bouncing epigastrium'. On the other hand, the contrasting phrase '*La sua sposa*' should be more legato and more cohesive. This would happen if he opened the [o] on the F4 and collected the [a] vowel on E4.

In the phrase '*Ed il publico applaude, e ride allegramente*', the larynx is too high, and the connection between the breath and the larynx is too tenuous. When singing '*Ma se Nedda sul serio sorprendessi*', Pavarotti uses a more solid and focused tone, which I prefer in a verismo role. In terms of the vocal line, I can say this is a better tone and a more appropriate laryngeal and focal position from which one can build dramatic tension. However, Pavarotti doesn't take advantage of it because in the next phrase, '*Altramente finirebbe*', he allows the larynx to rise on the [e] vowel F♯, giving the sound a more lyrical orientation and less substantive. This is a lovely tone per se, especially on the sustained F♯ on the [e] vowel, but it is too bright and lacking in gravitas for a dramatic role such as Canio. He should aim to maintain the previous position, building on the drama and tension by increasing breath energy to compensate for the dramatic tone. This would produce a forward, focused sound whilst maintaining amplitude, darker colour and a harmonically rich sound. Let us jump to the end of the aria '*Come e ver che vi parlo*' for which the larynx should be anchored and steadier for the A4, giving the tone more gravitas and a darker colour.

Vesti La Giubba

'Vesti la giubba' or *'On with the motley'* is the aria that marks the high-water mark both vocally and dramatically in *I Pagliacci* and is justly famous. Pavarotti's version is a lyrical rendition, as you would expect, but no less satisfying than the many more dramatic renditions of this aria. Nonetheless, even within the lyric paradigm, I would be less than honest if I didn't suggest a couple of improvements.

In the phrase *'Mentre preso dal delirio,'* the [e] vowel of *'preso'* is not anchored to the breath, causing the larynx, tongue and epiglottis to rise on the E natural, creating an overly bright tone, which is also a little unsteady. Further, the first [e] vowel in the phrase *'E quel che faccio'* has struck the correct emission, but again the breath *appoggio* is insufficient. The s*forzati* on the G4 is a lovely sound: it is collected, *appoggiato*, focused and exciting. I am sorry, but I can't say the same about the following phrase: *'E tu forse uom'.* Here Pavarotti sounds insecure, and the tone is too careful and contrived. He alters the [u] in *'sei tu',* raising the larynx in preparation for the A4, only to then give it a second lift on the actual A4 on the *'uom'.* This is followed by the heart-wrenching realisation that he really is a clown (*tu sei pagliaccio*). This has the effect of allowing the A4 to go back and become a little unsteady.

At the opening to the new section of the aria, *'Vesti la giubba, e la fascia in farina',* the tone on the E4 on the [e] vowel of *'vesti'* is far too open and bright for this particularly dramatic moment in the opera. In the following phrases, *'La gente pagha E rider vuole qua, e se Arlecchin ti invola Colombina, ridi Pagliaccio e ognun ti applaudira,'* there are several issues to be analysed in these few bars.

The first issue is the suspended straight sound that Pavarotti uses on the [a] vowel in *'qua'* on the E4, as there is no room for straight tone in verismo opera. He should be producing a vital vibrato tone that can withstand both a crescendo and a portamento to the [e] vowel on G4 on the *'e, se Arlecchin'*. This G4 displays a very narrow focus, relying too much on the subjective *appoggio* on the teeth rather than the objective breath *appoggio*. The [o] vowel in *Pagliaccio* on the G4 is excellent, but the A♭ on the [a] vowel of *spasm* is a dull sound lacking ring and brilliance. The final climax, *'Ah, ridi Pagliaccio, Sul tuo amore infranto',* is excellent, but the F♯ on the sustained *'Ah'* should possess more ring and more crescendo. In addition, the accented notes on the ascending scale *'Sul tuo amore infranto'* are all too careful and shallow. The whole sustained phrase needs more *appoggio*, titularly on the A4 on the [a] vowel of *'infranto,'* which requires more focus and more *appoggio*. These minor reservations aside, this is an excellent performance of a much-loved aria, as is Pavarotti's rendition of his last act aria, '*No Pagliaccio non son*'.

No Pagliaccio non son

Pavarotti begins this phrase with a forceful percussive tone, which, whilst lacking the amplitude and colour of a naturally dramatic tenor, remains rich in harmonics and retains the thrust and intent of the dramatic tenor both in colour and amplitude.

The phrase '*E il viso e pallido*' with its tricky *passaggio* notes is very well executed. The first two phrases that I would sing a little differently are the A♭ on '*Maledetta*'and the A flat on the [o] vowel of '*stolido*' in the phrase '*son quel che stolido*'. To my ear, both of these A♭ would benefit enormously from a slight lowering of the larynx and widening of the pharynx. This would create a flexible and malleable resonatory space capable of cradling the different vowels in the pharynx for the higher range.

An excellent example of *copertura* (collecting the tone) occurs on the phrase '*Ed una amor ch'era febre e follia*'. The G♭ on the [o] vowel of '*amor*' and [e] vowel of '*febre*' are beautifully collected. The same applies to the [a] vowel of '*sperai*' and the [o] vowel of '*ogni*', which are also beautifully collected.

The B♭ on the [E] of '*credeva*'and on the [E] vowel of '*abbietta*'both need to be opened out by lowering the larynx, maintaining a relatively high zygomatic arch and soft palate, with an increase in breath pressure to compensate for the extra load. Pavarotti opens the second B♭ on the [E] vowel right at the end of the note, so he knows it needs to be done, but without overdoing it.

Let me make it clear that I don't believe these notes are bad notes; instead, I feel that Pavarotti is undertaking a different journey. The latter constitutes a complete break from the past, consequently requiring the development of a different vocal paradigm, a different technique and a different psychology. In the past, he was singing all the high *tessitura* bel canto roles which required a lean and focused tone, with an emphasis on beauty of tone, flexibility and precision of execution. His new repertoire requires the wherewithal to execute a lower and more dramatic *tessitura* with its emphasis on amplitude, size of sound and vocal ring, which is capable of penetrating a much larger and more brass-oriented orchestration. This will not be easy for a tenor like Pavarotti, who is averse to being foolhardy, let alone reckless. Pavarotti's biggest fear was that he might overload the voice, causing the high range to open excessively and thereby shortening his career, which happened to his great hero and friend, Giuseppe di Stefano. There have been many tenors before and after Di Stefano who had short careers for various reasons. However there had never been a tenor with such a glorious natural voice as Di Stefano, such penetrating intelligence, innate musicality and intuitive feel for both the text and the drama as he displayed in his halcyon days. His early demise was a warning to most of us who were influenced by this great artist — a warning that Pavarotti took seriously. The richness and beauty of tone is undeniable and constant.

Pavarotti need not have worried about it because, in my interview with Mrs Pavarotti (Adua Veroni), we discussed the performances of I Pagliacci with James Levine at the Metropolitan Opera in 1994. She flew to New York for these performances, and after an elaborate discussion, we both concluded that this was a really convincing portrayal of the ill-fated Canio. This was a remarkable performance for a 59-year-old tenor who had by then sung not only all the lyric repertoire but also a fair slice of the dramatic repertoire.

True, the voice was occasionally under duress, but overall, it was a remarkable performance both vocally and dramatically.

I hope to analyse his incursions into the dramatic Verdian and Verismo repertoire such as *Andrea Chenier* and *La Gioconda,* as well as his excellent concert work in a second book on Pavarotti's technique. At any rate, the dramatic repertoire is not relevant to this book, which is dedicated to answering this question: 'Is Pavarotti the greatest lyric tenor of the twentieth century?' Whilst I have included in this study a couple of the Lirico spinto roles for analysis to give my reader an idea of how he coped with putting the voice under pressure, the Lirico spinto and dramatic repertoire are beyond the scope of this book.

Chapter 44

Turandot, Pavarotti/Sutherland/Mehta

We now come to the role of the Calef in Puccini's opera *Turandot*. This has become synonymous with Pavarotti, notwithstanding the fact that the part was not totally suited to his voice. This is very fitting, not least because Pavarotti's life story reads like a Goldoni fairy tale from which *Turandot* was derived.

Following a sensational performance of Nessun Dorma at the World Cup, Puccini's *Turandot* has become inexorably interwoven into the Pavarotti story, propelling that recording to number one in the most popular recording category.

Let us analyse this opera, more specifically, Pavarotti's role in more detail.

Act I

The opera opens in Peking's Imperial Palace as a herald reads an edict to the assembled crowd in the People's Square. It proclaims that any noble suitor wishing to marry Princess Turandot must divine the answers to three riddles set by Turandot herself. Any suitor who fails to answer correctly will be executed, which is the fate that awaits the Prince of Persia (Turandot's twenty-first failed suitor). Among the throng of people, we find the slave girl Liù, who is guiding and protecting her aged master Timur. At this point, the jostling from the crowd becomes so ferocious that the old man is bumped to the ground. Liu cries out for help and Prince Calàf steps forward only to recognise the old man as his exiled father, the vanquished King of Tartar. The old king has undoubtedly fallen on hard times, and only Liù remains loyal to him. Touched by her humanity, Calàf asks her why she cares so much for Timur. Her reply is both profound and inspirational: 'Once, a long time ago, you smiled upon me, Sire'.

With the rising of the moon and the fatal hour moving closer, the mob asks Turandot to spare the Prince of Persia. She appears on the palace balcony and, without a word, signals that the execution must proceed. Mesmerised by Turandot's unattainable beauty, Calef decides to tempt fate. Liù and Timur are horrified and try to dissuade him but to no avail. The three ministers of state — Ping, Pang, and Pong — also try to discourage his pursuit, but Calàf remains unmoved. He strikes the gong, thereby announcing his quest.

Act II

In their apartments, Ping, Pang, and Pong have gathered to discuss current events. They lament Turandot's thirst for blood and can only hope that someone will conquer her. In this famous trio the ministers indulge in a little wishful thinking, confessing that they long to return to their peaceful lives on their country estates. However, the clamour of the crowd assembled for the challenge of the riddles soon brings them back to earth.

We are now confronted with the unusual spectacle of the old emperor, Turandot's father, trying to save the young Calàf's life by persuading him to give up his quest for Turandot. However, Calàf will have none of it. In response to the clamour of the crowd Turandot makes an appearance. In her aria 'In questa reggia', she recounts the story of her beautiful ancestor, Princess Lou-Ling, who was abducted and killed by a conquering prince. Seeking revenge Turandot has turned against men and is determined that no man will possess her. Trumpets then herald the beginning of the riddles, and Turandot poses her first question to Calàf: 'What is born each night and dies each dawn'? 'Hope,' Calàf answers correctly. Turandot asks her second question: 'What flickers red and warm like a flame, yet is not a flame'? Calàf thinks for a moment, then with a flash of inspiration replies 'Blood'. Turandot is perturbed but, with great effort at nonchalance, asks the third riddle: 'What is like ice but burns, and if it accepts you as a slave, makes you a king'? An uncomfortable silence pervades the atmosphere until Calàf, as if inspired by the gods, calls out her name, 'Turandot!' While the populace is overjoyed with the turn of events, Turandot begs her father not to give her to the stranger, but her words are in vain. Calàf, being young and naive, offers Turandot a way out: 'If you can discover my name before dawn, then I will die for you'.

Act III

That night in the Imperial Gardens, Turandot announces a proclamation. On pain of death, no one in Peking shall sleep that night until someone discovers the stranger's name. Calàf has no doubt that he will be victorious, but Ping, Pang, and Pong attempt to bribe him into leaving the city. In response the mob threatens Calàf in order to learn his name. Soon, Liù and Timur are dragged in, and Calàf tries in vain to convince the crowd that neither of them knows his name. Turandot appears, demanding that Timur should divulge the stranger's name. Liù stands up for him, declaring that she alone knows his name and she will never reveal it. The imperial soldiers torture her, but she remains strong. Turandot is impressed by her fortitude and asks Liu what gives her the strength to resist. Liu simply replies that love makes her strong. Turandot demands more incredible torture, but Liù stands firm, telling her rival that she too is destined to know love's joy. Suddenly Liu grabs a dagger and thrusts it into her heart. The shocked crowd forms a funeral procession, and Timur follows Liu's body, lamenting the death of the only person who cared for him. Alone with Calàf, Turandot confronts him, but he grabs her and kisses her. Experiencing emotion for the first time, Turandot begins to weep, and Calàf finally reveals his identity. Turandot declares that she knows the stranger's name — his name is Love.

Critique of Pavarotti/Sutherland/Caballe in Turandot 1972

The first thing to say about this cast is that, although lyrical, it is nonetheless an excellent performance — proof positive that sometimes we give too much away for a few extra decibels. There is no doubt that there are some moments in which one may desire a little more colour, drama and/or *slancio*, especially in the middle register. However, it remains a fact that both Sutherland and Pavarotti give much more subtle and nuanced depictions of Turandot and Calaf, respectively, than we have heard on disc for a long time. Some of the soft singing and diminuendos are beautifully done, as is the intelligent and refined pointing of the text. Pavarotti presents us with a really remarkable performance — lyrical and lean, especially in the middle register, where he also maintains an excellent vocal line. This middle voice, as well as the width and openness that he demonstrates around the *passaggio* are the areas of most significant interest to us. This is a part of the voice in which Pavarotti has traditionally been assiduous in collecting (*voce coperta*) over many years. All of a sudden that does not seem to be as necessary around the *passaggio* as Italian singers often lack the kind of formal musical education that has become commonplace in the English-speaking world.

They do have one advantage however, as they know intuitively and through osmosis from a very young age how the music should sound and how a particular opera should be sung. Pavarotti knew that this music required more depth, roundness and amplitude around the *passaggio*, not to mention more *slancio* in the high register. (Let us recall that the young Pavarotti first sang '*Nessun Dorma*' on television at the age of eighteen, after which his mother sought out Leone Magiera, asking for his help.) He now delivered what has come to be recognised as not only an excellent performance of the role but one that was well-paced. Pavarotti displayed a beautifully collected but well-articulated tone in the lower and medium register, an exciting and unusually free and open tone at the *passaggio*, and a thrilling barrage of high notes. He also delivered some beautiful soft singing when required. It is not a perfect performance but even the odd aberration is essential to us in terms of our study. However, it would be many years before he felt sufficiently comfortable to sing the role on the stage, the first occasion being the 1977/78 season in San Francisco. (Fortunately for us, this performance was recorded and is still available, so we will discuss it in detail later.) For now, however, let us concentrate on this 1972 performance with Sutherland.

Pavarotti utilises three strategies from the International Italian School to develop this performance. The first is that he uses mainly *'voce chiusa'*: his voice is nicely collected, even in the lower and middle notes. This is the result of another strategy which the Italians refer to as *bocca raccolta*, referring to a collected mouth. Together they confer on the Pavarotti voice the primary strategy knows as *'Si canta come si parla'* — *you sing as you speak*.

From his very first entry, *'Padre mio padre'* on the F natural, Pavarotti announces that this is going to be a lyrical performance, nuanced and refined rather than concentrating on drama and volume. The tone is characterised by a 'voce *aperta'* (open tone), possessing a fresh, youthful bloom and a naturally thrilling high register. We soon discover an instead marked departure from the usual Pavarotti voice production. He collects the medium register rather carefully and then opens the voice around the *passaggio*, which had hitherto been assiduously collected in preparation for the *passaggio*.

A perfect example of this strategy is evident in his first act aria, 'Non piangere Liu'. The first part of the aria, which occupies a range of a major third, is, with the exception of a moderately opened [a] vowel, a beautifully collected tone. It is warm, round, and darkish with an excellent legato, and even the opening [a] vowel gives the tone more of a sense of spontaneity.

However, this all changes when we arrive at the phrase *'Non lo lasciare, portalo via con te*, a music excerpt of which appears below. As we can see, all the F naturals at the *passaggio* are open irrespective of the vowel. Indeed, for the phrase *'Non lo lasciare'* sung only on an F natural, Pavarotti lowers the larynx and firms the pharyngeal wall. Simultaneously he drops the jaw, opening his mouth for the [a] vowel of 'l'asciare', which automatically modifies towards the [aw] vowel. He then follows through with the open [e] vowel in a similar vocal tract position. Here, Pavarotti unusually demonstrates the traditional singer's formant.

Notwithstanding the fact that both Donald Miller and Kenneth Bozeman contend that Pavarotti actually tunes to the second formant, and I don't disagree with this proposition, I do believe that the relationship is much looser than it would be with a tenor such as Alfredo Kraus. However, in this instance I believe that he is tuning to the traditional laryngeal collar location. As already discussed, this strategy involves lowering the larynx, widening the pharynx, and widening the pyriform and ventricular sinuses. Later, Pavarotti places the [o] vowel in *'portalo via con te'* in a similar position and space, resulting in genuinely memorable singing.

Even more astounding is the fact that the G4 on the [a] vowel of *'portalo'* is also open. This is indeed a very unusual occurrence for Pavarotti, and to prove that it was no accident or aberration, he repeats the strategy in the second verse.

In the phrase *'chiede colui'*, all the F4 are open, as is the G♭ on the [o] vowel of *'colui'*. Again, this is something we rarely hear from Pavarotti. Generally, the [o] vowel is *coperta* even on the F natural, let alone the G♭. So, what are the consequences for the voice? We can say that the A♭ on the [o] vowel in *'non'* is a little dampened, but the B♭ that follows in the climax is glorious. He holds this climax for a decent length of time, even adding a crescendo at the end of it.

It is important to note that the crescendo is not just opening the mouth to make a more extensive and darker sound but rather an increase of breath pressure, creating a harmonically richer tone. He then opens the mouth slightly to accommodate the richer and more ample tone. Had he just increased the opening of his mouth without increasing breath pressure, the tone would have become dampened, and, as it occurred on a [o] vowel, it would have dropped back into his throat.

The scene we will discuss includes the duet at the end of *'In questa reggia'* and Pavarotti's response to the three enigmas. His rise to the high C5 with Sutherland is just splendid, whereas, in response to the enigmas, I find that Pavarotti produces a tone that is too edgy, too manufactured and excessively bright. The tone has temporarily lost some of its beauty. Nonetheless, he managed to produce an exciting high register.

Nessun Dorma

We finally arrive at the aria *Nessun Dorma*, the point in the opera for which every audience is waiting, no matter who the tenor may be. In this aria, Pavarotti reverses what he did with *'Non piangere Liu'*. Rather than opening the *passaggio* notes in this section, he now works diligently to collect them. This results in a slightly dampened *passaggio* around the F natural and F♯, mainly because Pavarotti typically and excessively modifies the [a] vowel towards the [o]. However, the benefits to the sequence of A4s that follow are pretty spectacular. This is more like the Pavarotti we have come to know and love: a glorious top register combined with a slightly longer vocal tract, giving the tone roundness, fullness and a lovely velvety colour (first formant or the *oscuro* element). There is a beautiful collaboration between the *bucco* (mouth) and pharyngeal resonating cavity (balanced *chiaroscuro*), as well as the matching of the glottal harmonics to their relative vocal tract formants.

Pavarotti begins the low and medium register with a collected tone produced by *una bocca raccolta*, a strategy that produces a moderately round, warm, *'oscuro'* tone and an even legato line. He then proceeds to a collected tone around the *passaggio (voce coperta)*. For instance, the F sharp on the [a] vowel of *'guardi le stelle'* and the [a] vowel of *'bacio'* in the phrase *'Ed il mio bacio scioglierà il silenzio'* are beautifully collected, as is the collected tone on the [e] vowel on the E4 of *'splendera'*. The G4 on the second *'Vincero'* is beautifully collected, facilitating the climax to the sustained B4. The sequence of A4s in both the first and second verse is nothing short of spectacular, as is the climax to the B4, which then drops to a sustained A4.

It is notable that in contrast to the first act aria, in the phrase *'Di legua notte,'* Pavarotti opens the [o] vowel in *'notte'*. However, he follows this with a penetrating and constricted [e] vowel in 'notte' rather than a similar resonatory space and manoeuvre as he did in the first act. I personally would prefer the sequence to be as seamless as possible, emphasising the similarities rather than the differences.

My only other suggestion in this aria is to consider producing a more lateral sound on the [a] vowels on the F♯ already alluded to above. This suggestion would facilitate the *passaggio* into head register, making it more natural than the excessively studied *passaggio* we have come to expect from Pavarotti. The other strategy I would adopt here is to sing the [e] vowel on the B4 as a more naturally lateral vowel, whilst also reinforcing the *appoggio*.

The singing in the last duet between Pavarotti and Sutherland is absolutely fantastic.

The tone is particularly exciting in the high register and beautifully touching in the softer singing. The only suggestion I would make would be to use a little more *slancio* and dramatic thrust in the angry phrases such as *'Principessa di morte, Principessa di gelo'*. Pavarotti's tone is lovely, but it lacks the necessary dramatic impetus that would then contrast with the soft singing in *'Mio fiore matutino'*. The singing in the last duet with Turandot is beautiful — an easy, mellifluous tone that displays a full and youthful bloom — Golden Age singing that we are not likely to hear again for a long time, if ever.

Conclusion for Turandot 1973 Pavarotti and Sutherland

The first thing we note in this opera is that Pavarotti has genuinely mastered his *appoggio* system. This applies to both his objective *appoggio* (breath management) and subjective *appoggio*. The guiding of sympathetic vibrations towards specific traditional focal points is now of a very high level. Note that I use the phrase 'guide the sound waves' which Pavarotti does so well. He gives the sound waves emanating from the glottis time and space to find their matching formants, thereby fulfilling their resonatory potential.

At the glottal level, Pavarotti is able to command a greater variety of colours without resorting to breathy phonation, employing a firm onset and equally firm glottal setting within a moderately low larynx. In fact, there are moments in this opera when the larynx takes a lower position than I had heard for a while. Even his soft singing has a lovely firm quality about it that was lacking in his earlier work.

In terms of the resonator, he uses a largely interactive resonating strategy, whereby the oral resonator and the pharyngeal resonator appear to be mainly on a continuum. That is, there is not as much distinction between the lateral or front vowels and the round, back vowels. Indeed, there are some phrases such as *'Non lo lasciare'* all on the F4 where he lowers the larynx, stretches and firms the pharyngeal wall, and simultaneously opens his mouth for the [a] vowel which automatically modifies towards the [aw] vowel. He then follows through with the [e] vowel in the some-position before placing the [o] vowel in the word *portalo* in a similar situation and space. This is decidedly memorable singing.

Critique of Turandot, Pavarotti/Caballe, San Francisco 1977

As I have argued above, Pavarotti really knew how a particular opera should sound, which is why he believed that *Turandot* was not within his purview. In his mind this was the domain of Mario Del Monaco and Franco Corelli; he didn't think that he would ever sing this opera. So, it required quite a shift in his mental processes and vocal psychology.

In general, we can say that the role of Calaf requires a more ample, more penetrating and darker-tinged voice than could be mustered by Pavarotti right up to November 1977.

Consequently, he was launching a new journey, a new adventure if you like, and no one knew the outcome, not even Pavarotti.

This performance of *Turandot* is characterised by a revamped technique displaying greater freedom, greater amplitude and generosity and a more natural emission. Even emotionally, Pavarotti does not seem to be as constrained by his technique as he had been previously. Consequently, this performance is much more spontaneous, enjoying greater amplitude and brilliance and a compelling expressivity.

Opening Scene

From the beginning of the opera, Pavarotti announces himself as a more heroic *lirico spinto* tenor. In fact, all the early interjections between Calaf and

Timur and Calaf and Liu are just fantastic, Pavarotti soars over the top of the orchestra and chorus to produce an inspiring heroic sound, which is also dramatically effective. This is especially so in the malediction scene in which Calaf curses Turandot.

Particularly beautiful is the change of sentiment, which is reflected in the tone after Turandot's appearance. Calaf is completely conquered by Turandot's beauty and his change of heart is reflected in the Phrases *'Non senti, il duo Profumo e nell'aria e nell'aria, sua divine bellezza meraviglia…. Io soffro padre soffro'*. This is lovely singing.

Non Pianger Liu

In the first part of his act 1 aria, *'Non piangere Liu'*, Pavarotti gives an admirable performance. The whole is beautifully done; if anything, the Pavarotti voice has grown not only stature, but also in size and shape. Overall, in the first part of this aria the tone is distinctive in its presence, compelling in its colour and penetration, and expressive in its humanity. The performance reveals some beautiful *piano* singing, some exciting *rubato* interspersed with practical *affrettando* and excellent text pointing.

The only thing that mars this performance for me is the senseless and indiscriminate insertion of an explosive release at the end of phrases. That notwithstanding, I like the overall singing so far. The second half of the aria could be more graceful and accomplished than the first part. In fact, up to this point, I was convinced that in line with his enormous natural gifts, Pavarotti was constitutionally incapable of making an ugly sound. Well, I am sorry to say that I was wrong. The [e] vowels in the phrase *'Al tuo piccolo cuore che non cade'* is not a beautiful sound.

However, there is one really positive outcome from Pavarotti's new venture into the more dramatic repertoire. He is finally doing what I have been calling for throughout this book: imbuing many of the rounder vowels with a more lateral shape and orientation. At the same time, he is not only opening the lateral vowels, but he is also modifying them towards the position of the [a] vowel. Well, I must confess that whilst I don't mind the [o] vowel moving more towards the open [aw] and the closed [u] moving towards a more relaxed [U] vowel, I do have a problem with the [e] vowel moving as far back in the resonating cavity as the position of the [a]. I understand that he is trying to create a tone with greater amplitude, but in this instance, he is compensating for one deficiency whilst creating another. Nonetheless, in general, the Pavarotti voice has gained in amplitude, width and distinctiveness.

Straniero Ascolta

Pavarotti manages the scene of the enigmas very well indeed. There is some excellent singing, and his responses are typically exciting both vocally and dramatically.

Nessun Dorma

Pavarotti begins this great aria with an uncharacteristic nasal and constricted tone. This is because he prolongs the [n] nasal continuant beyond its intended scope. In this type of manoeuvre, the soft palate is down, as is the uvula, allowing the vela pharyngeal port to remain open. The failure of the levator vela paletine and the tensor palato muscles to both rise and close the velarpharyngeal port ensures that some of the sound waves are diverted towards nasopharynx creating this nasal twang.

In addition, all the [a] vowels are too far back, simply because Pavarotti is aiming for too much width and amplitude. This shape can be excellent when it is accompanied by a concomitant level of breath (subglottal) pressure to direct the sound waves to follow through towards their natural focal point. This is different here.

Further, the [e] vowel in the phrase '*E chiuso in me*' is also too far back.

In the phrase beginning with '*Sulla too bocce lo diro,* ' Pavarotti adopts a defensive stance. Consequently, the tone is a little thin, a little back and a little under-supported. This tone requires greater *appoggio* of both the objective and subjective kind.

The E4 on the word '*Splendera*' is beautifully suspended (A type of voce finta), another innovation for Pavarotti.

The second sequence of high A4 on the '*Di legua o Notte tramontate stelle*' is much better. Greater *appoggio* and superior focus result in a more brilliant and exciting tone.

The second *Vincero* on the G4 is beautifully modulated, but the '*vincero*' on the B4 is under-energised and under-supported for the amplitude of sound Pavarotti is trying to produce. The more ample and intense the sound on a high frequency, the greater the appoggio required to support the vocal instrument. Consequently, the antagonistic action of the breathing muscles is insufficient to sustain the tone in the focal point Pavarotti was aiming for. Without this powerful impetus from the breath, the tone has no alternative but to fall back in the throat. It is still a good sound, but it lacks that forward trumpet tone that is required for the climax on '*Vincero*'.

Needless to say, this production of *Turandot* won Pavarotti had rave reviews and universal admiration, but he was always completely honest with himself, and he knew that this was not a role that he should sing too often in live performances.

At any rate, by the time Pavarotti had sung his first live performance of *Turandot* in San Francisco in 1977, he had been anointed as the greatest lyric tenor of his generation. In fact, following his phenomenal success in the 1976 season of *I Puritani* at the Metropolitan, many vocal authorities argued that he was already the greatest lyric bel canto tenor of all time.

Consequently, in 1976, he made his debut as Manrico in *Il Trovatore;* as we saw above, he followed this with the 1977 *Turandot* and, finally, in 1979, with *La Gioconda,* all with San Francisco Opera. Pavarotti had thus announced the beginning of an all-out assault on the *Lirico Spinto* repertoire. This would mark a complete break from the past and the beginning of a new era, and with it came new criteria and a different set of rules.

Chapter 45

Ballo in Maschera, Pavarotti/Solti May–June 1982

It was 1963 when Pavarotti was first introduced to Verdi's *Ballo in Maschera*. He was in Dublin singing the Duke in *Rigoletto* at the same time as the company was rehearsing its forthcoming production of *Ballo in Maschera*. As always Pavarotti was looking for opportunities to keep developing his craft. In this instance, he attended every rehearsal and later every performance, falling in love with this opera and determining that he would sing it in the latter part of his career. As it turned out, his voice was ready for Riccardo in *Ballo in Maschera* much earlier than he had expected. He debuted as Riccardo in 1969, recorded it in 1970, and has sung it everywhere since.

By 1981, he was able to report to William Wright that:

> There are several roles I have a special feeling for, the roles like Rodolfo and Nemorino for which I am well suited vocally and temperamentally — but if I were told that I would only be able to do that role for the rest of my life, that role would be Riccardo in Verdi's *Un Ballo in Maschera*.
>
> I love the part. Without doubt the opera belongs to the tenor, and the fantastic music that Verdi has given him provides the opportunity to display many different types of singing. As an example of the demands that *Ballo* makes for the tenor, look at the second scene of Act I, set in the fortune-teller Ulrica's den. In that scene, Riccardo has three excerpts of music alone and a difficult trio. Each calls for a different sound, a different phrasing, and a different dramatic mood. That is just one scene. The love duet in the second act is incredible. The only duet that matches it in intensity is the one in *Tristan und Isolde*. The love duet in Verdi's *Otello* is a masterpiece, of course, but a different kind of love is being expressed. For direct immediate passion, I know of nothing like the *Ballo* duet in Italian music [Pavarotti in Wright, 1981: 139].

I agree with everything that Pavarotti said above. Riccardo is absolutely a dream role and Verdi has indeed endowed Riccardo with not only wonderful vocal music of an incredibly varied style, but he also endowed him with tremendously human characteristics.

His love for his people seems boundless, and his love for Amelia remains absolutely pure. Here is a leader who is prepared to sacrifice his happiness for his principles, sending Amelia away with her husband so that she will remain safe and un-compromised.

At any rate, the beginning of the opera reveals a Pavarotti who is in absolutely majestic voice. As always, his tone is lovely, but this is more than a beautiful tone because if all we wanted was a beautiful tone, we would have settled for the 1970 recording.

This is much more about Pavarotti's technique which has changed enormously from his earlier days. Whereas the 1970 recording was more reliant on his natural gifts whilst still requiring a better technique and greater refinement, the 1982 performance is about harnessing nature and putting it in the service of art.

In this performance, Pavarotti has not only rectified the problems we identified in 1970 but has grown sufficiently confident to experiment.

Let us record the issues that have not yet been resolved:

- The first octave of the voice was sagging and variable — Pavarotti rectified it.

- The lack of dynamic buoyancy and sympathetic *'imposto'* tended to diminish the efficiency of focus, allowing the voice to become dark and heavy — Pavarotti rectified it.

- Pavarotti's double *'appoggio'* system is inefficient. Breath *appoggio* and subjective (sympathetic) *appoggio* have both been rectified.

- The majority of [e] vowels in the last recording were squeezed and narrow. This is no longer true — Pavarotti has rectified the problem.

- The [o] vowels in the head register were either overly squeezed or unfocused. Consequently, many of the [o] vowels were under the pitch or had dampened upper harmonics. This has been rectified but not completely eliminated.

- The lower register is very breathy and weak and still not fully developed. This was rectified.

This is quite an achievement for a singer who was already a great international tenor when he recorded the 1970 *'Ballo in Maschera',* so we were not starting from a low base. Pavarotti achieved all of the suggested improvements and then experimented with others.

This is undoubtedly a great voice, but we can't underestimate the fact that he possessed a very intelligent approach to his singing.

La rivedro nell'estasi

Pavarotti's singing of *'La rivedro nell'estasi'* is a splendid way to open this 1982 *Ballo in Maschera.* The tone is absolutely translucent, enjoying a sunny disposition whilst surrounded by a subtle and transparent velvet coating. Pavarotti forms a good legato line even if sometimes the [e] vowel becomes thinner than it should be in this role. However, there are times when the [e] vowel is open-throated and ample. The darker vowels have improved out of sight relative to his last recording. He really has achieved a wonderful *imposto*, although there is, from time to time, too much energy and lack of discipline for a character that has been brought up in a controlled and disciplined environment. The voice tends more towards '*voce aperta*' in this particular aria as opposed to '*voce chiusa*'.

What I have said about '*La rivedro nell'estasi*' applies equally to his second aria ', Di tu sei Fedele', except that he tends more towards '*voce chiusa,*' simply because he is exaggerating and acting up to make light of the situation. Deep down, he senses that Ulrica may be an authentic sybil, and he tries to lead her off the scent.

E scherzo ed e follia

Pavarotti is in splendid voice in this Solti recording, but the significant difference between this and the earlier recording is that the voice production is much firmer, more secure, more even, and more consistently forward and ringing than in his 1970 recording. It is mainly characterised by an emphatic ringing of the higher harmonics, giving the voice the proprioceptive sensation of a much more forward and higher sitting vocal production. The vocal quality and sympathetic sensation are the result of a higher laryngeal position, which elevates the tongue and hyoid bone. This configuration generally yields a more brilliant tone, often at the expense of the fundamental and lower harmonics. It is true that in this recording, the production can, at times, be too muscular and forceful, and yet at other times (especially in the soft singing and lower register), the tone can be a little feeble. I know that Pavarotti is doing this in order to create a contrast, but in accordance with Lamperti's maxim — 'Soft singing is in every way except for intensity the same as forte singing' [Lamperti, c.1883: 19].

Let me give you some specific examples.

In the opening scene, Riccardo is in the hall of the Governor's mansion when Oscar, his page, enters with a list of courtiers invited to the following function. A quick glance reveals that Amelia is coming with her husband Renato, who is the Governor's loyal secretary.

Riccardo's reaction shows that his heart skips a beat at the thought of seeing Amelia again. However, this wonderful moment is marred by the fact that Riccardo feels incredibly guilty about his feelings for his best friend's wife. In the aria '*La rivedro nell'estasi*', Riccardo extols Amelia's virtues and the ecstasy she brings into his life.

We are immediately aware that Pavarotti has diminished the load on the middle voice by lightening the first formant (*oscuro* aspects) and emphasising the second and third formants. The tone sounds brilliant — easy but *raccolto*. If anything, the first F natural is a little too open, and I would typically ask that he relax the larynx (which is too fixed) and think a little more [o] vowel. However, on this occasion, I believe that Pavarotti has an excellent reason to open with this colour, further demonstrating his uncontrollable passion for Amelia, leading him to irrational exhilaration. Just the thought of being in her presence makes his heart sing. Nothing is sensible about that, as she is married to his best friend. It is, therefore, a purely emotional reaction, and consequently, there can be nothing cerebral about his voice production.

Nonetheless, the singing is glorious. The first minor issue appears in the crescendo phrase '*Oh dolce notte*' in which he overemphasises the difference between the [o] and the [e] in '*notte*'. I believe this approach is undesirable because the [e] stands out; it breaks the legato line and destroys the already established smoothness. Given that the [o] vowel needs to be collected on the F♯, a better strategy would be to open the [e] vowel on the G♯ and slightly drop the jaw. This strategy requires a reinforcement of the breath whilst allowing the tongue to remain in the position of the [e] vowel. This would smooth the bumpy spots that are presently breaking the legato line.

He begins the phrase '*qui suonar d'amore*' quite well, but by the time he arrives at the

G♯, the tone is a trifle tight but eventually opens in a decent manner.

The [e] vowel in '*Stella*' is better but still a little tight, but the repeat is much improved. The chromatic passage at the reprise needs to be smoother. The G♯ in '*La tua parola*' and '*sonar d'amore*' is great both vocally and rhythmically.

The last B♭ in the phrase '*La sua parola udra*' is a little tight, mainly because Pavarotti is leaning a little too firmly, thus lowering both the diaphragm and the larynx.

I wouldn't wish to change anything because, in time, he will find a better balance and a more lyrical tone, the point being that you can't find a better balance until you find the breath. For the second time in his career Pavarotti is harnessing his respiratory resources very well in this performance. It is probably the most consistent '*voce appoggiata*' tone of his career, and his harnessing of the upper voice, keeping it closer to '*terra ferma*,' is a very interesting development. We may recall that just the year before this recording he told William Wright that his voice was flying a little too much but now he had it under control. This is precisely what he meant.

Di Tu Sei Fedele

This is really beautiful singing with just the right measure of roundness and brilliance.

Pavarotti is very firm on the breath, and in lowering the diaphragm, he also lowers the larynx; by bringing his excellent skills in focusing the voice, he manages very well with the *imposto*, except for the odd sequence.

So, the early part of this aria is a beautiful, burnished colour, well supported, with a larynx comfortably low and enough edge and brilliance in the tone to cut through.

There is a slight discolouration to the tone of the phrase, '*Con lacer vele e l'alma in tempesta, i solchi son franger dellonda funesta,*' caused by some laryngeal rigidity. He is conflicted about these phrases because he knows that traditionally there is broad agreement that moderately elevating the larynx makes it easier to execute fast staccato notes and ornamentation. This is true, but he has already chosen a strategy in the early phrases, knowing that it is absolutely possible to sing melismatic passages and ornamentation whilst maintaining a relatively low laryngeal position, as long as it is not excessively low or depressed. This requires a strong visualisation of what you want to achieve and the ability to trust the breath as the motivating force.

The A♭ on the [a] vowel of '*Irati*' is absolutely wonderful. On the other hand, the passage beginning with '*No, no, la morte e l'amor sviarmi del mar, la morte e l'amor sviarmi del mar*' is too aggressive, and consequently, the interval on the A♭s is out of focus — a little under the note and throaty. Well, you would think that with this undesirable outcome, I would condemn the experiment, but you would be wrong. Pavarotti miscalculates and overcompensates with the amount of pressure he is applying, but what he is attempting is just great. He is trying to realign the relationship between the breath and the sound, and he is not able to achieve it every time. However, Pavarotti is a quick learner and is able to equilibrate the emphasis between objective and subjective appoggio. This allows him to make amends with the same sequence in the second '*Nell'anime nostre non entra terror, Nell'anime nostre non entra terror*' — which is very well done! The final B♭ finds Pavarotti opening the vowel towards the [a]. It is an exciting sound, except at the very end when he opens the note just a little too much. However, this is purely for expressive reasons, and it does no harm.

Teco Io Sto: Love Duet

Amelia has consulted Ulrica to see if there is a way of breaking the love spell that seems to hold her fast to Riccardo. Ulrica says there is a way to break the spell by using an herb that is only available at the cemetery and must be picked at midnight. She is terribly frightened but decides to do it anyway. It is here that she is approached by Riccardo, who has heard everything and has learned that Amelia loves him.

The duet beginning with the phrase '*Teco io sto*' is energetic but much more mature than his previous recording and much more in keeping with the character's age and intent. Pavarotti goes a little beyond good taste, and the tone becomes too muscular in the phrase, '*Io lasciarti?*'. '*No giammai: non poss'io; che m'arde in petto immortal di te l'affetto.*' The vocal production in this duet needs to be firm, but neither percussive nor bombastic. Pavarotti is just a little too energetic. The breath should be dynamic and kinetic, but not to such a degree that the muscles are constantly in danger of losing control. You should think of sitting on a balloon of breath or wearing a lifebuoy around your waist (a constant reserve of breath), leaning down and out to increase breath pressure, and releasing the tension when you need less pressure. At all times the chest remains moderately high. The movements are relatively small, and the energy has to be carefully dosed out. There is absolutely no violence or jerkiness about this at all. It is the constant tension between airflow and breath pressure, as well as the inner and outer muscles, that constitute the support system. That notwithstanding, Pavarotti is in glorious voice. The tone has a beautiful blending of brilliance and velvety roundness, except when he pushes the high register into position (*impostazione*). Having said that, by the time he arrives at the F sharp of '*Cosi parli a chi t'adore,*' everything changes. From here on, he is singing — not just establishing character — and it is glorious. For instance, the '*Ah crudele a me rammemori*' is Riccardo's response to Amelia's reminder that she belongs to his best friend. In this touching but understated moment, Pavarotti is much more subtle, more authentic and infinitely more mature than he was in the 1970 performance.

The same is true of the next phrase, '*Non sai tu che se l'anima mia,*' which in this performance is more legato and controlled than previously. All the A4s and G4s are much firmer and more solidly underpinned by the breath, and the tone is far more open-throated than his previous performance. Pavarotti seems to have discovered the technique of lowering the larynx and supporting the whole instrument much more solidly than at any time since his recording of *La Boheme* with Von Karajan back in 1973. This newfound connection between the breath, tone and emotions has imbued the Pavarotti sound with richer harmonics, better legato, more consistent clarity of tone and diction, greater emotional involvement and more sophisticated interpretation. By the time we arrive at the '*Quante volte dal cielo implorai*', he opens the A4 as it is required by Verdi, something he failed to do in his first recording. Unfortunately, he forgets to reinforce the breath and find a more lateral position for this vowel. Consequently, the sound splays open and acquires an unfortunate movement in it, not to mention that it is a little throaty. The next A4 on '*La pieta che tu chiedei da me*' is much improved because Pavarotti focuses the [e] towards the zygomatic arch, altering the vowel toward the [i] whilst increasing the breath pressure a little, although not sufficiently. I don't like either of these responses. There is a better strategy for these A4s which is very simple: increase subglottal pressure as you ascend to the A4, slightly drop the jaw, but maintain the mouth and tongue in the lateral [e] position.

The Wagnerian-inspired '*Irradiami d'amore*' is just fantastic: beautiful, expressive singing with just the right amount of abandonment. What I have said about the 'Irradiami d'amor' applies equally to 'O qual soave brivido': just exquisite singing.

Forse La Soglia Attinse and Ma see Me Forsa Perderti

The opening phrase, '*Forse la soglia attinse*', has a beautiful tone, but Pavarotti spoils the next phrase ', *L'onor ed il dover*', by manufacturing the tone. The [o] vowel in '*onor*' is pitched too high on the zygomatic arch, allowing the tongue to retreat and creating a hollow mouth tone. It is only an E flat and there is no need to have such high *imposto, as* this serves to unbalance the vocal line long before he arrives at the modified G♭ on the [e] vowel of '*dover*' (which modification is too severe). I like the way Pavarotti juxtaposes the loud singing with some lovely soft singing. Hardly any two phrases are the same; it is not only technically proficient but also ingenious.

The G on the [o] vowel in the phrase '*e la sua sposa lo seguira*' could be more open, but the *piano* phrase '*e taccia il core*' is lovely. The '*Esito anchor*' is a good dramatic sound, as is the '*Ah! lo segnato*', which is juxtaposed with a lovely soft tone in '*Il sacrifizio mio*'.

The '*Ah*' is the only vowel that should be modified in this phrase but not as severely as Pavarotti modifies it here. The first '*Ah lo segnata*' is excellent, but the second is much more dramatic and probably the most dramatic sound I have heard from Pavarotti. He pitches the centre of the note quite low, using more vocalis muscle and less cricothyroid. I admire this experiment enormously, but I would not aim for such a dark tone here. The only assurance is that he is already a mature tenor, and his support is absolute — significantly better than anything he has done so far. His willingness to keep pushing himself in the quest for artistic perfection is in line with the great artists of the golden age.

This recitative '*Forse la soglia attinse*' is simply the most original, ingenious and innovative that Pavarotti has ever produced. I don't agree with everything he does. However, Pavarotti was in 1982-83 the greatest lyric tenor of the twentieth century and was still looking for ways to innovate, ways of performing our art more brilliantly. At about the same time he was working on

Mozart's *Idemoneo* and he had just debuted in the role of Radames in *Aida*. This was consistent with his philosophy which was dominated by the thought of beating his previous best.

The beginning of the aria proper, '*Ma se me forza perderti, per sempre, o luce mia,*' is a beautiful lyrical tone with just the right amount of energy. The centre tone is pitched fairly high against the zygomatic arch. The G4 on the [a] vowel in the phrase '*a te verra il mio palpito*' is much more interesting and superior to his last recording. The vowel is just a little more authentic and open, allowing the tone to ring freely. However, the [a] vowel on the A♭ in the phrase '*chiusa la tua memoria,*' which was too narrow in the last recording, begins a bit low but develops into a really wonderful tone in this performance. I also like the G♭ in '*quasi un desio fatale*' which again is a little different. Pavarotti approaches the entire phrase '*come se fosse l'ultima*' (marked *dolce*) quite softly. The same applies to the climatic phrase '*Come se fosse l'ultima*' in which the B♭ begins below the note and then opens up towards a decent tone. It's a trifle under the pitch because the resonatory space is too narrow.

The phrases '*Oh qual presagio m'assale*' and '*come se fosse l'ultima ora del nostro amor*' are both well produced. Pavarotti is a revelation in this recording. He does not achieve everything he attempts perfectly, but he produces a performance of outstanding beauty and variety in tone, all in keeping with his characterisation. Technically, he continues to try and improve he is more on the breath, his diction is fantastic, he is using a greater variety of vocal colours, and he remains creative in his interpretations. The voice is ample, darker, well supported and focused.

This performance, whilst occasionally flawed, is absolutely phenomenal: there is enormous depth and insight in this performance and vocal quality alters as the character develops and changes. *Bravo Luciano! Sei stato veramente Grande!*

Chapter 46

Conclusion — An Everlasting Legacy

Luciano Pavarotti was born under an auspicious star. His enormous gifts included not only a phenomenal voice but also his intelligence, natural musicality, personality and lust for life, tremendous willpower, and athleticism (he almost became a professional footballer).

These qualities combined to make him a perfect candidate for greatness. Pavarotti juxtaposed all of these qualities with his artistry, boyish openness, quick wit and good humour to create one of the greatest and most beloved artists of all time. Pavarotti was not just a voice for the ages. He was an extraordinary artist for the ages. However, even with these attributes, it is highly possible that his most significant competitive advantage was his cultural and musical environment and the unconditional love of his family and friends. We recall that Pavarotti and his father would walk to church hand in hand in order to sing at vespers when Pavarotti was only a young boy. Later, Pavarotti joined his father on the first tenor's line in the Corale Rossini. This was the choir that, in a never-to-be-forgotten occasion, won the choral Eisteddfod in Wales and inspired Luciano to become a professional tenor. Later still, he joined the chorus of the Teatro Comunale, where he was able to listen to and study all the great singers of the day. Pavarotti was by nature a gentle giant and people just loved him. From his humble but culturally rich background, he developed a strong personal philosophy centred around wisdom and a fundamental understanding of the human condition. Pavarotti was not a pretender, and he was enormously humble for a man of his achievements. Nor was he too proud to ask for help during his developmental years. The wisdom was in knowing both how and who to ask for help, and Pavarotti intuitively knew both.

He was grateful every day for his family, his teachers and his culture. We must not forget that the Pavarotti and Freni families went through some very difficult times during the war in Modena. Also, even with a magnificent voice, Pavarotti had great difficulty obtaining the technical proficiency that would allow him to express his great soul. He was demanding of himself and others where the art was concerned but enormously generous with friends and family, not to mention the next generation of singers. Moreover, he always appreciated and was thankful for the people who helped him in his ascent to the pinnacle of his art. He remained grateful to Arrigo Pola, Ettore Campogalliani, Mirella Freni, Leone Magiera, Joan Ingpen and Joan Sutherland for their help and mentorship in the early years.

We should also remind ourselves that Pavarotti's singing may be divided into four categories — his early years, the lyrical years, the beginning of the lyric spinto period and the full lirico-spinto tenor.

1. The early period is best characterised by a glorious voice with a magnificent top, but not yet in control of the breath or vocal clarity, diction or articulatory control. The voice may best be described as flow phonation. It is velvety, a little too dark and mellow, and the core of the sound is too far back. At this stage, the voice needs more brilliance and penetration. This period is represented by Beatrice di Tenda, L'amico Fritz and many of the 1965 live performances.

2. The second is characterised by a firmer onset (attack) and phonation, a firmer and more sustained breath management style, a more forward *imposto* with a more brilliant tone, greater penetration and a more balanced *chiaro/scuro*.

3. At the peak of this period, the *imposto* is placed high, the breath has gained in endurance (remaining more solid for longer), and it is more responsive. Consequently, the tone is firmer, more brilliant and penetrating, creating both a firmer onset and firmer sustained tone: *Rigoletto, La Boheme, La Fille du Regiment*, and *I Puritani*.

4. The fourth period refers to the full lirico-spinto repertoire, Turandot, Pagliacci, Trovatore, his 1982 Ballo in Maschera, La Gioconda, Andrea Chenier, and Aida

This is an extraordinarily wide-ranging repertoire, and my contention is that Pavarotti is the greatest lyric bel canto tenor of the twentieth century. There is simply no one that comes even close to Pavarotti's standard in the core lyric repertoire, including *La Boheme, Rigoletto, Lucia, Masked Ball, La Favorita, Maria Stuarda, L'Elisir d'amore, La Fille du Regiment, La Sonnambula, I Capuletti e Montecchi* and *I Puritani*.

I surmise that this is the reason why Von Karajan believed that his vocal folds had been kissed by God. Pavarotti later repaid the compliment when he declared that having worked with all the great conductors, Karajan was in a league of his own. In fact, he stated that there was Von Karajan and then all the others.

Having presented what I believe to be an exhaustive analysis of Pavarotti's stature in the rank of lyric tenors, I have come to the same conclusion about

Pavarotti's work. Having sung many of these roles and studied all the other tenors singing that repertoire, I have concluded beyond doubt that in the realm of the lyric bel canto tenors, there is Pavarotti, and then we have all the other excellent tenors. Even when I am particularly critical of him, I am still forced to reach the same conclusion.

In addition to the spirited dedication with which he pursued his vocal technique and his art, the management of his career was impeccable. He knew exactly when to take on a particular role, and above all, he knew when to say no to other roles. This was not just knowledge and intelligence but also instinct and intuition, coming from remaining close to his roots, not getting ahead of himself, and listening to his heart and the advice of those who loved him.

When he finally managed to conquer his technique, the magic happened naturally and spontaneously. Pavarotti just opened his arms and offered a warm embrace to all of humanity.

I ask myself whether we will ever see the likes of him again. As I fear the answer is a resounding no, let us pay homage to and enjoy Pavarotti's enormous and everlasting legacy to the world of opera.

Bibliography

Books

Adams, Brian (1986) 'La Stupenda '. Sydney: Random House.

Veroni, Adua (1992) 'Pavarotti: Life With Luciano'. New York, Rizzoli International Publishers.

Agur, A.M. R. & Lee, J. Ming (1999) 'Grant's Atlas of Anatomy'. Baltimore, Maryland: Lippicott, Williams & Wilkins.

Aikin, W.A. (1951) 'The Voice: an introduction to Practical Phonology'. London: Longmans Green.

Agricola, Johann Fredrich (1995) 'Introduction to the Art of Singing'. New York: Cambridge University Press. Lishing Company.

Alderston, Richard (1979)'The Complete Handbook of Voice Training'. New York: Parker Pub.

Alton, Everest & Pohlmann (2009) 'Master Handbook of Acoustics'. New York: McGraw Hill.

Alfred, John (1972) 'Manual of Sound Recording'. London: Fountain Press.

André, Naomi (2006) 'Voicing Gender'. Bloomington & Indianapolis: Indiana University Press.

Appelman, D. Ralph (1986) 'The Science of Vocal Pedagogy': Translated by Julianne Baird. Bloomington: Indiana. University Press.

Ardoin, John (1998) 'Callas At Juilliard: The Masterclasses'. Portland, Oregon: Amadeus Press Inc.

Ardoin, John (1988) 'The Calls Legacy'. London: Gerald Duckworth & Co. Ltd.

Bacilly, Benigne de (1968) 'Commentary upon the Art of Proper Singing'. New York: Institute of Medieval Studies.

Backus, John (1968) 'The Acoustical Foundation of Music'. New York:

Baudissone, Bruno (1989) 'Pricipessa turandot: La Voce e L'Arte di Gina Cigna'. Parma: Azzali Editore.

Bartholomew, Wilmer (1965) 'Acoustics of Music'. Englewood: Prentice-Hall.

_____ (1934) 'A Physical Definition of "Good Voice-Quality". Department of Research, Peabody Conservatory of Music, Baltimore Maryland.

Bassini, Carlo (2008) 'Art of Singing'. San Diego: Plural Publishing, Inc.

Batchelor, G. K. (2000) 'Introduction to Fluid Dynamics'. New York: Cambridge University Press.

Battaglia Damiani, Daniela (2003) 'Anatomia Della Voce'. Milano: Ricordi (BMG Publications.

Bayly, Anselm (1771)'A Practical Treatise on Singing and Playing with Just Expression and Real Elegance'. London: J. Ridley Publisher.

Behnke, Emil (1881)'The Mechanism of the Human Voice'. London: Curwen and Sons.

Behnke, E. and Browne, L. (1895) 'A Practical Guide For Singers and Speakers', London: Sampson, Low, Marston & Company Limited.

Behrman, Alison (2008) 'Speech and Voice Science'. San Diego: Plural Publishing Inc.

Benade, Arthur (1976) 'The Fundamentals of Musical Acoustics'. London: Oxford University Press.

Berard, Jean-Antoine (1755) 'L'Art du Chant'. Paris: Dessaint & Saillant.

Berg, Richard & Stork, David (2005) 'The Physics of Sound'. New Jersey: Pearson, Prentice Hall.

Bjorling, Anna-Lisa & Farks, Andrew 'Jussi'. Portland, Oregon: Amadeus Press

Bisogni, Vincenzo Ramon 'Franco Corelli — Irresistibili Tenore'. Varesi: Zecchini Editore.

Bloem – Hubatka, Daniela (2012) 'The Old Italian School of Singing: A Theoretical And Practical Guide'. North Caroline: McFarland and Company.

Boagno, Marina (1996) 'Corelli: A Man A Voice'. Forth Worth: Baskerville Publishers, Inc.

Bonvicini, Candido (1992) 'My Friend Pavarotti'. London: Omnibus Press.

Boone, Daniel R. et al. (2010) 'The Voice and Voice Therapy'. Boston: Allyn and Bacon -Pearson Education.

Bozeman, Kenneth W. (2013) 'Practical Vocal Acoustics: Pedagogical Applications for Teachers and Singers'. New York: Pendragon Press, Hillsdale, NY.

Bouhuys, Arend (1968) 'Sound production in man: annals of the New York Acadamy of Science'. New York: New York Academy of Science.

Bouhuys, Arend (1977) 'Physiology of Breathing'. London: Gune & Stratton.

Boynton, Joan Frey (2003) 'The Private Voice Studio Handbook: A Practical Guide to All Aspects of Teaching". Milwaukee: Hal-Leonard.

Brennan, Richard (2004) 'The Alexander Technique Manuel'. London: Connections Book Publishing Limited.

Breslen, Herbert & Midgette, Anne (2004) 'The King & I' London: Mainstream Publishing.

Brewer, David J. MD (1964) 'Research potential in Voice Physiology'. Syracuse: New York: University of New York.

Broad, David J. (1977) 'Topics in Speech and Science'. Los Angeles: Speech Communication Research Laboratory.

Brodnitz, Fredrich S. (1988) 'Keep Your Voice Healthy'. Austin, Texas: pro-ed Inc.

Brown, L. Oren (1996) 'Discover Your Voice: How to Develop Healthy Voice Habits'.

San Diego: Singular Publishing Group.

Brown, William Earl (1957) 'Vocal Wisdom: maxims of Giovanni Battista Lamperti'.

New York: Taplinger Publishing Company.

Brower, H. & Cooke, J. F. (1996) 'Great Singers on the Art of Singing'. Mineola N.Y.: Dover Publications.

Bruno, Giovanna & Paperi, Valerio (2001) 'La Voce Cantata: Fisiologia, patologia e pedagogia del canto artistico'. Roma: Verduci Editore.

Bukofzer, Manfred (1948) 'Music in the Baroque Era'. London: J. M. Dent & Sons.

Bunch, Meribeth (1997) 'Dynamics of the Singing Voice'. Wien: Springer-Verlag.

Bunch, Meribeth (2005) 'The Performers Voice: Realising Your Vocal Potential'. New York: W. W. Norton and Comp. Inc.

Burgin, John Carrol (1973) 'Teaching Singing'. Metuchen N. J.: Scarecrow Press.

Burney, Charles (1987) 'Viaggio Musicale In Italia'. Torino: E.D.T. Edizione Torino.

Bybee, Ariel and Ford, James E. (2004) 'The Modern Singing Master: Essays in honor of Cornelius L. Reid'. Marylands: Scarecrow Press, Inc.

Caccini, Giulio (1602) 'Le Nuove Musiche', Edited by H. Wiley Hitchcock. Madison: A-R Editions Inc.

Caesari, Herbert, E. (1936 Reprint 1968) 'The Science and Sensations of Vocal Tone'. London: J.M. Dent & Sons LTD.

Caesari, Herbert, E. (1965) 'The Alchemy of Voice'. London: Robert Hale.

Caesari, Herbert, E, (1969) 'The Voice of the Mind'. London: Robert Hale.

Caesari, Herbert, E. (1963) 'Tradition and Gigli'. London: Robert Hale.

Campbell, Agostini and Davis (1970) 'The Respiratory Muscles: Mechanics and Neural Control'. London: LLOYD-LUKE (Medical Books) LTD.

Callaghan, Jean (2000) 'Singing and Voice Science'. San Diego, California: Singular Publishing.

Callaghan, Jean (2014) 'Singing and Science, Body, Brain, & Voice'. Oxford, Compton Publishing Ltd.

Campbell, E. J. M.(1958) 'The Respiratory Muscles and the Mechanics of Breathing'. Chicago: Year Book (Medical) Publishers.

Campbell, Agostini, Davis (1970) 'The Respiratory Muscles and Neural Control'.

London: LLOYED-LUKE LTD.

Cappelletto, Sandro (1995) 'La Voce di Farinelli: vita di Farinelli Evirato Cantore'. Torino: E.D.T. Edizione di Torino.

Carboni, Giancarlo (2017) 'Manuale Professionale di Dizione e Pronuncia'. Milano: Ulrico Hoepli Editore.

Caruso, Enrico & Tetrazzini, Luisa (1909) 'Caruso and Tetrazzini on The Art of Singing', New York: Dover Publications Inc.

Casanova, Carlamaria (1885) 'Renata Tebaldi: The Voice of an Angel'. Forthworth: Baskerville Publishers, Inc.

Castiglione, Baldesar ((1967) The Book of the Courtier'. London: Penguin Books.

Celletti, Rodolfo (1991) 'A History of Bel Canto'. New York: Oxford University Press.

Celletti, Rodolfo (2000) 'La Grana Della Voce'. Milano: Baldini & Castoldi Publishers.

Chapin, Schuyler (1995) 'Sopranos, Mezzos, Tenors, Bassos, and Other Friends'. New York: Crown Publishers, Inc.

Chapman, Janice L. (2012) 'Singing And Teaching Singing: A Holistic Approach to Classical Voice'. San Diego: Plural Publishing Inc.

Christy, Van A. (1977) 'Expressive Singing'. Dubuque, Iowa: Wm. C. Brown Company Publishers.

Christiansen, Rupert (1995) 'Prima Donna'. London: Random House.

Cobelnzer, Horst and Muhar, Franz (2015) 'Respiro e Voce'. Roma: Dino Audino.

Coffin, Berton (1960) 'Singer's Repertoire: Lyric and Dramatic Tenors'. New York: Scarecrow Press, Inc.

Coffin, Berton (1980) 'Overtones of Bel Canto'. Lanham, Maryland: Scarecrow Press.

Coffin, Berton (1987) 'Coffin's Sounds of Singing'. Maryland: Scarecrow Press Inc.

Coffin, Berton (1989) "Historical Vocal Pedagogy Classics'. Maryland: Scarecrow Press.

Colton, Raymond & Caspar, Janina K. (1996) 'Understanding Voice Problems'. Baltimore, Maryland: Williams and Wilkins.

Conati, Marcello (1984) 'Interviews & Encounters with Verdi'. London: Victor Gollancz LTD.

Cooper, Morton (1999) 'Change your Voice, Change Your Life'. Los Angeles: Voice & Speech Co. of America Publisher.

Cunelli, Georges (1973) 'Voice no Mystery'. London: Staiber & Bell LTD.

Curtis, Henry Holbrook (1896) 'Voice Building And Tone Placing: Showing a New Method of Relieving Injured Vocal Cords By Tone Exercises. New York: D. Appleton and Company.

Delle Sedie, Enrico (n.d.) 'A Complete Method of Singing: A Theoretical And Practical Treatise On The Art Of Singing'. New York: G. Schirmer.

Dent, E. J. (1905) 'Alessandro Scarlatti: His Life and Works'. London: Edward Arnold.

Di Stefano, Giuseppe (1989) 'L'Arte Del Canto'. Milano: Rusconi Libri.

Domingo, Placido (1983) Placido Domingo: My First Forty Years'. London: Weidenfeld and Nicolson.

Doscher, Barbara (1988) 'The Functional Unity Of The Singing Voice'. Metuchen N.J.: Scarecrow Press Inc.

Douglas, Nigel (1992) 'Legendary Voices'. London: Andrea Deutsch Limited.

Drake, James A. (1997) 'Rosa Ponselle: A Centenary Biography'. Portland, Oregon: Amadeus Press.

Duey, Philip A. (1980) 'Bel Canto in Its Golden Age'. New York: Da Capo Press Inc.

Ellis, Alexander (1898) 'Speech and Song'. London: Novello.

Emmons, Shirlee (1990) 'Lauritz Melchior: Tristanissimo'. London: Schirmer Books Inc.

Ezzu, Alberto (2009) 'Il Canto degli Armonici'. Torino: Musica Pratica.

Fant, Gunnar (1970) 'Acoustic Theory of Speech Production'. The Hauge: Mouton Press.

Fant and Kruckenburg (1996) 'Voice source properties of the speech code'. TMH-QPSR

Fernandi, Franco (1994) 'Le Voci Piacentine: Due secoli di bel canto a Piacenza'. Parma: Azzali Editori.

Field Hyde, F.C. (1950) 'The Art and Science of Voice Training'. London: Oxford University Press.

Fields, Victor Alexander (1947) 'Training the Singing Voice'. New York: King's Crown Press.

Fields, Victor Alexander (1970) 'Foundation of the Singer's Art'. Reprint, 1984, 1984, New York: NATS Publications.

Fillebrown, Thomas (1911) 'Resonance in Singing and Speaking'. Bryn Mawr: Oliver Ditson.

Fischer-Dieskau, Dietrich (1976) 'Schubert: A Biographical Study of his Songs'. London: Cassell & Company Limited.

Fitzlyon, April (1987) 'Maria Malibran: Diva of the Romantic Age'. London: Souvenir Press (E & A).

Flanagan, James. L. (1972) 'Speech Analysis Synthesis and Perception'. New York: Springer Verlag.

Forman, Edward V. (1968) 'The Porpora Tradition'. Milwaukee: Pro Musica Press.

Forman, Edward V. (2006) 'How to Sing Italian Baroque Music Correctly'. Minnieapolis, Minessota: Pro Musica Press.

Forman, Edward Phd. (2006) 'The Art of bel canto in the Italian Baroque'. Minneapolis, Minessota: Pro Musica Press.

Forman, Edward (2006) 'A bel canto Method'. Minneapolis, Minnesota: Pro Musica Press.

Foster, Roland (1935) 'Vocal Success: A practical guide to the essentials of Good Singing'. Sydney: Paling's Music.

Freitas, Roger (2014) 'Portrait of a Castrato'. New York: Cambridge University Press.

Frisell, Anthony (1968) 'The Tenor Voice'. Massachusetts: Bruce Humphries Publishers.

Fuchs, Viktor (1967) 'The Art of Singing and Voice Technique'. London: Calder Boyars.

Fucito, S. & Beyer, J.B. (1922 Reprint 1995) 'Caruso and the Art of Singing'. Mineola New York: Dover Publications Inc.

Fussi, F. & Magnani, S. (1994) 'L'Arte Vocale'. Omega Edizione.

Fussi, F. & Magnani, S. (2003) 'Lo Spartito Logopedico'. Omega Edizione.

Fussi, F. & Magnani, S. (2010) 'Le Parole della Scena'. Omega Edizione.

Fussi, F. & Giraldone, M. (2009) 'Clinica della Voce'. Torino: Edizione di Cortina Torino.

Fussi, S. & Turli, E. (2008) 'Una Prospettiva per il metedo Estill VoiceCraft'. Omega Musica.

Galignano, M. (2013) 'Pedagogia e Sceinza della Voce'. Omega Edizione.

Garcia, Manuel 11 (a compilation of the 1841 & 1872 edit.) 'A complete Treatise on the Art of Singing: Part One'. New York: Da Capo Press (1984).

Garcia, Manuel 11 (1847) 'A Complete Treatise on the Art of Singing: Part Two'. New York: Da Capo Press (1975).

Garcia, Manuel (1894) 'Hints on Singing'. New York: Joseph Patelson Music House Ltd. (1982).

Gattey, Charles Neilson (1979) 'Queens of Song'. London: Barrie & Jenkins Ltd.

Gauffin & Hammarberg (1991) 'Vocal Fold Physiology; Acoustic, Perceptual And Physiological Aspects Of Voice Mechanisms.' San Diego, California: Singular Publishing Group Inc.

Gelb, Michael.J. (1995) 'Body Learning: An Introduction to the Alexander Technique'. New York: Henry Holt & Company LLC.

Gilardone, M. & Fussi, F. (1998) 'Le Voci di Puccini'. Omega Edizione.

Gilliland, Dale (2006) 'The teaching of Jean de Reske'. Minneapolis: Pro Musica Press.

Goldovsky, Boris (1968) 'Bringing Opera to Life'. New York: Appleton-Century-Crofts.

Gossett, P., Ashbrook, W., Budden, J., Lippman, F. Porter, A., Caner, M. (1980) 'The New Grove: Masters of of Italian Opera'. London: Macmillan Press.

Gosett, Philip (2006) 'Divas and Scholars: performing Italian Opera'. Chicago: University of Chicago Press.

Gray's Anatomy (1995) Peter L. Williams. Edinburgh: Churchill and Livingstone.

Grove, George (1973) 'Grove's Dictionary of Music And Musicians' in nine volumes and Supplementary, Edited by Eric Blom. London: Macmillan Press.

Grove, George (1985) 'The New Grove's Dictionary of Music', in 20 Volumes, Edited by Stanley Sadie. London: Macmillan Press.

Grove, George (1992) 'The New Grove's Dictionary of Opera', Edited by Stanley Sadie. London: Macmillan Press.

Hardcastle, W. & Laver, J. (1999) 'The Handbook of Phonetic Sciences'. Malden, Massachusetts: Blackwell Publishers.

Harpster, R (1984) 'Technique in Singing: A Program for Singers and Teachers'. New York: Schirmer Books, a division of Macmillan Inc.

Hedington, C., Westbrook, R., & Barfoot, T. (1991) 'Opera: A History'. London: Arrow Books Limited.

Helmholtz, Hermann (1877 Reprint 1954) 'On the Sensation of Tone'. New York: Dover Publications.

Heriot, Angus (1956) 'The Castrati in Opera'. London: Secker & Warburg.

Hiller, Johann Adam (1780) 'Treatise on Vocal Performance and Ornamentation'. (Reprint 2001). New York: Cambridge University Press.

Hines, Jerome (1994) 'Great Singers on Great Singing'. New York: Limelight Editions.

Hines, Jerome (1997) 'The Four Voices of Man'. New York: Limelight Editions.

Hirano, Minuro (1981) 'Clinical Examination of Voice'. Vienna: Springer-Verlag.

Hixon, Thomas J. (1991) 'Respiratory Function in Speech and Song'. San Diego, California: Singular Publishing Group.

Holden, Amanda (2001) 'The New Penguin Opera Guide'. London: Penguin Books.

Horne, Marilyn & Scovell, Jane (2005) 'Marilyn Horne: The Song Continues'. Fort Worth, Teases: Baskerville Publishers, Inc.

Jeans, James (1968) 'Science & Music'. New York: Dover Publications, Inc.

Joyner, James Richard (1998) 'Charles Amable Battaille: Pioneer in Vocal Science and the Teaching of Singing'. Lanham, Maryland: Scarecrow Press, Inc.

Harrison, Scott (2010) 'Perspective on Teaching Singing: Australian Vocal Pedagogues Sing Their Stories'. Bowen Hills Qld: Australian Academic Press.

Hemsley, Thomas (2013) 'Singing and Imagination'. Oxford: Oxford niversity Press.

Henderson, W. J. (1921) 'Early History of Singing'. New York: Longmans, Green And Co.

Hetherington, John (1973) 'Melba: A Biography'. London: Faber & Faber.

Hopkins, Bart (1996) 'Musical Instrument Design'. Tucson: Sharp Press.

Husler, F. & Rodd Marling, Y. (1965) 'Singing: The Physical Nature Of The Vocal Organ'. London: Faber & Faber Limited.

Jellinek, George (1986) 'Callas: Portrait of A Prima Donna'. New York: Dover Publication, Inc.

Jones, David L. (2017) 'A Modern Guide to Old World Singing'. David L. Jones.

Juvarra, Antonio (1987) 'Il Canto e le sue tecniche'. Milano: BMG Ricordi S.p.A.

Juvarra, Antonio (2015) 'Il Canto e le sue tecniche'. Milano: Casa Ricordi.

Juvarra, Antonio (2006) 'I segreti del belcanto'. Milano: Edizioni Curci.

Juvarra, A (2014) 'Canto Perduta Canto Ritrovato'. Roma:

Armando Editore.

Juvarra, A. (2014) 'La Tecnica Vocale Italiana'. Padova: Armelin Musica.

Kay, Elster (1963) 'Bel canto and the Sixth Sense'. London: Dobson.

Kayes, Gillyanne (2000) 'Singing and The Actor'. London: A.C. Black (Publishers) Limited.

Kelsey, Franklyn (1950) 'The Foundation of Singing'. London: Williams & Norgate.

Kendall, Alan (1992) 'Giocchino Rossini: The Reluctant Hero'. London: Victor Gollancz Ltd.

Kennedy-Fraser, Marjory (1887 reprinted 2010) 'David Kennedy; The Scottish Singer'.

Memphis Tennessee: General Books.

Kennedy Scott, Charles (1954) 'The fundamentals Of Singing'. London: Cassell And Company LTD.

Kesting, Jurgen ((1996) 'Luciamo Pavarotti: The Myth of the Tenor'. London: Robson Books LTD.

Klein, Hermann (1923) 'An Essay on Bel Canto and the Teachings of Manuel Garcia'. London: Oxford University Press.

Klein, Hermann (1903) 'Thirty Years of Musical Life in London'. New York: The Century Co.

Kolodin, Irving (1959) 'The Musical Life'. London: Victor Gollancz Ltd.

Lablache, Luigi (1842) 'Metodo Completo di Canto' (Reprint 1997). Milano: Casa Ricordi, BMG Ricordi.

Ladefoge, Peter (1966) 'Elements of Acoustics Phonetics'. Edinburgh: Oliver & Boyd.

Lamperti, Francesco (1864) 'Guida Teorica-Pratica- Elementare Per Lo Studio Del Canto'. Milano: Ricordi.

Lamperti, Francesco (circa 1983) 'The Art of Singing' translated by G Griffiths. New York: G. Schirmer.

Lamperti, G.B. (1905) 'The Techniques of Bel Canto'. New York: G. Schirmer.

Lanza Tomoasi, Gioacchino (1934) 'Vincenzo Bellini'. Palermo: Sellerio Editore.

Large, John Phd., (1980) 'Contributions of Voice Research to Singing'. Houston Texas: College-Hill Press.

Last, R. J. (1984) 'Anatomy Regional and Applied'. Edinburgh: Churchill Livingstone.

Lauri Volpi, Giacomo (1960) 'Voci Parallele'. Blogna: Bongiovanni Editore.

Lehmann, Lilli (1902) 'How to Sing'. (Reprint 1993). Mineola New York: Dover Publications Inc.

Lehmann, Lotte (1985) 'More Than Singing: The Interpretation of Songs'. New York: Dover Publications Inc.

Love, Harold (1981) 'The Golden Age of Australian Opera'. Sydney: Currency Press.

Love, Roger & Frazier Donna (1999) 'Set Your Voice Free'. New York: Little, Brown and Company.

Lovegrove Graziano, Susan (1999) 'Oggi si Canta: La Voce e il Canto nella didattica musicale'. Roma: BMG Ricordi.

Mackenzie, Sir Morell (1886) 'The Hygiene Of The Vocal Organs: A Practical Handbook For Singers and Speakers'. London: Macmillan and Co.

Mackenzie, Barbara & Mackenzie, Findlay (1967) 'Singers of Australia, from Melba to Sutherland'. Melbourne: Lansdowne Press.

Mackinlay, Malcom Sterling (1908) 'Garcia The Centenarian, and His Times'. New York: D. Appleton & Company.

McCoy, Scott DMA (2006) 'Your Voice: An Inside View". Princeton, New Jersey: Inside View Press.

McKinney, James C. (1994) 'The Diagnosis & Correction of Vocal Faults'. Long Grove, Illinois: Waveland Press Inc.

McMinn, R.M.H. (1998) 'A Concise Handbook of Human Anatomy'. London: Manson Publishing Ltd.

Magiera, Leone (2008) 'Pavarotti Up Close'. Milano: Universal Music, MGB Publications srl.

Magiera, Micaela (2018) 'The Girl Under the Piano'. Modena: Edizione Artestampa.

Magnani, S. & Fussi, F. (2015) 'Ascoltare la Voce'. Milano: FrancoAngeli.

Magnani, S. (2017) 'Curare la Voce: Diagnosi e terapia dei disturbi della Voce'. Milano: FrancoAngeli.

Magnani, S. (2017) 'Vivere di Voce: L'arte della manutenzione della voce per chi parla, rcita e canta'. FrancoAngeli, Milano.

Major, Norma (1987) 'Joan Sutherland'. London: Queen Anne Press.

Malmberg, Bertil (1968) 'Manuel of Phonetics'. Amsterdam: North-Holland Publishing Company.

Mancini, Giambattista (1774-1777) 'Practical Reflections On Figured Singing'. Champain, Illinois: Pro Musica Press.

Manén, Lucie (1974) 'The Art of Singing'. London: Faber Music LTD.

Manén, Lucie (1987) 'Bel Canto'. Oxford: Oxford University Press.

Mantovani, Nicoletta (2019) 'Luciano Pavarotti: Il Sole Nella Voce'. Bologna: Fondazione Luciano Pavarotti.

Manfredini, Vincenzo (1775) 'Regole Armoniche'. Venice 1775 facsimile New York: Broude Brothers.

Marafioti, Mario (1922 Reprint 1949) 'Caruso's Method of Voice Production: The Scientific Culture of The Voice'. New York: Dover Publishing Inc.

Marchesi, Mathilde (n.d. Reprint 1970) 'Theoretical & Practical Vocal Method'. New York: Dover Publications, Inc.

Marchesi, Mathilde (1897) 'Marchesi And Music: Passages From The Life Of A Famous Singing Teacher'. New York: Harper & Brothers Publishers.

Marchesi, Blanche (1923 reprint 1977) 'Singer's Pilgrimage: An Autobiography' New York: Arno Press.

Marchesi, Blanche (1931) 'The Singer's Catechism And Creed'. London: J.M. Dent.

Marek, Dan (2007) 'Singing The First Art'. Lanham, Maryland: Scarecrow Press Inc.

Mayer, Martin (1986) 'Grandissimo Pavarotti'. Double Day & Company, Garden City, New York.

Mari, Nanda (1970, Reprint 1987) 'Canto e Voce: Difetti Causati da un Errato Studio del Canto'. Milano: BMG Ricordi Music Publishers.

Matheopouos, Helena 'Diva: Great Soprano's and Mezzos Discuss Their Art'. London: Victor Gollancz.

Mayer, Marin (1986) 'Grandissimo Pavarotti'. New York: Doubleday & Company.

Meano, Carlo and Khoury, Adele (1967) 'The Human Voice in Speech and Song'. Springfield, Illinois: Charles C. Thomas Publisher.

Melba, Dame Nellie (1926) 'Melba Method'. London: Chapell.

Menicucci, Delfo (2011) Scuola di Canto Lirico e Moderno: indaggine sulla Tecnica di Affondo di Mario Del Monaco.' Torino: Omega Edizione.

Mensah, Karin (2009) 'L'Arte Di Cantare: Manuale Pratico di Canto Moderno'. Milano: Volenete & Co.

Miller, Donald Gray, PhD (2008) 'Resonance in Singing: Voice Building through Acoustic Feedback'. Princeton: Inside View Press.

Miller, Richard (1977 Reprint 1997) 'National Schools of Singing'. Lanham, Maryland: Scarecrow Press Inc.

Miller, Richard (1993)'Training Tenor Voices'. New York: Schirmer Books, an imprint of Macmillan Publishing Company.

Miller, Richard (1986 Reprint 1996)'The Structure of Singing'. New York, N.Y: Schirmer Books, an imprint of Macmillan Publishing Company.

Miller, Richard (1996) 'On The Art of Singing'. New York: Oxford University Press.

Miller, Richard (2000) 'Training Soprano Voices'. New York: Oxford University Press.

Miller, Richard (2004) 'Solutions For Singers: Tools For Performers And Teachers'.

New York: Oxford University Press.

Miller, Richard (2008) 'Securing Baritone, Bass-Baritone & Bass Voices'. New York: Oxford University Press.

Monahan, Brent Jeffrey (1978) 'The Art of Singing: A Compendium of Thoughts on Singing Published Between 1777 and 1927'. Metuchen, N.J.: The Scarecrow Press, Inc.

Monahan, Brent (2006) 'The Singer's Companion: A Guide to Improving Your Voice and Performance'. Pompton Plains, New Jersey: Limelight Editions.

Moore, Keith L. (1984) 'Clinically Oriented Anatomy'. Baltimore: Williams & Wilkins.

Mori, Rachele Maragliano (1970) 'Coscienza Della Voce Nella Scuola Italiana Di Canto'. Milano: Edizione Curci.

Myer, Edmund (1902) 'The Renaissance of the Vocal Art.' July 2004 [Ebook #12856].

_____(1891) 'Vocal Reinforcement.' Boston: Boston Music Co.

Osborne, Richard (2007) 'Rossini: His Life and Works'. New York: Oxford University Press.

Palisca, Claude V. (1968 Reprint 1991) 'Baroque Music'. Englewood Cliffs, New Jersey: Prentice-Hall Inc.

Panofka, Enrico (1871) 'Voci E Cantanti'. Florence: Arnaldo Forni Editore.

Parker, Roger (1994 Reprint 20001) 'The Oxford Illustrated History of Opera.' New York: Oxford University Press.

Pavarotti, Adua (1992) 'Life with Luciano'. Allen & Unwin, Australia.

Peraro, Walter (2004) 'Esercizi di Pronuncia'. Roma: Dino Audino.

Peri, Jacopo (1604) 'Le Varie Musiche And Other Songs', Edited by Tim Carter.' Madison: A-R Editions, Inc.

Phillips –Matz, Mary Jane (2001) 'Rosa Ponselle: An American Diva'. Boston: Northeastern University Press.

Pinksterboer, Hugo (2008) 'Tipbook Vocals: The Singing Voice'. Milwaukee: Hal Leonards Books.

Pisk, Litz (175) 'The Actor And His Body'. London: George Harrap & Co. Ltd.

Pleasants, Henry (1967 Reprint 1983) 'The Great Singers: From the Dawn of Opera to Our Own Time'. London: Papermac, A Division of Macmillan Publishers Limited.

Plunket Greene, Harry (1912 Reprint 1979) 'Interpretation In Song'. New York: Da Capo Press.

Potter, John (2001) 'The Cambridge Companion To Singing'. Edinburgh: Cambridge University Press.

Potter, John (2010) 'Tenor: A History Of A Voice'. New Haven: Yale University Press.

Porter, J.C. (1999) 'Baroque Naples: A Documentary History, 1600–1800'. New York: Italica Press.

Proctor, Donald F. (1980) 'Breathing, speech and Song'. Vienna: Spring-Verlag.

Proschowsky, Frantz (1926) 'The Way To Sing'. U.S.A: C.C. Birchard & Company.

Pullen, Robert & Taylor, Stephen (1994) 'Montserrat Caballe: Casta Diva'. London: Victor Gollancz.

Punt, Norman (1979) 'The Singer's and the Actor's Throat'. London: William Heinemann.

Raguenet, Francois (1709) (Reprint 1968) 'A Comparison Between the French and Italian Musick And Opera'. London: Gregg International Publishers Limited.

Randegger, Alberto (nd) 'Novello's Music Primers & Education Series: Singing'. London: Novello And Company, Limited.

Rasponi, Lanfranco (1994) 'The Last Prima Donnas'. New York: Limelight editors.

Reid, Cornelius L. (1972) 'The Free Voice: A Guide to Natural Singing'. New York: The Joseph Patelson Music House.

Reid, Cornelius L. (1974) 'Bel Canto: Principles and Practices'. New York: The Joseph Patelson Music House.

Reis, Cornelius (1984) 'The Free Voice: A Guide to Natural Singing'. New York: Joseph Patelson Music House.

Righini, Pietro (2008) 'L'Acustica Per Il Musicista: Fondamenti Fisici Della Musica'. Milano: Ricordi, BMG Publishing Scl.

Righini, Pietro (1980) 'Lessico Di Acustica E Tecnica Musicale'. Milano: BMG Ricordi Music Publishing S.p.A.

Rohmert, Giselle (2003) 'Il Cantante in Cammino Verso Il Suono'. Treviso: Diastemi Libri.

Roselli, John (1995) 'Singers of Italian Opera: The history of a profession'. Cambridge: Cambridge University Press.

Roselli, John (1996) 'The Life of Bellini'. Cambridge: Cambridge University Press.

Cambridge: Cambridge University Opera.

Rose, Arnold (1962 Reprint 1971) ' The Singer and the Voice'. London: Faber And Faber Limited.

Rossing, Moore and Wheeler 'The Science Of Sound'. San Francisco: Pearson Education, Inc., Publishing as Addison Wesley.

Rubboli, Danieli (1974) 'Le Voci Raccontate'. Bologna: Bongiovanni Editore.

Ruopolo, G. Schindler, A., Amitrano, A. Genovese, E. (2012) 'Manuale di Foniatria e Logopedia'. Roma: Societa Editrice Universo.

Ruopolo, G. and Amitrano, A. (2013) 'Disartria: Possiamo fare di Piu'. Torino: Omega Edizione.

Rushmore, Robert (1971) 'The Singing Voice'. London: Hamish Hamilton.

Sanchez Carbone, Maria Luisa (2005) 'Vox Arcana: Teoria e Pratica Della Voce'. Milano: Rugginenti Editore.

Sanchez carbone, Maria Luisa (2011) 'La Voce. Mille Esercizi e Vocalizzi per Educarla, Esercitarla, perfezionarla'. Milano: Rugginenti Editori

Sanchez Carbone, Maria Luisa (2017) 'Il Mondo del Canto: Vivere e Sopravvivere'. Milano: Rugginenti Editore.

San Carlo, Irene and Daniel, Patrick (1906) 'The Common-Sense of Voice Development'. London: Baillière, Tindall and Cox.

Schindler, Oskar & Mari, Nanda (1986) 'Il Canto Come Tecnica La Foniatrica Come Arte'. Milano: Universal Music Publishing Rocordi R.s.l.

Schnidler, O., Ruoppolo, G., and Schindler, A. (2011) 'Deglutologia'. Torino: Omega Edizione.

Oskar, Schnidler (2010) 'La Voce: Fisiologia, Patologia, Clinica e Terapia'. Padova: Piccin Nuova Libreria S.p.A.

Sataloff, Robert Thayer (1998) 'Vocal Health And Pedagogy'. San Diego: Singular Publishing Group Inc.

Sataloff, Robert Thayer (2005) 'Voice Science'. San Diego: Plural Publishing Company Inc.

Scholtz, Piotr O. (2001) 'Eunuchs and Castrati'. Princiton: Markus Wiener Publisher.

Scott, Michael (1992) 'Maria Meneghini Callas'. London: Simon & Schuster Ltd.

Scott, Michael (1993) 'The Record of Singing'. London: Gerald Duckworth & Co.

Seghers, Rene (2008) "Franco Corelli: Prince of Tenors". New York: Amadeus Press.

Seiler, Emma (1872) 'The Voice in Singing'. Philadelphia: Lippincott's Press.

Seikel, J., King, D., Drumright, D. (1997) 'Anatomy And Physiology For Speech And Language'. San Diego: Singular Publishing Group, Inc.

Shakespeare, William (1898) 'Art Of Singing'. London: Metzler & Co. Limited.

Shakespeare, William (1924) 'Plain Words on Singing'. London: G.P. Putnam's Sons.

Shaw, Bernard (1932) 'Music In London 1890-1894.' London: Constable And Company Limited.

Somerset Ward, Richard (2004) 'Angels And Monsters.' New Haven, Yale University Press.

Stanley, Douglas (1945) 'Your Voice: Applied Science of Vocal Art.' New York: Pitman Publishing Corporation.

Stark, James (1999) 'Bel Canto: A History Of Vocal Pedagogy.' Toronto: University Of Toronto Press Incorporated.

Stemple, Joseph et al. (2000) 'Clinical Voice Pathology: theory and Management.' New York: Delmar Cengage Learning.

Stendhal, (1823) 'The Life of Rossini'. Translated by Richhard N. Coe. Richmond, Surry: Alma Calssics.

Stevens, Kenneth N. (2000) 'Acoustic Phonetics'. Massachusetts: MIT Press Cambridge Massachusetts.

Stockhausen, Julius (1884), 'GESANGSMETHOD'. Provided by Saxon State And University Library.

Stockhausen, Julius (1886) "Singing method'. London: Dover Books.

Strunk, Oliver (1998) 'Source Readings in Music History'. London: W.W. Norton & Company Ltd.

Sundberg, Johan (1987) 'The Science of The Singing Voice'. Dekalb, Illinois: Northern Illinois University Press.

Sutcliff, Tom (2000) 'The Faber Book of Opera'. London: Faber and Faber Limited.

Sutherland, Joan (1997) The Autobiography: A Prima Donna's Progress'. Milson's Point: NSW, Random House Australia.

Taylor, David C. (1922) 'The Psychology of Singing'. New York: The Macmillan Company.

Tilmann, Bernhard N. (2007) 'Atlas of Human Anatomy'. New York: Mud Puddle Books.

Titze, Ingo (1994) 'Principles of Voice Production'. Englewood Cliffs New Jersey: Prentice Hall Inc.

Titze R. Ingo (2006) 'The Myoelastic Aerodynamic Theory of Phonation'. Iowa City: The National Centre for Voice Speech.

Toft, Robert (2013) 'Bel Canto: A Performer's Guide'. New York: Oxford University Press.

Tosi, Pier Franscesco (1723 English Edition 1743) 'Observations on The Florid Singing', Translated by Galliard. London: J. Wilcox.

Tosti, Francesco Paolo (1996) 'Il Canto Di Una Vita'. Torino: Edizione Di Torino.

Trovato, Elio (1996) 'Anita Cerquetti: Umilta e Fierezza'. Parma: Azzali Editore.

Vennard, William (1967) 'Singing the Mechanism and the Technic'. New York: Carl Fisher Inc.

Veneziano, Corrado (2013) 'Manuale di Dizione, Voce e Respirazione'. Abbruzzi: Salento Books.

Ulissi, Liliana (2000) 'Fedora Barbieri: Un Viaggio Nella Memoria'. Trieste: Balletto Stampatore.

Walker, Frank (1972) 'The Man Verdi'. New York: Alfred A. Knopf.

Ware, Clifton (1998) 'Basics of Vocal Pedagogy: The Foundation and Process of Singing'. Boston Massachusets: McGraw Hill,

Watson, Celeste R. (1999) 'Teaching the Mechanical Art Of Song'. South Minneapolis: Pro Musica Press.

Weiss, William (2002) 'Educare la Voce'. Roma: Dino Audino.

White, Ernest G. (1908 reprinted 1950) 'Science And Voice'. London: Boosey and Hawkes Ltd.

White, Ernest G. (1938) 'Sinus Tone Production'. London: Dent & Sons Ltd.

Wilson, K.J.W. & Waugh, A. (1998) 'Anatomy and Physiology in Health And Illness'.

London: Harcourt Brace and Company Limited.

Wilson, Pat (1997) 'The Singing Voice: An Owner's Manual'. Sydney: Currency Press Ltd.

Winckel, Fritz (1967) 'Music, Sound And Sensation: A Modern Exposition'. New York: Dover Press, Inc.

Wright, William (1981) 'Pavarotti: 'My Own Story'. London: Sedgwick & Jackson.

Wright, William (1995) 'Pavarotti: My World'. London: Chatto & Windus.

Zacconi, Lodovico (1592) 'Prattica Di Musica'. Florence: Arnaldo Forni Editore.

Zemlin, Willard (1988) 'Speech and Hearing Science: Anatomy & Physiology'. Englewood Cliffs, New Jersey: Prentice Hall.

Articles

Austin, Stephen (1996) 'Principles of Voice Science: Studio Applications', Australian Voice, 1996.

_____ (1997) 'I couldn't Understand a Single Word!' Australian Voice, 1997.

_____ (1999) 'Pedagogical Application of the Two-Register Theory'. Australian Voice January 2009.

_____ (2009) 'Stockhausen's Method of Singing.' Journal of Singing, Volume 66, No 1, September 2009.

_____ (2010) 'Carlo Bassini's The Art of Singing.' Journal of Singing, Volume 66, No. 5, May 2010.

_____ (2012) 'Awsome Voices!' Journal of Singing, Volume 68, No. 5, May 2012.

Baer, Thomas (1981) Observation of Vocal Fold Vibration: Measurement of Excised Larynges. Vocal Fold Physiology, Edited by Stevens & Hirano, University of Tokyo Press, 1981.

Bartholomew, Wilmer (1934) 'A Physical Definition of "Good Voice-Quality" in the Male Voice'. Journal of Acoustical Society of America, Vol. 6, 1934.

Bjorkner, Sundberg and Alku (2005) 'Subglottal Pressure and NAQ Variation in Voice Production of Classically Baritone Singers.'

Bouhuys, Proctor & Mead (1966) 'Kinetic aspects of singing.' Journal of Applied Physiology, 21 (2) 1966.

Brewer, David (1964) 'Research Potentials In Voice Physiology.' International Conference: State University Of New York: Syracuse.

Brodnitz, Friedrich (1975) 'The Age of the Castrato Voice.' The Journal of Speech and Hearing Disorders, Volume 40, 322-326.

Brown, Oren L. (2003), 'Register'. Volume 60, No. 2 December 2003.

_____ (2002), 'Sensations'. Journal of Singing, Volume 58, No. 3 January 2002.

_____ (2002) 'Glottal Valving'. Journal of Singing, Volume 59, No. 2, November 2002.

Bloothooft, Gerrit and Plomp, Reiner (1986) 'The sound level of the singer's formant in professional singing.' The Journal of Acoustical Society of America, Volume 79, No. 6.

Bozeman, Kenneth W. (2010), The Role of the First Formant in Training the Male Singing Voice. Journal of Singing, Volume 66, No 3 January 2010.

_____ (2012) 'New Technology for Teaching voice Science and Pedagogy: The Madde Synthesizer (Svante Grandvist)'. Journal of Singing, Volume 68, No/ 4, March 2012.

Broad, David (1979) 'The New Theories of Vocal Fold Vibration.' Speech and Language advances in Basic Research and Practice. Vol. 2, 1979.

Bunch, Meribeth and Sonninen, Aatto (1977) 'Some Further Observation On Covered and Open Voice Qualities.' The Nats Bulletin, October 1977.

Callaghan, Jean (1996) 'The Implications of Voice Science for the Teaching of Singing: Vocal Registers'. Australian Voice, Vol. 2, 1996.

Callaghan, Jean (1994), 'The Implications of Voice Science for Voice Pedagogy: The Singer's Formant'. The Nats Bulletin, Vol. 50, No. 5, May 1994.

Callaghan, Jean (1991) 'The Teaching of Vocal Technique for the twenty – first Century: current scientific Models Compared with Bel Canto Precepts'. AMEL, 13th Annual Conference, Hobart, September, 1991.

Callaghan, Jean (1994), 'Projection: Interdisciplinary Connections in the Professional Education of Singing Teachers'. AMEL, Proceedings of 16th Annual Conference, Melbourne, September 1994.

Callaghan, Jean (1996) 'The Implications of Voice Science for the Teaching of Singing: Vocal Registers. Australian Voice, ANATS, 1996.

Campbell, Agostinin & Davis (1970) 'The Respiratory Muscles: Mechanics and Neural Control.' LLOyd-Luke LTD, London 1970.

Casselman, Eugene (1950) 'The Secret of Bel Canto'. Etude, September 1950.

Chapman Byers, Margaret (1941) 'Sbriglia's Method of Singing.' The Etude, May 1942.

Cavagna and Camporesi (1970) 'Glottic Aerodynamics and Phonation'.

Childers, Yea, and Boccheri (1983) Source/Tract Interaction in Speech and Singing Synthesis.

Cleveland, Thomas (1993) 'Voice Pedagogy for the Twenty-First Century: Voice Classification (part II).' The Nats Journal, March 1993.

Coffin, Bertin (76) 'Articulation for Opera, Oratorio, and Recital' The Nats Bulletin, February 1976.

Colton, Raymond (1973) 'Some Acoustic Parameters related to the Perception of Modal-Falsetto Voice Quality.' Folia Phoniat. 25:302.

Colton & Hollien (1973) 'Perceptual Differentiation of the Modal and Falsetto Register.' Folia Phonat. 25:1973.

Collyer, Sally (2004) 'The Sound in Silence: Observations on Silent Singing as a Practice Technique.' Aus. Voice, Vol. 10, 2004.

Collyer, Sally (2009) 'Breathing in classical singing: Linking science and teaching.' Published by AEC.

Cyr, Mary (1977) 'On Performing 18th-Century Haute-Contre Roles'. The Musical Times, Vol. 118, April 1977.

Daniloff, Raymond (1980) 'Overview of Supraglottal Aspects of Voicing'. Transcripts of the Ninth Symposium Care of the Professional Voice, Van Lawrence M.D. Editor, Published by the Voice Foundation.

Darwin and Gardner (1986), 'Mistuning a harmonic of a vowel: Grouping and phase effects on vowel quality. 'Acoustical Society of America, 1986.

Delattre, Pierre (1958) 'Vowel Color and Voice Quality: An Acoustic and Articulatory Comparison'. The Bulletin, October 1958.

Dellattre and Howie (1962) 'An Experimental Study of the Effect of Pitch on Intelligibility of Vowels.' The Nats Bulletin, May 1962.

Draper, Ladefoged & Whitteridge (1959) 'Respiratory Muscles in Speech'. Journal of Speech and Hearing Research, Vol. 2.

Evans, Thomas (1973) 'Singing History'. Groves Dictionary of Music, Edited by Blom 1973.

Estill, Baer, Honda, and Harris (1988) 'Supralaryngeal Activity in a Study of Six Voice Qualities'. Haskins Laboratories, New Haven, CT, USA. The City University of New York, USA.

Fant, Gunnar & Lin, Q. (1988) 'Frequency Domain Interpretation And Derivation of Glottal Flow Parameters.' STL-QPSR, Vol. 29, No. 2-3].

Fant, Gunnar & Krukenberg, Anita (1996) 'Voice Source Properties of the Speech Code.' The Acoustical Society of America, December 1996.

Galliver, David (1974) 'Cantare Con La Gorga: The Coloratura Technique of the Renaissance Singer'.

_____(1976) 'Cantare Con Affetto: Keynote of the Bel Canto'.

Garcia, Manuel (1855) 'Observations on the Human Voice'. The Royal Society, March 1955.

Gaufin, Jan and Sundberg, Johan (1980) 'Data on the Glottal Voice Source Behaviour in Vowel production'. Paper given in Sydney, Australia, STL-QPSR 2-3/ 1980.

Gauffin, Jan & Sundberg, Johan (1989), 'Spectral Correlates of Glottal Voice Source Waveform Characteristics'. Journal of Speech and Hearing Research, Volume 32, September 1989.

Gould and Okamura (1974) 'Interrelationships Between Voice and Laryngeal Mucosal Reflexes.' In Ventilatory and Phonatory control systems, Wyke, London: Oxford University Press.

Griffin, Woo, Colton, Caspar, Brewer 'Physiological characteristics of the supported singing voice: a preliminary study.'

Gunter, Heather (2003) 'A Mechanical Model of Vocal-fold Collision with high Spatial and Temporal Resolution.' Acoustical Society of America, 113. No. 2, 2003.

Gunter, Horst (1992) Mental Concept In Singing: A Psychological Approach.' The Nats Journal, May 1992.

Hall, Karen (2007) 'Musical Theater and Classical Singing: at Odds Personally and Professionally'. Journal of Singing, Volume 63, No. 5, May 2007.

Helding, Lynn (2007) 'Voice Science and Vocal Art, Part One: In Search of Common Ground.' Journal of Singing, Volume 64, No. 2, November 2007.

Heman-Ackah, Yolanda (2005) 'Physiology of Voice Production: Considerations for the Vocal Performer.' Journal of Singing, Volume 62, No. 2, November 2005.

Hertegård, and Gauffin (1995) 'Glottal Area and Vibratory Patterns Studies with simultaneous stroboscopy, Flow Glotttography and Electroglottography. Journal of Speech and Hearing Research, Vol. 38.

Hirano, Minoru (1974) 'Morphological Structure of the Vocal Cord as a Vibrator and its vibrations'. Folia Phoniat, 26, (1974).

Hirano, Gould, Lambiase & kakita (1980) 'Movement of Selected Points on a Vocal Fold during Vibration.' Folia Phoniat, 32: 1980.

Hirano, Minoru (1988) 'Vocal Mechanism in Singing: Laryngological and Phoniatric Aspects.' Journal of Voice, Vol. 2, No. 1].

Hirosi and Gay (1973) 'Laryngeal Control in Vocal Attack.' Folia Phoniat., 25, 1973.

Hixon, T. J., & Weismer, G. (1995) 'Perspective on the Edinburgh Study of Speech Breathing.' Journal of speech and Hearing Research, Vol. 38, Feb.1995.

Hollien & Colton (1969) 'Four Laminagraphic Studies of Vocal Fold Thickness.' Folia Phoniat. 21,1969.

Hollien, Girard, Coleman (1977) Vocal Fold Vibratory Patterns of Pulse Register Phonation.' Folia Phoniat. 20, 1977.

Hollien, Brown and Weiss (1999) 'Another View of Vocal Mechanics.'

Journal of Singing, Volume 56, No. 1, September 1999.

Isshiki, Nobuhiko (1964) 'Regulatory Mechanism of Voice Intensity Variation'. Journal of Speech and Hearing Research, Vol. 7, 1964.

Jerold, Beverly (2005) 'Mystery In Paris, The German Connection and More: The Bèrard-Blanchet Controversy Revisited.' Eighteenth Century Music: Cambridge University Press.

Joliveau, Wolf, and Smith (2006) 'Sopranos tune resonances of their vocal tract when they sing in the high range'. Nature, 427, 116.

Joyner, James R. (1983) 'The Garcia Legacy: Charles Amable Battaille.'

The Bulletin, Vol. 39, No.5, May 1983.

Kelman, A. W. (1981) 'Vibratory Patterns of the Vocal Folds.' Folia Phoniat. 33.

Kelsey, Franklyn (1973) Voice Training: Mechanics — Technical History.

Groves, George, Blom Editor, Macmillan Press.

Kirkpatrick, Adam (2009) 'Chiaroscuro and the Quest for Optimal Resonance'. Journal of Singing, Volume 66, No. 1, September 2009.

_____(2008) 'Teaching Methods for Correcting Problematic Vibratos: Using Sustained Dynamic Exercises to Discover and Foster Healthy Vibrato. Journal of Singing, Volume 64, No. 5, May 2008.

Kob, Alhauser, Reiter (1999) 'Time-Domain Model of the Singing Voice.' Proceedings of the 2nd COST G-6 Workshop on Digital Audio Effects, NTNU, Trondheim, December 9-11, 1999.

Joiner, James Richard (1988) 'The Relationship of the Vocal Folds to Vowel Formation: A Study of Current Research.' Journal of Research in Singing September 1988.

Kaburagi, Tokihiko (2008) 'On the Viscous-inviscid interaction of the flow passing through the glottis.' The Acoustical Society of Japan.

Kenaston-French, Karen (2009) 'The Teachings of Jean-Antoine Berard:

Content, Context, and Legacy.' Journal of Singing, Volume 66, No 2 November 2009.

Keenze, Marvin & Bell, Donald (2005) 'Teaching Breathing'. Journal of Singing, Volume 61, No. 4, March 2005.

Kennedy-Dygas, Margaret (1999) 'Historical Perspective on the "Science" of Teaching Singing.' Journal of Singing, Volume 56, No 2 November 1999.

_____(2000) 'Historical Perspective on the Science of Teaching Singing Part III: Manuel Garcia II (1805–1806)'. Journal of Singing, Volume 56, No. 4 March 2000.

Kessler Price, Kathy (2011), Emma Seiler: A Pioneering Woman in the Art and Science of Teaching Voice. Journal of Singing, Volume 68, No. 1, September 2011.

Kiesgen, Paul (2005) 'Vocal Pedagogy: Breathing'. Journal of Singing, Volume 62, No 2, November 2005.

_____(2006) 'Vocal Pedagogy: Resonance.' Journal of Singing, volume 62, No. 4, March 2006.

_____(2006) 'Vocal Pedagogy: Registration.' Journal of Singing, Volume 62, No. 5, May 2006.

Ladefoged and Loeb (2002) 'Preliminary studies on respiratory activity in speech.' Linguistics Department, UCLA, Los Angeles 2002.

Large, John (1972) 'Towards an Integrated Physiologic-Acoustic Theory of Vocal Registers'. The Nats Bulletin, March 1972.

_____ (1973) 'Acoustic Study of Register Equalization in Singing.'

Folia Phoniat'. Volume 25.

Laukkanen, Lindholm, Vilkman Hataaja, Alku (1996) 'A Physiological and Acoustic Study on Voiced Bilabial Fricative / :/ as Vocal Exercise.'

Journal of Voice, Vol, 18, No. 1.

Laukkanen, Titze, Finnegan, Hoffman (2002) 'Laryngeal Muscle Activity in a Tonal Scale: Comparing Speech-like to Song-like Productions in a Mezzo-soprano.' Journal of Singing, Volume 59, No. 1, September 2002.

Leanderson, Sundberg and Von Euler (1987) 'Role of Diaphragmatic activity during singing: a study of transdiaphragmatic pressures.' PubMed 1987.

Lieberman, Philip (1968) 'Vocal Cord Motion in Man.' New York Academy of Sciences, Volume 155, Issue.

Lucero, Jorge (1997) 'Optimal Glottal Configuration for Ease of Phonation.' Journal of Voice, Vol. 12, No. 2.

_____(2005) 'Dynamics of the Vocal Fold Oscillation.'

National Congress on Applied Computational Mathematics CNMAC in Porto Alegre, September 2004.

McCoy, Scott (2003) 'Falsetto and the Male High Voice'.

_____(2008) 'The Seduction of Nasality.' Journal of Singing, 64 No 5, May 2008]. Journal of Singing, Volume 59, No. 5, May 2008.

_____(2010) 'Building the Foundation.' Journal of Singing, Volume 67, No.1, September 2010.

McCoy, Scott (2012) 'Some Thoughts on Singing and Science'. Journal of Singing, Volume 68, No. 5, May 2012.

McGowan, Richard, & Howe, Michael (2010) 'Comments on single-mass models of vocal fold vibrations'. Journals of Acoustical Society of America, April 2010.

McIver, William and Miller, Richard (1995) 'A Brief Study of Nasality in Singing'. Journal of Singing, Volume 52, No. 1, September 1995.

Mead, Hixon and Goldman (1970) 'The Configuration of the Chest Wall During Speech'. LLOyd-Luke LTD. London: 1970.

Mewburn Levien, John (1939-1941) 'The Decline of Singing'. Letters to the Editor of 'Musical Opinion'.

Miller, Bonnie & Alt, David (1989), 'Mathile Marchesi and the Ladies' Home Journal.' The Nats Journal, Volume 46, No 2, November 1989.

Miller, D, and Schutte, H. (2002) 'Characteristic Patterns Of Sub-And Supraglottal Pressure Variations Within The Glottal Cycle.' PAS-Conference October 2002.

Miller, R.L. (1959) 'Nature of the Vocal Cord Wave'. The Acoustical Society of America, Vol. 31, No. 6.

Miller, Richard (1980) 'Supraglottal Considerations and Vocal Pedagogy.' Transcripts of the Ninth Symposium, Care of the Professional Voice, Edited by Van Lawrence M.D., Published by the Voice Foundation.

Miller, Richard (1992) 'How Singing Is Not Like Speaking.' The NATS Journal, Volume 48, No. 5, May 1992.

Miller, Richard and Franco, Carlos (1991) Spectrographic Analysis of The Singing Voice. The Nats Journal, Volume 48, No. 1, Sept. 1991.

_____ (1992) A Brief Spectral Study of Vowel Differentiation and Modification in a Professional Tenor. The Nats Journal, Volume 49, No. 1, September 1992.

_____ (1994) 'Feeling, Hearing and Seeing the Voice.'

The NATS Journal, Volume 51, No. 2, November 1994.

_____ (1996) 'What Does Humming Accomplish'.

The NATS Journal, Volume 52, No. 3, February 1996.

Miller, Richard (1998) 'The Garcia Position.' Journal of Singing, Volume 55, No 2 November 1998.

Miller, Donald (2009) 'On Master Classes and the Olympic Games'. Journal of Singing, Volume, 65, No. 4, March 2009.

Millhouse, Thomas (2012) 'Observation of the higher formant structure in the male operatic vowel'. Macquarie University, Sydney, Australia.

_____ (2013) 'Perceptually motivated auditory interpretation of the singer's formant'. Asst. Voice, Vol. X 2013.

Morozov, V. P. (1956) 'Intelligibility in Singing as a Function of Fundamental Voice Pitch.' Soviet Physics-Acoustics, Vol. 10, 1956.

Myers, Myron (2008) 'The Legacy of Garcia.' Journal of Singing, Volume 64, No. 5, May 2008.

_____ (2008) 'The Legacy of Garcia, Part 2.' Journal of Singing, Volume 65, No 1, September 2008.

Newsom, Davis & Sears, T. (1970) 'The Proprioceptive Reflex Control Of The Intercostal Muscles During Their Voluntary Activation.' Journal of Physiology, (1970).

Nix, John (1995) 'The Vocal Method of Mathilde Marchesi: A Modern Evaluation.' The NATS Journal, Volume 51, No. 5, ay 1005.

_____ (1999) 'Lip Trills and Raspberries: "High Spit Factor" Alternatives to the Nasal Continuants Consonants.' Journal of Singing, Volume 55, No. 3, January 1999.

Nix, John (2004) 'Vowel Modification Revisited.'

Journal of Singing, Volume 61, No. 2 November 2004.

Pressman, Joel (1942) 'Physiology Of The Vocal Cords In Phonation And Respiration.' Archives of Otolaryngology, Volume 35, March 1942.

Pressman, Joel (1952) 'Sphincters of the Larynx.' The Academy of Ophthalmology and Otolaryngology, Chicago, October 1952.

Pressman and Kelemen (1955) 'Physiology of the Larynx.'

Dept. of Otolaryngology, Harvard Medical School, Boston Massachusetts, 1955.

Department of Otolaryngology, Harvard Medical School, Boston, Massachusetts, 1955.

Proctor, Donald (1980) 'Breath, the Power Source of the Voice.' The Bulletin, November 1980.

Radomski, Teresa (2005) 'A Bicentenary Reflection: The "Christopher Columbus of the larynx". Australian Voice: December 2005.

Reid, Cornelius (1997) 'Vocal Mechanics'. Journal of Singing, Volume 54, No. 1, September 1997.

Reid, Cornelius & Reid, Donna (2000) 'Eighteenth-Century Registration Concepts.' Journal of Singing, Volume 56, No. 4, March 2000.

Rezhevkin, S. N. 'Certain Results of the Analysis of a Singer's Voice.'

Soviet Physics-Acoustics, Vol. 2, 1956.

Rhodes Draayer, Suzanne (2007) 'Canciones de Espana: Manuel Garcia- Composer, Teacher, and Singer'. Journal of Singing, Volume 64, No. 2, November 2007.

Robinson, Clayne (2001) 'Beautiful Singing: What It Is and How to Do It'. Journal of Singing, Volume 58, No. 1 September 2001.

Rose, Arnold (1955) 'The Italian Method and the English Singer'. Musical Times, 96, December 1955.

Rothenberg, Martin (1968) 'The Breath Stream Dynamics of Simple-Released-Plosive.' www.rothenberg.org/breath-stream.

Rothenberg, Martin (1972) 'The Glottal Volume Velocity Waveform During Loose and Tight Voiced Glottal Adjustments.' Congress of phonetic Science . held at the University of Montreal and McGill University, Published by Mouton, The Hague 1972.

_____(1972) 'A new inverse-filter technique for deriving the glottal air flow waveform during voicing.' The Journal of the Acoustical Society of America, Vol. 53, No.6, 1972.

Rothenberg, Martin (1977) 'Measurement of Airflow in Speech'.

Publications of Dr. Martin Rothenberg, March 1977.

Rothenberg and Zahorian (1977) 'Nonlinear inverse filtering for estimating the glottal area waveform.' Acoustical Society of America, Vol. 61, No. 4, April 77.

_____(1980) 'Acoustic Interaction Between the Glottal Source and the Vocal Tract.' Vocal fold Physiology, K. Stevens & M. Hirano, Eds. University of Tokyo Press.

_____(1981) 'The Voice Source in Singing.' Research Aspects of Singing. Academy of Music, Stockholm, 1981.

_____(1981) 'An Interactive Model for the Voice Source.' Conference of Vocal fold Physiology, University of Wisconsin, June 1981.

_____(1984) 'Source-Tract Acoustic Interaction and Voice Quality.' The Voice Foundation, NY. 1984.

Rothenberg and Mahshie (1986) 'Induced transglottal pressure variations during voicing.' Journal of Phonetics, Academic Press Inc., 1986.

Rothenberg, Miller, Mollitor, Leffingwell (1987) 'The Control of Air Flow During Loud Soprano Singing.' Journal of Voice, Volume 1, No. 3, 1987.

_____(1988) 'Monitoring Vocal Fold Abduction Through Vocal Fold Contact Area.' Journal of Speech and Hearing Research, Vol. 31, September 1988.

_____(1988) 'Acoustic Reinforcement of Vocal Fold Vibratory Behaviour in Singing.' In Vocal Fold Physiology, New York 1988.

Rothenberg, M. (1988) 'Acoustic Reinforcement of Vocal Fold Vibratory Behaviour in Singing.' Raven Press, NY. 1988.

Rothenberg & Mashie (1988) 'Monitoring Vocal Fold Abduction Through Vocal Fold Contact Area.' Journal of Speech and Hearing Research, Vol. 31, September 1988.

_____(2002) 'Correct Low Frequency Phase Distortion.' Journal of Voice, Vol. 16, No. 1, 2002.

_____(2000) 'Nasal Resonance-Fact or Fiction?' Journal of Singing, Volume 57, No. 2, November 2000.

_____(2004) 'Register Unification-Give Me a Break'. Journal of Singing: Volume 61, No. 2, November 2004.

Austin, Stephen (2005) 'Treasure "Chest" – A Physiological and Pedagogical Review of the Low Mechanism.' Journal of Singing, Volume 61, No. 3, January 2005.

_____(2005) 'Like the Squawk of A capon: The Tenor do di Petto.' Journal of Singing, Volume 61, N0. 3, January 2005.

_____(2005) 'The Voce Chiusa.' Journal of Singing, Volume 61, No. 4 March 2005.

_____(2005) 'The Attack on the Coup de la Glotte.' Journal of Singing, Volume 61, No 5, May 2005.

_____(2005) 'Two-headed Llamas and the lutte vocale.' Journal of Singing, Volume 62, No. 1, September 2005.

_____(2006), 'There is a Whole in the Middle, the middle, the middle'. Journal of Singing, Volume 62, No. 3 January 2006.

_____(2006) 'Words from William Shakespeare'. Journal of Singing, Volume 63, No 1, September 2006.

_____(2006) 'Flapping Jaws and Acoustic Laws'. Journal of Singing, Volume 63, no. 2, November 2006.

_____(2007) 'Herman Klein: A Contemporary: Link to Mozart.' Journal of Singing, Volume 63, No. 4, March 2007.

_____(2008) 'Plugging the Holes.' Journal of Singing, Volume 64, No. 4, March 2008.

_____(2008) 'Filling the Gap with Giuseppe Aprile.' Journal of Singing, Volume 65, No. 2, November 2008.

_____(2009) 'Stockhausen's Method of Singing.' Journal of Singing, Volume 65, No 3, Jan

Italian Bel Canto in the Age of Vocal Science is a vital resource for voice teachers, vocal researchers, serious vocal students, and vocal connoisseurs. It is also a fitting conclusion to a profound and exhaustive study of singing that began with *A History of Vocal Pedagogy Intuition and Science (2017)*, followed by *Vocal Science for Elite Singers (2018)*.

(2004) 'The Control of Airflow during Singing.' Conference on the Physiology and Acoustics of Singing, Denver Colorado, 2004.

_____(2006) 'Some relations between glottal airflow and Vocal Fold Contact Area.' Rothenberg 2006.

_____(2008) 'The Source-Filter Model Lives (if you are careful).' The Voice Foundation, 37t^h Annual Symposium, May 2008.

Rubin, H., Hirt, C., & Le Cover, M. (1960) 'The Falsetto: A high Speed Cinematographic Study'.

Ruty, N., Van Hirtum, Pelerson, X. (2005) 'A Mechanical experimental setup to stimulate vocal fold vibration.' ZAS Papers in Linguistics 40, 2005.

Sanford, Sally (1995) 'A comparison of French and Italian Singing in the Seventeenth Century'. Journal of Seventeenth-Century Music, Vol. 1.

Saxon, K. & Berry, S. (2009) 'Vocal Exercise Physiology: Same Principles, New Training Paradigm'. Journal of Singing, Volume 66, No. 1, September 2009.

Schipp, Tom (1980) 'Vertical Laryngeal Position in Sighing.'

Transcripts of the Ninth Symposium Care of the Professional Voice', Edited by Van Lawrence M.D., Published by the Voice Foundation.

Schutte, Harm (1984) 'Efficiency of Professional Singing Voices in Terms of Energy'. Folia phoniat. 36: 1984.

Schutte, Harm K. (1989) 'Measurements of Vocal Function.' The Nats Journal, Volume 46, No 2 November 1989.

Schutte, H. and Miller, D. 'Characteristic Patterns of Sub-And-supraglottal Phase Variation within the Glottal cycle.' PAS-Conference, October 2002.

Schutte, Harm and Miller, Richard (1984) 'Breath management in repeated Vocal Onset.' Folia Phoniatrica, 36, 1984.

Schutte, Stark and Miller (2003) 'Change in Singing Voice Production, Objectively Measured.' Journal of Voice, vol. 17, no 4, 495–501].

Shore, Joseph (1995) 'A Great Singer on Great Singing: Jerome Hines Challenges Voice Scientists and Singers'. The Nats Journal, Volume 51 No 3, January 1995.

Sjoerdsma, Richard Dale (2011) 'Creativity and Imagination'. Journal of Singing, Volume 67, No. 5, May 2011.

Stark, James A. (1991) Garcia In Perspective: His Traite After 150 Years. JRS 20, 1991.

Stemple, Joseph et al (1994), Efficacy of Vocal Function Exercise as a Method of Improving Voice Production. Journal of Voice: Vol. 8, No 3.

Stevens, Robyn (2009) 'The Garcia Family: The Pedagogic Legacy of Romanticism's Premier Musical Dynasty'. Journal of Singing, Volume 65, No. 5.

Stone, Morrish, Sonies and Shawker 'Tongue Curvature: A Model of Shape during Vowel Production.' Folia Phoniat. 39. 302–315.

Stone, Cleveland, Sundberg, and Prokop (2002) 'Aerodynamic and acoustical measures of speech, operatic, and Broadway vocal styles in a professional female singer.' Speech, Music and Hearing, KTH, Stockholm, Vol. 43, 2002.

Story and Titze (1994) 'Voice simulation with a body-cover model of the vocal folds.' Journal of Acoustical Society of America, Vol. 97, No. 2.

Story, Titze and Hoffman (1996) 'Vocal Tract Area Function From Magnetic Resonance Imaging.' Journal of Acoustical Society of America, Vol.100, No.1.

Story, B., Laukkanen, A. Titze, I. (2000), 'Acoustic Impedance of an Artificially Lengthened and Constricted Vocal Tract.' Journal of Voice, Vol. 14, No. 4, 2000.

Story, Brad (2002), 'An overview of the physiology, physics and modeling of the sound source for vowels'. Department of Speech and Hearing Sciences, University of Arizona. Acoustic, Science & Technology. 23, 4 (2002),

Story, B. & Titze, I. (1994) 'Voice simulation with a body-cover model of the vocal folds.' Acoustical Society of America, Vol. 97. Feb. 1995.

Sundberg, Johan (1970) 'Formant Structure and Articulation of Spoken and Sung Vowels'. Folia Phoniatrica, vol. 22, 1970.

Sundberg, Johan (1973) 'The Source Spectrum in Professional Singing.'

Folia Phoniatrica, Vol. 25, 1971.

_____(1974) 'Articulatory Interpretation of the "Singing Formant".' J. Acoustical Society of America, Vol. 56, No. 4, April 1974.

Sundberg, Johan (1977) 'The acoustics of the Singing Voice.' Scientific America, March 77.

_____(1977) 'Studies of the Soprano Voice.' Journal of Research in Singing, 1, 1977.

Sundberg, Johan (1981) 'Research Aspects on Singing.' Publications Issued by the Royal Swedish Acadamy of Music No. 33, 1981.

_____ (1983) 'Chest Wall Vibrations in Singers.' American Speech-Language-Hearing Association, 1983.

Sundberg, Leanderson, von Euler and Lagercrantz (1984) 'Activation of the Diaphragm During Singing: A study of Transdiaphragmatic Pressures'.

Sundberg, Leanderson and von Euler (1988) 'Activity Relationship Between Diaphragm And Cricothyroid Muscles.' Journal STL-QPSR, 1988.

Sundberg, Elliot and Gramming (1991) 'How constant is subglottal pressure in singing?. Journal STL-QPSR, 1991.

Sundberg, Johan (1998) 'Vocal Tract Resonance In Singing'. The NATS Journal, March 1988.

_____ (1990) 'What's So Special About Singers?' Journal of Voice, Vol. 4, No. 2, 1990.

Sundberg, Elliot and Gramming (1988) 'How close is subglottal pressure in singing.' STL-QPSR.

_____ (1991) 'How constant is subglottal pressure in singing'. STL-QPSD, Vol. 32, No. 1.

_____ (1992) 'Phonatory Vibrations in Singers: A Critical Review'. Music Perception Spring 1992, Vol. 9, No.3.

_____ (1993) 'Breathing Behaviour during Singing.' The Nats Journal, Volume 49, No. 3, January 1993.

Sundberg, Johan, Skoog, Jorgen (1997), 'Dependence of Jaw Opening on Pitch and Vowel in Singers'. Dept. of Speech, Music, and Hearing, KTH, Stockholm, Sweden 1997.

Sundberg, Johan (2001) 'Level and Centre Frequency of the Singer's Formant'. Journal of Voice, Vol. 15, No. 2, 2001.

_____ (2003) 'Research on the Singing Voice in Retrospect.' Speech, Music and Hearing, KTH-QPSR Vol. 45, 2003.

Sundberg, Troven & Richter (2007) 'Sopranos with a singer's formant?' Historical, Physiological, and Acoustical Aspects of Castrato Singing. TMH-QPSR, KTH, Vol. 49, 2007.

Sundberg, La and Himonides (2013) 'Intonation and Expressivity: A Single Case Study of Classical Western Singing'. Journal of Voice, Vol. 27, No.3, 2013.

_____ (2013) 'Formant Tuning Strategies in Professional Male Opera Singers'. Journal of Voice, Vol. 27, No. 3, 2013.

Sutherland, Joan (1998) 'The Cornerstone of Singing: Breathing and Breath Support'. Opera News, 63 No. 5, November 1998.

Thomasson, Monica (2003) 'Effects of lung volume on the glottal voice source and the vertical laryngeal position in male professional opera singers'. Speech-Music-Hearing TMH-QPSR, KTH. Vol. 45: 2003.

Timberlake, Craig (1989), 'Thee Case of Manuel Garcia 11.' The NATS Journal, Volume 46, No 2, November1989.

Timberlake, Craig (1989), 'The Case of Manuel Garcia 11, Part 11.'

The Nats Journal, Volume 46, No 3, January 1990.

_____(1990) 'Terminological Turmoil – The Naming of Registers.' The Nats Journal, Volume 47, No. 1 September 1990.

_____(1990) 'The Quintessential Lieder Singer: Julius Stockhausen.' The Nats Journal, Volume 46, No. 4, March 1990.

_____(1990) 'Julius Stockhausen and His Method of Singing.' Nats Journal, Volume 46, No. 5, May 1990.

Timberlake, Craig (1991) 'Practica Musicae: Catching up on Caccini: Nuove Musiche.' The Nats Journal, Volume 47, No. 3, January 1991.

_____ (1991) 'The Caccini Collections Part 1.' The Nats Journal, Volume 47, No. 4, March 1991.

_____(1991) The Caccini Collection Part 11. The NATS Journal, Volume 47, No. 5, May 1991.

Timberlake, Graig (1993), Practica Musicae: 'Maffei – Medico e Musica.' The NATS Journal, Volume 45, No. 5, May 1993.

_____(1994) 'Pedagogical Perspectives, Past and Present: Laryngeal Positioning.' Volume 51, No 1 September 1994.

_____(1994) 'Pedagogical Perspectives, Past and Present: Apropos of Appoggio.' Volume 52, No 2 November 1994.

_____(1995) 'Pedagogical Perspectives, Past and Present: Apropos and Appoggio part II.' Volume 51, No 3 January 1995.

Titze and Strong, W. (1975) 'Normal Modes in Vocal Fold tissues.'

Titze, Ingo (1973) 'The Human Vocal Cords: A Mathematical Model, Part 1.' Phonetica 28, 129-170.

_____(1974) 'The Human Vocal Cords: A Mathematical Model, Part 11.' Phonetica 29, 1-21. Journal of Acoustics Society of America, Vol. 57, No. 3, March 1975.

Titze, Ingo (1980) 'Comments On The Myoelastic Aerodynamic Theory Of Phonation.' Journal of Speech and Hearing Research, September 1980.

_____(1981), 'Acoustic Interpretation of Resonant Voice'. Journal of Voice, Volume 15, No. 4, 2001.

Titze, Horii, and Scherer (1987) 'Some Technical Considerations in Voce Perturbation Measurements.' American Speech-Language-Hearing Association, Volume 30, June 1987.

_____(1988) 'The Physics of small-amplitude oscillation of the vocal folds.' Journal of Acoustics, Society of America, 83 (4), April 88.

_____(1988) 'Male-Female Differences in the Larynx.' The Nats Journal, January 1988.

_____(1988) 'A Framework for the Study of Vocal Registers.' Journal of Voice, Vol. 2, No. 3.

_____(1989) 'Physiologic and Acoustic differences between male and female voices.' Acoustical Society of America, Vol. 85 (4) April 1989.

Titze, Luchesi, and Hirano (1989) 'Role of the Thyrorytenoid Muscle in Regulation of Fundamental Frequency.' Journal of Voice, Vol. 3, No. 3.

Titze, Ingo (1992) 'Glottal Resistance.' The Nats Journal, Volume 48, No. 4, March 1992.

_____(1992), 'Acoustic Interpretation of the Voice Range Profile' (Phonetogram). Journal of Speech and Hearing Research, Vol. 35, 1992.

_____(1992) 'Voice Quality: Part I.' The NATS Journal, June 1992.

_____(1992) 'Voice Quality: Part II.' The NATS Journal, September 1992.

_____(1996) 'Lip and Tongue Trills — What do they do for us?

_____(1996) 'Vocal tract area functions from magnetic resonance imaging'. Journal of Acoustical Society of America, Volume 100, No. 1, July 1996.

_____(1998) 'The Wide Pharynx.' Journal of Singing Volume 55, No. 1, September 1998.

_____(1999) 'The Use of Low First Formant Vowels and Nasals to Train the Lighter Mechanism.' Journal of Singing, Volume 55, No. 4, March 1999.

_____(2001) 'Acoustic Interpretation of Resonant Voice.' Journal of Voice, Vol. 15, No. 4, 519-528: The Voice Foundation.

_____(2002), 'Regulating glottal airflow in phonation: Application of the maximum power transfer theorem to a low dimensional phonation model'. Acoustical Society of America, Volume 111, No. 1, Jan. 2002.

Titze & Story (2002) 'Rules for controlling low-dimensional vocal fold models with muscle activation'. Acoustical Society of America, Volume 112, No. 3, September 2002.

Titze, Laukkanen, Finnegan and Jaiswal (2002) 'Raising Lung Pressure and Pitch In Vocal Warm-Ups: The Use of Flow-Resistant Straws.' Journal of Singing, Volume 58, No. 4, March 2002.

_____ (2003) 'More About resonant Voice: Chasing the Formants but Staying Behind Them'. Journal of Singing, Volume 59, No. 5, May 2003.

_____ (2004) 'Theory of Glottal Airflow and Source-Filter Interaction in Speaking and Singing.' Acta Acoustical United with Acustica, Vol. 90, 2004.

_____ (2004) 'The Search for Efficient Voice Production: Where Is It Leading Us'. Journal of Singing, Volume 60, No. 4 April 2004.

Titze, Ingo and Storey, Brad (1997) 'Acoustic Interactions of the Voice Source with the Lower Vocal Tract.' Acoustical Society of America, Vol. 101, No. 4, April 1997.

Titze, and Talkin (1979), 'A theoretical study of the effects of various laryngeal configurations on the acoustics of phonation.' Acoustical Society of America, Vol. 66, No. 1, 1979.

Titze, Ingo (2004) 'The Search for Efficient Voice Production: Where Is It Leading Us.' Journal of Singing, Volume 60, No 4 March 2004.

_____ (2004) 'A Theoretical Study of Fo – F1 Interaction With Application to Resonant Speaking and Singing Voice.' Journal of Voice, Vol. 18, No. 3. 2004.

_____ (2004) 'What is Meant by Nonlinear and Interactive in Voice Science?' Journal of Singing, Volume 60, No. 3 January 2004.

_____ (2004) 'What makes A Voice Acoustically Strong?' Volume 61, No 1 September 2004.

_____ (2005) 'Space in the Throat and Associated Vocal Quality.' Journal of Singing, Volume 61, No 5, May 2005.

_____ (2005) 'How Loud is My Voice Inside My Mouth and Throat.' Journal of Singing, Volume 62, No. 2, November 2005.

_____ (2006) 'The Fo-F1 Crossover Exercises'. Journal of Singing, Volume 62, No. 3, January 2006.

_____ (2006) 'About Vocal Fold Thinning.' Journal of Singing, Volume 62, No. 4, March 2006.

_____ (2006) 'Voice Training and Therapy with a Semi-Occluded Vocal Tract: Rationale and Scientific Underpinning'. JSLHR, Vol. 49, 2006.

_____ (2007) 'Falsetto Register and Vowels.' Journal of Singing, Volume 63, N0. 4, March 2007.

_____(2007) 'Belting and a High Larynx Position.' Journal of Singing, Volume 63, No. 5, May 2007.

_____(2008) 'An Appeal for Patience and Long-suffering by Singing Teachers in Their Assessment of the Value of Voice Science.'

Journal of Singing, Volume 64, No. 5, May 2009.

_____(2009) 'How Are Harmonics Produced at the Voice Source'.

Journal of Singing, Volume 65, No. 5 May 2009.

_____(2009) 'What Signals Physical Strength in a Voice?' Journal of Singing, Volume 66, No. 2 November 2009.

_____ (2011) 'Introducing A Music Notation Scheme For Pitch-Vowel Interaction'. Journal of Singing, Volume 68, No. 1, September 2011.

Titze, Worley, and Story (2011) 'Source Vocal-Tract Interaction in Female operatic Singing and Theater Belting'. Journal of Singing, Volume 67, No.5, May 2011.

_____(2012), 'Why Do Classically Trained Singers Widen Their Throat.' Journal of Singing, Volume 60, No 2, November 2012.

_____(2013) 'A Short Tutorial on Sound Level and Loudness for Voice.' Journal of Singing, Volume 70, No. 2, November 2013.

Titze, Ingo (2003), 'More About Resonant Voice: Chasing the Formants But Staying Behind Them'. Journal of Voice, Volume 59, No. 5 May 2003.

Troup, Gordon (1982), 'The Physics of the Singing Voice.' Journal of research in Singing: Volume V1, No 1.

Troup, and Luke (1988) 'The Epiglottis As An Articulator In Singing'.

Journal of Research in Singing and Applied Vocal Pedagogy. December, 1988, XII No. I

Thomasson, Monica (2003) 'Effects of Lung Volume on the glottal voice source and the vertical laryngeal position in male professional opera singers.' Speech, Music and Hearing, KTH, Vol. 45, 2003.

Thomasson, Monica (2003) 'Effects of Inhalatory Behaviour and Lung Volume on Voice Function in Male Opera Singers.' Speech, Music and Hearing, KTH, Stockholm. TMH-QPSR-KTH, Vol. 45: 61-73.

Thorpe, Callaghan and Van Doorn (1999) 'Visual Feedback of Acoustic Voice Features: New Tool for the Teaching of Singing.' Nats, Australian Voice, Vol. 5, 1999.

Troupe and Luke (1985) 'Some Radiological Observations of Vocal Source-Vocal Tract Interaction.'Stockholm Music Acoustics Conference, July 1983, vol. 1.

Troupe, and Luke (1988) 'The Epiglottis as an Articulator in Singing'.Journal of Research in Singing and Applied Vocal Pedagogy.

Tunley, David (1984) 'The Union of Words and Music in Seventeenth- Century French Song-The Long and the Short of It.' Australian Journal of French Studies, Vol. 21, No. 3, 1984.

Van den Berg (1955) 'On the Role of the Laryngeal Ventricle in Voice Production.' Folia Phoniatr. 7, No. 2, 1955.

Van den Berg, Zantena & Doornenbal (1957) 'On the Air Resistance and the Bernoulli Effect of the Human Larynx.' The Acoustical Society of America, Vol. 29, No. 5, 1957.

Van den Berg, Janwillem (1958) 'Myoelastic-Aerodynamic Theory of Voice Production.' Journal of Speech and Hearing, Volume 1, No 3, September 1958.

_____(1956) 'Direct and Indirect Determination of the Mean Subglottal Pressure.' Folia Phoniatrica, Vol. 8, No.1, 1956.

_____(1963) 'Vocal Ligaments Versus Register.' The Nats Bulletin, February 1963.

Van den Berg (1968) 'Register Problems.' Croninigen, Laboratory of Medical Physics, University of Croningeng: 129-134.

_____(1968) 'Sound production in Isolated Human Larynges'. Croningen: Laboratory of Medical Physics, University of Croningen: 18-25.

Vasta, Stephen Francis (1999) 'The Rise of Little Voice'. Opera News, Vol. 64 No. 4, October 1999.

Verdolini, Druker, Palmer and Samawi (1998) 'Laryngeal Adduction in Resonant Voice'. Journal of Voice, Vol. 12, No. 3.

Von Leden, Hans (1961) 'The Mechanism of Phonation: A Search for a Rational Theory of Voice Production'. Archives of Otolaryngology: Vol. 74, Dec. 1961.

Von Leden, Hans (1992) 'A Cultural History Of The Larynx And Voice.'
In The Science and Art of Clinical Care, edited by Robert Thayer Sataloff. Singular Publishing Group Inc. San Diego.

Vennard, Hirano, and Ohala (1970) 'Laryngeal Synergy In Singing Chest, Head, And Falsetto.' The Nats Bulletin, October 1970.

Vennard, William and Hirano, Minoru (1971) Varieties of Voice Production. The Nats Bulletin, February 1971.

Vennard, William, Minoru Hirano, and Bjorn Fritzell (1971) 'The Extrinsic Laryngeal Muscles.' Bulletin, May 1971.

Vennard, William (1971), In Memorium. The Nats Bulletin, 1971.

Wadsworth, Stephen (1976) 'Bonynge on Bel Canto.'

Opera News, February1976.

Watson, Peter (2002) 'What Have Chest Wall Kinematics Informed Us about Breathing for Singing.' PAS-Conference October 2002.

Walker, Evan (2008) 'The Fable of Adolphe Nourit'. Journal of Singing, Volume 64, No. 4, March 2008.

Westerman Gregg, Jean (1990) 'From Song To Speech On Support'.

The NATS Journal, September 1990.

Westerman Gregg, Jean (2001) 'Resonation and Articulation-A New Concept.' Journal of Singing, Volume 58, No. 2, November 2001.

Winckel, F. (1969) 'Acoustical Foundation of Phonetics'. In Bertil Malmberg.

Winkworth, Davis, Ellis and Adams (1994), 'Variability and Consistency in Speech Breathing During Reading: Lung Volumes, Speech Intensity and Linguistic Factors.' Journal of Speech & Hearing, Vol. 37, June 1994.

Winkworth, and Davis (1997), 'Speech Breathing and the Lombard Effect.' Journal of Speech, Language and Hearing Research, Volume 40, February 1997.

Wolf, Stanley, and Sette (1935) 'Quantitave Studies on the Singing Voice.' Journal of Acoustical Society of America, Vol. 6, 1935.

Yanagisawa, Estill, Kmucha, and Leder (1989) 'The Contribution of Aryepiglottic Constriction to "Ringing" Voice Quality.' Journal of Voice Vol. 3, No. 4, 342–350.

Zanartu, Mongeau, Wodicka (2007), 'Influence of acoustic loading on an effective single mass model of the vocal folds.' Acoustical Society of America, vol. 121 (2) February 2007.

Zaslaw, Neal (1974) 'The Enigma of the Haute-Contre.' JSTOR: The Musical Times, Vol. 115, No. 1581, November 1974.

Zenker, Wolfgang (1964) 'Vocal Muscle Fibers And Their Motor-End Plates.' Research Potentials In Voice Physiology. State University of New York, Syracuse.

Bibliography

www.ingramcontent.com/pod-product-compliance
Lightning Source LLC
Chambersburg PA
CBHW052111010526
44111CB00036B/1637